IB World Schools

yearbook 2009

Editor: We

Editor in C

Acknowledgements

We are extremely grateful to the many people who have helped to compile this yearbook.

In particular, we are grateful to BBIS Berlin; Campion School, Greece; Collège du Léman, Switzerland; ISS Singapore; St George's College, Argentina; TASIS, The American School in England; and Wesley College, Melbourne, for allowing us to use their photographs on the cover of this book.

We also extend our warm gratitude to the many schools and colleges for providing us promptly and efficiently with the accurate information this yearbook contains.

Published in 2009 by John Catt Educational Ltd
12 Deben Mill Business Centre, Old Maltings Approach, Melton, Woodbridge, Suffolk IP12 1BL, UK.
Tel: +44 (0) 1394 389850   Fax: +44 (0) 1394 386893
Email: enquiries@johncatt.co.uk   Website: www.johncatt.com

To the publisher's knowledge all information contained in this yearbook was correct at the time of going to press. Any correspondence regarding incorrect information should be sent to the International Baccalaureate at the following address:

International Baccalaureate
Peterson House
Malthouse Avenue
Cardiff Gate
Cardiff
Wales CF23 8GL
United Kingdom

The Sex Discrimination Act 1975.
The publishers have taken all reasonable steps to avoid a contravention of Section 38 of the Sex Discrimination Act 1975. However, it should be noted that (save where there is an express provision to the contrary) where words have been used which denote the masculine gender only, they shall, pursuant and subject to the said Act, for the purpose of this publication, be deemed to include the feminine gender and vice versa.

British Library Cataloguing in Publication Data.

ISBN: 978-1-904724-60-5

Designed and typeset by John Catt Educational Ltd,
12 Deben Mill Business Centre, Old Maltings Approach, Melton, Woodbridge, Suffolk IP12 1BL, UK

Printed and bound in Great Britain by MPG Impressions,
Units E1-E4, Barwell Business Park, Leatherhead Road, Chessington, Surrey KT9 2NY

IB World Schools
yearbook 2009

CONTENT

Message from Chair and Director General

Dear members of the IB community

This is a particularly special time for the IB community. In 2008 we celebrated 40 years of the IB Diploma Programme and, as we review this Yearbook, it is astounding to see where we started in 1968 compared to where we are today.

The diversity among IB World Schools always serves as a reminder of how much has changed in the past 40 years. The Diploma Programme in the early days consisted of a common pre-university curriculum and a common set of external examinations for students in schools throughout the world, seeking to provide students with an internationally recognized qualification. The first IB World Schools were predominantly private international schools. This has changed over the years and today over half of all IB World Schools are state schools.

As chair of the International Baccalaureate (IB) Board of Governors and director general of the IB, we are always honoured to meet educators and IB advocates from around the world. IB teachers are at the heart of the IB's success, they are the ones instilling in our students the knowledge and values that will allow them to build tomorrow's world.

One of the ways we can support this is through the IB community theme 'sharing our humanity'. This initiative challenges the IB community to reflect and act upon six global issues. As always, IB World Schools have risen to that challenge and not only do students learn from one another in their classrooms as an example of school practice, but also from fellow students located in any of the 129 countries around the world. Through the IB community theme website they are learning and collaborating on topics such as global poverty, peace and conflict, and the digital divide.

Students from Regiopolis-Notre Dame Catholic High School in Kingston, Ontario, Canada, built a children's playground in the Dominican Republic.

Students at Bali International School, Indonesia, have developed the Taman Bacaan Community Library in Bali, which opened in February 2008 and provides books and computers for the local community. These are just two examples of the positive activity underway across the community.

Celebrating 40 years of the IB Diploma Programme has given us cause to reflect upon our past and our future. This Yearbook always serves as a reminder of how far we have come in that time and we are proud to present a group of schools who share in the values and philosophies of the IB and work towards its mission. We hope you will join them in this exciting journey.

Monique Seefried – Chair, IB Board of Governors
Jeffrey Beard – Director General

"The ideals aimed at building a better and more peaceful world that were part of the birth of the IB Diploma Programme have evolved over the past 40 years into something much bigger, into a whole education system from pre-school to completion of high school."

Monique Seefried, Chair, IB Board of Governors

Introduction

The International Baccalaureate (IB) offers three high quality and challenging educational programmes for a worldwide community of schools, aiming to develop internationally minded people who, recognizing their common humanity and shared guardianship of the planet, help to create a better, more peaceful world.

The IB works with schools around the world (both state and privately funded) that share the commitment to international education to deliver these programmes.

Schools that have achieved the high standards required for authorization to offer one or more of the IB programmes are known as 'IB World Schools'. There are more than 2400 IB World Schools (as at September 2008) and this number is growing annually.

The *IB World Schools Yearbook* is the official guide to schools authorized to offer the IB Primary Years, Middle Years and Diploma Programmes. It tells you where the schools are and what they offer, and provides up-to-date information about IB programmes and the International Baccalaureate.

This is an ideal reference for school administration, parents and education ministries worldwide as it:

- Provides a comprehensive reference of IB World Schools for quick and easy access.
- Raises the profile of schools within the IB World School community and beyond.
- Provides comprehensive information about the IB as well as the IB programmes.

How to use this Yearbook

The Yearbook has been designed to be as easy as possible to use and has been divided into five sections.

1. **General information** about the IB and IB programmes.
2. **Comprehensive information** about IB World Schools presented in alphabetical order by school name, coloured according to IB geographical region. In this section schools have been given the opportunity to highlight their best qualities by creating an enhanced profile of their school.
3. **Directory information** about every school authorized to offer one or more of the IB programmes as at September 2008. The directory is ordered by IB region and contains general and contact information about each school. Information about the four IB regions is also given in this section. (Schools that have elected to purchase a profile in the Yearbook will appear in capital letters in the directory.)
4. **Appendices** containing information and lists relevant to the IB. These include IB associations around the world, university acknowledgment of the Diploma Programme, universities offering IB scholarships, country representation, and a list of IB Diploma Programme subjects offered (in 2008).
5. **Index** of all schools listed geographically and alphabetically by name.

Are you looking for a specific IB World School?

If you know the name of the school but are unsure of its location, turn to the index on p. 399 where you will find an alphabetic listing of all IB World Schools.

Are you looking for an IB World School in a specific country?

Look first in the directory section; this will give you the basic information about all the schools in each region. More detailed information can be found in the profiles section for those schools marked with capitalized letters.

The IB website www.ibo.org also contains the most up-to-date information on IB World Schools. A school search option is available from every page on the site for people wanting to find an IB World School.

TILBURG UNIVERSITY

IB Mission Statement

The International Baccalaureate aims to develop inquiring, knowledgeable and caring young people who help to create a better and more peaceful world through intercultural understanding and respect.

To this end the organization works with schools, governments and international organizations to develop challenging programmes of international education and rigorous assessment.

These programmes encourage students across the world to become active, compassionate and lifelong learners who understand that other people, with their differences, can also be right.

Déclaration de mission de l'IB

Le Baccalauréat International (IB) a pour but de développer chez les jeunes la curiosité intellectuelle, les connaissances et la sensibilité nécessaires pour contribuer à bâtir un monde meilleur et plus paisible, dans un esprit d'entente mutuelle et de respect interculturel.

À cette fin, l'IB collabore avec des établissements scolaires, des gouvernements et des organisations internationales pour mettre au point des programmes d'éducation internationale stimulants et des méthodes d'évaluation rigoureuses.

Ces programmes encouragent les élèves de tout pays à apprendre activement tout au long de leur vie, à être empreints de compassion, et à comprendre que les autres, en étant différents, puissent aussi être dans le vrai.

Declaración de principios de IB

El Bachillerato Internacional tiene como meta formar jóvenes solidarios, informados y ávidos de conocimiento, capaces de contribuir a crear un mundo mejor y más pacífico, en el marco del entendimiento mutuo y el respeto intercultural.

En pos de este objetivo, la organización colabora con establecimientos escolares, gobiernos y organizaciones internacionales para crear y desarrollar programas de educación internacional exigentes y métodos de evaluación rigurosos.

Estos programas alientan a estudiantes del mundo entero a adoptar una actitud activa de aprendizaje durante toda su vida, a ser compasivos y a entender que otras personas, con sus diferencias, también pueden estar en lo cierto.

Global Education + Global Networks = Global Opportunities

International students have been welcomed at UNSW since the opening of the University in 1949. The international diversity of UNSW distinguishes the University from other major universities in Australia and globally.

The University of New South Wales (UNSW) is Australia's first international university.

- Ranked 44th in the world in the 2007 *Times Higher Education Report of World University Rankings*

- Ranked 1st in the world for accounting research in the international journal *Accounting and Finance*, June 2007 edition

- Consistently ranked as the leading Engineering Faculty in Australia

- A comprehensive teaching and research university offering over 400 degree programs across nine faculties

- One of the most international university campuses in the world with 120 nationalities represented in our student cohort

www.unsw.edu.au/international

UNSW International Office: Tel +61 2 9385 6996 ■ internationaloffice@unsw.edu.au

About the IB

The IB Diploma Programme was introduced in 1968. Its original purpose was to facilitate the international mobility of students, by providing schools with a curriculum and qualification recognized by universities around the world.

What started as a single programme grew into three programmes available to students aged three to 19, spanning the years from kindergarten to pre-university. IB programmes are taught in 2402 IB World Schools in 129 countries (as at September 2008). They can be offered individually, but a growing number of schools offer them as a continuum.

The **IB Primary Years Programme**, for students aged three to 12, focuses on the development of the whole child as an inquirer, both in the classroom and in the world outside.

The **IB Middle Years Programme**, for students aged 11 to 16, provides a framework of academic challenge that encourages students to embrace and understand the connections between traditional subjects and the real world, and become critical and reflective thinkers.

The **IB Diploma Programme**, for students aged 16 to 19, is an academically challenging and balanced programme of education with final examinations that prepares students for success at university and in life beyond.

IB programmes are available to students in a wide variety of schools and from a range of cultural, ethnic and socio-economic backgrounds. IB World Schools form a worldwide community in which there is no such thing as a 'typical' school (more than 50% of IB students are in state-funded schools).

Figure 1 : Types of IB World Schools

Diploma Programme

	Africa, Europe, Middle East	Asia Pacific	Latin America	North America	Total
private	364	222	194	87	867
state	1214	24	15	661	914
Total	**578**	**246**	**209**	**748**	**1781**

Middle Years Programme

	Africa, Europe, Middle East	Asia Pacific	Latin America	North America	Total
private	85	67	46	41	239
state	25	38	0	360	423
Total	**110**	**105**	**46**	**401**	**662**

Primary Years Programme

	Africa, Europe, Middle East	Asia Pacific	Latin America	North America	Total
private	99	111	57	35	302
state	11	10	0	150	171
Total	**110**	**121**	**57**	**185**	**473**

Total number of programmes:	2916	
Total number of private programmes:	1408	**48.29% of all IB programmes**
Total number of state programmes:	1508	**51.71% of all IB programmes**

IB World Schools:
- Share the mission and commitment of the IB to quality international education.
- Play an active and supporting role in the worldwide community of IB schools.
- Share their knowledge and experience in the development of IB programmes.
- Are committed to the professional development of teachers.

Funding for IB programmes comes from the fees paid by IB World Schools, with additional income from workshops and publication sales. Donors provide support for development projects that otherwise cannot be implemented from the organization's budget.

Figure 2: IB World Schools

Total number of IB World Schools: 2402 in 129 countries (September 2008)

Breakdown by regions

Africa/Europe/Middle East	79 countries	630 schools
Asia-Pacific	24 countries	338 schools
Latin America	17 countries	240 schools
North America and the Caribbean	9 countries	1194 schools

Breakdown by programmes

	PYP	MYP	DP
Africa/Europe/Middle East	110	110	578
Asia-Pacific	121	105	246
Latin America	57	46	209
North America	185	401	748

At September 2008 over 656,000 students are enrolled in one of the three IB programmes at schools in 129 countries. Over the past ten years, the number of students has grown between 10% and 20% each year, resulting in remarkable levels of sustained growth.

Compound annual growth rates for the three IB programmes demonstrate strong year-on-year growth.

Figure 3: Growth of the three IB Programmes

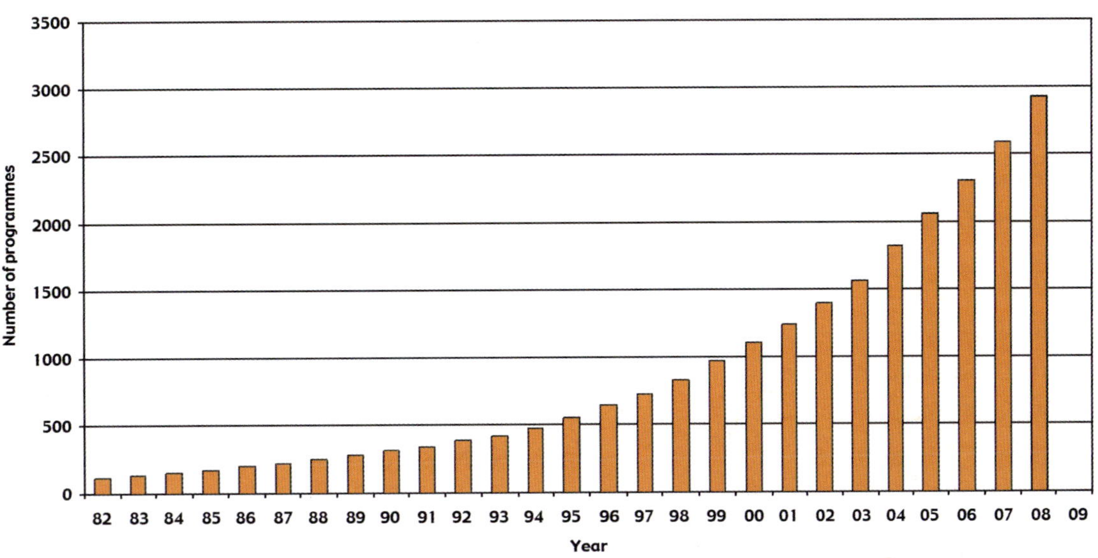

Forty Years of Education for a Better World

The IB is motivated by a mission. The founders of the IB Diploma Programme in the 1960s were a group of forward-thinking teachers at the International School of Geneva, with assistance from several other international schools, who truly believed that education should encourage an understanding and appreciation of other cultures, languages and points of view.

Carrying forward the ideals and dreams of the IB founders, the organization exists to provide high quality education for a better world, as expressed in our mission statement.

The IB community in 2008 recognizes that what has been accomplished is due to a small group of generous individuals, schools, institutions and governments working together in a true spirit of cooperation. Despite geographical, language and cultural differences, they have created a programme of international education that has become a role model for education in the 21st century.

The following schools participated in trial examinations of the IB diploma in 1968:

Atlantic College, Wales
International College, Beirut
International High School, Copenhagen
International School of Geneva
Iranzamin International School, Tehran
North Manchester High School for Girls
United Nations International School (UNIS), New York

The IB Diploma Programme

The IB Diploma Programme was created, originally in English and French, by teachers at a number of international schools. The aims of this new programme were:

- To provide a world perspective.
- To promote intercultural understanding.
- To develop world citizenship.
- To promote critical thinking skills.
- To facilitate access to higher education worldwide.

The programme consisted of a common pre-university curriculum and set of external examinations for students in schools throughout the world and sought to provide students with a truly international education – an education that encouraged an understanding and appreciation of other cultures, languages and points of view. Schools that first offered the IB Diploma Programme were predominantly private international schools, but they included a very small number of private national institutions and schools belonging to state education departments. This has changed over the years and today more than 50% of all IB students attend state-funded schools.

IB Primary Years Programme and IB Middle Years Programme

To give younger students access to an IB education, in 1994 the IB added the Middle Years Programme, a curriculum for students aged 11–16, and in 1997 it offered for the first time the Primary Years Programme for students aged three to 12. As with the Diploma Programme, the IB Primary Years and Middle Years Programmes seek to help students gain an international perspective and critical thinking skills.

IB regions

The IB opened four regional offices between the mid-1970s and the early 1980s. The first was IB North America in 1977, located in New York and working with schools in the US, Caribbean and Canada. In 1982, under the leadership of the head of an international school in Uruguay, the IB established a regional office in Buenos Aires to promote the IB Diploma Programme in Latin America. That same year it created an office in Singapore for Asia Pacific that was headed by a senior official with the United World College in Singapore. The IB's Africa, Europe and Middle East regional office first opened in London in 1978. After several interim moves the office settled in Geneva in 1994.

Chairs of the IB Board of Governors (formerly Council of Foundation)

1968–1981	John Goormaghtigh	Director of the European office of the Carnegie Endowment for International Peace
1981–1984	Seydou Madani Sy	Rector of the University of Dakar, Senegal, and later minister for justice and special advisor to the president of Senegal
1984–1990	Piet Gathier	Director general of secondary education, the Netherlands
1990–1996	Thomas Hagoort	International lawyer, USA
1996–1997	Bengt Thelin	Director general of education, Sweden
1997–2003	Greg Crafter	Former minister for education in South Australia, lawyer
2003–2009	Monique Seefried	Former executive director, Center for the Advancement and Study of International Education, USA

IB directors general

Alec Peterson	1968–77	Derek Blackman	1998–99
Gérard Renaud	1977–83	George Walker	1999–2006
Roger Peel	1983–98	Jeffrey Beard	2006–

"So, as it was being formed in the 1960s, IB international education wanted students to recognize that people share a common heritage, to adopt positive attitudes about other cultures, to respect all human beings, to understand that nations are interdependent, to know about history and the present on a world scale, to be able to commit themselves to a society where one could hold opinions freely and to engage in critical thinking, physical exercise and community service."

Ian Hill, IB Deputy Directory General

IB Learner Profile

Introduced in March 2006, the IB learner profile is the IB mission statement translated into a set of learning outcomes for the 21st century. The attributes of the profile express the values inherent to the IB continuum of international education: these are values that should infuse all elements of the IB Primary Years Programme, IB Middle Years Programme and IB Diploma Programme and, therefore, the culture and ethos of all IB World Schools. The learner profile provides a long-term vision of education. It is a set of ideals that can inspire, motivate and focus the work of schools and teachers, uniting them in a common purpose.

The attributes and descriptors of the learner profile define the type of learner the IB hopes to develop through its programmes. It originated in the IB Primary Years Programme (PYP) where it was called the 'PYP student profile', but practitioners from all three programmes identified it as a set of qualities that could also enhance learning in the IB Middle Years and IB Diploma Programmes – learning that should not come to a stop at the age of 11, but should carry through to the completion of the Diploma Programme. It is now called the 'IB learner profile' to make it applicable to all students and adults involved in the implementation of IB programmes.

It is the IB's intention that the learner profile will help develop coherence within and across the three programmes. It provides a clear and explicit statement of what is expected of students, teachers and school administrators in terms of learning, and what is expected of parents in terms of support for that learning.

This symbol, created in 2008, identifies the learner profile as something that is relevant to the entire worldwide community of people that support our mission.

A video that helps to bring the IB mission to life by showing the learner profile in action in IB World Schools is available on www.ibo.org and is an ideal introduction or finale to a presentation about the IB at information evenings, board meetings or other school events. It is available in English, French and Spanish versions and in a number of formats for use in PowerPoint presentations or on your school website. Download a high quality version in WMV format from: www.ibo.org/communications/

Reflective

Thinkers

Caring

Inquirers

The IB Learner Profile

IB learners strive to be:	
Inquirers	They develop their natural curiosity. They acquire the skills necessary to conduct inquiry and research and show independence in learning. They actively enjoy learning and this love of learning will be sustained throughout their lives.
Knowledgeable	They explore concepts, ideas and issues that have local and global significance. In so doing, they acquire in-depth knowledge and develop understanding across a broad and balanced range of disciplines.
Thinkers	They exercise initiative in applying thinking skills critically and creatively to recognize and approach complex problems, and make reasoned, ethical decisions.
Communicators	They understand and express ideas and information confidently and creatively in more than one language and in a variety of modes of communication. They work effectively and willingly in collaboration with others.
Principled	They act with integrity and honesty, with a strong sense of fairness, justice and respect for the dignity of the individual, groups and communities. They take responsibility for their own actions and the consequences that accompany them.
Open-minded	They understand and appreciate their own cultures and personal histories, and are open to the perspectives, values and traditions of other individuals and communities. They are accustomed to seeking and evaluating a range of points of view, and are willing to grow from the experience.
Caring	They show empathy, compassion and respect towards the needs and feelings of others. They have a personal commitment to service, and act to make a positive difference to the lives of others and to the environment.
Risk-takers	They approach unfamiliar situations and uncertainty with courage and forethought, and have the independence of spirit to explore new roles, ideas and strategies. They are brave and articulate in defending their beliefs.
Balanced	They understand the importance of intellectual, physical and emotional balance to achieve personal well-being for themselves and others.
Reflective	They give thoughtful consideration to their own learning and experience. They are able to assess and understand their strengths and limitations in order to support their learning and personal development.

IB Programmes

The IB offers a continuum of education, consisting of three individual programmes. The programmes span the years from kindergarten to a pre-university diploma.

The three IB programmes share a common philosophy and common characteristics. They develop the whole student, helping students to grow intellectually, socially, aesthetically and culturally. They provide a broad and balanced education that includes science and the humanities, languages and mathematics, technology and the arts. The programmes teach students to think critically, and encourage them to draw connections between areas of knowledge and to use problem-solving techniques and concepts from many disciplines. They instill in students a sense of responsibility towards others and towards the environment. Lastly, and perhaps most importantly, the programmes give students an awareness and understanding of their own culture and of other cultures, values and ways of life.

All three programmes:
- Have a strong international dimension.
- Draw on content from educational cultures around the world.
- Require study across a broad range of subjects.
- Include both individual subjects and transdisciplinary areas.
- Give special emphasis to learning languages.
- Focus on developing the skills of learning.
- Provide opportunities for individual and collaborative planning and research.
- Encourage students to become responsible members of their community.

IB programmes include:
- A written curriculum or curriculum framework.
- Student assessment appropriate to the age range.
- Professional development and networking opportunities for teachers.
- Support, authorization and programme evaluation for the school.

The IB Primary Years Programme

The IB Primary Years Programme, for students aged three to 12, focuses on the development of the whole

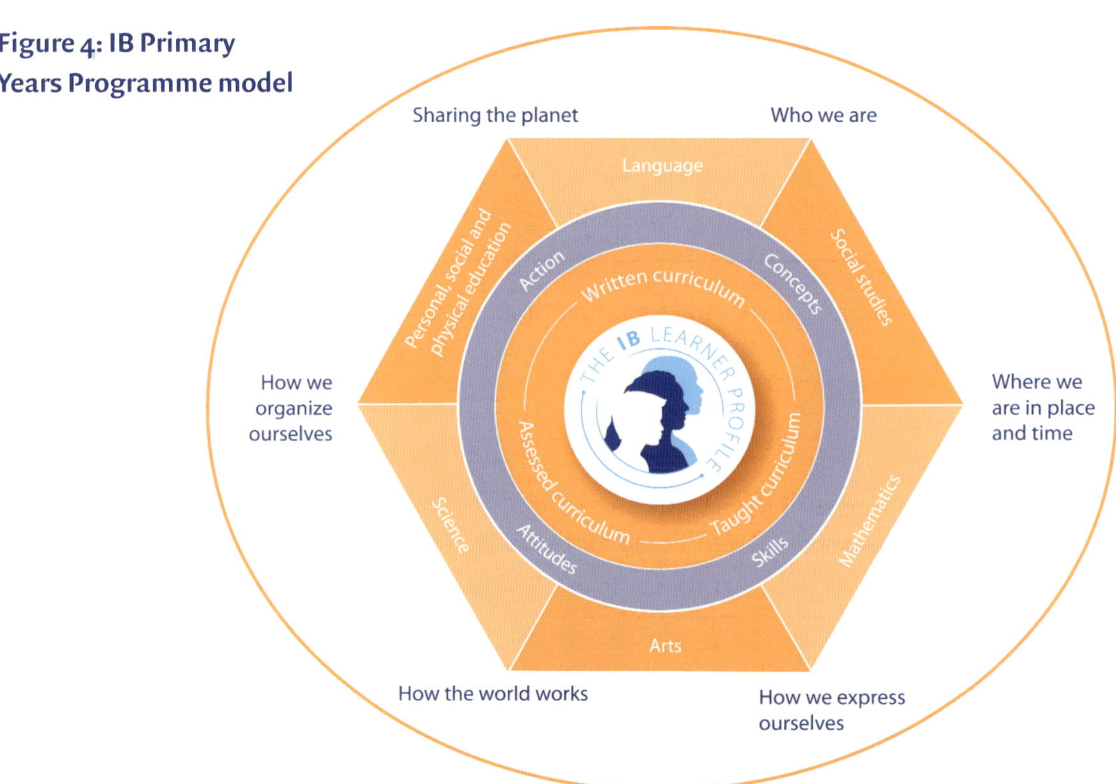

Figure 4: IB Primary Years Programme model

child as an inquirer, both in the classroom and in the world outside. It is a framework consisting of five essential elements (concepts, knowledge, skills, attitude, action) and guided by six transdisciplinary themes of global significance, explored using knowledge and skills derived from six subject areas (language, social studies, mathematics, science, arts, and personal, social and physical education) with a powerful emphasis on inquiry-based learning.

The most significant and distinctive feature of the IB Primary Years Programme is the six transdisciplinary themes. These themes are about issues that have meaning for, and are important to, all of us. The programme offers a balance between learning about or through the subject areas, and learning beyond them. The six themes of global significance create a transdisciplinary framework that allows students to 'step up' beyond the confines of learning within subject areas:

- Who we are.
- Where we are in place and time.
- How we express ourselves.
- How the world works.
- How we organize ourselves.
- Sharing the planet.

The IB Primary Years Programme exhibition is the culminating activity of the programme. It requires students to analyse and propose solutions to real-world issues, drawing on what they have learned through the programme. Evidence of student development and records of PYP exhibitions are reviewed by the IB as part of the programme evaluation process.

Assessment is an important part of each unit of inquiry as it both enhances learning and provides opportunities for students to reflect on what they know, understand and can do. The teacher's feedback to the students provides the guidance, the tools and the incentive for them to become more competent, more skilful and better at understanding how to learn.

Unique characteristics of the programme include the following:

- It encourages international-mindedness in IB students.
- It encourages a positive attitude to learning by engaging students in inquiries and developing their awareness of the process of learning so that they become lifelong learners.
- It reflects real life by encouraging learning beyond and through traditional subjects with meaningful, in-depth inquiries into real issues.
- Through the learner profile, it emphasizes the development of the whole student – physically, intellectually, emotionally and ethically.

The IB Middle Years Programme

The IB Middle Years Programme, for students aged 11 to 16, provides a framework of academic challenge that encourages students to embrace and understand the connections between traditional subjects and the real world, and to become critical and reflective thinkers. Students are required to study their mother tongue, a second language, humanities, sciences, mathematics, arts, physical education and technology. In the final year of the programme, students also engage in a personal project, which they will use to demonstrate the understandings and skills they have developed throughout the programme.

Students study subjects from each of the eight subject groups through the five areas of interaction: approaches to learning, community and service, human ingenuity (formally *homo faber*), environments, and health and social education.

- **Approaches to learning** is concerned with developing the intellectual discipline, attitudes, strategies and skills that will result in critical, coherent and independent thought and the capacity for problem solving and decision-making.
- **Community and service** starts in the classroom and extends beyond it, requiring students to participate in the communities in which they live. The emphasis is on developing community awareness and concern, a sense of responsibility, and the skills and attitudes needed to make an effective contribution to society.
- **Human ingenuity** allows students to focus on the evolution, processes and products of human creativity. It considers their impact on society and on the mind. Students learn to appreciate the human capacity to influence, transform, enjoy and improve the quality of life. This area of interaction encourages students to explore the relationships between science, aesthetics, technology and ethics.

Figure 5: IB Middle Years Programme model

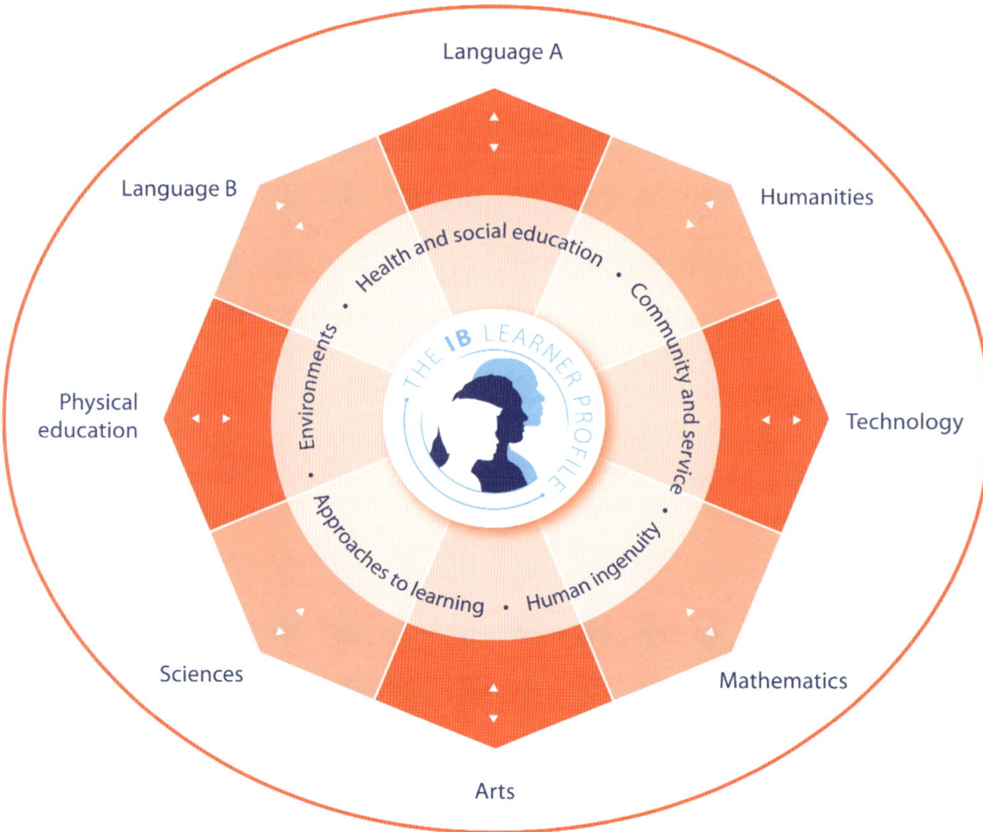

- **Environments** aims to make students aware of their interdependence with the environment so that they become aware of their responsibility, and may take positive, responsible action for maintaining an environment fit for the future.
- **Health and social education** prepares students for a physically and mentally healthy life, aware of potential hazards and able to make informed choices. It develops in students a sense of responsibility for their own well-being and for the physical and social environment. Assessment is criterion referenced, so students around the world are measured against pre-specified criteria for each subject group. Teachers may modify these criteria to be age-appropriate in the earlier years of the programme.

Teachers set assessment tasks that are assessed internally in the school. External checks (either moderation or monitoring of assessment by IB examiners) are carried out on this internal assessment to ensure worldwide consistency of standards. For schools that require official IB certification for their students, moderation is carried out every year.

Unique characteristics of the programme include the following:

- It encourages international-mindedness in IB students, starting with a foundation in their own language and culture.
- It encourages a positive attitude to learning by challenging students to solve problems, show creativity and resourcefulness and participate actively in their communities.
- It reflects real life by providing a framework that allows students to see the connections among the subjects themselves, and between the subjects and real issues.
- It supports the development of communication skills to encourage inquiry, understanding, language acquisition, and to allow student reflection and expression.
- Through the learner profile, it emphasizes the development of the whole student – physically, intellectually, emotionally and ethically.

The IB Diploma Programme

The IB Diploma Programme, for students aged 16 to 19, is an academically challenging and balanced programme of education with final examinations that prepares students for success at university and life beyond.

IB Diploma Programme students study six courses

at higher level or standard level. Students must choose one subject from each of groups 1 to 5, thus ensuring breadth of experience in languages, social studies, the experimental sciences and mathematics. The sixth subject may be an arts subject chosen from group 6, or the student may choose another subject from groups 1 to 5. At least three and not more than four subjects are taken at higher level (recommended 240 teaching hours), the others at standard level (150 teaching hours). Students can study these subjects, and be examined, in English, French or Spanish.

In addition, three core elements – the extended essay, theory of knowledge and creativity, action, service – are compulsory and central to the philosophy of the programme.

Students take written examinations at the end of the programme, which are marked by external IB examiners. Students also complete assessment tasks in the school, which are either initially marked by teachers and then moderated by external moderators or sent directly to external examiners.

The marks awarded for each course range from 1 (lowest) to 7 (highest). Students can also be awarded up to three additional points for their combined results on theory of knowledge and the extended essay. The diploma is awarded to students who gain at least 24 points, subject to certain minimum levels of performance across the whole programme and to satisfactory participation in the creativity, action, service requirement. The highest total that a Diploma Programme student can be awarded is 45 points.

Unique characteristics of the programme include the following:

- It provides a package of education that balances subject breadth and depth, and considers the nature of knowledge across disciplines through the unique theory of knowledge course.
- It encourages international-mindedness in IB students, starting with a foundation in their own language and culture.
- It develops a positive attitude to learning that prepares students for university education.
- It has gained a reputation for its rigorous external assessment with published global standards, making this a qualification welcomed by universities worldwide.
- It emphasizes the development of the whole student – physically, intellectually, emotionally and ethically.

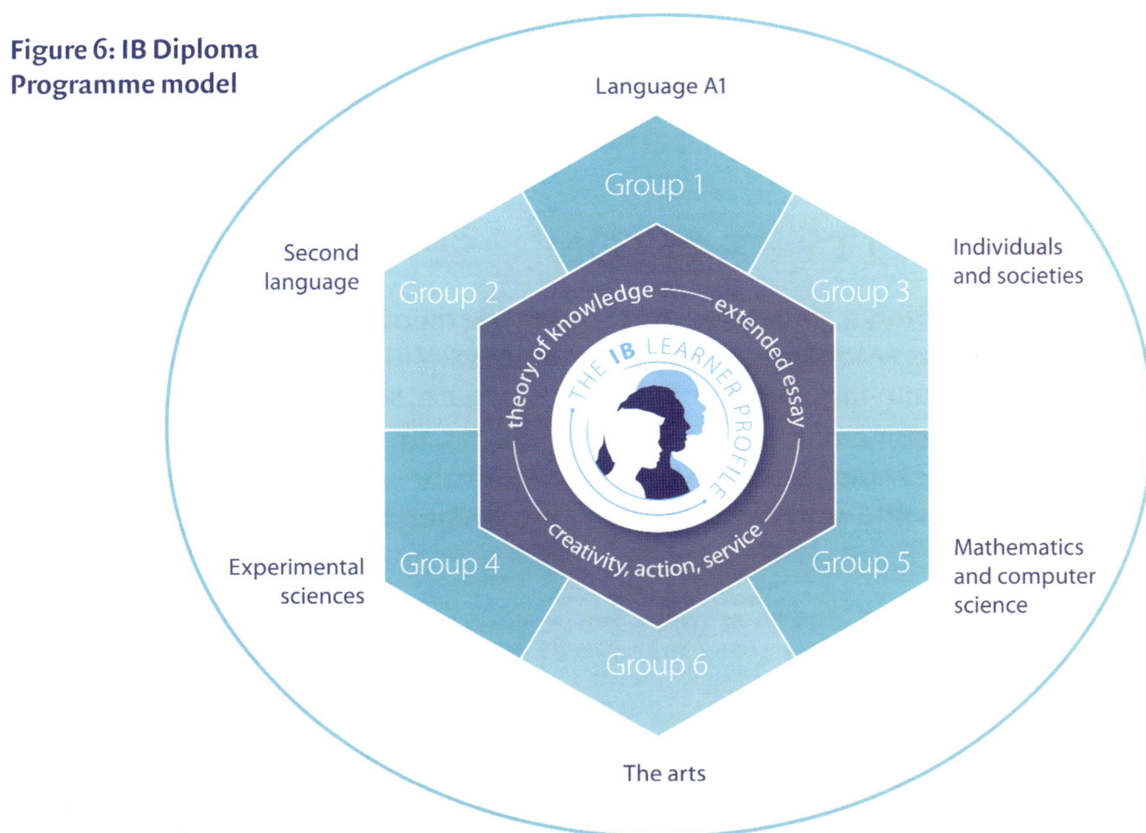

Figure 6: IB Diploma Programme model

FAST TRAIN

PROGRAMS FOR INTERNATIONAL EDUCATORS

Licensure/Master's Degree Programs:
Elementary PK–6   or   ESOL PK–12

Online Certificate Program in Special Education (15 credits)

Certificate in Advanced IB Studies (15 credits, IB recognized)

HIGHLIGHTS OF PROGRAMS
In-state tuition rates for all applicants
Combinations of online course work and intensive
 summer study
Practical course work taught by experienced mentors

REQUIREMENTS
Bachelor's degree
3.00 GPA in last 60 hours of undergraduate course work
Three letters of recommendation
Goal statement
Official transcript

RECRUITMENT FAIR
**Council of International Schools, International
School Services and George Mason University
Recruitment Fair**
WHEN: Each June
LOCATION: George Mason University, Fairfax, Virginia
CONTACT: www.cois.org

PROGRAM INFORMATION
Lynn Walker Levy, Coordinator
FAST TRAIN Programs
Center for International Education
fastrain@gmu.edu
http://gse.gmu.edu/fasttrain

GEORGE
MASON
U N I V E R S I T Y

College of
Education and
Human
Development

CREATIVITY   ACTION   SERVICE

With Les Elfes International you have access to dedicated staff in our own properties in Verbier, Crans-Montana, La Tzoumaz and Villars in Switzerland, and Faraya-Mzaar in Lebanon for your future ski trips.

You can tailor your CAS requirements using our projects in Tanzania, India, China, Thailand, Cambodia, Vietnam Australia, France, Italy and 35 destinations worldwide with Les Elfes International.

info@leselfes.ch
www.leselfes.com
Tel. +41 (0) 27 775 35 90
Fax. +41 (0) 27 775 35 99

Universities and governments

In an environment of increasing competitiveness among institutions of higher education, and taking account of the growing mobility of students, university admissions tutors and academic staff around the world recognize the benefits of recruiting IB graduates for their universities and colleges. The benefits include:

- The admission of students from a rigorous academic background, who know how to think and learn.
- The absence of any concerns about grade inflation.
- The knowledge that state and national standards are being met and exceeded through effective teaching and learning; IB standards and grading practices are the same around the world, which means the criteria for achieving each grade are the same for all IB World Schools.
- The rich diversity of experience and perspective that IB Diploma Programme students bring to their university or college.

IB students routinely gain admission to some of the best known universities in the world. Most of these institutions have established recognition policies for the IB diploma. (See Appendix 3 (page 367) for a list of universities around the world recognizing the IB diploma.)

The IB and government

Engaging regional and national governments is at the centre of the IB's commitment to diversity and inclusivity. There is a growing awareness among governments that education systems have to work in an international society, not just a national one. The IB engages with many governments about either creating more IB World Schools or influencing national education systems. The IB is defined by its values and those include pedagogical leadership and international-mindedness. Across the world, the IB is working hand-in-hand with regional and national governments to ensure state access to IB programmes.

Examples of this work include the Canadian province of Nova Scotia who is working with the IB to ensure its students enjoy all the benefits of an internationally focused education.

In Ecuador the president has made education a priority as he seeks to advance the economy, and ensuring more students have access to IB programmes is seen as essential to this.

"One of the advantages of an IB curriculum is its structure and quality. It's a coordinated programme, well established, well known and well respected."
Christoph Guttentag,
Duke University

The IB Around the World

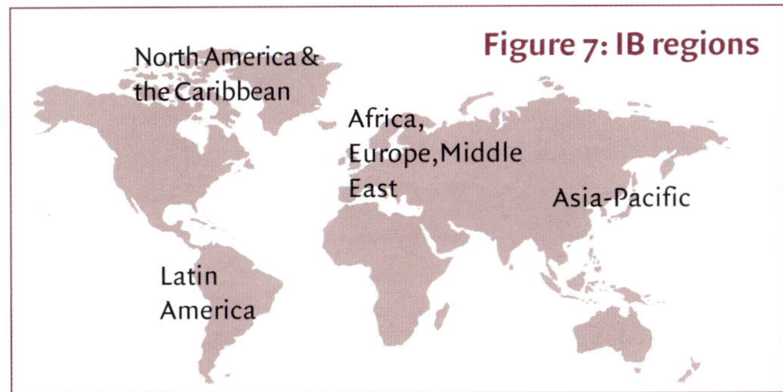

Figure 7: IB regions

Today the IB works with IB World Schools in 129 countries. Its headquarters are in Geneva, Switzerland, but there are offices in Cardiff, Bath, New York, Sydney, Buenos Aires, Geneva and Singapore.

The largest office is situated in Cardiff, UK, and houses the academic, assessment, ICT, strategy and planning, global communications, finance and human resources directorates and the publications department.

The IB regional offices represent the three regions: Africa, Europe, Middle East; Asia Pacific; Latin America and North America and the Caribbean. As at September 2008, over 444 IB staff are located in 11 centres around the world.

The **regional offices** and **regional representatives** work closely with schools that are interested in applying to become IB World Schools, with those that are candidate schools and with existing IB World Schools. They are also responsible for establishing contact with ministries of education, universities and other international institutions in the educational world.

Services provided by IB regional offices

For interested or candidate schools:

- Introductory or orientation workshops.
- Consultation, advice and materials on the application and authorization process.
- Training workshops.
- Arrangement of authorization visits by the IB.

For IB World Schools:

- Teacher training programmes for new and experienced IB teachers.
- Regional conferences.
- Periodic evaluations of a school's IB programmes.
- Monitoring and assisting with the implementation of creativity, action and service projects.

For universities:

- Information on the philosophy, structure and requirements of the IB Diploma Programme.
- Access to the content and requirements of the IB Diploma Programme curriculum and assessment.
- Advice on establishing an IB recognition policy.

For governments:

- Advice on how to integrate IB programmes into state educational systems.
- Consultation regarding recognition of the IB diploma.

2020 Vision Project

It is anticipated that there will be 2.5 million students at 10,000 IB World Schools by 2020. The IB recognizes the requirement to evolve to meet the needs of its rapidly expanding global community and has set up the 2020 vision project to address this. The 2020 vision project will transform the way the IB is structured, managed and resourced.

The organization aims to strengthen its infrastructure by investing in technology, people and systems and introducing methods that reflect its service-oriented spirit and facilitate forward-planning.

Part of this work includes a change in structure of IB North America and the Caribbean and the IB Latin America regions. Effective 1 January 2009 the regions will merge to form the IB Americas. The current offices in Buenos Aires, New York and Vancouver will continue to operate and provide schools with high quality service in the near term. As the 2020 vision project evolves, more local offices will open in the IB Americas region. These local offices will provide direct customer support in local languages and time zones throughout the region.

The aim of this initiative is to culturally enrich the experience of schools and teachers throughout the Americas and improve connectivity between countries ensuring a higher profile of language skills, experience and understanding of the whole region.

As the 2020 vision project develops further, more information about changes to the organization's structure will be communicated to stakeholders via the IB website.

IB Community Theme: Sharing Our Humanity

In an effort to strengthen its large and growing community and the IB mission, the IB has initiated an IB community theme.

This idea was conceived in 2006 and the first theme, sharing our humanity, was officially launched in April 2007.

The theme, lasting three years, is intended to serve as a focus for the IB and IB World Schools, to capture the excellent initiatives that are already underway in many schools and encourage and inspire new activities, in and out of the classroom.

The following issues are being addressed by the IB community:

- Global poverty.
- Education for all.
- Peace and conflict.
- Global infection diseases.
- Digital divide.
- Disasters and emergencies.

The IB is addressing these issues through presentations by key speakers at regional conferences, articles in major publications and by sharing examples of the positive action underway in the community.

A dedicated online environment was launched in January 2008 and is the first IB website available to all members of the community, including parents and students. The website is intended to be a resource for the community where people can:

- Post materials and links to other relevant websites from other organizations relating to global issues.
- Post materials developed by IB teachers relating to the theme.
- Post reports by the community on examples of action taken.
- Join in discussion forums.

The IB encourages to schools to join in the theme through:

- PYP projects.
- Professional development activities for teachers.
- IB global lessons.
- School conferences and events.
- Raising awareness to students on global issues.
- Service and fundraising action.
- Adjustments to lessons to incorporate references to the six global issues.

In October 2008 a global lesson took place across the community where IB World Schools were encouraged to teach a lesson on global poverty. An outline lesson and accompanying materials were developed for the IB Diploma Programme theory of knowledge course and the IB Middle Years Programme humanities course.

Ultimately the IB community theme can become a catalyst for vital small-scale changes across the world which, when added together, make a genuine difference to tackling global issues.

IB Governance

IB Board of Governors

The IB is governed by a Board of Governors, whose members are elected by the Board on nominations presented by the governance committee. Membership comprises a minimum of four IB World School heads; two IB alumni; two from each IB region; and a diversity of gender, culture and geography with experience from both the business and academic worlds. Board members (with the exception of the director general) are volunteers and receive no payment for their time or work on the Board.

Members as at September 2008

President: Dr Monique Seefried, founder of the Center for the Advancement and Study of International Education (CASIE), France/USA.

Vice president: Dr Indu Shahani, principal, HR College of Commerce and Economics, India.

Treasurer: Dr Michael Obermayer, chairman, European American Investment Bank, Austria.

Secretary: Ms Graciela Borrás de Xanthopoulos, director general, Saint Mary of the Hills School, Argentina.

Members:

Ms Izamar Álvarez, executive director of FUNDACEA, Venezuela.

Dr Carl Amrhein, Provost and Vice-President (Academic) University of Alberta, Canada.

Mr Jeffrey Beard, director general, IB, Switzerland.

Mr Ibrahim Betil, chair, Community Volunteers Foundation, Turkey.

Dr Masood Faizullah, trustee to IB Asia Pacific, Singapore.

Prof Eleri Jones, head, Welsh School of Hospitality, Tourism and Leisure Management, University of Wales Institute, UK.

Dr Shamsh Kassim-Lakha, former Minister for Education, Science and Technology, Pakistan.

Mr Michael Matthews, head, Inter-Community School Zurich, Switzerland.

Ms Katy Ricks, Head, Sevenoaks School, UK.

Mr Stephen Spahn, Chancellor/Headmaster, The Dwight School, NY, USA.

Ms Roshan Thomas, director, Sparks Academy Kabul, Afghanistan.

Ms Tammy Wan, director, corporate finance and advisory, Standard Chartered Bank Ltd, Hong Kong.

Heads of IB World Schools

Heads of IB World Schools play an important advisory role in the IB. They serve on IB committees, advise the IB on its programmes and services and contribute to an ongoing discussion about the philosophy, objectives and methodologies of international education.

All heads of IB World Schools automatically belong to the IB heads standing association (HSA). HSA's role is to:

- Advise and cooperate with the IB on matters of concern to IB World Schools, with particular reference to educational philosophy, curriculum development and finance, and to offer practical support whenever possible.
- Provide opportunities for discussion of matters of interest to heads.
- Give assistance to the heads of newly authorized schools.
- Further the cause of international education.

Each IB region has a Regional Council that serves as a strategic sounding board for the regional director and provides information and assistance related to IB issues in various parts of the region. The Heads Council is an advisory group to the director general to keep him in touch with issues that affect IB World Schools around the world. It is made up of 12 members, three from each region to serve a three-year term.

The IB Online

IB website

Each year, over 20 million pages are downloaded from www.ibo.org – it is the largest, most comprehensive and most widely used source of information about the International Baccalaureate.

Almost one third of all the pages (more than seven million) are downloaded by people searching for IB World Schools. The school search option is available from every page on the site because we know that many people, having read about the IB programmes, want to find a local IB World School.

Every IB World School has its own page on www.ibo.org that is automatically created and maintained using data from our administrative website (IBIS). Features on the website include:

- Customized home pages containing information and links for IB coordinators, educators, students, parents and our other main stakeholder groups.
- An online store at http://store.ibo.org where publications, merchandise and gift items can be purchased.
- A 'Find a School' function, to enable quick and easy searching for IB World Schools.
- IB HeadNet, a password-protected section containing information for heads of schools.
- A workshops and conferences calendar, showing details of teaching training workshops and other events around the world.
- Advertising of teaching posts worldwide.
- Regional sections maintained by the four IB regional offices.

Online Curriculum Centre

The online curriculum centre is a password-protected IB website designed to support teachers of the three IB programmes. The site includes:

- IB publications for all curriculum areas across the three IB programmes.
- News items and important information.
- Discussion forums (organized by subject/curriculum area) for teachers to communicate freely with other IB teachers.
- Teacher-generated resources.
- Support areas for special educational needs, second-language and mother-tongue support, librarians, academic honesty and calculators.
- Online subject specialists (online faculty members) to answer curriculum and assessment queries.
- A real-time chat facility.

IBIS

IBIS is a collection of electronic services for IB coordinators and is only available to IB Primary Years, Middle Years and Diploma Programme coordinators in IB World Schools. IBIS allows coordinators to:

- Register candidates, change registrations and produce reports about candidate registrations.
- Produce invoice/fees reports.
- Receive examination results.
- Submit electronic forms.
- View and search the latest school directory.
- Participate in electronic conferencing with other IB members.
- Create an electronic query.

Digital Space Initiative (DSI)

The International Baccalaureate's Digital Space Initiative (DSI) aims to enhance the experiences and functionality that the IB offers its community in an online, web-based environment.

The organization hopes to integrate digital technology more and more into the IB experience, in line with the increased use around the world of web-based communities to share educational and social experiences.

A result of DSI will be a more cohesive, more effective and more user-friendly web presence by aligning existing websites. For example, an IB teacher will eventually see relevant, highlighted news, resource and e-newsletter links when logging into the IB website, and will have convenient access to sites such as the OCC and the IB Community Theme site.

Explaining and Promoting IB Programmes

For schools that have achieved the high standards required for authorization, one of the benefits is to be known as an IB World School and to make use of the IB identity. This helps to reinforce the reputation and credibility of your school by associating with the globally recognized quality and values of the IB.

IB World School identity

IB World Schools can use this logo in connection with the programmes for which they are authorized. The design uses the same core as the main IB logo. It is available to download from www.ibo.org/communications/ in a wide variety of formats (EPS, GIF, JPEG). It is also available in English, French or Spanish.

Your page on the IB website

Each year, over 20 million pages are downloaded from www.ibo.org, it is the largest, most comprehensive and most widely used source of information about the IB. Almost one third of all the pages (more than seven million) are downloaded by people searching for IB World Schools. The school search option is available from every page on the site because we know that many people, having read about the IB programmes, want to find a local IB World School.

To increase the number of visitors to your page on www.ibo.org we automatically ensure that Google and other major search engines index your page regularly. We include your page in our own site search engine and the site A to Z index. You can also opt to be included in the 'IB World Schools' feature that appears throughout www.ibo.org. Pages that have this feature display details of a different school each time they are displayed. You will find 'Focus on a School' on the home page, every country page, and many regional pages throughout the site. To be included, please write to: web@ibo.org.

The IB brochure *Education for a Better World* is a 12 page, high impact, full-colour brochure available in English, French and Spanish. It is ideal for anyone who needs a high level introduction to the International Baccalaureate and its work.

Three IB programme flyers support the brochure. Each full-colour flyer provides an introduction to one of the IB programmes. They have been written with audiences such as parents in mind and are ideal for distribution at information evenings.

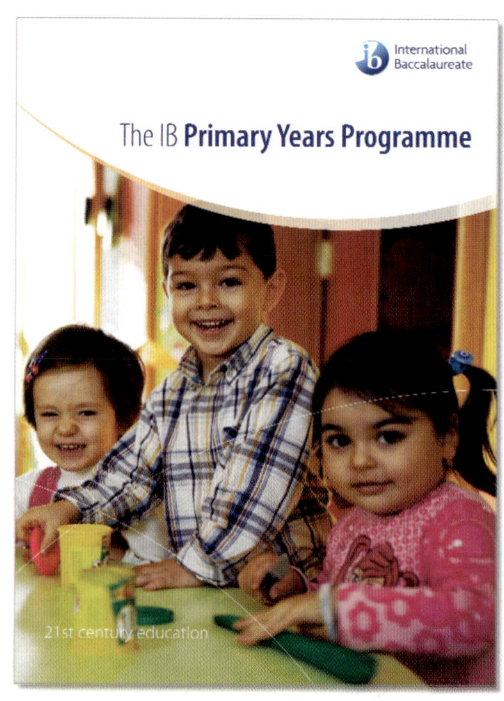

What can I be?

The IB is often a complex thing to understand. It keeps growing and developing.

This book has been written to help you make sense of the IB. It will help you tell the IB story in a more powerful and consistent way, whether you are writing, speaking or just using the logo.

IB screensaver and desktop

The IB screensaver and desktop image are based on an animation of the IB logo. They help to reinforce the IB identity and to promote IB programmes. IB World Schools are welcome to download these from www.ibo.org/communications/
to use on computers within the school or distribute among the school community.

IB PowerPoint presentations

A number of standard PowerPoint presentations are available to download at:
www.ibo.org/communications/
These presentations aim to help schools explain and promote IB programmes to diverse audiences.

IB World

IB World magazine is the official magazine of the International Baccalaureate, published three times a year. The magazine aims to keep everyone informed about the stories happening across the ever-widening IB community. The articles vary widely, from teachers writing about classroom experiences and students sharing their community service projects to more philosophical articles about the role of education. There are single

subscription and bulk subscription offers on this magazine making it possible to distribute the magazine to parents, teachers, board members and others who are interested in IB programmes. Place your order online at:
www.themagazineshop.com/Group-IB_World.aspx

Support available

Information about the supporting materials available to help you promote your programmes is outlined in the booklet 'promoting and explaining your IB programmes'. This and all the materials presented are available to download in PDF format from:
www.ibo.org/communications.

Alternatively, if you have any other questions, please contact the IB communications team by email at: communications@ibo.org
or by calling: +44 (0) 29 2054 7777.

IB Developments

Diploma Programme online

The IB has announced its intention to develop an online version of the Diploma Programme to be offered to communities of learners in collaboration with IB World Schools. Online learning has the potential to both enrich the curriculum and learning experience for students at IB World Schools, while opening access to those who cannot physically attend an IB World School.

The Diploma Programme Online project will allow students to study a variety of Diploma Programme subjects with other students from around the world led by an IB teacher at a distance via the World Wide Web. Teachers and students will learn together in virtual classrooms. Experienced IB teachers will provide the instruction online and students will complete courses that have been authorized by the IB. Authorized online courses will have the same status as face-to-face courses and students will undertake the same internal and external assessments.

The IB will maintain the quality of the Diploma Programme Online courses through authorization and evaluation processes and standards for course development, delivery, instruction and assessment. The project will be carefully studied for its impact on students, schools, and the Diploma Programme.

The Diploma Programme Online will begin as a pilot and expand over time. Through the pilot the organization will investigate offering online courses from all six subject groups and support for the core Diploma Programme requirements. Certain courses are available now but the full pilot is dependent on external funding.

IB World Schools wishing to register their interest in this pilot are invited to contact: dp.online@ibo.org

Career-related education

The International Baccalaureate Career-related Certificate (IBCC) is a new IB initiative (not a new IB programme) that aims to work with, and support schools and colleges, that wish to add an international dimension to their vocational offerings.

The IBCC incorporates the educational principles, vision and learner profile of the IB, into local school and college vocational programmes, and specifically addresses the needs of students engaged in career-related education. The IB's involvement allows these students to be exposed to elements of an IB education, through a selection of Diploma Programme subjects and an adapted IBCC core.

The IB's requirements in terms of the certificate are, a Diploma Programme group 2 subject (a foreign language), one other subject from any of the six Diploma Programme groups, and an adapted core that includes a critical thinking course, community and service and a reflective project (based on the students' vocational studies).

Assessment will be a blend of direct IB and local assessment. The IB is not involved in any assessment associated with the local vocational course, and is not involved in any certification other than the IBCC. The IB will assess the DP subjects and the reflective project. An IB certificate (the IBCC) will be issued subject to satisfactory completion of these IB requirements. The IBCC is an adaptation of the IB's existing Diploma Programme certificates.

The IBCC was introduced by the IB to help achieve its strategic aim of accessibility, enabling more students to experience and benefit from an IB education, regardless of personal circumstances. It also meets a growing desire of schools to offer an alternative to the full Diploma Programme.

From September 2007, a total of six schools from around the world (Finland, Canada, Hong Kong, Dubai, USA and the UK) took part in the pilot with another school from Mauritius entering the pilot in January 2008. The pilot is expected to finish in 2011.

For more information about this project, see the IB website at: www.ibo.org/mission/ibcareercertificate/

An A to Z of School Leadership

by George Walker

Drawing on 30 years of experience in schools and as a former director general of the International Baccalaureate, Professor George Walker OBE has written a unique compendium about leadership.

A prominent figure in international education, George Walker shares his understanding of many aspects of school management in an engaging, penetrating and accessible book.

- Insightful, informative and packed full of practical knowledge and good sense
- Covers all aspects of leading a school
- Advice and guidance from a leading international educator
- Accessible and entertaining A to Z style

£15.95

"George Walker is an educator of exceptional experience and wisdom… Leaders from all sectors of life will profit from this book, and educational leaders will place it on the small shelf of indispensable guides."
— Howard Gardner

Now Available

Creating Lifelong Learners
by Ian Andain and Ged Murphy

A practical teacher reference relating approaches to learning and teaching to the IB programmes and philosophy.

To purchase a copy, or for further information about IB publications, products and services, please visit
http://store.ibo.org

Phone: +44 29 2054 7746
Fax: +44 29 2054 7779
Email: sales@ibo.org

School Profiles

These are provided by schools electing to purchase an enhanced profile.
For a complete listing of all IB World Schools at September 2008,
see the directory section, page 165.

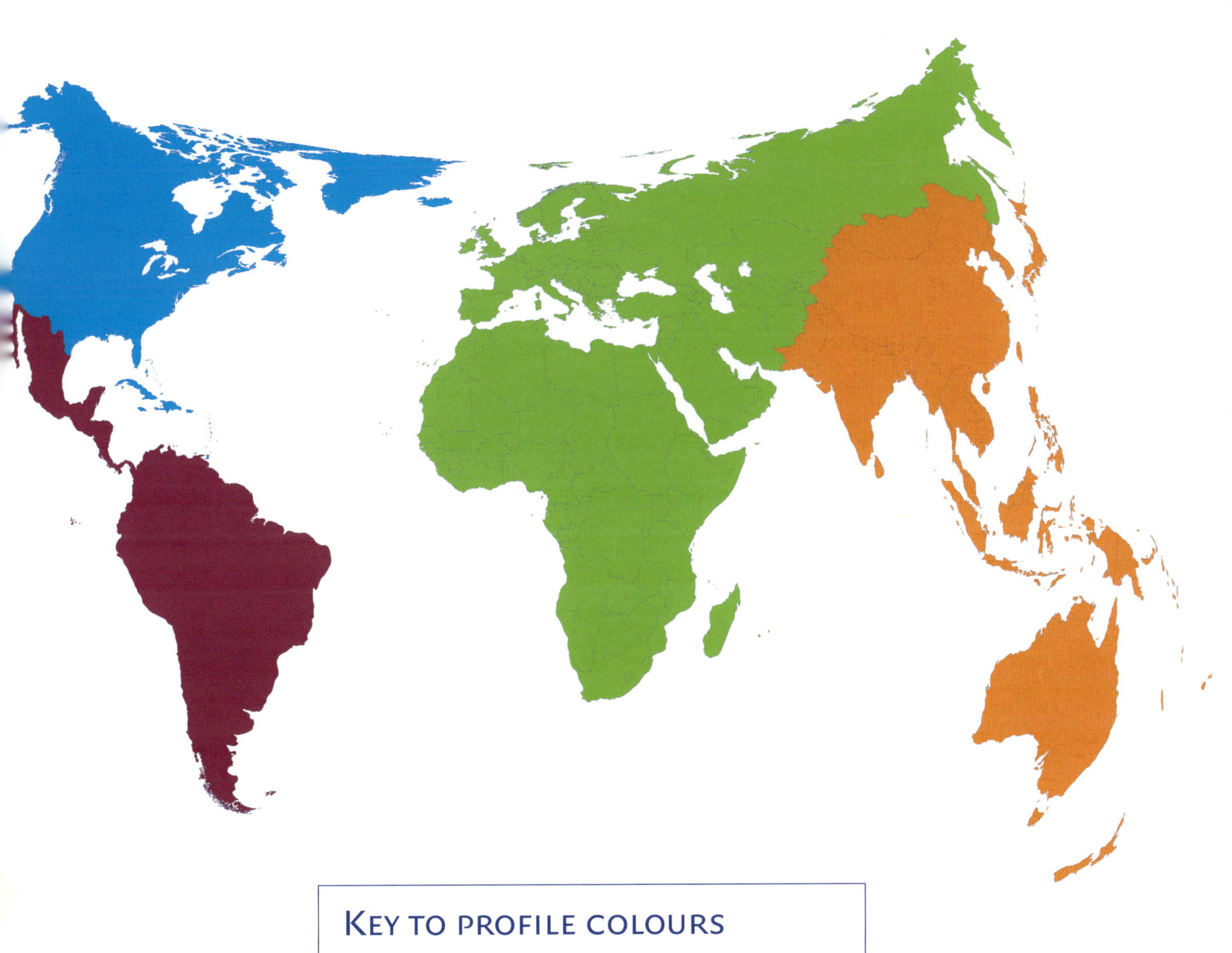

ACS (International), Singapore

(Founded 1886)

Principal
Rev Dr John C Barrett

Diploma coordinator
Daniel Toyne

Status Private

Boarding/day Mixed

Gender Coeducational

Language of instruction
English

Programmes offered Diploma

Age range of pupils 13-18

Fees per annum
Day: S$18,000-S$21,000;
Boarding: S$9500-S$10,700

Address
61 Jalan Hitam Manis
Singapore
278475 | SINGAPORE

TEL +65 6472 1477

FAX +65 6472 0477

Email
john.barrett@acs
international.com.sg

Website
www.acsinternational.com.sg

ACS (International) was established in 2005 as a response to the Singapore government's policy to make Singapore an 'educational hub' in the region of South East Asia. From its founding, it was always intended to become an IB World School and, following its authorization in August 2006, began teaching its first IB Diploma Programme cohort in January 2007 offering the full range of subjects. There are currently 250 students studying an increasing number of subjects on the IB Diploma Programme.

The school is an independent, non-profit, coeducational Singaporean international school offering an all-round, secondary education for students from Year 1 (post-primary) through to Year 6 (pre-university). Our students are of equally Singaporean and international backgrounds. Our student population comes from 28 different countries. ACS (International) is not regulated by the MOE and has the freedom to offer its own curriculum.

ACS (International) is approved by the Singapore Methodist Church as well as the Singapore Ministry of Education and is accredited by British based CIE (University of Cambridge International Examinations) as well as the IB. The Singapore Ministry of Education has named the school an 'Institution of Public Character' for its role in community commitment and service and also short listed it for the Singapore Education Award for the Best Host of International Students studying in Singaporean schools (2008). We are now embarking on the accreditation process for CIS (Council of International Schools).

The parents of ACS (International) students come from a variety of business, government and other professional backgrounds. The school currently numbers 700 students in total with each year group consisting of a maximum of 125 students. There are 25 students in each tutor group and most subject teaching groups average 15-20 students at IGCSE and IB levels.

The school's first IB Diploma Programme cohort sat their examinations in November 2008. A preparation course for SATs is provided for students aiming for entrance into US universities.

The school has a full wireless LAN campus and all students have their own laptops. The library resources are extensive and being developed to provide a fully comprehensive collection. Full, up-to-date sports facilities are scheduled to be completed early in 2009 and new provision for drama will subsequently be created. The school employs a full-time tertiary educational adviser and has strong links with universities around the world.

All students from Years 1-6 participate in our ACAS (Academic, Creativity, Action and Service) Programme which reflects the aims and values of the IB and offers opportunities to develop a wide range of skills including sports, drama, music, service (local and international) and participation in international competitions *ie* Model United Nations. Students have many opportunities through our pastoral system to develop leadership skills. IB Diploma Programme students take part in an overseas service trip as well as joint seminars and inter-school conferences on IB Diploma Programme areas such as TOK in Singapore and beyond.

ACS Cobham International School

Head of School
Mr T Lehman

Diploma coordinator
Craig Worthington

Status Independent

Boarding/day Mixed

Gender Coeducational

Language of instruction
English

Programmes offered Diploma

Age range of pupils 2-18

Number of pupils enrolled 1365

Fees per annum
Day: £8310-£18,280
Boarding: £26,890-£32,040

Address
Heywood
Portsmouth Road
Cobham
Surrey
KT11 1BL | UK

TEL +44 (0)1932 867251
FAX +44 (0)1932 869789

Email
cobhamadmissions@
acs-england.co.uk

Website
www.acs-england.co.uk

ACS Cobham International School enrols students from nearly 60 countries (American and British students represent well over half the population), speaking more than 30 languages, all seeking an education which prepares them for a global future. Our goal is to encourage critical thinkers, responsible global citizens and students who are prepared to achieve the highest standards, both in their subsequent education and throughout their careers. Although there is no formal entrance exam, ACS Cobham is a university-preparatory school, sending students to many of the finest universities in the world.

Academic programme

- ACS Cobham is an International Baccalaureate (IB) World School, offering the IB Diploma Programme.
- ACS Cobham offers a traditional American High School Diploma, including prestigious Advanced Placement (AP) courses.
- ACS Cobham graduates attend leading universities around the world including: Cambridge, Oxford, Imperial College London and London School of Economics in the UK; Stanford, Harvard, Princeton and Yale in the USA; and leading universities in other countries such as Canada, Japan, the Netherlands and Sweden.

Faculty The faculty includes 139 full-time teachers, all holding university degrees; approximately one-half have advanced degrees. The student to teacher ratio is approximately 9:1.

Boarding The school offers coeducational boarding with separate-wing accommodation for 110 students aged between 12 (7th grade) and 18 (12th grade). All student rooms are ergonomically designed for two with en suite facilities and internet connections.

The campus

- ACS Cobham is located 23 miles south of central London on a beautiful 128-acre site, giving students plenty of space and acting as a useful learning resource.
- Superb purpose-built teaching facilities now include a state-of-the-art interactive learning centre, complete with video conferencing. Campus sports facilities include: soccer and rugby fields, softball and baseball diamonds, an all-weather Olympic-sized track, tennis courts, golf course, and a sports centre, with a basketball/volleyball show court, competition-class swimming pool, dance studio and fitness suite.

Student activities

- ACS Cobham offers extensive and varied extracurricular clubs, sports and community service activities both locally and internationally, encouraging students to participate in the richness of school life.
- Students also participate in international theatre art programmes, competitive sports tournaments, maths, literature and music competitions in the UK and across Europe.

Admissions Admissions officers are available throughout the year to speak about possible enrolment. Applicants do not need to sit a formal entrance exam. Students are accepted in all grades throughout the year. Application forms, previous school records and teacher references are required for entry.

ACS Egham International School

Head of School
Moyra Hadley

PYP coordinator
Colin Sercombe

MYP coordinator
Victoria Ryan

Diploma coordinator
Justin McCarthy

Status Independent

Boarding/day Day

Gender Coeducational

Language of instruction
English

Programmes offered
PYP, MYP, Diploma

Age range of pupils 2-18

Number of pupils enrolled 584

Fees per annum
Day: £8310-£18,050

Address
Woodlee
London Road
Egham
Surrey
TW20 0HS | UK

TEL +44 (0)1784 430 800
FAX +44 (0)1784 430 626

Email
eghamadmissions@
acs-england.co.uk

Website
www.acs-england.co.uk

Enrolling students from 40 countries (American and British students represent well over half the population), ACS Egham International School is known as a friendly and caring international community which values a holistic approach to education. The school's philosophy is based on developing the individual potential of each student by providing an engaging and challenging educational programme. We promote high standards of scholarship, responsibility and citizenship through our International Baccalaureate (IB) Programmes so that all our students can be successful learners. Although there is no formal entrance exam, ACS Egham is a university-preparatory school, sending its students to many of the finest universities in the world.

Academic programme

- ACS Egham is an International Baccalaureate World School and one of only three schools in the UK to offer the IB Primary Years Programme (three to 11), the IB Middle Years Programme (11-16) and the IB Diploma Programme (17-18).
- ACS Egham graduates attend leading universities around the world including: Oxford, University College London, King's College London, Royal Holloway and University of Warwick in the UK; Boston University, Texas A&M, and Universities of Kansas, Oklahoma and Southern California in the USA; and other fine universities in Australia, Canada, Norway and Singapore.

Faculty The faculty includes over 78 full-time teachers, all holding university degrees, approximately one-third have advanced degrees. The student to teacher ratio is approximately 9:1.

The campus

- ACS Egham is located 25 miles south-west of central London on a 20 acre site.
- The campus offers superb teaching, sports and extracurricular facilities including a newly opened Visual Arts & Design Technology Centre.

Student activities

- Extensive and varied extracurricular clubs, sports, and community service activities both locally and internationally encourage students to benefit from the richness of school life.
- Students also participate in international theatre art programmes, competitive sport tournaments, maths, literature, and music competitions in the UK and across Europe.

Admissions Admissions officers are available throughout the year to speak with families about possible enrolment. Visits can be arranged on weekdays or weekends.

- Applicants do not need to sit a formal entrance exam.
- Students are accepted in all grades throughout the year.
- Application forms and previous school records are required for entry.

Head of School
Ginger Apple

Diploma coordinator
Chris Green

Status Independent

Boarding/day Day

Gender Coeducational

Language of instruction
English

Programmes offered Diploma

Age range of pupils 4-18

Number of pupils enrolled 584

Fees per annum
Day: £8310-£17,410

Address
Hillingdon Court
108 Vine Lane, Hillingdon
Uxbridge
Middlesex
UB10 0BE | UK

TEL +44 (0)1895 259 771
FAX +44 (0)1895 818 404

Email
hillingdonadmissions@
acs-england.co.uk

Website
www.acs-england.co.uk

Enrolling students from 40 countries, ACS Hillingdon International School strongly values partnerships among parents, teachers and students. Our philosophy actively encourages a sense of teamwork and aims to set a challenging yet achievable academic standard. We believe in meeting the developmental needs of our students by providing a balanced educational programme and preparing them to take their places in our ever-changing world. Although there is no formal entrance exam, ACS Hillingdon is a university-preparatory school, sending its students to many of the finest universities in the world.

Academic programme

- ACS Hillingdon is an International Baccalaureate (IB) World School, offering the IB Diploma Programme.
- ACS Hillingdon offers a traditional American High School Diploma, including prestigious Advanced Placement (AP) courses.
- ACS Hillingdon graduates attend leading universities around the world including: Cambridge, Imperial College, King's College, London School of Economics, Royal Veterinary College and St George's Hospital Medical School in the UK; Pennsylvania State University, Purdue, Texas A & M, Tufts University and the US Air Force Academy in the USA; and leading universities in other countries such as Canada, Japan, the Netherlands and Sweden.

Faculty The faculty includes 78 full-time teachers, all holding university degrees; approximately one-third have advanced degrees. The student to teacher ratio is approximately 9:1.

The campus

- ACS Hillingdon is located 15 miles west of Central London with underground rail access, on an 11-acre site set in parkland.
- The excellent facilities are augmented by a new music centre, complete with digital recording studio, rehearsal rooms, practice studios and a computer lab for music technology.
- The campus has on-site playing fields, tennis courts and playgrounds with additional off-site soccer, rugby, track, baseball, softball, swimming and golf facilities available.
- Door-to-door and shuttle bus services are available for much of Central London, West London and Middlesex from Maidenhead to Westminster.

Student activities

- A full range of sports including basketball, tennis, soccer, rugby, swimming, baseball, softball, track and field, cross country and volleyball.
- Extracurricular activities include Student Council, Model United Nations yearbook, music, art, drama, computers, languages and recycling.

Admission Admissions officers are available throughout the year to speak with families about possible enrolment. Applicants do not need to sit a formal entrance exam. New students are accepted in all grades throughout the year. Application forms and previous school records are required for entry.

Aloha College

(Founded 1982)

Senior School Headmaster
Mr Robert Clarence

Diploma coordinator
Eugenio López

Status Private

Boarding/day Day

Gender Coeducational

Language of instruction
English, Spanish

Programmes offered Diploma

Age range of pupils 3-18

Number of pupils enrolled 845

Fees per annum For 2009 fees please contact the Registrar Susan Robson de Morales

Address
Urbanización el Angel
Nueva Andalucía
29660 Marbella
(MÁLAGA) | SPAIN

TEL +34 95 281 41 33
FAX +34 95 281 85 23

Email
info@aloha-college.com

Website
www.aloha-college.com

Academic Excellence

A non-profit-making organisation owned by a charitable trust and administered by two headteachers, a Business Manager and a Board of Governors, all of whom are parents.

- Aloha College was the first IB World School in Spain; academic excellence is our foremost goal.
- Students study English and Spanish and can gain qualifications in both educational systems.
- Fully coeducational day school, unique atmosphere, highly creative and innovative.
- Students go on to the world's leading universities such as Oxford, Warwick, Bath, Navarra, ICADE and London University.

Purpose-built Facilities

In the senior school building there is an arts block, a science block and a media centre which holds the library. The laboratories, IT and art suites are equipped with the most up-to-date facilities. Aloha College has wireless computer connections in all of its buildings. The sixth form has its own study area and lounge.

Dual Curriculum

The college provides a British style education for the international community but has developed a dual curriculum. Regular inspections are conducted under the auspices of the British Council and the Spanish Ministry of Education. College statutes limit class size to a maximum of

12 pupils in the sixth form and 20 in the rest of the school. There is a pupil to staff ratio of better than 10:1. Aloha College is an official examination centre for the American SAT exams.

The Arts

Aloha College places great emphasis on art, drama and music. Aloha is an official examination centre for the prestigious LAMDA awards (London Academy of Music and Dramatic Arts). Facilities include a drama studio with tiered seating and a spacious music studio. There is a dedicated sixth form art room. Individual tuition is available in the piano and other instruments. Classes are available in a variety of dance disciplines as well as in public speaking.

Extra Activities

The sixth form is fully involved with the MUN (Model United Nations), attending three conferences per year. The college organises an extensive programme of extracurricular activities. The Duke of Edinburgh's Award Scheme and Activities Week are strong features of the college's outdoor pursuits provision.

The Aims of Aloha College

The primary aims of Aloha College are to enlarge each student's knowledge, experience and imagination and to enable each of our students to develop a set of moral principles, within a spirit of international understanding and interchange. Thus we expect that the alumni of Aloha will play an active and leading role in the world beyond school.

American Community Schools of Athens

(Founded 1945)

Director
Dr Stefanos Gialamas

PYP coordinator
Dina Pappas

Diploma coordinator
Julia Tokatlidou

Status Private

Boarding/day Day

Gender Coeducational

Language of instruction
English

Programmes offered
PYP, Diploma

Age range of pupils JK-12

Number of pupils enrolled 792

Fees per annum €6000-13,000

Address
129 Aghias Paraskevis
Ano Xalandri
Athens
GR 152 34 | GREECE

TEL +30 210 639 3200
FAX +30 210 639 0051

Email
acs@acs.gr

Website
www.acs.gr

Since 1945, ACS Athens has been committed to providing excellence in education to the children of the international, American, and local communities in Athens. Admitted on the basis of a selective admissions process, the 792 students at ACS Athens represent over 52 countries from all parts of the world. Committed to promoting high standards of academic, social, cultural, civic, and athletic achievement, ACS Athens was the first school in Greece, and one of the first worldwide, to offer the IB Diploma Programme in 1976. ACS Athens is fully accredited by the Middle States Association of Schools and Colleges in the US. It has been authorized to offer the IB Primary Years Programme since 2002.

Embracing both the American and the IB philosophy in education, the school promotes interdisciplinary, student-centered, and inquiry-based learning. Students' individual skills and talents are celebrated and enhanced, while addressing their individual needs. Our objective is to invest in individual talents and strengths in order to achieve the objectives of the IB Diploma Programme. Parallel to the rigorous academic programs are extensive activities, athletics, and community service programs which allow all students to develop a well-rounded personality and to become caring and responsible citizens, not only in school, but beyond the limits of the classroom as well.

ACS houses the largest English language library in Greece, seven computer labs, electronic boards in more than half of our classrooms, PCs in all classrooms, a state-of-the-art performing arts center, a tournament quality gymnasium, an Olympic swimming pool, tennis courts and soccer fields. These provide students with ample opportunities to explore and develop their academic, artistic, athletic skills, and talents.

All ACS graduates earn an American High School Diploma. In addition, they may earn the IB Diploma, or one or more IB Certificates in the subjects of their choice. Students may also earn equivalency to the Greek *Apolytirion* (State Public High School Diploma). All ACS graduates go on to further education in universities around the world and many of them have been accepted to top universities like Yale, Columbia, Harvard, Imperial, Cambridge, Oxford, Duke, and the University of Athens, among hundreds of others. We are proud of our students' successes.

Admissions: contact Mr John Papadakis.

American International School of Johannesburg

(Founded 1982)

Head of School
Dr Robert E Beck

Diploma coordinator
Sophie Hall

Status Private

Boarding/day Day

Gender Coeducational

Language of instruction
English

Programmes offered Diploma

Age range of pupils 4-19

Number of pupils enrolled 713

Address
Private Bag X4
Bryanston
2021 | SOUTH AFRICA

TEL +27 11 464 1505
FAX +27 11 464 1327

Email
rbeck@aisj-jhb.com

Website
www.aisj-jhb.com

AISJ offers the IB Diploma Programme in South Africa. The school serves a diverse community of students from around the world. We provide a challenging education emphasizing academic excellence through a collaborative partnership with families and staff. Our programme inspires and prepares the students to become responsible world citizens with a passion for lifelong learning.

AISJ is located on a beautiful 58 acre campus on the northern end of the greater Johannesburg area, and relatively close to Pretoria.

The campus includes an all-purpose gymnasium, 25 meter swimming pool, outdoor tennis and basketball courts and three soccer fields. There are separate laboratories for biology, physics, chemistry and environmental science. The school has a fine arts center that includes a 200 seat theater. The secondary library has over 12,000 volumes, 1200 videotapes and DVDs, magazine and newspaper subscriptions, 24 networked internet workstations with access to the EBSCO Host electronic database, and two web-based databases for full-text periodical and encyclopedia reference. The high school also has a technology laboratory with 20 workstations.

The school is accredited in the United States through the Middle States Association of Colleges and Secondary Schools. AISJ is also a member of the Association for the Advancement of International Education (AAIE), the Association of International Schools in Africa (AISA), and is an IB World School.

AISJ is a pre-kindergarten through 12th grade coeducational school founded in 1982. Currently the school offers an American Diploma Program, the International Baccalaureate (IB) Diploma Programme and IB Certificate courses.

IB courses are taught over two years in grades 11 and 12. IB non-Diploma candidates can earn IB Certificates in each IB subject completed. Approximately one-half of the seniors and three quarters of the juniors are enrolled in the IB Diploma Programme. All IB courses are open to non-Diploma candidates and every graduating student has taken at least one IB course.

The pre-K – Grade 12 enrollment of 713 students represents 60 nationalities with the largest national group being American citizens (40% of total enrollment).

AISJ has an excellent faculty of 90 teachers (40 American, 25 South African, four Canadian and 21 others). Over one third hold master degrees and five hold doctoral degrees. Average class-size in the HS is 12. This allows for significant personal attention.

The school has active co-curricular and extracurricular programs. The Student Council represents the student body to the school administration.

Our service program involves students in a variety of AISJ and local South African service projects. We have an active National Honor Society (NHS) chapter. The school hosts an annual Model United Nations Conference (JOMUN) and also participates in MUN conferences in The Hague, Cairo and Russia.

There are also sponsored fine arts and foreign language trips to Europe. Varsity sports teams compete with local schools as well as international school leagues. Sports include soccer, volleyball, basketball, tennis, swimming and horseback riding.

American International School of Kuwait

The American International School of Kuwait opened 17 years ago when Kuwait was liberated after the Iraqi invasion. From its humble beginnings with only 300 students on opening day, the school has grown into an internationally recognized and fully authorized IB World School with more than 1500 students from the Middle East and around the world. AIS is a private independent day school serving students from pre-kindergarten through grade 12. It has an excellent academic reputation and provides a demanding and challenging environment for students, many of whom attend top universities around the world.

Almost one half of the student population at AIS is Kuwaiti. Another 25% are Arabic first-language speakers from elsewhere in the Middle East, and the remainder of the population comes from around the world. The ethnic diversity of the Middle East, layered with the complexity of an otherwise international student body provides a stimulating and endlessly fascinating environment in which we attempt to live the IB Learner Profile.

In sports, soccer is without doubt the favourite, but AIS students take part in a wide range of athletic and cultural activities through the Kuwait Schools Activities Association (KSAA) and the Eastern Mediterranean Activities Conference (EMAC) of which AIS is a full member. In addition, there is an active Model United Nations (MUN), through which our students travel annually for the international event in The Hague.

Facilities

The brick walled campus contains more than one hundred teaching spaces in three buildings that surround two interior courts. As part of the improvement plan put forth in 2003, there has been a massive refurbishment of the school's facilities. This includes the addition of new classrooms, music rooms, a 1200 seat theatre, strength training and aerobics rooms, a new indoor and outdoor gymnasium, as well as a soccer field on the roof.

Curriculum & accreditation

AIS was authorized by the International Baccalaureate Organization (IB) to offer the Diploma Programme in 1993. Since then, AIS has added the IB Middle Years Programme in 2006 and the Primary Years Programme in 2008. AIS is accredited to award American High School Certification by the Middle States Association of Colleges and Schools. In addition, it is a member of the Association for Advancement of International Education (AAIE) and of International School Services (ISS).

American School of Bombay

(Founded 1981)

Head of School
Dr Paul Fochtman

PYP coordinator
Khushnuma Ferzandi

Diploma coordinator
Dr Rob Allison

Status Private

Boarding/day Day

Gender Coeducational

Language of instruction
English

Programmes offered
PYP, Diploma

Age range of pupils 3-17

Number of pupils enrolled 680

Address
SF2, G-Block
Bandra Kurla Complex Road,
Bandra East
Mumbai
400 098 | INDIA

TEL +91 22 6772 7272
FAX +91 22 2652 1234

Email
asb@asbindia.org

Website
www.asbindia.org

The American School of Bombay (ASB) was founded as an independent, coeducational day school in 1981. The school offers an educational program from early childhood through grade 12 for approximately 680 students from over 43 nationalities. ASB serves the international and expatriate community of Mumbai and is recognized with full accreditation from the Middle States Association of Colleges and Secondary Schools, and The Commission on International and Trans-Regional Accreditation. ASB has been an IB World School since 1998 and is authorized to offer both the Primary Years and Diploma Programmes.

The school offers a college preparatory curriculum that awards graduates an American high school diploma and/or the International Baccalaureate Diploma and focuses on the development of the whole child. ASB challenges students to become lifelong learners pursuing their dreams while caring and sensitive to the needs of others. The school's curriculum is enhanced with a widely recognized laptop program where all students in grades 6 through 12 own a Tablet PC and gain technological fluency from the earliest years.

ASB offers a number of extracurricular learning opportunities including a comprehensive after-school activities program. All middle and high school students participate in a Week Without Walls program that is directly linked with the curriculum. ASB is a member of the South Asia Inter-School Association athletic conference, which provides student athletes the opportunity to compete in sports with other international schools. Students also participate in Model United Nations, International Schools Theater Association, and international choral and instrumental concerts.

The school is housed in a specially designed campus in Mumbai. The school facility includes well-equipped classrooms, wireless laptop access, premier industry standard science labs, a multipurpose gymnasium, two libraries, cafeteria, heated swimming pools, climbing wall, and playground area. The outdoor sports ground includes a running track, soccer field, basketball, and tennis courts.

ASB graduates have been accepted at the world's finest colleges and universities, including Amherst College, Harvard University, Boston University, Columbia University, John Hopkins University, Princeton University, Purdue University, and University of Paris and have gone on to contribute personally and professionally across a diversity of fields.

AMERICAN SCHOOL OF THE HAGUE

Director
Dr Richard Spradling

Diploma coordinator
Victor Ferreira

Status Private

Boarding/day Day

Gender Coeducational

Language of instruction
English

Programmes offered Diploma

Age range of pupils 4-18

Number of pupils enrolled 1100

Fees per annum €15,625-18,500

Address
Rijksstraatweg 200
2241BX Wassenaar |
NETHERLANDS

TEL +31 70 512 1080

FAX +31 70 51 12400

Email
admissions@ash.nl

Website
www.ash.nl

The American School of The Hague (ASH) serves the educational needs of the American and international corporate and diplomatic communities in the Netherlands. ASH's 1000 students, ages four to 18, represent over 60 cultures; half are from North America. While ASH reflects the American educational philosophy, the diverse backgrounds of the students foster teaching and learning in the context of international understanding and global citizenship. ASH is a school with a rigorous academic program. The high school curriculum emphasizes preparation for university studies in all countries of the world. All graduates earn a US high school diploma. Students are given the opportunity to choose the IB Diploma Programme, or combine IB courses with AP or regular curriculum subjects to earn IB certificates in subject specialties. IB offerings at ASH are given across the curriculum at both standard and higher levels. A variety of IB language courses, including mother tongue tutorials, are offered. Students at ASH who choose the IB Diploma Programme enjoy a 95% or higher success rate, and ASH posts scores higher than the world average.

In addition ASH students move with confidence to new schools throughout the world, and more than 98% of each graduating class enters university. The academic program includes a wide range of fine and applied arts courses, with a curriculum that is technologically competitive throughout the disciplines. A full sports program and extracurricular activities are an important part of student life. The Hague International Model United Nations, a major event for many ASH High School students, is sponsored by the school each January for more than 3000 international participants. The arts program offers individual and group instruction and performance opportunities in vocal and instrumental music, and the ASH Jazz Band is well known throughout Europe. Athletic teams in ten sports travel throughout Europe competing with other international schools. The 11-acre campus has spacious classrooms, specialized teaching areas, and multiple science and multi-media labs. The grounds include outdoor sports areas for all age groups, including soccer and baseball fields.

Amman Baccalaureate School

(Founded 1981)

Principal
Dr Samia Al Farra

MYP coordinator
Iman Awad

Diploma coordinator
Cathy Souob

Status Private

Boarding/day Day

Gender Coeducational

Language of instruction
English, Arabic

Programmes offered
MYP, Diploma

Age range of pupils 4-18

Number of pupils enrolled 961

Address
PO Box 441
Sweileh 11910
Amman | JORDAN

TEL +962 6 541 1572/1191

FAX +962 6 5412603

Email
proffice@abs.edu.jo

Website
www.abs.edu.jo

The Amman Baccalaureate School (ABS) is a private, fee-paying day school, licensed by the Jordanian Ministry of Education. It is coeducational and prepares its students for the International Baccalaureate Diploma and Certificates as school leaving qualifications. In addition to providing an academic education of high quality, the school attaches considerable importance to creative, physical and community service activities, and offers a wide and developing range of facilities and opportunities in these areas.

ABS was founded in 1981 with the aim of providing a bilingual education which would meet, in quality and breadth, the highest international standards, whilst remaining firmly rooted in the Arab heritage. At the same time, the school has increasingly attracted students from the international community who wish to take advantage of the opportunity offered in the Middle Years School (MYP) and IB Diploma College (Diploma Programme) to pursue an education in English which, nonetheless, sustains close contact with the culture of the host country.

The Amman Baccalaureate School is a school where modern educational theory and practice are implemented and enthusiastically embraced. In its officially recognized role as a 'pioneer school', ABS pilots new materials, methods and approaches, and so paves the way for other schools to follow. Emphasis on bilingualism at every stage promotes knowledge of different cultures, traditions and values, and this fosters openness, understanding and tolerance.

Involvement with each and every student as an individual is a guiding principle at ABS. The high proportion of teachers to students (1:7) allows this principle to be a reality. This compares very favorably with institutions of similar academic standing, both nationally and internationally.

From its modest beginnings in rented premises with 100 pupils, it now has about 961 students and its own purpose-built campus, with a strong staff, a wide and varied curriculum and impressive technical, sporting and educational resources.

ABS is accredited by the Council of International Schools (CIS) and the New England Association of Schools and Colleges (NEASC).

Amsterdam International Community School

(Founded 2003)

Principal
Kees van Ruitenbeek

Diploma coordinator
Elizabeth Ann Young

Status State

Boarding/day Day

Gender Coeducational

Language of instruction
English

Programmes offered Diploma

Age range of pupils 4-19

Number of pupils enrolled 382

Fees per annum €3800-€5800

Address
Prinses Irenestraat 59
1077 WV Amsterdam |
NETHERLANDS

TEL +31 20 577 1240

FAX +31 20 577 1249

Email
info@aics.eu

Website
www.aics.eu

In September 2003, the Amsterdam International Community School opened its doors for the first time. Today, we have over 380 students and together our students and staff come from more than 40 countries around the world. The AICS is subsidised by the Dutch Government and this enables us to offer a low-cost alternative while maintaining the high quality of the education we provide.

The AICS offers international education for four to 19 year olds by using internationally recognised curricula (International Primary Curriculum, IB Middle Years Programme (candidate status) and the IB Diploma Programme). We facilitate community based, international learning for students of all nationalities, abilities and socio-economic backgrounds.

The school strongly believes in being part of the community. From an educational point of view, this makes the children's learning 'real' and relevant. We encourage all our students and parents to embrace the Dutch living experience. All students receive four Dutch language and culture lessons each week, as we feel it is important for them to have opportunities to integrate with other Dutch children. Our students participate in swimming lessons, sports days, museum visits and ice-skating along with other Dutch schools. For our secondary school students, we also offer an established Community and Service Programme.

Non-native speakers receive extra English language lessons (EAL), and we also offer an English immersion programme (ELIP). We have a Student Support Department for special educational needs and learning support, a School Counsellor and a Career Counsellor.

Our primary students participate in various after-school clubs including the Art Club, Animation Club and Music Club. For our secondary students we offer Science Club, Electronic Learning Environment Club, volleyball, basketball, School Yearbook Committee and The Hague International Model United Nations.

We are associated with a day-care centre on the premises which also offers before and after-school care.

The AICS is located in a quiet residential area of Amsterdam and is within five minutes of all public transport facilities (train, tram, metro and bus).

The AICS doesn't just offer education – we offer worthwhile experiences.

Ardingly College

(Founded 1858)

Headmaster
Mr Peter Green

Diploma coordinator
John Langford

Status Private

Boarding/day Mixed

Gender Coeducational

Language of instruction
English

Programmes offered Diploma

Age range of pupils 13-18

Fees per annum
Day: £17,700;
Boarding: £22,800-£23,400

Address
College Road
Ardingly
Haywards Heath
West Sussex
RH17 6SQ | UK

TEL +44 (0)1444 893000

FAX +44 (0)1444 893001

Email
registrar@ardingly.com

Website
www.ardingly.com

Ardingly College is an independent, coeducational boarding school located on almost three hundred acres of delightful Sussex countryside. Just 20 minutes from Gatwick airport and 45 minutes by train to London, it is ideally placed to offer a first class education. Essentially a traditional English boarding school, Ardingly has the added benefit of a strong international perspective, with 20% of the students coming from Europe, Africa, Asia, Australia or America.

The school's primary focus is on individual students, who are helped to fit in quickly and make friendships that may well last a lifetime. Class sizes are small, the range of activities and opportunities on offer is quite extraordinary and the atmosphere is friendly and caring.

Curriculum

The senior school of Ardingly College has 470 students ranging from 13 to 18 years of age. Students prepare for the English GCSE exams at age 16 (Year 11) and then choose between the IB Diploma Programme and A levels in the sixth form. Currently, the courses are evenly split, with approximately 50 students in the lower sixth form taking on either the IB or A levels each year. Class sizes are small and although the maximum for IB classes is 15, actual class sizes tend to range from eight to 12.

Our IB results are outstanding, and recently one of our students was the top IB Diploma student in England and fourth outright worldwide. Consistently good results are achieved by all of our students, who then go on to the top universities in the UK, the USA, Europe or Australia. A full range of IB subjects is offered while the languages available are Latin, French, German and Spanish.

As well as an outstanding range of activities including music, art, drama, sailing, CCF and games, the school also offers an innovative choice of community service projects for the CAS component of the IB, including a fortnight spent teaching young African children in The Gambia.

Entry requirements

Intake is for September each year and tests and interviews are held throughout the year for those students wishing to enter the school at all levels.

Entry into the IB Diploma Programme is by GCSE results (currently at least six B grades or better) or by our own entrance examination, along with school reports and interview. A Pre-IB programme is also offered for overseas students, usually for one year before they would normally start the main IB Diploma Programme.

There are two scholarships worth up to 50% remission of fees available each year for outstanding applicants, with testing taking place in February or March each year.

Further details of Ardingly College can be obtained from the school website or by phoning the Registrar, who will be happy to provide a prospectus and arrange a visit.

Ardingly College is a Registered Charity (No. 1076456) to promote and extend education in accordance with the principles of the Woodard Corporation.

Australian International Academy

(Founded 1983)

Head of the Academy
Mr Salah Salman

PYP coordinator
Mrs Leyla Mohamoud

MYP coordinator
Mrs Gafiah Dickinson

Diploma coordinator
Mrs Maha Elsayegh

Status Private

Boarding/day Day

Gender Coeducational

Language of instruction
English

Programmes offered
PYP, MYP, Diploma

Age range of pupils 4-18

Number of pupils enrolled
2370

Fees per annum Local students:
AUS$3125-7935; International
students: AUS$10,000-16,000

Address
56 Bakers Road
North Coburg
VIC 3058 | AUSTRALIA

TEL +61 3 9350 4533
FAX +61 3 9354 4731

Email
aia@aia.vic.edu.au

Website
www.aia.vic.edu.au

Academy Vision Statement

The Academy offers a broad and well-balanced curriculum with global perspectives to students in primary, secondary and post compulsory levels. The Academy offers the IB Primary and Middle Years Programmes to students from prep to Year 10. In the senior years the Academy offers the Victorian Certificate of Education, High School Certificate, and IB Diploma Programme. AIA is committed to academic success and is open for all denominations.

Academy Profile

The Australian International Academy is a diverse, international and multicultural school with a total of approximately 2400 students from prep to Year 12 on four campuses: Melbourne Senior Campus, King Khalid Coburg Campus, Sydney Campus, and Australian School of Abu Dhabi-UAE Campus.

The Academy population has a wide range of students from different ethnic backgrounds consisting of local and international students.

Academic, Spiritual and Moral Development Aim

To provide students with the education that will inculcate in them moral values while providing a quality secular education that will equip them for life in Australia and overseas. The academy aims at the development of the whole person, intellectually, spiritually, socially and physically and the development of individual talents and abilities.

Social Aim

To develop in all students the acquisition of social skills that will enable them to function effectively and harmoniously in Australia's multi-cultural and multi-faith society.

Cultural Aim

- To develop a realisation that different cultures make up our society and accept others, whilst encouraging the development of pride in being Australian citizens.
- Whilst retaining pride in the child's own faith, to develop pride in being Australian and an ability to adapt and fit within any cultural context.

Co-curricular Programme

AIA provides a wide range of co-curricular activities that extend and complement the academic programme, enrich students' lives, and develop their skills. Such activities include interfaith and intercultural programmes, environmental projects, sport, camps, outdoor educations, debating, oration, competitions, chess, school productions and publications, leadership training, community and service.

Grupo Alexander Bain

Head José Francisco Uribe Gaudry, MYP, DP
Bachillerato Alexander Bain (ages 12-18)
Las Flores 497, Tlacopac +(52 55)5683 2911

Head Ana María Palacios Boix, PYP, MYP
Colegio Alexander Bain (ages three to 12)
Barranca de Pilares 29, Tlacopac +(52 55)5595 0493

Head Lourdes Córdoba de Aburto, PYP, MYP
Escuela Alexander Bain (ages three to 12)
Barranca de Pilares 4, Tlacopac +(52 55)5683 3255

Head Ofelia Arriaga de Nájera, PYP, MYP
Instituto Alexander Bain (ages three to 12)
Cascada 320, Jardines del Pedregal +(52 55)5595 6579

Status
Private

Gender
Coeducational

Language of instruction
Spanish, English, French

PYP Coordinator
Teresa Yáñez Clavel
tyanez@alexanderbain.edu.mx

MYP Coordinator
Gloria E. Prian Arroyo
gloria.prian@alexander-bain.edu.mx

Diploma Coordinator
Adriana Rodríguez Reyes
adriana.rodriguez@alexander-bain.edu.mx

Website
www.alexander-bain.edu.mx

Founded 50 years ago, Alexander Bain schools have always been ahead of their time in Mexico. Since then, we have offered bilingual coeducation in a friendly environment where each student counts as an individual, our main goal being to strengthen his or her abilities.

Located in the affluent residential southern part of Mexico City, our schools house 2500 students in four campuses which fulfill different age needs.

Alexander Bain programs are accredited by the Mexican Ministry of Public Education, Secretaría de Educación Pública (SEP) and Universidad Nacional Autónoma de México (UNAM). Alexander Bain is also an IB World School authorized by the International Baccalaureate to provide the IB Primary, Middle Years, and Diploma Programmes. Alexander Bain welcomes families of all faiths and cultures. We value expressing different points of view.

An extensive attitudes program, involving staff, students and their families, provides support and develops meaningful relationships within our school community. We aim to make sure that all of its members actions and attitudes reflect the IB learner profile. We provide a self-learning environment where inquiry leads to develop critical thinking skills. Students understand themselves and their teachers as learners.

Our high school is careful that our students are prepared for university studies in Mexico, United States and around the world. Alumni have attended prestigious universities such as Yale University, Massachusetts Institute of Technology (MIT), New York University (NYU), Harvard University, Stanford University, Columbia University, La Sorbonne in Paris, among others.

Our staff meets the highest national accreditations and participates in an ongoing teachers development program that includes IB training, as well as training from Mexico's most renowned universities and educational institutions. ESL teachers are currently engaging in an online program 'Teaching for Understanding' offered by Harvard University. Collaborative teacher planning leads to building understanding and stresses the importance of breadth and depth of answers to inquiry.

Facilities include swimming pools for preschool and elementary school, and several courts for different sports activities. The middle and high schools have access to a spinning gym and a fitness program. The Alexander Bain Group hosts an athletic meet with other schools in Mexico City and has been proud to produce olympic athletes. We also have science laboratories, art workshops, an auditorium, and wired libraries.

Our curricula is complemented by extracurricular activities including athletic meets, performing arts, visual arts and a chess club. After school activities are considered as the time when children discover or develop new abilities that go beyond the academics. These activities are available for all ages. We have choirs that give presentations throughout the year. Our Christmas and spring concerts are a tradition where parents, students, staff and grandparents from all our campuses are invited to participate. We also host a dance festival where junior and high school students in Mexico City participate in different categories. Chinese (Mandarin) is being offered as an optional subject after school. Students that study Chinese throughout their stay at the Alexander Bain will become fluent speakers of a fourth language.

Students are also engaged in national and international camps and trips which encourage young people to be independent, committed, confident, open minded and unique. Every year each grade has the opportunity of traveling within our country.

Every trip relates to one of the units of inquiry from our program. Some groups may visit archaeological or historic sites while others may set up a biology lab on the beach to study the ecosystem. International trips are an opportunity to practice second and third languages taught in school and to develop international-mindeness. Some international trips include attending another IB World School abroad.

We encourage through action, service to both local communities and national NGOs, fulfilling individual potential and recognizing individual responsibilities as global citizens. Each grade has a special assignment whose purpose is contributing to improve our community. Helping others will encourage our students to become better persons who will influence their surroundings positively.

Alexander Bain's high school students participate yearly in the Latinamerican InterCAS project. Students and teachers from Latin American IB World Schools come together to benefit a needy community. Last year this event took place in Mexico, and our students hosted, in their own homes, participants and their families from Peru and Argentina.

Barton Court Grammar School

Headteacher
Dr Stephen Manning

Diploma coordinator
Moira Driscoll

Status State

Boarding/day Day

Gender Coeducational

Language of instruction
English

Programmes offered Diploma

Address
Longport
Canterbury
Kent
CT1 1PH | UK

TEL +44 (0)1227 464600

FAX +44 (0)1227 781399

Email
office@bartoncourt.org

Website
www.bartoncourt.org

Barton Court is stunningly situated in the centre of the world famous historical city of Canterbury. Its beautiful buildings and leafy grounds are next to the World Heritage Site of St Augustine's Abbey and within sight of the cathedral. As well as the amazing sense of history throughout the city, Canterbury is a vibrant modern place of learning, with two universities and a renowned art college. In relation to its relatively small size, the city accommodates more university students than any other city in the world. Foreign students who come to Barton Court receive help in finding accommodation. We are a non-fee paying school for EU students.

Canterbury is 60 miles from London and is well served by the M2 and M20 with easy access to the Port of Dover, the Channel Tunnel and Gatwick, Heathrow and Stansted airports plus two railway links.

Barton Court has approximately 1000 students from a wide variety of backgrounds, over 250 of whom are in the sixth form. Our students sit GCSEs in Year 11 with over 98% gaining five plus A*-C grades. We are among the most successful at sixth form level in the county of Kent.

We have many outstanding facilities including a brand new IB Diploma centre, an amazing new two tier library and a new sports hall will be completed in the spring 2009.

As we have moved totally over to the International Baccalaureate Diploma Programme, we are able to offer the full range of Diploma Programme subjects. 39 of our staff have been trained in IB methodology and subject specifications. We are totally committed to the IB.

Entrance requirements are an average of seven GCSEs at B grade or equivalent. If you are interested in attending Barton Court please contact us for more information or look at our website for the IB Diploma Programme prospectus and application form.

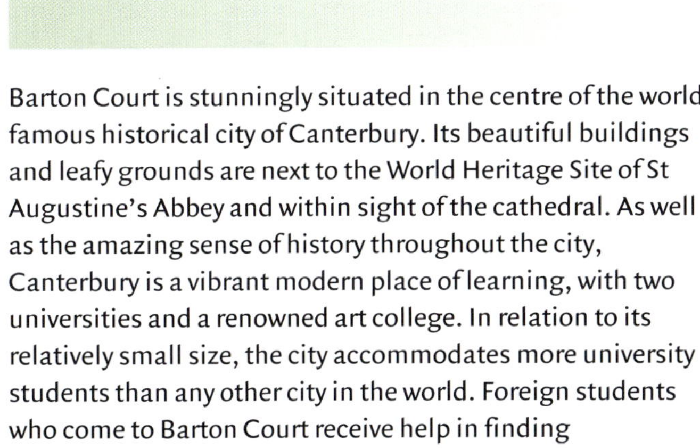

Bavarian International School e.V.

(Founded 1990)

Director
Bryan Nixon

PYP coordinator
Angela Hoelzl

Diploma coordinator
Siegfried Joseph

Status Private

Boarding/day Day

Gender Coeducational

Language of instruction
English

Programmes offered
PYP, Diploma

Age range of pupils 4-18

Address
Schloss Haimhausen
Hauptstrasse 1
Haimhausen
D-85778 | GERMANY

TEL +49 8133 917111
FAX +49 8133 917115

Email
director@bis-school.com

Website
www.bis-school.com

The Bavarian International School was established in 1990 to offer an English language education to children from the international community in the north of Munich.

Set in a green and peaceful park-like environment, the impressive and historic mansion known as Schloss Haimhausen houses upper school classrooms and offices. Adjacent modern, purpose-built buildings house middle and lower school classrooms. Science laboratories, music rooms, libraries, computer suites, a sports hall (with adjoining track and field complex) cafeterias and a Performing Arts Centre enhance the facility, which opens onto a vista of field and forest.

The lower school, which includes pre-reception to Grade 5, is authorized to offer the IB Primary Years Programme. Maximum class sizes in lower school range from 20 in pre-reception to 24 in reception to Grade 5. Maximum class size for both the middle school (grades 6-8) and the upper school (grades 9-12) is also 24 students.

BIS has been authorized to offer the IB Diploma Programme since 1995. The school strongly encourages and supports all upper school students who possess the necessary aptitude and motivation to complete the requirements of the IB Diploma Programme in Grades 11-12.

The school's current enrolment of 750 students represents over 40 nationalities, with approximately 40 students in each graduating class since 2005. Over 95% of all BIS graduates go on to continue their education at leading colleges and universities around the world.

The 78 full time teachers at BIS come from 14 different nations. All are university graduates, and on average they have ten years of teaching experience. 18 of them hold a Master's degree, and one a Doctorate. Teachers are offered regular professional development opportunities in Germany and abroad, to support them in their ongoing quest for excellence.

The BIS mission is to 'inspire young minds and challenge young individuals to achieve their intellectual and personal potential within a caring international environment'. This mission informs all choices made by the school, and unites students, parents, teachers and administrators into a community of learners.

BBIS Berlin Brandenburg International School GmbH

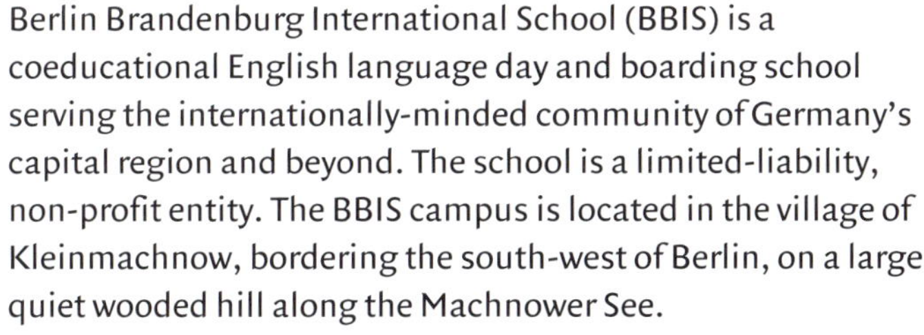

(Founded 1990)

Head of School
Thomas Schaedler

PYP coordinator
Lisa Roy

MYP coordinator
Michaela Jung

Diploma coordinator
Karin Schnoor

Status Private

Boarding/day Both

Gender Coeducational

Language of instruction
English

Programmes offered
PYP, MYP, Diploma

Age range of pupils 3-19

Number of pupils enrolled 650

Fees per annum
Day: €8,700-€13,800;
Boarding: + €16,200

Address
Am Hochwald 30
14532 Kleinmachnow |
GERMANY

TEL +49 33203 8036 0
FAX +49 33203 8036 121

Email
office@bbis.de

Website
www.bbis.de

Berlin Brandenburg International School (BBIS) is a coeducational English language day and boarding school serving the internationally-minded community of Germany's capital region and beyond. The school is a limited-liability, non-profit entity. The BBIS campus is located in the village of Kleinmachnow, bordering the south-west of Berlin, on a large, quiet wooded hill along the Machnower See.

Founded in 1990, BBIS is fully authorized by the International Baccalaureate (IB) organization in Geneva, Switzerland, to offer all three IB Programmes covering the three to 19 age range. The school is also fully accredited by the Council of International Schools (CIS) and the Middle States Association of Colleges and Schools (MSA).

From Early Childhood to grade 12, BBIS is truly an international school, with about 650 students representing 50 different nationalities. In grades 11 and 12 students have the opportunity to earn the IB Diploma, a qualification recognized by top universities throughout the world, or a BBIS High School Diploma. BBIS teachers are certified, experienced professionals from all over the world, but mostly from the United States of America, the United Kingdom, and Germany.

BBIS offers excellent facilities and an extensive extracurricular programme for students of all ages. Classes are small, usually with fewer than 18 students, enabling teachers to know each student well and address his or her individual needs. In addition, specific support is provided for students with special needs and those for whom English is not a first language.

The BBIS Boarding School, located in Potsdam-Babelsberg about 20 minutes from the campus, houses international BBIS students from grades 6 through 12. Young people come together from all over the world who are determined to nurture their own strong minds, bodies, and spirits, and to further international understanding and tolerance. In the heart of Europe, BBIS boarding students learn many different languages with a special focus on English and German. Through this unique living and learning opportunity, the BBIS Boarding School encourages its students to widen their perspectives and prepare for future challenges in today's dynamically growing global society.

Beaumont School (BeauSandVer)

(Founded 1938)

Head of School
Elizabeth Hitch

Diploma coordinator
Morag McCrorie

Status State

Boarding/day Day

Gender Coeducational

Language of instruction
English

Programmes offered Diploma

Address
Oakwood Drive
St Albans
Hertfordshire
AL4 0XB | UK

TEL +44 (0)1727 854 726
FAX +44 (0)1727 847 971

Email
morag.mccrorie@beaumont.
herts.sch.uk

Website
www.beaumont.herts.sch.uk

Beaumont is part of the BeauSandVer consortium of three successful schools situated in St Albans just north of London. The consortium is made up of two mixed 11-18 schools (Sandringham and Beaumont) and one 11-18 boys school with a coeducational sixth form (Verulam). We are non-selective state schools with a proven track record of delivering high quality education to all students. The majority of our sixth form students go on to good quality universities including Oxbridge.

IB students are taught in small classes which enable a tutorial style of learning tailored to individual needs. Students have a personal tutor who oversees their progress and provides academic mentoring. The school has excellent facilities including new computer suites, well-stocked libraries, drama studios, a sports hall and extensive playing fields.

We are committed to the development of the whole person and have well-established links with groups in the UK and overseas, who work with us in our CAS programme. Curriculum enrichment is a central tenet of our ethos with students being offered trips to galleries, museums and theatres, exchange visits with partner schools abroad, work experience at home and overseas, as well as expeditions to countries as diverse as Belize, Iceland, Lesotho, Burkina Faso

and China. Students can also choose to get involved in our many school based groups for music and sport amongst others.

Most of our students live locally but some commute from London via excellent communication links with the capital. The entry requirement for the IB Diploma Programme is an average GCSE point score of at least 43 (or similar).

Our IB Diploma subjects include English, French, German, Spanish (including *ab initio*), economics, geography, history, philosophy, psychology, biology, chemistry, physics, maths, computing science, visual arts, drama and music. These are offered at both higher and standard levels. Next year will see the introduction of other subjects.

You will be highly motivated through well-prepared lessons taught by well-qualified staff. You will expect to go on to study at university in Britain or anywhere in the world, in the knowledge that you have high academic ability, you are a well-rounded, articulate young person with a sound understanding of the international community.

For more information please contact us via our own website www.beaumont.herts.sch.uk or our consortium website www.beausandver.org.uk

Bedford High School for Girls

(Founded 1882)

Headmistress
Mrs Julie Eldridge

Diploma coordinator
Philip Herrick

Status Private

Boarding/day Mixed

Gender Female

Language of instruction
English

Programmes offered Diploma

Age range of pupils 7-18

Number of pupils enrolled 800

Fees per annum
Day: £7524-£10,611;
Boarding: £19,884

Address
Bromham Road
Bedford
Bedfordshire
MK40 2BS | UK

TEL +44 (0)1234 360221

FAX +44 (0)1234 353552

Email
admissions@bedfordhigh.co.uk

Website
www.bedfordhigh.co.uk

At Bedford High School for Girls academic excellence and happy pupils are equally important goals. By providing a supportive and caring environment, every girl is able to develop her talents, achieve her potential and leave us as a confident young woman ready to take her place in society.

Opportunities abound throughout the school, whether in the range of musical, sporting, dramatic or extracurricular activities on offer. Bedford High School for Girls was recently placed eighth in the *Financial Times' Top IB Schools* ranking.

If your daughter joins us for our sixth form, she will find it is quite different from her earlier time at school. She will have more independence, which brings greater personal responsibility for managing her time and undertaking independent study. Girls in the sixth form also play a significant role in the School Council and are expected to take greater responsibility for the day-to-day running of the school.

The sixth form have their own centre, Watkins House, where there is a bright and lively culture. There are a number of common rooms, and a kitchen, where the atmosphere is more relaxed and where your daughter will form many friendships while also developing a degree of independence. The house also has quiet areas available for private study.

The sixth form also play a significant role in supporting the life of the school and regularly show visitors around, help with activities for younger girls and take on roles of leadership and responsibility. The sixth form elect their team of School Officers from whom a Head Girl and three deputies help to coordinate activities for the year groups, including the organisation of the Leavers' Ball which is held annually at the end of the upper sixth examination period.

We will continue to encourage your daughter to enrich her experience during her time with us through her ongoing participation in extracurricular activities. Subject-based societies are also a key feature of the sixth form, and a significant aid to learning through practice and discussion.

Binus School Simprug

(Founded 1998)

Head of School
Peter Matthew Saidi

PYP coordinator
Richel Langit-Dursin

MYP coordinator
Tommy Mangoendaan

Diploma coordinator
Erdolfo L Lardizabal

Status Private

Boarding/day Day

Gender Coeducational

Language of instruction
English

Programmes offered
PYP, MYP, Diploma

Number of pupils enrolled 1200

Address
Jl Sultan Iskandar
Muda Kav G-8, Simprug
Jakarta Selatan
12220 | INDONESIA

TEL +62-21-724-3663
FAX +62-21-7278-3939

Email
psaidi@binus.edu

Website
www.binus-school.net

BINUS SCHOOL Simprug is a coeducational, multi-denominational day school catering for the early years to high school age groups.

Teaching at BINUS SCHOOL Simprug is about inspiring one another to achieve personal bests. We are committed to the pursuit of academic excellence. At the same time, learning is more than just the academic knowledge and skills. It is about building hearts as well as minds. We place great focus on student commitment and character – what we call 'fighting spirit'. All lessons across the school inspire students towards desirable lifelong work habits and the school-wide values of being respectful, ready and responsible.

Teaching and assessment strategies are planned and delivered so that we nurture leaders who are creative, self-confident and principled. Our strategic alliances with the best schools in other countries help develop the cultural intelligence of our students, preparing them to be global citizens ready to make important contributions to the world around them.

Our commitment to being a world-class community means that we benchmark using international curriculums, international competitions, worldwide examinations, and world-class enterprises.

We became an authorized International Baccalaureate (IB) World School in October 2006. We are also proud to offer, under one roof, all of the three internationally-recognised and world-renowned IB Programmes: Primary Years (PYP), Middle Years (MYP) and Diploma (DP).

Supported by highly qualified, experienced and professional expatriate and local teaching staff, BINUS SCHOOL Simprug provides international standard teaching and learning facilities, large and bright classrooms, science laboratories, technology laboratories, learning centres, indoor sports centres, music studios, a visual and performing arts centre, and student support services.

These programmes and facilities are provided to enable each child to develop intellectually, socially, culturally, emotionally, physically and spiritually as a reflection of BINUS SCHOOL Simprug's commitment to the pursuit of proud and outstanding achievements.

Blackfriars Priory School

Head of School
Brian Turner

PYP coordinator
John Niedzwiecki

Status Private

Boarding/day Day

Gender Male

Language of instruction
English

Programmes offered PYP

Address
17 Prospect Road
Prospect
SA 5082 | AUSTRALIA

TEL +61 (0) 8 8269 6333
FAX +61 (0) 8 8269 7846

Email
jniedzwiecki@bps.sa.edu.au

Website
www.bps.sa.edu.au

Blackfriars Priory School is a Catholic Dominican school for boys from Reception through to Year 12 which promotes the spiritual, intellectual, physical and social development of each member of the school community.

The dynamic International Baccalaureate Primary Years Programme at Blackfriars is aligned with the South Australian Curriculum Standards and Accountability Framework. With literacy and numeracy considered to be of prime importance, we challenge students to ask important questions, conduct in-depth research, analyse findings, report in a variety of ways and reflect on their responsibility as global citizens. We seek to develop higher order thinking skills, positive attitudes toward learning and an active sense of compassion.

Boys have particular learning styles. Blackfriars' teachers design differentiated learning tasks that meet these needs, employing kinaesthetic learning experiences and 'visual' learning opportunities. Being on a shared campus, our primary students have regular access to facilities such as extensive playing fields, gymnasium, music suite, two libraries and scientific laboratories. All classrooms are also equipped with interactive whiteboards and students have ready access to computer suites and classroom stations. A structured co-curricular program gives our students the opportunity to engage in a wide variety of physical activities and musical pursuits.

The care and well being of every boy is more than a responsibility at Blackfriars, it is central to our mission as a school. In the primary years the nurture ethic lies at the core of classroom relationships. It is promoted by teachers, expected of boys and is a living reality. Daily reflection, prayer, liturgies and the sacramental program are central to our mission. Compassionate values are further developed in social service programs such as the International Dominican Missions Project, Global Connections Program, Moore Street Day Centre Soup Kitchen Support Project and the St Vincent de Paul Winter and Christmas Appeals.

The school strives to highlight the importance of the search for truth or *Veritas*, the Dominican motto, which promotes a view of knowledge that has its origin and intent centred in the search for God in our daily lives. A search that is shared within the 40 or so nationalities and 17 religious traditions that makes up the Blackfriars Priory School Community.

Bladins International School

(Founded 1987)

Principal
Niklas Anderberg

PYP coordinator
Ingrid Hortin

MYP coordinator
Debbie Thoresson

Status Private

Boarding/day Day

Gender Coeducational

Language of instruction
English

Programmes offered
PYP, MYP

Age range of pupils 3-16

Number of pupils enrolled 256

Fees per annum Please contact
the school for information

Address
Box 20093
S-200 74 Malmö | SWEDEN

TEL +46 40 300885
FAX +46 40 910885

Email
sandra@bladins.se

Website
www.bladins.se

Bladins school is a unique independent school with a strong tradition of empowering students to reach their full potential as responsible people in today's and tomorrow's world. Its family oriented community nurtures a sense of community with mutual respect. The school's competent and caring staff works in partnership with parents to enrich the learning experience for all students in a secure and inspiring environment.

At Bladins emphasis is placed on fully developing the students' intellectual, aesthetic, emotional, physical and moral potential and, as a school, serve as an example of educational excellence. By having a comprehensive view of the students, Bladins creates long-term and trusting relationships with students, parents and staff.

As responsible individuals in society, Bladins students respect the value of others and have personal values, self-understanding and positive self-image, ethical attitudes toward work and social relations, sound decision-making skills, think and act critically, creatively and independently; leading to a positive and healthy lifestyle. Students learn how to learn, discover the joy of learning, develop the capacity to solve problems independently and in co-operation with others and acquire knowledge and sensitive awareness of universal ethical and moral issues.

Bladins school is run as a foundation governed by a board composed of parents. Key members of management and teachers attend board meetings allowing full benefit and broad representation of the parties' needs. The school encourages parent involvement in support of their children's education through involvement in classroom activities, the Parents' Association and the Board.

Bladins has a Swedish section which is one of the oldest private schools in Sweden. Located on the same campus, the International School benefits from direct exposure to Swedish culture and cross-curricular courses and programmes. The school is fully recognized by the Swedish Department of Education and receives both national and local grants.

Curriculum

Committed to the continued development of the IB the school offers high quality education through the PYP and MYP. In this way Bladins prepares students for the demands of higher education and of life. Our graduates have gone on to attend universities worldwide including Yale in USA; and London, Cambridge and Oxford in the UK.

Bladins extended curriculum includes courses in health, research report writing and life experiences; a course intended to give older students an insight into adult life through hearing speakers' own experiences of the world of work and leisure. Students from MYP2 to MYP5 join with the equivalent Swedish classes for one session per week of integrated electives where they elect to take practical and creative courses together, communicating in both English and Swedish, thus fostering the aim of intercultural awareness. All students develop ICT skills through integration into the curriculum and as separate courses. For non-native English students, Bladins offers English as an Additional Language (EAL). Swedish courses are required from PYP1; foreign language courses begin in MYP1. Our special needs department takes extra care of students with a range of learning difficulties including dyslexia.

Branksome Hall

BRANKSOME HALL

(Founded 1903)

Head of School
Karen Murton

PYP coordinator
Anne Beveridge

MYP coordinator
Heather Friesen

Diploma coordinator
David Mindorff

Status Independent

Boarding/day Mixed

Gender Female

Language of instruction
English

Programmes offered
PYP, MYP, Diploma

Number of pupils enrolled 875

Fees per annum C$24,000

Address
10 Elm Avenue
Toronto ON
M4W 1N4 | CANADA

TEL +1 416 920 9741
FAX +1 416 920 5390

Email
kmurton@branksome.on.ca

Website
www.branksome.on.ca

From Junior Kindergarten to IB2 (Grade 12), the girls and young women of Branksome Hall are passionate, powerful learners and leaders. Ours is a community of inquirers; of knowledgeable, principled students and skilled, caring teachers. Graduates proceed to esteemed universities worldwide, the great majority as scholarship recipients.

An IB World School, Branksome is committed to a liberal arts curriculum that emphasizes critical thinking and values diverse perspectives. We offer boarding to students from Grade 8 to IB2 (Grade 12), who are supervised in small groups by residence dons, with a varied and enriching weekend program that explores Toronto's social and cultural scene.

All students benefit from academic and social support at every level, and balance classroom life with a broad selection of clubs and societies, and athletic, artistic and leadership development activities. Our international and local community service projects engage every student and are praised as a model for schools across the province and the country.

Above all, we are a welcoming community, grounded in 105 years of tradition, and actively supported by alumnae across the globe. Branksome encourages our students to become women of confidence and compassion, ready to shape their futures in our ever-changing world.

Brighton Primary School

An Internationally Accredited School

(Founded 1875)

Head of School
Gordon Pratt

PYP coordinator
Patrice Shadbolt

Status State

Boarding/day Day

Gender Coeducational

Language of instruction
English

Programmes offered PYP

Age range of pupils 5-12

Number of pupils enrolled 740

Address
Wilson Street
Brighton
Victoria
3186 | AUSTRALIA

TEL +61 39592 0177
FAX +61 39593 1642

Email
brighton.ps@brighton.vic.edu.au

Website
www.brighton.vic.edu.au

Brighton Primary School has been serving the educational needs of our community for over 130 years and is acknowledged for its dedicated teachers, progressive curriculum, excellent facilities and bright students.

As an authorized IB World School and accredited by the Council of International Schools together with its excellent facilities and progressive curriculum, Brighton Primary School is recogised as one of the foremost of its type in the State of Victoria. The dedicated staff continue to ensure the maintenance of high standards for the benefit of the learning community.

Our differentiated curriculum provides a challenging and engaging program which enables students to reach their potential and develop lifelong learning skills. Recognising that each child has the potential to exceed expectations, students are encouraged to question, to think independently and to be receptive to new and different views. They are guided not only to learn but to apply what they have learned. The IB

PYP curriculum is both engaging and relevant and enables our school to foster a love of learning as a solid platform for our students' present and future development.

A contributing factor to the progressive curriculum is the provision of excellent resources to maximise individual and group learning outcomes. These include:

Networked digital technology in all teaching spaces including interactive whiteboards, purpose built centres for music, art, science and technology, sport and library.

In addition, the school is located in extensive and versatile grounds. These provide our students with a safe and pleasant environment in which to explore and enjoy outdoor learning and physical activity. Our structured sports track and facilities for junior and senior physical education feature prominently in our curriculum.

Brighton Primary has developed a culture of continuous learning and improvement aimed at creating global citizens of the future.

British International School – Istanbul

Director
Brian Smith

Diploma coordinator
Richard Robinson

Status Private

Boarding/day Day

Gender Coeducational

Language of instruction
English

Programmes offered Diploma

Age range of pupils 2 -18

Number of pupils enrolled 620

Address
PDI-ER Uluslararasi Ozel
Egitim, Hizmetleri Ticaret AS
Maslak Meydan SK.
Spring Giz Plaza
K-5 No: 30/B Istanbul
MASLAK VD 723 012 2635 |
TURKEY

TEL +90 212 202 7027
FAX +90 212 257 76 28

Email
directorofsecondary@bis.k12.tr

Website
www.bis.k12.tr

Eruditio Limites Permeat – Education Transcends Boundaries

The British International School Istanbul has a worldwide reputation for educational excellence. It is a leading private international school in Turkey, offering the English and Welsh National Curriculum, IGCSE and the International Baccalaureate Diploma Programme. This provides students with a broad ranging and challenging academic programme.

Pupils are assessed and accepted throughout the academic year, space permitting. The language of instruction is English.

We offer German, Italian, Spanish, French and Turkish in a coeducational community that includes students from over 55 nationalities, from the ages of 2½ to 18 years. EFL and ESL (English as a Foreign, or Second Language) support is also available.

Our ethos is welcoming and embracing. We aim to inspire student enthusiasm, confidence, and independence. From pre school to secondary we promote fundamentals of the IB Diploma Programme: awareness and esteem of different cultures, beliefs, skills, values and personalities. The starting point of this international wisdom is a grasp of each individual's own personal culture. Istanbul is the perfect location for such exploration, a prerequisite to success in the 21st century.

Academic performance is high, with excellent external results in both primary and secondary schools. Primary SAT results are well above average. Tertiary entry by recent IB Diploma graduates includes such universities as British Columbia, Edinburgh, Durham and New York.

There is a full time student advisor/college counsellor and a special needs and counselling specialist supporting student learning and pastoral care.

There is a strong creative arts programme with cross curricular programmes involving visual art, drama and music.

BISI has a strong commitment to PE which extends well beyond the curriculum with coached sports programmes for soccer, swimming, athletics, cross-country, volleyball, orienteering, tennis, basketball, rugby, hockey, netball and gymnastics. There is an extensive range of after school activities ranging from chess to glass painting, photography, *Dungeons and Dragons*, aikido, horse riding, fitness to ballet.

BISI expects parents to play an integral part in the education of their children. A strong partnership between school and home is actively encouraged.

Through a vibrant and caring environment and excellent academic programme, we aim to inspire each child to reach their maximum potential and become confident young people.

British International School, Phuket

(Founded 1996)

Head of School
Prof Dr George Hickman

Diploma coordinator
Michele Watson

Status Private

Boarding/day Mixed

Gender Coeducational

Language of instruction
English

Programmes offered Diploma

Age range of pupils
18 months–18 years

Number of pupils enrolled 850

Address
59 Moo 2, Thepkrasattri Road
Koh Kaew
Muang
PHUKET 83000 | THAILAND

TEL +66 76 238711
FAX +66 76 238750

Email
info@bcis.ac.th

Website
www.bcis.ac.th

The British International School, Phuket, is an English medium, coeducational, day and boarding school providing an education of the highest quality to national and international students between the ages of 18 months and 18 years. The school offers an English and international curriculum to 850 students of 33 nationalities, from pre-school to pre-university.

External examinations are offered in IB Diploma Programme, IGCSE, GCSE, Cambridge ESOL and ICDL.

Situated on the beautiful island of Phuket in Thailand, the extensive 35-acre campus includes high quality boarding accommodation and comprehensive sporting and recreational facilities.

The school is jointly accredited by the Council of International Schools (CIS) and the New England Association of Schools and Colleges (NEASC). It is also a member of the International Schools Association of Thailand (ISAT), the Federation of British International Schools in South and East Asia (FOBISSEA) and the Boarding Schools Association of the United Kingdom (BSA).

British Schools of Washington and Houston

Principal
Peter Harding (BSW)
Alison Norris (BSH)

Diploma coordinator
Scott Hussey (BSW)
Simon Porter (BSH)

Status Private

Boarding/day Day

Gender Coeducational

Language of instruction
English

Programmes offered
Diploma

Age range of pupils
3-18

Fees per annum
$17,425-$22,475

Address
BSW
2001 Wisconsin Ave NW
Washington
DC 20007 | USA

TEL +1 202 829 3700

FAX +1 202 829 6522

Address
BSH
4211 Watonga Boulevard
Houston
TX 77092 | USA

TEL +1 713 290 9025

FAX +1 713 290 9014

Email
headbsw@britishschool.org
headbsh@britishschool.org

Website
www.britishschool.org

The British School of Houston (BSH) and The British School of Washington (BSW) are authorized to offer the International Baccalaureate Diploma Programme. The British School of Washington began offering the Diploma in 2003 and the British School of Houston in 2005.

The British Schools of America (BSA) have five schools across the US – in Boston, Charlotte, Chicago, Houston and Washington. Each of our schools began as primary schools and has expanded their senior programme as they grow. BSW and BSH, the oldest of our schools, are through schools offering the IB Diploma Programme.

BSA schools offer British-style international education to pupils from ages three to 18. Each year, BSA educates over 1400 pupils from over 45 countries around the world. We provide high quality education to both international expatriates in the United States and to American pupils. It is our pupils that truly make us international. They bring a wealth of experience and knowledge with them and their learning at BSA allows them to excel and learn wherever life leads them.

Pupils follow the British National Curriculum through GCSE in Year 11 which provides them with a strong international foundation for the IB Diploma Programme. All pupils in Years 12 and 13 follow courses leading to the IB Diploma. The small teaching groups at BSA schools give a tutorial atmosphere to all instructional sessions. There is a maximum of 20 pupils in any class, but within the IB programme groups are typically much smaller. Our small group of graduates are studying at some of the finest universities and colleges in the United States and abroad.

Course offerings for the IB Diploma Programme include English, biology, chemistry, physics, mathematics, mathematics studies, French, history, European history, geography, German, Spanish, Latin, visual arts, theatre arts, film, music, and design technology.

Cambridge High School

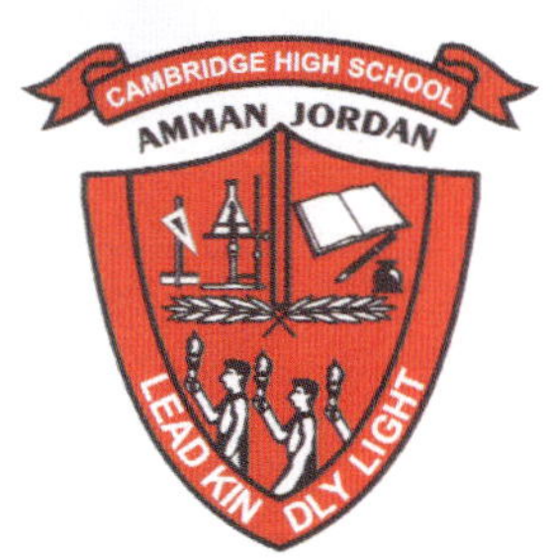

(Founded 2000)

Head of School
Diana Afranji

Diploma coordinator
Kathleen Awwad

Status Private

Boarding/day Day

Gender Coeducational

Language of instruction
English

Programmes offered Diploma

Number of pupils enrolled 1300

Fees per annum
JDnr 1000-4000

Address
Al Rabia
Abdel Kareem Al Dabbas Street,
PO Box 851771
Amman
11185 | JORDAN

TEL +962 6 5512556
FAX +962 6 5512558

Email
cambridge@cambridge.edu.jo

Website
www.cambridge.edu.jo

Cambridge High School was founded at the onset of the new millennium, based on a philosophy of progressiveness, both in educational and behavioral aspects. Our aim is clear; to help our students (from an early age) to develop an eagerness for knowledge, to explore the small community around them and become assets towards its growth, ultimately taking its place (and theirs!) in our ever emergent global community. Therefore, in a few years we have taken strides in establishing a bilingual syllabus for grades KG-12 (Arabic and English). This has encouraged families of all faiths and cultures from more than 25 countries to enroll their children of all ages into the different programs offered.

The curriculum is complemented by a wide-ranging array of co-curricular and extracurricular activities that discover and enhance each student's strengths, aptitudes and talents. A comprehensive counseling program offers support to students, teachers, as well as parents. This, in turn, complements our belief in involving our secondary students in helping around the school grounds and inside the classrooms of younger students.

In their senior school, students study the IGCSE curriculum doing the coursework and practicals, this encourages independent study and an environment of external assessment, thus preparing them for the International Baccalaureate (IB) Diploma Programme. In grades 11 & 12 students move on to the IB Diploma Programme. They may choose between the IB Diploma Programme or Certificate, offering a range of subjects both in Higher and Standard levels. Subjects on offer are: English, Arabic, business and management, information technology, biology, chemistry, physics, mathematics and visual arts.

Facilities at the Cambridge High School campus include two outdoor playgrounds, fully equipped science laboratories, a drama room, and three art studios, as well as five computer labs. We are also in the process of concluding the construction of our state of the art indoor swimming pool, gymnasium, theatre and multi-purpose hall.

Campion School

(Founded 1970)

Head
Stephen Atherton

Diploma coordinator
Fred Clough

Status Private

Boarding/day Day

Gender Coeducational

Language of instruction
English

Programmes offered Diploma

Age range of pupils 3-18

Number of pupils enrolled 485

Address
PO Box 67484
Pallini
15302 | GREECE

TEL +30 210 6071700

FAX +30 210 6071780

Email
fclough@campion.edu.gr

Website
www.campion.edu.gr

Campion School is a kindergarten to 18+ international school, offering a curriculum modelled on the English National Curriculum, and preparing students for the IGCSE and the IB Diploma. Since the year 2000 the school has been situated on a new purpose-built campus, in open countryside outside Athens close to the Attica Highway. We make good use of our location in Greece, enriching pupils' experience in the classroom with a programme of educational visits and excursions for subjects in the arts, life sciences and classics; and these are complemented by a varied extracurricular programme of sporting and cultural activities.

Our admissions policy is non-selective, and we aim to develop the various talents of every member of our diverse student body. All students in the final two years of school follow the IB Diploma, and we are proud of the consistently good quality of our results since we began teaching the programme in 2001. Our top students over the past two years have achieved the highest possible score of 45. These impressive top scores, together with our high IB Diploma pass rate and average score (33 over the past three years), are an indication of how the IB Diploma Programme enables all our students to succeed in making the most of their abilities.

Despite our modest size, we offer a wide range of subjects: English and Greek (in groups 1 and 2), French, Spanish and Arabic; history, geography, economics, psychology, information technology, and a special school-based syllabus in group 3, classical Greek and Roman studies; chemistry, physics, biology, and environmental systems and societies; mathematics at both higher and standard level, and mathematical studies; and music, theatre and visual arts. All students take a short course in research and presentation skills at the start of their IB years, and their progress in all respects is carefully monitored at every stage of their studies.

We offer expert guidance to students in their applications to university and in planning their future careers. Most of our graduates go on to universities in the UK, a few to other European countries, the United States or Canada, and many successfully apply for highly competitive courses at leading universities. The destinations of this last year's graduates, for example, include (in the UK) the universities of Oxford, St Andrews and Warwick and (across the Atlantic) Georgetown University, Washington DC and the University of Toronto.

Carey Baptist Grammar School

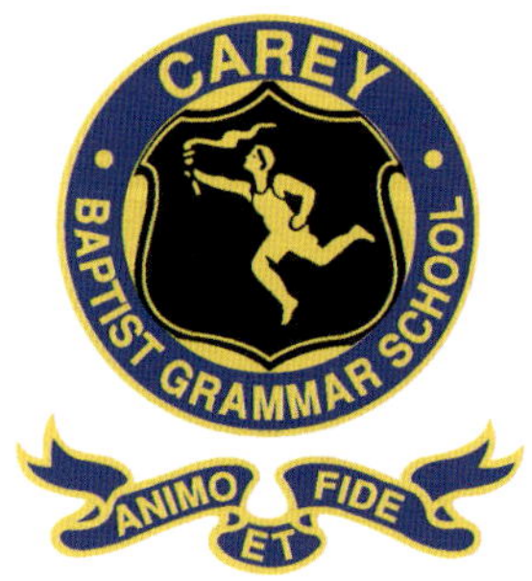

(Founded 1923)

Principal
Phil De Young

Diploma coordinator
David Hamer

Status Private

Boarding/day Day

Gender Coeducational

Language of instruction
English

Programmes offered Diploma

Age range of pupils 3–18

Number of pupils enrolled
2282

Fees per annum For 2009 fees please contact the Registrar via email: registrar@carey.com.au or go to www.carey.com.au

Address
349 Barkers Road
Kew
VIC 3101 | AUSTRALIA

TEL +61 39816 1222
FAX +61 39816 1263

Email
david.hamer@carey.com.au

Website
www.carey.com.au

Carey is an international school accredited by the Council of International Schools and authorised to offer the IB Diploma Programme. It regularly records excellent academic results, with Year 12 students achieving university entrance scores in the top 10% of the State.

Carey's main Kew campus is situated close to the CBD in one of Melbourne's most attractive suburbs, and caters for students from three-year-old kindergarten to Year 12.

Senior school's pre-tertiary environment encourages independent study and the development of research skills. Students may choose the Victorian Certificate of Education (VCE) or International Baccalaureate (IB) Diploma Programme and a range of advanced studies.

Subjects offered are biology, business and management, chemistry, Chinese, economics, English, French, geography, German, history, Indonesian, information technology in a global society, mathematics, music, philosophy, physics, psychology, Spanish, theatre arts, visual arts and other languages by arrangement.

Facilities include specialist science laboratories, a lecture theatre, humanities classrooms and studios for fine art, visual arts and media. Adjoining the canteen is a large covered area for use by senior school students for private study, discussion and relaxation.

An extensive co-curricular programme of sports, drama, music, debating, theatre production and media is designed to complement the curriculum and provide balance with academic studies. The broad range of the activities on offer explores individual strengths and interests and offers opportunities for involvement with the potential for lifelong enjoyment. Facilities at the Carey Sports Complex include swimming and diving pools, a gymnasium, games courts and several ovals.

Founded on Christian principles, Carey welcomes families from 30 countries of all faiths and cultures into a community that celebrates its own diversity. At all levels students are encouraged to see themselves as citizens of the world, and to serve local, national and global communities to the best of their abilities through a range of social service programmes, many of which support the service component of the IB's CAS programme.

Comprehensive pastoral care at Carey provides support and allows for the development of meaningful relationships between staff, the students and their families.

CATS Canterbury

(Founded 1952)

Principal
Ms Marie-Louise Banning

Diploma coordinator
Mr Noel Ensoll

Status Private

Boarding/day Mixed

Gender Coeducational

Language of instruction
English

Programmes offered Diploma

Age range of pupils 15-18

Number of pupils enrolled 185

Fees per annum £22,725

Address
68 New Dover Road
Canterbury
Kent
CT1 3LQ | UK

TEL +44 (0)1227 866540
FAX +44 (0)1227 866550

Email
admissions@catscanterbury.com

Website
www.catscanterbury.com

Welcome to CATS Canterbury – a world class college

CATS Canterbury is an independent, coeducational sixth form college located in the beautiful cathedral city of Canterbury. An hour from London and two hours from Paris, the city is a dynamic modern town with two universities and a prestigious art school.

CATS academic achievements lie in its student university destinations, with 77% gaining acceptance at first choice UK universities such as Cambridge, Manchester and UCL. Since the establishment of CATS in 1952, students have performed well academically – in 2008 97% achieved A level grades at A-C. In total, there are about 200 students in the college aged 15-19 and over 35 nationalities.

CATS Canterbury is a challenging place to be. Students for the IB Diploma will need to have a good amount of enthusiasm, ambition and motivation as they will live and learn in an environment founded on high teaching standards and a rigorous two system approach. The first, teaching in small groups, to ensure individual attention to help develop skills and confidence, and the second a personal tutor to guide, advise and support students throughout their time at the college. We combine academic rigour with an understanding attitude that respects the individual, the highest standards with the maximum of personal flexibility.

We pride ourselves on our informal and friendly style, which ensures that there is always time for the individual.

All our facilities have recently been refurbished, dedicated teaching space, an impressive and well resourced library, large common room and a number of quiet rooms on campus for private study.

Balancing work with play is vital and at CATS students have the chance to join in a range of sporting activities including football, badminton and volleyball. Students are encouraged to be active in all aspects of college life and contribute to the local and global community.

Preparatory IB Course: This course is designed to prepare students fully for the rigours of the IB Diploma Programme. Students aged 15 or more can join CATS Canterbury Preparation for the IB Diploma Programme (Pre-IB). Students may start at different times during the year, depending on their individual academic requirements.

Admissions to CATS Canterbury is by interview and assessment. If you live in China, Russia, Korea, or Turkey you will be able to apply through our local office. Students wishing to study the IB Diploma can apply from the age of 16. The college can consider also transfers from other IB World Schools.

Centro Escolar Instituto La Paz, SC

(Founded 1950)

Head of School
Francisco Javier González García

PYP coordinator
Liliana Muñoz López

MYP coordinator
José Luis García Ramírez

Status Private

Boarding/day Day

Gender Coeducational

Language of instruction
English, Spanish

Programmes offered PYP, MYP

Age range of pupils 3-15

Number of pupils enrolled 1200

Fees per annum US$4000

Address
Av Plan de San Luis 445
Col Nueva Santa María
México City
02800 | MEXICO

TEL +52 55 55 56 66 46
FAX +52 55 55 56 66 46

Email
institutolapaz@infosel.net.mx

Website
www.institutolapaz.edu.mx

Founded in 1950, Instituto La Paz has always stood for the best quality in education. Our mission is: to be an educational institution that helps to develop young men and women who have the highest human values and who are active promoters of the development of the society to which they belong. Our institutional values are: HONESTY, RESPONSIBILITY AND RESPECT.

Constructive critical thinking is built up in daily activities in order to form more respectful and integrated human beings who can be competitive in today's complex world.

Our co-curricular activities are:

- Arts: which include dancing, theater, choir and art workshops.
- Sports: soccer, basketball, Tae Kwon Do and cheerleading are practiced in integral programs that enhance skills development.
- Language acquisition with internal certification: English (ESOL Cambridge) and French, support intercultural and international awareness.
- La Paz MUN: a junior model of debates from the United Nations, in which students not only develop their language B skills (English), but also their tolerance, respect and ability to work with others in order to find possible solutions to current world problems.

Partnership with parents starts with a permanent calendar of workshops and conferences that enables them to establish better communication in relation to their children's educational goals.

We administer national and international exchanges, sending our delegation accompanied by teachers, to one of the members of the ISSE (International School to School Experience). They are hosted by different families and attend school daily; at a later date we house the exchange delegation. Some of the countries that have participated are: USA, Canada, El Salvador, Ecuador, Costa Rica, Bermuda, India and Australia.

The school also participates with the SEP (Mexican Educational Program) and the SRE (International Relations Secretary) in a Bi-National Program which is focused on international cooperation in order to support Mexican children to establish a link with their national identity in an international context.

Finally, the school curriculum is designed to form fully rounded individuals who will be able to face the current world with confidence and ability.

Collège du Léman International School

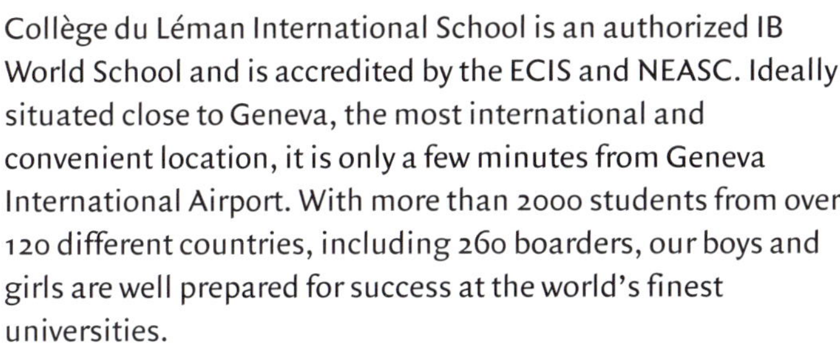

Collège du Léman International School is an authorized IB World School and is accredited by the ECIS and NEASC. Ideally situated close to Geneva, the most international and convenient location, it is only a few minutes from Geneva International Airport. With more than 2000 students from over 120 different countries, including 260 boarders, our boys and girls are well prepared for success at the world's finest universities.

The high level of education offered at our school results from nearly half a century of sound pedagogical experience. For our students aged three to 18 years, we offer two academic programmes. One is taught in English, preparing for entrance into colleges and universities in North America, Europe and throughout the world, through the International Baccalaureate (IB Diploma), Advanced Placement examinations and the International General Certificate of Secondary Education (IGCSE).

Our IB Diploma Programme offers a wide range of subjects, taught by specialists, including economics, *ab initio* Chinese and all three sciences. Several of these subjects, adapted to demand on a yearly basis, can be taken in French, thereby giving the possibility of gaining a bilingual diploma.

The French language programme prepares students for the French Baccalauréat and the Swiss Federal Maturité – including the bilingual French-English Maturité leading to entrance into universities worldwide. Our experienced educators also prepare students for SAT and TOEFL examinations and our college counsellors assist students in their university applications. Most students are required to study French and many of our students leave us as multi-lingual. For non-English speakers our teachers have a vast experience of teaching ESL (English as a Second Language).

With average class sizes of 20 and a student to teacher ratio of 10:1 our teachers can take the time to understand every child's unique learning style and provide the individual attention they need to achieve their maximum developmental potential. Our excellent resources include state of the art science laboratories, two auditoriums, two language laboratories, a computer suite and excellent library facilities. With all of our students from kindergarten to high school and both boarding and day students working together on the one campus our students have a great experience of living in a truly international society.

Deira International School

Head of School
John Bastable

Diploma coordinator
Jenny Bastable

Status Private

Boarding/day Day

Gender Coeducational

Language of instruction
English

Programmes offered Diploma

Age range of pupils 3-18

Fees per annum
AED 26,600-53,600

Address
PO Box 79043
Dubai | UNITED ARAB EMIRATES

TEL +9714 2325552
FAX +9714 2325151

Email
jbastable@disdubai.ae

Website
www.disdubai.ae

Deira International School is an authorised IB World School offering English, Spanish, French, Arabic, business & management, economics, ITGS, history, geography, biology, chemistry, physics, environmental systems, mathematics, music, theatre arts, visual arts and NEW this year – film studies.

DIS is also authorised to pilot the International Baccalaureate Career-Related Certificate (IBCC) – a new IB initiative.

IBCC incorporates the educational principles, vision and learner profile of the IB with a local vocational programme provided by the Al-Futtaim Training Centre. IBCC offers a different and exciting pathway for students to engage in work related studies whilst gaining an IB education. Currently DIS offers a business oriented course with practical experience in the retail sector. Students take three IB Diploma Programme Certificates, study approaches to learning, write a reflective project and participate in the CAS programme.

DIS has a beautiful 80,000 sq.m. campus situated in Dubai Festival City, UAE.

'Forever learning, forever achieving'

Dhirubhai Ambani International School

(Founded 2003)

Head of International Curriculum
Dermot Keegan

Diploma coordinator
Riad Rojoa

Status Private

Boarding/day Day

Gender Coeducational

Language of instruction
English

Programmes offered Diploma

Age range of pupils 4-18

Number of pupils enrolled 1012

Address
Bandra-Kurla Complex
Bandra (East)
Mumbai – 400098 | INDIA

TEL +91 22 40617000
FAX +91 22 40617099

Email
info@da-is.org

Website
www.da-is.org

Dhirubhai Ambani International School was founded in 2003 and prepares students for the Indian Certificate of Secondary Education, the IGCSE and the IB Diploma.

The school's goal is to provide a unique experience that enables children to enjoy the learning process and bring out their full potential. Its motto **'Dare to Dream…Learn to Excel'** embodies the ethos that children should be encouraged to aim high and be guided to do their best in everything they do. As much as equipping them to think and act critically, to be creative in their responses and to be able to engage with the forces of change, the school aims to help students to develop a strong awareness of their history and traditions, as well as their place in a global context. In achieving this, the school synthesizes internationally acclaimed pedagogical practices with India's rich educational heritage and seeks to cultivate ethical and responsible citizenship.

Current enrolment is 1012, with 177 taking the IB Diploma in Years 11 and 12. The school has 143 faculty members, with most of them having experience at leading schools in India and international schools worldwide.

Our first four graduating classes achieved an average IB Diploma score of 36 points. They have gained admission to prestigious universities such as Harvard, Stanford, Princeton, Yale, U Penn-Wharton, Oxford, Cambridge and the London School of Economics, to name a few. Some have received full scholarships at Harvard, Yale, Stanford and Princeton, among others. Graduates have also gained admissions to universities in Singapore, Hong Kong and Germany, as well as in India. Our first three classes of ICSE and IGCSE students also earned superb results.

The school complements its core curriculum with a strong emphasis on co-curricular programmes and an eclectic mix of activities. DAIS is accredited by The Hague International Model United Nations and, in 2008, earned Regional Membership of Round Square and Regular Membership of the Council of International Schools. In working towards promoting internationalism, peace and friendship, the school encourages exchange programmes in learning, sports, culture, and service to the community.

Dulwich College Beijing

DULWICH COLLEGE BEIJING

(Founded 2005)

Headmaster
Brian McDouall

Diploma coordinator
Kevin Huntley

Status Private

Boarding/day Day

Gender Coeducational

Language of instruction
English

Programmes offered Diploma

Age range of pupils 1-18

Number of pupils enrolled 1090

Fees per annum
RMB25,900-182,000

Address
89 Capital Airport Road
Shunyi District
Beijing 101300 | PR CHINA

TEL +86 10 6454 9000
FAX +86 10 6454 9001

Email
info@dulwich-beijing.cn

Website
www.dulwich-beijing.cn

Dulwich Beijing is a member of the family of Dulwich Colleges in China and a partner to Dulwich College, London, a prestigious UK independent school dating back to the early seventeenth century.

Situated in the villa district on the north-eastern fringes of China's capital city, just ten minutes from the airport, the Dulwich campus is set amidst extensive sports grounds next to the Wen Yu river and boasts world class facilities to support all aspects of its broad curricular and co-curricular programmes.

The Dulwich educational philosophy places equal emphasis on the intellectual and personal development of students. To this end we focus on four core areas: academic excellence; a commitment to sport; the provision of a wide range of musical, dramatic and artistic opportunities; and a commitment to the community – school, local, regional and global.

Academic study

Dulwich students are challenged academically, acquiring the skills to be successful in life. They learn to develop ideas over a period of time; to work alone and in groups; to be flexible; to use technology effectively; to be able to problem solve and to perform in a variety of situations; and to commit to a life of continued learning.

Sports

At Dulwich students can try their hand at a wide variety of sports, competing at high levels. In addition to the obvious benefits of promoting fitness and a healthy lifestyle, involvement in sport is one of the best ways to develop social, team and leadership skills.

The arts

Performance and the development of self-expression is at the heart of our school. We give every student the opportunity to perform for themselves, their friends and their families. Some will be soloists, others will shine as part of a group, but all will have the reward of being a part of a community that is proud of what it does. Our standards are high and the development of this area of school life is a high priority.

Community

Our community stretches beyond the borders of family and school, and our students must accept a responsibility to make a difference to the world in which they live. To be givers rather than takers.

As our motto 'Building Bridges to the World' implies, we offer our students structure, direction, support, pathways, and connections, and ultimately the confidence and opportunity to build bridges for themselves.

Dulwich College Shanghai

<table>
<tr><td>

(Founded 2003)

Headmaster
Brian McDouall

Diploma coordinator
Michelle Brinn

Status Private

Boarding/day Day

Gender Coeducational

Language of instruction
English

Programmes offered Diploma

Age range of pupils 2-18

Number of pupils enrolled 1250

</td><td>

Fees per annum
ENC: 152,000RMB-
195,000RMB; IGCSE: 203,000;
IB Diploma: 205,000

Address
266 Lan An Road
JinQiao, PuDong
Shanghai 201206 | PR CHINA

TEL +8621 5899 9910
FAX +8621 5899 9810

Email
info@dulwich-shanghai.cn

Website
www.dulwich-shanghai.cn

</td></tr>
</table>

Dulwich College Shanghai is a prestigious private academic institution delivering an enhanced English National Curriculum to an international group of children from kindergarten to Year 9, IGCSE in Years 10 and 11 and the International Baccalaureate Diploma Programme in Years 12 and 13.

The Dulwich College mission is the pursuit of excellence: excellence in the academic sphere, excellence on the sporting field, and excellence in the arts. The primary goal of Dulwich College is to develop all aspects of each student's intellectual, physical, creative and social character.

Dulwich College benefits from a rich history. One of Britain's most prestigious independent schools, Dulwich College was founded in 1619. Dulwich College has a distinguished tradition of inspired teaching and genuine scholarship. Students come from a wide range of backgrounds with diverse interests that enrich the life of the college. Almost one sixth of all students at Dulwich College London are accepted at Oxford, Cambridge or top tier North American Universities.

In 2003, Dulwich College London founded its first international school in China in Shanghai forging strong and valuable links to Asia. Based on the success of Dulwich College Shanghai, Dulwich College has since opened schools in Beijing and Suzhou. All Dulwich Colleges share a similar ethos and curriculum which are grounded in close partnership with Dulwich College London.

Dulwich College Shanghai has state-of-the-art facilities and technologies to aid students in all areas of work, helping them succeed to their best ability and enjoy the school environment. Indoor facilities include art rooms, a graphics and textiles room and kiln, a DT workshop, science laboratories each with their own prep rooms, wireless network access, interactive white boards, a humanities resource centre, a mathematics suite, a dedicated ICT suite, a well-resourced and equipped library, two indoor sports halls, a fitness suite, dance room and dining halls. Outdoor facilities include rugby, cricket and football fields as well as access to a 25m swimming pool, tennis courts and squash courts.

Having been authorized as an IB World School in 2007, the newly created IB Programme at Dulwich College Shanghai provides the best of both worlds – our 400 years of experience educating students to be the best that they can be, with the international recognition of the IB Diploma.

Ecole Active Bilingue Jeannine Manuel

(Founded 1954)

Principal
Elisabeth Zéboulon

Diploma coordinator
Shirley Burchill

Status Private

Boarding/day Day

Gender Coeducational

Language of instruction
English, French

Programmes offered Diploma

Age range of pupils 4-18

Number of pupils enrolled 3000

Fees per annum
€1290–€1320 per term;
IB Classes: €4090 per term

Admission Office
Florence Bosc
Director of Admissions
Tel: +33 01 44 37 00 80

Address
Théâtre
70 rue du Théâtre
75015 Paris | FRANCE

Dupleix
15, Rue Edgar Faure
75015 Paris | FRANCE

Suffren
141, Avenue de Suffren
75007 Paris | FRANCE

Tel: +33 01 44 37 00 80
Fax: +33 01 45 79 88 02

Lille (Day and Boarding)
418 bis rue Albert Bailly
59700 Marq-en-Baroeul
LILLE | FRANCE

Tel +33 03 20 65 90 50
Fax +33 03 20 98 06 41

Email
admissions@eabjm.net

Website
www.eabjm.org

EABJM is a non-profit pre-K-12 coeducational college and preparatory school founded in 1954 with the mission to develop international understanding through bilingual (French/English) education.

Today, EABJM has become the largest non-denominational independent school in France, with 2900 students representing 66 nationalities and every major cultural tradition.

EABJM is recognized by UNESCO as an 'associated' school. The school's academic excellence matches its diversity: EABJM is regularly ranked among the top five of all 121 Paris high schools (public and independent) for its overall academic performance.

Each year, EABJM welcomes more than 100 new non-French speaking students who enroll in 'adaptation classes' where they follow a French immersion programme.

THE LOWER AND MIDDLE SCHOOL follow the national curriculum with several exceptions: English is taught every day and, in middle school sciences, history and geography are taught in English. The curriculum is enriched at all levels, not only with a more advanced English language and literature curriculum, but also, for example, with Chinese language instruction (compulsory in grades 3-4-5), an integrated science programme in Lower School, and independent research projects in middle school.

IN THE UPPER SCHOOL 10th graders follow the national curriculum. In 11th grade, students choose between the standard French Baccalaureate, the French OIB (International Option within the French Baccalaureate) and the IB Diploma Programme. The IB Diploma Programme is not subsidized and tuition is more than twice the French curriculum tuition.

Out of the last two EABJM Paris graduating classes (349) students, 28 percent took the IB, 37 percent opted for the French OI Baccalaureate, and the balance sat the standard French Baccalaureate without 'Option internationale'.

Over the past four years, 16 per cent of our Paris graduates have gone to US colleges or universities, 24 per cent chose the UK, 12 per cent opted for Canada, 45 per cent entered the French higher education system, and the remaining three per cent pursued their higher education all over the world

Admission

Although applications typically exceed available spaces by a ratio of 4:1, every effort is made to reserve space for international applicants, including children of families who expect to remain in France for a limited period of time and wish to combine a cultural immersion in French education with the ability to re-enter their own school systems and excel.

Ecole Oasis Internationale

Head of School
Mrs Esmat Lamei

PYP coordinator
Naira Hamdi

MYP coordinator
Chérine Zaytoun

Diploma coordinator
Fatma Hussein

Status Private

Boarding/day Day

Gender Coeducational

Language of instruction French

Programmes offered
PYP, MYP, Diploma

Age range of pupils 3-18

Number of pupils enrolled 771

Address
Zahraa El Maadi
Quarter no 3 and no 7 part A
and B
Cairo | EGYPT

TEL +2 02 25162608

FAX +2 02 27545280

Email
admission @oasisdemaadi.com
hr@oasisdemaadi.com

Website
www.oasisdemaadi.com

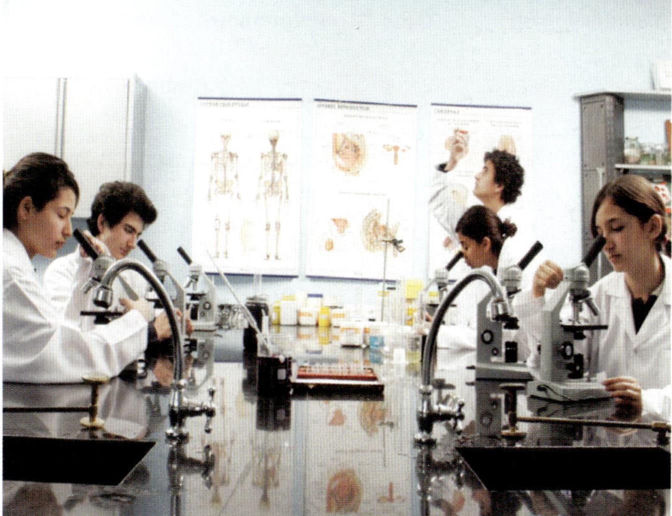

Curriculum

Oasis International School was the first school in the world authorized to teach the three IB programmes in French: the Primary Years Programme (PYP) and the Middle Years Programme (MYP) since 2002 and the IB Diploma Programme since 2004.

Facilities

We have two different campuses (one for the PYP and a second for the MYP and the IB Diploma Programme) integrating new technologies, high standard of teaching methods and material, required for being well prepared for their future.

Events

- Model United Nations Conference (10 -14/03/2009).
- International Summer School – July 2009.

Oasis School Group was established with a vision.

This vision is to offer young Egyptians the best possible education to form the new generations with confidence and knowledge to build and serve modern Egypt and prepare them for their bright professional careers.

Today this vision is a reality. Our graduates were all admitted to prestigious universities in Egypt and abroad (France, Canada, New Zealand). They are now ambassadors of the education they have received in our establishment.

We don't only instil knowledge but we also try to develop the personality of our students, awaken their intellect to having their own points of view and give them a sense of belonging to their culture while maintaining a global vision of the world.

In this way, at a young age, we develop in our students the regulations that accompany them all their life: discipline, respect, integrity, perseverance, enthusiasm and understanding the value of work.

All these skills build the personality of our students and their capacity to adapt in different life situations.

We satisfy their natural curiosity through the skills learned in our curriculum which features the academically rigorous IB programmes at all levels.

Our students learn their talents in different branches: arts, languages, mathematics, sciences, sports, social studies, technology and service to community.

Our students acquire competencies that allow them to analyze, reflect, develop critical thinking and advanced research skills.

The variety of activities available give them the opportunity to develop necessary skills needed today and in the future.

Nourished by the years of education based on our culture, integrity, tolerance, and international culture, our students are ready to be the ambassadors of the education they have received. They are also able and fond of participating in the development of their own country.

Eyüboglu High School

(Founded 1985)

Head of School
Burçak Eyüboglu

PYP coordinator
Tuna Mengü

MYP coordinator
Asli Bali

Diploma coordinator
Gaye Önol

Status Private

Boarding/day Day

Gender Coeducational

Language of instruction
English, Turkish

Programmes offered
PYP, MYP, Diploma

Age range of pupils 2-18

Address
Namik Kemal mah
Dr Rüstem Eyüboglu sok 3,
Ümraniye
Istanbul
34762 | TURKEY

TEL +90 216 522 12 12

FAX +90 216 335 71 98

Email
sema.ozkaya@eyuboglu.com

Website
www.eyuboglu.com

Eyüboglu Educational Institutions are a group of private, coeducational schools founded in 1985. EEI is comprised of three kindergardens, three elementary sections, a secondary, and a science secondary section and offers a bilingual education to students aged two to 18. School philosophy is based on academic excellence, internationalism, intercultural and social awareness. Eyüboglu Schools was the first Turkish institution to have achieved authorization to offer all three IB Programmes: Diploma, Middle Years and Primary Years. With this unique feature, the school's internationally recognized high standards of academic excellence enable the Eyüboglu graduates to further their studies in the finest universities, both locally and in the US, Canada and the UK. There is a strong ESL program in all sections, leading our students to, in addition to IB qualifications, UCLES and TOEFL English proficiency examinations. Starting from Grade 5, German, French and Spanish are taught as a second foreign language. Elective subjects offer more intensive and specialized study in the fields of social sciences, sciences, arts, music, computer and astronomy. Individualized instruction is part of the curriculum. There is a wide variety of extracurricular activities in art, music, humanities and drama. Besides traditional sports activities, archery, horse riding, fencing, swimming, folk dancing, and modern dance are also offered.

Teachers have an average of ten years of teaching experience, and 42% of the subject teachers hold postgraduate degrees. The average tenure at the school is seven years.

Facilities on the campus, which is situated on the Asian side of Istanbul, include an arts and sports complex with a swimming pool, various art studios and sports areas for handball, volleyball, athletics, basketball, archery, ballet and folk-dancing. A theatre hall seating 480, a full-sized gymnasium, four smaller multi-purpose PE halls, activity rooms, four art and ceramics studios, four libraries with 56,000 volumes, tennis, basketball and handball courts, a bocce field, and a general playing field. There are eleven science laboratories. The two observatories are equipped with powerful telescopes which enable the school and wider community to make astronomical observations.

Admission to Eyüboglu is offered on the basis of a school-administered examination for the elementary section and according to Turkish Ministry of Education regulations for the secondary sections.

(Founded 1942)

Head of School
Francisco Galicia Ortega

PYP coordinator
Rosario Pérez Lozano

MYP coordinator
Sofía Dolega Zakrzewski

Diploma coordinator
Erika Würfl Marx

Status Private

Boarding/day Day

Gender Coeducational

Language of instruction
Spanish, English

Programmes offered
PYP, MYP, Diploma

Age range of pupils
7 months-19 years

Number of pupils enrolled
2325

Address
9 Poniente 2709
Puebla
72160 | MEXICO

TEL +52 222 30 30 400

FAX +52 222 230 15 15

Email
info@cap.edu.mx

Website
www.cap.edu.mx

The American School of Puebla, located in the city of Puebla, in central Mexico, was founded in 1942, with the purpose of providing educational services with an international and intercultural focus to students of all nationalities. The school is a private, non-sectarian institution for boys and girls from pre-K through preparatory school (senior high school) for students aged seven months to 19 years. We were the first school in the state authorized by the International Baccalaureate to teach its three programmes: the Primary Years Programme (PYP), the Middle Years Programme (MYP) and the Diploma Programme. The primary and secondary schools are accredited by the Mexican Ministry of Education in the state of Puebla (SEP) and the University of Puebla (BUAP) accredits the preparatory school. We are a member of the Tri-Association of American Schools (Mexico, Central America and the Caribbean) and ASOMEX (Association of American Schools in Mexico).

Affiliations and Accreditations

The American School of Puebla is, according to its corresponding needs and levels, accredited by the Ministry of Education and the local public university as well as by associations to which membership is voluntary, in programs that enhance the educational experience for our students.

- Our affiliation with the Association of American Schools in Mexico, (ASOMEX, www.asomex.org) offers us the opportunity for creative, cultural, artistic, athletic, educational and professional development, through conferences, workshops and tournaments.
- The Tri-association (www.tri-association.org) is an organization of American Schools from Mexico, Central America, Colombia and the Caribbean that meets throughout the year for conferences and workshops offered to teachers and administrators.
- Private School authorization code from the Ministry of Education (SEP), ES547-11.
- Training Center Code, 21PES0024R.
- Authorized for the Middle Years Programme by the International Baccalaureate, April 3, 2006.
- Authorized for the Diploma Progarmme in 1998 and the PYP in 2004.

George Green's School

(Founded 1828)

Principal
Kenny Frederick

Diploma coordinator
Geraldine Naughten

Status State

Boarding/day Day

Gender Coeducational

Language of instruction
English

Programmes offered
Diploma

Age range of pupils 11-19

Number of pupils enrolled 1250

Address
100 Manchester Road
Isle of Dogs
London
E14 3WE | UK

TEL +44 (0)207 987 6032

FAX +44 (0)207 538 2316

Email
enquiries@georgegreens.com

Website
www.georgegreens.com

Situated on the River Thames, George Green's Sixth Form benefits from the transport facilities, buildings, attractions and views in the surrounding area. Students can take full advantage of Greenwich, with its museums, university and historic locations directly to the south and the Canary Wharf business district to the north.

George Green's School was authorized to deliver the IB Diploma Programme in September 2008, it is one of the few coeducational state schools in London offering this International Baccalaureate Programme. The international nature of the Diploma Programme and its philosophy particularly meets the needs of our humanities status school and our student body that reflects the ethnic and cultural diversity found in East London. The Diploma Programme runs alongside a limited range of traditional A levels as well as BTEC Diplomas and Entry Level courses.

The IB Diploma Programme is a Post-16 programme of study of the highest academic standing, offering a challenging and academically stimulating pre-university education. Internationally renowned as the 'gold-standard', the breadth of study and depth of intellectual engagement, it is particularly suitable for highly motivated, hard-working, able students. The programme equips students with the skills sand attitudes necessary for success at university and in employment. Students are encouraged to become well-rounded independent thinkers, who will take on an active role in the global society. For this reason, George Green's Sixth Form takes pride in its extensive enrichment programme that builds on the IB Diploma Programme curriculum. By offering a wide range of opportunities to participate in creative activities and sports as well as service to the school and wider community, we believe students are well prepared for university life and beyond. Students regularly participate in various extracurricular activities including – the European Youth Parliament, Millennium Volunteering and Fulcrum Challenge.

The European Youth Parliament is an annual competitive debating event held at the Foreign and Commonwealth Office, designed to introduce students to competitive negotiation and representation – all fundamentals of any modern democracy. Students from George Green's also regularly participate in the Fulcrum Leadership Challenge and have participated in overseas cultural visits to India, Kenya and Tanzania as part of this programme designed to nurture leadership and management skills. Past participants described it as a life-changing experience – ideal for students interested in leadership, senior management and professional careers. Based in the UK, the Millennium Volunteering scheme is a nationally recognised programme of voluntary and community-based projects involving two hundred hours of work. This popular programme encourages students to partake in local community and social work, another important aspect of Creativity, Action and Service (CAS).

German School Beirut

(Founded 1954)

Director
Omar Salloum

Diploma coordinator
Hadi Bou Hassan (English)
Angela Haddad (German)

Status Private

Boarding/day Day

Gender Coeducational

Language of instruction
English

Programmes offered Diploma

Age range of pupils 3-20

Number of pupils enrolled 1000

Fees per annum US$4000

Address
PO Box 11-3888
Beirut | LEBANON

TEL +96 1174 0523
FAX +96 1174 0523

Email
germanschoolb@gmail.com

Website
www.deutscheschule
beirut.edu.lb

The German School Beirut is a liberal educational institution. It strives to be a racially and culturally diverse community of students, parents, and teachers dedicated to creating a peaceful environment where each person is treated with unconditional patience, regard and acceptance. Within such an environment each student will be empowered and inspired to reach his/her full academic, emotional, physical, and spiritual potential. (Mission Statement)

With this mission statement in mind, our school is proud to offer a variety of academic programs in an attempt to attend to the different learning styles of our students, especially as the school consists of around 1000 students from 46 different nationalities. We have sustained our long tradition of high quality education in Lebanon by offering the International Baccalaureate (IB) Diploma Programme and the new German International Baccalaureate, aligned with the Lebanese Baccalaureate and the Deutsches Sprachdiplom.

The school thus combines the well founded solidity of German and Lebanese education along with the open modern principles of the International Baccalaureate.

The German International Baccalaureate (GIB) is fully recognized by German universities as well as universities all around the world as equivalent to the *Abitur*.

The IB Diploma Programme subjects currently offered are: German (A1, A2 and *ab initio*), English (A1 and B), Arabic (A2, B and *ab initio*), French, physics, biology, chemistry,

environmental systems and societies, philosophy, geography, history, economics, Informational Technology in a Global Society (ITGS), mathematics and math studies. We do have future plans to give courses in visual arts, business and management and psychology.

In the German IB, biology and history are taught in the German language.

The German School Beirut prides itself in being a school that cares for the students' best interest. We believe that preparing students for life in the best possible way is one of our top priorities. In this regard, the school faculty and administration has carefully studied the requirements of the Lebanese Baccalaureate and that of the International Baccalaureate and was able to exclusively design the 'Double Program' where students are able to graduate with both the Lebanese Baccalaureate and IB diplomas.

Throughout their scholastic years, students practice the spirit of open-mindedness, tolerance and mutual respect. Starting from the lower elementary, students are exposed to three languages: English, German and Arabic. They begin to study French at the age of nine since we believe that multilingual competence is a precondition of individual success and higher careers in the globalizing world.

The German School does not only emphasize students' potential and progress, teacher's professional development is highly accentuated. This takes place by supporting and sending teachers to workshops nationally and abroad. We help our staff remain updated on the latest educational methodologies.

Campus & Facilities

The 18000m^2 school campus is situated above the Mediterranean Sea in the south of Beirut. The greens, flowers, trees and splendid view overlooking the blue Mediterranean provide an atmosphere of calmness and tranquility. This ambiance helps reduce stress and improve concentration in order to study essential knowledge. In addition to the main campus outside Beirut, the DSB holds a second smaller campus near the American University of Beirut. The Beirut city branch enrolls children from the kindergarten up to grade 3, making it more convenient for young pupils living in Beirut city.

There are many clubs for hobbies and leisure offered on campus. A well rounded student is one who is not only academically competent but also able to be involved in a variety of activities. In light of this, the German School offers clubs that cover a range of hobbies and activities. By enrolling students are not only enjoying their time after school, but developing a talent or a hobby into a series of achievements and a skill of enjoyment.

Along with the outdoor campus, students enjoy the facilities of three science labs and a computer lab which are used for conducting lessons in addition to students' own project work.

The school library also offers a huge collection of books in the four languages of study at the school, with different genres to match students' interest. Students also refer to the library for their research work, where references and sources are offered and are accessible.

Our school pays special attention to the arts: students are encouraged to express their artistic talents in all their forms around campus and with their peers. Students leave their artistic touches through drawings and a variety of paintings and sculptures can be found around campus.

The arts area is not only viewed as an entity of its own, it is also considered as a major constituent of all subjects, where students produce the outcomes and creative manipulation of their lessons.

Such projects are noted as part of the curriculum and also considered as CAS projects.

CAS is also integrated with all subjects, where students implement the three aspects of CAS in various contexts in and outside the school premises.

Admission Policy

Our school follows a non selective admission policy. We believe that every student has the potential to succeed, however it is the role of educators to see that this potential is effectively channeled to achieve the desired results.

Students of the German School Beirut have achieved distinguishable results in the programs we are offering. They have shown competence and aptness to manipulate all specifications and requirements of these curricula.

Graduates of the German School Beirut not only study in Germany, every year our students are able to enroll at the world's top universities, with majors that range from medicine, engineering, literature, communication arts, fine art and law.

Projects: Education for Sustainable Development

International orientation and ethics of responsibility are practiced and emphasized in the German School Beirut. Therefore, the school has decided to implement the objective of 'Education for Sustainable Development' according to the proclamation by the General Assembly of the United Nations of the 'Decade of Education for Sustainable Development 2004 to 2014'.

In social service activities (CAS) students learn to practice the ethics of responsibility by taking care of others and in environmental projects they learn to protect the ecological balance of the one world we have to live in.

(Founded 1996)

Director General
Amr Ahmed Mokhtar

PYP coordinator
Françoise Mokhtar-Bencteux

MYP coordinator
May Fathi Waly

Diploma coordinator
Amr Ahmed Mokhtar

Status Private

Boarding/day Day

Gender Coeducational

Language of instruction
English, French, Arabic

Programmes offered
PYP, MYP, Diploma

Age range of pupils 3-18

Address
405 Gezirat Mohamed Street
Giza | EGYPT

TEL +20 (02) 35 40 58 90/91

FAX +20 (02) 37 49 44 06

Email
mail@greenlandschool.org

Website
www.greenlandschool.org

Green Land International School

GPIS Mission Statement

GPIS aims at providing its students with high quality international education in a local environment. The education places a strong emphasis on fostering respect for international, as well as national cultures, histories and societies.

GPIS

GPIS is an IB World School accredited by the reputable worldwide educational organization (IB) and authorized to offer the three IB programmes:

- Primary Years Programme (three to 11 years old)
- Middle Years Programme (11-15 years old)
- Diploma Programme (15-18 years old)

All students in GPIS master two languages (French-English) besides their mother tongue (Arabic). All IB diploma graduates earn a bilingual diploma.

Beautiful and Safe Environment

The school is a model of greenery and security. Students enjoy the beauty of the green unpolluted environment. These perfect conditions secure a stable and more enjoyable educational process.

The Quality Assurance Certificate BS EN ISO 9001: 2000

This certificate is an assurance to all parents that the school has an efficient administrative and educational system conforming to ISO standards under the umbrella of British Standard Institute BSI -UK.

2007 Robert Blackburn Award for the best Community and Service Project in Africa

GPIS is collaborating with Green Land Charity Association in eight developmental projects in a poor village near the school called Gezirat Mohamed village. One of these projects was the restoration of a polyclinic in the village. GPIS students have won the IB '2007 Blackburn Award' for this community and service project.

IB Diploma Results

We are proud to announce that IB diploma students' results in session May 2007 were exceeding **35 points as an average**. Moreover 40% of GPIS students' results were among **best 5% worldwide**.

GPIS Staff Development Unit

In GPIS we believe in continuous development that is why the school has created a staff development unit to provide both academic and soft skills trainings to ensure the best learning prospect for students. Moreover GPIS teachers attend regularly IB international workshops.

GPIS IB coordinators as well as some of GPIS teachers are IB examiners, leaders or moderators in the three IB programmes.

Ecole Internationale du Pré Vert
Déclaration de Mission de GPIS

L'objectif de GPIS est de procurer à ses élèves une éducation internationale de qualité dans un environnement local. Cette éducation met l'accent sur le respect des valeurs et de toutes les cultures internationales et nationales.

GPIS

GPIS est une école du monde BI accréditée par l'organisation du Baccalauréat international (IB) à dispenser les trois programmes du BI

- Le Programme Primaire – PP (trois to 11 ans)
- Le Programme du Premier Cycle Secondaire – PPCS (11-15 ans)
- Le Programme du Diplôme – DP (15-18 ans)

Tous les élèves GPIS maîtrisent parfaitement deux langues (le français et l'anglais) parallèlement à leur langue maternelle (l'arabe). Les étudiants de GPIS obtiennent un diplôme bilingue.

Un environnement Sûr et Agréable

Le cadre verdoyant, la nature environnante loin de toute pollution ainsi que le calme de l'école fournissent au personnel de GPIS les meilleures conditions de travail.

Le certificat d'assurance de qualité BS EN ISO 9001: 2000

Ce certificat garantit à tous les parents l'efficacité et le sérieux du système administratif et éducatif. Ce système est conforme aux normes de qualité du ISO sous le chapiteau de L'organisation du British Standard Institute BSI du Royaume Uni.

Le Prix International Blackburn 2007 pour le meilleur projet de service communautaire en Afrique

GPIS, en collaboration avec l'association de charité Green Land, participe activement au développement de huit projets socioéducatifs et de santé publique dans le village de Gezirat Mohammed avoisinant à l'école. Les élèves de GPIS ont reçu l'un des prix les plus prestigieux : Le prix international Blackburn 2007 pour leur participation active dans un de ces projets. Les élèves ont aménagé une polyclinique dans une zone rurale très démunie dans ce village.

Les résultats du Diplôme

Nous sommes fières d'annoncer les résultats des élèves du Diplôme de la session Mai 2007. Ces résultats ont dépassé **35 points de moyenne** . D'autre part 40 % des élèves de GPIS se trouvaient classes parmi **les 5% des meilleurs élèves du BI au monde.**

L'unité de développement professionnel de GPIS

À GPIS, nous croyons que le développement professionnel et les formations intenses peuvent seuls permettre et garantir la qualité de l'enseignement ainsi que l'acquisition des compétences nécessaires à l'expansion de tout projet pédagogique de qualité. Tout le personnel enseignant de GPIS assistent régulièrement a des formations internationales de l'OBI.

Les Coordinateurs de GPIS ainsi que quelques professeurs occupent la position de formateurs ou d'examinateurs de l'IBO dans les trois programmes du BI.

Gresham's School

(Founded 1555)

Headmaster
Mr Philip John

Diploma coordinator
Mr Mark Abbott

Status Private

Boarding/day Mixed

Gender Coeducational

Language of instruction
English

Programmes offered Diploma

Age range of pupils 13-18

Number of pupils enrolled 474

Fees per annum
Day: £17,490
Boarding: £22,785

Address
Cromer Road
Holt
Norfolk
NR25 6EA | UK

TEL +44 (0)1263 714511
FAX +44 (0)1263 712028

Email
headmaster@greshams.com

Website
www.greshams.com

Founded in 1555 by Sir John Gresham, the school is located in the historic Georgian market town of Holt near the North Norfolk coast, an Area of Outstanding Natural Beauty and World Heritage site. The school is easily accessible by road with intercity rail and international air connections at Norwich 40 minutes away. Our warm community, committed staff, wide range of opportunities, outstanding facilities and rural environment combine to provide a unique educational experience. Gresham's is primarily a full boarding school with all the associated benefits of academic and sporting excellence in addition to a wide range of extracurricular activities.

Our alumni have made significant contributions to human endeavour. Poets W H Auden and Sir Stephen Spender, composer Lord Benjamin Britten and theatre director Sir Peter Brook, have had a profound effect on the arts, Lord Reith and Sir John Tusa have been innovative in the field of media and communication, while hovercraft inventor Sir Christopher Cockerell and entrepreneur Sir James Dyson have had an equally significant influence on science and technology.

Gresham's has a long tradition of service and has been wholeheartedly involved in the Duke of Edinburgh's Award Scheme from its beginning, we have a well supported Combined Cadet Force and a strong and varied programme of both individual and team sports, which allow students to engage in a healthy and active lifestyle. Visual and performing arts are particularly well resourced and students have a wide range of opportunities to express their creativity.

We offer the following IB subjects at Higher and Standard Level: English A1 and A2, German A1, French B, Spanish B and *ab initio*, Latin, history, economics, geography, environmental systems & societies, biology, chemistry, physics, mathematics, mathematical studies and visual arts. A one year pre-IB course is available to students who require an accelerated learning environment before entering the IB Diploma Programme.

Gresham's School is in the care of the Worshipful Company of Fishmongers and is a registered charity for the purposes of education. Charity number 1105500.

Haileybury

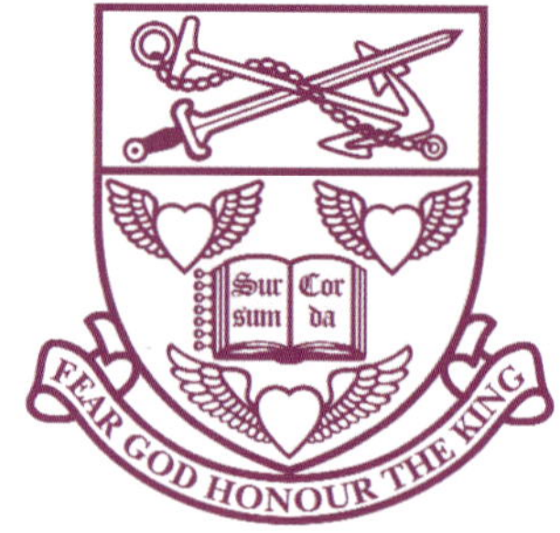

(Founded 1862)

The Master
S A Westley MA

Diploma coordinator
Laura Pugsley MA, PhD

Status Private

Boarding/day Mixed

Gender Coeducational

Language of instruction
English

Programmes offered Diploma

Age range of pupils 11-18

Number of pupils enrolled 755

Fees per annum
Day: £12,630-£19,005
Boarding: £16,050-£25,305

Address
Haileybury
Hertford
Hertfordshire
SG13 7NU | UK

TEL +44 (0)1992 462507
FAX +44 (0)1992 470663

Email
registrar@haileybury.com

Website
www.haileybury.com

For girls and boys looking for a typical British education with an international flavour, Haileybury, the independent coeducational boarding school in Hertfordshire, could prove to be the perfect fit.

Haileybury has offered the International Baccalaureate Diploma Programme since 1999 and it has been embraced wholeheartedly by staff and pupils alike.

IB students' results for 2008 were the best for quite a few years, with the average points score 35.4 out of a maximum 45 points. Out of the 59 candidates entered, ten were awarded 40 points or more.

In 2008/2009, 93 pupils are studying the Diploma Programme at Haileybury. In September 2003, the range of subjects offered was extended by the inclusion of theatre arts, design, technology and music, and we now boast more than 20 subject choices for pupils studying the IB.

Haileybury is primarily a boarding school and a successful one at that, as is demonstrated by the fact that our numbers are up dramatically compared with seven years ago. This is in direct contrast to the national trend which indicates that boarding in general is in the doldrums, with the total number of boarders nationally continuing to decline in four of the last six years.

In September 1999 there were 372 boarders at the school, and 515 in September 2007. This is almost a 40% rise in eight years.

The Master, Stuart Westley, attributes Haileybury's success to the fact that the school provides its boarders with a fulfilling, happy experience.

Adding to Haileybury's international flavour are the 150 or so pupils from over 30 countries, many of whom are studying the IB Diploma Programme. The thriving International Society within the school brings all pupils together and helps those from different countries to settle in more easily.

To find out more information about the courses offered, please contact Dr Laura Pugsley, IB coordinator, on email: l.pugsley@haileybury.com

About Haileybury

Haileybury is a coeducational boarding school, situated 20 miles north of London and 30 miles south of Cambridge in rural Hertfordshire. Set in spacious grounds and enjoying unrivalled facilities, Haileybury combines traditional values with a progressive outlook, aiming to provide the very best all-round education for 11- to 18-year-olds.

Renowned for community spirit and vibrant atmosphere, Haileybury was described in its successful 2006 Inspection Report as providing 'a wide-ranging, high quality experience which caters well for pupils' intellectual, physical and aesthetic needs'.

Haileybury has a flourishing academic reputation, and was ranked at Number 28 in the 2006 *Times* league tables.

Haileybury is a Registered Charity No. 310013.

Hasseris Gymnasium

Principal
Anders Bach Jensen

Diploma coordinator
Lars Nielsen

Status State

Boarding/day Both

Gender Coeducational

Language of instruction
English

Programmes offered Diploma

Address
Hasserisvej 300
DK-9000 Aalborg | DENMARK

TEL +45 9632 7117/
+45 2330 3409
FAX +45 9818 6312

Email
ib@hasseris-gym.dk

Website
www.hasseris-gym.dk

Hasseris Gymnasium is situated in the southern part of Aalborg, the capital of the Northern Jutland region. Plenty of green areas surround the school and it is not far away from Limfjorden. In these beautiful settings and stimulating learning environment Hasseris Gymnasium has offered the IB Diploma Programme since its authorisation in 2003, along with the Danish national high school programme.

Our teaching staff is a committed group of highly qualified teachers. Everybody contributes strongly to the implementation of the school's set of values with keywords such as professionalism, creativity, innovation, open-mindedness and tolerance.

Students applying to Hasseris Gymnasium can either join our preparatory programme, equivalent to the first year of the national programme, or they can apply directly for the IB Diploma Programme. We educate students from a large variety of cultural backgrounds, and each year we normally accommodate up to 20 different nationalities.

In our IB programme we offer the following subjects: Danish A1/B, English A1/A2/B, self-taught A1, French B, German B, Spanish *ab initio*, history, geography, biology, chemistry, physics, three levels of math, visual arts and music.

It is our aim that IB students participate in all school activities together with the students in the national programme. This includes music, art and sports events, and of course school cafés and parties. We also have a special IB committee, run by IB students, who arrange different kinds of after-school activites.

We work closely together with Aalborg BK Sports College in order to provide boarding facilities to those of our students who live in the city on their own.

International education is highly regarded in the region, and English school programmes for students aged five to 16 are taught at Aalborg International School. In addition to this, the local university and other educational institutions also offer a broad variety of courses with English as the language of instruction.

Experience the world in Aalborg at Hasseris Gymnasium

High School Affiliated To Nanjing Normal University

(Founded 1902)	**Number of pupils enrolled** 2494
Head of School Zhanbao Wang	**Fees per annum** 60,000 RMB
Diploma coordinator Gong Yan	**Address** 37 Chahaer Road Jiangsu Province Nanjing 210003 | PR CHINA
Status State	
Boarding/day Mixed	
Gender Coeducational	TEL +86 25 8346 9052
Language of instruction English	FAX +86 25 8346 9052
Programmes offered Diploma	**Email** wzb@nsfz.net
	Website www.nsfz.net

High School Affiliated To Nanjing Normal University, a school with more than 100 years of history, has been enjoying great popularity in China. It admits top students through the Nanjing High School Entrance Exam. Over 95% of its graduates each year are admitted to top Chinese universities and colleges and more and more students in recent years are admitted to universities abroad.

The philosophy of the school is to help develop each of its students from good to great. Students are expected to bear the characteristics of being responsible and creative.

The school provides two curriculums to its students – the Chinese National Curriculum and the IB Diploma Programme. Besides those, there is a range of optional courses covering subject areas from language, science, humanity, art and computer science and technology for students, taking the National Curriculum and the International Baccalaureate Diploma Programme, to choose from.

Varieties of extracurricular activities add to the richness of student life in the campus. There are annual school activities like Singing Fest, Science and Tech Fest, Sports Meet, *etc.* Our one-week Social Experience is an exciting period, when students visit factories, department stores, the army and meet and learn from countryside workers, salesmen, soldiers and farmers.

Besides that, students have opportunities to join in some international exchange programs. Being involved in AFS (American Field Service), and being once the AFS China training center, the school sends students to and welcomes students from abroad every year. Other programs are YFU (Youth For Understanding), AYA (Academic Year in America) and SIG (Summer Institute For The Gifted).

The school faculty team takes a leading role in both teaching and academic research among local schools. There are national curriculum revisers, national entrance examination chief examiners, subject teaching material chief editors among the team. More opportunities of professional development and bilingual teachers are another two shining points, which make the school stand out from local schools.

The school is a nominated pilot school for the Chinese National Curriculum reform by the Chinese Education Administration and one of the ten model schools of Chinese fundamental education.

Holy Trinity College

(Founded 1989)

Heads
Marcela Stewart de Tovo and
Stella Barbuzzi de Suárez

Diploma coordinator
Valeria Tommasi de Ruival

Status Private

Boarding/day Day

Gender Coeducational

Language of instruction
English, Spanish

Programmes offered Diploma

Age range of pupils 2-18

Number of pupils enrolled 637

Address
Gascón 544
Mar del Plata
7600 | ARGENTINA

TEL +54 223 486 3471
FAX +54 223 451 0168

Email
trinity@trinity.esc.edu.ar

Website
www.trinity.esc.edu.ar

Holy Trinity College was founded in 1989 with the ultimate goal of providing our students with a curriculum that integrates a strong Catholic education, a deep love for their country, and a bilingual education that combines traditional values with solid, yet modern instruction.

Well-rounded education

The curriculum is aimed at providing a bilingual and international educational experience. As a part of our educational goals, we are able to asses our students' progress through the many international exams we offer. Among them are the Trinity College Oral Exams from London, the Cambridge University IGSCE exams, and finally the International Baccalaureate Diploma Programme. Upon graduation, the students receive 'The National Bilingual Certificate in Secondary Education for Sciences and Humanities'.

Holy Trinity's athletic programs represent an important part of student life. Pupils participate in hockey, rugby, track and field, and swimming, competing in national and international tournaments.

The school also has a choir and a very enthusiastic orchestra that play in and out of school.

Values

Our school nurtures and maintains the principles and values of the Schoenstatt spirituality. Holy Trinity College is formed by a group of families that maintain a very strong and active relationship with the school, and support what Trinity stands for. They organize activities and athletic events, which always draw enthusiastic participation.

Holy Trinity has well-established links with schools within the country, as well as with schools in England, New Zealand, South Africa, Scotland, the United States, and France. We aspire to stimulate curiosity and consciousness of their local area and to help them broaden their views to new horizons.

Objectives

Holy Trinity College aims to enable their students with the necessary knowledge, skills and attitudes to embark into a university career within the country or abroad. We believe that education is the key element for a good quality of life. It is our aim to generate the necessary opportunities to provide our students access to a globalized world, and help them develop an awareness of the key role they will play in shaping the future of the world in years to come.

Hørsholm International School

(Founded 1996)

Director
Mr Jan Thrane

PYP coordinator
Karen Johansen

MYP coordinator
Karen Johansen

Status Private

Boarding/day Day

Gender Coeducational

Language of instruction
English

Programmes offered
PYP, MYP

Age range of pupils 4-16

Number of pupils enrolled 220

Fees per annum
Kindergarten 1: 48,400 DKK;
Kindergarten 2-Grade 10:
19,690 DKK

Address
Cirkelhuset
Christianshusvej 16
DK 2970 Hørsholm | DENMARK

TEL +45 45 57 26 16

FAX +45 45 57 26 69

Email
his@ngg.dk

Website
www.his.dk

Hørsholm International School is an IB World School offering international education in the English language for non-permanent international families. Students from all cultures and faiths are welcomed.

Hørsholm International School (HIS) is located in a green belt 25 km north of the capital city of Copenhagen and is easily accessible by car and public transportation.

There are 220 students with 46 nationalities from around the globe. No one nationality is dominant at HIS.

The international teachers are qualified in their home countries and represent 15 nationalities.

Students are supported as English Language Learners in our language support unit. Single subject teachers cover: the arts (music, drama, visual art), physical education, technology and Danish. Middle Years students are offered a choice of modern languages including French, German and Spanish.

Hørsholm International School is the international department of the largest private school in Denmark, Nordsjællands Grundskole & Gymnasium with a total of 1400 students.

The school day begins at 8:55 for all students and finishes at 14:30 for all Primary Year students. Middle Years students may finish at 15:15 or 16:00 on some days.

Indoor facilities include a canteen, two gymnasium rooms, a before and after school care facility for students up to grade 4, state of the art science laboratories, a computer laboratory and a library.

Outdoor facilities include soccer pitches, science experimental area, hockey mini arena, basketball, and play areas for younger and older students.

As one part of community and service students from grades 3-10 are elected by peers to represent their classes on the student council.

Institut Le Rosey

(Founded 1880)

Headmaster
Rob Gray

Diploma coordinator
Steve Cranville

Status Private

Boarding/day Boarding

Gender Coeducational

Language of instruction
English, French

Programmes offered Diploma

Age range of pupils 7-18

Number of pupils enrolled 402

Fees per annum
Juniors: SFr 63,000;
Secondary: SFr 84,000
(Boarding), 88,100 (IB)

Address
Château du Rosey
1180 Rolle | SWITZERLAND

TEL +41 21 822 5500

FAX +41 21 822 5555

Email
rosey@rosey.ch

Website
www.rosey.ch

Founded in 1880, Institut Le Rosey is a coeducational international boarding school, offering a rounded bilingual education in English and/or French for students aged eight to 18, leading to the IB Diploma and French baccalauréat. It also offers a unique two-campus system through its move from an attractive 75-acre château setting by Lake Geneva to the school's alpine campus in Gstaad every winter term.

An International Mission

Le Rosey is an extraordinarily international boarding community, with well over 50 nationalities in its student body, and over 20 on the teaching staff. The cultural and linguistic diversity of 400 students is guaranteed by highly selective admissions with quotas of no more than 10% per nationality. Students choose either English or French as their principal academic language but dual-language programmes enable and encourage all to become bilingual or polyglot. This multinational mix naturally creates a special campus atmosphere, and enhances global awareness and international understanding.

Academics

The IB Diploma Programme and the school's middle- and lower-school programmes are offered in English and French. As well as promoting English-French bilingualism and biculturalism, Le Rosey also offers a broad academic programme and range of IB and 'Pre-Bac' subjects, with a particularly strong tradition in foreign languages. Through its mother-tongue programme, over a dozen A1 languages are taught every year for the IB and lower down the school; well over 20 have been taught since 2000 when the school adopted the IB. University admissions in the USA, UK and elsewhere (including the Ivy League, Oxbridge and the LSE) testify to high academic standards.

Sports, Arts and Expeditions

Le Rosey is committed to holistic educational principles. An exceptionally varied sports, arts and cultural programme takes full advantage of facilities which include riding stables, a sailing centre, as well as indoor and outdoor swimming pools. At weekends, students participate in a demanding expeditions programme – linked to the Duke of Edinburgh's Award Scheme – and many take part in cultural visits to European capitals. Most distinctively, Le Rosey's winter term, on its complete campus in the exclusive alpine resort of Gstaad, guarantees the physical and psychological benefits of winter sports and a mountain environment.

The Rosey Spirit

Through adherence to a strong set of ethical values, small class sizes and close relationships between staff and students, and a policy of accepting only boarders, Le Rosey creates an enduring sense of community and solidarity between a unique mix of nationalities, races and cultures. An entirely independent alumni association, the AIAR, provides a global network of friends and connections, justifying Le Rosey's motto of 'a school for life'.

(Founded 1973)

Headteacher
Maria Teresa Compeán
de Carrera

PYP coordinator
Claudia Ghigliazza

MYP coordinator
María Cristina Beltrán
Aguerrebere

Diploma coordinator
María Concepción Sacristán
de García

Status Private

Boarding/day Day

Gender Coeducational

Language of instruction
Spanish, English, French

Programmes offered
PYP, MYP, Diploma

Age range of pupils 2-19

Number of pupils enrolled 1600

Address
Periférico Sur 5170
Col Pedregal de Carrasco,
Delegación Coyoacán
04700 México DF | MEXICO

TEL +52 5 55 606 3113
FAX +52 5 55 665 7613

Email
buzon@olinca.edu.mx

Website
www.olinca.edu.mx

The Olinca Mission 'To Become Better human Beings' is based on academic and formative excellence.

Talent, enthusiasm and rigorous dedication is clearly evident in the results of the programs of the Mexican educative authorities, SEP and UNAM, IB, and our own Institutional Programs.

Olinca pioneered the three IB Programmes in Mexico in 1980. We have developed these programmes in kindergarten, primary, middle school, and high school.

Olinca's Institutional Programs:

1 Technology of Information: computers, technology and robotics.
2 Art: all forms of artistic expression.
3 Languages: Spanish, English and French with international certification.
4 Nationalism – Internationalism: 'One Family, Mankind; One Home, the Earth', school to school exchange programs in Mexico and the world over.
5 Sports and Physical Education: soccer, basketball, cheerleading, karate, chess and other.
6 Community Service: 14 community projects with excellent results.
7 Formation and Development: definition and clarification of values: responsibility, generosity and joyous celebration in attitudes, deeds and objectives.
8 Academics: stimulation of intellectual inquisitiveness, strengthening and buttressing justified logical and critical reasoning.

Facilities

- 17,000m² facilities
- Science, robotic, art labs
- Ceramic workshop
- Radio lab
- Afternoon activities
- Sports
- Guided homework
- Reinforcement classes

We have three campuses in:

Coyoacán

Altavista

Cuernavaca

International College Spain

International College Spain (ICS), founded in 1980, is the leading international school in Spain. It is a day school with approximately 650 students, from three- to 18-years-old, on the roll. The students originate from 48 different countries. The language of instruction is English. ICS has been an IB World School since 1980 and offers an international curriculum throughout the whole age range (Kindergarten to Grade 12), by means of the three prestigious International Baccalaureate Programmes.

The school year, from September to June with winter and spring breaks, is divided into three academic terms. The school has no religious or any other affiliation, and is governed by an independent Board of Trustees. ICS is accredited by both the New England Association of Schools and Colleges and the Council of International Schools, and is approved by the Spanish Ministry of Education as a foreign school for the education of both Spanish and foreign students.

The school campus is situated on three hectares of land in La Moraleja, ten kilometres north of the centre of Madrid. The installations include two separate buildings for primary and secondary schools, four science laboratories, a large art room, a music room, two computer labs and a computer resource centre, an auditorium, a gymnasium, a cafeteria and outdoor sports areas. ICS also has a field centre, La Perla, situated in the province of Toledo, where groups of students gather to participate in cross curricular activities.

The school has acquired a reputation for encouraging high academic achievement within a caring and stimulating environment. ICS IB Diploma Programme students consistently obtain a more than satisfactory overall average score with a handful of students achieving 40+ points. Our students continue their studies in top universities all over the world but principally in the UK, USA and Spain.

ICS has an excellent extracurricular activities programme covering a wide range of sports: football, basketball, golf, horse riding, swimming, volleyball, judo, karate, skiing; as well as dance, games and language classes.

Central to the educational philosophy of International College Spain is the desire to promote international understanding whilst preparing its students for the challenges of life in a multicultural global society. Through its international programmes and its many activities the school strives not only to prepare its students for higher education, but also tries to teach them self-confidence, self-reliance and the ability to cope with the diversity of life in the modern world.

Further information can be obtained from the Admissions Officer on admissions@icsmadrid.org

'Learning Together for a Better World'

International School Manila

(Founded 1920)	**Number of pupils enrolled** 1878
Head of School David Toze	**Address** University Parkway, Fort Bonifacio, Global City, Taguig PO Box 1526 MCPO, 1255 Makati City | PHILIPPINES
Diploma coordinator Sandy Van Nooten	TEL +63 2 8488440 FAX +63 2 8408489
Status Private	
Boarding/day Day	**Email** tozed@ismanila.org
Gender Coeducational	**Website** www.ismanila.org
Language of instruction English	
Programmes offered Diploma	
Age range of pupils 3-18	

The International School Manila (ISM) is a private independent school for students from Pre-School through Grade 12 and is incorporated under the laws of the Republic of the Philippines as a non-profit, non-stock organization. It was founded in 1920 as the American School, but the name was officially changed in 1970 to reflect its diverse student population. In February 2008 ISM received dual accreditation by the Council of International Schools and the US based Western Association of Schools and Colleges (WASC). ISM is certified to award the traditional US High School Diploma and the International Baccalaureate Diploma.

ISM students represent some 60 different nations with approximately 25% North American, 8% European, 60% Asian-Pacific and the remaining 7% from other countries. ISM is a college preparatory school where instruction is primarily in English. We aim to prepare our students for higher education institutions around the world, with the majority of our students attending universities in the US, Canada, the UK, Japan, Korea, Europe and Australia.

The IB Programme was introduced into the curriculum in 1976 and currently ISM offers 41 IB courses. Based on the number of exams written by our students, ISM is ranked first in the Philippines, ninth in the Asia Pacific Region and 47th in the world as of May 2008. Our records reflect that our students score well-above world averages in most subjects.

The IB programme at the International School Manila offers open enrolment to all students for both the Diploma Programme and the Certificate Programme. Currently we have 70% of our 12th year students taking the Diploma Programme with the remainder opting for IB Certificate study.

ISM is located on a 7.5 hectare site in the new Global City development in Metro Manila. Our purpose-built campus accommodates the dynamic curricular and co-curricular programs being offered to our elementary, middle and high school student population.

International School of Berne

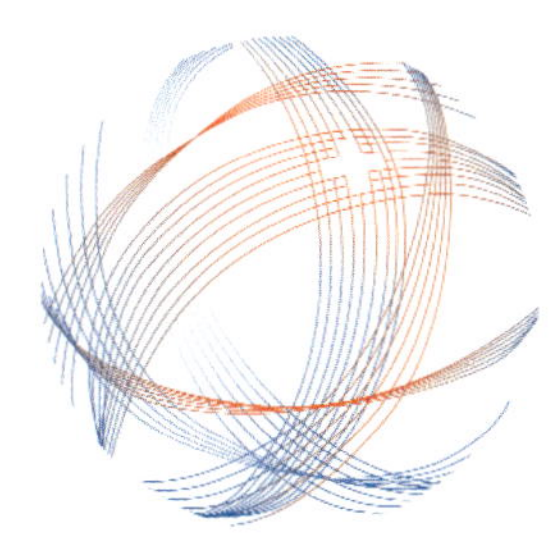

International
School
of Berne

(Founded 1961)

Head of School
Kevin Page

PYP coordinator
Alyson Rees

MYP coordinator
James Cairns

Diploma coordinator
Eric Mace-Tessler

Status Private

Boarding/day Day

Gender Coeducational

Language of instruction
English

Programmes offered
PYP, MYP, Diploma

Age range of pupils 3-19

Number of pupils enrolled 280

Fees per annum
CHF 7990-28,850

Address
Mattenstrasse 3
Gümligen
Berne
3073 | SWITZERLAND

TEL +41 31 951 23 58
FAX +41 31 951 17 10

Email
office@isberne.ch

Website
www.isberne.ch

The International School of Berne (ISBerne), founded in 1961, is a day school providing an international education in English for children from the diplomatic and multinational community of Berne and the surrounding cantons.

ISBerne is accredited by the Council of International Schools and the New England Association of Schools and Colleges.

ISBerne is one of approximately 2400 IB World Schools, and one of only 118 authorized to offer all three prestigious International Baccalaureate (IB) Programmes:

- the **IB Primary Years Programme** in the Early Learning Centre and KG – Grade 5 (ages three to 11),
- the **IB Middle Years Programme** in Grades 6 – 10 (ages 11-16) and
- the **IB Diploma Programme**, a comprehensive pre-university course, in Grades 11 and 12 (ages 16-19).

ISBerne has 280 students aged three to 19. Staff and students from over 40 nations create a multicultural and welcoming family atmosphere. Small classes and dedicated teachers ensure an individualized approach to learning. The local environment enables ISBerne to provide a unique and rich learning experience in the heart of Switzerland. The school language is English and French and/or German are compulsory from elementary school. The spirit of ISBerne and its international programmes make the school unique in the region.

All students from ELC to Grade 12 participate in whole school activities such as assemblies, theatre productions, music ensemble, choir, sports events and tournaments. The school's sports teams participate in tournaments and meets throughout Switzerland.

As part of the Physical Education Programme, the school provides skiing or snowboarding days for Grades 2-12 and ice-skating mornings for Kindergarten and Grade 1 from January to March. These ski days are an unforgettable experience for students and teachers, who travel together to the ski area in a private train. The children are taught by professional ski teachers. Parents have the opportunity to join these outings.

Located in the suburb of Muri-Gümligen, the school is easily accessible by private and public transport. It is situated about one hour from the beautiful Swiss Alps and from the French-speaking part of Switzerland, with its lakes and vineyards.

International School of Bremen

(Founded 1998)

Director
Mr Malcolm Davis

Diploma coordinator
Mr Kim Walton

Status Private

Boarding/day Day

Gender Coeducational

Language of instruction
English

Programmes offered Diploma

Age range of pupils 3-18

Number of pupils enrolled 270

Fees per annum €7750-€11,550

Address
Thomas-Mann Strasse 6-8
D-28213 Bremen | GERMANY

TEL +49 421 337 9272
FAX +49 421 337 9273

Email
office@isbremen.de

Website
www.isbremen.de

The International School of Bremen was established in 1998 to serve the international community of Bremen. The school occupies a purpose-built German school in the Schwachhausen area of Bremen close to the city centre in a quiet residential area. Classes are taught in refurbished classrooms with appropriate furniture, books and materials. Classes are generally small and teachers are able to provide individual assistance.

The students range in age from three to 18 years and are placed in grades – preschool through grade 12. The students come from 35 different countries around the world. The school is governed by a five member Executive Board representing the corporate sponsors of the school. The Director is the chief executive officer of the school and makes all decisions in conjunction with the Executive Board. The teachers are from the United States, Germany, India, UK, Canada and Australia.

All of the teachers are certified according to the standards of their home countries.

ISB offers an international curriculum drawing upon best practice from the UK, USA, Australia and the host country, with all instruction in English except for foreign language classes. The curriculum in the elementary school is the International Primary Curriculum. In the early part of secondary the focus is on IGCSE and in the last two years the International Baccalaureate Diploma Programme. Specialist teachers provide instruction in music, physical education, art, drama and language. An ESL programme is offered for those students who need assistance with English. A school counsellor is available to assist both with social and emotional development as well as academic matters. Parenting classes are offered, the school is non-selective – however, SEN support is limited.

International School of Curaçao

(Founded 1968)

Director
Margie Elhage-Cancio PhD

Diploma coordinator
Suhasini M Iyengar

Status Private

Boarding/day Day

Gender Coeducational

Language of instruction
English

Programmes offered Diploma

Age range of pupils 3-19

Number of pupils enrolled 528

Fees per annum Contact Mrs Loraine van Rosberg at vanrosbergl@isc.an

Address
PO Box 3090
Koninginnelaan z/n
Curaçao | NETHERLANDS ANTILLES

TEL +599 9 737 3633
FAX +599 9 737 3142

Email
muralis@isc.an

Website
www.isc.an

The International School of Curaçao (ISC) educates students from diverse cultures to have the skills to think creatively, communicate effectively, reason critically and act compassionately.

ISC has pledged to achieve this by providing a high quality English medium education using United States and internationally recognized standards.

The elementary school begins with kindergarten for three-year-olds and extends to grade 5. Each classroom is self-contained with students taking core subjects from their homeroom teacher. Students receive instruction in art, music, computers, library and PE from K3 and begin taking Dutch and Spanish classes in 2nd grade. Elementary school builds a foundation of academic skills and personal competency that will prepare children to succeed in later grades. Our elementary program emphasizes fundamental skills in language arts and mathematics.

Our middle school offers a program tailored to the unique social and learning needs of students in grades 6, 7 and 8. We encourage students to solve problems, apply organizational skills, research important questions, and most importantly to celebrate the differences within themselves and those around them.

Our high school offers a vigorous liberal arts education for every student and fosters international understanding. Advanced Placement (AP) courses are offered in Spanish and Spanish literature. We also offer students the full International Baccalaureate (IB) Diploma Programme in the 11th and 12th grade or the option of pursuing individual certificates in the different subject areas.

Other special curriculum features include: English as a second language (ESL), learning resource (LR), as well as guidance counseling and college placement.

The International School of Curaçao is a member of the Association of American Schools in South America (AASSA), a Member of the College Board and the National Association for College Admission Counseling and is fully accredited by the Southern Association of Colleges and Schools (SACS) since 1990.

An international education today for the global citizens of tomorrow.

International School of London

(Founded 1972)

PYP coordinator
Hala Fadda

MYP coordinator
Paul Morris

Diploma coordinator
Huw Davies

Status Private

Boarding/day Day

Gender Coeducational

Language of instruction
English

Programmes offered
PYP, MYP, Diploma

Age range of pupils 3-18

Number of pupils enrolled 350

Fees per annum
£13,000-£18,250

Address
139 Gunnersbury Avenue
Acton
London
W3 8LG | UK

TEL +44 (0)20 8992 5823
FAX +44 (0)20 8993 7012

Email
mail@islondon.com

Website
www.islondon.com

The International School of London (ISL) was established in 1972. The school accepts girls and boys of all nationalities from pre-school age up to the IB Diploma Programme.

Students may join ISL at any time during the academic year and enter the year level as may be appropriate to their age groups. Because of the international nature of our school we have new students joining and leaving our school each year.

At primary level, we offer the IB Primary Years Programme (PYP) from the Early Childhood Programme to Year 6. Using the PYP we are able to provide students with an international curriculum, which focuses on developing the whole child. We have one class per year group.

In the middle school we offer the IB Middle Years Programme, providing a learning environment, which enables students to develop and fulfil their potential. To this end we have created a teaching approach that fosters individual responsibility for learning in an atmosphere of cooperation amongst students. As an international school based in the heart of London we promote appreciation of cultural diversity within the school as well as encourage meaningful integration with the surrounding community.

At IB Diploma Programme level, we offer a broad range of choices within each subject group but we do need to ensure that class sizes are efficient so that, while we do our best to meet each student's need, it may not be possible to offer every combination. During the last two years ISL students have achieved places at some of the most prestigious universities around the world including: University of Oxford – UK; University of Chicago – USA; Keio University – Japan; Universita Commerciale 'Luigi Bocconi' – Italy.

Non-English speaking students are admitted at PYP and MYP levels and given special English language support through Intensive English or English as a Second Language courses. Transfer to the full range of subjects takes place progressively when the student is ready.

Mother tongue is valued highly at ISL and instruction is made available in many languages according to need. The Home Languages programme is an integral part of the curriculum from Year 1 to Year 13. Currently the school offers: Arabic, Czech, Danish, Dutch, French, German, Finnish, Icelandic, Italian, Japanese, Norwegian, Portuguese, Russian, Spanish and Turkish.

The school was purpose-built in the 1930s and has recently undergone a large scale refurbishment with new classrooms, improved library, outdoor play area and two IT suites.

Gunnersbury Park is adjacent with facilities for outdoor sports, and a gymnasium and swimming pool complex is nearby at the Brentford Leisure Centre. A door-to-door bus service covers most of central, west and south London, and underground stations are within ten minutes' walk.

Parents

The ISL Parent Teacher Association (PTA) is a non-profit organisation involving all ISL parents and staff and aims to stimulate communication and create a better understanding between the school and parents; to encourage the growth and reputation of the school; to promote its policies and provide support where appropriate. Parental involvement at ISL is highly valued and encouraged. The PTA Chair is an ex-officio member of the ISL School Board. Regular PTA activities include a welcome BBQ, weekly cookery demonstrations in the kitchen, English language classes, a Book Club, coffee mornings, theatre visits and guided walks in London.

In the ISL classrooms the learning environment created is of support. Students are encouraged to express their viewpoints in a variety of forms (orally, wall display, drawings, roleplaying, written form, modelling, artefact production *etc*). These viewpoints are valued as worthwhile contributions to the learning experience. This environment creates an atmosphere of respect and trust where ideas are brought into the open, discussed, experimented with and challenged. ISL teachers are aware that learning is a gradual, non-linear and affective process; by following a 'spiral curriculum scheme' with an emphasis on formative assessment we offer ample opportunities for students to revisit and to rethink their ideas in new contexts.

By giving time for the students to think through new learning experiences they are able to internalise and to express deeper conflicting ideas and articulate their views more coherently. The combination of a spiral curriculum scheme, differentiated teaching strategies and teacher support are proving ideally suitable for integrating the newly arrived student whilst we maintain the demands of an academically ambitious curriculum.

International School of Tianjin

(Founded 1994)

Director
Steve Moody

PYP coordinator
Josianne Fitzgerald

MYP coordinator
Barbara Wrightson

Diploma coordinator
Susan Hall

Status Private

Boarding/day Day

Gender Coeducational

Language of instruction
English

Programmes offered
PYP, MYP, Diploma

Age range of pupils 3-18

Number of pupils enrolled 500

Address
Weishan Road, Shuanggang
Jinnan District
Tianjin
300350 | PR CHINA

TEL +86 22 2859 2001
FAX +86 22 2859 2007

Email
info@istianjin.net

Website
www.istianjin.org

For over fourteen years, the International School of Tianjin (IST) has provided an education of distinction to young global citizens while serving the needs of our communities. Established as an international school to realize the need for premier education that meets rigorous global standards, IST is accredited to teach students from nursery through grade 12 and is the only IB World School in Tianjin. Since our first graduating class in 2005, IST students have been accepted at numerous universities. A partial listing includes Bowdoin College, Purdue University, Singapore Management University, Seoul National University, University of Southern California, University of Toronto, Pennsylvania State University, Ateneo De Manila University and University of British Columbia.

At IST we provide a truly international education, celebrating the diversity of world cultures with a student population of more than 500 from 26 countries. The teaching staff at IST numbers over 65 and reflects the internationalism of our student body and parent community. They are well trained and certified in their respective fields and have an average of over 13 years teaching experience.

Curriculum

Based on the International Baccalaureate Programmes, our curriculum offers three stages spanning the primary, middle, and secondary school years and integrating a common philosophy and characteristics throughout the entire educational experience.

Student Admissions

Students are admitted based on an assessment of the student's ability to benefit both from the school's academic programme and also from the student life environment, which emphasizes care for the person, development of self-discipline, and responsibility to the community. English is the language of instruction and to this end the school provides a comprehensive and dynamic English as a Second Language (ESL) programme. Because of our experienced special needs department, IST is also able to accept students with mild to moderate learning difficulties.

Facilities

Located along a major access point that is central to both Tianjin and Tanggu communities, our 13-acre purpose built campus is surrounded by spacious green playing fields, parks and gardens. We have over 70 classrooms, gymnasium, two full-size basketball courts, a climbing wall, an outdoor soccer pitch, a 21,000+ volume English-based library, three well-equipped IT labs, multiple mini IT labs, four state-of-the-art science labs and networked and wireless IT facilities – all of which enhance both curriculum related and extracurricular activities. Our outstanding theatre, art and music facilities were also specifically designed to heighten the artistic learning process. We also have an in-house clinic, staffed during regular school hours and during on-site extracurricular activities. Transportation services to and from school are available from several different locations within Tianjin and Tanggu.

(Founded 2002)

Head of School
Rhonda L Mott-Hill

PYP coordinator
Alex Cardona

Status Private

Boarding/day Day

Gender Coeducational

Language of instruction
English

Programmes offered PYP

Age range of pupils 3-17

Address
Zum Park 5
CH-8404 Winterthur |
SWITZERLAND

TEL +41 52 269 5900
FAX +41 52 269 5902

Email
administration@iswinterthur.ch

Website
www.iswinterthur.ch

Our students and families represent more than 34 nationalities. We offer a full day school to all students with the choice of half-day or full day school for Early Years 1 and a full day programme for all students from EY2 to grade 10.

The breadth and depth of our curricular programmes, delivered in a nurturing environment, follows the Early Years 1 and 2 (ages three to four), the IB Primary Years Programme (PYP) (ages five to 11) and the IB Middle Years Programme (MYP) (ages 11-16). These programmes combine the best research and practice from a range of national systems with a wealth of knowledge and expertise from international schools to create a relevant and engaging educational experience. We are officially recognized as an IB World School having received PYP authorization in May 2006, and are a candidate school for the MYP.

The ISW Primary Years Programme has designed a transdisciplinary curriculum framework that draws the individual disciplines together into a coherent whole while preserving the essence of each subject. Furthermore, the programme accommodates traditional academic subjects yet emphasizes the interrelatedness of knowledge and skills. Students develop a deep understanding of important concepts through inquiry, conduct research into knowledge which has local and global significance, acquire and practice a range of essential skills, develop positive attitudes towards learning, the environment and other people, and have the opportunity for involvement in responsible action and social service.

The ISW Middle Years Programme aims to help students develop the knowledge, understanding, skills and attitudes they need to participate actively and responsibly in an ever changing world. Our students are encouraged to question, evaluate, think critically and independently. They work collaboratively, investigate and explore the connections between subjects, and develop a sense of their own place in the world. We seek to give the students an international perspective – to help them develop a sensitivity to the experiences of people and cultures throughout the world, while at the same time fostering a commitment to help others and act as responsible members of the community at local, national, and international levels.

ISS International School Singapore

(Founded 1981)

Headmaster
Anthony Race

PYP coordinator
George Piacentini

MYP coordinator
Elizabeth Carrick

Diploma coordinator
Stuart Jones

Status Private

Boarding/day Day

Gender Coeducational

Language of instruction
English

Programmes offered
PYP, MYP, Diploma

Age range of pupils 3-18

Number of pupils enrolled 850

Fees per annum
S$11,000-S$23,000

Address
21 Preston Road
Singapore
109355 | SINGAPORE

TEL +65 6475 4188
FAX +65 6273 7065

Email
admissions@iss.edu.sg

Website
www.iss.edu.sg

ISS International School Singapore was founded in 1981 to serve the expatriate community in Singapore. Our focus is to nurture every child to develop his or her maximum potential. ISS also places strong emphasis on holistic learning, focusing on every student's personal and social development.

ISS International School Singapore is:

- An experienced PYP, MYP and DP authorized IB World School, with years of experience offering each programme.
- The ONLY IB World School in Singapore that specializes in the IB. Due to a curriculum re-structure, we are able to offer the three IB Programmes to their fullest potential without competing pedagogical interference from other curricula or programs.
- A truly international school with a multi-cultural environment, comprising of students from over 45 countries with no dominant culture.
- Outstanding student support services such as counseling, personal focus and attention, university advising, *etc.*
- Well known for our activities program, including field trips, and our adventurous activity week programs held each year.
- Please read our ISS High School Profile for more details www.iss.edu.sg/hsprofile.pdg.

Our Academic Programme

ISS is an authorized International Baccalaureate World School offering Primary Years Programme (Kindergarten – Grade 5), Middle Years Programme (Grade 6 – Grade 10) and Diploma Programme (Grade 11-12). Our accreditation with the Western Association of Schools and Colleges (WASC) also enables us to offer a High School Diploma to our IB Diploma and IB Certificate graduates.

Academic Year – August to June (Semester 1 mid-August to mid-December, Semester 2 mid-January to early June).

Faculty

- Teachers from 17 different countries.
- Predominantly trained in United States, Britain, Canada, New Zealand, and Australia. Many faculty members are moderators, examiners and workshop leaders (CIS team members) for the IB organization.

Student Information – Students from over 45 countries.

Class sizes – elementary school: 15-20 students; middle school: 20-24 students; high school: 15-20 students

Admissions

Our admissions staff are available year round to meet with you regarding admissions for all three schools.

- Applications are accepted year round, subject to places being available.
- As part of the admissions procedure, we would like to review the applicant's school reports/transcripts for the past three years, as well as a letter of reference to be completed by the principal or teacher about the applicant's overall conduct and abilities.
- Students must pass our English language proficiency test to be eligible for admission.

itgymnasiet

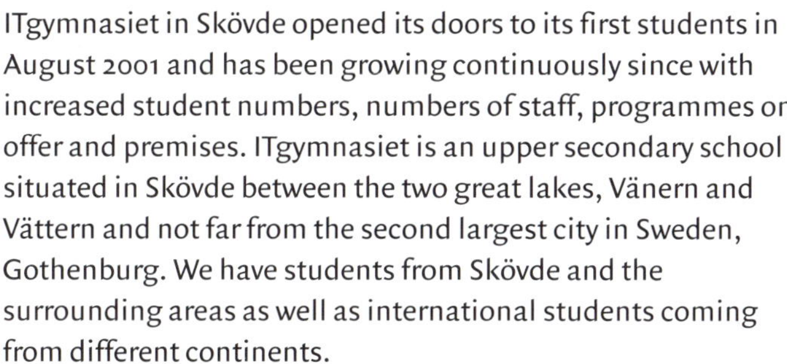

Head of School
Sven Ove Johansson

Diploma coordinator
Carl Liwell

Status State

Boarding/day Day

Gender Coeducational

Language of instruction
English

Programmes offered Diploma

Number of pupils enrolled 320

Address
Box 399
Skövde
54128 | SWEDEN

TEL +46 500 416990

Email
info@itgymnasiet.nu

Website
www.itgymnasiet.nu

ITgymnasiet in Skövde opened its doors to its first students in August 2001 and has been growing continuously since with increased student numbers, numbers of staff, programmes on offer and premises. ITgymnasiet is an upper secondary school situated in Skövde between the two great lakes, Vänern and Vättern and not far from the second largest city in Sweden, Gothenburg. We have students from Skövde and the surrounding areas as well as international students coming from different continents.

ITgymnasiet is a small but modern school with the latest equipment when it comes to computers and other technology. Two programs are running at the school, an ITprogramme and the International Baccalaureate Diploma Programme. In October 2004 the school was given authorisation to teach the IB Diploma Programme – an acknowledgement that the school lives up to internationally high demands for quality. The first group started in 2005 and had their exams in May 2008.

At ITgymnasiet we can see that one of the best features of the IB Diploma Programme is that it gives students the tools for participating actively in a global community, through their developing knowledge of, and respect for, different cultures, democracy, freedom, justice, equality and human rights. What is more, the programme leads to an internationally accepted examination which creates an interest in other peoples and cultures and issues of the global environment. One of our goals with the programme is that, once they have completed their studies, students will feel that the international experience is a natural part of everyday life, that they are aware of global issues and that they perceive that their ambitions are not limited by national frontiers.

Since the IB Diploma Programme is a two-year programme, we therefore have the opportunity to provide the students with a preparatory year so that they can get the most out of their IB studies.

For more information and pictures please visit our website!

John Paul I High School

(Founded 1979)

Principal
Liboria Amato

MYP coordinator
Anne-Marie Delisle

Status State

Boarding/day Day

Gender Coeducational

Language of instruction
English (56%), French (44%)

Programmes offered MYP

Number of pupils enrolled 685

Address
8455 Pre-Laurin
St Leonard QC
H1R 3P3 | CANADA

TEL +1 514 328 7171
FAX +1 514 328 7804

Email
amdelisle@emsb.qc.ca

Website
www.emsb.qc.ca/johnpauli

John Paul I is a junior high school consisting of Secondary 1 and 2 pupils. Our sister school Laurier Macdonald completes the other three years of the Middle Years Programme. The selection of students is based on an entrance exam, a student's profile, and teachers' comments. The school year, from September to June with winter and spring breaks, is divided into four academic terms. The curriculums followed are set by the Quebec Ministry of Education and the IB standards.

John Paul I challenges students academically and promotes life skills. Its focus is on students becoming inquirers, finding meaning, and being enthusiastic about discovering knowledge on their own. Pupils at this age go through many physical and emotional changes; consequently health education is a priority.

John Paul I is a community school easily accessed by public transportation. The MYP is one of three programs that our school offers, the other two being Bilingual (English-French) and English Core. These programs and the rigorous pedagogical demands are what makes our school appealing to parents and students in the community.

John Paul I has excellent extracurricular activities covering a range of sports: football, soccer, volleyball, bocci, world cup tournament, rock climbing; as well as Leadership Group, Photo Club, and Yearbook Club. Many do community service beyond the required hours. Our students are active in their churches, elementary schools, community centers, and local organisations.

John Paul I has a first-rate visual arts/media curriculum. Great productions have been put forth by students. Enrichment activities to complement our programs are emphasised. For example, students learn Spanish as a third language. As an enrichment activity, a trip to Spain is organized, which puts forward a great opportunity to apply the knowledge and language skills that they have previously acquired. Students are also committed and dedicated to embellishing their school, making it a very welcoming environment for all.

However successful John Paul I programs are, the emphasis is on exploring new possibilities and doing one's personal best.

Laurier Macdonald High School

(Founded 1984)

Principal
Eileen Kelly

MYP coordinator
Anne-Marie Delisle

Status State

Boarding/day Day

Gender Coeducational

Language of instruction
English (77%), French (23%)

Programmes offered
MYP

Age range of pupils 14-18

Number of pupils enrolled 1000

Address
7355 Boulevard Viau
St Leonard QC
H1S 3C2 | CANADA

TEL +1 514 374 6000

FAX +1 514 374 7220

Email
amdelisle@emsb.qc.ca

Website
www.lauriermacdonald.ca

Laurier Macdonald Senior High School is an inclusive learning community committed to the achievement of student excellence within a dynamic global landscape. Personal and academic accomplishment is developed through creative thought, rigorous intellectual inquiry, the ideal of citizenship, and a deepening respect for oneself and others.

Success is promoted through the teaching and exploration of multiple literacies, the Media Production Program, Community Learning Center, and the diversification of learning pathways: an International Baccalaureate Middle Years Programme, Bilingual Studies, or a Core English Syllabus.

Along with expectations of academic inquiry, students benefit from its school-wide media production program. The curriculum focuses on media production methods as a way to prepare students to be active participants in tomorrow's world today. Media is experienced as a way of life, a means of exploring and refashioning the world as they see it. Lessons learned in the arts, humanities, sciences and mathematics find real world application through production methods.

Students also follow enrichment programs in ethics education as well as physical fitness. We believe our students have reached a critical point in moral and intellectual development. Our rich ethics program provides students with the opportunity to discuss, debate, and argue important global issues.

Health and well-being are essential aspects within the curriculum. The school promotes lifelong health and positive attitudes towards physical activity. Current studies in brain development suggest physical activity helps improve academic achievement. Our physical education facilities include two gymnasia and a swimming pool.

Engagement in extracurricular activities is a school requirement. A sense of involvement is essential for student growth. Adolescents need to be involved in activities that develop organization and social skills. Our student life program helps our students learn these essential life skills. The Laurier Macdonald Rams represent the school in a wide array of sporting events; soccer, basketball, swimming, track and field, and volleyball.

Entry Requirements

Good standing in the programme (our students begin their course of MYP studies at John Paul 1 Junior High School) and/or recommendation of teaching teams.

(Founded 2003)

Academic Director
Mrs A K Chan

Diploma coordinator
Jonathon Shaw

Status Private

Boarding/day Day

Gender
Coeducational

Language of instruction
English

Programmes offered
Diploma

Address
No 5 & 7, Jalan Teknologi 2/1
Kota Damansara
47800 Daerah Petaling
SELANGOR | MALAYSIA

TEL +60 03 6157 8123/6145 3888
FAX +60 03 6156 9011/6145 3838

Email
info@srikdu.edu.my

Website
www.srikdu.edu.my

Sekolah Sri KDU® is a private coeducational school offering the Malaysian National Curriculum at primary and secondary levels. It is also an IB World School offering the International Baccalaureate Diploma Programme.

Established in 2003, Sekolah Sri KDU® enrols approximately 1400 students in the secondary school and the IB Diploma Programme. The school has an outstanding academic record and is recognized as a leader in education in Malaysia.

The 12-acre school campus in Kota Damansara was the 'Winner 2005' in the FIABCI – Malaysia Property Awards 2005 and the 1st Runner Up in the Specialised Project Category of the world level FIABCI Prix d' Excellence 2006.

The campus provides an excellent range of facilities including those for stage performances and a sports complex.

Our priorities are to provide opportunities for students to achieve their academic and personal potential. Students are coached to develop and practice higher order skills including theorising, analysis, prioritisation and presentation skills. The school actively implements the IB Learner Profile.

Sri KDU® employs a highly qualified and professionally trained team of local and international teachers for the IB Diploma Programme. Specialist teachers are provided for Spanish, French, English and theatre arts. The teacher student ratio of 1:8 provides for personal attention and bonding.

IB coordinator Jonathon Shaw who has more than 30 years of teaching experience is an examiner in Theory of Knowledge and has organised international events including IB Workshops.

Commencing in 2007, there are currently 72 students registered with this programme. They have performed a Phantasmagorias of Julius Caesar and in solidarity with the UN Day for the Elimination of Racial Prejudice, Sri KDU® IB students held a poetry and literary reading to introduce the work of American poet, William Stafford. The IB faculty also regularly invites guest speakers, conducts study tours and recently hosted visitors from the United World College of the Atlantic.

Many of the students are sponsored by state scholarship agencies including Petronas, Malaysia's state-owned Oil and Gas Company. Sri KDU® is a May School and students are accepted each year for the IB Diploma Programme in June.

King Edward's School Witley

(Founded 1553)

Head
P Kerr Fulton-Peebles MA

Diploma coordinator
Christine Meharg

Status Private

Boarding/day Mixed

Gender Coeducational

Language of instruction
English

Programmes offered Diploma

Age range of pupils 11–18

Number of pupils enrolled 435

Fees per annum
Day: £16,140
Boarding: £22,470

Address
Petworth Road
Wormley
Godalming
Surrey
GU8 5SG | UK

TEL +44 (0)1428 686768

FAX +44 (0)1428 682850

Email
admissions@kesw.surrey.sch.uk

Website
www.kesw.surrey.sch.uk

King Edward's School Witley is an independent, coeducational school for approximately 440 boarders and day pupils between the ages of 11 and 18.

The school is situated in extensive grounds in the heart of the Surrey countryside, but only 12 miles from Guildford and 45 miles from London. Easy access to the school is provided by road and by rail as the local mainline to London station is only five minutes' walk away. The school is 45 minutes by car from both Gatwick and Heathrow airports.

Founded in 1553, King Edward's is steeped in history, but combines its traditional strengths with a modern outlook. The school is proud to be one of the first English boarding schools in the area to offer the International Baccalaureate Diploma Programme. Since introduction, the students have all gained their Diploma, and with an average points score of 34 over the last three years. Our results place us in the top ten UK schools, and the top three boarding schools. The rigour of the programme is strongly supported by King Edward's excellent academic facilities. The library is well-resourced and students have access throughout the school and boarding houses to computers and intranet facilities. Students can choose from the broad range of subjects on offer, and receive tuition in small classes, with one-to-one tutor support, a feature of our tutorial programme.

Well-qualified teaching and boarding staff aim to educate the whole individual, to give each student an opportunity to build on his or her strengths. The school's strong pastoral and caring philosophy creates an environment in which students can thrive and develop.

The co-curricular programme provides the opportunity for students to participate in a wide range of cultural and sporting activities. Educational visits, both in and out of the UK, feature frequently in the school's calendar. These range from watching local and London theatre productions to scuba-diving in the Caribbean or spending three weeks in Malawi to support the 'Home of Hope' orphanage there.

Although a British boarding school where 80% of the students are English native speakers, King Edward's welcomes students from the international community, and in fact has young men and women of 30 different nationalities. The school offers a range of scholarships to help those with particular academic, artistic or musical abilities, and bursaries to those who are specifically in need of boarding education.

Subjects available:

Group 1: English A1, German A1, language A1 self taught

Group 2: French B, German B, English A2, Latin, Greek, Spanish *ab initio*

Group 3: Economics, geography, history, philosophy

Group 4: Biology, chemistry, physics

Group 5: Mathematics HL, mathematics standard, mathematics studies

Group 6: Visual arts

King Edward's School Witley is a registered charity (No. 311997) to provide education for children with a boarding need.

King William's College

(Founded 1833)

Principal
S J Welch MA, PhD

Diploma coordinator
Dr Rene Filho

Status Private

Boarding/day Mixed

Gender Coeducational

Language of instruction
English

Programmes offered Diploma

Age range of pupils 11-18

Number of pupils enrolled 370

Fees per annum
Day: £16,659
Boarding: £24,264

Address
Castletown
Isle of Man
IM9 1TP | UK

TEL +44 (0)1624 820428

FAX +44 (0)1624 820401

Email
principal@kwc.sch.im

Website
www.kwc.im

King William's College is a coeducational school located by the sea on the beautiful Isle of Man and provides education from three to 18. Boarding is available from age 11. Pastoral care is excellent thanks to a fully supportive tutorial system. A wide range of subjects is available at GCSE and results are excellent, averaging 100% pass and over 50% A* and A grades.

All students in the sixth form take the IB Diploma Programme. Over the past five years, over 95% of candidates have been awarded the full Diploma with 100% having achieved full certification. The college regularly appears in the top 5% of the best British schools in various league tables (18th position our best over the past five years) and over 90% of our students are offered a place at their first choice university. The average score for the sixth form entries is 35 points.

There are around 60 students in each of the two sixth form years and the average class size is 11.

College boarding facilities are regularly upgraded and all sixth formers are in single or twin rooms. There are two boarding houses on campus, one for boys and one for girls. Brand new sixth form and fifth form centres have recently been completed providing modern facilities in relaxed surroundings. The college has first class IT facilities and the campus is wi-fi throughout.

The school has a very strong record in art, drama and music. Over 50% of all pupils seek specialist tuition in a musical instrument. Sporting facilities are very good and our teams compete successfully in hockey, rugby, football, golf, sailing and a wide variety of other sports. The college runs a very successful Duke of Edinburgh's Award Scheme.

Academic scholarships are available and details can be obtained from the Admissions Registrar. Bursary support may also be available and information on this can be sought from the Bursar (bursar@kwc.sch.im).

The Isle of Man is a jewel set in the Irish Sea: easily accessible while retaining a tranquil charm and unique spirit. The island is a microcosm of rural Britain and has beautiful scenery and excellent walks while having modern shopping and tourism facilities. It is a very safe place to live in as crime is very low and the pace of life is generally less frenetic than in mainland Britain. The island has a key role in the offshore finance industry. The Isle of Man is a Crown Dependency and has associate member status of the European Union.

The college is near Ronaldsway airport and has direct daily flights to a wide range of destinations including London, Glasgow, Manchester and Dublin and onward links worldwide.

King William's College is an excellent independent school with a genuine international dimension in the education it provides, and is justifiably proud of its status as a leading British IB World School.

King William's College is a registered charity for the education of children. (IOM No. 335)

(Founded 2000)

Principal
Ms Tracy Brazier

Diploma coordinator
Nick Clay

Status State

Gender Coeducational

Language of instruction
English

Programmes offered Diploma

Age range of pupils 11-18

Number of pupils enrolled 800

Address
Southway
Guildford
Surrey
GU2 8DU | UK

TEL +44 (0)1483 458 956
FAX +44 (0)1483 458 957

Email
info@kingscollegeguildford.com

Website
www.kingscollegeguildford.com

Kings College is one of a few English state schools and a growing number of private schools to offer the world-renowned alternative to A levels, the International Baccalaureate Diploma Programme. However, unlike private schools, at Kings College there are no tuition fees. We have been fully authorized as an IB World School by the IB organisation for seven years and praised by inspectors from the UK. The college welcomes students who are interested in a broad-based and challenging course accepted by universities not only in the UK but also around the world.

Kings College was opened in December 2000 and provides high-quality teaching and learning for students from the age of 11-18. The college prepares all of its students to play their part as highly-skilled and adaptable individuals in a global community. Our first aim is for all of our students to be confident individuals, believing in themselves and realising that they can achieve more than they think possible. Our curriculum focuses on both the arts and technology. We were formally designated a Technology College in January 2002, and gained the Artsmark Silver Award in May 2003 and the Artsmark Gold in May 2006.

In 2006 the college underwent a five-year review evaluation by the IB. It concluded that we were offering a strong IB Diploma Programme and that we had made excellent progress in the last five years. It concluded 'much of what you do is exemplary and it is hoped that other schools will increasingly look to you for advice'. We are proud to offer the exam that is now widely held to be the gold standard in Post-16 education. Ofsted reported in October 2007 that the students enjoy being in the sixth form, that it is well led and managed and that students are very well supported academically.

Kings College is a modern and vibrant learning community and we warmly invite you to join us. For further information on the course, or to visit the college to discuss possible entry, please call Dr Mark Taylor on +44 (0) 1483 484847 or email m.taylor@kingscollegeguildford.com

Lauriston Girls' School

(Founded 1901)

Head of School
Meg Hansen

Diploma coordinator
Eirwen Stevenson

Status Private

Boarding/day Day

Gender Female

Language of instruction
English

Programmes offered Diploma

Age range of pupils 3-18

Number of pupils enrolled 1040

Fees per annum
AU$11,340-21,980

Address
38 Huntingtower Road
Armadale VIC 3143 | AUSTRALIA

TEL +61 3 9864 7555
FAX +61 3 9822 7950

Email
admissions@lauriston.vic.edu.au

Website
www.lauriston.vic.edu.au

Lauriston Girls' School is an independent non-denominational school for girls from Kindergarten to Year 12. Founded in 1901, Lauriston has a proud tradition of excellence in educational, sporting and cultural pursuits.

Lauriston comprises: Kindergarten – for three- and four-year-old boys and girls, based on the Reggio Emilia philosophy; Junior School – with an emphasis on numeracy and literacy; the unique Year 9 Howqua Program, a residential year at the magnificent Howqua campus in the Victorian high country; and Senior School – where students choose from the Victorian Certificate of Education (VCE) or the globally-recognised International Baccalaureate Diploma Programme.

The Armadale campus is located close to the city centre in one of Melbourne's attractive tree-lined suburbs. The facilities are modern and well-equipped and convenient to public transport.

Lauriston has an open entry policy where all students are welcome to study the IB Diploma Programme or the local curriculum. Lauriston's academic results are outstanding: 18% of the 2007 IB Diploma Programme class achieved a score of 40+. Since the introduction of the IB in 1991, Lauriston has had 12 perfect Diploma scores, two in the 2007 examinations.

The school balances outstanding academic results with a range of exciting co-curricular activities: sports, arts, music and drama and community service. Lauriston is an internationally minded school which encourages cultural exchange and welcomes students from all over the world.

Underpinning every aspect of school life are five core values: relationships, courage, creative reflection, intellectual enquiry and engagement in life. Lauriston's values are perfectly aligned with the IB philosophy of 'developing inquiring, knowledgeable and caring people who create a better world through intercultural understanding'. Students learn in an environment which nurtures important life skills thus ensuring that students leave Lauriston as well-rounded, self reliant and confident individuals.

We are participating in the IB Schools to Schools Project and are supporting a school in Aceh. Another student-initiated community project is the Benjamin Andrew Footpath Library, providing books to homeless people. IB Diploma Programme subjects offered are English A1, Chinese A1, Mandarin B, French B, Spanish *ab Initio*, economics, history, geography, information technology in a global society, biology, chemistry, physics, mathematics, mathematical studies, visual arts, music, theatre arts and other languages by arrangement. Many students are successfully studying Chinese, Thai or Korean as their first language and English as their second.

Marymount International School

(Founded 1955)

Headmistress
Sister Kathleen Fagan RSHM

MYP coordinator
Nicholas Marcou

Diploma coordinator
Brian Johnson

Status Private

Boarding/day Both

Gender Female

Language of instruction
English

Programmes offered
MYP, Diploma

Age range of pupils 11-18

Number of pupils enrolled 248

Fees per annum
Day: £14,895-£16,945;
Weekly boarding: £25,135-£27,185; Boarding: £26,340-£28,390

Address
George Road
Kingston upon Thames
Surrey
KT2 7PE | UK

TEL +44 (0)20 8949 0571
FAX +44 (0)20 8336 2485

Email
admissions@
marymountlondon.com

Website
www.marymountlondon.com

Located on a private residential estate, twenty minutes from Central London and within easy reach of the airports and all transport links, Marymount International School offers both boarding and day places to girls between 11 and 18.

International Baccalaureate Diploma results and their equivalent UCAS scores have put this independent girls school, tucked away on seven private acres in the Coombe estates area of Kingston, at the top of the school rankings. Recent league tables in *The Times* recognized the outstanding achievement of Marymount International School students by placing the school in the top 3.5% of the 1000 UK schools listed. Two of our recent graduates received perfect scores of 45 points for their IB Diploma.

Among the top twenty schools ranked by *The Times* seven are International Baccalaureate Diploma Programme schools. The internationally acclaimed IB Diploma Programme is recognised globally by universities, as a benchmark of quality in education.

Our student body is made up of about 248 girls aged 11-18 years and approximately half of these attend as boarders. Classes are small and study programmes are planned to meet the needs of individual students.

Our boarding students are offered a full range of extra curricular activities both in the evenings and at weekends.

Boarding staff organise trips, visits, activities and the attractions of London and surrounding areas are close by.

Recent overseas destinations for educational tours for all students have included Austria, China, Cyprus, Czech Republic, France, Germany, Greece, Italy, Iceland, Mexico, Morocco, Russia, Spain and Switzerland!

The student body at present represents over 48 different nationalities – the largest groups in the school include students from the UK, the US, Japan, Germany, China (including Hong Kong) and Korea. We also have others from many different countries which makes this school a truly international experience.

Sister Kathleen Fagan, the Headmistress at Marymount, shares the good news: "As long-time practitioners and believers in the high academic quality of the IB, it is wonderful to see our girls getting the recognition and commendation they deserve for all their hard work. We must also thank our teachers for their commitment and dedication to the success and achievement of our students."

Providing excellent facilities and an experienced teaching faculty, our students work hard and have fun!

Marymount International School is a registered charity providing education to international students. Charity No. 1117786.

Meadowridge School

(Founded 1985)

Head of School
Mr Hugh Burke

PYP coordinator
Mr Terry Donaldson

MYP coordinator
Ms Kuldeep Thendal

Status Independent

Boarding/day Day

Gender Coeducational

Language of instruction
English

Programmes offered
PYP, MYP

Number of pupils enrolled 503

Fees per annum Domestic Fees:
C$11,000-12,400; International
Fees: C$17,800-18,900

Address
12224 240th Street
Maple Ridge BC
V4R 1N1 | CANADA

TEL +1 604 467 4444
FAX +1 604 467 4989

Email
info@meadowridge.bc.ca

Website
www.meadowridge.bc.ca

Situated in the shadow of the Golden Ears Mountains on a 16.4 acre campus in beautiful Maple Ridge, British Columbia, Meadowridge is an interdenominational, coeducational, university preparatory day school serving students from Junior Kindergarten (age four) to Grade 12.

With an emphasis on the development of well-rounded individuals, our students learn to live well, with others and for others, as citizens of a just community. The foundation of that learning is the safe and supportive environment of the school. Our class sizes are small in order to provide more individual instruction and to permit the full participation of every student. The strong motivation, diligence, and respect for others shown by Meadowridge students is certainly due in part to these learning conditions.

We also believe in maintaining both an overall student teacher ratio of 10:1, and a maximum student population of 545 students. Studies have shown that overall school population size, is of equal, if not greater importance than class size as a predictor of student success.

At Meadowridge, we know every child's name, their hobbies, their families, their friends, their challenges and their successes. We believe that excellence is developed through warm and caring relationships between adults and children, so that students can meet challenges with support and confidence.

Meadowridge is one of only seven IB World Schools in Canada accredited to offer both the PYP and MYP Programmes. We are also the only IB School in British Columbia to adhere to the principles of accreditation outlined by the Canadian Educational Standards Institute (www.cesi.edu), Canada's only internationally recognized school accreditation agency.

In 2008, we completed a new building expansion, which includes six new classrooms, a cafeteria, theatre, and two new state-of-the-art science labs, bringing our total facility size to 103,000 square feet. We also have additional space to house the largest school library collection in the province, and plans are under way for a second athletic field, which will serve as an international sized soccer pitch in 2009.

MEF International School

Primary School Principal
Felicity Hewett

Secondary School Principal
Alexandra Conchard

PYP coordinator
Lisa Hughes

Diploma coordinator
Malcolm Ringo

Status Private

Boarding/day Day

Gender Coeducational

Language of instruction
English

Programmes offered
PYP, Diploma

Age range of pupils
3-18

Number of pupils enrolled 325

Fees per annum
US$7975-19,444

Address
Dereboyu Caddesi
Ortaköy
34340 Istanbul | TURKEY

TEL +90 (212) 287 6900 ext 1340
FAX +90 (212) 287 4681

Email
contact@mef.k12.tr

Website
www.mefinternationalschool.com

"Building Bridges between Countries and Cultures"

Our Vision

To be a world-class school with a vision to the future.

Our Mission Statement

MEFIS offers a stimulating education program that strives to meet the individual learning needs of its students. The school provides equality in opportunities, so that each child is guided to discover and develop intellectual, creative, social and physical potentials. In doing so, the school endeavors to empower its students with a lifelong passion for learning. Students are encouraged to become confident, balanced and socially responsible individuals who will contribute positively to local and global communities.

Our School

MEF International School was founded in 1998 by a Turkish science teacher and businessman as a private coeducational institution for the expatriate community in Istanbul.

MEF International School is structured to provide quality education for ages three to 18 through its authorized Primary Years Programme from its early childhood center to its IB Diploma Programme in the secondary school. MEF International School is a fully authorized Cambridge International Centre (CIE/CIC) offering Checkpoint and IGCSE in the secondary school.

The focus is on students constructing meaning, becoming inquirers and being enthusiastic about discovering knowledge on their own. The school provides a first class English-medium international education, complemented throughout the school by French, Spanish and Turkish Host Country Studies. The Learning Support Team provides support to students who have special leaning needs. The programs cater to students for their needs through English as an Additional Language (EAL), Learning Support, Enrichment/Extension, Guidance Counseling and College Counseling.

Our Students

As for the Turkish Ministry of Education requirements, all enrolled students at MEF International School hold a passport other than Turkish through Grade 10. However, our IB Diploma Programme, known as MEF Schools of Turkey, accommodates international and some Turkish national students. The MEF International School student body represents 45 different nationalities. At MEF International School, we understand that by developing holistic learning, intercultural awareness and communication we are helping our students to learn to manage emotions, predict consequences, develop optimistic thinking habits, and set goals that are also skills that improve student achievement and wellbeing. Students are therefore encouraged through various aspects of the curriculum to engage in varied activities.

Community and Service: Throughout the school students participate in charity events, including food drives, clothes drives, fundraising activities. Secondary school students (grade 6-12) have an active role in helping the community by attending local amenities.

Model European Parliament: High School pupils have the opportunity to join other young people across Europe to get involved in politics and debate the issues affecting the continent today, as well as coming up with possible solutions to those pressing problems. Every year, MEF International School students are the only young people in the country selected to represent Turkey.

Student Council: The philosophy behind student council is to give empowerment to the students and allow them to take responsibility. The student council allows the students to have a voice, with opportunities to contribute to many aspects of school activities and development. The student council has an impact on the social and personal development of the students of the school. They are also actively involved in the wider community raising money through fundraising events for local charities. There is both a Primary and Secondary Student Council.

Academic Success

MEFIS academic success is outstanding and every year our graduating students are admitted to high ranked Universities in the UK, USA and Canada. At IGCSE, 75% of our students score A* -C. Since IB Diploma Programme accreditation in September 1998, 90% of our students successfully obtained their IB Diploma. In the 2007-8 academic year, students obtained their IB Diplomas with an average points score of 37.25. The highest score by an individual student was 42 points.

Our Faculty

There are 63 full-time members of staff, representing 13 different nationalities. All teachers hold a university degree as well as a teaching certificate in their field of instruction. In addition 20% of the faculty hold higher degrees. The student to teacher ratio is 5:1 over the whole school.

Our Facilities

The school is situated in the heart of Istanbul. The facilities are on a four acre campus nestling in the hills above Ortaköy, only minutes away from the Bosphorus straits and residential locations preferred by the expatriate community. MEF International School shares the campus and facilities with the MEF National School.

The facilities are designed with modern educational methodologies in mind. Our campus facilities include the following: over 30 classrooms, equipped specialists rooms, individual learning support rooms, four modern science labs, a library center, two fully networked IT labs, two soft surface playgrounds, an indoor swimming pool, a gymnasium, three sport centers, a dance studio, an outdoor football court, a tennis court, a concert auditorium, an outdoor amphitheatre.

For further information, please contact our admissions officer (contact@mef.k12.tr) or visit our school website at: www.mefinternationalschool.com

Modern Montessori School

(Founded 1994)

Principal
Randa Hasan

Diploma coordinator
Kawther Saa'd AlDin

Status Private

Boarding/day Day

Gender Coeducational

Language of instruction
English

Programmes offered Diploma

Age range of pupils 3-18

Number of pupils enrolled 1300

Address
PO Box 1941
Khilda
Amman
11821 | JORDAN

TEL +9626 5535190

FAX +9626 5535831

Email
ksd@montessori.edu.jo

Website
www.montessori.edu.jo

The Modern Montessori School (MMS) aims to provide a rich and stimulating environment where children can develop to their full potential. Understanding and appreciating the differences that make every student unique, each child is valued as an independent thinker and encouraged to make choices on his or her own.

Our system of personalised education encourages every student to develop his or her own talent, to respect the differences in others, and to be a respectable member of a community, thus achieving the finest possible holistic education. This aims to instil a pride in accomplishments, providing the students with the confidence needed to use their abilities to the fullest and enabling them to define and achieve success in college, career and, above all, in life.

To this end, the IB Diploma Programme at the Modern Montessori School is designed largely to cater for the needs of individuals, rather than for the collective needs of a group; our subject menu is varied and enjoys a degree of flexibilty, which in turn allow students to choose the subjects which appeal to their different learning preferences and future university courses.

Furthermore, the MMS has devised an extracurricular, three-level award scheme which has the IB CAS programme perched atop its golden level. The Amin Hasan Award (AHA) programme provides students from grade 7-12 with the ability to participate in enjoyable yet beneficial and thought-provoking activites which foster a sense of compassion, teamwork, and mutual respect among students in addition to promoting the principles of model citizenship and the importance of solidarity and togetherness among people, irrespective of their ethnic, religious, or gender differences.

At MMS, we also believe in the inherent ability of each student to achieve their best. This is why our Learning Support Department works hand-in-hand with administrators, programme coordinators, and teachers to cater for students who have special learning needs through the application of an inclusion programme.

We also believe that cooperation between home and school is required to ensure the personal and intellectual development of each student. Consequently, we have designed an E-school portal where both parents and students are kept up-to-date with everything they need from report cards and academic calendars to forums and E-learning material.

Prior to their joining the IB Diploma Programme, all students undergo an internally-devised two-year preparation programme, the Bridge Years. By the end of these two years, students will have been exposed to the requirements of the Diploma Programme and completed their pre-IB assessments, which play an integral role in determining the students' IB Diploma Programme subjects.

The Modern Montessori School is accredited by the International Centre for Montessori Education (ICME), Cambridge and Edexcel International Examinations' syndicates and is an authorized IB World School.

Mulgrave Independent School

(Founded 1995)

Head of School
Tony Macoun

PYP coordinator
Patricia Jolley

Diploma coordinator
Isobel Willard

Status Private

Boarding/day Day

Gender Coeducational

Language of instruction
English

Programmes offered
PYP, Diploma

Number of pupils enrolled 750

Address
2330 Cypress Lane
West Vancouver BC
V7S 3H9 | CANADA

TEL +1 604 922 3223
FAX +1 604 922 3328

Email
tmacoun@mulgrave.com

Website
www.mulgrave.com

Mulgrave School is a non-denominational, coeducational IB World School (Kindergarten to Grade 12). With established programmes in the PYP and the Diploma Programme, the school is in the final stages of authorisation for the Middle Years Programme. Mulgrave, a day school, is located on the forested slopes of Vancouver's North Shore, overlooking the magnificent Burrard Inlet and the Pacific Ocean. Highly valued for its positive community spirit and for its vibrant atmosphere, the school encourages its students to reach their highest goals in a Renaissance approach to education. Academic rigour and breadth of educational experiences are fundamental to student success. Action, service, leadership and independence in learning are inherent to the school's ethos, as is a culture of caring and intrinsic discipline. Celebrating cultural diversity, developing intellectual abilities, and promoting athletic and artistic promise underlie a Mulgrave education.

To enhance the delivery of curricula, Mulgrave utilises wireless technology throughout the school. Smart Boards are used extensively through all grades to enable students to approach their learning in different ways. Students from

Grades 6 to 12 benefit from a laptop programme, where they are encouraged to explore global perspectives and expand the boundaries of their learning. The school's commitment to athletics, outdoor education, arts, leadership and co-curricular programmes provides a wide opportunity for students to find and develop their unique passions. Ethics, morals and principles are firmly entrenched in a Mulgrave education and our talented faculty model the qualities that we value for our students.

Experienced teachers from around the world provide a comprehensive and challenging IB curriculum to an equally diverse student body of 750 young people. Within the framework of the three International Baccalaureate Programmes, the teachers develop the unique skills required to succeed in our ever-changing human environment. Students are inspired to be creative problem-solvers, effective communicators and lifelong learners. At Mulgrave School, we foster the development of young leaders who demonstrate international understanding and meaningful action as responsible citizens of the global community.

Munich International School

(Founded 1966)

Head of School
Dr Mary Seppala

Status Private

Boarding/day Day

Gender Coeducational

Language of instruction
English

Programmes offered
PYP, MYP, Diploma

Age range of pupils 4-18

Number of pupils enrolled 1300

Fees per annum €12,340-15,400

Address
Schloss Buchhof
Percha
Starnberg
82319 | GERMANY

TEL +49 8151 366 0
FAX +49 8151 366 119

Email
admissions@mis-munich.de

Website
www.mis-munich.de

Munich International School (MIS) is a non-profit, coeducational school serving students from Early Childhood (ages four and five) through Grade 12. More than 1300 students represent around fifty nationalities at MIS.

Founded in 1966, MIS serves the international community in and around Munich, as well as those from the local community who wish to take advantage of the unique MIS educational experience. The 26-acre MIS campus lies near scenic Lake Starnberg, 12 miles south of Munich. School buses serve the cities of Munich and Starnberg as well as the surrounding region.

As an exemplary English language, IB World School, MIS inspires students to be interculturally aware and achieve their potential within a stimulating and caring learning environment. The curriculum follows the framework of the International Baccalaureate (IB) Primary Years Programme (PYP) and the IB Middle Years Programme (MYP), which culminate in the final two years with the IB Diploma Programme. The IB Middle Years Programme overarches the two-year International General Certificate of Secondary Education (IGCSE) Programme in Grades 9 and 10.

In the belief that students will best benefit from the experience of living in Germany if they are able to communicate effectively and take part in local culture, MIS offers German language instruction to all students.

Furthermore, comprehensive instruction in English as a second language (ESL) is offered to serve students who come to MIS with little or no English language.

The school's internationally recognized academic standards enable students to transfer smoothly to other international or national schools. MIS graduates attend some of the finest colleges and universities around the world, including Brown, Cambridge, Columbia, Georgetown, Harvard, The London School of Economics, MIT, Oxford, Princeton and Yale.

MIS offers competitive and non-competitive sports with numerous teams participating in renowned international sports tournaments. A variety of activities in the fine arts, ranging from painting, drawing, and ceramics to handicrafts, drama, and dance are offered after school. There are several school choirs, bands, and orchestral groups. Students participate in the International School Theatre Festival, the Speech and Debate Team, mathematics contests and other prestigious international school events.

MIS encourages high standards of academic achievement, ongoing personal development, and the freedom to create and explore. Students are encouraged to be independent thinkers and to accept and appreciate the validity of other people's perspectives and cultures.

(Founded 1992)

Headmaster
Mr Simon Leslie

PYP coordinator
Kate Grant

MYP coordinator
Pia Bergqvist

Diploma coordinator
Helen Stanton

Status Private

Boarding/day Day

Gender Coeducational

Language of instruction
English

Programmes offered
PYP, MYP, Diploma

Age range of pupils 3-18

Number of pupils enrolled 1410

Fees per annum
US$13,860-26,910

Address
36 Soi 15 Sukhumvit Road
Wattana
Bangkok
10110 | THAILAND

TEL +66 2 651 2065
FAX +66 2 253 3800

Email
nist@nist.ac.th

Website
www.nist.ac.th

Welcome to The New International School of Thailand (NIST), a non-profit school which offers a truly international education to culturally diverse students aged three to 18. NIST is dually-accredited by both the Council of International Schools (CIS) and by the New England Association of Schools and Colleges, USA (NEASC). NIST was the first school in Thailand authorized to run all three International Baccalaureate (IB) Programmes: the IB Primary Years Programme (PYP), the IB Middle Years Programme (MYP), and the IB Diploma Programme.

For students aged three to 12, the PYP focuses on the development of the whole child, in the classroom and in the world outside, through other environments where children learn. It offers a framework that meets children's multiple needs: academic, social, physical, emotional and cultural. The MYP provides a framework of academic challenge and life skills for students aged 11-16 years. The five-year programme offers an educational approach that embraces yet transcends traditional school subjects. It leads on from the PYP and serves as excellent preparation for the Diploma Programme. The IB Diploma Programme is an academically rigorous, broad and diverse education curriculum which encompasses the final two years of secondary school, grades 12 and 13. IB Diploma holders have access to the world's leading universities – our students have been accepted into such well-known universities as Stanford, London School of Economics and MIT.

NIST has an extensive World Language Programme for all students over the age of six. Languages offered include French, Spanish, Hindi, Japanese, Mandarin, Korean, German, Thai and many more – a total of 19 languages are offered at NIST. But NIST is more than just a school, a place where students sit in classrooms, learning their lessons, our students are also encouraged to pursue other activities, such as community service and sports. As part of the IB Diploma Programme, students are required to participate in a compulsory programme called Creativity, Action and Service (CAS). The service portion encourages students to contribute to a variety of community-based activities, helping them understand the demands of the global society they will eventually become an integral part of.

Amid all this, NIST has committed itself to IT excellence and innovation. NIST is proud to offer students the use of tablet laptops, a completely wireless campus, and LCD equipped classrooms, to name but a few IT developments.

Through NIST's rigorous academic curriculum, challenging sports programme, enriched arts programme and access to cutting-edge technology, our students are equipped to join the global marketplace, well-prepared as world citizens.

North London Collegiate School

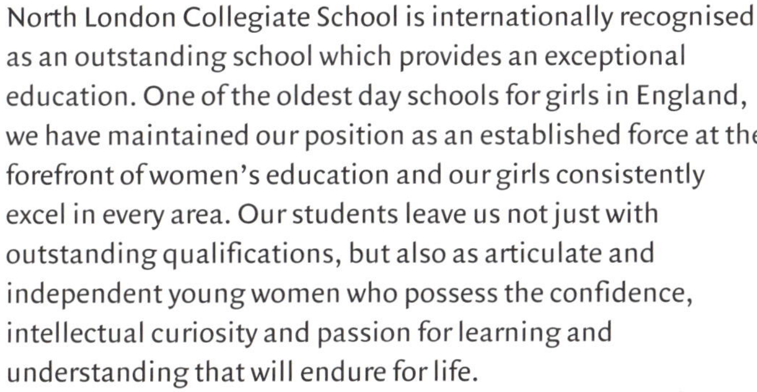

(Founded 1850)

Headmistress
Mrs Bernice McCabe

Diploma coordinator
Michael Burke

Status Private

Boarding/day Day

Gender Female

Language of instruction
English

Programmes offered Diploma

Age range of pupils 4-18

Number of pupils enrolled 1060

Fees per annum
£10,116-£11,925

Address
Canons
Canons Drive
Edgware
Middlesex
HA8 7RJ | UK

TEL +44 (0)20 8952 0912

FAX +44 (0)20 8951 1391

Email
office@nlcs.org.uk

Website
www.nlcs.org.uk

North London Collegiate School is internationally recognised as an outstanding school which provides an exceptional education. One of the oldest day schools for girls in England, we have maintained our position as an established force at the forefront of women's education and our girls consistently excel in every area. Our students leave us not just with outstanding qualifications, but also as articulate and independent young women who possess the confidence, intellectual curiosity and passion for learning and understanding that will endure for life.

At the heart of our school is a desire to nurture a genuine love of learning and spirit of enquiry, enabling each girl to recognise academic excellence and realise that it is attainable. Alongside this, we want school to be a place where each girl can achieve a real sense of self-esteem by making the most of her talents, learning the value of responsibility and service to others and participating in an exciting programme of extracurricular activities in areas such as sport, music, drama, dance and art.

Ever conscious of this spirit of education which we have cherished at the school for over 150 years, we are pleased to offer the IB Diploma Programme as an obvious and natural development of our sixth form provision. We are delighted that our students have consistently achieved an average Diploma score in excess of 40 points, and that nine of our students in the past three years have achieved the maximum 45 points. All of our students go on to study at selective universities in the UK and around the world, many at Oxbridge and Ivy League institutions, and we have an outstanding programme of support in place as girls make their decisions about higher education.

The combination of breadth, scholarship and academic rigour offered by the IB Diploma Programme ensures that students at North London Collegiate School enjoy an exciting and academically stimulating sixth form experience, providing them with an excellent preparation for life at university and in the wider world beyond.

Qatar Leadership Academy

Head of School
Bruno Behr

Diploma coordinator
Andrew S Frezuldeen

Status Private

Boarding/day Boarding

Gender Male

Language of instruction
English, Arabic

Programmes offered Diploma

Age range of pupils 11-17

Number of pupils enrolled 90

Fees per annum QR50,000

Address
PO Box 24421
Doha | QATAR

TEL +974 474 2222

FAX +974 474 2173

Email
bbehr@qf.org.qa

Website
www.qla.edu.qa

Qatar Leadership Academy is an English language medium school which aims to provide a high quality, internationally recognised programme, for its male students aged between 11 and 17 years. It is a unique concept in education, as it combines the IB Diploma Programme with Leadership and Heritage Programmes. QLA is part of the Qatar Foundation family which is a driving force behind educational development within Qatar.

All programmes are complemented by a rigorous athletic programme aimed at promoting fitness, good health and teamwork. The academy encourages local and international field trips. Recent trips have included: Tanzania, Turkey, UK, Portugal and Pakistan.

As QLA is a boarding school our cadets come from a wide variety of backgrounds and cultures: from other GCC countries, from the Gulf area and even from Canada and Australia, if their Arabic speaking parents are coming back to the Middle East. Students are housed in comfortable rooms which are shared by no more than four students. These rooms all have internet access for each student, a lounge area and an en suite bathroom. Recreational facilities are provided in the accommodation area. The campus also boasts a swimming pool, gym, fitness room, outdoor running track, abseiling tower, football field and volleyball and basketball courts.

QLA has been authorized to offer the IB Diploma Programme since March 2007. At present, QLA is also an IB Middle Years Programme candidate school.

Our IB Middle Years Programme (candidate status only) includes: Arabic (Language A), English (Language A or B), French (Language B), Islamic studies, humanities which incorporates Arabic cultural studies, leadership, integrated science (physics, chemistry and biology), maths, personal management (Grade 6), visual arts, technology and physical education.

At IB Diploma level we offer Arabic or English (Language A1), English (Language A1/A2 or B), French (Language *ab initio*), history, business management, mathematics and maths studies, environmental science, physics, chemistry and design technology. Additionally, students follow the Theory of Knowledge (TOK) course, complete 150 hours of CAS (Creativity, Action and Service) and complete an extended essay (EE).

Our unique Leadership Programme is an integral part of QLA's educational programme. It aims to develop the individual potential of every student by building self-esteem, self-discipline and character. Students' leadership capacity is developed through community service activities, lessons on emotional management and development of effective skills as a team leader or team member. Leadership complements the IB Programmes through additional development of effective communication skills. The Leadership Programme is also designed to develop a sense of personal responsibility and of accomplishment. Throughout the course students become familiar with styles of leadership using local and international leaders as role models. Additionally, the students learn about leadership theory and its application through practical tasking and logical thinking. They also have the opportunity to learn about personal wellness and fitness, first aid, the principles of marksmanship, map reading skills and finally orienteering.

Our Heritage Programme celebrates Islamic and Arabic culture and values. Through the Heritage Programme students develop an appreciation and understanding of their past, helping to maintain the values and traditions for the future. QLA has specially designated areas for heritage: stables for camels and horses, a falconry area and *al Majlis*. Students also practice traditional dancing (*al Aarda*) and marine heritage. They learn to appreciate not only the value of their own country and culture but are also encouraged to be aware and understand the cultures of other people.

Graduates from Qatar Leadership Academy have enhanced opportunities to further their education through well known international universities based at Qatar Foundation such as: Carnegie Melon, Weil Cornell, Texas A&M, Georgetown and Virginia Commonwealth. They can also enter Qatar University or embark on a military career either within the Qatar Armed Forces at the military college or other internationally well known military colleges. Additionally, students may choose to study abroad either in Europe, England or USA.

Queenwood School for Girls

Head of School
James Harpur

Diploma coordinator
Judy Tenzing

Status Private

Gender Female

Language of instruction
English

Programmes offered
Diploma

Address
Locked Bag 1
Mosman
NSW 2088 | AUSTRALIA

TEL +61 2 89687777
FAX +61 2 89687778

Email
q@queenwood.nsw.edu.au

Website
www.queenwood.nsw.edu.au

Queenwood encourages the highest fulfillment of personal academic potential through self-discipline, self-reliance, and independent and cooperative learning. The school offers a wide experience of sporting and cultural activities, together with a focus on social responsibility and commitment to helping others.

We offer the opportunity for students to make sound progress in academic achievement. Students are treated as individuals and staff, specialised in their disciplines, teach at differentiated levels. This approach to education means that special programs are offered for gifted children, for those from non-English-speaking backgrounds, and for those with learning difficulties. Virtually all students in Year 7 go on to complete Year 12 of whom 98% choose to further their education at university or another tertiary institution. The school has a published discipline policy but no formal rule book. Each student is expected to evaluate her behaviour according to the following guidelines: is it safe for all who might be affected; is it considerate of all concerned; does it reflect well on you, your family and your school? The Pastoral Care Program at Queenwood aims to support each student. Counseling is available and a Peer Support Program is in operation.

IB Success: Queenwood students have risen to this challenge with relish and their results speak for themselves. Since its inception at Queenwood in 2001 our students have consistently scored 30 (from a possible 45) and above (over 90 in the HSC system) with 65% scoring over 34 (above 95) and 20% scoring 40 or above (99 in the HSC gradings). IB Diploma Programme results are measured against a global cohort rather than at a state or national level.

Extracurricular activities: camping program, chess, competitions, dance, debating, drama productions, Duke of Edinburgh's Award Scheme, fitness, Model United Nations, music, student exchanges, study tours (*eg* Cambodia, Thailand, Vietnam, Japan, Nepal, France, Italy and Peru), Shakespeare Festival, and Tournament of Minds.

Sports: athletics, cross country, basketball, gymnastics, hockey, indoor hockey, netball, rowing, skiing and snowboarding, soccer, softball, touch football, swimming, tae kwan do, tennis, water polo and yoga.

Ravenswood

(Founded 1901)

Principal
Ms Vicki Steer BA(Hons), MA,
DipEd, GradDipEd(Admin),
MACE, MACEL

Diploma coordinator
Robin Julian

Status Private

Boarding/day Mixed

Gender Female

Language of instruction
English

Programmes offered Diploma

Age range of pupils 5-18

Number of pupils enrolled 1120

Fees per annum
Day: AU$11,890-20,020
Boarding: AU$17,040

Address
1B Cecil Street
Gordon
NSW 2072 | AUSTRALIA

TEL +61 2 9498 9808
FAX +61 2 9498 9999

Email
enrol@ravenswood.nsw.edu.au

Website
www.ravenswood.nsw.edu.au

A Kindergarten to Year 12 school, Ravenswood provides a challenging and diverse curriculum which ensures girls have the opportunity to grow and develop in core areas, while at the same time pursuing individual interests.

Ravenswood follows the NSW Board of Studies curriculum as its learning framework. Its core curriculum includes English, mathematics, science, geography, history, physical education and health, and religious education.

During junior school, in addition to core studies girls experience music, French, visual arts, speech, information technology and information resources. Their learning also encompasses thinking, reading, writing, sport, creative arts and play.

The specialised Learning Enrichment Department at Ravenswood supports girls across the school, ranging from those who are gifted or talented through to those who have special needs.

A uniquely tailored middle school programme recognises the different learning needs of girls in the early stage of adolescence. The programme is structured to include experiential learning to enhance the skills and knowledge required for girls to move into their senior school years.

In Year 7 all girls study a core curriculum plus music, two languages, drama, visual arts and technology and applied studies. As girls progress through Years 7 to 10 their study choices increase as they choose subjects of interest to them.

In Years 11 and 12, girls are offered a choice of study paths: the International Baccalaureate (IB) Diploma Programme or the NSW Higher School Certificate (HSC). This choice and flexibility allows girls to tailor their studies to their own interests, skills and needs. It also encourages them to be independent and to take responsibility for the development of their future path, be it through further study or in life generally.

Redlands

(Founded 1884)

Principal
Dr Peter Lennox

Diploma coordinator
Hugh King

Status Private

Boarding/day Day

Gender Coeducational

Language of instruction
English

Programmes offered Diploma

Age range of pupils 3-19

Address
272 Military Road
Cremorne
NSW 2090 | AUSTRALIA

TEL +61 2 9908 6479
FAX +61 2 9909 3228

Email
hking@redlands.nsw.edu.au
registrar@redlands.nsw.edu.au

Website
www.redlands.nsw.edu.au

Redlands is a leading Australian independent school that offers an educational experience designed to inspire individual achievement and confidence for life.

Redlands provides an extensive range of opportunities – academic, sports, creative, outdoor education, service – for students to learn, to achieve and to develop their unique skills and talents.

The rich and balanced education program is aimed at developing well-rounded, confident and compassionate young adults who are prepared for life after school, ready to meet challenges and embrace opportunities and change in the 21st Century.

Redlands students work together within an inclusive, real world, coeducational environment, complemented by a comprehensive leadership and service programme, to develop the knowledge, capability and confidence to let their light shine – at school and beyond.

At Redlands students receive an outstanding academic education as a result of the school's individual approach, committed teachers and world-class learning programmes and resources.

Redlands has offered the International Baccaluareate for Years 11-12 since 1988, longer than any other school in New South Wales. The twenty year association with the IB has helped the school build its reputation as a leading provider of a well-rounded global education.

In embarking on the IB Diploma Programme at Redlands, students will commit themselves to:

- a two year journey of discovery and self-awareness
- an experience that will be ultimately both rewarding and empowering
- an outcome that will enable a smooth transition between school and university.

As a non-selective school, students at Redlands have the opportunity to study for the IB Diploma Programme if they so wish. Careful counselling is undertaken in considering course structure and styles of learning to assist students in making the right choice for them. Each year between 20% and 33% of Redlands students select the IB.

Redlands IB Results

- Over the past five years, three Redlands students have achieved the perfect IB score – 45/45.
- In 2007, 12 students (six boys and six girls) achieved an IB score between 40 and 45, equating to a UAI score of 99 and above.
- In each of 2006 and 2007, six students were awarded rare bilingual diplomas – in German, French, Chinese, Korean and Arabic.

At Redlands, all components of the IB Diploma Programme are delivered by a strong team of IB teachers, including assistant examiners and moderators in their subject areas, IB trained workshop leaders and teachers who are involved in curriculum review.

For more information about Redlands please contact the Registrar or visit our website www.redlands.nsw.edu.au.

Renaissance College
Hong Kong

啓新書院

(Founded 2006)

Head of School
Mr Peter Kenny

PYP coordinator
Ms Rosario Colet

MYP coordinator
Mr Grant Rogers

Diploma coordinator
Ms Carol Larkin

Status Private

Boarding/day Day

Gender Coeducational

Language of instruction
English

Programmes offered
PYP, MYP, Diploma

Age range of pupils 5-18

Number of pupils enrolled 1600

Fees per annum
Primary School: HK$68,400
Secondary School: HK$92,400

Address
5 Hang Ming Street
Ma On Shan
New Territories
HONG KONG | PR CHINA

TEL +852 3556 3556
FAX +852 3556 3446

Email
info@renaissance.edu.hk

Website
www.renaissance.edu.hk

Renaissance College Hong Kong (RCHK) is a world-class coeducational independent school and an IB World School. Located in the heart of Hong Kong's New Territories, the college was established in 2006 as the flagship of the English Schools Foundation (ESF) to serve the needs of the local and international expatriate community in Hong Kong.

Students are educated from year one to university entrance on the one site, guided and encouraged by international educators. Our student body comprises 38 nationalities, with 25 languages represented. English is the medium of instruction.

The Renaissance College Scholarship Programme provides pathways for motivated and talented secondary students, who strive for academic excellence and are empowered to take progressive action in their lives.

Apple Asia describes Renaissance College as a leading school in the region. Technology is integrated college-wide throughout the curriculum.

Our Creativity, Action and Service (CAS) programme is integral to college life. Students participate in a myriad of artistic, musical, sporting, and service activities conducted on-site and off-campus.

Renaissance College encourages young people to be curious and caring global citizens. Our aim is to prepare well-educated young people to lead future generations to seek and create an environment of intercultural understanding and respect for others.

We believe and expect that our students will pursue knowledge, learn through service, and strive to build a better world through action.

Facilities

Our purpose built campus provides the context for students to excel. State-of-the-art facilities include our Performing Arts Centre, Black Box Theatre, 25 metre indoor swimming pool, music rooms, library, science laboratories, gymnasiums, artificial turf tennis courts, outdoor basketball courts, cafeterias.

Curriculum

Renaissance College is a fully authorized IB World School offering the Primary Years Programme (PYP) from Year 1 to Year 6, the Middle Years Programme (MYP) from Year 7 to Year 11, and the Diploma Programme (DP) in Year 12 and Year 13. We focus on developing students as lifelong learners by building research skills, promoting personal responsibility, and encouraging independence.

Entry requirements

Entrance assessments and interview: Year 1 to Year 13

Richmond upon Thames College

(Founded 1977)

Principal
Kevin Watson

Diploma coordinator
Stephen Winfield

Status State

Boarding/day Day

Gender Coeducational

Language of instruction
English

Programmes offered
Diploma

Age range of pupils 16-18

Number of pupils enrolled
4000 (IB 70-90)

Fees per annum Free to under
19s in EU; Non-EU: £6050

Address
Egerton Road
Twickenham
Middlesex
TW2 7SJ | UK

TEL +44 (0)20 8607 8000/8294
FAX +44 (0)20 8744 9738

Email
SWinfield@rutc.ac.uk

Website
www.rutc.ac.uk

Welcome to the IB Diploma Programme at Richmond upon Thames College (RuTC) in Twickenham, twenty minutes by train from Central London. Founded in 1977, RuTC is a state funded college offering courses to 16-19 and adult learners, and we are the largest provider of students (over 1000 in 2007) to higher education in the UK. The diversity of our curriculum is unrivalled by any institution, with 4000 students drawn from the local community, from across London, and a comprehensive range of international backgrounds. We are particularly proud of our successes with the IB Diploma Programme, introduced in 2004, which has quickly established itself as a vital presence in the college's life: its commitment to academic excellence and adventure, and the energy and creativity of the IB students themselves, are a continual learning experience for us all.

RuTC's Diploma Programme students in the past three years gained places in universities throughout the UK, including Oxford and Cambridge,(five students in 2008 alone), Edinburgh, UCL, Imperial College, the London School of Economics, Exeter and Leeds, in subjects ranging from medicine to French, Japanese, international relations, veterinary science, and architecture. Others have gone to universities abroad, including the United States. Our pass rates, consistently well above the global level, mean that in 2008 we were in third position among state providers of the IB in the UK, and high on the national listing of all top IB schools.

If these results are important, the two years of a young person's life spent with us are equally so. Weekly specialist tutorials and CAS consultations are central to the Diploma Programme, as is the sense of belonging to a 'family' of like-minded, motivated individuals within the larger, dynamic space of RuTC. As befits its size and status, the college offers outstanding, accredited sports facilities, comprehensive theatre, music, art and design resources, full ICT support, a dedicated careers service with experienced higher education advisors, and an infinite variety of student clubs and societies. Above all, our broad range of subjects – sciences, humanities, languages and liberal arts – gives each student the opportunity to pursue a flexible, tailor-made combination of subjects and to develop intellectually and vocationally towards the IB's own ideal of an informed, inquiring, fully rounded citizen of the world.

Rossall School

(Founded 1844)

Headmaster
Dr Stephen Winkley

Diploma coordinator
Dr Doris Dohmen

Status Private

Boarding/day Mixed

Gender Coeducational

Language of instruction
English

Programmes offered Diploma

Age range of pupils 2-18

Number of pupils enrolled 620

Fees per annum
Day: £6510-£10,500
Boarding: £16,560-£26,490

Address
Broadway
Fleetwood
Lancashire
FY7 8JW | UK

TEL +44 (0)1253 774260
FAX +44 (0)1253 772052

Email
enquiries@
rossallcorporation.co.uk

Website
www.rossallschool.org.uk

A Traditional British Boarding School With An International Reputation

With its gothic architecture, manicured lawns and traditions dating back to the reign of Queen Victoria, Rossall School is every inch the quintessential boarding school, yet despite its thoroughly English packaging, there's a whole world of difference on its 164 year old campus.

With children from aged two to 18 on campus, Rossall School is a vibrant and lively community of 620 boarding and day pupils. As one of only nine schools in the UK with a separate International Study Centre, Rossall boasts a truly cosmopolitan outlook, and with 32 different nationalities represented on the 160 acre campus, it's hardly surprising.

Academic Excellence

Rossall currently provides one of the broadest curriculum programmes available in the UK independent school market. Rossall junior school is a candidate school for the IB Primary Years Programme whilst the senior school continues to follow the British National Curriculum culminating with GCSE examinations at the end of Year 11. At sixth form, pupils have the choice of studying either A levels, the International Baccalaureate Diploma Programme or the BTEC National Diploma in Design.

The school's academic success is based upon small class sizes and a tutorial system ensuring that all pupils receive regular support and guidance on academic matters. 95% of Rossall pupils proceed to higher education at universities around the world each year with excellent Oxbridge success.

Outstanding Facilities

Rossall's enviable on-campus facilities include 150 acres of outdoor grassed sports pitches for cricket, football, rugby and athletics plus floodlit all-weather surfaces for hockey, a gymnasium, heated indoor swimming pool, Fives courts, a shooting range and an archery range. A secure wireless internet network is operational campus wide in addition to computer facilities provided in two state-of-the-art IT suites. The school is also home to the Lawrence House Astronomy & Space Science Centre, the only centre of its kind in Britain, which specialises in astronomy education and incorporates a space observatory and planetarium for year round viewing of the night sky.

Boarding

Renowned for its standard of pastoral care, Rossall provides a 'family structure' for girls and boys age seven plus, with 24 hour support to enable pupils to get used to life at boarding school. Separate accommodation exists for boys and girls in one of the ten boarding houses which are in the process of being sensitively modernized to the highest standard.

Extracurricular Activities

A huge range of extracurricular activities are offered to pupils during the week. The Combined Cadet Force (CCF) also plays an important part in school life and enables pupils to gain flying, sailing and outdoor pursuit qualifications and expertise.

Rossall also excels at music and the performing arts. In addition to sport, music and drama over 30 clubs are offered in a variety of areas from chess to environmental groups.

Rossall School is a registered charity (No. 526685) which exists to provide education for children.

Rydal Penrhos

Headmaster
Mr P A Lee-Browne MA

Diploma coordinator
Mr W Williams

Status Private

Boarding/day Mixed

Gender Coeducational

Language of instruction
English

Programmes offered Diploma

Age range of pupils 11-18

Number of pupils enrolled 472

Fees per annum
Day: £9945-£14,190; Weekly
boarding: £17,415-£21,555;
Boarding: £19,350-£21,555

Address
Pwllycrochan Avenue
Colwyn Bay
Conwy
LL29 7BT | UK

TEL +44 (0)1492 530155
FAX +44 (0)1492 531872

Email
info@rydal-penrhos.com

Website
www.rydal-penrhos.com

Location
- Situated on the Bay of Colwyn and on the edge of the Snowdonia National Park, Rydal Penrhos is ideally placed to combine a rigorous academic curriculum with a rich variety of outdoor activities.
- There are excellent transports links to London, the Midlands and Manchester and Liverpool airports within 70 minutes allow easy access from Europe and beyond.

Ethos
- Scholarship and intellectual fulfilment are vital to allow pupils to move on to the next stage in their lives, and these are the starting point for all members of the school.
- As an IB World School, we expect pupils from an early age to think and work for themselves within a global dimension, and we set great store by self-development through independent reflection and learning.
- Member of HMC, IAPS, SHMIS and Methodist Independent Schools.

Curriculum
- Offers a wide range of subjects at GCSE, IGCSE, A level and IB Diploma Programme, and our recent Estyn (Welsh Schools Inspectorate) inspection identified the breadth of the sixth form curriculum as 'outstanding'.
- In addition to the examined curriculum, there is a PSHE programme for pupils throughout the school that includes careers, work experience and university guidance, and timetabled activities and games periods for all.
- EFL and learning support are well resourced, our philosophy being to encourage pupils to develop their own strategies for learning and development.

Facilities
- Recent developments to the schools have included a new dining hall, fitness suite, dance studio, sports centre and Learning Resource Centre, as well as a new Sixth form Centre.
- The swimming pool, drama studio, music, art and D&T schools and excellent rugby, hockey and cricket pitches are in constant use. Tennis, skiing, sailing and outdoor pursuits are well supported.

Boarding
- The boarding houses enjoy excellent standards of decoration and facilities in common, but have plenty of individual character.
- Each house has its dedicated team of houseparents supported by tutors, and there is a wide range of weekend boarding activities, as well as inter-house competitions (involving day and boarding pupils) throughout the year.
- Full, weekly and flexi boarding is available from seven years upwards for boys and girls.

Saint Edmund Preparatory High School

Head of School
John P Lorenzetti

Diploma coordinator
Raffaele Malafronte

Status Private

Boarding/day Day

Gender Coeducational

Language of instruction
English

Programmes offered Diploma

Address
2474 Ocean Avenue
Brooklyn
New York
NY 11229 | USA

TEL +1 718 743 6100

FAX +1 718 743 5243

Email
rmalafronte@stedmundprep.org

Website
www.stedmundprep.org

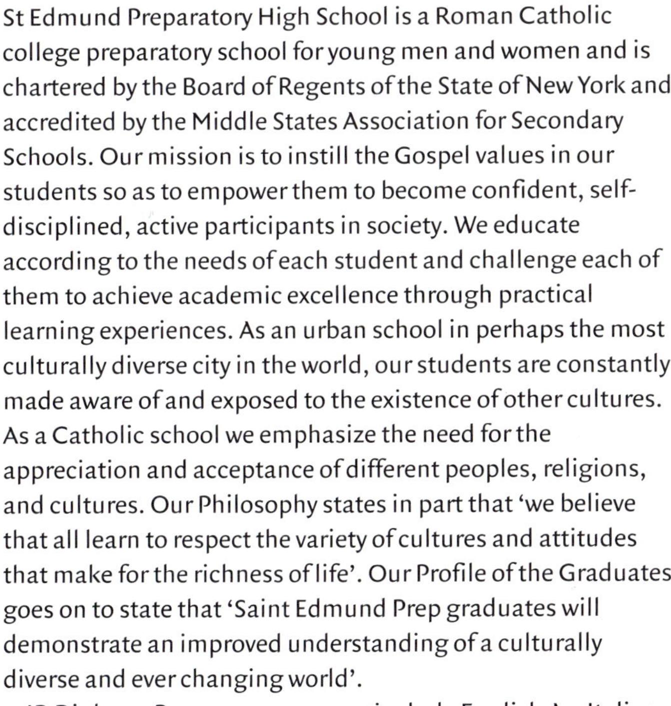

St Edmund Preparatory High School is a Roman Catholic college preparatory school for young men and women and is chartered by the Board of Regents of the State of New York and accredited by the Middle States Association for Secondary Schools. Our mission is to instill the Gospel values in our students so as to empower them to become confident, self-disciplined, active participants in society. We educate according to the needs of each student and challenge each of them to achieve academic excellence through practical learning experiences. As an urban school in perhaps the most culturally diverse city in the world, our students are constantly made aware of and exposed to the existence of other cultures. As a Catholic school we emphasize the need for the appreciation and acceptance of different peoples, religions, and cultures. Our Philosophy states in part that 'we believe that all learn to respect the variety of cultures and attitudes that make for the richness of life'. Our Profile of the Graduates goes on to state that 'Saint Edmund Prep graduates will demonstrate an improved understanding of a culturally diverse and ever changing world'.

IB Diploma Programme courses include English A1, Italian B, Spanish B, history of the Americas, biology, math, music, psychology and visual arts. The school recently opened a new 15,000 square foot addition to the present building which houses a new library and media centre, a band room, an art studio, a weight training room and a dance studio. The main building also contains two computer labs and three, recently constructed, state-of-the-art science labs. In order to provide for each student's emotional and spiritual growth we provide three full-time guidance counsellors, a full-time campus minister, a part-time chaplain, our Emmaus Retreat Program and a Christian Service Program. Our extracurricular program includes more than thirty-five clubs and activities, a rich and varied sports program for both boys and girls comprised of twenty-seven teams in sixteen sports, and award-winning student publications including a newspaper, yearbook and literary magazine. We are proud of the fact that more than seventy percent of the student body participates in at least one extracurricular activity.

Saint Edmund Preparatory High School has been preparing students for life for more than seventy-five years. Our success and longevity have resulted from a commitment to academic excellence and the conviction that we are a family guided by the same Catholic values.

Sandringham School (BeauSandVer)

Head of School
Alan Gray

Diploma coordinator
Graeme Swann

Status State

Boarding/day Day

Gender Coeducational

Language of instruction
English

Programmes offered Diploma

Address
The Ridgeway
St Albans
Hertfordshire
AL4 9NX | UK

TEL +44 (0)1727 759 240

FAX +44 (0)1727 759 242

Email
graeme.swann@
sandringham.herts.sch.uk

Website
www.sandringham.herts.sch.uk

Sandringham is part of the BeauSandVer consortium of three successful schools situated in St Albans just north of London. The consortium is made up of two mixed 11-18 schools (Sandringham and Beaumont) and one 11-18 boys school with a coeducational sixth form (Verulam). We are non-selective state schools with a proven track record of delivering high quality education to all students. The majority of our sixth form students go on to good quality universities including Oxbridge.

IB students are taught in small classes which enable a tutorial style of learning tailored to individual needs. Students have a personal tutor who oversees their progress and provides academic mentoring. The school has excellent facilities including new computer suites, well-stocked libraries, drama studios, a sports hall and extensive playing fields.

We are committed to the development of the whole person and have well-established links with groups in the UK and overseas, who work with us in our CAS programme. Curriculum enrichment is a central tenet of our ethos with students being offered trips to galleries, museums and theatres, exchange visits with partner schools abroad, work experience at home and overseas, as well as expeditions to countries as diverse as Belize, Iceland, Lesotho, Burkina Faso and China. Students can also choose to get involved in our many school based groups for music and sport amongst others.

Most of our students live locally but some commute from London via excellent communication links with the capital. The entry requirement for the IB Diploma Programme is an average GCSE point score of at least 43 (or similar).

Our IB Diploma subjects include English, French, German, Spanish (including *ab initio*), economics, geography, history, philosophy, psychology, biology, chemistry, physics, maths, computing science, visual arts, drama and music. These are offered at both higher and standard levels. Next year will see the introduction of other subjects.

You will be highly motivated through well-prepared lessons taught by well-qualified staff. You will expect to go on to study at university in Britain or anywhere in the world, in the knowledge that you have high academic ability, you are a well-rounded, articulate young person with a sound understanding of the international community.

For more information please contact us via our own website www.sandringham.herts.sch.uk or our consortium website www.beausandver.org.uk

Santiago College

(Founded 1880)

Head of School
Lorna Prado Scott

PYP coordinator
Jessica Allen

MYP coordinator
Andrea Strauszer

Diploma coordinator
Luz Maria Garcelón

Status Private

Boarding/day Day

Gender Coeducational

Language of instruction
Spanish, English

Programmes offered
PYP, MYP, Diploma

Age range of pupils 4-18

Number of pupils enrolled 1825

Address
Lota 2465
Providencia
Santiago | CHILE

TEL +56 2 7513800

FAX +56 2 7513802

Email
master@scollege.cl

Website
www.scollege.cl

Santiago College is a bilingual, independent, coeducational day school, founded as a non-sectarian institution in 1880 with support from the US Methodist Church.

The educational programme at Santiago College meets the requirements of the Chilean Ministry of Education and is authorized to deliver the three International Baccalaureate Programmes. It holds accreditation and is a member of ECIS/CIS (European Council of International Schools/Council of International Schools) and NEASC (New England Association of Schools and Colleges).

Students normally enter Santiago College at PK level and stay until they graduate from 12th Grade. The students are mainly Chilean but a number of students come from other countries and priority admission is given to overseas applicants. Approximately 90% of the graduating class enters Chilean universities and the rest pursue studies in the USA or Europe. The school operates a 180-day minimum calendar starting in early March and ending in mid-December. PK and kindergarten children have a half-day schedule. All other grades have a full school day beginning at 08:00 and ending at 15:35.

The school campus of 3.3 hectares is located close to the city centre. Facilities include a library of 30,000 volumes, 62 classrooms, AV rooms, gymnasiums, playing fields, science labs and computer labs, music and art studios and a dining room. The school owns an 11.2-hectare campus at La Dehesa, a suburb of Santiago, where most sports and physical education activities take place in large playing fields and sporting facilities.

Santiago College is a leader in education that offers a distinctive tradition of bilingual academic excellence grounded on solid values and respect for diversity. The mission of the school is to develop students who can contribute to a global world in constant change.

Scarborough College

(Founded 1901)

Headmaster
Jonathan S Lee

Diploma coordinator
Amanda Evirgen

Status Private

Boarding/day Mixed

Gender Coeducational

Language of instruction
English

Programmes offered Diploma

Age range of pupils 3-18

Number of pupils enrolled 450

Fees per annum
Day: £5580-£9360
Boarding: £16,140-£17,340

Address
Filey Road
Scarborough
North Yorkshire
YO11 3BA | UK

TEL +44 (0)1723 360620
FAX +44 (0)1723 377265

Email
admin@scarboroughcollege.co.uk

Website
www.scarboroughcollege.co.uk

Friendly atmosphere in a beautiful location

The beautiful campus of IB World School Scarborough College overlooks the spectacular North Yorkshire coast. The school has a warm, friendly environment, which is frequently commented upon by visitors. There is good access to the cities of York, Leeds, Manchester and Newcastle, and easy transfers from Manchester, Leeds, Bradford and all northern UK airports.

Outstanding pastoral care

The happiness and welfare of students is the college's top priority. Here is a school where the Head knows every child personally.

Pastoral care was judged by ISI Inspectors to be outstanding (January 2006). Study, recreation and boarding facilities are all of the highest modern standards. There are high expectations for both behaviour and dress, which contribute towards the positive learning environment.

Broad curriculum

The school has a strong reputation for offering a broad and stimulating education. Underpinned by traditional principles, the school has always championed innovation, which led it to

be the first school in North Yorkshire to introduce the exclusive study of the International Baccalaureate Diploma Programme. At its heart are the traditional disciplines of English, mathematics, science and modern foreign languages. In Year 10 these subjects form the 'core' at GCSE, leaving room for three or four 'option' subjects. Extra English language tuition is given, where necessary, to international students. A Learning Support department exists to help everyone make the most of his or her potential. Sixth form students study the IB Diploma Programme, which is a rigorous two-year course of study that prepares students for life after school and university. The Diploma Programme is a comprehensive and balanced qualification that is recognised throughout the world.

A vigorous programme of activities takes place outside the classroom, and all students are expected to participate fully. The college's particular strengths lie in drama, music, art, with a full and varied sporting programme including tennis, hockey and outdoor adventure.

Spectacular location by the sea and a friendly community; a breath of fresh air.

Sevenoaks School

(Founded 1432)

Head
Mrs Katy Ricks MA

Diploma coordinator
Nick Alchin

Status Private

Boarding/day Mixed

Gender Coeducational

Language of instruction
English

Programmes offered Diploma

Age range of pupils 11-18

Number of pupils enrolled 985

Fees per annum
Day: £15,936-£18,102 Boarding:
£25,554-£27,720

Address
Sevenoaks
Kent
TN13 1HU | UK

TEL +44 (0)1732 455133
FAX +44 (0)1732 456143

Email
nsa@sevenoaksschool.org

Website
www.sevenoaksschool.org

Sevenoaks School has been offering the IB Diploma Programme for 30 years and it is now studied by all 400+ pupils in the sixth form. The school provides pupils with a balanced and intellectually demanding education while promoting international understanding.

Founded in 1432, the school is situated on an attractive 100-acre campus adjoining Knole Park on the edge of town. It is only 30 minutes from central London and is conveniently close to Gatwick, Heathrow, the Channel Tunnel and continental Europe. Sevenoaks is an international community offering a unique boarding experience for young people from the UK and all over the world.

Curriculum

A wide range of subjects is offered at GCSE, with setting in core subjects. In the sixth form all pupils study the IB Diploma Programme.

Academic results are outstanding, and each year a significant number of pupils gain places in both arts and sciences at Oxford, Cambridge and the Ivy League universities, as well as other leading universities. The school regularly has a number of pupils achieving the maximum 45 points in the IB Diploma (nine in 2008). Special emphasis is placed on the teaching of modern languages (with an exceptional exchange programme). There is a large range of sport on offer, and pupils regularly achieve honours in rugby, cricket, basketball, sailing, shooting and tennis. There is also a strong emphasis on music, drama and art, and pupils are encouraged to participate in other co-curricular activities. The school is proud of its strong tradition of community service and involvement in the Duke of Edinburgh's Award Scheme.

Facilities

An ambitious development programme has ensured that facilities are first class. A new fully equipped sports centre was completed in early 2005 and a state-of-the-art performing arts centre is in the final planning stages. Other developments in recent years include a new dining hall and language centre and a new specialist teaching centre for mathematics. There are seven boarding houses, including a coeducational junior house (11-13), four single-sex houses (13-18) and two sixth form houses (16-18), attracting both British and overseas pupils. Accommodation ranges from a charming Queen Anne house to the more modern, purpose-built International Centre.

Entrance

At age 11, 13 and 16, by examination and interview;
Year 7 (11+): entrance examination;
Year 9 (13+): entrance examination or Common Entrance;
Sixth Form (16+): entrance examination and GCSE results or equivalent national grades.

Up to 50 scholarships are awarded annually at 11, 13 and 16, for academic excellence, music, sport and art.

Sevenoaks School is a registered charity for purposes of education. Charity No. 1101358.

Sotogrande International School

(Founded 1978)

Head
Christopher T J Charleson

PYP coordinator
Emma Butler

Diploma coordinator
Carmelo Mancera

Status Private

Boarding/day Mixed

Gender Coeducational

Language of instruction
English, Spanish

Programmes offered
PYP, Diploma

Age range of pupils 3-18

Number of pupils enrolled 680

Fees per annum
Day: €5616-€12,549
Boarding: €8892-€12,192

Address
Apartado 15
Sotogrande
PROVINCIA DE CÁDIZ, 11310 |
SPAIN

TEL +34 956 795 902
FAX +34 956 794 816

Email
info@sis.ac

Website
www.sis.ac

Sotogrande International School is a community of learners that has at its core the SIS Values. These values, based on the IB learner profile, shape our behaviour, inform our decision-making and provide a focus for all our actions. Members of our community are encouraged to open their hearts and minds to the joy of learning, to discover their strengths, identify their passions and develop outstanding learning skills.

Our school:

• Focuses on the whole person

SIS has a philosophy of student-focused, inquiry-based, multi-disciplinary, integrated learning. We believe in developing an enduring love of learning, based on the attitudes and attributes of the SIS Values.

• Offers a rich cultural diversity

SIS has a rich curricular and co-curricular programme of intercultural activities, events and exchanges that are designed to develop a deep understanding of what it means to be a global citizen. We aim to instil an intercultural and environmental responsibility and a commitment to global solidarity and community service.

• Focuses on academic success

We celebrate achievement and aim for the highest academic standards: our IB Diploma graduates have entered top universities worldwide. This reflects strong academic and guidance programmes and high quality teaching and pastoral care.

• Provides outstanding facilities for learning

Our purpose-built, high technology campus reflects our commitment to collaborative learning, designed to meet the needs of young adults entering a global 21st century society.

Founded in 1978, SIS is a leading international, coeducational day and boarding school. We are in the process of becoming an all-through IB school offering the PYP, MYP (candidate status) and Diploma Programmes. We are an inclusive community offering English language and special educational needs support throughout the school where required.

SIS is fully accredited by CIS and NEASC and authorised by NABSS. Our programme is fully convalidated by the Spanish Ministry of Education, allowing our IB Diploma graduates direct access to Spanish universities. This unique combination provides independent, external assurance of the quality of education at SIS.

St Andrew's College

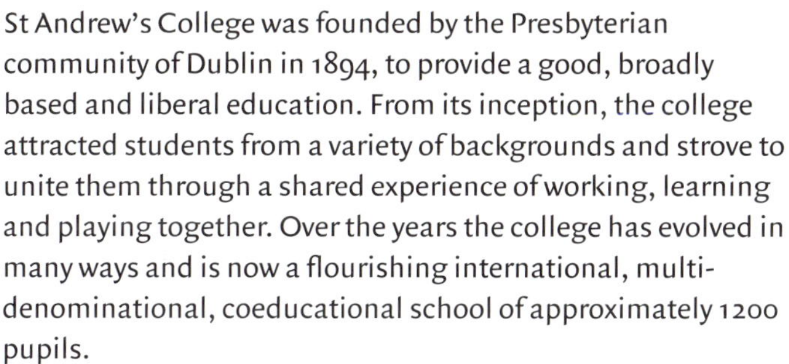

(Founded 1894)

Principal
Mr Arthur Godsil

Diploma coordinator
Monica Docherty

Status Private

Boarding/day Day

Gender Coeducational

Language of instruction
English

Programmes offered Diploma

Age range of pupils 4-18

Address
Booterstown Avenue
Blackrock
COUNTY DUBLIN | IRELAND

TEL +353 1 288 2785
FAX +353 1 283 1627

Email
information@st-andrews.ie

Website
www.st-andrews.ie

St Andrew's College was founded by the Presbyterian community of Dublin in 1894, to provide a good, broadly based and liberal education. From its inception, the college attracted students from a variety of backgrounds and strove to unite them through a shared experience of working, learning and playing together. Over the years the college has evolved in many ways and is now a flourishing international, multi-denominational, coeducational school of approximately 1200 pupils.

In 1985, St Andrew's College became the first school in Ireland to offer the International Baccalaureate Diploma Programme. Since then, it has built up a well-deserved reputation for its excellent results and for its distinctive multicultural environment. The philosophy on which the college was founded, and from which it still draws its inspiration, is that a well-resourced, rounded education is essential to the moral, social, cultural and academic development of every student. This philosophy is mirrored in the IB Diploma Programme which combines academic rigour with a strong extracurricular dimension and various community service projects. The IB Diploma Programme students at St Andrew's participate in a wide range of activities, playing team sports such as hockey, rugby, tennis, basketball and badminton, taking part in activities such as the Model United Nations and Model European Parliament, being involved in environmental projects, assisting in the school library and local communities and helping various charities by fundraising and doing voluntary work.

The IB Diploma Programme was developed to create acceptable matriculation qualifications for students attending international schools. Since 1985, St Andrew's IB students have been accepted into many universities and other institutions of higher learning throughout the world. In recent years these have included MIT, Yale, Berkeley and Columbia (USA), Cambridge, Durham, Edinburgh and the LSE (UK), the Universities of Tokyo and Keio (Japan), the National University of Ireland and the University of Dublin. These students frequently acknowledge the extent to which their studies in the IB Diploma Programme have helped them in their university careers.

The IB student profile at St Andrew's College is a truly international one, with students coming from all continents. This ethnic and cultural diversity enriches the school community in many ways and provides a wealth of knowledge and experience which is of great benefit to other students in the school.

St Andrew's College Dublin Limited is a registered charity which exists to provide education for children between the ages of four and 18. (No. CHY 4055.)

St Christopher's School

Principal
Edward Goodwin

Diploma coordinator
Stephen Martin

Status Private

Boarding/day Day

Gender Coeducational

Language of instruction
English

Programmes offered Diploma

Age range of pupils 3-18

Number of pupils enrolled 2150

Fees per annum
IB/A level: BD6021
(Others: BD2140-5550)

Address
PO Box 32052
Isa Town | KINGDOM OF
BAHRAIN

TEL +973 17 788101
FAX +973 17 788120

Email
office.seniors@st-chris.net

Website
www.st-chris.net

St Christopher's is a large, internationally renowned, not-for-profit school with over 2100 students representing 70 nationalities. Children from the age of three to 18 years benefit from the excellence, dedication and hard work of our teachers and support personnel who work together to create an environment in which each student can learn effectively.

St Christopher's Senior School provides students with a genuinely welcoming start to secondary education. The special atmosphere and style of the senior school is difficult to define but is ever present: academic certainly, but thoughtful and sensitive; competitive but good humoured; capable of inspiring passion and skill in the arts; with a certain independence of spirit but set in a strong sense of community. Success is measured not only in academic achievement but also in terms of growth in maturity, the development of social awareness, self-discipline and motivation, and a respect for the individual. The school promotes an environment in which it is considered natural to help and support others within the school, and to give service to the wider community.

Facilities

The facilities on the senior school campus include a large library, 11 science laboratories, three art rooms, a drama hall and a music suite with practice rooms. In addition there is a large sports hall, swimming pool, garden and recreational areas as well as the normal specialist rooms. Sixth form students have a dedicated study centre with their own social area.

Curriculum

St Christopher's teaches the National Curriculum at Key Stages 1, 2, 3 and offers GCSE at Key Stage 4. Sixth form students follow either an IB Diploma Programme or an A level programme.

Entry Requirements

Year 7 to 11: Entrance Examination
Sixth Form: conditional on students achieving at least five GCSE passes at Grade C or an equivalent qualification.

(Founded 1975)

Principal
Maria do Rosário Empis

PYP coordinator
Amanda Jones

MYP coordinator
Sharon Thompson

Diploma coordinator
Richard Parker

Status Private

Boarding/day Day

Gender Coeducational

Language of instruction
English

Programmes offered
PYP, MYP, Diploma

Age range of pupils 3-18

Number of pupils enrolled 702

Fees per annum
€7,247-€17,869

Address
Rua Maria Brown
Outeiro de Polima
2785-816 S Domingos de Rana |
PORTUGAL

TEL +351 21 444 0434
or +351 21 448 0550
FAX +351 21 444 3072

Email
school@dominics-int.org

Website
www.dominics-int.org

Veritas – Search for Truth

The Dominican motto, truth, is the inspiration of Dominican Schools. Dominican education has always been concerned with the development of the whole person. Respect and appreciation of all cultures, nationalities and religions are essential. These principles are the foundation upon which the Dominican Sisters established St Dominic's International School in Lisbon, Portugal, in 1964. This commitment has remained as St Dominic's has become an IB World School, using the three programmes: PYP, MYP and Diploma.

The International Baccalaureate Diploma Programme (DP) grants direct entry into the most prestigious institutions in the world due to its intellectual rigour and high academic standards. The Creativity, Action and Services components of the IB programmes reinforce St Dominic's core values.

St Dominic's International School, Portugal, is in the Cascais area, a suburb of Lisbon. It is conveniently close to the A5 motorway (which connects Lisbon with its suburbs) and the Marginal (the coastal road along the Tejo River).

Applications for admissions are accepted throughout the year. Families seeking admission for their children should make an appointment with the Vice Principals/Heads of junior or senior schools.

Minimum age requirements per class have to be completed by 31 December. Admission of students is dependent on reports from previous schools and an interview, conducted by the respective Vice-Principal/Head of School.

Initial placement is tentative. Tests in English and maths can be required to place students in different levels of class.

St Edward's, Oxford

(Founded 1863)

Warden
Andrew Trotman MA

Diploma coordinator
Jesse Elzinga

Status Private

Boarding/day Mixed

Gender Coeducational

Language of instruction
English

Programmes offered Diploma

Age range of pupils 13-18

Number of pupils enrolled 658

Fees per annum
Day: £21,609
Boarding: £27,015

Address
Woodstock Road
Oxford
Oxfordshire
OX2 7NN | UK

TEL +44 (0)1865 319323
FAX +44 (0)1865 319242

Email
registrar@stedwards.oxon.sch.uk

Website
www.stedwards.oxon.sch.uk

St Edward's, Oxford, is a coeducational boarding school from 13-18 situated in the north of the city providing an excellent all-round education for each individual in its care.

With approximately 100 academic scholars and exhibitioners, St Edward's offers a challenging environment where every pupil has the chance to be a leader. In its recent ISI inspection St Edward's was described as a 'remarkable school' which 'offers a very high quality of education' and produces pupils that 'are well prepared for higher education and service to the wider community'.

Academic rigour is the cornerstone of the development of St Edward's: the school has a one in eight teacher/pupil ratio and in the last five years 50 pupils have won places to Oxford, Cambridge and Harvard Universities. The inspectorate described the teaching at St Edward's as 'enabling pupils of all abilities to think for themselves and enjoy success'.

St Edward's is undergoing an exciting programme of development: The North Wall Arts Centre is an inspirational new building dedicated to an array of cultural events, educational opportunities and world class performances for the people of Oxford and beyond, whilst the new science building is a flagship in sustainable design setting new eco-standards for schools. The laboratories boast state-of-the-art equipment rarely found in British schools.

Music is a great strength at St Edward's and many pupils are members of national orchestras and choirs. The school delivers 500 instrumental music lessons every week, taught by highly qualified and experienced staff, and the department holds in excess of 60 concerts during the academic year.

St Edward's has always had a strong sporting tradition allowing pupils with the potential to become elite sportsmen and women. The number of boys and girls reaching county and national levels continues to grow. Around 40 pupils each year are successful in gaining gold/silver Duke of Edinburgh Awards.

76% of pupils are full boarders and so the school buzzes with life in the evenings and at weekends. Day pupils are fully integrated into the 11 boarding houses which are single sex and vertically grouped.

St Francis College

(Founded 2003)	**Age range of pupils** 2-18
College Principal Shirley Hazell	**Number of pupils enrolled** 500
PYP coordinator Agustin Onsari	**Fees per annum** US$9,795-17,247
MYP coordinator Sean Quinn	**Address** Rua Bélgica 399 Jardim Europa Sao Paulo 01448-030 SP | BRAZIL
Diploma coordinator Luis Prado	
Status Private	TEL +55 11 3082 7640 FAX +55 11 3898 2891
Boarding/day Day	**Email** office@stfrancis.com.br
Gender Coeducational	
Language of instruction English, Portuguese	**Website** www.stfrancis.com.br
Programmes offered PYP, MYP, Diploma	

Mission Statement

St Francis College is an international school which strives for excellence providing the solid foundation for passionate lifelong learning. We empower pupils within a warm and friendly community to become proactive and responsible citizens of the world by fostering moral and intellectual autonomy.

Beliefs and Values

We believe that:

- We have a responsibility towards society as advocators of the next generations.
- Pupils have the potential to develop in all areas within a well thought, balanced and stimulating curriculum.
- Everyone in the community has an important role in the achievement of our mission.
- Learning is best achieved through inquiry, significant experimenting, and meaningful problem solving.
- Pupils best develop in an environment which is a reflection of a safe and supportive community.
- Pupils are unique and active agents of their own learning.
- Teachers are active leaders and role models who guide pupils to achieve their innate potential.
- Pupils should understand and respect their home and host cultures and heritages.
- In the world of today, pupils must be prepared for a global scenario where the acquisition and fluency in English is an essential tool for the future.

Curriculum

The curriculum offered is an international one with English as one of the main languages of instruction. An important element in the curriculum is the Portuguese language subjects which include Brazilian literature, Portuguese language as well as the history and geography of Brazil. A broad approach of processes based learning will also encompass the humanities, arts, sciences, mathematics and information technology. The formal curriculum is guided by the Brazilian and British National Curriculum and the IB Programmes. The college provides students with academic challenge and key life skills in a flexible and transdisciplinary programme. Throughout the primary school the college offers the IB Primary Years Programme and in the secondary school it offers the IB Middle Years Programme and the IB Diploma Programme in the last two years. IGCSE exams are also offered in the main subjects in Year 10. Pupils will conclude their secondary education having also obtained their Brazilian Studies degree.

Entry requirements

Due to the international nature of the school children are accepted at different times during the year. Evaluations and interviews are held before acceptance. Previous school reports and IGCSE results, if applicable, are taken into account.

However the school will give the needed support in English to those international children who might need it. Entrance from the primary school into the secondary school is automatic. Parents are invited to contact the school via email or telephone the intake officer for a prospectus or to arrange a visit.

St George's College

Founded 1898

(Founded 1898)

Head
Mr Derek Pringle

PYP coordinator
Mabel Orlando

Diploma coordinator
Chris Gregory

Status Private

Boarding/day Mixed

Gender
Coeducational

Language of instruction
English, Spanish

Programmes offered
PYP, Diploma

Age range of pupils 3-18

Number of pupils enrolled 810

Address
Guido 800
B1878WAA Quilmes
Buenos Aires | ARGENTINA

TEL +54 11 4257 3472 ext 146
FAX +54 11 4253 0030

Email
info@stgeorge.com.ar

Website
www.stgeorge.com.ar

St George's College consists of two private, non-profit, IB World Schools offering a national programme of education fully integrated with the IB PYP, MYP and Diploma Programmes and the IGCSE: St George's College North, located inside the San Jorge Village in Los Polvorines some 35 kms north of Buenos Aires and St George's College, Quilmes, 20 kms south of Buenos Aires. Both schools follow a very similar educational programme and the pastoral and sporting activities are virtually the same.

Our mission is to provide students with a bilingual education that integrates the Argentine and international curricula. We strive for the continual improvement in the quality of the teaching and learning, management and school resources in order that students may develop their potential to the full. Our environment nurtures individual development, independent thinking, sportsmanship and an extensive and close interaction with the community.

Situated just 25 minutes outside the city of Buenos Aires, St George's College, Quilmes, has a beautiful and safe 27 hectare campus which allows students to participate in extracurricular activities that are an integral part of our IB syllabus and school philosophy. While academics drive the school programme, attention is also focused on the physical, artistic, social and spiritual needs of our students. A further strength is the continuing commitment to high quality boarding which maintains the very special community spirit of this outstanding school.

The school consists of three sections, kindergarten (three to six years), preparatory school (six to 11 years) and secondary (11-18 years). Each section has its own Head and this senior management team are responsible to the overall Headmaster of the school for the day-to-day running and strategic development of their section.

The Headmaster is a member of the Headmaster's Conference; the teaching staff is of high quality and well qualified. Most are at least bilingual and over 15 of them, including the Headmaster, are native English speakers. A high proportion of lessons are conducted in English.

St George's will always seek to maintain its boarding facilities (about 15% of the pupils board) as we see it as a valuable contribution to the pastoral support we offer. Boarders will generally be admitted from sixth grade upwards. The boarding housemaster and housemother maintain a watchful eye on the development and general happiness of those students under their care, and communicate matters of concern directly to parents and tutors.

The overall aim of the college sports programme is to provide enjoyment, coupled with competition and a sense of success. Students throughout the whole school participate in the following major activities during the academic year: gym; swimming; aerobics; diving; hockey; rugby; athletics; football; cricket; handball; softball; volleyball; tennis and golf.

St George's is a happy community in which young people really can flourish and develop their talents.

St Helen's School

(Founded 1899)

Head
Mrs Mary Morris BA

Diploma coordinator
Mary Bowman

Status Private

Boarding/day Day

Gender Female

Language of instruction
English

Programmes offered Diploma

Age range of pupils 3-18

Number of pupils enrolled 1140

Fees per annum £11,995

Address
Eastbury Road
Northwood
Middlesex
HA6 3AS | UK

TEL +44 (0)1923 843210
FAX +44 (0)1923 843211

Email
enquiries@sthn.co.uk

Website
www.sthn.co.uk

Located across 20 acres of grounds in Northwood, Middlesex, close to Hertfordshire and Buckinghamshire and with easy access by underground from central London, St Helen's School offers day places to girls aged three to 18.

The school offers both the International Baccalaureate Diploma Programme and A levels to sixth form students. Our sixth form is a vibrant community of approximately 170 girls. Class sizes are small with study programmes tailored to meet individual needs. Girls consistently achieve excellent results, going on to prestigious universities of their first choice.

League tables in *The Times* in 2008 placed St Helen's in the top four IB schools in the UK, with 25% of our recent IB graduates achieving 40 points or more and one student achieving the perfect score of 45 points.

Girls go on to pursue a wide variety of courses and opportunities at university, with our recent graduates studying subjects such as architecture, Chinese, dentistry, geography, history, medicine, pharmacy and veterinary medicine at universities including Oxford, Cambridge, Durham, Imperial College, UCL and Nottingham.

Classroom-based work is complemented by a wide range of extracurricular activities including concerts, plays, the Combined Cadet Force organised jointly with Merchant Taylors' School, and the Duke of Edinburgh's Award Scheme, as well as a huge variety of clubs and societies. Trips and visits complement and enrich learning and we place a high priority on careers education, with all girls doing work experience in the UK or in Europe.

St Helen's offers every pupil an academic, innovative and stimulating education, enabling each girl to develop her intellectual, creative and physical talents to the full. Students are encouraged to develop lifelong skills in a diverse range of areas and to pursue their individual talents and ambitions, in a friendly, supportive and well-ordered environment, ready to take their place in the adult world.

St Helen's is a registered charity which exists to provide education for able children (Charity No. 312762).

Taejon Christian International School

(Founded 1958)

Headmaster
Dr Thomas J Penland

PYP coordinator
Liz Harder

Diploma coordinator
Ken Gunther

Status Private

Boarding/day Mixed

Gender
Coeducational

Language of instruction
English

Programmes offered
PYP, Diploma

Number of pupils enrolled 594

Address
201-1 O-Jung Dong
Daedeok-Gu
Daejeon
306-819 | REPUBLIC OF KOREA

TEL +82 042 633 3663
FAX +82 042 631 5732

Email
hdmst@tcis.or.kr

Website
www.tcis.or.kr

Become a part of a nurturing community that cares. TCIS prides itself on community and taking care of each and every student. The school offers a differentiated curriculum serving ELL students and special needs students while still matriculating a significant number of each graduating class to highly selective universities around the world. TCIS is an outstanding IB World School for grades Pre-K to 12th (with a boarding program from grades 6-12). The student population has grown to just under 600 students with 200 students in our highly nurturing residence program.

Curriculum

The school is authorized to offer the IB Diploma Programme and the IB Primary Years Programme within the context of quality, traditional Christian education. Almost all of the 11th and 12th grade students are IB Diploma candidates and many of our graduates attend highly selective universities in North America. TCIS is accredited not only by the IB but also has a long, excellent history of accreditation with the Western Association of Schools and Colleges. The school participates in activities with the KAIAC conference and also in the Asia Pacific Activities Conference with exchanges in sports, music,

drama, and academics with some of the other leading international schools in East Asia. The school is certified as a foreign school by the Korea Ministry of Education.

Facilities

The attractive ten acre garden campus is equipped with a high school building, an elementary building, info-tech building and multiple middle school classrooms located in a designated area on the campus. The facilities also include a school performing arts auditorium, seven dorms in total both on and off campus, three cafeteria areas, a gymnasium, tennis courts, and lighted soccer field. Daejeon, 'the most livable' city in Korea is just 50 minutes by high-speed rail from downtown Seoul.

Entry Requirements

A foreign passport, green (permanent residence) card or if you are a Korean citizen then five-years documented living outside of Korea is required for admissions. A personal boarding interview is required with the student and parents or guardians.

The school is governed by a not-for-profit Christian foundation board.

TASIS The American School in England

(Founded 1976)

Head
Dr James Doran

Diploma coordinator
Chantal Gordon

Status Private

Boarding/day Mixed

Gender Coeducational

Language of instruction
English

Programmes offered Diploma

Age range of pupils 3-18

Number of pupils enrolled 750

Fees per annum
Day: £5500-£17,500
Boarding: £26,750

Address
Coldharbour Lane
Thorpe
Surrey
TW20 8TE | UK

TEL +44 (0)1932 565252
FAX +44 (0)1932 564644

Email
ukadmissions@tasisengland.org

Website
www.tasis.com/England

TASIS England offers its widely respected university-preparatory curriculum to day students, ages three to 18, and to boarding students, ages 14-18. Located on a beautiful and historic estate 18 miles south-west of London and eight miles from Heathrow Airport, TASIS England's spacious campus combines Georgian mansions and 17th century cottages with new, purpose-built facilities.

The TASIS experience prepares young people from over 50 nations to meet the challenges of a demanding world. Small classes and a dedicated, experienced faculty, numbering in excess of 100, provide an outstanding environment for learning. Individualised college counselling assists students in every step of the university selection and application process.

Success in the International Baccalaureate Diploma Programme and American College Board Advanced Placement courses (similar to A levels) has resulted in acceptances to some of the finest universities in the United States, the United Kingdom, Canada and worldwide.

While academics are emphasised, sports, the arts, extracurricular activities, and community service are essential to the school's mission of ensuring a balanced education.

TASIS England comprises three divisions: Lower (ages three to 10), Middle (ages 11-13) and Upper (ages 14-18). Students in each division regularly benefit from the opportunity to work closely with visiting artists, actors, musicians and sports professionals.

The school takes full advantage of its location, and students enjoy numerous field trips, cultural excursions, weekend activities and travel to London, throughout the UK and abroad as extensions to classroom learning.

Admissions decisions for the academic school year are made on a rolling basis upon receipt of a completed application form together with the application fee, three teachers' recommendations and three years of transcripts. Standardised test scores and a student questionnaire are required. An interview is recommended unless distance is a prohibiting factor. Contact Bronwyn Thorburn-Riseley, Director of Admissions: ukadmissions@tasisengland.org

Accredited by the Council of International Schools (CIS) and the New England Association of Schools and Colleges (NEASC), TASIS England is an IB World School and was inspected by Ofsted in 2004. The school is a member of The Association of Boarding Schools (TABS) and the National Association of Independent Schools (NAIS).

The Awty International School

(Founded 1956)

Principal
Mr Sam Waugh

Diploma coordinator
Carol Case PhD

Status Private

Boarding/day Day

Gender Coeducational

Language of instruction
English

Programmes offered Diploma

Age range of pupils 3-18

Number of pupils enrolled 1192

Address
7455 Awty School Lane
Houston
TX 77055-7222 | USA

TEL +1 713 686 4850

FAX +1 713 686 1351

Email
admissions@awty.org

Website
www.awty.org

The Awty International School, a non-profit private school located in west Houston provides a world-class education on a welcoming campus, within a unique environment that challenges and inspires all of its students to fulfill their potential through a solid educational program leading to either the International Baccalaureate or French Baccalauréat diplomas. Students in both programs must meet the requirements for an American high school diploma which includes credits in fine arts, computer science and American history.

In a diverse international culture, the school creates well-educated and responsible world citizens who become lifelong learners. Teachers encourage students to be independent thinkers prepared to live in a global society and to continue to perform community service. A dedication to the Learning Profile in all facets of the Awty community contributes to the intellectual growth and academic success of all the students. Extracurricular activities include: newspaper, orchestra, Model UN, Interscholastic Athletics and student government, among others. The International Baccalaureate Diploma Programme at Awty School is consistently among the highest performing worldwide with an average success rate of 95% and a mean IB score of 34.

In small class settings the Awty curriculum concentrates on all areas of the IB hexagon. Group One and Two languages are taught by native speakers. Among the available languages offered at various levels are: Arabic, Chinese, Dutch, English, French, German, Norwegian, Portuguese and Spanish. All students must take two languages and may study a third if desired.

Group Three allows students to select either history or economics. In Group Four students may choose among four sciences: biology, chemistry, physics and environmental science. In Group Five mathematics is offered at three levels. The Group Six elective offers all of the following of which the student may take one subject: art, music, theatre, computer science, chemistry, economics, or a third language: Chinese, French or Spanish. All other requirements for the IB Diploma, Theory of Knowledge, Extended Essay and CAS are addressed with the same level of instruction and guidance.

The British School, Rio de Janeiro

(Founded 1924)

Directors
Paul Wiseman OBE and
Therezinha Pientznauer

Diploma coordinator
Ralph Jennings

Status Private

Boarding/day Day

Gender Coeducational

Language of instruction
English

Programmes offered Diploma

Age range of pupils 2-18

Number of pupils enrolled 1600

Fees per annum US$20,000

Address
Rua Real Grandeza 87
Botafogo
Rio de Janeiro-RJ
22281-030 | BRAZIL

TEL +55 21 2539 2717
FAX +55 21 2244 5591

Email
edu@britishschool.g12.br
admissions@britishschool.g12.br

Website
www.britishschool.g12.br

Founded in 1924, we are a non-profit, independent and coeducational day school offering a complete and coherent curriculum for pupils of all nationalities from ages two to 18.

The school is an IB World School and accredited by the Council of International Schools (CIS). The Director Paul Wiseman is a member of the Latin American Heads Conference (LAHC).

The school has 1600 pupils located on three sites. Botafogo houses a primary school and the first year of secondary school. The secondary school is based at Urca, close to the Sugar Loaf. The Barra site opened in February 2006. It is a major project to establish a school in the Barra suburb. For 2009, the intake of pupils will be from age two (pre-nursery) to age 12 (Class 6). Subsequent year groups will be opened annually.

We aim to cultivate well-informed, open-minded, confident, caring and enquiring young people who strive to do their best. The emphasis on academic achievement is balanced by our concern to meet our pupils' physical, emotional and social needs and to ensure that they are prepared for active and well-balanced citizenship.

English is the language of teaching and learning. From pre-nursery to Class 9 the programme broadly follows the English National Curriculum. Secondary students are prepared for the International General Certificate of Secondary Education (IGCSE) examinations and the International Baccalaureate (IB) Diploma. The school has a history of creditable results in both IGCSE and IB and evident success in university entrance worldwide.

Classes are generally small and the school environment is pleasant, well resourced and stimulating, with a strong focus on health, safety and security. Performing arts, sports, Model United Nations, Duke of Edinburgh's Award Scheme and work experience provide a wide range of co-curricular opportunities. Experiences beyond the school include numerous local day visits and national or international residential trips for most year groups from Class 3 upwards.

Our teachers are well qualified (some 25% being recruited from overseas) and supported by a robust and effective programme of continuing professional development.

Extracurricular activities

The extracurricular activities offered include football, capoeira, volleyball, basketball, ballet, artistic gymnastics, judo, choir, music (instruments and singing), cooking, drama and arts. Depending on the age and interest of the students, hiking and climbing, rowing and sailing lessons are also offered.

Facilities

Air-conditioned classrooms, some with interactive white boards and computers connected to the internet, five science laboratories and six computer laboratories, five libraries, open spaces for sports and games, playgrounds with a variety of toys, three auditoriums for classes, drama presentations and art exhibitions, four sickbays and three dining halls.

The Dwight School

Chancellor
Stephen H Spahn

PYP coordinator
Elaine Natalicchi

MYP coordinator
Dianne Drew

Diploma coordinator
Anthony Foster

Status Private

Boarding/day Mixed

Gender Coeducational

Language of instruction
English

Programmes offered
PYP, MYP, Diploma

Age range of pupils 2-18

Number of pupils enrolled 480

Fees per annum $32,200

Address
291 Central Park West
New York
NY 10024 | USA

TEL +1 212 724 6360
FAX +1 212 874 4232

Website
www.dwight.edu

The Dwight School, founded in 1872, is the first school in the US to offer the three International Baccalaureate (IB) Programmes, grades K-12. With the opening of Woodside Preschool in the fall of 2005, Dwight became the first school to offer the IB Primary Years Programme for children ages two to four. The school motto is 'use your spark of genius to build a better world'. The school's mission is to develop each student's unique capabilities. The programme incorporates academic excellence and a commitment to educate a diverse student population in leadership and responsibility to others. Nearly 40 nationalities are represented at Dwight.

Dwight students aim to become confident, self-motivated, disciplined, knowledgeable and open-minded inquirers, as well as caring, principled and responsible citizens. Dwight co-founded the Institute for Civic Leadership in order to construct a school model for civic leadership, continuing the tradition of graduates Mayor Fiorello La Guardia, Robert Moses, Walter Lippman, Governor Herbert Lehman and Secretary of the Treasury Henry Morganthau.

The school is organized into five divisions, each with a Dean. In Timothy House (K-five) students master traditional math, reading and writing skills, as well as geography, humanities and science. Students study French and Chinese, and small classes allow each child to reach his full intellectual, physical and social potential. More than fifteen after-school programs are offered.

In the Bentley House (six to eight), students study the major academic disciplines, and they also learn study skills, technology, environmental studies, civics, community activities and health and social education across all academic disciplines. After school there are teams, clubs and activities. Trips to England, France and Peru are another aspect of the Dwight international experience.

Franklin House (nine to ten) and Anglo House (11-12) place special emphasis on the IB Diploma Programme. Students study Diploma Programme subjects with the expectation that many will complete the full Diploma by grade 12. Rich course offerings from theater, art and music extend to unique programmes in design technology, environmental studies, economics and business management. Special field expeditions to India, Peru, Mexico and Kenya are part of the international mission of the school.

Dwight is an authorized IB World School and is accredited by the European Council of International Schools and the Middle States Association of Colleges and Secondary Schools. Students enter leading universities in the United States and abroad.

Financial aid is granted on the basis of need and academic promise.

(Founded 1984)

General Director
Jean-Marc Gobbi

Diploma coordinator
Trevor Alan Tricker

Status Private

Boarding/day Mixed

Gender Coeducational

Language of instruction
English, French

Programmes offered Diploma

Age range of pupils 3-19

Number of pupils enrolled 500

Fees per annum
Day: €6,300-8,550
Boarding: €17,320-18,770

Address
500 Route de Bouc-Bel-Air
Domaine des Pins, Luynes
Aix en Provence
13080 | FRANCE

TEL +33 (0)4 4224 0340

FAX +33 (0)4 4224 0981

Email
info@ibsofprovence.com

Website
www.ibsofprovence.com

The International Bilingual School of Provence, an independent coeducational secondary school located near Aix-en-Provence in the south of France, owes its international character to the diversity of its student population. The school, established since 1984, has an annual enrolment of 500 students from more than 30 different countries in its day and boarding sections. In addition to the French students who make up 45% of the student population, IBS welcomes pupils from the five continents desiring to pursue their education in English, French or both.

A particularity of the school is that the international section is not dominated by any one nationality and new students are made to feel at home immediately. Committed to French-English bilingualism, the school offers both the International Baccalaureate Diploma Programme and the French Baccalaureate. Mother tongue classes are also provided to ensure that the student maintains his/her own language skills.

Philosophy

Small classrooms, qualified teachers, modern facilities in a tranquil, calm environment help ensure the success of each student. The campus is concentrated around the main building, a typical 'Mas' which is perfectly adapted to the daily activities of the school. IBS offers its students the most modern boarding houses and our campus includes: an audio-visual centre, fully-equipped science laboratory, newly designed dining hall, computer labs, library, swimming pool, tennis courts, soccer field, and dance/martial arts/table tennis hall. Involvement in various extracurricular activities is expected and enhances the development of each individual's character within the spirit of the school. Politeness, respect and consideration for others are important values at IBS. Students leave IBS, the majority for university placements, as caring, responsible young citizens.

Summer school

During the spring and summer holidays, IBS offers intensive French as a Foreign Language and English immersion programmes. Over 250 students from all over the world join IBS every summer to develop their language skills while discovering the beauty of the Provence region.

Admissions

Admission applications are accepted throughout the year for interested students. For more information, contact Mr Trevor Alan Tricker, Head of International Studies, or consult the school website at www.ibsofprovence.com.

The International School Of Penang (Uplands)

(Founded 1955)

Acting Head
Alan Smith

PYP coordinator
Ali Nicholson

Diploma coordinator
Isabel Henriques Davis

Status Private

Boarding/day Mixed

Gender Coeducational

Language of instruction
English

Programmes offered
PYP, Diploma

Age range of pupils 4-19

Number of pupils enrolled 600

Fees per annum
RM10,395-37,500

Address
Jalan Sungai Satu
Batu Feringgi
11100 Penang | MALAYSIA

TEL +604 8819 777
FAX +604 8819 778

Email
info@uplands.org

Website
www.uplands.org

Our motto: Respect for self; respect for others

We are a coeducational secular, non-profit day and boarding educational institution offering quality international education to children aged between four- and 19-years-old. As an IB World School our students' examination results have consistently been above global averages for the last six years, in the IB Diploma, IGCSE and GCSE categories.

The school was originally founded in 1955 by the Incorporated Society of Planters (ISP) to provide expatriate planters a place to school their children. Over 50 years later we still provide a safe and caring environment for expatriates and Malaysian students alike, and for some, a 'home away from home' at our boarding houses.

The International School Of Penang still retains the name 'Uplands' to preserve our long heritage and history on this island. Upland's roots are firmly in Penang, an island itself rich in the history of dynamic international and interethnic exchange. Educating young people of over 30 nationalities, we are fully committed to the concept of Universal Values and International Ideals, and believe that hope for peace in the future lies in an interdependent international community where 'respect for self; respect for others' is paramount.

Learning support

The Learning Support Department aims to support those who are struggling to meet the demands of mainstream curriculum. It tailors individual programs called Individualised Education Programs (IEPs) for students who need help.

Extracurricular activities (ECAs)

There are many opportunities for all students to excel in and enjoy ECAs. Our annual performing arts events and visual exhibitions, successes in the sports field at state and international level are our testament to educating a person as a whole.

The campus

A purpose built four-acre campus is conveniently situated in the resort township of Batu Feringgi, Penang Island. The school features 36 classrooms, five science laboratories, a multi purpose hall with gymnasium, a new artificial-turf sports field and a 25-metre swimming pool. The modern classroom buildings encircle a beautiful garden courtyard creating a peaceful environment conducive for learning.

The North London International School

(Founded 1885)

Head of School
Mr David Rose MA(Ed),
BA, CertEd

PYP coordinator
Theresa Heath

MYP coordinator
Yukesha Makhan

Diploma coordinator
Edith van der Linden

Status Private

Boarding/day Day

Gender Coeducational

Language of instruction
English

Programmes offered
PYP, MYP, Diploma

Age range of pupils 2-19

Number of pupils enrolled 400

Fees per annum £2985-£14,280

Address
Friern Barnet Lane
London
N11 3LX | UK

TEL +44 (0)20 8920 0600
FAX +44 (0)20 8211 4605

Email
admissions@nlis.org

Website
www.nlis.org

Curriculum

Students follow the International Baccalaureate Programmes, starting at aged three with the Primary Years Programme, moving onto the Middle Years Programme at age 11 and the Diploma Programme at age 16. The programmes are designed to encourage the development of learning skills and to meet a child's academic, social, physical, emotional and cultural needs. Through enquiry based learning and various disciplines, subject interrelatedness is accentuated, preparing students for the pre-university Diploma Programme. Within the Diploma Programme students must study six subjects, a research project, leading to a 4000 word essay, The Theory of Knowledge course, and Creativity, Action, Service (CAS). The CAS programme is a fundamental part of the Diploma Programme, requiring students to participate in 150 hours of activities both in and out of school.

Entry Requirements

Kindergarten and Lower School (ages two to 11): students are invited to attend for half a day and may be asked to complete a basic assessment. Upper School (ages 11 – 15): students are interviewed by the Head of the school, invited to visit the school for a day and may be required to complete a basic assessment. Diploma Programme applicants are invited for interview with the programme co-ordinator. Students would be expected to have five or six GCSE passes, with B, A or A* grades for subjects to be studied at Higher Level.

Aims and Objectives of the School

The school aims to create a secure, well-ordered and happy environment with the learning process at its core with emphasis placed on the successful development of the whole individual. Importance is placed on students learning to work as team members and, where appropriate, as leaders. The school serves a cosmopolitan community of both local and international students. Empathy and understanding of differing cultures, religions and backgrounds are encouraged.

The school recognises that students can have a variety of different learning styles. The Quest Programme is designed for students who need help developing strategies to assist them to study effectively. Through one-to-one tuition from specialist staff in skills such as effective reading, time management, planning of work and revision and exam techniques, students can reach their full potential, further enhanced by the school's teacher-student ratio.

Students at The North London International School receive a thorough preparation for university and adult life, with skills in learning independently, leadership, adapting confidently to new situations and becoming active members of an international society.

The Stephen Perse Sixth Form College

Head of School
Miss Patricia Kelleher

Diploma coordinator
Simon Armitage

Status Private

Boarding/day Day

Gender Coeducational

Language of instruction
English

Programmes offered Diploma

Age range of pupils 16-18

Number of pupils enrolled 95

Fees per annum £12,105

Address
Shaftesbury Road
Cambridge
Cambridgeshire
CB2 8AA | UK

TEL +44 (0)1223 488430
FAX +44 (0)1223 467420

Email
office@stephenperse.com

Website
www.stephenperse.com

The Stephen Perse Sixth Form College aims to foster a love of learning, developing inquiring, reflective, open-minded young people, prepared for the opportunities of the twenty-first century and equipped to play an active role in an increasingly international world.

The college was established by The Perse School for Girls, one of the most successful schools in the UK. It was authorized in 2007 as an IB World School and opened its doors to its first group of students in September 2008. The college provides over 2000 square metres of brand new, dedicated facilities for students aged 16-19, giving an inspirational environment in which to learn. The building is fully networked and every student has his or her own wireless laptop. The teaching classrooms are complemented by four purpose-built laboratories, a language laboratory and a multimedia suite, ensuring we make the very best use of the latest technology. Our common room facility comprises a cafeteria-style dining area as well as general relaxation space.

Our relationship with the senior school of Perse Girls is another unique attraction of the college. It means that you benefit from the same team of teaching staff who have helped to create one of the UK's highest achieving schools; it also gives you access to some amazing specialist facilities, including a new Visual Arts Centre that gives our art students the dedicated space they need to pursue their studies. In addition, music and drama benefit from the purpose-built rehearsal and performance space at the Perse Girls' site.

In subject classes with a maximum size of 15 students, we place great emphasis on discussion, interaction and enquiry. The atmosphere is one that fosters lively group discussion whilst also allowing you to develop at your own pace. We are keen to help you find the inquisitiveness that characterises the best in sixth form education.

We have a strong outward-looking approach that is about far more than visiting places and speaking languages. An appreciation of the diversity and richness of other cultures and environments is central. We hold an International School Award from the British Council in recognition of our impressive range of international activities. In recent years our historians have gone to Berlin and Istanbul, Moscow and St Petersburg, classicists to Rome and Pompeii, drama students to Greece, musicians to Australia and the Rhineland, and our geographers to Morocco – not forgetting the sports tours and the annual ski-trip, and exchange programmes with work experience and study visits abroad for modern linguists.

The Sultan's School

(Founded 1977)	**Number of pupils enrolled** 1200
Principal Antony Cashin	**Fees per annum** RO1300-3000
Diploma coordinator Ray Zinsli	**Address** PO Box 665 Seeb 121 | SULTANATE OF OMAN
Status Private	**TEL** +968 24536 777 **FAX** +968 24536 997
Boarding/day Mixed	
Gender Coeducational	**Email** principle@sultansschool.org
Language of instruction English	**Website** www.sultansschool.org
Programmes offered Diploma	
Age range of pupils 3-18	

"The Sultan's School is a coeducational school offering a bilingual education from early childhood to pre-university. The school seeks to provide a broad and balanced education to the highest quality which reflects and strengthens the Omani and Islamic culture while encouraging an international perspective and developing critical, creative thinking in its students."

The school was established in 1977 under the sponsorship of His Majesty Sultan Qaboos bin Said. The school seeks to provide a superior education which will lead directly to leading western or Arab universities. Combining the best of the old with the best of the new, the school strives to develop those habits and attitudes necessary for success in an increasingly interdependent world, including traits of responsibility, tolerance, integrity, initiative, perseverance and cooperation.

The garden-like setting of the spacious 250,000 square metre campus is unique among private schools in Oman, offering a pleasant and tranquil environment in which each student can have every opportunity to develop to his or her fullest potential.

The school's excellent facilities, top-quality staff and impressive academic record have made it the 'Premier Private School' in Oman for the past 30 years. The student roll is around 1200, from kindergarten through to Year 13 and comprises students from 25 different nationalities.

The curriculum is bilingual for Omanis, with Arabic, Islamic Education and social studies taught in Arabic and mathematics, English and the sciences taught in English; music, PE and information technology are taught in both languages. The curriculum in the elementary school is based on the British National Curriculum and the Arabic curriculum follows the Ministry of Education's Basic Education Programme.

In the secondary school, the curriculum is aimed towards preparation for the International General Certificate of Secondary Education (IGCSE) examinations studied in Years 10 and 11. A range of options are offered outside of the core, including information technology, business studies, economics, geography, physical education, drama, art, and music.

The International Baccalaureate Diploma Programme is studied in Years 12 and 13 with around 70-80 students in each year, pursuing the full and varied range of IB Diploma Programme options on offer.

The Sultan's School offers an extensive programme of extracurricular activities throughout the academic year. The schedule changes twice each semester, offering students from Years 5-13 a wide variety of activities from which to choose. All in all, our extracurricular programme allows students to enrich themselves in areas outside the normal academic curriculum, to become more well-rounded, interested and interesting people.

Applications to study at The Sultan's School are considered throughout the year and we welcome visits by families of prospective applicants both Omani and expatriate.

The York School

(Founded 1965)

Head of School
Ezio Crescenzi

PYP coordinator
Patricia Jerred

MYP coordinator
Eric Robertson

Diploma coordinator
David Hanna

Status Private

Boarding/day Day

Gender Coeducational

Language of instruction
English

Programmes offered
PYP, MYP, Diploma

Age range of pupils 3-17

Number of pupils enrolled 593

Fees per annum Grades 1 to 12:
$21,700 tuition, $4000 one time
registration fee; Junior and
Senior Kindergarten: $18,100
tuition, $4000 one time
registration fee

Address
1320 Yonge Street
Toronto ON
M4T 1X2 | CANADA

TEL +1 416-646-5275
(Admissions) +1 416-926-1325
(Main switchboard)
FAX +1 416-926-9592

Email
ezio_crescenzi@tys.on.ca

Website
www.yorkschool.com

As a non-denominational, coeducational, university preparatory school, The York School's mission is to develop inquiring, knowledgeable and caring young people who are engaged citizens of the world.

We offer an education marked by individual attention, progressive methods and a climate of collaboration and excellence. In 2005, we became the first school in Canada accredited to offer the three International Baccalaureate (IB) Programmes.

'Experience Teaches' is more than our motto. It is a day-to-day operating philosophy. It means learning by asking important questions, and learning through action where teachers engage and guide students in their discovery of the self and exploration of the world around them.

As an IB World School, we cultivate the acquisition of skills such as time management, research and creative thinking, which are the cornerstones of academic excellence. Our progressive approach to technology includes laptops for all students, smartboards, online collaboration tools, the latest learning software and a wireless environment.

To complement our comprehensive academics, we offer drama, art, music, athletics and engage our students in community service from an early age so they become internationally minded and engaged citizens of the world. We reach across borders to offer our students local, national and international learning opportunities.

Our school is located at the epicentre of Toronto with easy access to public transportation. Supervised activities enable our students to experience all that Toronto affords from world-class music and theatre to renowned museums and galleries. In addition, they also enjoy field study at our northern campus, Camp Oochigeas, and develop an appreciation for learning in the great outdoors.

We see the IB Diploma as the ultimate passport. It takes our graduates to the university of their choice, usually with offers of early acceptance, choice in admission to residence, and advance standing.

All of our graduates pursue post-secondary education. Some of the universities they have chosen to attend include Cornell University, Bryn Mawr College, Barnard College, Berklee College of Music, Duke, London School of Economics, Queen's University, McGill University, the University of Toronto, and the University of Western Ontario.

Tollbar Business & Enterprise College

Principal
Mr D J Hampson BSc, BA

Diploma coordinator
Mrs D Shelton

Status State

Boarding/day Day

Gender Coeducational

Language of instruction
English

Programmes offered Diploma

Age range of pupils 11-18

Number of pupils enrolled
2094

Address
Station Road
New Waltham
Grimsby
North-East Lincolnshire
DN36 4RZ | UK

TEL +44 (0)1472 500505

FAX +44 (0)1472 500506

Email
sixform@tollbarbec.co.uk

Website
www.tbecib.co.uk

Tollbar BEC Sixth Form is committed to providing students with an education that enables them to compete with the world's best. Now studying the International Baccalaureate Diploma Programme, sixth formers enjoy an independent learning experience, which promotes social awareness and gives them the skills and confidence to compete.

Students come to Tollbar to study in a purposeful but relaxed environment. They enjoy unrivalled facilities in state-of-the-art surroundings, which are affiliated to north-east Lincolnshire's largest and most successful Business and Enterprise College.

Tollbar Sixth Form offers an exciting and very creative climate for learning, and prepares its students for active, local, national and global citizenship. The richness of the IB programme promotes international understanding and prepares students for university life and/or the world of work far better than any other currently available education.

With a 2008 OFSTED inspection declaring the college 'outstanding' in 25 out of 26 categories, we invite you to come along and see for yourselves what we have to offer.

Curriculum

As all our sixth form students study the IB Diploma Programme we are able to offer a wide range of subjects from each group.

Facilities

The sixth form campus is completely independent from the main school.

Specialist facilities include:
- Three fully-equipped science labs with data-logging facilities.
- A fully-equipped computer room for ICT.
- Computer-based listening facilities for languages to complement the two Divace language labs.
- High-specification sewing machines with computer-aided design facilities for textiles and CADCAM facilities, together with a laser-cutting machine for resistant materials technology.
- A newly-refurbished and equipped photography suite with darkroom and high-specification colour printer and a large, purpose-built art studio.
- A state-of-the-art gymnasium.
- Conference-style accommodation for business studies, supported by three computer suites.
- A study area and library equipped with 20 networked computers specifically for student use.
- Café Express for hot and cold food in a relaxed atmosphere.
- Common Room containing pool tables, table football and a large wall-mounted plasma screen.

Further expansion is now taking place for September 2009 which consists of a new block of eight classrooms together with office and meeting rooms.

Universal American School, Dubai

(Founded 2005)

Head of School
Ray Taylor

Diploma coordinator
Courtney Malone

Status Private

Boarding/day Day

Gender Coeducational

Language of instruction
English

Programmes offered Diploma

Age range of pupils 3-18

Number of pupils enrolled 1100

Fees per annum
AED 23,500-56,000

Address
PO Box 79133
Dubai Festival City
Dubai | UNITED ARAB EMIRATES

TEL +971 4232 5222

FAX +971 4232 5545

Email
rtaylor@uasdubai.ae

Website
www.uasdubai.ae

Introduction:

On September 10, 2005, the Universal American School in Dubai welcomed 250 students to a purpose-built, state-of-the art, 65,000 square meter campus in Dubai Festival City. UAS is now in its fourth year of existence, with over 1100 students from over 70 countries.

UAS has gained full accreditation from the Middle State Association of Colleges and Schools, and Council of International Schools, and is authorized to offer the International Baccalaureate Diploma Programme (IBDP).

UAS is managed by Educational Services Overseas Limited (ESOL), a school management organization that operates some of the region's leading American and British schools.

Curriculum:

The school's education program is based on the New York State standards leading to the American High School Diploma. Arabic is taught from grades (KG-12) while Spanish and French are offered from grades 7-12. The curriculum is designed to ensure easy transferability to other countries.

The school also offers the International Baccalaureate Diploma Programme (IBDP) as an option in Grades 11 and 12.

Facilities:

The UAS campus is amongst the finest in the Middle East. The campus includes an indoor gymnasium, Olympic size track and soccer field, art and music rooms, computer and science laboratories, libraries, and a swimming pool.

Faculty:

UAS employs approximately 120 full-time faculty members. The teachers at UAS are predominantly North American, from the United States and Canada, and all have been carefully selected and screened. The teachers hold North American teaching certification or an equivalent credential in their field of instruction, in addition to a university degree. Many of the faculty hold post-graduate degrees, including doctorates. Teachers from Arab countries teach Arabic, AFL, and Islamic studies.

Students:

Students at UAS enjoy the privilege of an education that is nurturing, holistic and inspires respectful relationships.

Students are empowered to use multiple perspectives to address ways and means for developing a sustainable and peaceful world.

Utahloy International School Guangzhou

(Founded 1998)

Head of School
Elaine Whelen

MYP coordinator
Jacqui Cussen

Diploma coordinator
Urs Jungo

Status Private

Boarding/day Day

Gender Coeducational

Language of instruction
English

Programmes offered
MYP, Diploma

Age range of pupils 2-18

Number of pupils enrolled 820

Fees per annum
RMB78,400-130,100

Address
6km Sha Tai Highway
JinBao Gong, Tong He
Guangzhou
GUANGDONG 510515 | PR CHINA

TEL +8620 87202019

FAX +8620 87044296

Email
uis@utahloy.com

Website
www.utahloy.com

Located on the edge of beautiful Golden Lake, surrounded by forested hillsides Utahloy is only 20 minutes from Guangzhou's CBD. The school has spacious and attractive grounds, creating a healthy, safe and pleasant environment for students. Utahloy has been providing a rigorous academic programme for the international community since 1998. The school offers an international K-12 education for more than 800 expatriate students who represent 49 nationalities. The school has become known for its stimulating, supportive, and caring environment.

Utahloy is an IB World School and member of the Council of International Schools. It is authorised to provide the IB Middle Years and Diploma Programmes. We have candidate status to implement the PYP. Academic rigour is assured due to the high calibre of international teachers employed. The diverse faculty is recruited from: Australia, Canada, China, France, Germany, India, Japan, Korea, the Netherlands, New Zealand, South Africa, Switzerland, the UK and the USA.

Mother tongue languages are sustained and developed within the curriculum. Students develop an academic vocabulary, expand their language usage, and study literature and culture in their mother tongue. Languages currently offered to mother tongue speakers include: Chinese, French, Spanish, German, Japanese and Korean. The arts are celebrated through music, drama, dance and visual art. Students can study these subjects to IB Diploma level.

The host country language and culture is studied through specialist Chinese language classes, integrated units of work in the classroom, and field trips in the region. Global citizenship is developed through: community service projects; environmental sustainability action and awareness; Model United Nations participation; and through our emphasis on multilingual communication. We are proud of Utahloy's commitment to the development of internationally-minded students who will benefit from their global connections and help create a better world.

Verulam School (BeauSandVer)

Head of School
David Kellaway

Diploma coordinator
Susan Turner

Status State

Boarding/day Day

Gender Coeducational

Language of instruction
English

Programmes offered
Diploma

Address
Brampton Road
St Albans
Hertfordshire
AL1 4PR | UK

TEL +44 (0)1727 766 100

FAX +44 (0)1727 766 256

Email
sue.turner@
verulam.herts.sch.uk

Website
www.verulamschool.net

Verulam is part of the BeauSandVer consortium of three successful schools situated in St Albans just north of London. The consortium is made up of two mixed 11-18 schools (Sandringham and Beaumont) and one 11-18 boys school with a coeducational sixth form, (Verulam). We are non-selective state schools with a proven track record of delivering high quality education to all students. The majority of our sixth form students go on to good quality universities including Oxbridge.

IB students are taught in small classes which enable a tutorial style of learning tailored to individual needs. Students have a personal tutor who oversees their progress and provides academic mentoring. The school has excellent facilities including new computer suites, well-stocked libraries, drama studios, a sports hall and extensive playing fields.

We are committed to the development of the whole person and have well-established links with groups in the UK and overseas, who work with us in our CAS programme. Curriculum enrichment is a central tenet of our ethos with students being offered trips to galleries, museums and theatres, exchange visits with partner schools abroad, work experience at home and overseas, as well as expeditions to countries as diverse as Belize, Iceland, Lesotho, Burkina Faso and China. Students can also choose to get involved in our many school based groups for music and sport amongst others.

Most of our students live locally but some commute from London via excellent communication links with the capital. The entry requirement for the IB Diploma Programme is an average GCSE point score of at least 43 (or similar).

Our IB Diploma subjects include English, French, German, Spanish (including *ab initio*), economics, geography, history, philosophy, psychology, biology, chemistry, physics, maths, computing science, visual arts, drama and music. These are offered at both higher and standard levels. Next year will see the introduction of other subjects.

You will be highly motivated through well-prepared lessons taught by well-qualified staff. You will expect to go on to study at university in Britain or anywhere in the world, in the knowledge that you have high academic ability, you are a well-rounded, articulate young person with a sound understanding of the international community.

For more information please contact us via our own website www.verulamschool.net or our consortium website www.beausandver.org.uk

Warminster School

Founded 1707

(Founded 1707)

Headmaster
Martin Priestley

Diploma coordinator
Olivia Bourne

Status Private

Boarding/day Mixed

Gender Coeducational

Language of instruction
English

Programmes offered Diploma

Age range of pupils 3-18

Number of pupils enrolled 630

Fees per annum
Day: £12,000
Boarding: £21,000

Address
Church Street
Warminster
Wiltshire
BA12 8PJ | UK

TEL +44 (0)1985 210160
FAX +44 (0)1985 210154

Email
admin@warminsterschool.org.uk

Website
www.warminsterschool.org.uk

Warminster is a coeducational school of over 630 students aged three to 18, located in the south-west of England. Founded in 1707, the school is a member of the Society of Headmasters and Headmistresses of Independent Schools and has been an authorized IB World School since December 2005. Warminster School prides itself on its ability to combine a strong academic record and excellent facilities with a warm, friendly family ethos. A comprehensive pastoral care programme, centred around the role of the tutor, provides appropriate levels of support at all times.

In 2008, Warminster School's IB students averaged 32 points, with some pupils achieving over 40 points. The A level pass rate in 2007 was 100%. 95% of our students go on to study at leading universities around the world including Oxford and Cambridge, where the IB Diploma is particularly well received. Over the last few years we have opened a refurbished sixth form centre and a humanities building (2001), a new dining hall (2002), a new science centre and library (January 2005), and a new design technology centre (March 2006).

Warminster School welcomes students from over ten different countries into a community that celebrates its own diversity and encourages service to local, national and global societies. With a talented and enthusiastic staff and a diverse range of subjects and activities on offer, pupils are able to develop their potential to the full. The wide range of extracurricular activities include music, drama, a comprehensive range of sports and opportunities to go on challenging international visits to LED countries.

Experienced resident house staff provide a supportive environment for boarding students in comfortable, well-equipped boarding houses. Recreational activities and trips are arranged each weekend. For medical care there is a school nursing sister on duty every day.

Subjects offered are: biology, chemistry, economics, English A1 and A2, French B, geography, German A1, history, mathematics, music, physics, social and cultural anthropology, Spanish B and *ab initio*, visual arts.

Warminster School is a registered charity which exists to provide education for children. (No 1042204.)

Wesley College, Melbourne

(Founded 1866)

Principal
Helen Drennen

PYP coordinator
Kathy Saville

Diploma coordinator
Isaac Quist

Status Private

Boarding/day Day

Gender Coeducational

Language of instruction
English

Programmes offered
PYP, Diploma

Age range of pupils 3-18

Number of pupils enrolled 3100

Fees per annum
AU$19,000

Address
577 St Kilda Road
Melbourne
VIC 3004 | AUSTRALIA

TEL +61 3 8102 6888
FAX +61 3 9510 6284

Email
principal@wesleycollege.net

Website
www.wesleycollege.net

Since its beginnings in 1866, Wesley has held a significant place in Australian social and educational history, and is widely recognised for its standards of excellence and its pioneering role as an instigator in many areas of education. An open entry, coeducational and Uniting Church school, the culture of Wesley College is underpinned by an open and broad Christian philosophy that welcomes and embraces children of all faiths and celebrates a diversity of cultures. In all areas of educational endeavour, Wesley's results rank with the best in Australia and, in the case of the International Baccalaureate Diploma, with the best in the world. Every year Wesley's students readily gain admission into the most prestigious tertiary institutions within Australia and around the world.

The blend of innovation with tradition, of freedom with self-discipline, of formal learning with creativity, of breadth balanced with specialisation, characterises the Wesley experience. The extensive range of programs on offer demonstrates a firmly held belief in the power of learning to change lives and to develop active, compassionate, enquiring, and knowledgeable individuals who are alive to their responsibilities as members of wider and interconnected local, national and international communities. At Wesley College students have the opportunity to learn to live as part of a close-knit community, to experience the lives of others and to make an enduring difference. The pastoral care program is well integrated and characterised by a system of mutual support based on respect and understanding. It plays a key role in Wesley's strategies to ensure that every child has a unique opportunity to discover what it is to be a human being, through learning to know, to do, to live with, and ultimately, to be.

The St Kilda Road campus is located in Prahran, and close to Melbourne's attractive and vibrant CBD. It caters for students from kindergarten to Year 12 (ages three to 18). The Glen Waverley campus, set in the calm, leafy and expansive surroundings of the beautiful suburb of Glen Waverley also caters for students from kindergarten to Year 12 (ages three to 18). The Elsternwick campus, the smallest of the three, is situated in one of Melbourne's well established suburbs and offers a close family and home feel to students from kindergarten to Year 9 (ages three to 15). Clunes, the historic gold mining town 35km north of Ballarat, is home to Wesley's purpose built Residential Learning Village for Year 9 students. A well-developed Outdoor Education program is facilitated through the Chum Creek Camp (a bush property at the foot of the Great Divide, approximately 80km north-east of Melbourne), Lochend (a coastal property nestling between freshwater lakes and the sand dunes and seas of the wild west coast) and Mallana (on the edge of the Gippsland Lakes).

A large number of Wesley's highly experienced teachers are involved in the delivery of both the PYP and the DP. Many are regularly invited to mark examination scripts, lead teacher training workshops, and to participate in such important IB and Victoria Curriculum and Assessment Authority (VCAA) processes as school evaluation and authorization as well as curriculum review and development. As Wesley College students make the transition from the IB PYP and the comprehensive Wesley Middle Years course, they are well prepared and equipped to make an informed choice between the two main senior years courses undertaken at the College – the Victorian Certificate of Education (VCE) and the IB Diploma Programme. At all levels Wesley's teachers adopt pedagogical practices that develop and reinforce the skills and attitudes needed for critical thinking, enquiry, independent learning and international mindedness among students.

Subjects offered include biology, business & management, chemistry, Chinese, economics, English, environmental systems & societies, film, French, geography, German, history, Indonesian, Japanese, mathematics, music, philosophy, physics, psychology, Spanish, theatre arts, and visual arts. In addition students are able to study different languages in line with their needs and interests.

Wesley College also provides a broad range of co-curricular activities including community service, debating, music, sports, and theatre. These play a significant role in the overall personal development of our students as confident individuals

alive to the responsibilities they have to themselves and to the diverse communities within which they operate.

To enrich the curriculum as a whole and enhance its delivery, Wesley provides an extensive range of modern, state of the art facilities including a comprehensive infrastructure for ICT use and development, specialist classrooms, laboratories, libraries, visual arts and music studios, lecture theatres, multimedia centres, study centres, sports complexes, canteens and leisure spaces.

Whitgift School

(Founded 1596)

Headmaster
Dr Christopher Barnett

Diploma coordinator
Stewart Cook

Status Private

Boarding/day Day

Gender Male

Language of instruction
English

Programmes offered Diploma

Age range of pupils 10-18

Number of pupils enrolled 1251

Fees per annum £12,816

Address
Haling Park
South Croydon
Surrey
CR2 6YT | UK

TEL +44 (0)20 8688 9222
FAX +44 (0)20 8760 0682

Email
office@whitgift.co.uk

Website
www.whitgift.co.uk

Whitgift School is an independent boys' day school set in the beautiful estate of Haling Park in South Croydon, Surrey. The school was founded by Archbishop John Whitgift in 1596 and moved to its present site in 1931. It is academically strong, and is regularly highly placed in national league tables for examination results; this year *The Times* ranked the school in the top four independent boys schools nationally. The first three IB Diploma Programme cohorts averaged over 37 points and one third of students averaged over 40 points. The recent ISI inspection report acknowledged its standing as 'one of the leading schools in the country', offering 'outstanding educational opportunities'.

Whitgift is also fortunate to possess some of the finest school facilities anywhere. Its dedicated teaching rooms, laboratories, art studios and workshops are arranged around two attractive quadrangles and are superbly resourced, with two libraries, six computer suites and a purpose-built Music School with concert hall. A Water Garden, containing several rare species and providing unique study opportunities, was opened last year. An impressive range of playing fields, all on site, supports an enormous variety of sporting activity. The school regularly wins national sporting competitions. The school's patron, HRH the Duke of York, in 2005 opened a magnificent new Sports Centre, providing unrivalled opportunities for pupils.

Whitgift is a forward-thinking, innovative institution, introducing many curricular and co-curricular initiatives such as its bilingual programme for pupils in French, German and from 2005, Spanish, and its Strings and Brass schemes to introduce younger pupils to new instruments. The school has strong multi-cultural and internationalist perspectives, with unequalled language provision in the curriculum, an impressive array of trips and exchanges abroad, and a growing number of overseas partner schools.

The adoption of the IB Diploma Programme as an alternative to A levels in the sixth form was thus a natural decision resulting from the already established ethos of the school under Headmaster Dr Christopher Barnett. A rich programme of study is offered, in classes with an excellent teacher/student ratio. The Theory of Knowledge is placed at the heart of learning. A full and varied programme for CAS is followed.

Admission to Whitgift is by competitive examination; the major points of entry are at 10+ (Year 6) and 11+ (Year 7) although some pupils are still accepted for 12+ and 13+ entry. Sixth form places are offered on the basis of previous or predicted academic achievement; an entrance paper is sat in a subject of the applicant's choice. Scholarships are awarded for the academically very able, and also for a range of co-curricular abilities such as sport, music, drama, art and design technology. The Whitgift Foundation operates a generous bursary scheme for those requiring financial assistance.

Whitgift School is a registered charity (No. 271320) to advance the education of pupils of the school.

(Founded 1996)

Head of School
Svetlana Kulichenko

MYP coordinator
Elena Nikeryassova

Diploma coordinator
Evgeny Mironov

Status Private

Boarding/day Day

Gender Coeducational

Language of instruction
English

Programmes offered
MYP, Diploma

Number of pupils enrolled 250

Fees per annum €10,000

Address
Building 3
Stroginsky Boulevard 7
Moscow
123592 | RUSSIAN FEDERATION

TEL +7 495 750 3102
FAX +7 495 750 0197

Email
kulichenkos@newmail.ru

Website
www.integration21.ru

The Moscow XXI Century Integration International Secondary School was founded in 1996. It is a private independent school administrated by Mrs Svetlana Kulichenko. Being a fee-paying school, it is run as a non-commercial enterprise, with educational development and social wellbeing as the primary objective.

In 2002 the school acquired the status of School with Advanced English Studies. The school conducts a lot of activities in cooperation with The High School of Economics, The Spivacov Foundation and other local and international organizations and universities.

The school's aim is to develop students as unique individuals, as active, free-thinking people who live in close touch with the surrounding world and its history, who know and are able to evaluate its national culture and fit in with intercultural environment.

The school provides various learning opportunities, as well as applying the latest technological devices, modern educational techniques. The school integrates the National and the European approach to school education.

In 2003 the school was authorized to offer the International Baccalaureate (IB) Middle Years Programme. In 2006 the school was authorized to offer the IB Diploma Programme. Both programmes will allow the school to integrate successfully into the world's educational system which is gradually becoming more and more unified. In the 2008/2009 school year the school offers the following Diploma Programme courses: Russian A1, English B, history, business and management, social and cultural anthropology, physics, environmental systems, mathematics.

Since 2008 the XXI Century Integration International Secondary School offers an exclusive summer programme providing international school students (aged ten-18) with the unique opportunity to combine learning, creative enrichment and action-packed adventure in the historic and picturesque seaside town of Karlobag, Croatia. Students who gain a place at the XXI Century Integration International Secondary School summer camp are able to create a personalised two-week programme to suit both their academic needs and extracurricular tastes. Students choose up to four academic courses and one elective course. Students have a unique opportunity to come to our summer camp together with their parents or other relatives, whose personal interests will be catered for as well, since the school offers a tailor-made summer programme for adults who might wish to accompany their children.

The IB Middle Years and Diploma Programmes in the school are run by experienced educators and taught by the first class teachers. Each student has an individual programme. Classes are kept small (ten-12 students). Syllabus content is constantly reviewed and updated. The school provides educational programmes not only for domestic students, but also for a wide range of students coming from the English speaking countries.

International quality of education in the school, firstly, implies studying such foreign languages as English, French, German, Spanish and Chinese. In addition to standard courses on vocabulary and grammar, there are special classes of oral practice with native speakers and special courses in everyday English, math in English, biology in English, which allow the students to acquire bilingual skills in the chosen subjects.

Secondly, international textbooks and computer programmes are used in the educational process.

Finally, the school staff take regular courses in the partner schools in Great Britain, such as Marlborough College and Alexanders International School. They also attend the workshops and seminars arranged by the International Baccalaureate regional office.

The school has two main buildings, fulfilling the requirements of the primary and secondary education respectively. There are approximately 120 students aged 11-16 in the secondary school. Grade 6 is the first year of the IB Middle Years Programme (IB MYP), while Grade 5 is a preparatory year.

Although every student and class has their own respective timetable, it is a rule that the school day is divided into two main sections:

- from 09.00 to 14.30 the 'core features' of the curriculum are covered – those being, Language A (Russian), Language B (English), Language C (French, German, Spanish, Chinese), maths, science, humanities, arts, physical education and technology;
- the latter part of the day is devoted towards 'special courses'. The students have a wide choice in this area, and are required to select the appropriate number of academic classes and sporting activities.

The school day can vary from six to nine lessons (each lesson being 40 minutes long), depending upon the choices made by an individual. This schedule includes PE, art, drama and music, and also allows time for students to do their homework and to take some fresh air.

IB

Schools Directory

IB

Africa | Europe | Middle East

Africa, Europe and Middle East

The IB Africa, Europe and Middle East office, located in Geneva (Switzerland), currently provides services for the three IB programmes to schools in the following countries.

Angola	Hungary	Mauritius	Slovakia
Austria	Iceland	Monaco	Slovenia
Azerbaijan	Iran, Islamic Republic of	Morocco	South Africa
Bahrain	Ireland	Mozambique	Spain
Belgium	Isle of Man	Namibia	Sudan
Bosnia and Herzegovina	Israel	Netherlands	Swaziland
Botswana	Italy	Nigeria	Sweden
Bulgaria	Jordan	Norway	Switzerland
Croatia	Kazakhstan	Occupied Palestinian	Syrian Arab Republic
Cyprus	Kenya	Territory	Tanzania
Czech Republic	Kuwait	Oman	Togo
Denmark	Latvia	Poland	Tunisia
Egypt	Lebanon	Portugal	Turkey
Estonia	Lesotho	Qatar	Uganda
Ethiopia	Libyan Arab Jamahiriya	Romania	Ukraine
Finland	Lithuania	Russian Federation	United Arab Emirates
France	Luxembourg	Rwanda	United Kingdom
Germany	Macedonia	Saudi Arabia	Uzbekistan
Ghana	Malawi	Senegal	Zambia
Greece	Malta	Serbia	Zimbabwe

Regional Tasks

The range of services offered by the IBAEM regional office are grouped under the following activities: authorization and evaluation processes; professional development of teachers and administrators for IB World Schools; recognition of the IB programmes by national authorities; promotion.

Schools Associations in IBAEM

There are formal and/or informal associations for IB schools in the following countries. The associations in countries which are marked with an asterisk (*) also include the membership of non-IB schools:

CIS (Commonwealth of Independent States)

Germany *

Kenya

Middle East

Netherlands *

Nordic countries as a whole and in each Nordic country

Poland

Switzerland *

Spain

South Africa

Turkey

UK

Some facts about this region

As at September 2008

IBAEM serves 630 schools located in 79 countries and offers 798 programmes in total.

DP programmes:	578
MYP programmes:	110
PYP programmes:	110
Schools offering all three programmes:	47
Schools offering DP and MYP:	34
Schools offering DP and PYP:	23
Schools offering MYP and PYP:	16
State school programmes	250
Private school programmes	548

ANGOLA

Luanda International School
Status Private
Programme PYP, MYP, Diploma
Diploma Coordinator Roger Groenink
MYP Coordinator Tony Martin
PYP Coordinator Felicity Hewett
Gender Coeducational
Languages English
Boarding/day Day
PO Box 1566, Luanda, Angola
TELEPHONE: +244 222 460752
FAX: +244 222 460782
EMAIL: director@lisluanda.com
WEBSITE: www.lisluanda.com

AUSTRIA

American International School
Status Private
Programme Diploma
Diploma Coordinator Cheryl Augustine
Gender Coeducational
Languages English
Boarding/day Day
Salmannsdorferstrasse 47, Vienna 1190,
Austria
TELEPHONE: +43 1 401320
FAX: +43 1 401325
EMAIL: e.stern@ais.at
WEBSITE: www.ais.at

Danube International School
Status Private
Programme MYP, Diploma
Diploma Coordinator Giles Pope
MYP Coordinator Mark Brierley
Gender Coeducational
Languages English
Boarding/day Day
Josef Gall Gasse 2, 1020 Vienna, Austria
TELEPHONE: +43 1 7203110
FAX: +43 1 7203110-40
EMAIL: pdefty@danubeschool.at
WEBSITE: www.danubeschool.at

Linz International School Auhof (L.I.S.A)
Status State
Programme Diploma
Diploma Coordinator Karl Mühlstein
Gender Coeducational
Languages English
Aubrunnerweg 4, Linz A-4040, Austria
TELEPHONE: +43 732 245867 0
FAX: +43 732 245867 17
EMAIL: k.hoetzenecker@auhof.eduhi.at

Vienna International School
Status Private
Programme PYP, Diploma
Diploma Coordinator Alan Honeyman
PYP Coordinator Kate Dalton
Gender Coeducational
Languages English
Boarding/day Day
Strasse der Menschenrechte 1, Vienna 1220,
Austria
TELEPHONE: +43 1 203 5595
FAX: +43 1 203 0366
EMAIL: visinfo@vis.ac.at
WEBSITE: www.vis.ac.at

AZERBAIJAN

The International School of Azerbaijan, Baku
Status Private
Programme PYP, MYP, Diploma
Diploma Coordinator Michael Foxmann
MYP Coordinator Gillian Ashworth
PYP Coordinator David Tigchelaar
Gender Coeducational
Languages English
Boarding/day Day
AIOC-TISA, c/o BP Azerbaijan, Chertsey Road,
Sunbury on Thames TW16 7LN, UK
TELEPHONE: +994 12 973028
FAX: +994 12 4972194
EMAIL: director@aioctisa.az
WEBSITE: www.tisa.az

BELGIUM

Antwerp International School
Status Private
Programme Diploma
Diploma Coordinator Nigel Gardner
Gender Coeducational
Languages English
Boarding/day Day
Veltwijcklaan 180, 2180 Ekeren, Antwerpen
2180, Belgium
TELEPHONE: +32 3 543 93 00
FAX: +32 3 541 8201
EMAIL: smurray@ais-antwerp.be
WEBSITE: www.ais-antwerp.be

International Montessori School Tervuren
Status Private
Programme MYP
MYP Coordinator Rinze Hoekstra
Gender Coeducational
Languages English, French
Boarding/day Day
Rotselaerlaan 1, Tervuren 3080, Belgium
TELEPHONE: +32 2 767 6360
FAX: +32 2 767 6360
EMAIL: annie.hoekstra@skynet.be
WEBSITE: http://international-montessori.org

International School of Brussels
Status Private
Programme Diploma
Diploma Coordinator Thomas Smith
Gender Coeducational
Languages English
Boarding/day Day
19 Kattenberg, Boitsfort, Brussels 1170,
Belgium
TELEPHONE: +32 2 661 4221
FAX: +32 2 661 4200
EMAIL: admissions@isb.be
WEBSITE: www.isb.be

Scandinavian School of Brussels
Status Private
Programme Diploma
Diploma Coordinator Marianne Hafvenström
Gender Coeducational
Languages English
Boarding/day Mixed
Square d'Argenteuil 5, Waterloo 1410,
Belgium
TELEPHONE: +32 2 357 06 70
FAX: +32 2 357 06 80
EMAIL: t.aberg@ssb.be
WEBSITE: www.ssb.be

St John's International School
Status Private
Programme PYP, Diploma
Diploma Coordinator Marleen Robberechts
PYP Coordinator Helen Saunders
Gender Coeducational
Languages English
Boarding/day Day
146 Drève Richelle, Waterloo 1410, Belgium
TELEPHONE: +32 2 352 0610
FAX: +32 2 352 0620
EMAIL: twalters@stjohns.be
WEBSITE: www.stjohns.be

The British School of Brussels
Status Private
Programme Diploma
Diploma Coordinator John Knight
Gender Coeducational
Languages English
Boarding/day Day
Leuvensesteenweg 19, 3080 Tervuren, Belgium
TELEPHONE: +32 2 766 0430
FAX: +32 2 767 8070
EMAIL: admissions@britishschool.be
WEBSITE: www.britishschool.be

BOSNIA & HERZEGOVINA

Druga Gimnazija Sarajevo
Status State
Programme MYP, Diploma
Diploma Coordinator Vedad Lihovac
MYP Coordinator Tarik Hadziahmetovic
Gender Coeducational
Languages English
Boarding/day Day
Sutjeska 1, Sarajevo 71000, Bosnia &
Herzegovina
TELEPHONE: +387 33667438
FAX: +387 667438
EMAIL: aaida@smartnet.ba
WEBSITE: www.2gimnazija.edu.ba

Gimnazija Banja Luka
Status State
Programme Diploma
Diploma Coordinator Rastko Vukovic
Gender Coeducational
Languages English
Boarding/day Day
Zmaj Jovina 13, Banja Luka, Republic of
Srpska 78000, Bosnia & Herzegovina
TELEPHONE: +387 51 213 259/283/249
FAX: +387 51 223 571
EMAIL: gimn@inecco.net
WEBSITE: www.gimnazijabl.rs.ba

UWC in Mostar
Status Private
Programme Diploma
Diploma Coordinator Mark Sylvester
Gender Coeducational
Languages English
Boarding/day Mixed
Spanjolski Trg 1, Mostar 88000, Bosnia &
Herzegovina
TELEPHONE: +387 36 320 601
FAX: +387 36 320 601
EMAIL: p.reg7@yahoo.co.uk
WEBSITE: www.uwc-ibo.org

BOTSWANA

Westwood International School
Status Private
Programme PYP, Diploma
Diploma Coordinator Jannie Kleynhans
PYP Coordinator Janet Lewis
Gender Coeducational
Languages English
Boarding/day Day
PO Box 2446, Gaborone, Botswana
TELEPHONE: +267 3906736
FAX: +267 3906734
EMAIL: westwood@info.bw
WEBSITE: www.ecis.org/westwood

BULGARIA

American College Arcus
Status Private
Programme Diploma
Diploma Coordinator Camellia Antonova
Gender Coeducational
Languages English
Boarding/day Mixed
16 Dragoman Street, 5000, Veliko Turnovo,
Bulgaria
TELEPHONE: +359 62 619959
FAX: +359 62 619961
EMAIL: info@ac-arcus.com
WEBSITE: www.ac-arcus.com

American College of Sofia
Status Private
Programme Diploma
Diploma Coordinator Joseph Rosevear
Gender Coeducational
Languages English
Boarding/day Mixed
PO Box 873, Sofia 1000, Bulgaria
TELEPHONE: +359 2 434 1008
FAX: +359 2 974 3129
EMAIL: acs@acs.bg
WEBSITE: www.acs.bg

Anglo-American School of Sofia
Status Private
Programme Diploma
Diploma Coordinator Ana Leahy
Gender Coeducational
Languages English
Boarding/day Day
PO Box 31, Sofia 1784, Bulgaria
TELEPHONE: +359 2 923 8810
FAX: +359 2 923 8859
EMAIL: jleahy@aas-sofia.org
WEBSITE: www.aas-sofia.org

Professor Vassil Zlatarski Private School – Sofia
Status Private
Programme Diploma
Diploma Coordinator Tsvetanka Kardasheva
Gender Coeducational
Languages English
Boarding/day Day
49 Kliment Ohridski Boulevard, BG-Sofia
1756, Bulgaria
TELEPHONE: +359 2 974 36 66
FAX: +359 2 962 71 64
EMAIL: kardasheva@gmail.com
WEBSITE: www.zlatarskischool.org

CROATIA

American International School of Zagreb
Status Private
Programme Diploma
Diploma Coordinator Jasna M Kolbah
Gender Coeducational
Languages English
Boarding/day Day
Vorcarska 106, Zagreb 10000, Croatia
TELEPHONE: +385 1 4680 133
FAX: +385 1 4680 171
EMAIL: robin.heslip@aisz.hr
WEBSITE: www.aisz.hr

Matija Gubec Primary School
Status State
Programme MYP
MYP Coordinator Boris Vampula
Gender Coeducational
Languages English
Boarding/day Day
Davorina Bazjanca 2, Zagreb 10000, Croatia
TELEPHONE: +385 1364 9133
EMAIL: os-zagreb-066@skole.htnet.hr
WEBSITE: www.skole.htnet.hr/
os-zagreb-066/skola/

Prva Gimnazija Vara din
Status State
Programme Diploma
Diploma Coordinator Miljenka Stimec
Gender Coeducational
Languages English
Boarding/day Day
P Preradovica 14, Vara din 42000, Croatia
TELEPHONE: +385 42 302 123
FAX: +385 42 320 420
EMAIL: rajka.pticek@vz.t-com.hr
WEBSITE: http://public.srce.hr/gimvaraz/

XV. Gimnazija
Status State
Programme MYP, Diploma
Diploma Coordinator Ljiljana Crnkovic
MYP Coordinator Vlasta Sabljak
Gender Coeducational
Languages English
Boarding/day Day
Jordanovac 8, Zagreb 10000, Croatia
TELEPHONE: +385 1 230 2255
FAX: +385 1 2321 564
EMAIL: vjavor@zagreb.mioc.hr

CYPRUS

PASCAL English School – Larnaka
Status Private
Programme Diploma
Diploma Coordinator Despina Lioliou
Gender Coeducational
Languages English
Boarding/day Day
PO Box 45077, Aradippou 7110, Cyprus
TELEPHONE: +357 24 813 900
FAX: +357 24 534 232
EMAIL: liolioud@pascal.ac.cy
WEBSITE: www.pascal.ac.cy

PASCAL English School – Nicosia
Status Private
Programme Diploma
Diploma Coordinator Ariana Milutinovic
Gender Coeducational
Languages English
Boarding/day Day
PO Box 24746, Nicosia 1303, Cyprus
TELEPHONE: +357 22 590 900
EMAIL: andreas@pascal.ac.cy
WEBSITE: www.pascal.ac.cy

The American International School in Cyprus
Status Private
Programme Diploma
Diploma Coordinator Christiane Camacho
Gender Coeducational
Languages English
Boarding/day Mixed
PO Box 23847, 11 Kassos Str, Nicosia 1686, Cyprus
TELEPHONE: +357 22 316345
FAX: +357 22 316549
EMAIL: aisc@aisc.ac.cy
WEBSITE: aisc.ac.cy

CZECH REPUBLIC

International School of Prague
Status Private
Programme Diploma
Diploma Coordinator Karen Ercolino
Gender Coeducational
Languages English
Boarding/day Day
Nebusicka 700, Prague 6, Nebusice 16400, Czech Republic
TELEPHONE: +420 2 203 84111
FAX: +420601209849
EMAIL: rlandau@isp.cz
WEBSITE: www.isp.cz

The English College in Prague
Status Private
Programme Diploma
Diploma Coordinator Colin Beet
Gender Coeducational
Languages English
Boarding/day Day
Sokolovska 320, 190 00 Prague 9, Czech Republic
TELEPHONE: +420 2 8389 3113
FAX: +420 2 8389 0118
EMAIL: headmaster@englishcollege.cz
WEBSITE: www.englishcollege.cz

The English International School, Prague
Status Private
Programme Diploma
Diploma Coordinator Marie-France Labelle
Gender Coeducational
Languages English
Boarding/day Day
Na Okruhu 395, 14400 Prague 4, Czech Republic
TELEPHONE: +420 2 6191 2368/2371
FAX: +420 2 6191 0074
EMAIL: eisp@volny.cz
WEBSITE: www.eisp.cz

The Prague British School
Status Private
Programme Diploma
Diploma Coordinator Tom Nagel
Gender Coeducational
Languages English
Boarding/day Day
K Lesu 558/2, 142 00 Prague 4, Czech Republic
TELEPHONE: +420 226 096 200
FAX: +420 226 096 201
EMAIL: info@pbschool.cz
WEBSITE: www.pbschool.cz

DENMARK

Birkerod Gymnasium
Status State
Programme Diploma
Diploma Coordinator Christina Rye Tarp
Gender Coeducational
Languages English
Boarding/day Mixed
Söndervangen 56, Box 220, Birkeröd 3460, Denmark
TELEPHONE: +45 45 81 02 56
FAX: +45 45 82 02 57
EMAIL: ib@birke-gym.dk
WEBSITE: www.birke-gym.dk

Copenhagen International School
Status Private
Programme PYP, MYP, Diploma
Diploma Coordinator Anna Weston
MYP Coordinator Josée Band
PYP Coordinator Paulette Johnson
Gender Coeducational
Languages English
Boarding/day Day
Hellerupvej 22 -26, Hellerup 2900, Denmark
TELEPHONE: +45 39463300
FAX: +45 3961 2230
EMAIL: cis@cisdk.dk
WEBSITE: www.cis-edu.dk

Grenaa Gymnasium & HF
Status State
Programme Diploma
Diploma Coordinator Kirsten Bech Hansen
Gender Coeducational
Languages English
Boarding/day Mixed
Postbox 109, Grenaa 8500, Denmark
TELEPHONE: +45 87 58 4050
FAX: +45 87 58 4060
EMAIL: of@ggadm.aaa.dk
WEBSITE: www.grenaa-gym.dk

HASSERIS GYMNASIUM
Status State
Programme Diploma
Diploma Coordinator Lars Nielsen
Gender Coeducational
Languages English
Boarding/day Both
Hasserisvej 300, DK-9000 Aalborg, Denmark
TELEPHONE: +45 9632 7117/+45 2330 3409
FAX: +45 9818 6312
EMAIL: ib@hasseris-gym.dk
WEBSITE: www.hasseris-gym.dk
see full details on page 89

Herlufsholm Skole
Status Private
Programme Diploma
Diploma Coordinator Cecilia Karlström
Gender Coeducational
Languages English
Boarding/day Mixed
Herlufsholm Allé 170, Naestved 4700, Denmark
TELEPHONE: +45 55 75 35 00
FAX: +45 55 75 35 14
EMAIL: eusebius@herlufsholm.dk

DENMARK

HØRSHOLM INTERNATIONAL SCHOOL
Status Private
Programme PYP, MYP
MYP Coordinator Karen Johansen
PYP Coordinator Karen Johansen
Gender Coeducational
Languages English
Boarding/day Day
Cirkelhuset, Christianshusvej 16, DK 2970 Hørsholm, Denmark
TELEPHONE: +45 45 57 26 16
FAX: +45 45 57 26 69
EMAIL: his@ngg.dk
WEBSITE: www.his.dk
see full details on page 92

Kolding Amstsgymnasium og HF-Kursus
Status State
Programme Diploma
Diploma Coordinator Bo Skibelund
Languages English
Boarding/day Day
Skovvangen 10, Kolding DK 6000, Denmark
TELEPHONE: +45 7633 9600
FAX: +45 7633 9600
EMAIL: rk@kolding-gym.dk
WEBSITE: www.kolding-gym.dk/

Nörre Gymnasium
Status State
Programme Diploma
Diploma Coordinator Mrs Jutta Rüdiger
Gender Coeducational
Languages English
Boarding/day Day
Mörkhöjvej 78, 2700 Brönshöj, Denmark
TELEPHONE: +45 44 94 27 22
FAX: +45 44 94 26 69
EMAIL: jb@norreg.dk
WEBSITE: www.norreg.dk

Nyborg Gymnasium
Status State
Programme Diploma
Diploma Coordinator Helene Bendorff Kristensen
Gender Coeducational
Languages English
Boarding/day Boarding
Skolebakken 13, Nyborg 5800, Denmark
TELEPHONE: +45 6531 0217
FAX: +45 6531 7886
EMAIL: hj@nyborg-gym.fyns-amt.dk

Struer Gymnasium og HF
Status State
Programme Diploma
Diploma Coordinator Ariane Bräuninger Tang
Gender Coeducational
Languages English
Boarding/day Mixed
Jyllandsgade 2, Struer 7600, Denmark
TELEPHONE: +45 9785 4300
FAX: +45 9785 4133
EMAIL: je@stgym.dk
WEBSITE: www.struer-gym.dk

EGYPT

American International School in Egypt
Status Private
Programme Diploma
Diploma Coordinator Susan Eby
Gender Coeducational
Languages English
Boarding/day Day
PO Box 8090, Masaken, Nasr City, Cairo 11371, Egypt
TELEPHONE: +20 22 617 4001
FAX: +20 22 617 4002
EMAIL: ais@aisegypt.com

Cairo American College
Status Private
Programme Diploma
Diploma Coordinator Theresa Hurley
Gender Coeducational
Languages English
Boarding/day Day
PO Box 39, Maadi, Cairo 11431, Egypt
TELEPHONE: +20 2 2755 5555
FAX: +20 2519 6584
EMAIL: mgreeley@cacegypt.org
WEBSITE: www.cacegypt.org

ECOLE OASIS INTERNATIONALE
Status Private
Programme PYP, MYP, Diploma
Diploma Coordinator Maurice Hébert
MYP Coordinator Chérine Zaytoun
PYP Coordinator Nayera Hamdi
Gender Coeducational
Languages French
Boarding/day Day
Zahraa El Maadi, Quarter no 3 and no 7 part A and B, Cairo, Egypt
TELEPHONE: +2 02 25162608
FAX: +2 02 27545280
EMAIL: admission @oasisdemaadi.com
WEBSITE: www.oasisdemaadi.com
see full details on page 79

GREEN LAND PRÉ VERT INTERNATIONAL SCHOOL – EGYPT
Status Private
Programme PYP, MYP, Diploma
Diploma Coordinator Amr Ahmed Mokhtar
MYP Coordinator May Fathi Waly
PYP Coordinator Françoise Mokhtar-Bencteux
Gender Coeducational
Languages English, French, Arabic
Boarding/day Day
405 Gezirat Mohamed Street, Giza, Egypt
TELEPHONE: +20 (02) 35 40 58 90/91
FAX: +20 (02) 37 49 44 06
EMAIL: mail@greenlandschool.org
WEBSITE: www.greenlandschool.org
see full details on page 85

The British International School of Cairo
Status Private
Programme Diploma
Diploma Coordinator Georgia Trotter
Gender Coeducational
Languages English
Boarding/day Day
PO Box 137, Gezira, Cairo, Egypt
TELEPHONE: +20 22 735 6674
FAX: +20 22 736 4168
EMAIL: principal@bisc.edu.eg
WEBSITE: www.bisc.edu.eg

The Modern English School, Cairo
Status Private
Programme Diploma
Diploma Coordinator Chris O'Connell
Gender Coeducational
Languages English
Boarding/day Day
PO Box 5, Tagamoa Khamis, New Cairo 11835 Cairo, Egypt
TELEPHONE: +20 2 2617 0005 11
FAX: +20 2 2617 0020
EMAIL: mescairo@mescairo.com
WEBSITE: www.mescairo.com

ESTONIA

International School of Estonia
Status Private
Programme PYP, Diploma
Diploma Coordinator Randal Eplin
PYP Coordinator Dee Broussard
Gender Coeducational
Languages English
Boarding/day Boarding/day
Juhkentali 18, Tallinn 10132, Estonia
TELEPHONE: +372 666 4380
FAX: +372 666 4383
EMAIL: ise@ise.edu.ee
WEBSITE: www.ise.edu.ee

ETHIOPIA

German Embassy School Addis Ababa
Status Private
Programme Diploma
Diploma Coordinator Anne Symank
Gender Coeducational
Languages English, German
Boarding/day Day
c/o Deutche Botschaftsschule Addis Ababa, Auswärtiges Amt, D-11020 Berlin, Germany
TELEPHONE: +251 11 553 4465
FAX: +251 11 553 4418
EMAIL: dsaddis@ethionet.et
WEBSITE: www.ds-addis.de

International Community School, Addis Ababa
Status Private
Programme Diploma
Diploma Coordinator Mark Robertson-Jones
Gender Coeducational
Languages English
Boarding/day Day
PO Box 70282, Addis Ababa, Ethiopia
TELEPHONE: +251 113 711544
FAX: +251 113 710722
EMAIL: ics@icsaddis.edu.et
WEBSITE: http://addis.ecis.org/

Sandford International School
Status Private
Programme Diploma
Diploma Coordinator Stephen Marshall
Gender Coeducational
Languages English
Boarding/day Day
PO Box 30056 MA, Addis Ababa, Ethiopia
TELEPHONE: +251 1 552 275
FAX: +251 1 551 945
EMAIL: sandford@telecom.net.et

FINLAND

Helsingin Suomalainen Yhteiskoulu
Status Private
Programme Diploma
Diploma Coordinator Minna Ankkuri
Gender Coeducational
Languages English
Boarding/day Day
Isonnevantie 8, Helsinki 00320, Finland
TELEPHONE: +358 94774 1814
FAX: +358 9 477 418 10
EMAIL: Anja-Liisa.Alanko@edu.hel.fi
WEBSITE: www.syk.fi

Imatran yhteislukio
Status State
Programme Diploma
Diploma Coordinator Anne Lindell
Gender Coeducational
Languages English
Boarding/day Day
Koulukatu 2, Imatra 55100, Finland
TELEPHONE: +358 5 6815 820
EMAIL: aapo.ropponen@imatra.fi
WEBSITE: www.koulut.imatra.fi/yhtlukio

International School of Helsinki
Status Private
Programme PYP, MYP, Diploma
Diploma Coordinator Brian Ellum
MYP Coordinator Andrew Mitchell
PYP Coordinator Tania Wilson
Gender Coeducational
Languages English
Boarding/day Day
Selkämerenkatu 11, Helsinki 00180, Finland
TELEPHONE: +358 9 686 6160
FAX: +358 9 685 6699
EMAIL: bobw@ish.edu.hel.fi
WEBSITE: www.ish.edu.hel.fi

Joensuun Lyseon Lukio
Status State
Programme Diploma
Diploma Coordinator Jukka Hurskainen
Gender Coeducational
Languages English
Boarding/day Day
Koskikatu 8, Joensuu 80100, Finland
TELEPHONE: +358 13 267 5631
FAX: +358 13 267 5561
EMAIL: petri.lehikoinen@jns.fi
WEBSITE: www.lyseo.jns.fi

Jyväskylän Lyseon Lukio
Status State
Programme Diploma
Diploma Coordinator Kaija Kiraly
Gender Coeducational
Languages English
Yliopistonkatu 13, Jyväskylä 40100, Finland
TELEPHONE: +358 1462 4680
EMAIL: jorma.lempinen@jkl.fi

Kupion Lyseon Lukio
Status State
Programme Diploma
Diploma Coordinator Suvi Tirkkonen
Gender Coeducational
Languages English
Boarding/day Day
Puijonkatu 18, Kuopio 70110, Finland
TELEPHONE: +358 17 184 562
FAX: +358 17 184 561
EMAIL: leena.auvinen@kuopio.fi
WEBSITE: www.koulut.kuopio.fi/ffiLyseo/

Lyseonpuiston Lukio
Status State
Programme Diploma
Diploma Coordinator Eija Koivuranta
Gender Coeducational
Languages English
Boarding/day Day
IB section, Ruokasenkatu 18, Rovaniemi 96200, Finland
TELEPHONE: +358 16 322 2541
FAX: +358 16 322 3032
EMAIL: risto.kuoksa@rovaniemi.fi
WEBSITE: www.rovaniemi.fi/kouluv/omat/lyska

Mattlidens Gymnasium
Status State
Programme Diploma
Diploma Coordinator Annika Lindblom
Gender Coeducational
Languages English
Boarding/day Day
Mattliden 1, Esbo FIN-02230, Finland
TELEPHONE: +358 50 346 6884
FAX: +358 9 81643083
EMAIL: gunmaj.roiha@mattliden.fi
WEBSITE: www.mattliden.fi/gym

Oulu International School
Status State
Programme PYP, MYP
MYP Coordinator Raija Johnson
PYP Coordinator Kelvey Marden
Gender Coeducational
Languages English
Boarding/day Day
Kasarmintie 4, Oulu 90100, Finland
TELEPHONE: +358 44 7035418
FAX: +358 8 558 49430
EMAIL: raija.perttunen@ouka.fi
WEBSITE: www.oulu-ois.fi

Oulun Lyseon Lukio
Status State
Programme Diploma
Diploma Coordinator Pirkko Viro
Gender Coeducational
Languages English
Boarding/day Day
Kajaaninkatu 3, Oulu 90100, Finland
TELEPHONE: +358 8 5584 9455
FAX: +358 8 558 49459
EMAIL: teuvo@lyseo.edu.ouka.fi
WEBSITE: www.lyseo.edu.ouka.fi

Ressu Comprehensive School
Status State
Programme PYP, MYP
MYP Coordinator Heidi Halkilahti
PYP Coordinator Niko Lewman
Gender Coeducational
Languages English, Finnish
Boarding/day Day
Lapinlahdenkatu 10, FIN-00180 Helsinki, Finland
TELEPHONE: +358 9 3108 2101
EMAIL: erja.hoven@edu.hel.fi
WEBSITE: www.ressuy.edu.hel.fi

Ressun Lukio
Status State
Programme Diploma
Diploma Coordinator Tiina Nurmi
Gender Coeducational
Languages English
Boarding/day Day
PO Box 3809, City of Helsinki FIN-00099, Finland
TELEPHONE: +358 9 604 849
FAX: +358 9 603 905
EMAIL: ari.huovinen@edu.hel.fi
WEBSITE: www.ressunlukio.fi

Tampereen Lyseon lukio
Status State
Programme Diploma
Diploma Coordinator Tuija Laurila
Gender Coeducational
Languages English
Boarding/day Day
F E Sillanpään Katu 7, PL 29, Tampere 33231, Finland
TELEPHONE: +358 3 0207146311
FAX: +358 3 0207146310
EMAIL: Kaisa.Kuoppala@tampere.fi
WEBSITE: www.info.tampere.fi/l/lyseo

IB AFRICA | EUROPE | MIDDLE EAST

Tikkurilan Lukio
Status State
Programme Diploma
Diploma Coordinator Maarit Berg
Gender Coeducational
Languages English
Boarding/day Day
Valkoisenlahteentie 53, Vantaa 01370, Finland
TELEPHONE: +358 9 8392 5119
FAX: +358 9 8392 5123
EMAIL: risto.vayrynen@vantaa.fi
WEBSITE: www.koulut.vantaa.fi/tilu/alku.htm

Turun Normaalikoulu
Status State
Programme MYP, Diploma
Diploma Coordinator Raimo Junnikkala
MYP Coordinator Pirjo Lammila-Raisanen
Gender Coeducational
Languages English
Boarding/day Day
PL 13, Turku 20611, Finland
TELEPHONE: +358 2 33371
FAX: +358 2 333 7800
EMAIL: marjut.kleemola@utu.fi

Vasa Ovningsskola
Status State
Programme Diploma
Diploma Coordinator Anna Martikainen
Gender Coeducational
Languages English
Boarding/day Day
Skolhusgatan 31, Vasa FIN-65100, Finland
TELEPHONE: +358 6 3247610
FAX: +358 6 324656
EMAIL: ulla.granfors@abo.fi
WEBSITE: www.vasa.abo.fi/vos/

FRANCE

American School of Paris
Status Private
Programme Diploma
Diploma Coordinator Phil Jones
Gender Coeducational
Languages English
Boarding/day Day
41 rue Pasteur, BP 82, Saint-Cloud Cedex
92216, France
TELEPHONE: +33 1 41 12 82 82
FAX: +33 1 46 02 23 90
EMAIL: head@asparis.fr
WEBSITE: www.asparis.org

EAB International – The Victor Hugo School
Status Private
Programme Diploma
Diploma Coordinator Jonathan Benison
Gender Coeducational
Languages English
Boarding/day Day
The Victor Hugo School, 23 rue de Cronstadt,
Paris 75015, France
TELEPHONE: +33 (0)1 5656 6070
EMAIL: conchard@eab.fr
WEBSITE: www.eab.fr

ECOLE ACTIVE BILINGUE JEANNINE MANUEL
Status Private
Programme Diploma
Diploma Coordinator Shirley Burchill
Gender Coeducational
Languages English, French
Boarding/day Day
70 rue du Théâtre, Paris 75015, France
TELEPHONE: +33 1 44 37 00 80
FAX: +33 1 45 79 06 66
EMAIL: admissions@eabjm.net
WEBSITE: www.eabjm.org
see full details on page 78

ECOLE ACTIVE BILINGUE JEANNINE MANUEL (LILLE)
Status Private
Programme Diploma
Diploma Coordinator Sybille Lambert
Gender Coeducational
Languages French
Boarding/day Mixed
418 bis, rue Albert Bailly, Marcq-en-Baroeul
59700, France
TELEPHONE: +33 3 2065 9050
FAX: +33 3 20 98 06 41
EMAIL: f.gianni@eabjm.net
see full details on page 78

International School of Lyon
Status Private
Programme PYP, Diploma
Diploma Coordinator Mike Ford
PYP Coordinator Susan Foster
Gender Coeducational
Languages English
Boarding/day Day
80 Chemin du Grand Roule, 69110 Sainte Foy
Lès Lyon, France
TELEPHONE: +33 (0) 478 866 190
FAX: +33 (0) 478 866 198
EMAIL: dphilip@islyon.org
WEBSITE: www.islyon.org

International School of Nice
Status Private
Programme Diploma
Diploma Coordinator Eugene Stevelberg
Gender Coeducational
Languages English
Boarding/day Day
15 avenue Claude Debussy, Nice 06200,
France
TELEPHONE: +33 4 93 21 04 00
FAX: +33 4 93 21 84 90
EMAIL: michael.wylie@cote-azur.cci.fr
WEBSITE: www.isn-nice.org

International School of Paris
Status Private
Programme PYP, MYP, Diploma
Diploma Coordinator Phil Anderson
MYP Coordinator Stacey Chandler
PYP Coordinator Fiona Symons
Gender Coeducational
Languages English
Boarding/day Day
6 rue Beethoven, Paris 75016, France
TELEPHONE: +33 1 4224 0954
FAX: +33 1 4527 1593
EMAIL: apeverelli@isparis.edu
WEBSITE: www.isparis.edu

International School of Toulouse
Status Private
Programme Diploma
Diploma Coordinator Nicholas Fretwell
Gender Coeducational
Languages English
Boarding/day Day
Route de Pibrac, Colomiers 31770, France
TELEPHONE: +33 562 74 26 74
FAX: +33 562 74 26 75
EMAIL: ist@intst.net
WEBSITE: www.intst.net

Ombrosa, Lycée Multilingue de Lyon
Status Private
Programme Diploma
Diploma Coordinator Wendy O'Mahony
Gender Coeducational
Languages English
Boarding/day Day
95 Quai Clemenceau, Caluire 69300, France
TELEPHONE: +33 4 78 23 22 63
FAX: +33 4 78235622
EMAIL: lvezin@ombrosa.com
WEBSITE: www.ombrosa.com

THE INTERNATIONAL BILINGUAL SCHOOL OF PROVENCE
Status Private
Programme Diploma
Diploma Coordinator Trevor Alan Tricker
Gender Coeducational
Languages English, French
Boarding/day Mixed
500 Route de Bouc-Bel-Air, Domaine des Pins,
Luynes, Aix en Provence 13080, France
TELEPHONE: +33 (0)4 4224 0340
FAX: +33 (0)4 4224 0981
EMAIL: info@ibsofprovence.com
WEBSITE: www.ibsofprovence.com
see full details on page 149

GERMANY

BAVARIAN INTERNATIONAL SCHOOL E.V.
Status Private
Programme PYP, Diploma
Diploma Coordinator Siegfried Joseph
PYP Coordinator Angela Hoelzl
Gender Coeducational
Languages English
Boarding/day Day
Schloss Haimhausen, Hauptstrasse 1, Haimhausen D-85778, Germany
TELEPHONE: +49 8133 917111
FAX: +49 8133 917115
EMAIL: director@bis-school.com
WEBSITE: www.bis-school.com
see full details on page 56

BBIS BERLIN BRANDENBURG INTERNATIONAL SCHOOL GMBH
Status Private
Programme PYP, MYP, Diploma
Diploma Coordinator Karin Schnoor
MYP Coordinator Michaela Jung
PYP Coordinator Lisa Roy
Gender Coeducational
Languages English
Boarding/day Both
Am Hochwald 30, 14532 Kleinmachnow, Germany
TELEPHONE: +49 33203 8036 0
FAX: +49 33203 8036 121
EMAIL: office@bbis.de
WEBSITE: www.bbis.de
see full details on page 57

Berlin British School
Status Private
Programme Diploma
Diploma Coordinator Donna McRudden
Gender Coeducational
Languages English
Boarding/day Day
Dickensweg 17-19, Berlin 14055, Germany
TELEPHONE: +49 30 35109190
FAX: +49 30 35109189
EMAIL: bbs.enq@t-online.de
WEBSITE: www.berlinbritishschool.de

Berlin International School
Status Private
Programme PYP, Diploma
Diploma Coordinator Emma Moffatt
PYP Coordinator Angeline Aow
Gender Coeducational
Languages English
Boarding/day Day
Lentzeallee 8/14, Berlin 14195, Germany
TELEPHONE: +49 (0) 30 8200 7790
FAX: +49 (0) 30 8200 7799
EMAIL: director@berlin-international-school.de
WEBSITE: www.berlin-international-school.de

Bonn International School EV
Status Private
Programme PYP, MYP, Diploma
Diploma Coordinator Lorraine Heinrichs
MYP Coordinator Naranda Mehrotra
PYP Coordinator Shireen Appana
Gender Coeducational
Languages English
Boarding/day Day
Martin-Luther-King Str 14, Bonn/Bad Godesburg 53175, Germany
TELEPHONE: +49 228 308 540
FAX: +49 228 30854 351
EMAIL: info@bis.bonn.org
WEBSITE: www.bis.bonn.org

Dresden International School e.V
Status Private
Programme PYP, MYP, Diploma
Diploma Coordinator Timothy Thomas
MYP Coordinator Chris Mordue
PYP Coordinator Matthew Robinson
Gender Coeducational
Languages English
Boarding/day Day
Annenstr 9, 01067 Dresden, Germany
TELEPHONE: +49 351 3400 428
FAX: +49 351 3400 430
EMAIL: csorenson@dresden-is.de
WEBSITE: www.dresden-is.de

Felix-Klein-Gymnasium
Status State
Programme Diploma
Diploma Coordinator Dietmar Freimann
Gender Coeducational
Languages English
Boarding/day Day
Böttingerstr 17, 37073 Göttingen, Germany
TELEPHONE: +49 551 400 2909
FAX: +49 551 400 2067
EMAIL: fkg@goettingen.de
WEBSITE: www.fkg-goettingen.de

Franconian International School
Status Private
Programme Diploma
Diploma Coordinator Liam Browne
Gender Coeducational
Languages English
Boarding/day Day
Christoph-Dassler Str 1, 91074, Herzogenaurach, Germany
TELEPHONE: +49 9132 797910
FAX: +49 9132 797912
EMAIL: info@the-fis.de
WEBSITE: www.ecis.org/fis

Frankfurt International School
Status Private
Programme PYP, Diploma
Diploma Coordinator David Morgan
PYP Coordinator Caroline Joslin-Callahan
Gender Coeducational
Languages English
Boarding/day Day
An der Waldlust 15, Oberursel 61440, Germany
TELEPHONE: +49 6171 20240
FAX: +49 6171 2024 384
EMAIL: mark_ulfers@fis.edu
WEBSITE: www.fis.edu

Friedrich-Ebert-Gymnasium
Status State
Programme Diploma
Diploma Coordinator Jutta Hoenow
Gender Coeducational
Languages English
Boarding/day Day
Ollenhauerstrasse 5, Bonn 53113, Germany
TELEPHONE: +49 228 777520
FAX: +49 228 777524
EMAIL: juttahoenow@hotmail.com

Friedrich-Wilhelm-Gymnasium Köln
Status State
Programme Diploma
Diploma Coordinator Brigid Hoffmann
Gender Coeducational
Languages English
Boarding/day Day
Severinstraße 241, Köln 50676, Germany
TELEPHONE: +49 221 2219 1628
FAX: +49 221 2219 1584
EMAIL: jansen@fwg-koeln.de
WEBSITE: www.fwg-koeln.de

Goethe-Gymnasium
Status State
Programme Diploma
Diploma Coordinator Rolf Theis
Gender Coeducational
Languages English
Boarding/day Day
Friedrich-Ebert-Anlage 22-24, Frankfurt 60325, Germany
TELEPHONE: +49 69 2123 3525
FAX: +49 69 2123 0717
EMAIL: RDTheis@aol.com

Goetheschule
Status State
Programme Diploma
Diploma Coordinator Joachim Pieper
Gender Coeducational
Languages English
Boarding/day Day
Ruschenstrasse 1, Essen 45133, Germany
TELEPHONE: +49 201 841170
FAX: +49 201 8411726
EMAIL: vera.bittner@schule.essen.de
WEBSITE: www.goetheschule-essen.de

Heidelberg International School
Status Private
Programme PYP
PYP Coordinator Allyn Raw
Gender Coeducational
Languages English
Boarding/day Day
Villa Heinstein, Wieblinger Weg 9, 69123 Heidelberg, Germany
TELEPHONE: +49 6221 75 90 600
FAX: +49 6221 7590 6099
EMAIL: info@hischool.de
WEBSITE: www.hischool.de

Helene-Lange-Gymnasium
Status State
Programme Diploma
Diploma Coordinator Bernd Flügge
Gender Coeducational
Languages English
Boarding/day Day
Bogenstr 32, Hamburg 20144, Germany
TELEPHONE: +49 40 428 9810
FAX: +49 40 428 98110
EMAIL: a.bluetener@hlg-hamburg.de
WEBSITE: www.hh.schule.de/hlg

International School Hamburg
Status Private
Programme Diploma
Diploma Coordinator Anthony Martin
Gender Coeducational
Languages English
Boarding/day Day
Holmbrook 20, Hamburg 22605, Germany
TELEPHONE: +49 40 883 0010
FAX: +49 40 881 1405
EMAIL: info@ishamburg.org
WEBSITE: http://international-school-hamburg.de

International School Hannover Region
Status Private
Programme PYP, MYP, Diploma
Diploma Coordinator Meera Phatarfod
MYP Coordinator Naomi Rasmer
PYP Coordinator Darran Litchfield
Gender Coeducational
Languages English
Boarding/day Day
Bruchmeister Allee 6, Hannover 30169, Germany
TELEPHONE: +49 511 270 41650
FAX: +49 511 270 41651
EMAIL: pat-baier@is-hr.de
WEBSITE: www.is-hr.de

INTERNATIONAL SCHOOL OF BREMEN
Status Private
Programme Diploma
Diploma Coordinator Mr Kim Walton
Gender Coeducational
Languages English
Boarding/day Day
Thomas-Mann Strasse 6-8, D-28213 Bremen, Germany
TELEPHONE: +49 421 337 9272
FAX: +49 421 337 9273
EMAIL: office@isbremen.de
WEBSITE: www.isbremen.de
see full details on page 98

International School of Düsseldorf
Status Private
Programme PYP, MYP, Diploma
Diploma Coordinator Colin Blake
MYP Coordinator Laura Maly-Schmidt
PYP Coordinator Amanda Jones
Gender Coeducational
Languages English
Boarding/day Day
Niederrheinstrasse 336, 40489 Düsseldorf, Germany
TELEPHONE: +49 210 639 3200
FAX: +49 210 639 0051
WEBSITE: www.isdedu.de

International School of Stuttgart
Status Private
Programme PYP, MYP, Diploma
Diploma Coordinator Neil Byrom
MYP Coordinator Eva Wilke
PYP Coordinator Anja Junginger
Gender Coeducational
Languages English, German in Kindergarten
Boarding/day Day
Sigmaringer Str 257, Stuttgart 70597, Germany
TELEPHONE: +49 711 769 6000
FAX: +49 711 769 600 10
EMAIL: iss@issev.de
WEBSITE: www.international-school-stuttgart.de

International School Wiesbaden
Status Private
Programme PYP
PYP Coordinator Andrea Rosinger
Gender Coeducational
Languages English, German
Boarding/day Day
Rudolf Dietz Strasse 14, 65207 Wiesbaden/Naurod, Germany
TELEPHONE: +49 6127 994053
FAX: +49 6127 994099
EMAIL: mark_ulfers@fis.edu
WEBSITE: www.isw.fis.edu

ISF International Schule Frankfurt-Rhein-Main Verwaltungs-GmbH
Status Private
Programme Diploma
Diploma Coordinator Vivian Papfakli-Strouza
Gender Coeducational
Languages English
Boarding/day Day
Strasse zur Internationalen Schule 33, 65931 Frankfurt am Main, Germany
TELEPHONE: +49 69 954 3190
FAX: +49 69 954 31920
EMAIL: isf@sabis.net

Leipzig International School eV
Status Private
Programme Diploma
Diploma Coordinator Mark Collier
Gender Coeducational
Languages English
Boarding/day Day
Koenneritzstrasse 47, Schleussig, Leipzig 04229, Germany
TELEPHONE: +49 341 421 0574
FAX: +49 341 421 2154
EMAIL: m-webster@intschool-leipzig.com
WEBSITE: www.intschool-leipzig.com

Lessing-Gymnasium
Programme Diploma
Diploma Coordinator Andrea Meinecke
Gender Coeducational
Languages English
Boarding/day Day
Heerstr 7, 51143 Koeln, Germany
TELEPHONE: +49 2203 99201 66
FAX: +49 2203 99201 68
EMAIL: headteacher_lessing@hotmail.com
WEBSITE: www.lessing-gymnasium.eu

MUNICH INTERNATIONAL SCHOOL
Status Private
Programme PYP, MYP, Diploma
Diploma Coordinator John McMurtry
MYP Coordinator Angela Brassington
PYP Coordinator Angela Steinmann
Gender Coeducational
Languages English
Boarding/day Day
Schloss Buchhof, Percha, Starnberg 82319, Germany
TELEPHONE: +49 8151 366 0
FAX: +49 8151 366 119
EMAIL: admissions@mis-munich.de
WEBSITE: www.mis-munich.de
see full details on page 119

Nelson Mandela State International School Berlin
Status State
Programme Diploma
Diploma Coordinator Charles Spiller
Gender Coeducational
Boarding/day Day
Kastanienallee 12-13, Berlin 14050, Germany
TELEPHONE: +49 30 9029 23913
FAX: +49 030 902 928 02
EMAIL: hertzens@yahoo.de
WEBSITE: www.sisberlin.de

Schule Schloss Salem
Status Private
Programme Diploma
Diploma Coordinator Anne-Claere Gurlitt
Gender Coeducational
Languages English
Boarding/day Boarding
Schloss Salem (Castle District), Salem
D-88682, Germany
TELEPHONE: +49 75 53 919 0
FAX: +49 75 53 919 380
WEBSITE: www.salem-net.de

St George's School
Status Private
Programme Diploma
Diploma Coordinator Mr J Doyle
Gender Coeducational
Languages English
Boarding/day Day
Anton Antweiler Strasse 4, Cologne 50938,
Germany
TELEPHONE: +49 221 297 8990
FAX: +49 221 297 89914
EMAIL: info@stgeorgesschoolcologne.de
WEBSITE: www.stgeorgesschoolcologne.de

St Leonhard Gymnasium
Status State
Programme Diploma
Diploma Coordinator Christine Bludau
Gender Coeducational
Languages French
Boarding/day Day
Jesuitenstr. 9, Aachen 52062, Germany

Stiftung Louisenlund
Status Private
Programme Diploma
Diploma Coordinator A Tegen
Güby 24357, Germany
TELEPHONE: +49 4354 999685
FAX: +49 4354 999352
EMAIL: info@louisenlund.de
WEBSITE: www.louisenlund.de

Theodor-Heuss-Gymnasium
Status State
Programme Diploma
Diploma Coordinator Heike Maass
Gender Coeducational
Languages English
Boarding/day Day
Freyastr 10, Ludwigshafen 67059, Germany
TELEPHONE: +45 621 504 431 710
EMAIL: davidwadle@thg-lu.de
WEBSITE: www.thg-lu.de

Thuringia International School – Weimar
Status Private
Programme Diploma
Diploma Coordinator Jana Schlichtenberg
Gender Coeducational
Languages English
Boarding/day Day
Bonhoefferstrasse 26, Weimar 99427,
Germany
TELEPHONE: +49 (0)3643 776904
FAX: +49 3643 776 905
EMAIL: info@this-weimar.de
WEBSITE: www.this-weimar.de

Werner-Heisenberg-Gymnasium
Status State
Programme Diploma
Diploma Coordinator Birgit Krämer
Gender Coeducational
Languages English
Boarding/day Day
Werner-Heisenberg-Str 1, Leverkusen 51381,
Germany
TELEPHONE: +49 2171 70670
FAX: +49 2171 706741
EMAIL: mgerling@t-online.de
WEBSITE: www.whg.schulen-lev.de

GHANA
Lincoln Community School
Status Private
Programme PYP, MYP, Diploma
Diploma Coordinator Jonathan Lorence
MYP Coordinator Victoria Rio
PYP Coordinator Rebecca Grace Phillips
Gender Coeducational
Languages English
Boarding/day Day
N126/21 Dedeibaa St, Abelenkpe, Accra,
Ghana
TELEPHONE: +233 21 774 018
FAX: +233 21 774 018
EMAIL: jroberts@lincoln.edu.gh
WEBSITE: www.lincoln.edu.gh

SOS-Hermann Gmeiner International College
Status Private
Programme Diploma
Diploma Coordinator Julian H Kitching
Gender Coeducational
Languages English
Boarding/day Boarding
Private Mail Bag, Community 6, Tema, Ghana
TELEPHONE: +233 22 204267
FAX: +233 22 202916
EMAIL: nkrumah_m@soshgic.edu.gh

Tema International School
Status Private
Programme Diploma
Diploma Coordinator Trevor Trumper
Gender Coeducational
Languages English
Boarding/day Mixed
PO Box CO 864, Tema, Ghana
TELEPHONE: +233 22 301 358
EMAIL: etorto@tis.edu.gh
WEBSITE: www.tis.edu.gh

GREECE
AMERICAN COMMUNITY SCHOOLS OF ATHENS
Status Private
Programme PYP, Diploma
Diploma Coordinator Julia Tokatlidou
PYP Coordinator Dina Pappas
Gender Coeducational
Languages English
Boarding/day Day
129 Aghias Paraskevis, Ano Xalandri, Athens
GR 152 34, Greece
TELEPHONE: +30 210 639 3200
FAX: +30 210 639 0051
EMAIL: acs@acs.gr
WEBSITE: www.acs.gr
see full details on page 44

Anatolia College
Status Private
Programme Diploma
Diploma Coordinator Theodoros Filaretos
Gender Coeducational
Languages English
Boarding/day Mixed
PO Box 21021, Pylea, Thessaloniki 55510,
Greece
TELEPHONE: +30 231 0 398222
FAX: +30 231 0 301076
EMAIL: rjackson@ac.anatolia.edu.gr
WEBSITE: www.anatolia.edu.gr

GREECE

CAMPION SCHOOL
Status Private
Programme Diploma
Diploma Coordinator Fred Clough
Gender Coeducational
Languages English
Boarding/day Day
PO Box 67484, Pallini 15302, Greece
TELEPHONE: +30 210 6071700
FAX: +30 210 6071780
EMAIL: fclough@campion.edu.gr
WEBSITE: www.campion.edu.gr
see full details on page 69

Costeas-Gitonas School
Status Private
Programme Diploma
Diploma Coordinator Zoi Geitona
Gender Coeducational
Languages English
Boarding/day Day
Pallini - Attikis, Athens 15351, Greece
TELEPHONE: +30 210 6030 411
FAX: +30 210 6030 570
EMAIL: cgeitonas@costeas-geitonas.gr
WEBSITE: www.cgs.gr

Doukas School SA
Status Private
Programme Diploma
Diploma Coordinator George Drivas
Gender Coeducational
Languages English
Boarding/day Mixed
151 Mesogion Street, 15125 Paradissos,
Marousi, Athens 15125, Greece
TELEPHONE: +30 210 618 6000
FAX: +30 210 6186 020
EMAIL: ibyp@doukas.gr
WEBSITE: www.doukas.gr

Geitona School
Status Private
Programme Diploma
Diploma Coordinator Vangelis Symeonidis
Gender Coeducational
Languages English
Boarding/day Day
PO Box 74128, Sternizes, Koropi Attiki 166 02,
Greece
TELEPHONE: +30 210 9656200-10
FAX: +30 210 9655920
EMAIL: esym@geitonas-school.gr
WEBSITE: www.geitonas-school.gr

H.A.E.F (Psychico College)
Status Private
Programme Diploma
Diploma Coordinator John Woodcock
Gender Coeducational
Languages English
Boarding/day Day
Psychico College, PO Box 65005, Psychiko,
Athens 15410, Greece
TELEPHONE: +30 210 6798208
FAX: +30 210 6756762
EMAIL: kokla@haef.gr
WEBSITE: www.haef.gr

IM Panayotopoulos School
Status Private
Programme Diploma
Diploma Coordinator Stavros Triantafillidis
Gender Coeducational
Languages English
Boarding/day Day
14 Nikiforou Lytra St, 15452 Psychico, Athens
GR-154 52, Greece
TELEPHONE: +30 210 677 6010
FAX: +30 210 677 7552
EMAIL: ibimpa@impanagiotopoulos.gr
WEBSITE: www.impanagiotopoulos.gr

International School of Athens
Status Private
Programme PYP, MYP, Diploma
Diploma Coordinator Arthur Kattavenos
MYP Coordinator Meg Matsaganis
PYP Coordinator Chris Grant-Bear
Gender Coeducational
Languages English
Boarding/day Day
PO Box 51051, Kifissia, Athens 14510, Greece
TELEPHONE: +30 210 6233 888
FAX: +30 210 6233 160
EMAIL: info@isa.edu.gr
WEBSITE: www.isa.edu.gr

Moraitis School
Status Private
Programme Diploma
Diploma Coordinator Spiros Molfetas
Gender Coeducational
Languages English
Boarding/day Day
A Papanastasiou & Ag Dimitriou, Paleo
Psychico, Athens 15452, Greece
TELEPHONE: +30 210 679 5000
FAX: +30 210 679 5090
EMAIL: aldimar@moraitis.edu.gr
WEBSITE: www.moraitis.edu.gr

Nea Genia Ziridi
Status Private
Programme Diploma
Diploma Coordinator Emmanuela Kantzia
Gender Coeducational
Languages English
Boarding/day Day
21 Plateia Filikis Etairias, Athens 106 71,
Greece
TELEPHONE: +30 210 3612 800
EMAIL: kmitsiou@hotmail.com
WEBSITE: www.ziridis.gr

Pinewood Schools of Thessaloniki
Status Private
Programme Diploma
Diploma Coordinator Morris Lando
Gender Coeducational
Languages English
Boarding/day Mixed
PO Box 21001, Pilea, Thessaloniki GR-55510,
Greece
TELEPHONE: +30 2310 301 221
FAX: +30 2310 323 196
EMAIL: pbbaiter@otenet.gr
WEBSITE: www.pinewood.gr

St Catherine's British Embassy School
Status Private
Programme Diploma
Diploma Coordinator Stuart Bond
Gender Coeducational
Languages English
Boarding/day Day
PO Box 51019, Kifissia, Athens 14510, Greece
TELEPHONE: +30 210 2829 750
FAX: +30 210 2826 415
EMAIL: headmaster@stcatherines.gr
WEBSITE: www.stcatherines.gr

HUNGARY

American International School of Budapest
Status Private
Programme Diploma
Diploma Coordinator Karen Kish
Gender Coeducational
Languages English
Boarding/day Day
PO Box 53, Budapest 1525, Hungary
TELEPHONE: +36 26 556 000
FAX: +36 26 556 003
EMAIL: admissions@nk.aisb.hu
WEBSITE: www.aisb.hu

Karinthy Frigyes Gimnázium
Status State
Programme Diploma
Diploma Coordinator Szilvia Cserép
Gender Coeducational
Languages English
Boarding/day Day
Thököly utca 7, Budapest 1183, Hungary
TELEPHONE: +36 1 291 2072
FAX: +36 1 291 2367
EMAIL: hutus@karinthy.hu
WEBSITE: www.karinthy.hu

SEK Budapest International School
Status Private
Programme Diploma
Diploma Coordinator Gabriella Gidró
Gender Coeducational
Languages English
Boarding/day Day
Hüvösvölgyi út 131, Budapest 1021, Hungary
TELEPHONE: +36 1 394 2968
EMAIL: mhinojosa@sekmail.com
WEBSITE: www.sek.hu

The British International School, Budapest

Status Private
Programme Diploma
Diploma Coordinator Rachel Batty
Gender Coeducational
Languages English
Boarding/day Day
Kiscelli koz 17, Budapest 1037, Hungary
TELEPHONE: +36 1 200 8488
FAX: +361 200 9969
EMAIL: admissions@bisb.hu
WEBSITE: www.bisb.hu

ICELAND

Menntaskolinn vid Hamrahlid

Status State
Programme Diploma
Diploma Coordinator Soffía Sveinsdóttir
Gender Coeducational
Languages English
Boarding/day Day
Hamrahlí 10, Reykjavik 105, Iceland
TELEPHONE: +354 595 5200
FAX: +354 595 5250
EMAIL: rektor@mh.is
WEBSITE: www.mh.is

IRAN

Tehran International School

Status State
Programme Diploma
Diploma Coordinator Nasrin Barootchi
Gender Coeducational
Languages English
Boarding/day Day
East Sarv Street, Kadj Sq Saadat Abad, Tehran 19816, Iran
TELEPHONE: +98 21 22065 648
FAX: +98 21 206 5447
EMAIL: ibo.iran@gmail.com
WEBSITE: www.tisschool.com

IRELAND

ST ANDREW'S COLLEGE

Status Private
Programme Diploma
Diploma Coordinator Monica Docherty
Gender Coeducational
Languages English
Boarding/day Day
Booterstown Avenue, Blackrock, County Dublin, Ireland
TELEPHONE: +353 1 288 2785
FAX: +353 1 283 1627
EMAIL: information@st-andrews.ie
WEBSITE: www.st-andrews.ie
see full details on page 137

ISRAEL

Anglican International School

Status Private
Programme Diploma
Diploma Coordinator Nancy Jenkins
Gender Coeducational
Languages English
Boarding/day Day
PO Box 191, 82 Rechov Haneviim, Jerusalem 91001, Israel
TELEPHONE: +972 2 567 7200
FAX: +972 2 538 4874
EMAIL: phil.billing@aisj.ico.il
WEBSITE: www.aisj.co.il

ITALY

ACAT-IST: International School of Turin

Status Private
Programme PYP, MYP, Diploma
Diploma Coordinator Cy Webber
MYP Coordinator Jennifer Hahn
PYP Coordinator Clare Muir
Gender Coeducational
Languages English
Boarding/day Day
Vicolo Tiziano 10, Moncalieri, Torino 10024, Italy
TELEPHONE: +39 011 645 967
FAX: +39 011 643 298
EMAIL: info@acat-ist.it
WEBSITE: www.acat-ist.it

American International School in Genoa

Status Private
Programme Diploma
Diploma Coordinator Elizabeth Rosser Boiardi
Gender Coeducational
Languages English
Boarding/day Day
Via Quarto, 13-c, Genova 16148, Italy
TELEPHONE: +39 010 386528
FAX: +39 010 3740274
EMAIL: director@aisge.it
WEBSITE: www.aisge.it

American Overseas School of Rome

Status Private
Programme Diploma
Diploma Coordinator Belinda Fiochi
Gender Coeducational
Languages English
Boarding/day Mixed
Via Cassia 811, Rome 00189, Italy
TELEPHONE: +39 06 334 381
FAX: +39 06 3326 2608
EMAIL: info@aosr.org
WEBSITE: www.aosr.org

American School of Milan

Status Private
Programme MYP, Diploma
Diploma Coordinator Samer Khoury
MYP Coordinator Valeria Meroni
Gender Coeducational
Languages English
Boarding/day Day
Via Carl Marx 14, Noverasco di Opera, Milano 20090, Italy
TELEPHONE: +39 02 530 00020
FAX: +39 02 5760 6274
EMAIL: aaustin@asmilan.org
WEBSITE: www.asmilan.org

Deledda International School

Status State
Programme Diploma
Diploma Coordinator Elizabeth Rice
Gender Coeducational
Languages English
Boarding/day Day
IB Diploma Course, Via Bertani, 6, Castelletto, Genova, Liguria 16125, Italy
TELEPHONE: +39 010 811634
FAX: +39 010 839 1360
EMAIL: venzano@gmx.net
WEBSITE: www.deleddainternational.it

International School of Como

Status Private
Programme PYP
PYP Coordinator Becky Taylor
Gender Coeducational
Languages English
Boarding/day Day
Via per Cernobbio 19, Como 22100, Italy
TELEPHONE: +39 031 57 6186
FAX: +39 031 57 2289
EMAIL: tcunningham@iscomo.com
WEBSITE: www.iscomo.com

International School of Florence

Status Private
Programme Diploma
Diploma Coordinator Debra Williams
Gender Coeducational
Languages English
Boarding/day Day
Via del Carota 23/25, Bagno a Ripoli, Florence 50012, Italy
TELEPHONE: +39 055 6461 007
FAX: +39 055 644 226
EMAIL: head.aisf@interbusiness.it
WEBSITE: www.aisfitaly.org

International School of Milan
Status Private
Programme PYP, MYP, Diploma
Diploma Coordinator David Towe
MYP Coordinator Adam Brown
PYP Coordinator Julia Woollacott
Gender Coeducational
Languages English
Boarding/day Day
Via G Bellini, 1, Milan 20146, Italy
TELEPHONE: +39 02 4229 0577
FAX: +39 02 4235 428
EMAIL: thaywood@ism-ac.it
WEBSITE: www.ism-ac.it

International School of Milan-Monza Section
Status Private
Programme PYP
PYP Coordinator Jamie Schmitz
Gender Coeducational
Languages English
Boarding/day Day
Via Ramazzotti 28/A, Monza 20052, Italy
TELEPHONE: 39 039 249 6015
EMAIL: thaywood@ism-ac.it
WEBSITE: www.ism-ac.it

Marymount International School
Status Private
Programme Diploma
Diploma Coordinator James Romano
Gender Coeducational
Languages English
Boarding/day Day
Via di Villa Lauchli, 180, (Via Cassia) km 7, Rome 00191, Italy
TELEPHONE: +39 06 3629101
FAX: +39 06 3630 1738
EMAIL: yhennigan@marymountrome.it
WEBSITE: www.marymountrome.org

Sir James Henderson British School of Milan
Status Private
Programme Diploma
Diploma Coordinator Andrew Watson
Gender Coeducational
Languages English
Boarding/day Day
Via Pisani Dossi 16, Milan 20134, Italy
TELEPHONE: +39 02 210941
FAX: +39 02 21094225
EMAIL: info@sjhschool.com
WEBSITE: www.sjhschool.com

St George's British International School
Status Private
Programme Diploma
Diploma Coordinator Gayle Haywood
Gender Coeducational
Languages English
Boarding/day Day
Via Cassia, La Storta, Roma 00123, Italy
TELEPHONE: +39 06 30860021
FAX: +39 06 30892490
EMAIL: principal@stgeorge.school.it
WEBSITE: www.stgeorge.school.it

St Stephen's School
Status Private
Programme Diploma
Diploma Coordinator Jennifer Ferrara
Gender Coeducational
Languages English
Boarding/day Mixed
Via Aventina 3, Rome 00153, Italy
TELEPHONE: +39 06 575 0605
FAX: +39 06 574 1941
EMAIL: ststephens@ststephens-rome.com
WEBSITE: www.ststephens-rome.com

The English International School of Padua
Status Private
Programme Diploma
Diploma Coordinator Martin Daly
Gender Coeducational
Languages English
Boarding/day Day
Via Forcellini 168, Padova, Veneto, Italy
TELEPHONE: +39 049 8022503
FAX: +39 049 8020660
EMAIL: eisp@eisp01.com
WEBSITE: www.eisp01.com

United World College of the Adriatic
Status Private
Programme Diploma
Diploma Coordinator Helen White
Gender Coeducational
Languages English
Boarding/day Boarding
Via Trieste 29, Duino, Trieste 34011, Italy
TELEPHONE: +39 040 3739 111
FAX: +39 040 3739 225
EMAIL: uwcad@uwcad.it
WEBSITE: www.uwcad.it

VIS Vicenza International School
Status Private
Programme Diploma
Diploma Coordinator Mary Bussino Cappellari
Gender Coeducational
Languages English
Boarding/day Day
Contra San Marcello, 9, Vicenza 36100, Italy
TELEPHONE: +39 0444 525080
FAX: +39 0444 528083
EMAIL: head@internationalyceum.it

Vittoria International School
Status Private
Programme Diploma
Diploma Coordinator Giovanni Casavecchia
Gender Coeducational
Languages English
Boarding/day Day
Piazza Vittorio Veneto 13, Turin 10124, Italy
TELEPHONE: +39 011 889870
FAX: +39 011 8123486
EMAIL: info@vittoriaweb.it
WEBSITE: www.vittoriaweb.it

JORDAN

Amman Academy
Status Private
Programme Diploma
Diploma Coordinator Ruba Rabadi
Gender Coeducational
Languages English
Boarding/day Day
PO Box 840, Khalda 11821, Jordan
TELEPHONE: +962 6 535 4118
FAX: +962 6 5331760
EMAIL: rjfakhoury@ammanacademy.edu.jo
WEBSITE: www.ammanacademy.edu.jo

AMMAN BACCALAUREATE SCHOOL
Status Private
Programme MYP, Diploma
Diploma Coordinator Cathy Souob
MYP Coordinator Iman Awad
Gender Coeducational
Languages English, Arabic
Boarding/day Day
PO Box 441, Sweileh 11910, Amman, Jordan
TELEPHONE: +962 6 541 1572/1191
FAX: +962 6 5412603
EMAIL: proffice@abs.edu.jo
WEBSITE: www.abs.edu.jo
see full details on page 49

Amman National School
Status Private
Programme Diploma
Diploma Coordinator Diana Dahleh
Gender Coeducational
Languages English
Boarding/day Day
PO Box 140565, Amman 11814, Jordan
TELEPHONE: +962 654 11067/8
FAX: +962 654 11067
EMAIL: ans@ans.edu.jo
WEBSITE: www.ans.edu.jo

CAMBRIDGE HIGH SCHOOL
Status Private
Programme Diploma
Diploma Coordinator Kathleen Awwad
Gender Coeducational
Languages English
Boarding/day Day
Al Rabia, Abdel Kareem Al Dabbas Street, PO Box 851771, Amman 11185, Jordan
TELEPHONE: +962 6 5512556
FAX: +962 6 5512558
EMAIL: cambridge@cambridge.edu.jo
WEBSITE: www.cambridge.edu.jo
see full details on page 68

Mashrek International School
Status Private
Programme MYP, Diploma
Diploma Coordinator Mirna Al-Jouzi
MYP Coordinator Suha Lallas Kassisieh
Gender Coeducational
Languages English
Boarding/day Day
PO Box 1412, Amman 11118, Jordan
TELEPHONE: +962 6541 2979
FAX: +962 6541 1143
EMAIL: administration@mashrek.edu.jo
WEBSITE: www.mashrek.edu.jo

MODERN MONTESSORI SCHOOL
Status Private
Programme Diploma
Diploma Coordinator Kawther Saa'd Al Din
Gender Coeducational
Languages English
Boarding/day Day
PO Box 1941, Khilda, Amman 11821, Jordan
TELEPHONE: +9626 5535190
FAX: +9626 5535831
EMAIL: ksd@montessori.edu.jo
WEBSITE: www.montessori.edu.jo
see full details on page 117

The Ahliyyah School for Girls
Status Private
Programme Diploma
Diploma Coordinator Suha Ziadeh Fasheh
Gender Female
Languages English
Boarding/day Day
PO Box 2035, Jabal Amman, Amman 11181, Jordan
TELEPHONE: +962 646 498 61
FAX: +962 646 215 49
EMAIL: h.najjar@asg.edu.jo
WEBSITE: www.asg.edu.jo

KAZAKHSTAN

International College of Continuous Education, Astana
Status Private
Programme PYP, MYP
MYP Coordinator Anatoliy Kuznetsov
PYP Coordinator Svetlana Gavrilova
Gender Coeducational
Languages English, Russian
Boarding/day Day
2 Molodezhny Microdistrict, Astana 0100000 473000, Kazakhstan
TELEPHONE: +7 3172 224593
FAX: +7 3172 224 590
EMAIL: mkno@kepter.kz
WEBSITE: www.mkno.kz

International College of Continuous Education, Almaty
Status Private
Programme PYP, MYP
MYP Coordinator Oxana Akimova
PYP Coordinator Tamara Markina
Gender Coeducational
Languages English, Russian
Boarding/day Day
69A Zheltoksan Street, Almaty 480004, Kazakhstan
TELEPHONE: +7 3272 399736
FAX: +7 3272 799273
EMAIL: icce@netexecutive.com
WEBSITE: www.icce-kazakhstan.kz

International School of Almaty
Status State
Programme MYP
MYP Coordinator Roza Bazarbayeva
Gender Coeducational
Languages English
Boarding/day Day
40b Satpayev street, Almaty 480057, Kazakhstan
TELEPHONE: +7 3272 744808
FAX: +7 3272 748189
EMAIL: international_school@nursat.kz

Miras International School Almaty
Status Private
Programme PYP, MYP, Diploma
Diploma Coordinator Adam Armanski
MYP Coordinator Rosa Matayeva
PYP Coordinator Terance Tiplady
Gender Coeducational
Languages English, Kazakh, Russian
Boarding/day Day
190 Al-Farabi, Almaty 050043, Kazakhstan
TELEPHONE: +7 3272 55 1025
FAX: +7 3272 55 1151
EMAIL: principal@almaty.miras.kz
WEBSITE: www.miras.kz

Miras International School, Astana
Status Private
Programme PYP, MYP
MYP Coordinator Paul Harrison
PYP Coordinator Maira Kunanbayeva
Gender Coeducational
Languages English, Russian
Boarding/day Mixed
30 Ablai Khan Avenue, Astana 010009, Kazakhstan
TELEPHONE: +7 3172 369867
FAX: +7 3172 369868
EMAIL: principal@miras-astana.kz
WEBSITE: www.miras-astana.kz

KENYA

Aga Khan Academy, Mombasa
Status Private
Programme PYP, Diploma
Diploma Coordinator Helene Caillet
PYP Coordinator Andrea Mwunla
Gender Coeducational
Languages English
Boarding/day Day
PO Box 90066, Mombasa, Kenya
TELEPHONE: +254 41 2220 360
FAX: +254 41 227 982
EMAIL: slakahani@hotmail.com

Aga Khan Academy, Nairobi
Status Private
Programme Diploma
Diploma Coordinator Fidelis Nthenge
Gender Coeducational
Languages English
Boarding/day Day
PO Box 44424, Nairobi 00100, Kenya
TELEPHONE: +254 20 374 9495/2266
FAX: +254 20 374 6886
EMAIL: hahmed@aka.ac.ke

Braeburn College
Status Private
Programme Diploma
Diploma Coordinator Benson Kairu
Gender Coeducational
Languages English
Boarding/day Mixed
PO Box 45112, 0100 GPO, Nairobi, Kenya
TELEPHONE: +254 20 8561144/8013737
FAX: +254 20 8562450
EMAIL: headmaster@braeburn.ac.ke
WEBSITE: www.braeburn.com

International School of Kenya
Status Private
Programme Diploma
Diploma Coordinator Robert Blanchard
Gender Coeducational
Languages English
Boarding/day Day
End of Peponi Road/Kirawa Road, PO Box 14103-00800, Nairobi 00800, Kenya
TELEPHONE: +254 20 418 3622
FAX: +254 20 418 3272
EMAIL: awilliams@isk.ac.ke
WEBSITE: www.isk.ac.ke/

St Mary's School
Status Private
Programme Diploma
Diploma Coordinator Francis Kimweli
Gender Coeducational
Languages English
Boarding/day Day
PO Box 40580, Rhapta Road, Nairobi 00100, Kenya
TELEPHONE: +254 20 4444 569
FAX: +254 20 4444 754
WEBSITE: www.stmarys.ac.ke

KINGDOM OF BAHRAIN

Abdul Rahman Kanoo International School
Status Private
Programme Diploma
Diploma Coordinator Mohamed Reza
Gender Coeducational
Languages English
Boarding/day Day
PO Box 2512, Manama, Kingdom of Bahrain
TELEPHONE: +973 17 875 055
FAX: +973 17 877 000
EMAIL: principal@kanooschool.edu.bh
WEBSITE: www.kanooschool.edu.bh

Bahrain Bayan School
Status Private
Programme Diploma
Diploma Coordinator Majdi El Hajj
Gender Coeducational
Languages English
Boarding/day Day
Road 4111, Building 230, PO Box 32411, Isa Town 841, Kingdom of Bahrain
TELEPHONE: +973 177 801 66
FAX: +973 177 800 19
EMAIL: nwehbe@bayan.edu.bh
WEBSITE: www.bayan.edu.bh

Bahrain School
Status Private
Programme Diploma
Diploma Coordinator Trevor Burt
Gender Coeducational
Languages English
Boarding/day Mixed
PO Box 934, Manama, Kingdom of Bahrain
TELEPHONE: +973 17719822
FAX: +973 17728583
EMAIL: alice.berard@eu.dodea.edu
WEBSITE: www.bahr-ehs.eu.dodea.edu/localib.htm

IBN Khuldoon National School
Status Private
Programme Diploma
Diploma Coordinator Ayman Zanoun
Gender Coeducational
Languages English
Boarding/day Day
PO Box 20511, Manama, Kingdom of Bahrain
TELEPHONE: +973 17780 661
FAX: +973 17689 028
EMAIL: s.chammaa@ikns.edu.bh

Modern Knowledge Schools
Status Private
Programme Diploma
Diploma Coordinator David Bailey
Gender Coeducational
Languages English
Boarding/day Day
PO Box 15826, Manama, Kingdom of Bahrain
TELEPHONE: +973 17 727724
FAX: +973 17 827 449
EMAIL: deweybahrain@hotmail.com
WEBSITE: www.mks.edu.bh

Naseem International School
Status Private
Programme PYP, Diploma
Diploma Coordinator Fuad Prins
PYP Coordinator Trish Berry
Gender Coeducational
Languages English, Arabic
Boarding/day Day
PO Box 28503, Rifa, Kingdom of Bahrain
TELEPHONE: +973 689 684
FAX: +973 687 166
EMAIL: merbati1@batelco.com.bh
WEBSITE: www.naseemschool.com.bh

Shaikha Hessa Girls' School
Status Private
Programme Diploma
Diploma Coordinator Yasmeen Al-Khalifa
Gender Female
Languages English
Boarding/day Day
PO Box 37799, Riffa, Kingdom of Bahrain
TELEPHONE: +973 17 756 111
FAX: +973 17 750 700
EMAIL: Adrine.Katchadurian@shgs.edu.bh
WEBSITE: www.shgs.edu.bh

ST CHRISTOPHER'S SCHOOL
Status Private
Programme Diploma
Diploma Coordinator Stephen Martin
Gender Coeducational
Languages English
Boarding/day Day
PO Box 32052, Isa Town, Kingdom of Bahrain
TELEPHONE: +973 17 788101
FAX: +973 17 788120
EMAIL: office.seniors@st-chris.net
WEBSITE: www.st-chris.net
see full details on page 138

KUWAIT

American Creativity Academy
Status Private
Programme Diploma
Diploma Coordinator Linda Tom Marling
Gender Coeducational
Languages English
Boarding/day Day
PO Box 1740, Hawalli 32018, Kuwait
TELEPHONE: +965 2673333
FAX: +965 2632478
EMAIL: gertrude@aca.edu.kw
WEBSITE: www.aca.edu.kw

AMERICAN INTERNATIONAL SCHOOL OF KUWAIT
Status Private
Programme PYP, MYP, Diploma
Diploma Coordinator Cheryl Hordenchuk
MYP Coordinator Rosalee Van Staalduinen
PYP Coordinator Stephanie Moynan
Gender Coeducational
Languages English
Boarding/day Day
PO Box 3267, Salmiya 22033, Kuwait
TELEPHONE: +965 2225 5155
FAX: +965 2225 5156
EMAIL: director@aiskuwait.org
WEBSITE: www.aiskuwait.org
see full details on page 46

LATVIA

International School of Latvia
Status Private
Programme PYP, MYP, Diploma
Diploma Coordinator William Elman
MYP Coordinator Eleanor Surridge
PYP Coordinator Stan Krause
Gender Coeducational
Languages English
Boarding/day Day
Viestura iela 6A, Jurmala LV 2010, Latvia
TELEPHONE: +371 7755 146
FAX: +371 7755 009
EMAIL: lmolacek@isl.edu.lv
WEBSITE: www.isl.edu.lv

International School of Riga
Status Private
Programme PYP
PYP Coordinator Arita Lauka
Gender Coeducational
Languages English
Boarding/day Day
Zvejnieku iela 12, Riga 1048, Latvia
TELEPHONE: +371 7624 622
EMAIL: director@isriga.lv
WEBSITE: www.isriga.lv

Riga State Gymnasium No.1
Status State
Programme Diploma
Diploma Coordinator Liga Reitere
Gender Coeducational
Languages English
Boarding/day Day
Raina bulv 8, Riga 1050, Latvia
TELEPHONE: +371 7 228 607
FAX: +371 7 228 607
EMAIL: marisbrasla@inbox.lv
WEBSITE: www.r1g.edu.lv

LEBANON

American Community School at Beirut
Status Private
Programme Diploma
Diploma Coordinator Ghada Jaber
Gender Coeducational
Languages English
Boarding/day Day
PO Box 8129, Riad Solh, Beirut 11072260, Lebanon
TELEPHONE: +961 1 374 310
FAX: +961 1 366050
EMAIL: gdamon@acs.edu.lb

GERMAN SCHOOL BEIRUT
Status Private
Programme Diploma
Diploma Coordinator Hadi Bou Hassan (English), Angela Haddad (German)
Gender Coeducational
Languages English
Boarding/day Day
PO Box 11-3888, Beirut, Lebanon
TELEPHONE: +96 1174 0523
FAX: +96 1174 0523
EMAIL: germanschoolb@gmail.com
WEBSITE: www.deutscheschulebeirut.edu.lb
see full details on page 83

International College, Ain Aar
Status Private
Programme PYP
PYP Coordinator Nayla Serhal
Gender Coeducational
Languages Arabic, English, French
Boarding/day Day
Bliss Street, PO Box 11, Riad El Solh, Beirut 2020, Lebanon
TELEPHONE: +96 149 28468
FAX: +96 149 11247
EMAIL: jjohnson@ic.edu.lb
WEBSITE: www.ic.edu.lb

International College, Ras Beirut
Status Private
Programme PYP, Diploma
Diploma Coordinator Rasha Daouk
PYP Coordinator Ghada Maalouf
Gender Coeducational
Languages English, Arabic, French
Boarding/day Day
PO Box 11-0236, Riad El Solh, Beirut 1107-2020, Lebanon
TELEPHONE: +961 1 371 294
FAX: +961 1 362 500
EMAIL: jjohnson@ic.edu.lb
WEBSITE: www.ic.edu.lb

Sagesse High School
Status Private
Programme Diploma
Diploma Coordinator Lady Maalouf
Gender Coeducational
Languages English
Boarding/day Mixed
Aïn Saadeh, Metn, Lebanon
TELEPHONE: +961 1 872 145
FAX: +961 1 872 149
EMAIL: sagessehs@sagessehs.edu.lb
WEBSITE: www.sagessehs.edu.lb

LESOTHO

Machabeng College, International School of Lesotho
Status Private
Programme Diploma
Diploma Coordinator Martin Thompson
Gender Coeducational
Languages English
Boarding/day Mixed
PO Box 1570, Maseru 100, Lesotho
TELEPHONE: +266 2231 3224
FAX: +266 2231 6109
EMAIL: machabhm@lesoff.co.za
WEBSITE: www.machcoll.co.ls

LITHUANIA

Siauliai Didzdvaris gymnasium
Status State
Programme Diploma
Diploma Coordinator Rima Morkuniene
Gender Coeducational
Languages English
Boarding/day Day
Vilniaus g 188, Siauliai 76299, Lithuania
TELEPHONE: +370 41 431 424
EMAIL: vaidas@dg.su.lt
WEBSITE: www.dg.su.lt

Vilnius Lyceum
Status State
Programme Diploma
Diploma Coordinator Vilija Balciunaité
Gender Coeducational
Languages English
Boarding/day Day
Sirvintu 82, Vilnius LT-08216, Lithuania
TELEPHONE: +370 5 2775836
FAX: +370 5 2775836
EMAIL: adm@licejus.lt
WEBSITE: www.licejus.lt

LUXEMBOURG

Fräi-Öffentlech Waldorfschoul Lëtzebuerg
Status Private
Programme Diploma
Diploma Coordinator Camille Putz
Gender Coeducational
Languages French
Boarding/day Day
45 rue de l'Avenir, Luxembourg 1147
TELEPHONE: +352 466932
FAX: +352/220208
EMAIL: waldorf-bacinternational@ecole.lu
WEBSITE: www.waldorf.lu

International School of Luxembourg
Status Private
Programme Diploma
Diploma Coordinator Peter Jenks
Gender Coeducational
Languages English
Boarding/day Day
36 Boulevard Pierre Dupong, Luxembourg 1430
TELEPHONE: +352 26 04 40
FAX: +352 26 04 47 04
EMAIL: information@islux.lu
WEBSITE: www.islux.lu

Lycée Technique du Centre
Status State
Programme Diploma
Diploma Coordinator Netty Maas
Gender Coeducational
Languages French
Boarding/day Day
106 avenue Pasteur, Luxembourg L-2309
TELEPHONE: +352 47 38 11 1
FAX: +352 47 38 11 333
EMAIL: admin@ltc.lu
WEBSITE: www.ltc.lu

MACEDONIA

Josip Broz Tito – High School
Status State
Programme Diploma
Diploma Coordinator Gordiana Gjorgova
Gender Coeducational
Languages English
Boarding/day Day
Dimitrije Cupovski bb, Skopje 1000, Macedonia
TELEPHONE: +389 2 3214 314
FAX: +389 2 3211 082
EMAIL: ibjbtsk@mt.net.mk

NOVA International Schools
Status Private
Programme Diploma
Diploma Coordinator Lidija Stankovic
Gender Coeducational
Languages English
Boarding/day Day
Ul Praska BB, Skopje 1000, Macedonia
TELEPHONE: +389 2 3061 907
EMAIL: vnovakovska@nova.edu.mk
WEBSITE: www.nova.edu.mk

MALAWI

Bishop Mackenzie International Schools
Status Private
Programme Diploma
Diploma Coordinator Janice Todd
Gender Coeducational
Languages English
Boarding/day Day
PO Box 102, Lilongwe, Malawi
TELEPHONE: +265 1 756 984
FAX: +265 1 751 374
EMAIL: p.todd@bmismw.com
WEBSITE: www.bmismw.com

MALTA

Verdala International School
Status Private
Programme Diploma
Diploma Coordinator Lawrence Simpson
Gender Coeducational
Languages English
Boarding/day Mixed
Fort Pembroke, Pembroke PBK 1641, Malta
TELEPHONE: +356 21375133
FAX: +356 21372387
EMAIL: headmaster@verdala.org
WEBSITE: www.verdala.org

MAURITIUS

Clavis Primary School
Status Private
Programme PYP
PYP Coordinator Dr Gloria Kauffman
Gender Coeducational
Languages English, French
Boarding/day Day
Montagne Ory, Moka, Mauritius
TELEPHONE: +230 433 4439/4337708
FAX: +230 433 4274
EMAIL: n.j.hamer@clavis.mu
WEBSITE: www.clavis.mu

Le Bocage International School
Status Private
Programme Diploma
Diploma Coordinator Rasika Khadun
Gender Coeducational
Languages English
Boarding/day Day
Montagne Ory, Moka, Mauritius
TELEPHONE: +230 433 0941
FAX: +230 433 4914
EMAIL: lbis@lbis.intnet.mu
WEBSITE: www.lebocage.net

Northfields International High School
Programme Diploma
Diploma Coordinator Camelia Ramsamy
Gender Coeducational
Languages English
Boarding/day Day
Labourdonnais Village, Mapou, Mauritius
TELEPHONE: +230 266 9448/9
FAX: +230 266 9447
EMAIL: cameliaramsamy@yahoo.co.uk
WEBSITE: www.northfieldsonline.com

MONACO

International School of Monaco
Status Private
Programme PYP, MYP, Diploma
Diploma Coordinator Ms Natasha Chisholm
MYP Coordinator Stuart Findlay
PYP Coordinator Kay Scarlett
Gender Coeducational
Languages English
Boarding/day Day
12 quai Antoine 1er, Monte Carlo 98000, Monaco
TELEPHONE: +377 9325 6820
FAX: +377 9325 6830
EMAIL: director@ibo.org
WEBSITE: http://ismonaco.org

MOROCCO

Casablanca American School
Status Private
Programme Diploma
Diploma Coordinator John Maressa
Gender Coeducational
Languages English
Boarding/day Day
Route de la Mecque, Lotissement Ougoug, Quartier Californie, Casablanca 20150, Morocco
TELEPHONE: +212 22 21 41 15/16
FAX: +212 22 21 24 88
EMAIL: dhughes@cas.ac.ma
WEBSITE: www.cas.ac.ma

Écoles Al Madina
Status Private
Programme MYP, Diploma
Diploma Coordinator Roger Guillemette
MYP Coordinator Nadia Lahrim
Gender Coeducational
Languages French
Boarding/day Day
Lotissement Bellevue 11, Rue 3 Californie, Casablanca, Morocco
TELEPHONE: +212 22 50 50 97
FAX: +21222 50 49 60
EMAIL: a.lahlou@almadina.ac.ma
WEBSITE: www.almadina.ac.ma

Groupe Scolaire La Résidence
Status Private
Programme MYP
MYP Coordinator Nawal Hefiri
Gender Coeducational
Languages French
87-89 Avenue 2 mars, Casablanca, Morocco
TELEPHONE: +212 22809050/51
FAX: +212 22809052
EMAIL: gsr@gsr.ac.ma
WEBSITE: www.gsr.ac.ma

Rabat American School
Status Private
Programme Diploma
Diploma Coordinator Gail MacMillan
Gender Coeducational
Languages English
Boarding/day Day
c/o US Embassy, BP 120 Rabat, Morocco
TELEPHONE: +212 3 671 476
FAX: +212 3 670 963
EMAIL: info@ras.ma
WEBSITE: www.ras.ma

MOZAMBIQUE

American International School of Mozambique
Status Private
Programme Diploma
Diploma Coordinator Lea-Carol Glennon
Gender Coeducational
Languages English
PO Box 2026, Maputo, Mozambique
TELEPHONE: +258 2 1491 994
EMAIL: director@aism-moz.com
WEBSITE: www.aism-moz.com

NAMIBIA

Windhoek International School
Status Private
Programme PYP, Diploma
Diploma Coordinator Mark McLennan
PYP Coordinator Bruce Parcher
Gender Coeducational
Languages English
Boarding/day Day
P/Bag 16007, Windhoek, Namibia
TELEPHONE: +264 61 241 783
FAX: +264 61 243 127
EMAIL: kjarman@wis.edu.na
WEBSITE: www.wis.edu.na

NETHERLANDS

American International School of Rotterdam
Status Private
Programme Diploma
Diploma Coordinator Evelyn Armstrong
Gender Coeducational
Languages English
Boarding/day Day
Verhulstlaan 21, Rotterdam WJ 3055, Netherlands
TELEPHONE: +31 10 422 5351
FAX: +31 10 422 4075
EMAIL: queries@aisr.nl
WEBSITE: www.aisr.nl

AMERICAN SCHOOL OF THE HAGUE
Status Private
Programme Diploma
Diploma Coordinator Victor Ferreira
Gender Coeducational
Languages English
Boarding/day Day
Rijksstraatweg 200, 2241BX Wassenaar, Netherlands
TELEPHONE: +31 70 512 1080
FAX: +31 70 51 12400
EMAIL: admissions@ash.nl
WEBSITE: www.ash.nl
see full details on page 48

AMSTERDAM INTERNATIONAL COMMUNITY SCHOOL
Status State
Programme Diploma
Diploma Coordinator Elizabeth Ann Young
Gender Coeducational
Languages English
Boarding/day Day
Prinses Irenestraat 59, 1077 WV Amsterdam, Netherlands
TELEPHONE: +31 20 577 1240
FAX: +31 20 577 1249
EMAIL: info@aics.eu
WEBSITE: www.aics.eu
see full details on page 50

Arnhem International School
Status State
Programme MYP, Diploma
Diploma Coordinator Mieke Ensink
MYP Coordinator Rubin Borges
Gender Coeducational
Languages English
Boarding/day Day
Groningensingel 1245, Arnhem HZ 6835 HZ, Netherlands
TELEPHONE: +31 26 3200111/4
FAX: +31 26 3200113
EMAIL: avanlanen@lorentzlyceum.nl
WEBSITE: www.arnheminternationalschool.nl

International School Eerde
Status Private
Programme Diploma
Diploma Coordinator Heidi Lenoir
Gender Coeducational
Languages English
Boarding/day Mixed
Kasteellaan 1, Ommen PJ 7731, Netherlands
TELEPHONE: +31 529 451452
FAX: +31 529 456377
EMAIL: info@eerde.nl
WEBSITE: www.eerde.nl

International School Hilversum 'Alberdingk Thijm'
Status State
Programme MYP, Diploma
Diploma Coordinator Glyn Jones
MYP Coordinator Sannerijn Jansen
Gender Coeducational
Languages English
Boarding/day Day
Emmastraat 56, Hilversum 1213 AL, Netherlands
TELEPHONE: + 31 35 6729931
FAX: + 31 35 6729939
EMAIL: j.vandriel@klg.nl
WEBSITE: www.ishilversum.nl

International School Maastricht
Status State
Programme Diploma
Diploma Coordinator Maurice Tonnacr
Gender Coeducational
Languages English
Boarding/day Day
PO Box 1187, 6201 BD Maastricht, Netherlands
TELEPHONE: +31 43 367 4666
FAX: +31 43 367 0809
EMAIL: admin@ism.portamosana.nl
WEBSITE: www.ismaastricht.nl

International School of Amsterdam
Status Private
Programme PYP, MYP, Diploma
Diploma Coordinator Donald LeBeau
MYP Coordinator Helen Forde
PYP Coordinator Susan Loban
Gender Coeducational
Languages English
Boarding/day Day
PO Box 920, Amstelveen 1180 AX, Netherlands
TELEPHONE: +31 20 347 1111
FAX: +31 20 347 1222
EMAIL: egreene@isa.nl
WEBSITE: www.isa.nl

International School The Rijnlands Lyceum
Status State
Programme MYP, Diploma
Diploma Coordinator Jonathan Symmons
MYP Coordinator Leonore Kromhout
Gender Coeducational
Languages English
Boarding/day Mixed
Apollolaan 1, Oegstgeest BA 2341, Netherlands
TELEPHONE: +31 71 5193 555
FAX: +31 71 5193 550
EMAIL: j.swieringa@rijnlandsluceum-rlo.nl
WEBSITE: www.isrlo.nl

International Secondary School Eindhoven
Status State
Programme MYP, Diploma
Diploma Coordinator Ian Rutherford
MYP Coordinator Ann Cloutier
Gender Coeducational
Languages English
Boarding/day Day
Venetiestraat 43, Eindhoven RM 5632, Netherlands
TELEPHONE: +31 40 242 68 35
FAX: +31 40 256 63 44
EMAIL: mwatts@issehv.nl
WEBSITE: www.issehv.nl

Laar en Berg
Status State
Programme MYP
MYP Coordinator Beata Hitchcock
Gender Coeducational
Languages English
Boarding/day Day
Langsakker 4, Laren GB 1251, Netherlands
TELEPHONE: +31 3553 95422
FAX: +31 3553 18046
EMAIL: r.stoelinga@klg.nl
WEBSITE: www.laarenberg.nl

Maartenscollege
Status Private/state
Programme MYP, Diploma
Diploma Coordinator Joke Jansma
MYP Coordinator Michael Weston
Gender Coeducational
Languages English
Boarding/day Day
PO Box 6105, Groningen HC 9702,
Netherlands
TELEPHONE: +31 50 534 0084
EMAIL: m.b.weston@maartens.nl
WEBSITE: www.maartenscollege.nl

Rotterdam International Secondary School
Status State
Programme Diploma
Diploma Coordinator Jane Forrest
Gender Coeducational
Languages English
Boarding/day Day
Bentincklaan 280, Rotterdam 3039 KK,
Netherlands
TELEPHONE: +31 10 890 7744
FAX: +31 10 890 7755
EMAIL: admin.riss@wolfert.nl
WEBSITE: www.wolfert.nl/riss

The British School in The Netherlands
Status Private
Programme Diploma
Diploma Coordinator Bridget van de Pol
Gender Coeducational
Languages English
Boarding/day Day
Jan van Hooflan 3, 2252 BG Voorschoten,
Netherlands
TELEPHONE: +31 (0) 71 560 2222
FAX: +31 (0) 71 560 2200
EMAIL: senior@britishschool.nl
WEBSITE: www.britishschool.nl

The International School of The Hague
Status State/private
Programme MYP, Diploma
Diploma Coordinator Mr K Mythen
MYP Coordinator Marian Cunnane
Gender Coeducational
Languages English
Boarding/day Day
Wijndaelerduin 1, The Hague 2554 BX,
Netherlands
TELEPHONE: +31 70 328 1450
FAX: +31 70 328 2049
EMAIL: p.kotrc@ishthehague.nl
WEBSITE: www.ishthehague.nl

Violenschool International Primary School
Status State
Programme PYP
PYP Coordinator Judy Blundell
Gender Coeducational
Boarding/day Day
Rembrandtlaan 30, Hilversum BH 1213,
Netherlands
TELEPHONE: +31 35 6216 053
FAX: +31 35 6246 878
EMAIL: info@ipsviolen.nl
WEBSITE: ipsviolen.nl

NIGERIA

American International School of Lagos
Status Private
Programme Diploma
Diploma Coordinator Carla Massoud
Gender Coeducational
Languages English
Boarding/day Day
c/o Sandy Hackbarth, Tacoma Public Schools,
601 South 8th Street, PO Box 1357, Tacoma
WA 98401, USA
TELEPHONE: +234 1 461 0985
FAX: +234 1 461 0986
EMAIL: info@aislagos.com
WEBSITE: www.aislagos.com

D-Ivy College
Status Private
Programme Diploma
Diploma Coordinator Oyinlola Ilo
Gender Coeducational
Languages English
Boarding/day Mixed
32 Allen Avenue, Ikeja, Lagos, Nigeria
TELEPHONE: +234 1 7914447
FAX: +234 4971329
EMAIL: omoilo@hotmail.com
WEBSITE: www.d-ivycollege.com

Ibadan International School
Status Private
Programme PYP
PYP Coordinator Valerie Aimakhu
Gender Coeducational
Languages English
Boarding/day Day
c/o Busi & Stephenson, 101-103 Bold Street,
Liverpool L1 4HL, UK
TELEPHONE: +234 2 231 0742
FAX: +234 2 231 0759
EMAIL: motunige2004@yahoo.co.uk
WEBSITE:
www.ibadaninternationalschool.com

NORWAY

Arendal Videregående Skole
Status State
Programme Diploma
Diploma Coordinator Liina Bårdsen
Gender Coeducational
Languages English
Boarding/day Day
Postboks 325, Arendal 4803, Norway
TELEPHONE: +47 37 00 02 00
FAX: +47 37 00 02 01
EMAIL: Dag.Samuelsen@arendal.vgs.no
WEBSITE: www.arendal.vgs.no

Ås videregående skole
Status State
Programme Diploma
Diploma Coordinator Margrethe Hall
Christensen
Gender Coeducational
Languages English
Boarding/day Day
Postboks 10, Ås N - 1430, Norway
TELEPHONE: +47 64 97 57 00
FAX: +47 64 97 57 01
EMAIL: per.lien@aas.vgs.no
WEBSITE: www.aas.vgs.no

Berg Videregående Skole
Status State
Programme Diploma
Diploma Coordinator Jean H Lundberg
Gender Coeducational
Languages English
Boarding/day Day
John Colletts allé 106, Oslo 0870, Norway
TELEPHONE: +47 22 58 72 00
FAX: +47 22 95 07 85
EMAIL: berit.hetland@ude.oslo.kommune.no
WEBSITE: www.berg.vgs.no

Bergen Katedralskole

Status State
Programme Diploma
Diploma Coordinator Erik Thomassen
Gender Coeducational
Languages English
Boarding/day Day
Postboks 414, Bergen 5828, Norway
TELEPHONE: +47 55 33 8200
FAX: +47 5 5338201
WEBSITE: www.hordaland-f.kommune.no/bks

Finnfjordbotn Vidaregåande Skole

Status State
Programme Diploma
Diploma Coordinator Vivian Jakobsen
Gender Coeducational
Languages English
Boarding/day Mixed
Finnsnes 9300, Norway
TELEPHONE: +47 77 85 08 00
FAX: +47 77 85 08 01
EMAIL: margoth.hovda.lien@tromsfylke.no
WEBSITE: www.finnfjordbotn.vgs.no

Frederik II videregående skole

Status State
Programme Diploma
Diploma Coordinator Carsten Dyndale
Gender Coeducational
Languages English
Boarding/day Day
PB 523, Merkurveien 2, Fredrikstad 1612, Norway
TELEPHONE: +47 69 36 64 00
FAX: +47 69 36 64 01
EMAIL: frederikii.vgs@ostfold-f.kommune.no
WEBSITE: www.frederikii.vgs.no

Gjøvik videregående skole

Status State
Programme Diploma
Diploma Coordinator Ivar Brandt
Gender Coeducational
Languages English
Boarding/day Day
PO Box 534, 2803 Gjøvik, Oppland, Norway
TELEPHONE: +47 6113 1300
EMAIL: aase.sletten@oppland.org
WEBSITE: www.gjovik.vgs.no

International School of Bergen

Status Private
Programme MYP
MYP Coordinator Gillian Boniface
Gender Coeducational
Languages English
Boarding/day Day
Vilheim Bjerknesvei 15, Bergen 5081, Norway
TELEPHONE: +47 55 306330
FAX: +47 55 306331
EMAIL: june@isob.no

International School of Stavanger

Status Private
Programme Diploma
Diploma Coordinator Lynn Park
Gender Coeducational
Languages English
Boarding/day Day
Treskeveien 3, Hafrsfjord 4043, Norway
TELEPHONE: +47 51554300
FAX: +47 51554301
EMAIL: lduevel@isstavanger.no
WEBSITE: www.isstavanger.no

International School Telemark

Status Private
Programme MYP
MYP Coordinator Robert Browne Laverick
Gender Coeducational
Languages English
Boarding/day Day
Tormod Gjestlandsvei 52, Porsgrunn 3936, Norway
TELEPHONE: +47 3592 7100
FAX: +47 3592 7101
EMAIL: paul@istelemark.no
WEBSITE: www.istelemark.no

Kongsberg International School

Status State
Programme PYP, MYP
MYP Coordinator Andrew Gregory
PYP Coordinator Heikki Soini
Gender Coeducational
Languages English
Boarding/day Day
Dyrmyr gate 41, Kongsberg 3611, Norway
TELEPHONE: +47 32 2993 80
FAX: +47 32 2993 81
EMAIL: catherine.jolly@kischool.org
WEBSITE: www.kischool.org

Kongsberg videregående skole

Status State
Programme Diploma
Diploma Coordinator Jan Stokseth
Gender Coeducational
Languages English
Boarding/day Day
Postboks 424, Kongsberg 3604, Norway
TELEPHONE: +47 3286 7600
FAX: +47 3286 7650
EMAIL: kirsten.bockman@skole.bfk.no
WEBSITE: www.kongsberg.vgs.no

Lillestrom Videregaende Skole

Status State
Programme Diploma
Diploma Coordinator Brit Jordet
Gender Coeducational
Languages English
Boarding/day Day
Postboks 333, Lillestrom, Akershus 2001, Norway
TELEPHONE: +47 63 89 06 00
FAX: +47 63 89 06 10
EMAIL: tor.nakstad@lillestrom.vgs.no

Nesbru Videregaende Skole

Status State
Programme Diploma
Diploma Coordinator Knut Gundersen
Gender Coeducational
Languages English
Boarding/day Day
Halvard Torgersensvei 8, Postbox 38, Nesbru 1378, Norway
TELEPHONE: +47 66 854 400
FAX: +47 66 854 410
EMAIL: inger-marit.oymo@nesbru.vgs.no
WEBSITE: www.nesbru.vgs.no

Oslo International School

Status Private
Programme Diploma
Diploma Coordinator Peter Luitjens
Gender Coeducational
Languages English
Boarding/day Day
PO Box 53, Bekkestua 1318, Norway
TELEPHONE: +47 67 8182 90
FAX: +47 2 214 4044
EMAIL: director@oslois.no
WEBSITE: www.oslointernationalschool.no

Red Cross Nordic United World College

Status Private
Programme Diploma
Diploma Coordinator Dr Alistair Robertson
Gender Coeducational
Languages English
Boarding/day Boarding
N - 6968 Flekke, Fjaler, Norway
TELEPHONE: +47 5773 7005
FAX: +47 5773 5555
EMAIL: info@rcnuwc.no
WEBSITE: www.rcnuwc.no

Sandefjord Videregaende Skole

Status State
Programme Diploma
Diploma Coordinator Finn Röijen
Gender Coeducational
Languages English
Boarding/day Day
Postboks 2006, Sandefjord 3202, Norway
TELEPHONE: +47 33 488 690
FAX: +47 33 488 621
EMAIL: annesm@vfk.no
WEBSITE: www.svgs.vfk.no

Skagerak International School

Status Private
Programme Diploma
Diploma Coordinator Michael Meszaros
Gender Coeducational
Languages English
Boarding/day Day
Framnesveien 7, Sandefjord 3222, Norway
TELEPHONE: +47 33 42 38 10
FAX: +47 33 46 93 63
EMAIL: lars.ask@skagerak.org
WEBSITE: www.skagerak.org

Skagerak Primary and Middle School
Status Private
Programme PYP, MYP
MYP Coordinator Janet Field
PYP Coordinator Jon Davidson
Gender Coeducational
Languages English
Boarding/day Day
Kjellbergveien 2, Sandefjord 3213, Norway
TELEPHONE: +47 33423800
EMAIL: janet.field@skagerak.org
WEBSITE: www.skagerak.org/

St Olav Videregaende Skole
Status State
Programme Diploma
Diploma Coordinator Heather Arneson
Gender Coeducational
Languages English
Boarding/day Day
PO Box 590, Stavanger 4001, Norway
TELEPHONE: +47 5 184 9904
FAX: +47 5 184 9950
EMAIL: gafi@rfk.rogaland-f.kommune.no
WEBSITE: www.st-olav.vgs.no/

Trondheim International School
Status Private
Programme PYP, MYP
MYP Coordinator Shane Tastad
PYP Coordinator Shane Tastad
Gender Coeducational
Languages English
Boarding/day Day
Festningsgata 2, Trondheim 7014, Norway
TELEPHONE: +47 7351 4800
FAX: +47 7352 4801
EMAIL: office@this.no
WEBSITE: www.this.no

Trondheim Katedralskole
Status State
Programme Diploma
Diploma Coordinator Elin Øksnes
Gender Coeducational
Languages English
Boarding/day Day
Munkegaten 8, Trondheim 7013, Norway
TELEPHONE: +47 73 54 01 00
FAX: +47 73 54 01 01
EMAIL: anne.lise.drege@stft.no
WEBSITE: www.trondheim-katedral.vgs.no

Vardafjell Videregående Skole
Status State
Programme Diploma
Diploma Coordinator Åse Lønø Amlie
Gender Coeducational
Languages English
Boarding/day Day
Spannaveien 25, Haugesund 5532, Norway
TELEPHONE: +47 5270 9910
FAX: +47 5270 9915
EMAIL: asbjoern.velde@rogfk.no
WEBSITE:
www.rogaland-f.kommune.no/ffivardafje/

PALESTINE

Friends School
Status Private
Programme Diploma
Diploma Coordinator Luai Awwad
Gender Coeducational
Languages English
Boarding/day Day
PO Box 66, West Bank, Palestine, via Israel
TELEPHONE: +972 229 56230
FAX: +972 229 56231
EMAIL: amra@palfriends.org

POLAND

33 Liceum im M Kopernika
Status State
Programme Diploma
Diploma Coordinator Grazyna Kania
Gender Coeducational
Languages English
Boarding/day Day
ul Bema 76, Warsaw 01-225, Poland
TELEPHONE: +48 22 632 75 70
FAX: +48 22 632 1376
EMAIL: astoma@kopernik.edu.pl

American School of Warsaw
Status Private
Programme Diploma
Diploma Coordinator Malgosia Hydzik
Gender Coeducational
Languages English
Boarding/day Day
Bielawa, ul Warszawska 202, Konstancin-Jeziorna 05-520, Poland
TELEPHONE: +48 22 702 8500
FAX: +48 22 702 8516
EMAIL: admissions@asw.waw.pl
WEBSITE: www.asw.waw.pl

British International School of Cracow
Status Private
Programme Diploma
Diploma Coordinator Stanislaw Kwiecinski
Gender Coeducational
Languages English
Boarding/day Day
Ul Smolensk 25, 31-108 Kraków, Poland
TELEPHONE: +48 12 292 64 80
FAX: +48 12 2926 481
EMAIL: admin@bisc.krakow.pl
WEBSITE: www.bisc.krakow.pl

High School No 111 in Gdansk
Status State
Programme Diploma
Diploma Coordinator Alina Spychala
Gender Coeducational
Languages English
Boarding/day Day
ul Topolowa 7, Gdansk 80255, Poland
TELEPHONE: +48 5834 10671
FAX: +48 5234 10671
EMAIL: gbogusz@lo3.gdansk.ids.pl
WEBSITE: www.lo3.gdansk.ids.pl

I Liceum Ogólnoksztalcace im St Staszica w Lublinie
Status State
Programme Diploma
Diploma Coordinator Monika Trznadel
Gender Coeducational
Languages English
Boarding/day Boarding
Al Raclawickie 26, Lublin 20043, Poland
TELEPHONE: +48 81 441 1460
EMAIL: monikat@bachus.1lo.lublin.pl
WEBSITE: www.1lo.lublin.pl

I Prywatne Liceum Ogolnoksztalcace
Status Private
Programme Diploma
Diploma Coordinator Iwona Richter
Gender Coeducational
Languages English
Boarding/day Day
ul Dabrowskiego 262/280, Poznan PL-60-406, Poland
TELEPHONE: +48 618 477 435
FAX: +48 618 477 456
EMAIL: iplo@main.amu.edu.pl

I SLO im Jam Saheba Digvijay Sinhji
Status State
Programme Diploma
Diploma Coordinator Ewa Stawecka
Gender Coeducational
Languages English
Boarding/day Day
Ul Raszyñska 22, Warszawa 02 026, Poland
TELEPHONE: +48 22 822 25 15
EMAIL: secretariat@neuron.bednarska.ed.pl
WEBSITE: www.bednarska.edu.pl

II Liceum Ogólnoksztalcace im Stefana Batorego
Status State
Programme Diploma
Diploma Coordinator Joanna Szczesniak
Gender Coeducational
Languages English
Boarding/day Day
ul Mysliwiecka 6, Warsawa 00459, Poland
TELEPHONE: +48 22 628 2101
EMAIL: mzielicz@poczta.onet.pl
WEBSITE: www.batory.edu.pl

II LO im Gen Zamoyskiej i H Modrzejewskiej

Status State
Programme Diploma
Diploma Coordinator Barbara Wieloch
Gender Coeducational
Languages English
Boarding/day Day
Matejki 8/10, Poznan 60760, Poland
TELEPHONE: +48 61 866 2892
FAX: +48 61 866 2892
WEBSITE: www.2lo.poznan.pl

III Liceum Ogolnoksztalcace, Gdynia

Status State
Programme MYP, Diploma
Diploma Coordinator Zofia Krakowiak-Michlewicz
MYP Coordinator Hanna Goworowska - Adamska
Gender Coeducational
Languages English, Polish
Boarding/day Mixed
Legionów 27, Gdynia 81-405, Poland
TELEPHONE: +48 58 622 1833
FAX: +48 58 622 1529
EMAIL: sako@lo3.gdynia.pl
WEBSITE: www.lo3.gdynia.pl

International American School

Status Private
Programme Diploma
Diploma Coordinator Andrzej Cichy
Gender Coeducational
Languages English
Boarding/day Day
Ul Dembego 18, Warszawa 02-796, Poland
TELEPHONE: +48 22 649 1442
EMAIL: principal@ias.edu.pl
WEBSITE: www.ias.edu.pl

International European School Warsaw

Status Private
Programme Diploma
Diploma Coordinator Irena Chrzanowska
Gender Coeducational
Languages English
Boarding/day Day
Wiertnicza 75, Warsaw 02-952, Poland
TELEPHONE: +48 842 44 48
FAX: +48 842 44 48 ext 108
EMAIL: mira@ies.waw.pl
WEBSITE: http:/www.ies-warsaw.pl

International School of Poznan

Status Private
Programme Diploma
Diploma Coordinator Iwona Richter
Gender Coeducational
Languages English
Boarding/day Day
Ul Taczanowskiego 18, Poznan 60-147, Poland
TELEPHONE: +48 61 646 37 60
FAX: +48 61 646 37 65
EMAIL: info@isop.pl
WEBSITE: www.isop.pl

IV Liceum Ogolnoksztalcace im.Emilii Szczanieckiej

Status State
Programme Diploma
Diploma Coordinator Agnieszka Bojkow
Gender Coeducational
Languages English
Boarding/day Day
ul Pomorska 16, Lodz 91-416, Poland
TELEPHONE: +48 42 6336293
FAX: +48 42 6336293
EMAIL: k.felde@interia.pl
WEBSITE: www.4liceum.pl

Kolegium Europejskie

Status Private
Programme Diploma
Diploma Coordinator Joanna Pillans
Gender Coeducational
Languages English
Boarding/day Day
Kazimierza Wielkiego 33, Krakow 30-074, Poland
TELEPHONE: +48 12 632 46 29
FAX: +48 12 632 46 29
EMAIL: kolegium@ke.edu.pl
WEBSITE: www.ke.edu.pl

Liceum Ogólnoksztalcace Ekola

Status State
Programme Diploma
Diploma Coordinator Adriana Kurowska-Mitas
Gender Coeducational
Languages English
Boarding/day Day
Ul Zielinskiego 56, Wroclaw 53534, Poland
TELEPHONE: +48 71 3614 370
EMAIL: fundacja@ekola.edu.pl
WEBSITE: www.ekola.edu.pl

Liceum Ogólnoksztalcace Nr V in Wroclaw

Status State
Programme Diploma
Diploma Coordinator Aleksandra Podolska-Strycharska
Gender Coeducational
Languages English
Boarding/day Day
ul Grochowa 13, Wroclaw PL 53-523 53523, Poland
TELEPHONE: +48 713 619266
FAX: +48 713 619266
EMAIL: ssocha@lo5.wroc.pl
WEBSITE: www.lo5.wroc.pl

LIV Prywatne Liceum Ogólnoksztalcace

Status Private
Programme Diploma
Diploma Coordinator Joanna Majorek
Gender Female
Languages English
Boarding/day Mixed
ul Czerniakowska 137, Warszawa 00-720, Poland
TELEPHONE: +48 22 841 3854
EMAIL: ruth.kawa@gmail.com
WEBSITE: www.nazaretanki.edu.pl

Meridian International School

Status Private
Programme Diploma
Diploma Coordinator Arif Erkol
Gender Coeducational
Languages English
Boarding/day Day
ul Radarowa 6, Warsaw 02-137, Poland
TELEPHONE: +48 22 868 2503
EMAIL: principal@meridian.edu.pl
WEBSITE: www.meridian.edu.pl

Paderewski Private Grammar School

Status Private
Programme MYP, Diploma
Diploma Coordinator Danuta Paterek
MYP Coordinator Dorota Smedek
Gender Coeducational
Languages English
Boarding/day Day
ul Symfoniczna 1, Lublin 20-853, Poland
TELEPHONE: +48 81 740-75-43
FAX: +48 81 441 9936
EMAIL: akademos@akademos.com.pl
WEBSITE: www.paderewski.lublin.pl

Prywatne Liceum Ogólnoksztalcace im. Melchiora Wankowicza

Status Private
Programme Diploma
Diploma Coordinator Justyna Proksza
Gender Coeducational
Languages English
Boarding/day Day
ul. Witosa 18, Katowice 40832, Poland
TELEPHONE: +48 322549194
FAX: +48 322015152
EMAIL: jolakaluza@wp.pl
WEBSITE: www.szkolajakdom.szkolnastrona.pl

Prywatne Liceum Ogólnoksztalcace nr 32

Status Private
Programme Diploma
Diploma Coordinator Jolanta Choinska-Mika
Gender Coeducational
Languages English
Boarding/day Day
Ul Górska 7, Warsaw 00740, Poland
TELEPHONE: +48 22 841 1572
FAX: +48 22 841 1572
EMAIL: hannaplo32@interia.pl
WEBSITE: www.plo32pg33.edu.pl

Szczecin International School
Status Private
Programme Diploma
Diploma Coordinator Jeremy Clark
Gender Coeducational
Languages English
Boarding/day Day
ul A Mickiewicza 49, Szczecin 70385, Poland
TELEPHONE: +48 91 4240 300
EMAIL: maria.sawka@sis.info.pol
WEBSITE: www.sis.info.pl

Szkola Europejska – Gimnazjum/Liceum
Status Private
Programme Diploma
Diploma Coordinator Beata J Biala
Gender Coeducational
Languages English
Boarding/day Day
ul Tuszynska 31, Lódz 93 - 020, Poland
TELEPHONE: +48 42 682 12 10
EMAIL: u.moryc@wp.pl
WEBSITE: www.szkolaeuropejska.pl

The British School
Status Private
Programme Diploma
Diploma Coordinator Mary Donnellan
Gender Coeducational
Languages English
Boarding/day Day
Ul Limanowskiego 15, Warsaw 02 943, Poland
TELEPHONE: +48 22 842 32 81
FAX: +48 22 842 32 81
EMAIL: tmcgrath@thebritishschool.pl
WEBSITE: www.thebritishschool.pl

VI Liceum Ogólnoksztalcace im J Slowackiego w Kielcach
Status State
Programme Diploma
Diploma Coordinator Malgorzata Kulakowska
Gender Coeducational
Languages English
Boarding/day Day
ul Gagarina 5, Kielce 25031, Poland
TELEPHONE: +48 41 361 55 56
FAX: +48 41 361 34 73
EMAIL: slowacki@6lo-kielce.edu.pl
WEBSITE: www.6lo-kielce.edu.pl

Zespol Szkol Numer 4 – IX Liceum Ogólnoksztalcace
Status State
Programme Diploma
Diploma Coordinator Malgorzata Kozielewicz
Gender Coeducational
Languages English
Boarding/day Day
Ul Zofii Nalkowskiej 9, Bydgoszcz 86866, Poland
TELEPHONE: +48 52 3610 885
EMAIL: ewanow17@o2.pl
WEBSITE: www.lo9gim17.pl

Zespól Szkól Ogólnoksztalcacych im. Pawla z Tarsu
Status Non-profit Funded By Social Society
Programme Diploma
Diploma Coordinator Agnieszka Kantorowicz
Gender Coeducational
Languages English
Boarding/day Day
ul Piotra Skargi 24, Jozefow 05-420, Poland
TELEPHONE: +48 22 789 5969
EMAIL: rylskab@interia.pl
WEBSITE: www.schola-konwalia.iq.pl

PORTUGAL

Carlucci American International School of Lisbon
Status Private
Programme Diploma
Diploma Coordinator Ana Almeida
Gender Coeducational
Languages English
Boarding/day Day
Rua Antonio dos Reis, 95, Linhó, Sintra 2710-301, Portugal
TELEPHONE: +351 21 923 9800
FAX: +351 21 923 9899
EMAIL: info@caislisbon.org
WEBSITE: www.caislisbon.org

Colegio Planalto
Status Private
Programme Diploma
Diploma Coordinator Jose Manuel Ferrão
Gender Male
Languages English
Boarding/day Day
Rua Armindo Rodrigues, 28, Lisbon 1600-414, Portugal
TELEPHONE: +351 21 754 15 30
FAX: +351 21 754 15 15
EMAIL: director@colegioplanalto.pt
WEBSITE: www.colegioplanalto.pt

Oporto British School
Status Private
Programme Diploma
Diploma Coordinator Paul Stedman
Gender Coeducational
Languages English
Boarding/day Day
Rua da Cerca 326/338, 4150-201, Porto 4150-201, Portugal
TELEPHONE: +351 22 616 6660
FAX: +351 22 616 6668
EMAIL: obs.school@mail.telepac.pt
WEBSITE: www.obs.edu.pt

ST DOMINIC'S INTERNATIONAL SCHOOL
Status Private
Programme PYP, MYP, Diploma
Diploma Coordinator Richard Parker
MYP Coordinator Sharon Thompson
PYP Coordinator Amanda Jones
Gender Coeducational
Languages English
Boarding/day Day
Rua Maria Brown, Outeiro de Polima, 2785-816 S Domingos de Rana, Portugal
TELEPHONE: +351 21 444 0434 (or 448 0550)
FAX: +351 21 444 3072
EMAIL: school@dominics-int.org
WEBSITE: www.dominics-int.org
see full details on page 139

St Julian's School
Status Private
Programme Diploma
Diploma Coordinator Zelia Pereira
Gender Coeducational
Languages English
Boarding/day Day
Secondary School, Quinta Nova, Carcavelos Codex 2776-601, Portugal
TELEPHONE: +351 21 4585300
FAX: +351 21 4585313
EMAIL: headmaster@stjulians.com
WEBSITE: www.stjulians.com

QATAR

Al Bayan Educational Complex for Girls
Status Private
Programme Diploma
Diploma Coordinator Rana Naji
Gender Female
Languages English
Boarding/day Day
PO Box 23533, Doha, Qatar
TELEPHONE: +974 436 7824
FAX: +974 436 7851
EMAIL: n_almutawa@yahoo.com
WEBSITE: www.albayan.edu.com

Al Jazeera Academy
Status Private
Programme Diploma
Diploma Coordinator Fiona Littlewood
Gender Coeducational
Languages English
Boarding/day Day
PO Box 22250, Mesaimeer, Doha, Qatar
TELEPHONE: +974 469 3777
FAX: +974 468 2555
EMAIL: director@aja.edu.qa
WEBSITE: www.aja.edu.qa

Al Wakra Independent Secondary School

Status Private
Programme Diploma
Diploma Coordinator Ghassan N Bedwan
Gender Male
Languages English
Boarding/day Day
PO Box 80150, Al Wakrah, Qatar
TELEPHONE: +974 464 3739
FAX: +974 464 1019
EMAIL: wissfb@wakra.edu.qa
WEBSITE: www.wakra.edu.qa

Qatar Academy

Status Private
Programme PYP, MYP, Diploma
Diploma Coordinator Ron Smith
MYP Coordinator Chad Schwaberow
PYP Coordinator Roula Fallaha
Gender Coeducational
Languages English
Boarding/day Day
PO Box 1129, Al Luqta Street, Doha, Qatar
TELEPHONE: +974 482 6666
FAX: +974 4802769
EMAIL: ghedger@qf.org.qa
WEBSITE: www.qataracademy.edu.qa

QATAR LEADERSHIP ACADEMY

Status Private
Programme Diploma
Diploma Coordinator Andrew S Frezuldeen
Gender Male
Languages English, Arabic
Boarding/day Boarding
PO Box 24421, Doha, Qatar
TELEPHONE: +974 474 2222
FAX: +974 474 2173
EMAIL: bbehr@qf.org.qa
WEBSITE: www.qla.edu.qa
see full details on page 122

The Gulf English School

Status Private
Programme Diploma
Diploma Coordinator Bob Turrell
Gender Coeducational
Languages English
Boarding/day Day
PO Box 2440, Doha, Qatar
TELEPHONE: +974 4873865 / 69
EMAIL: headteacher@gulfenglishschool.com
WEBSITE: www.gulfenglishschool.com

ROMANIA

American International School of Bucharest

Status Private
Programme PYP, MYP, Diploma
Diploma Coordinator Tiffany Hay
MYP Coordinator Tracy Arnold
PYP Coordinator Jimena Zalba
Gender Coeducational
Languages English
Boarding/day Day
Sos Pipera-Tunari 196, Voluntari, Jud Ilfov, Bucharest 077190, Romania
TELEPHONE: +40 (21) 204 4300
FAX: +40 (21) 211 0104
EMAIL: dottaviano@aisb.ro
WEBSITE: www.aisb.ro

Mark Twain International School

Status Private
Programme PYP, Diploma
Diploma Coordinator Florin Droc
PYP Coordinator Irene Popa-Scurtu
Gender Coeducational
Languages English, Romanian
Boarding/day Day
25b Erou Iancu Nicolae Street, Voluntari - Ilfov, Ilfov 077190, Romania
TELEPHONE: +4021 267 8912
FAX: +4021 267 8985
EMAIL: directors@marktwainschool.ro
WEBSITE: www.marktwainschool.ro

RUSSIAN FEDERATION

Anglo-American School of Moscow

Status Private
Programme PYP, Diploma
Diploma Coordinator Theressa Smith
PYP Coordinator Tracy France-George
Gender Coeducational
Languages English
Boarding/day Day
c/o American Embassy, Box M, 00140 Helsinki Finland
TELEPHONE: +7 495 231 4488
FAX: +7 495 231 4475
EMAIL: drew.alexander@aas.ru
WEBSITE: www.aas.ru

British International School, Moscow

Status Private
Programme Diploma
Diploma Coordinator Peter Giddens
Gender Coeducational
Languages English
Boarding/day Day
Novoyasenevsky prospekt 19/5, Moscow 117593, Russian Federation
TELEPHONE: +7 495 425 5100
FAX: +7 495 426 5400
EMAIL: richard.naylor@bismoscow.com
WEBSITE: www.bismoscow.com

Education through Dialogue School

Status Private
Programme Diploma
Diploma Coordinator Olga Suvorkova
Gender Coeducational
Languages English
Boarding/day Day
Nekrasova Street, 19, St Petersburg 191014, Russian Federation
TELEPHONE: +7 812 272 0360
FAX: +7 812 275 0257
EMAIL: pilotextern@mail.ru
WEBSITE: www.shod.ru

Educational Centre 'Gamma' #1404

Status State
Programme MYP
MYP Coordinator Elena Andreeva
Gender Coeducational
Languages English
Boarding/day Day
3/5 Boljshaya Olenjay Street, Moscow 107014, Russian Federation
TELEPHONE: +8 495 268 46 86
FAX: +8 495 268 46 30
EMAIL: zolidia@rambler.ru
WEBSITE: www.gamma1404.ru

European Gymnasium

Status Private
Programme MYP, Diploma
Diploma Coordinator Gyulnar Zamaletdinova
MYP Coordinator Elena Vlasova
Gender Coeducational
Languages English, Russian
Boarding/day Day
House 3, 3rd Sokolnicheskaya St, Moscow 107014, Russian Federation
TELEPHONE: +7 495 268 4404
FAX: +7 495 268 4404
EMAIL: info@eurogym.ru
WEBSITE: www.eurogym.ru

Krasnoyarsk Gimnazia "Univers" #1

Status State
Programme Diploma
Diploma Coordinator Evgenia Skuratovich
Gender Coeducational
Languages English
Boarding/day Day
Korneeva Street, 50, Krasnoyarsk 66001, Russian Federation
TELEPHONE: +7 3912 43 63 56
FAX: +7 3912 43 63 56
EMAIL: bvv@univers.krasu.ru
WEBSITE: www.univers.krasu.ru

Linguistic School 1531
Status State
Programme MYP
MYP Coordinator Svetlana Ushakova
Gender Coeducational
Languages English
Boarding/day Day
Godovikov Street 4, Moscow RU-129085, Russian Federation
TELEPHONE: +7 495 287 25 71
FAX: +7 495 287 02 20
EMAIL: sch1531.edu@mtu-net.ru

Medical Technical Lyceum
Status State
Programme Diploma
Diploma Coordinator Natalia Bodyagina
Gender Coeducational
Languages English
Boarding/day Day
Polevaya str 74, Samara 443002, Russian Federation
TELEPHONE: +7 846 237 0343
FAX: +7 846 237 0343
EMAIL: alex@mtlic.samara.ru

Moscow Economic School
Status Private
Programme PYP, MYP, Diploma
Diploma Coordinator Alla Skvorkina
MYP Coordinator Elena Efimova
PYP Coordinator Tatiana Savelieva
Gender Coeducational
Languages English
Boarding/day Day
29 Zamorenova Street, Moscow 123022, Russian Federation
TELEPHONE: +7 495 252-24-06
FAX: +7 495 253-43-23
EMAIL: yuris@mes.ru
WEBSITE: www.mes.ru

Moscow Economic School, Campus Zaitsevo
Status Private
Programme PYP, MYP
MYP Coordinator Madlena Shaginyan
PYP Coordinator Larisa Zaitseva
Gender Coeducational
Languages English, Russian
Boarding/day Day
29 Zamorenova Street, Moscow 123022, Russian Federation
TELEPHONE: +7 495 780 5230
FAX: +7 495 780 5235
EMAIL: natalyak.mes.ru
WEBSITE: www.mes.ru

Moscow School 45
Status State
Programme MYP, Diploma
Diploma Coordinator Larissa Korabelshchikova
MYP Coordinator Alexander Kisin
Gender Coeducational
Languages English
Boarding/day Day
8 Grimau Str, Moscow 117036, Russian Federation
TELEPHONE: +7 (495) 1263382
FAX: +7 495 1264405
EMAIL: mshneyder@nm.ru
WEBSITE: http://schools.techno.ru/ms45

President School
Status Private
Programme Diploma
Diploma Coordinator Natalia Lyubomirskaya
OK Sosny, PO Uspenskoye, Odintsovski r-n Moscow Region 143030, Russian Federation
TELEPHONE: +7 495 786 7306
FAX: +7 495 786 7326
EMAIL: la-m@mail.ru
WEBSITE: www.president.edu.ru

School Premier
Status Private
Programme PYP, MYP, Diploma
Diploma Coordinator Natalia Lyubomirskaya
MYP Coordinator Alexey Mashkovtsev
PYP Coordinator Kholodkova Lioubov
Gender Coeducational
Languages English
Boarding/day Day
40/2 Shipilovskaya Str, Moscow 115653, Russian Federation
TELEPHONE: +7 495 393 0818
FAX: +7 4 95 3930711
EMAIL: lubow@premier.edu.ru
WEBSITE: www.premier.edu.ru

Vladivostok Boarding School for Gifted Children
Status State
Programme Diploma
Diploma Coordinator Natalia Nikolayevna Tischenko
Gender Coeducational
Languages Russian
Boarding/day Boarding
41 Gogolya Street, Primorskiy Krai, Vladivostok 690990, Russian Federation
TELEPHONE: +7 4232 31 61 36
FAX: +7 4232 31 61 36
EMAIL: koskaus@yahoo.com
WEBSITE: www.vvsu.ru/giftedschool

XXI CENTURY INTEGRATION INTERNATIONAL SECONDARY SCHOOL
Status Private
Programme MYP, Diploma
Diploma Coordinator Evgeny Mironov
MYP Coordinator Elena Nikeryassova
Gender Coeducational
Languages English
Boarding/day Day
Building 3, Stroginsky Boulevard 7, Moscow 123592, Russian Federation
TELEPHONE: +7 495 750 3102
FAX: +7 495 750 0197
EMAIL: kulichenkos@newmail.ru
WEBSITE: www.integration21.ru
see full details on page 163

RWANDA

Green Hills Academy
Status Private
Programme Diploma
Diploma Coordinator Alpana Mukherjee
Gender Coeducational
Languages English, French
Boarding/day Day
PO Box 6419, Nyarutarama, Kigali, Rwanda
TELEPHONE: +250 519 765
EMAIL: ronwallace@shaw.ca
WEBSITE: www.greenhillsacademy.rw

SAUDI ARABIA

American International School – Riyadh
Status Private
Programme Diploma
Diploma Coordinator Cristina Pennington
Gender Coeducational
Languages English
Boarding/day Day
PO Box 990, Riyadh 11421, Saudi Arabia
TELEPHONE: +966 1 491 4270
FAX: +966 1 491 7101
EMAIL: dgordon@ais-r.edu.sa
WEBSITE: www.ais-r.org

King Faisal School
Status Private
Programme Diploma
Diploma Coordinator Tawfiq Saleh
Gender Male
Languages English
Boarding/day Day
PO Box 94558, Riyadh 11614, Saudi Arabia
TELEPHONE: +966 1 482 0802
FAX: +966 1 482 1521
EMAIL: kfs@kfs.sch.sa
WEBSITE: www.kfs.sch.sa

The British International School of Jeddah
Status Private
Programme Diploma
Diploma Coordinator Jemma De Smidt
Gender Coeducational
Languages English
Boarding/day Day
PO Box 6453, Jeddah 21442, Saudi Arabia
TELEPHONE: +966 2 699 0019
FAX: +966 2 699 1943
EMAIL: conti@conti.sch.sa
WEBSITE: www.continentalschool.com

SENEGAL

West African College of the Atlantic
Status Private
Programme Diploma
Diploma Coordinator Karima Abbott
Gender Coeducational
Languages French
Boarding/day Day
BP 24340, Ouakam, Dakar, Senegal
TELEPHONE: +221 820 4929
FAX: +221 820 4929
EMAIL: wacadlih@telecomplus.sn

SERBIA

Crnjanski High School
Status Private
Programme Diploma
Diploma Coordinator Mirjana Krstulovic
Gender Coeducational
Languages English
Boarding/day Day
Djordja Ognjanovica 2, 11030 Belgrade, Serbia
TELEPHONE: +381 11 3548 825
EMAIL: krstulmi@sezampro.yu
WEBSITE: www.crnjanski.edu.yu

Gimnazija Ruder Boskovic
Status Private
Programme Diploma
Diploma Coordinator Ivana Vukmirica
Gender Coeducational
Languages English
Boarding/day Boarding
Kneza Vi eslava 17, Beograd, Srbija i Crna Gora 11000, Serbia
TELEPHONE: + 381 11 35 407 86
EMAIL: mladen.sarcevic@boskovic.edu.yu
WEBSITE: www.boskovic.edu.yu

International School of Belgrade
Status Private
Programme PYP, MYP, Diploma
Diploma Coordinator Aleka Novitski Bilan
MYP Coordinator Branka Sreckovic-Minic
PYP Coordinator Doriane Marvel
Gender Coeducational
Languages English
Boarding/day Day
Temi varska 19, Belgrade 11040, Serbia
TELEPHONE: +381 11 206 9999
FAX: +381 11 265 2619
EMAIL: esands@isb.co.yu
WEBSITE: www.isb.co.yu

SLOVAKIA

Gymnazium Jura Hronca
Status State
Programme Diploma
Diploma Coordinator Matej Gonda
Gender Coeducational
Languages English
Boarding/day Mixed
Novohradská 3, Bratislava 821 09, Slovakia
TELEPHONE: +421 2 555 711 22
EMAIL: zitna@gjh.sk
WEBSITE: www.gjh.sk

QSI International School of Bratislava
Status Private
Programme Diploma
Diploma Coordinator Michelle Lake
Gender Coeducational
Languages English
Boarding/day Day
Karloveská 64, Bratislava 4 84220, Slovakia
TELEPHONE: +421 2 6542 2844
FAX: +421 2 6541 1646
EMAIL: merrywade@qsi.org
WEBSITE: www.qsi.sk

The British International School
Status Private
Programme Diploma
Diploma Coordinator Ingrid Mornarova
Gender Coeducational
Languages English
Boarding/day Day
Peknikova 6, Bratislava 84102, Slovakia
TELEPHONE: +421 2 69307081/2
FAX: +421 2 69307083
EMAIL: info@bisb.sk
WEBSITE: www.bis.sk

SLOVENIA

Danila Kumar Primary School
Programme PYP, MYP
MYP Coordinator Barbara Gostisa
PYP Coordinator Kristina Fuerst
Gender Coeducational
Boarding/day Boarding
Godezeva 11, Ljubljana 1000, Slovenia
TELEPHONE: +386 01 5636 834
FAX: +386 01 5614 105
EMAIL: group2.osljdk@guest.arnes.si
WEBSITE: www.gimb.org

Druga Gimnazija Maribor
Status State
Programme Diploma
Diploma Coordinator Vesna Senica
Gender Coeducational
Languages English
Boarding/day Mixed
Trg Milosa Zidanska 1, 2000 Maribor 02, Slovenia
TELEPHONE: +386 2 3318004
FAX: +386 2 3324880
EMAIL: ivan.lorencic@guest.arnes.si

Gimnazija Bezigrad
Status State
Programme MYP, Diploma
Diploma Coordinator Mirko Mrcela
MYP Coordinator Barbara Gostisa
Gender Coeducational
Languages English
Boarding/day Day
Periceva 4, Ljubljana 1000, Slovenia
TELEPHONE: +386 1 3000 400
FAX: +386 1 3000 440
EMAIL: janez@gimb.org
WEBSITE: www.gimb.org

SOUTH AFRICA

AMERICAN INTERNATIONAL SCHOOL OF JOHANNESBURG
Status Private
Programme Diploma
Diploma Coordinator Sophie Hall
Gender Coeducational
Languages English
Boarding/day Day
Private Bag X4, Bryanston 2021, South Africa
TELEPHONE: +27 11 464 1505
FAX: +27 11 464 1327
EMAIL: rbeck@aisj-jhb.com
WEBSITE: www.aisj-jhb.com
see full details on page 45

International School of Hout Bay
Status Private
Programme Diploma
Diploma Coordinator Michele Marnitz
Gender Coeducational
Languages English
Boarding/day Day
Suite 164, Private Bag X14, Hout Bay, Cape Town 7872, South Africa
TELEPHONE: +27 21 790 6285
FAX: +27 21 790 5814
EMAIL: pelham.lindfield@iesedu.com
WEBSITE: www.sekhoutbay.org.za

SPAIN

ALOHA COLLEGE
Status Private
Programme Diploma
Diploma Coordinator Eugenio López
Gender Coeducational
Languages English, Spanish
Boarding/day Day
Urbanización el Angel, Nueva Andalucía, 29660 Marbella (Málaga), Spain
TELEPHONE: +34 95 281 41 33
FAX: +34 95 281 85 23
EMAIL: info@aloha-college.com
WEBSITE: www.aloha-college.com
see full details on page 43

American School of Barcelona
Status Private
Programme Diploma
Diploma Coordinator Lori J Lauscher
Gender Coeducational
Languages English
Boarding/day Day
Calle Balmes 7, 08950 Esplugues de Llobregat, Barcelona, Spain
TELEPHONE: +34 93 371 4016
FAX: +34 93 473 4787
EMAIL: info@a-s-b.com
WEBSITE: www.a-s-b.com

American School of Madrid
Status Private
Programme Diploma
Diploma Coordinator Johannah Eklund
Gender Coeducational
Languages English
Boarding/day Day
Apartado 80, Madrid 28080, Spain
TELEPHONE: +34 91 740 19 00
FAX: +34 9 1 357 26 78
EMAIL: williamohale@asmadrid.org
WEBSITE: www.asmadrid.org

American School of Valencia
Status Private
Programme Diploma
Diploma Coordinator Marc Boyer
Gender Coeducational
Languages English
Boarding/day Day
Urbanización Los Monasterios, Apartado de Correos 9, Puzol, Valencia 46530, Spain
TELEPHONE: +34 96 140 5412
FAX: +34 96 140 5039
EMAIL: saaratatem@asvalencia.org
WEBSITE: www.asvalencia.org

Bell-lloc Del Pla
Status Private
Programme Diploma
Diploma Coordinator Manel Montoliu Bargalló
Gender Male
Languages Spanish
Boarding/day Day
Can Pau Birol 2-6, 17005, Girona 17005, Spain
TELEPHONE: +34 972 232 111
FAX: +34 972 230 023
EMAIL: miquel.riera@bell-lloc.org

Centre Cultural I Esportiu XALOC
Status Private
Programme Diploma
Diploma Coordinator Martí Curiel
Gender Male
Languages Spanish
Boarding/day Day
Gran Vía 100, L'Hospitalet de Llobregat, Barcelona 08902, Spain
TELEPHONE: +34 93 335 1600
FAX: +34 93 335 0493
EMAIL: miquelan@xaloc.org
WEBSITE: www.xaloc.org

Colegio Arena Atlántico
Status Private
Programme Diploma
Diploma Coordinator David Arbelo Llorente
Gender Coeducational
Languages Spanish
Boarding/day Day
Paseo San Patricio, No 20, Gran Canaria 35416, Spain
TELEPHONE: +34 928 629 140
FAX: +34 928 634 764
EMAIL: pino_afonso@colegioarenas.es
WEBSITE: www.colegioarenas.es

Colegio de San Francisco de Paula
Status Private
Programme MYP
MYP Coordinator Víctor M Jiménez Suárez
Gender Coeducational
Languages Spanish
Boarding/day Day
C/ Santa Angela de la Cruz, 11, Sevilla 41003, Spain
TELEPHONE: +34 95 422 4382
FAX: +34 9 5 4214047
EMAIL: director@sfpaula.com
WEBSITE: www.sfpaula.com

Colegio Gaztelueta
Status Private
Programme Diploma
Diploma Coordinator Ibon Estrada
Gender Male
Languages Spanish
Boarding/day Day
PO Box 2, Las Arenas, Vizcaya 48930, Spain
TELEPHONE: +34 94 463 3000
FAX: +34 94 480 1403
EMAIL: icires@gaztelueta.com
WEBSITE: www.gaztelueta.com

Colegio Heidelberg
Status Private
Programme Diploma
Diploma Coordinator Soraya Mashlab del Rosario
Gender Coeducational
Languages Spanish
Boarding/day Day
Apartado de Correos 248, Las Palmas de Gran Canaria 35080, Spain
TELEPHONE: +34 928 350 462
FAX: +34 928 351 604
EMAIL: msolaesa@colegioheidelberg.com

Colegio Internacional Meres
Status Private
Programme Diploma
Diploma Coordinator Oscar Luis Bernardo Fernández
Gender Male
Boarding/day Day
Meres S/N, (Siero) 33.199, Asturias 33199, Spain
TELEPHONE: +34 985 792 427
FAX: +34 985 794 582
EMAIL: meres01@teleline.es
WEBSITE: www.colegiomeres.com

Colegio Internacional Peñacorada
Status Private
Programme Diploma
Diploma Coordinator Antonio G de la Pisa
Gender Coeducational
Languages Spanish
Boarding/day Day
Calle Bandonilla 32, CP Armunia León 24009, Spain
TELEPHONE: +34 987 202352
FAX: +34 987 208305
EMAIL: colegiopenacorada@colegiopenacorada.es
WEBSITE: www.colegiopenacorada.es

Colegio Internacional SEK-Alborán
Status Private
Programme MYP, Diploma
Diploma Coordinator Belén Ortega Sánchez
MYP Coordinator Luis Carlos Jiménez
Gender Coeducational
Languages Spanish
Boarding/day Day
Almerimar, 04700 El Ejido, Almeria, Spain
TELEPHONE: +34 950 497273
FAX: +34 950 497898
EMAIL: sek-alboran@sek.es
WEBSITE: www.sek.es

Colegio Internacional SEK-Catalunya

Status Private
Programme MYP, Diploma
Diploma Coordinator Jordi Ros Sabaté
MYP Coordinator Alfonso Fernández
Gender Coeducational
Languages Spanish
Boarding/day Day
Av Els Tremolencs, 24-26, La Garriga,
Barcelona 08530, Spain
TELEPHONE: +34 938 71 84 48
FAX: +34 938 71 77 17
EMAIL: mclagar@sek.es
WEBSITE: www.sek.es

Colegio Internacional SEK-Cuidalcampo

Status Private
Programme MYP, Diploma
Diploma Coordinator Marisol Martin
MYP Coordinator Alicia Martinez
Gender Coeducational
Languages Spanish
Avd. de las Perdices, No 2, San Sebastián de
los Reyes, Madrid 28707, Spain
TELEPHONE: +34 91 659 6303
FAX: +34 91 6596304
EMAIL: cmvizoso@sek.es
WEBSITE: www.sek.es

Colegio Internacional SEK-EL Castillo

Status Private
Programme MYP, Diploma
Diploma Coordinator Encarnación Pérez
Morales
MYP Coordinator Elvira Menchén
Gender Coeducational
Languages Spanish
Boarding/day Mixed
C/Castillo de Manzanares, S/N, Urbanizción
Villafranca del Castillo, Villanueva de la
Cañada, Madrid 28692, Spain
TELEPHONE: +34 91 815 0892
FAX: +34 91 815 1140
EMAIL: sek-castillo@sek.es
WEBSITE: www.sek.es

Colegio Marcote

Status Private
Programme Diploma
Diploma Coordinator Saturnino Alborja
Garcia
Gender Coeducational
Languages Spanish
Boarding/day Day
Avda del Puente, 80 (Cabral), Vigo,
Pontevedra 36318, Spain
TELEPHONE: +34 986 251 511
FAX: +34 986 277 534
EMAIL: unipri@arrakis.es

Colegio Obradoiro

Status Private
Programme Diploma
Diploma Coordinator Pedro-Jesus R García
Gender Coeducational
Languages Spanish
Boarding/day Day
Feáns 152, La Coruña 15190, Spain
TELEPHONE: +34 981 281 888
FAX: +34 981 131 034
EMAIL: bijrubal@eresmas.com
WEBSITE: www.colegioobradoiro.es

Colegio Retamar

Status Private
Programme Diploma
Diploma Coordinator Anthony Matthews
Gender Male
Languages Spanish
Boarding/day Day
Madrid España, c / Pajares 22, Madrid 28223,
Spain
TELEPHONE: +34 91 714 10 22
FAX: +34 91 714 10 23
EMAIL: jl_alier@retamar.com

El Plantio International School

Status Private
Programme Diploma
Diploma Coordinator José E García Cebrián
Gender Coeducational
Languages English
Boarding/day Day
Calle 233 No36 Urb El Plantío, La Cañada,
Paterna, Valencia 46182, Spain
TELEPHONE: +34 96 132 14 10
FAX: +34 96 132 18 41
EMAIL: plantio@plantiointernational.com
WEBSITE: plantiointernational.com

ESCAAN International School

Status Private
Programme Diploma
Diploma Coordinator Neus Roig
Gender Coeducational
Languages English
Boarding/day Day
Passeig Isaac Albeniz, Vallpineda, Sitges
08870, Spain
TELEPHONE: +34 93 894 20 40
FAX: +34 93 894 20 72
EMAIL: information@escaan.com
WEBSITE: www.escaan.com

I.E.S. Alfonso X 'el Sabio'

Status State
Programme Diploma
Diploma Coordinator J M Q Cervantes
Gender Coeducational
Languages Spanish
Boarding/day Day
Avda D Juan de Borbón 3, Murcia 30007,
Spain
TELEPHONE: +34 968 232 040
FAX: +34 968 270 068
EMAIL: carlos.collado@educarm.es
WEBSITE: www.centros5.pntic.mec.es
/ies.alfonso.x.el.sabio/

I.E.S. Juan de la Cierva y Codorníu

Status State
Programme Diploma
Diploma Coordinator M Cañizares Millán
Gender Coeducational
Languages Spanish
Boarding/day Day
C/San Antonio, 84, Totana (Murcia) 30850,
Spain
TELEPHONE: +34 968 42 19 19
EMAIL: juande14@centros5.pntic.mec.es
WEBSITE: www.juandelacierva.org

I.E.S. Maestro Matías Bravo

Status State
Programme Diploma
Diploma Coordinator Daniel Pescador Morán
Gender Coeducational
Languages Spanish
Boarding/day Day
Avenida Mar Egeo S/N, Valdemoro, Madrid
28300, Spain
TELEPHONE: +34 91 801 8044
FAX: +34 91 808 7061
EMAIL: javier.lizasoain@madrid.org
WEBSITE: www.educa.madrid.org/web/
ies.maestromatiasbravo.valdemoro

IES Bachiller Sabuco

Status State
Programme Diploma
Diploma Coordinator Cecilia García Pascual
Gender Coeducational
Languages Spanish
Boarding/day Day
Albacete, Avenida de España 9, Albacete
02002, Spain
TELEPHONE: +34 967 229 540
FAX: +34 967 506 626
EMAIL: director@sabuco.com
WEBSITE: www.sabuco.com

IES Cardenal López de Mendoza

Status State
Programme Diploma
Diploma Coordinator C Mulas Sánchez
Gender Coeducational
Languages Spanish
Boarding/day Day
Plaza Luis Martin Santos s/n, Burgos 09002,
Spain
FAX: +34 947 257649
EMAIL: calzadas87c@terra.es

IES Carlos III de Toledo

Status State
Programme Diploma
Diploma Coordinator Angel Valero Lumbreras
Gender Coeducational
Languages Spanish
Avenida de Francia 5, Toledo 45005, Spain
TELEPHONE: +34 925 212 967
FAX: +34 925 254 747
EMAIL: 4500556.ies@edu.jccm.es

IES Castilla
Status State
Programme Diploma
Diploma Coordinator R Mª García Muñoz
Gender Coeducational
Languages English
Boarding/day Day
Calle Alonso Velázquez s/n, 42003, Soria 42003, Spain
TELEPHONE: +34 975 221 283
FAX: +34 975 213 777
EMAIL: vagudo@roble.pntic.mec.es

IES Jaume Vicens Vives
Status State
Programme Diploma
Diploma Coordinator M L G Vall-llovera
Gender Coeducational
Languages Spanish
Boarding/day Day
Prov Girona estado España, c/Ferrandiz I de Bellés s/n, Girona, Catalunya 17004, Spain
TELEPHONE: +34 972 200 130
FAX: +34 972 227 018
EMAIL: ramoned@pie.xtec.es

IES Lucas Mallada
Status State
Programme Diploma
Diploma Coordinator P Vallés de las Cuevas
Gender Coeducational
Languages Spanish
Boarding/day Day
C/Torre Mendoza No 2, Huesca 22005, Spain
TELEPHONE: +34 (974) 244 834
FAX: +34 (974) 241 770
EMAIL: ieslmahuesca@educa.aragob.es
WEBSITE: www.ieslucasmallada.com

IES Marqués de Santillana
Status State
Programme Diploma
Diploma Coordinator J M Piñeiro Moratinos
Gender Coeducational
Languages Spanish
Boarding/day Day
Avenida de España, 2, Torrelavega, Cantabria 393000, Spain
TELEPHONE: +34 942 88 16 00
FAX: +34 942 89 13 40
EMAIL: director@iesmarquesdesantillana.com
WEBSITE: www.iesmarquesdesantillana.com

IES Martinez Montanes
Status State
Programme Diploma
Diploma Coordinator Rosario Parejo del Valle
Gender Coeducational
Languages Spanish
Boarding/day Day
Fernández de Ribera s/n, Seville 41005, Spain
TELEPHONE: +34 955 623 877
FAX: +34 954 634 138
EMAIL: iesmmontanes@terra.es

IES Mateo Sagasta
Status State
Programme Diploma
Diploma Coordinator P Valer Melchor
Gender Coeducational
Languages Spanish
Boarding/day Day
Glorieta del Doctor Zubia s/n, La Rioja, Logroño 26003, Spain
TELEPHONE: +34 941 256 500
FAX: +34 941 255 050
EMAIL: ies.sagasta@larioja.org
WEBSITE: www.arrakis.es/ffisagasta/

IES Miguel de Cervantes Saavedra
Status State
Programme Diploma
Diploma Coordinator Nuria Cortina García
Gender Coeducational
Languages Spanish
Boarding/day Day
Ciudad Real, Avda Jesús de Haro, s/n, 13600 Alcazar de San Juan, Spain
TELEPHONE: +34 926 540 956
FAX: +34 926 540 990
EMAIL: bi.cervantes@terra.es
WEBSITE: www.jccm.es/edu/ies/cervantes

IES Ramiro de Maeztu
Status State
Programme Diploma
Diploma Coordinator Laura Salto Díaz
Gender Coeducational
Languages Spanish
Boarding/day Day
C/ Serrano 127, Madrid 28006, Spain
TELEPHONE: +34 91 561 7838
FAX: +34 91 411 0865
EMAIL: coral@madrid.org

IES Real Instituto de Jovellanos
Status State
Programme Diploma
Diploma Coordinator L D Romero de la Cruz
Gender Coeducational
Languages Spanish
Boarding/day Day
Avenida de la Constitución s/n, Gijón, Asturias 33071, Spain
TELEPHONE: +34 985 387 703
FAX: +34 985 990884
EMAIL: jovellan@netcom.es
WEBSITE: www.netcom.es/jovellan

IES Rosalia de Castro
Status State
Programme Diploma
Diploma Coordinator J A Filgueira Cobos
Gender Coeducational
Languages Spanish
Boarding/day Mixed
Calle San Clemente, 3, Santiago de Compostela, La Coruña 15705, Spain
TELEPHONE: +34 981 569650
FAX: +34 981 586 271
EMAIL: ies.rosalia.castro@edu.xunta.es

IES Santa Clara
Status State
Programme Diploma
Diploma Coordinator J L Suárez de la Fuente
Gender Coeducational
Languages Spanish
Boarding/day Day
c/ Santa Clara 13, Santander, Cantabria 39001, Spain
TELEPHONE: +34 942 216 550
FAX: +34 942 361 788
EMAIL: silvino_1@infonegocio.com

IES Usandizaga-Peñaflorida-Amara
Status State
Programme Diploma
Diploma Coordinator Alberto Salvador
Gender Coeducational
Languages Spanish
Boarding/day Day
Calle Felipe IV nº 1A, San Sebastián, Guipúzcoa 20011, Spain
TELEPHONE: +34 943 454 366
FAX: +34 943 450112
EMAIL: asalvador-bi@euskalnet.net
WEBSITE: www.usandizaga.com

Instituto de Educación Secundaria do Castro
Status State
Programme Diploma
Diploma Coordinator Luis Otero Gutiérrez
Gender Coeducational
Languages Spanish
Boarding/day Day
C/Posada Curros 1, Vigo 36203, Spain
TELEPHONE: +34 986422974
FAX: +34 986423063
EMAIL: ies.docastro@edu.xunta.es
WEBSITE: http://centros.edu.xunta.es/iesdocastro

INTERNATIONAL COLLEGE SPAIN
Status Private
Programme PYP, MYP, Diploma
Diploma Coordinator Esther Espinal
MYP Coordinator Ursula Garcia
PYP Coordinator Jennifer Barnett
Gender Coeducational
Languages English
Boarding/day Day
Apartado 1271, Alcobendas, Madrid 28108, Spain
TELEPHONE: +34 91 650 2398
FAX: +34 91 650 1035
EMAIL: admissions@icsmadrid.org
WEBSITE: www.icsmadrid.org
see full details on page 95

Les Alzines
Status Private
Programme Diploma
Diploma Coordinator T Barnadas Vilamitjana
Gender Girls
Languages Spanish
Boarding/day Day
La Creu de Palau 2, Girona 17003, Spain
TELEPHONE: +34 972 212162
FAX: +34 972 226286
EMAIL: tbarnadas.lesalzines@institucio.org
WEBSITE: www.institucio.org/lesalzines

Newton College
Status Private
Programme MYP, Diploma
Diploma Coordinator Malén Ferrer Tomas
MYP Coordinator Jorge Sevilla Esclapez
Gender Coeducational
Languages English, Spanish
Boarding/day Day
Camino Viejo Elche Alicante km3, Partida de
Maitino P-1, Elche (Alicante) 03295, Spain
TELEPHONE: +34 965 451 428
FAX: +34 965 451 428
EMAIL: diplomaib@ya.com

**SOTOGRANDE INTERNATIONAL
SCHOOL**
Status Private
Programme PYP, Diploma
Diploma Coordinator Carmelo Mancera
PYP Coordinator Emma Butler
Gender Coeducational
Languages English, Spanish
Boarding/day Mixed
Apartado 15, Sotogrande, Provincia de Cádiz,
11310, Spain
TELEPHONE: +34 956 795 902
FAX: +34 956 794 816
EMAIL: info@sis.ac
WEBSITE: www.sis.ac
see full details on page 136

Swans International Sierra Blanca
Status Private
Programme Diploma
Diploma Coordinator Jose Prieto Borrego
Gender Coeducational
Languages English
Boarding/day Day
Swans School, Urbanización El Capricho,
Marbella 29600, Spain
TELEPHONE: +34 952902755
FAX: +34 952900914
EMAIL: admin@swansschool.net
WEBSITE: www.swansschool.net/secondary

SUDAN

**Khartoum International Community
School**
Status Private
Programme PYP, Diploma
Diploma Coordinator Darren Acomb
PYP Coordinator Myna Anderson
Gender Coeducational
Languages English
Boarding/day Day
PO Box 1840, Khartoum, Sudan
TELEPHONE: +249 183 215 000
FAX: +249 183 215 215
EMAIL: principal@kics.sd
WEBSITE: wwww.kics.sd

SULTANATE OF OMAN

American-British Academy
Status Private
Programme PYP, MYP, Diploma
Diploma Coordinator Terry Storer
MYP Coordinator Trina Bonetti
PYP Coordinator Stephen Madden
Gender Coeducational
Languages English
Boarding/day Day
PO Box 372, Post Code 115, Medinat Al Sultan
Qaboos 115, Sultanate of Oman
TELEPHONE: +968 24 603 646
FAX: +968 24 603 544
EMAIL: admin@abaoman.edu.om
WEBSITE: www.abaoman.edu.om

THE SULTAN'S SCHOOL
Status Private
Programme Diploma
Diploma Coordinator Ray Zinsli
Gender Coeducational
Languages English
Boarding/day Mixed
PO Box 665, Seeb 121, Sultanate of Oman
TELEPHONE: +968 24536 777
FAX: +968 24536 997
EMAIL: principle@sultansschool.org
WEBSITE: www.sultansschool.org
see full details on page 153

SWAZILAND

**Waterford Kamhlaba United World
College of Southern Africa**
Status Private
Programme Diploma
Diploma Coordinator Anna Marsden
Gender Coeducational
Languages English
Boarding/day Mixed
PO Box 52, Mbabane, Swaziland
TELEPHONE: +268 42 20866
FAX: +268 42 20088
EMAIL: principal@waterford.sz
WEBSITE: www.waterford.sz

SWEDEN

Aranäsgymnasiet
Status State
Programme Diploma
Diploma Coordinator John Stanish
Gender Coeducational
Languages English
Gymnasiegatan, Kungsbacka 43442, Sweden
TELEPHONE: +46 (0) 300 83 34 00
FAX: +46 (0) 300 83 33 50
EMAIL: john.stanish@kungsbacka.se
WEBSITE:
www.aranasgymnasiet.kungsbacka.se

Åva Gymnasium
Status State
Programme Diploma
Diploma Coordinator Rolf Öberg
Gender Coeducational
Languages English
Boarding/day Day
Box 1450, Täby 18314, Sweden
TELEPHONE: +46 (0) 855 55 8000
EMAIL: larsake.sandberg@ava.taby.se
WEBSITE: www.ava.taby.se

Björknäsgymnasiet
Status State
Programme Diploma
Diploma Coordinator Eva Jansson
Gender Coeducational
Languages English
Björknässkolan, Idrottsgatan 4, Boden 96164,
Sweden
TELEPHONE: +46 921 625 13
EMAIL: mikael.seva@edu.boden.se
WEBSITE: www.bjorknasgymnasiet.se

BLADINS INTERNATIONAL SCHOOL
Status Private
Programme PYP, MYP
MYP Coordinator Debbie Thoresson
PYP Coordinator Ingrid Hortin
Gender Coeducational
Languages English
Boarding/day Day
Box 20093, S-200 74 Malmö, Sweden
TELEPHONE: +46 40 300885
FAX: +46 40 910885
EMAIL: sandra@bladins.se
WEBSITE: www.bladins.se
see full details on page 62

Ehrensvärdska gymnasiet
Status State
Programme Diploma
Diploma Coordinator Sten Bernhardsson
Gender Coeducational
Languages English
Boarding/day Day
Utbildningsförvaltningen, Karlskrona
Kommun, Karlskrona, Ehrensvärdska
gymnasiet 37183, Sweden
TELEPHONE: +46 455 304081
FAX: +46 455 303373
EMAIL: johan.melin@karlskrona.se
WEBSITE: http://chapman.karlskrona.se/

Europaskolan

Status State
Programme MYP
MYP Coordinator Ulf Jonsson
Gender Coeducational
Languages English
Boarding/day Day
Gotlandsgatan 43, Stockholm 11665, Sweden
TELEPHONE: +46 8 335054
FAX: +46 8 335028
EMAIL: anette.parts@europaskolan.nu
WEBSITE: www.europaskolan.nu

Filbornaskolan

Status State
Programme Diploma
Diploma Coordinator Monika Cramborn
Gender Coeducational
Languages English
Boarding/day Day
Filbornavägen 101, Helsingborg S-256 61, Sweden
TELEPHONE: +46 (0) 42 444 2400
FAX: +46 (0) 423 887 19
EMAIL: info.filbornaskolan@helsingborg.se
WEBSITE:
www.helsingborg.se/filbornaskolan

Grennaskolan Riksinternat

Status State
Programme Diploma
Diploma Coordinator Jessica Humphreys
Gender Coeducational
Languages English
Boarding/day Mixed
Borgmästargården, Gränna SE-563 22, Sweden
TELEPHONE: +46 390 56150
FAX: +46 390 56151
EMAIL: info@grennaskolan.se
WEBSITE: www.grennaskolan.se

Hvitfeldtska Gymnasiet

Status State
Programme Diploma
Diploma Coordinator Maria Nicolai
Gender Coeducational
Languages English
Boarding/day Day
Rektorsgatan 2, Göteburg 41133, Sweden
TELEPHONE: +46 31 36 70 623
FAX: +46 31 36 70 602
EMAIL: agneta.santesson@educ.goteborg.se
WEBSITE: www.hvitfeldt.educ.goteborg.se

IB School South

Status State
Programme Diploma
Diploma Coordinator K Henrekson Ahlberg
Gender Coeducational
Languages English
Boarding/day Day
Box 203, Skärholmen 12724, Sweden
TELEPHONE: +46 8 680 7200
FAX: +46 8 680 7222
EMAIL: ann-christin.wangler@
utbildning.stockholm.se
WEBSITE: www.skn.edu.stockholm.se

International School of Helsingborg

Status State
Programme PYP, MYP, Diploma
Diploma Coordinator Gideon Boulton
MYP Coordinator Roseanne McCormack
PYP Coordinator Carla Johansson
Gender Coeducational
Languages English
Boarding/day Day
Västra Allén 7, Helsingborg 25451, Sweden
TELEPHONE: +46 42 105 742
FAX: +46 42 134 190
EMAIL: ishelsingborg@helsingborg.se
WEBSITE: www.is-hbg.se

International School of the Gothenburg Region

Status State/private
Programme PYP, MYP, Diploma
Diploma Coordinator Lee Brown
MYP Coordinator Jayson Williams
PYP Coordinator Marilyn James
Gender Coeducational
Languages English
Boarding/day Day
PO Box 2667, Gothenburg 403 14, Sweden
TELEPHONE: +46 31 367 29 00
FAX: +46 31 367 29 01
EMAIL: tage@isgr.se
WEBSITE: www.isgr.se

Internationella Skolan Atlas

Status State
Programme PYP
PYP Coordinator Reenie Lee
Gender Coeducational
Languages English, Swedish, Turkish
Boarding/day Day
Brigadgatan 18, Linköping 581 81, Sweden
TELEPHONE: +46 13 20 7510
FAX: +46 13 20 5276
EMAIL: karin.lang@linkoping.se
WEBSITE: www.isatlas.com

ITGYMNASIET I SKÖVDE

Status State
Programme Diploma
Diploma Coordinator Carl Liwell
Gender Coeducational
Languages English
Boarding/day Day
Box 399, Skövde 54128, Sweden
TELEPHONE: +46 500 416990
EMAIL: info@itgymnasiet.nu
WEBSITE: www.itgymnasiet.nu
see full details on page 105

Katedralskolan in Linköping

Status State
Programme Diploma
Diploma Coordinator Ingrid Norling
Gender Coeducational
Languages English
Boarding/day Day
Platensgatan 20, Linköping 58220, Sweden
TELEPHONE: +46 132 07549
FAX: +46 132 07531
EMAIL: britt-marie.andersson@linkoping.se
WEBSITE: www.linkoping.se/katedral

Katedralskolan in Lund

Status State
Programme Diploma
Diploma Coordinator Åsa Björkman
Gender Coeducational
Languages English
St. Södergatan 22, Lund 22223, Sweden
TELEPHONE: +46 4635 76 15
FAX: +46 4635 76 44
EMAIL: ulrika.wiman@lund.se
WEBSITE: www.katedralskolan.lund.se

Katedralskolan in Uppsala

Status State
Programme Diploma
Diploma Coordinator Sven Jonsson
Gender Coeducational
Languages English
Boarding/day Day
Skolgatan 2, Uppsala S-753 12, Sweden
TELEPHONE: +46 18 5681 30
FAX: +46 18 5681 01
EMAIL: gunnar.salomonson@katedral.se
WEBSITE: www.katedral.se

Katedralsskolan in Skara

Status State
Programme Diploma
Diploma Coordinator Kerstin Persson
Gender Coeducational
Languages English
Boarding/day Day
Brunsbogatan 1, Skara 532 88, Sweden
TELEPHONE: +46 511 32600
FAX: +46 511 32330
EMAIL: marianne.perserius@skara.se
WEBSITE: www.katedralskolan.nu

Kungsholmen's Gymnasium, International Section

Status State
Programme Diploma
Diploma Coordinator Mike Powers
Gender Coeducational
Languages English
Boarding/day Day
Hantverkargatan 67-69, PO Box 12601, Stockholm 11292, Sweden
TELEPHONE: +46 8 508 38 003
FAX: +46 8 508 38 001
EMAIL:
agneta.karlsson@utbildning.stockholm.se

Malmö Borgarskola
Status State
Programme Diploma
Diploma Coordinator Anders Carlsson
Gender Coeducational
Languages English
Boarding/day Day
Box 17029, Malmö 200 10, Sweden
TELEPHONE: +46 4034 1000
FAX: +46 4011 3650
EMAIL: nicola.sarac@pub.malmo.se
WEBSITE: www.malmo.se/borgarskolan

Naturvetargymnasiet
Status State
Programme Diploma
Diploma Coordinator Malin Söderberg
Gender Coeducational
Languages English
Boarding/day Day
Västergatan 4, Södertälje 15145, Sweden
TELEPHONE: +46 8 55021336
FAX: +46 8 55022088
EMAIL: stefan.sidusgard@sodertalje.se
WEBSITE:
www.sodertalje.se/naturvetargymnasiet

Ostra Gymnasieskolan
Status State
Programme Diploma
Diploma Coordinator Neil Gosser-Duncan
Gender Coeducational
Languages English
Boarding/day Day
Fridhemsvägen 2, Umeå 90337, Sweden
TELEPHONE: +46 90 162 900
FAX: +46 90 143 791
EMAIL: ellinor.hareskog@umea.se

Per Brahegymnasiet
Status State
Programme Diploma
Diploma Coordinator Hakan Jakobson
Gender Coeducational
Languages English
Boarding/day Day
Residensgatan, Jönköping 553 16, Sweden
TELEPHONE: +46 36 105 472
FAX: +46 36 166 775
EMAIL: gun-ann.oholm.Jansson@
sbf.jonkoping.se
WEBSITE: www.pb.edu.jonkoping.se

Rudbeck
Status State
Programme Diploma
Diploma Coordinator Runar Krantz
Gender Coeducational
Languages English
Boarding/day Day
Box 423, Sollentuna 191 24, Sweden
TELEPHONE: +46 8 5792 1800
FAX: +46 8 5792 1777
EMAIL: info@rudbeck.se
WEBSITE: www.rudbeck.se

Sannarpsgymnasiet
Status State
Programme Diploma
Diploma Coordinator Gerd Nyholm Jansson
Languages English
Frennarpsvägen 1, Halmstad 30244, Sweden
TELEPHONE: +46 35 13 9798
FAX: +46 35 13 76 98
EMAIL: lars.berg@halmstad.se
WEBSITE:
www.sannarpsgymnasiet.halmstad.se

Sigtunaskolan Humanistiska Läroverket
Status Private
Programme MYP, Diploma
Diploma Coordinator Alan Hobson
MYP Coordinator Lena Månsson
Gender Coeducational
Languages English
Boarding/day Mixed
Box 508, Sigtuna 19328, Sweden
TELEPHONE: +46 8 592 571 00
FAX: +46 8 592 572 50
EMAIL: rune.svaninger@sshl.se
WEBSITE: www.sshl.se

Söderportgymnasiet
Status State
Programme Diploma
Diploma Coordinator Göte Paulsson
Gender Coeducational
Languages English
Boarding/day Mixed
Västra Boulevarden 53, Kristianstad 291 31, Sweden
TELEPHONE: +46 4413 5919
FAX: +46 4410 1825
EMAIL: nils.truedsson@kristianstad.se
WEBSITE: www.edu.kristianstad.se/soderport

St Eskils Gymnasium
Status State
Programme Diploma
Diploma Coordinator Kevin Rogers
Gender Coeducational
Languages English
Boarding/day Day
Smedjegatan 3-5, Eskilstuna 631 86, Sweden
TELEPHONE: +46 16 710 2780
EMAIL: sonny.lundgren@eskilstuna.se
WEBSITE: www.eskilstuna.se

Stockholm International School
Status Private
Programme MYP, Diploma
Diploma Coordinator Christopher Mockrish
MYP Coordinator Aaron Nussbaum
Gender Coeducational
Languages English
Boarding/day Day
Johannesgaten 18, Stockholm 11138, Sweden
TELEPHONE: +46 8 4124000
FAX: +46 8 412 4001
EMAIL: j.foulkes-jones@intsch.se
WEBSITE: www.intsch.se

Sven Eriksonsgymnasiet
Status State
Programme Diploma
Diploma Coordinator Monica Tengling
Gender Coeducational
Languages English
Boarding/day Day
Sven Eriksonplatsen, Borås SE-50180, Sweden
TELEPHONE: +46 33 35 80 48
FAX: +46 33 35 81 11
EMAIL: lars-goran.norven@boras.se
WEBSITE: www.utb.boras.se/uk/se

The English School of Almhult
Status State
Programme PYP
PYP Coordinator Patricia Hudson
Gender Coeducational
Boarding/day Day
Skolgatan 1, Almhult 34323, Sweden
TELEPHONE: +46 0476 55188
FAX: +46 0476 55188
EMAIL: vivien.bjornestrand@almhult.se
WEBSITE:
www.almhult.se/utbild/skola/english.htm

Tingvallagymnasiet
Status State
Programme Diploma
Diploma Coordinator Annelie Fräjdin
Gender Coeducational
Languages English
Boarding/day Day
Karlbergsgatan 2A, Karlstad 65184, Sweden
TELEPHONE: +46 54 296953
FAX: +46 54 296910
EMAIL: eva.hallonsten@karlstad.se
WEBSITE: www.tingvalla.karlstad.se/
utbild/nyib/pres.html

Torsbergsgymnasiet
Status State
Programme Diploma
Diploma Coordinator Ylva Tidén
Gender Coeducational
Languages English
Boarding/day Day
Läroverksgatan 36, Bollnäs 82133, Sweden
TELEPHONE: + 46 278 254 91
FAX: +46 278 194 70
EMAIL: eva.hildebrand@bollnas.se
WEBSITE: www.torsbergsgymnasiet.se

Växjö Katedralskola
Status State
Programme Diploma
Diploma Coordinator Charlotte Mechura
Gender Coeducational
Languages English
Boarding/day Day
Samuel Ödmans Väg 1, Växjö 35239, Sweden
TELEPHONE: +46 470 41732
FAX: +46 470 19337
EMAIL: Yngve.Filipsson@katedral.vaxjo.se
WEBSITE: www.katedral.vaxjo.se

Young Business Creatives
Status State
Programme Diploma
Diploma Coordinator Peter Morris
Gender Coeducational
Languages English
Boarding/day Day
Marcusplatsen 7, Nacka 131 34, Sweden
TELEPHONE: +46 8 718 7710
FAX: +46 87 188 202
EMAIL: info@ybc-nacka.se
WEBSITE: www.ybc-nacka.se

SWITZERLAND

Collège Alpin Beau Soleil
Status Private
Programme Diploma
Diploma Coordinator Helen Cevey
Gender Coeducational
Languages English
Boarding/day Boarding
Avenue Centrale, Villars sur Ollon 1884,
Switzerland
TELEPHONE: +41 24 496 2620
FAX: +41 24 496 2627
EMAIL: dlineham@beausoleil.ch
WEBSITE: www.beausoleil.ch

COLLÈGE DU LÉMAN INTERNATIONAL SCHOOL
Status Private
Programme Diploma
Diploma Coordinator Rossella Cosso
Gender Coeducational
Languages English, French
Boarding/day Mixed
74 route de Sauverny, Versoix, Geneva 1290,
Switzerland
TELEPHONE: +41 22 775 5555
FAX: +41 22 775 5559
EMAIL: info@cdl.ch
WEBSITE: www.cdl.ch
see full details on page 73

Ecole Nouvelle de la Suisse Romande – Chailly
Status Private
Programme Diploma
Diploma Coordinator Jean-Luc Terzolo
Gender Coeducational
Languages French, English
Boarding/day Mixed
Chemin de Rovéréaz 20, CP 161, 1000
Lausanne 12, Switzerland
TELEPHONE: +41 21 654 65 00
FAX: +41 21 652 65 05
EMAIL: info@ensr.ch
WEBSITE: www.ensr.ch

Haut-Lac, International Bilingual School
Status Private
Programme MYP, Diploma
Diploma Coordinator Alistair Knight
MYP Coordinator Denise Coates
Gender Coeducational
Languages English
Boarding/day Day
14 route du Tirage, St-Légier-la Chiesaz 1806,
Switzerland
TELEPHONE: +41 21 943 06 60
FAX: +41 21 943 06 61
EMAIL: ibcoordinator@haut-lac.ch
WEBSITE: www.haut-lac.ch

INSTITUT LE ROSEY
Status Private
Programme Diploma
Diploma Coordinator Steve Cranville
Gender Coeducational
Languages English, French
Boarding/day Boarding
Château du Rosey, 1180 Rolle, Switzerland
TELEPHONE: +41 21 822 5500
FAX: +41 21 822 5555
EMAIL: rosey@rosey.ch
WEBSITE: www.rosey.ch
see full details on page 93

Institut Montana
Status Private
Programme Diploma
Diploma Coordinator Kevin O'Brien
Gender Coeducational
Languages English
Boarding/day Mixed
Zugerberg, Zug 6300, Switzerland
TELEPHONE: +41 41 729 1177
FAX: +41 41 711 5465
EMAIL: df@montana-zug.ch
WEBSITE: www.montana-zug.ch

Inter-Community School Zurich
Status Private
Programme PYP, MYP, Diploma
Diploma Coordinator Philomena Marchetti
MYP Coordinator Graham Gardner
PYP Coordinator Brett Penny
Gender Coeducational
Languages English
Boarding/day Day
Strubenacher 3, 8126 Zumikon, Switzerland
TELEPHONE: +41 44 919 8300
FAX: +41 44 919 8353
EMAIL: mmatthews@icsz.ch
WEBSITE: www.icsz.ch

International School Basel
Status Private
Programme PYP, MYP, Diploma
Diploma Coordinator Stephen Sims
MYP Coordinator Zuzana Cox
PYP Coordinator Patricia Whataran
Gender Coeducational
Languages English
Boarding/day Day
Fleischbachstrasse 2, Reinach BL 2 4153,
Switzerland
TELEPHONE: +41 61 715 33 62
FAX: +41 61 715 33 15
EMAIL: lesley.barron@isbasel.ch
WEBSITE: www.isbasel.ch

INTERNATIONAL SCHOOL OF BERNE
Status Private
Programme PYP, MYP, Diploma
Diploma Coordinator Eric Mace-Tessler
MYP Coordinator James Cairns
PYP Coordinator Alyson Rees
Gender Coeducational
Languages English
Boarding/day Day
Mattenstrasse 3, Gümligen, Berne 3073,
Switzerland
TELEPHONE: +41 31 951 23 58
FAX: +41 31 951 17 10
EMAIL: office@isberne.ch
WEBSITE: www.isberne.ch
see full details on page 97

International School of Geneva (Campus des Nations)
Status Private
Programme PYP, MYP, Diploma
Diploma Coordinator Conrad Hughes
MYP Coordinator Fiona Davison
PYP Coordinator Christine DeLuca
Gender Coeducational
Languages English, French
Boarding/day Day
11 route des Morillons, CH-1218 Grand
Saconnex, Switzerland
TELEPHONE: +41 22 770 4760
FAX: +41 22 770 4710
EMAIL: andrew.hand@ecolint.ch
WEBSITE: www.ecolint.ch

International School of Geneva (La Châtaigneraie)
Status Private
Programme PYP, Diploma
Diploma Coordinator Fred Piderit
PYP Coordinator Ann Le Diraison
Gender Coeducational
Languages English
Boarding/day Day
La Châtaigneraie, Founex, Vaud 1297,
Switzerland
TELEPHONE: +41 22 776 2431
FAX: +41 22 960 9120
EMAIL: chris.binge@ecolint.ch
WEBSITE: www.ecolint.ch

International School of Geneva (La Grande Boissière)
Status Private
Programme Diploma
Diploma Coordinator Stephen Burke
Gender Coeducational
Languages English
Boarding/day Day
LGB campus, La Grande Boissière, 62 route de Chêne, Geneva 1208, Switzerland
TELEPHONE: +41 22 787 2400
FAX: +41 22 787 2410
EMAIL: michael.featherstone@ecolint.ch
WEBSITE: www.ecolint.ch

International School of Kreuzlingen Konstanz
Status Private
Programme PYP
PYP Coordinator Stefan Preisig
Gender Coeducational
Languages English
Boarding/day Day
Villa Doldenhof, Hauptstrasse 27, Kreuzlingen, Thurgau 8280, Switzerland
TELEPHONE: +41 71 672 2727
FAX: +41 71 672 2717
EMAIL: s.preisig@iskk.ch
WEBSITE: www.iskk.ch

International School of Lausanne
Status Private
Programme PYP, MYP, Diploma
Diploma Coordinator Simon Foley
MYP Coordinator David Harrison
PYP Coordinator Lief Erickson
Gender Coeducational
Languages English
Boarding/day Day
Chemin de la Grangette 2, 1052 Le Mont-sur-Lausanne, Switzerland
TELEPHONE: +41 21 560 0200
FAX: +41 21 560 0203
EMAIL: info@isl.ch
WEBSITE: www.isl.ch

International School of Schaffhausen
Status Private
Programme PYP
PYP Coordinator Victoria Roberts
Gender Coeducational
Languages English
Boarding/day Day
Mühlenstrasse 87, Schaffhausen 8200, Switzerland
TELEPHONE: +41 052 624 1707
FAX: +41 052 624 1756
EMAIL: info@issh.ch
WEBSITE: www.issh.ch

International School of Zug & Luzern, Riverside Campus
Status Private
Programme MYP, Diploma
Diploma Coordinator Susan Canobie
MYP Coordinator Nicola Cook
Gender Coeducational
Languages English
Boarding/day Day
Artherstrasse 55, Zug 6300, Switzerland
TELEPHONE: +41 41 726 0450
FAX: +41 41 724 0452
EMAIL: info@iszl.ch
WEBSITE: www.iszl.ch

International School of Zug & Luzern, Zug Campus
Status Private
Programme PYP
PYP Coordinator Jacqueline Webb
Gender Coeducational
Boarding/day Day
Walterswil, Baar 6340, Switzerland
TELEPHONE: +41 41 768 1188
FAX: +41 41 768 1189
EMAIL: office@isoz.ch
WEBSITE: www.isoz.ch

International School Rheintal
Status Private
Programme PYP, MYP, Diploma
Diploma Coordinator Steve Bavaro
MYP Coordinator Jim Connor
PYP Coordinator John Urquhart
Gender Coeducational
Languages English
Boarding/day Day
Aeulistrasse 10, Buchs 9470, Switzerland
TELEPHONE: +41 81 750 6300
FAX: +41 81 750 6301
EMAIL: meg.sutcliffe@isr.ch
WEBSITE: www.isr.ch

INTERNATIONAL SCHOOL WINTERTHUR
Status Private
Programme PYP
PYP Coordinator Alex Cardona
Gender Coeducational
Languages English
Boarding/day Day
Zum Park 5, CH-8404 Winterthur, Switzerland
TELEPHONE: +41 52 269 5900
FAX: +41 52 269 5902
EMAIL: administration@iswinterthur.ch
WEBSITE: www.iswinterthur.ch
see full details on page 103

Leysin American School
Status Private
Programme Diploma
Diploma Coordinator Daniel Spiegel
Gender Coeducational
Languages English
Boarding/day Boarding
Leysin 1854, Switzerland
TELEPHONE: +41 24 493 3704
FAX: +41 24 493 3790
EMAIL: admission@las.ch
WEBSITE: www.las.ch

Literargymnasium Rämibühl
Status State
Programme Diploma
Diploma Coordinator M Schneckenburger
Gender Coeducational
Languages English
Boarding/day Day
Rämistrasse 56, Zürich 8001, Switzerland
TELEPHONE: +41 1 265 62 11
FAX: +41 1 265 62 14
EMAIL: christoph.baumgartner@krl.bid.zh.ch
WEBSITE: www.lgr.ch

Lyceum Alpinum Zuoz
Status Private
Programme Diploma
Diploma Coordinator M Cristina Cavalli
Gender Coeducational
Languages English
Boarding/day Mixed
CH-7524, Zuoz, Switzerland
TELEPHONE: +41 81 851 30 00
FAX: +41 81 851 30 99
EMAIL: beat.sommer@lyceum-alpinum.ch
WEBSITE: www.lyceum-alpinum.ch

Mutuelle d'etudes Secondaires
Status Private
Programme Diploma
Diploma Coordinator Marie-Claude Zerbini
Gender Coeducational
Languages French
Boarding/day Day
7bis boulevard Carl-Vogt, Genève 1205, Switzerland
TELEPHONE: +41 22 741 0001/52
FAX: +41 22 741 2125
EMAIL: michel.dubret@free.fr

Realgymnasium Rämibühl
Status State
Programme Diploma
Diploma Coordinator Christian Maurer
Gender Coeducational
Languages English
Boarding/day Day
Rämistrasse 56, Zürich 8001, Switzerland
TELEPHONE: +41 44 265 63 12
FAX: +41 44 265 63 14
EMAIL: ch.sommer@rgzh.ch
WEBSITE: www.rgzh.ch

SWITZERLAND

SIS Swiss International School
Status Private
Programme Diploma
Diploma Coordinator Alfons Würms
Gender Coeducational
Languages English
Boarding/day Day
Scheuchzerstrasse 2, Zürich 8006, Switzerland
TELEPHONE: +41 44 368 4020
FAX: +41 44 388 9949
EMAIL:
steingruber.rodolfo@minervazuerich.ch
WEBSITE: www.minervazuerich.ch

St George's School in Switzerland
Status Private
Programme Diploma
Diploma Coordinator Mr Tim Jupp
Gender Coeducational
Languages English
Boarding/day Mixed
Chemin de St Georges 19, CH 1815
Clarens/Montreux, Switzerland
TELEPHONE: +41 21 964 3411
FAX: +41 21 964 4932
EMAIL: office@st-georges.ch
WEBSITE: www.st-georges.ch

Swiss International School – Zurich North
Status Private
Programme PYP
PYP Coordinator Rachael Lewis
Gender Coeducational
Languages English
Boarding/day Day
Industriestrasse 50, Wallisellen CH-8304,
Switzerland
TELEPHONE: +41 44 830 7000

The American School in Switzerland
Status Private
Programme Diploma
Diploma Coordinator Howard Stickley
Gender Coeducational
Languages English
Boarding/day Mixed
Via Collina D'Oro, Montagnola-Lugano 6926,
Switzerland
TELEPHONE: +41 91 960-5151
FAX: +41 91 994 23 64
WEBSITE: http://tasis.ch

Zurich International School
Status Private
Programme PYP, Diploma
Diploma Coordinator Joseph Amato
PYP Coordinator David Sargeant
Gender Coeducational
Languages English
Boarding/day Day
Steinacherstr 140, Wädenswil 8820,
Switzerland
TELEPHONE: +41 58 750 2500
FAX: +41 58 750 2201
EMAIL: pmott@zis.ch
WEBSITE: www.zis.ch

SYRIA

ICARDA International School of Aleppo
Status Private
Programme PYP, Diploma
Diploma Coordinator Peter Krader
PYP Coordinator Gillian Assi
Gender Coeducational
Languages English
Boarding/day Day
PO Box 5466, Aleppo, Syria
TELEPHONE: +963 21 574 3104
FAX: +963 21 744 622
EMAIL: rettga@yahoo.com
WEBSITE: www.icarda.org

TANZANIA

Aga Khan School, Dar-es-Salaam
Status Private
Programme Diploma
Diploma Coordinator Ann Breuer
Gender Coeducational
Languages English
Boarding/day Day
PO Box 125, Dar-es-Salaam, Tanzania
TELEPHONE: +255 22 215 0700/215 0406
FAX: +255 22 2150701
EMAIL: sheila.clitheroetieszen@akest.org
WEBSITE: www.akdn.org/agency/akes.html

International School Moshi, Arusha Campus
Status Private
Programme PYP, MYP
MYP Coordinator Steve Brown
PYP Coordinator Betty Brown
Gender Coeducational
Languages English
Boarding/day Day
PO Box 2691, Arusha, Tanzania
TELEPHONE: +255 27 250 5029
FAX: +255 27 250 5031
EMAIL: adrianm@ismac.ac.tz
WEBSITE: www.ismoshi.org

International School Moshi, Moshi Campus
Status Private
Programme PYP, MYP, Diploma
Diploma Coordinator Alastair Brandon
MYP Coordinator Jeff Holcomb
PYP Coordinator Sarah Hopkins
Gender Coeducational
Languages English
Boarding/day Mixed
PO Box 733, Lema Road, Moshi, Kilimanjaro,
Tanzania
TELEPHONE: +255 27 275 5004
FAX: +255 27 275 2877
EMAIL: school@ismoshi.net
WEBSITE: www.ismoshi.net

International School of Tanganyika
Status Private
Programme PYP, MYP, Diploma
Diploma Coordinator Steve Maine
MYP Coordinator Claudia Kennedy
PYP Coordinator Jill Lawson
Gender Coeducational
Languages English
Boarding/day Day
United Nations Road, PO Box 2651, Dar-es-
Salaam, Tanzania
TELEPHONE: +255 22 2151817
FAX: +255 22 2152077
EMAIL: director@istafrica.com
WEBSITE: www.istafrica.com

TOGO

British School of Lomé
Status Private
Programme Diploma
Diploma Coordinator Andrew Joy
Gender Coeducational
Languages English
Boarding/day Mixed
c/o Hellman House, Lakeside Industrial
Estate, Colnbrook, Slough SL3 0EL, UK
TELEPHONE: +228 226 46 06
FAX: +228 226 49 89
EMAIL: admin@bsl.tg
WEBSITE: www.bsl.tg

École Internationale Arc-en-Ciel
Status Private
Programme Diploma
Diploma Coordinator Philip J Smith
Gender Coeducational
Languages French
Boarding/day Mixed
BP 2985, Lomé, Togo
TELEPHONE: +228 222 0329
FAX: +228 222 0329
EMAIL: ecole_arcenciel@yahoo.fr

TUNISIA

American Cooperative School of Tunis
Status Private
Programme Diploma
Diploma Coordinator Elizabeth Thornton
Gender Coeducational
Languages English
Boarding/day Day
c/o American Embassy, Zone Nord-Est des
Berges du La, Nord de Tunis, La Goulette
2045, Tunisia
TELEPHONE: +216 71 760 905
FAX: +216 71 761 412
EMAIL: director@acst.intl.tn
WEBSITE: www.acst.net

TURKEY

Aka School
Status Private
Programme Diploma
Diploma Coordinator Sydney Bulbul
Gender Coeducational
Languages English
Boarding/day Day
Radyum Sok No 21 Basin Sitesi, Bahcelievler, Istanbul, Turkey
TELEPHONE: +90 2125572772
FAX: +90 2125532698
EMAIL: oinanc@akakolji.K12.tr
WEBSITE: www.akakoleji.k12.tr

American Collegiate Institute
Status Private
Programme Diploma
Diploma Coordinator Mine Erim
Gender Coeducational
Languages English
Boarding/day Day
Inonu Caddesi, No 476, Goztepe, Izmir 35290, Turkey
TELEPHONE: +90 232 285 3401
FAX: +90 232 246 1674
EMAIL: etrujillo@aci.k12.tr
WEBSITE: www.aci.k12.tr

Ar-El Primary & High Schools
Status Private
Programme PYP, MYP
MYP Coordinator Aylin Ergin
PYP Coordinator Hulya Aydiner Salt
Gender Coeducational
Languages English
Boarding/day Day
Ar-El Egitum Kurumlari, A S Gunesli Yolu, Ataturk Caddesi, Radar Karsisi, Yenibosna, Bahçelievler, Istanbul 34530, Turkey
TELEPHONE: +90 212 550 4930
FAX: +90 212 550 7782
EMAIL: ayhandoganli@ar-el.k12.tr
WEBSITE: www.ar-el.k12.tr/en

Bilkent International School
Status Private
Programme Diploma
Diploma Coordinator Dr Hande Gürel
Gender Coeducational
Languages English
Boarding/day Day
Bilkent International School, East Campus, Ankara 06533, Turkey
TELEPHONE: +90 312 266 4961
FAX: +90 312 266 4963
EMAIL: jswetz@bups.bilkent.edu.tr
WEBSITE: www.bups.bilkent.edu.tr

BRITISH INTERNATIONAL SCHOOL - ISTANBUL
Status Private
Programme Diploma
Diploma Coordinator Richard Robinson
Gender Coeducational
Languages English
Boarding/day Day
PDI-ER Uluslararasi Ozel Egitim, Hizmetleri Ticaret AS, Maslak Meydan SK. Spring Giz Plaza, K-5 No: 30/B Istanbul, Maslak VD 723 012 2635, Turkey
TELEPHONE: +90 212 202 7027
FAX: +90 212 257 76 28
EMAIL: directorofsecondary@bis.k12.tr
WEBSITE: www.bis.k12.tr
see full details on page 65

Enka Schools
Status Private
Programme PYP, Diploma
Diploma Coordinator Peter Howard
PYP Coordinator Muge Selcuk
Gender Coeducational
Languages Turkish, English
Boarding/day Day
Sadi Gülçelik Spor Sitesi, Istinye, Istanbul 34460, Turkey
TELEPHONE: +90 212 276 05 45 ext 106
FAX: +90 212 276 82 94
EMAIL: mailbox@enkaschools.com
WEBSITE: www.enkaschools.com

EYÜBOGLU HIGH SCHOOL
Status Private
Programme PYP, MYP, Diploma
Diploma Coordinator Gaye Önol
MYP Coordinator Asli Bali
PYP Coordinator Tuna Mengü
Gender Coeducational
Languages English, Turkish
Boarding/day Day
Namik Kemal mah, Dr Rüstem Eyüboglu sok 3, Ümraniye, Istanbul 34762, Turkey
TELEPHONE: +90 216 522 12 12
FAX: +90 216 335 71 98
EMAIL: sema.ozkaya@eyuboglu.com
WEBSITE: www.eyuboglu.com
see full details on page 80

Irmak School
Status Private
Programme PYP
PYP Coordinator Eda Ceylan
Cemil Topuzlu Cad No 112, Caddebostan, Istanbul 34728, Turkey
TELEPHONE: +90 216 411 39234/5
FAX: +90 216 411 3926
EMAIL: atilla.kucukkayikci@irmak.k12.tr
WEBSITE: www.irmak.k12.tr

Istanbul International Community School
Status Private
Programme PYP, MYP, Diploma
Diploma Coordinator Charles Soprano
MYP Coordinator Heather Shepherd
PYP Coordinator Jonathan Twigg
Gender Coeducational
Languages English
Boarding/day Day
Karaagac Koyu, Hadimkoy, Istanbul 34866, Turkey
TELEPHONE: +90 212 857 8264
FAX: +90 212 857 8270
EMAIL: headmast@iics.k12.tr
WEBSITE: www.iics.k12.tr

Istanbul Prof. Dr Mümtaz Turhan Sosyal Bilimler Lisesi
Status State
Programme Diploma
Diploma Coordinator Ilkay Aydin
Gender Coeducational
Languages English
Boarding/day Mixed
Fevzi Çakmak Cad. Fatih Mah., No:2 Yenibosna, Bahçelievler, Istanbul, Turkey
TELEPHONE: +902 1255 16146
FAX: +902 1250 36391
EMAIL: aerdogan@ istanbulsosyalbilimlerlisesi.k12.tr
WEBSITE: www.isbl.k12.tr

Kultur 2000 College
Status Private
Programme MYP, Diploma
Diploma Coordinator Gökçe Kitapli
MYP Coordinator Gökçe Kitapli
Gender Coeducational
Languages English, Turkish
Boarding/day Day
Alkent 2, Faz yani, Karaagaç Koyu Yolu, Buyukçekmece, Istanbul 34500, Turkey
TELEPHONE: +90 212 889 1929
FAX: +90 212 889 1949
EMAIL: kultur2000@kultur2000.k12.tr
WEBSITE: www.kultur2000.k12.tr

Kultur High School
Status Private
Programme Diploma
Diploma Coordinator Douglas Norman
Gender Coeducational
Languages English
Boarding/day Boarding
Incirli Yolbasi Sok No1, Bakirkoy, Istanbul 34730, Turkey
TELEPHONE: +90 212 5705444
FAX: +90 212 5838619
EMAIL: bahattins@kultur.k12.tr
WEBSITE: www.kultur.k12.tr

Marmara Education Group

Status Private
Programme MYP, Diploma
Diploma Coordinator Fikret Özgenç
MYP Coordinator Gamze Çakar
Gender Coeducational
Languages English
Boarding/day Day/mixed
Marmara Egitim Köyü, Basibüyük, Maltepe,
Istanbul 34857, Turkey
TELEPHONE: +90 216 626 10 00
FAX: +90 216 626 10 28
EMAIL: markol@mek.k12.tr
WEBSITE: www.mek.k12.tr

MEF INTERNATIONAL SCHOOL

Status Private
Programme PYP
PYP Coordinator Lisa Hughes
Gender Coeducational
Languages English
Boarding/day Day
Dereboyu Caddesi, Ortaköy, 34340 Istanbul,
Turkey
TELEPHONE: +90 (212) 287 6900 ext 1340
FAX: +90 (212) 287 4681
EMAIL: contact@mef.k12.tr
WEBSITE: www.mefinternationalschool.com
see full details on page 115

MEF Schools of Turkey

Status Private
Programme Diploma
Diploma Coordinator Dilara-Jane Sougstad
Gender Coeducational
Languages English
Boarding/day Mixed
Amberlidere Mevkii -Dereboyu, Cad-Ortakoy,
Ortaköy, Istanbul 34340, Turkey
TELEPHONE: +90 212 2876900/237
EMAIL: ibdp@mef.k12.tr
WEBSITE: www.mef.k12.tr

Ozel Kultur Ilkogretim Okulu

Status Private
Programme MYP
MYP Coordinator Fatih Karadagli
Gender Coeducational
Boarding/day Day
9-10 Kisim, Atakoy, Istanbul 34750, Turkey
TELEPHONE: +90 212 559 0488
FAX: +90 212 560 4779
EMAIL: bahar-gunver@kultur.k12.tr
WEBSITE: www.kultur.k12.tr

Ozel Yüzyil Isil Okullari

Status Private
Programme Diploma
Diploma Coordinator Patrick Swann
Gender Coeducational
Languages English
Boarding/day Day
Bahçeköy Valide Sultan Cd, Alay Yolu No: 2,
Sariyer-Istanbul 34473, Turkey
TELEPHONE: +90 212 226 23 53
FAX: +90 212 226 22 30
EMAIL: mdizdar@yuzyilisil.k12.tr
WEBSITE: www.yuzyilisil.k12.tr

Private Yuce Schools, Yuce High School

Status Private
Programme Diploma
Diploma Coordinator Sencer Dönmez
Gender Coeducational
Languages English
Boarding/day Day
Ozel Yuce Okullari, Zuhtu Tigrel Caddesi,
Ismet Eker Sokak No 5, Oran-Ankara 06450,
Turkey
TELEPHONE: +90 312 490 02 02
FAX: +90 312 490 87 90
EMAIL: kagank@yuce.k12.tr
WEBSITE: www.yuce.k12.tr/

Privatschule Der Deutschen Botschaft Ankara

Status Private
Programme Diploma
Diploma Coordinator A Wilhelm-Reyhan
Gender Coeducational
Languages English, German
Boarding/day Day
Tunus Cad 56, Cankaya, Ankara, Turkey
TELEPHONE: +90 312 426 63 82
FAX: +90 312 426 45 57
EMAIL: ers@dsankara.com
WEBSITE: www.dsankara.com

Tarsus American School

Status Private
Programme Diploma
Diploma Coordinator Müfide van der Hoeven
Gender Coeducational
Languages English
Boarding/day Mixed
Cengiz Topel Caddesi, Caminur Mahallesi No
66, Tarsus, Mersin 33440, Turkey
TELEPHONE: +90 324 613 54 02/3/4
FAX: +90 324 624 63 47
EMAIL: info@tac.k12.tr
WEBSITE: www.tac.k12.tr

TED Ankara College Foundation High School

Status Private
Programme Diploma
Diploma Coordinator Mustafa Ustunusik
Gender Coeducational
Languages English
Boarding/day Day
Taspinar Koyu Yumrubel Mevkii No 310, Incek,
Golbasi, Ankara 06830, Turkey
TELEPHONE: +90 (312) 5869043/4
FAX: +90 (312) 5869070
EMAIL: mtoklucu@tedankara.k12.tr
WEBSITE: www.tedankara.k12.tr

TED Bursa College

Status Private
Programme Diploma
Diploma Coordinator Zeynep Karslioglu
Gender Coeducational
Languages English
Boarding/day Day
21 Yüzyil Cad Mürsel, Köyü Mevkii, Bademli,
Bursa, Turkey
TELEPHONE: +90 224 549 2100
EMAIL: kayhankarli@tedbursa.k12.tr
WEBSITE: www.tedbursa.k12.tr

Tev Inanc Turkes High School For Gifted Students

Status Private
Programme Diploma
Diploma Coordinator David Helliwell
Gender Coeducational
Languages English
Boarding/day Boarding
Muallimkoy Mevkii, PK 125, Gebze, Kocaeli
41490, Turkey
TELEPHONE: +90 262 759 11 95
EMAIL: aozkardes@tevitol.k12.tr
WEBSITE: www.tevitol.k12.tr

The Koç School

Status Private
Programme Diploma
Diploma Coordinator Gautam Sen
Gender Coeducational
Languages English
Boarding/day Mixed
PO Box 60, Tuzla, Istanbul 34941, Turkey
TELEPHONE: +90 216 304 1017
FAX: +90 216 304 1024/48
EMAIL: onurja@kocschool.k12.tr

UGANDA

Aga Khan High School, Kampala

Status Private
Programme Diploma
Diploma Coordinator Christopher Onyango
Gender Coeducational
Languages English
Boarding/day Day
PO Box 6837, Kampala, Uganda
TELEPHONE: +256 414 300208
EMAIL: margaret.bell@akesu.org
WEBSITE: www.agakhanschools.org

International School of Uganda

Status Private
Programme PYP, MYP, Diploma
Diploma Coordinator Janet Groves
MYP Coordinator Claudia Kennedy
PYP Coordinator Daniel Todd
Gender Coeducational
Languages English
Boarding/day Day
PO Box 4200, Kampala, Uganda
TELEPHONE: +256 41 200 374/8 / 9
FAX: +256 41 200 303
EMAIL: dgroves@isumail.ac.ug
WEBSITE: www.lincoln.ac.ug

Kampala International School
Status Private
Programme Diploma
Diploma Coordinator Marie Kamure
Gender Coeducational
Languages English
Boarding/day Day
PO Box 2020, Bukoto, Kampala, Uganda
TELEPHONE: +256 41 530 472
FAX: +256 41 543 444
EMAIL: principal@kisu.com
WEBSITE: www.kisu.com

UK

ACS COBHAM INTERNATIONAL SCHOOL
Status Independent
Programme Diploma
Diploma Coordinator Craig Worthington
Gender Coeducational
Languages English
Boarding/day Mixed
Heywood, Portsmouth Road, Cobham, Surrey KT11 1BL, UK
TELEPHONE: +44 (0)1932 867251
FAX: +44 (0)1932 869789
EMAIL: cobhamadmissions@acs-england.co.uk
WEBSITE: www.acs-england.co.uk
see full details on page 40

ACS EGHAM INTERNATIONAL SCHOOL
Status Independent
Programme PYP, MYP, Diploma
Diploma Coordinator Justin McCarthy
MYP Coordinator Victoria Ryan
PYP Coordinator Colin Sercombe
Gender Coeducational
Languages English
Boarding/day Day
Woodlee, London Road, Egham, Surrey TW20 0HS, UK
TELEPHONE: +44 (0)1784 430 800
FAX: +44 (0)1784 430 626
EMAIL: eghamadmissions@acs-england.co.uk
WEBSITE: www.acs-england.co.uk
see full details on page 41

ACS HILLINGDON INTERNATIONAL SCHOOL
Status Independent
Programme Diploma
Diploma Coordinator Chris Green
Gender Coeducational
Languages English
Boarding/day Day
Hillingdon Court, 108 Vine Lane, Hillingdon, Uxbridge, Middlesex UB10 0BE, UK
TELEPHONE: +44 (0)1895 259 771
FAX: +44 (0)1895 818 404
EMAIL: hillingdonadmissions@acs-england.co.uk
WEBSITE: www.acs-england.co.uk
see full details on page 42

Alton College
Status State
Programme Diploma
Diploma Coordinator Martin Savery
Gender Coeducational
Languages English
Boarding/day Day
Old Odiham Road, Alton, Hampshire GU34 2LX, UK
TELEPHONE: +44 (0)1420 592200
FAX: +44 (0)1420 592253
EMAIL: enquiries@altoncollege.ac.uk
WEBSITE: www.altoncollege.ac.uk

Anglo-European School
Status State
Programme Diploma
Diploma Coordinator Jane Strachan
Gender Coeducational
Languages English
Boarding/day Day
Willow Green, Ingatestone, Essex CM4 0DJ
TELEPHONE: +44 (0)1277 354 018
FAX: +44 (0)1277 355 623
EMAIL: enquiries@aesessex.co.uk
WEBSITE: www.aesessex.co.uk

ARDINGLY COLLEGE
Status Private
Programme Diploma
Diploma Coordinator John Langford
Gender Coeducational
Languages English
Boarding/day Mixed
College Road, Ardingly, Haywards Heath, West Sussex RH17 6SQ, UK
TELEPHONE: +44 (0)1444 893000
FAX: +44 (0)1444 893001
EMAIL: registrar@ardingly.com
WEBSITE: www.ardingly.com
see full details on page 51

BARTON COURT GRAMMAR SCHOOL
Status State
Programme Diploma
Diploma Coordinator Moira Driscoll
Gender Coeducational
Languages English
Boarding/day Day
Longport, Canterbury, Kent CT1 1PH, UK
TELEPHONE: +44 (0)1227 464600
FAX: +44 (0)1227 781399
EMAIL: office@bartoncourt.org
WEBSITE: www.bartoncourt.org
see full details on page 55

BEAUMONT SCHOOL (BEAUSANDVER)
Status State
Programme Diploma
Diploma Coordinator Morag McCrorie
Gender Coeducational
Languages English
Boarding/day Day
Oakwood Drive, St Albans, Hertfordshire AL4 0XB, UK
TELEPHONE: +44 (0)1727 854 726
FAX: +44 (0)1727 847 971
EMAIL: morag.mccrorie@beaumont.herts.sch.uk
WEBSITE: www.beaumont.herts.sch.uk
see full details on page 58

BEDFORD HIGH SCHOOL FOR GIRLS
Status Private
Programme Diploma
Diploma Coordinator Philip Herrick
Gender Female
Languages English
Boarding/day Mixed
Bromham Road, Bedford, Bedfordshire MK40 2BS, UK
TELEPHONE: +44 (0)1234 360221
FAX: +44 (0)1234 353552
EMAIL: admissions@bedfordhigh.co.uk
WEBSITE: www.bedfordhigh.co.uk
see full details on page 59

Bedford School
Status Private
Programme Diploma
Diploma Coordinator Colin Marsh
Gender Male
Languages English
Boarding/day Mixed
De Parys Avenue, Bedford, Bedfordshire MK40 2TU, UK
TELEPHONE: +44 (0)1234 362200
FAX: +44 (0)1234 362283
EMAIL: info@bedfordschool.org.uk
WEBSITE: www.bedfordschool.org.uk

Bexhill College
Status State
Programme Diploma
Diploma Coordinator Ian Mowat
Gender Coeducational
Languages English
Boarding/day Day
Penland Road, Bexhill-on-Sea, East Sussex TN40 2JG, UK
TELEPHONE: +44 (0)1424 214545
FAX: +44 (0)1424 215050
EMAIL: enquiries@bexhillcollege.ac.uk
WEBSITE: www.bexhillcollege.ac.uk

Bexley Grammar School

Status State
Programme Diploma
Diploma Coordinator Ken Brown
Gender Coeducational
Languages English
Boarding/day Day
Danson Lane, Welling, Kent DA16 2BL, UK
TELEPHONE: +44 (0)20 8304 8538
FAX: +44 (0)20 8304 0248
EMAIL: enquiries@bexleygs.co.uk
WEBSITE: www.bexleygs.co.uk

Bishop Ramsey Church of England School

Status State
Programme Diploma
Diploma Coordinator Carole Watson
Gender Coeducational
Languages English
Boarding/day Day
Hume Way, Ruislip, Middlesex HA4 8EE, UK
TELEPHONE: +44 1895 639227
FAX: +44 1895 62242
EMAIL: awilcock@hillingdongrid.org
WEBSITE:
www.bishopramsey.hillingdon.sch.uk

Blackpool Sixth Form College

Status State
Programme Diploma
Diploma Coordinator Philip Benson
Gender Coeducational
Languages English
Boarding/day Day
Blackpool Old Road, Blackpool FY3 7LR, UK
TELEPHONE: +44 (0) 1253 394911
FAX: +44 (0) 1253 300459
EMAIL: enquiries@blackpoolsixth.ac.uk
WEBSITE: www.blackpoolsixth.ac.uk

Box Hill School

Status Private
Programme Diploma
Diploma Coordinator Monica Pengilley
Gender Coeducational
Languages English
Boarding/day Mixed
Mickleham, Dorking, Surrey RH5 6EA, UK
TELEPHONE: +44 (0)1372 373382
FAX: +44 (0)1372 363942
EMAIL: enquiries@boxhillschool.org.uk
WEBSITE: www.boxhillschool.org.uk

Brentwood School

Status Private
Programme Diploma
Diploma Coordinator Timothy Woffenden
Gender Coeducational
Languages English
Boarding/day Mixed
Ingrave Road, Brentwood, Essex CM15 8AS
TELEPHONE: +44 (0)1277 243243
FAX: +44 (0)1277 243299
EMAIL: headmaster@brentwood.essex.sch.uk
WEBSITE: www.brentwoodschool.co.uk

Bridgwater College

Status State
Programme Diploma
Diploma Coordinator Martyn Aldridge
Gender Coeducational
Languages English
Boarding/day Mixed
Bath Road, Bridgwater, Somerset TA6 4PZ, UK
TELEPHONE: +44 (0)1278 455464
FAX: +44 (0)1278 444363
EMAIL: information@bridgwater.ac.uk
WEBSITE: www.bridgwater.ac.uk

Broadgreen High School

Status State
Programme Diploma
Diploma Coordinator Martina Hedges
Gender Coeducational
Languages English
Boarding/day Day
Queens Drive, Liverpool, Merseyside L13 5UQ
TELEPHONE: +44 (0)151 228 6800
FAX: +44 (0)151 220 9256
EMAIL: enquiries@broadgreenhig.org.uk
WEBSITE: www.broadgreenhigh.org.uk

Brockenhurst College

Status State
Programme Diploma
Diploma Coordinator Patricia Harriss
Gender Coeducational
Languages English
Lyndhurst Road, Brockenhurst, Hampshire
SO42 7ZE, UK
TELEPHONE: +44 (0)1590 625555
FAX: +44 (0)1590 625526
EMAIL: enquiries@brock.ac.uk
WEBSITE: www.brock.ac.uk

CATS CANTERBURY

Status Private
Programme Diploma
Diploma Coordinator Mr Noel Ensoll
Gender Coeducational
Languages English
Boarding/day Mixed
68 New Dover Road, Canterbury, Kent CT1
3LQ, UK
TELEPHONE: +44 (0)1227 866540
FAX: +44 (0)1227 866550
EMAIL: admissions@catscanterbury.com
WEBSITE: www.catscanterbury.com
see full details on page 71

Cheltenham Bournside School

Status State
Programme Diploma
Diploma Coordinator David Proudlove
Gender Coeducational
Languages English
Boarding/day Day
Warden Hill Road, Cheltenham,
Gloucestershire GL51 3EF, UK
TELEPHONE: +44 1242 235555
FAX: +44 1242 226742
EMAIL: head@bournside.gloucs.sch.uk
WEBSITE: www.bournside.gloucs.sch.uk

Cirencester College

Status State
Programme Diploma
Diploma Coordinator Katy Albiston
Gender Coeducational
Languages English
Boarding/day Day
Fosse Way Campus, Stroud Road, Cirencester,
Gloucestershire GL7 1XA, UK
TELEPHONE: +44 (0)1285 640994
FAX: +44 (0)1285 644171
EMAIL: student.services@cirencester.ac.uk
WEBSITE: www.cirencester.ac.uk

City of Stoke-on-Trent Sixth Form College

Status State
Programme Diploma
Diploma Coordinator Michael Casey
Gender Coeducational
Languages English
Boarding/day Day
Victoria Road, Fenton, Stoke-on-Trent ST4
2RR, UK
TELEPHONE: +44 (0)1782 854 222
FAX: +44 (0)1782 747 456
EMAIL: helen.pegg@stokesfc.ac.uk
WEBSITE: www.stokesfc.ac.uk

City Technology College, Kingshurst

Status State
Programme Diploma
Diploma Coordinator Roz Trudgon
Gender Coeducational
Languages English
Boarding/day Day
PO Box 1017, Cooks Lane, Kingshurst,
Birmingham, West Midlands B37 6NZ, UK
TELEPHONE: +44 (0)121 329 8300
EMAIL: ann.jones@kingshurst.ac.uk
WEBSITE: www.kingshurst.ac.uk

Coleg Llandrillo

Status State
Programme Diploma
Diploma Coordinator Melanie Monteith
Gender Coeducational
Languages English
Boarding/day Day
Llandudno Road, Rhos on Sea, Conwy LL28
4HZ, UK
TELEPHONE: +44 (0)1492 546 666
FAX: +44 (0)1492 543052
EMAIL: admissions@llandrillo.ac.uk
WEBSITE: www.llandrillo.ac.uk

Cowley Language College

Status State
Programme Diploma
Diploma Coordinator Matthew Hesketh
Gender Coeducational
Languages English
Boarding/day Day
Hard Lane, St Helens, Merseyside WA10 6LB
TELEPHONE: +44 (0)1744 678 030
EMAIL: cameron.sheeran@sthelens.org.uk
WEBSITE:
www.cowleylanguagecollege.org.uk

Dallam School

Status State
Programme Diploma
Diploma Coordinator Richard Doyle
Gender Coeducational
Languages English
Boarding/day Mixed
Milnthorpe, Cumbria LA7 7DD, UK
TELEPHONE: +44 (0)15395 65165
FAX: +44 (0)15395 65175
EMAIL: enquiries@dallam.eu
WEBSITE: www.dallam.eu

Dane Court Grammar School

Status State
Programme Diploma
Diploma Coordinator Steven Sunderland
Gender Coeducational
Languages English
Boarding/day Day
Broadstairs Road, Broadstairs, Kent CT10 2RT
TELEPHONE: +44 (0) 1843 864941
FAX: +44 (0) 1843 608811
EMAIL: admin@danecourt.kent.sch.uk
WEBSITE: www.danecourt.kent.sch.uk

Dartford Grammar School

Status State
Programme MYP, Diploma
Diploma Coordinator Peter Fidczuk
MYP Coordinator Peter Fidczuk
Gender Coeducational
Languages English
Boarding/day Day
West Hill, Dartford, Kent DA1 2HW, UK
TELEPHONE: +44 (0)1322 223039
FAX: +44 (0)1322 291426
EMAIL: info@dartfordgrammar.kent.sch.uk
WEBSITE: www.dartfordgrammar.kent.sch.uk

De Ferrers Specialist Technology College

Status State
Programme Diploma
Diploma Coordinator Paul Galloway
Gender Coeducational
Languages English
Boarding/day Day
St Mary's Drive, Trent Campus, Burton upon Trent, Staffordshire DE13 0LL, UK
TELEPHONE: +44 (0) 1283 239936
EMAIL: office@deferrers.staffs.sch.uk
WEBSITE: www.deferrers.com

Doncaster College

Status State
Programme Diploma
Diploma Coordinator Ms Jo Burgess Stokes
Gender Coeducational
Languages English
Boarding/day Day
The Hub, Chapell Drive, Doncaster, South Yorkshire DN1 2RF, UK
TELEPHONE: +44 (0)1302 553553
FAX: +44 (0)1302 553559
EMAIL: infocentre@don.ac.uk
WEBSITE: www.don.ac.uk

Dover Grammar School for Boys

Status State
Programme Diploma
Diploma Coordinator Aidan Cruttenden
Gender Male
Languages English
Boarding/day Day
Astor Avenue, Dover, Kent CT17 0DQ, UK
TELEPHONE: +44 (0) 1304 206117
FAX: +44 (0) 1304 206074
EMAIL: office@dovergramboys.kent.sch.uk
WEBSITE: www.dovergramboys.kent.sch.uk

Ellesmere College

Status Private
Programme Diploma
Diploma Coordinator Helen T Scarisbrick
Gender Coeducational
Languages English
Boarding/day Mixed
Ellesmere, Shropshire SY12 9AB, UK
TELEPHONE: +44 (0)1691 622321
FAX: +44 (0)1691 623286
EMAIL: hmsecretary@ellesmere.com
WEBSITE: www.ellesmere.com

Exeter College

Status State
Programme Diploma
Diploma Coordinator Betty Woodfin
Gender Coeducational
Languages English
Boarding/day Day
Hele Road, Exeter, Devon EX4 4JS, UK
TELEPHONE: +44 (0)845 111 6000
FAX: +44 (0)1392 279972
EMAIL: busschool@exe-coll.ac.uk
WEBSITE: www.exe-coll.ac.uk

Felsted School

Status Private
Programme Diploma
Diploma Coordinator Paul Clark
Gender Coeducational
Languages English
Boarding/day Mixed
Felsted, Great Dunmow, Essex CM6 3LL, UK
TELEPHONE: +44 (0) 1371 822600
FAX: +44 (0) 1371 822607
EMAIL: info@felsted.org
WEBSITE: www.felsted.org

Fettes College

Status Private
Programme Diploma
Diploma Coordinator John Fern
Gender Coeducational
Languages English
Boarding/day Mixed
Carrington Road, Edinburgh EH4 1QX, UK
TELEPHONE: +44 (0)131 311 6744
FAX: +44 (0)131 311 6714
EMAIL: enquiries@fettes.com
WEBSITE: www.fettes.com

Finham Park School

Status State
Programme Diploma
Diploma Coordinator Victoria Chandley
Gender Coeducational
Languages English
Boarding/day Day
Green Lane, Coventry, West Midlands CV3 6EA, UK
TELEPHONE: +44 (0)2476 418 135
FAX: +44 (0)2476 840 803
EMAIL: headteacher@finhampark.co.uk
WEBSITE: www.finhampark.co.uk

Formby High School

Status State
Programme Diploma
Diploma Coordinator Nicola Davies
Gender Coeducational
Languages English
Boarding/day Day
Freshfield Road, Formby, Liverpool, Merseyside L37 3HW, UK
TELEPHONE: +44 (0) 1704 835650
FAX: +44 (0) 1704 835657
EMAIL: admin.formbyhigh@ schools.sefton.gov.uk
WEBSITE: www.formbyhigh.org

George Dixon International School & Sixth Form Centre

Status State
Programme Diploma
Diploma Coordinator Colin McKenzie
Gender Coeducational
Languages English
Boarding/day Day
City Road, Edgbaston, Birmingham, West Midlands B17 8LF, UK
TELEPHONE: +44 (0)121 675 44 88

GEORGE GREEN'S SCHOOL

Status State
Programme Diploma
Diploma Coordinator Geraldine Naughten
Gender Coeducational
Languages English
Boarding/day Day
100 Manchester Road, Isle of Dogs, London E14 3WE, UK
TELEPHONE: +44 (0)207 987 6032
FAX: +44 (0)207 538 2316
EMAIL: enquiries@georgegreens.com
WEBSITE: www.georgegreens.com
see full details on page 82

GRESHAM'S SCHOOL
Status Private
Programme Diploma
Diploma Coordinator Mr Mark Abbott
Gender Coeducational
Languages English
Boarding/day Mixed
Cromer Road, Holt, Norfolk NR25 6EA, UK
TELEPHONE: +44 (0)1263 714511
FAX: +44 (0)1263 712028
EMAIL: headmaster@greshams.com
WEBSITE: www.greshams.com
see full details on page 87

HAILEYBURY
Status Private
Programme Diploma
Diploma Coordinator Laura Pugsley MA, PhD
Gender Coeducational
Languages English
Boarding/day Mixed
Haileybury, Hertford, Hertfordshire SG13 7NU, UK
TELEPHONE: +44 (0)1992 462507
FAX: +44 (0)1992 470663
EMAIL: registrar@haileybury.com
WEBSITE: www.haileybury.com
see full details on page 88

Halesowen College
Status State
Programme Diploma
Diploma Coordinator Mick Grant
Gender Coeducational
Languages English
Boarding/day Day
Whittingham Road, Halesowen, West Midlands B63 3NA, UK
TELEPHONE: +44 (0)121 602 7777
FAX: +44 (0)121 585 0369
EMAIL: info@halesowen.ac.uk
WEBSITE: www.halesowen.ac.uk

Harrogate Grammar School
Status State
Programme Diploma
Diploma Coordinator Michael Bailey
Gender Coeducational
Languages English
Boarding/day Day
Arthurs Avenue, Harrogate, North Yorkshire HG2 0DZ, UK
TELEPHONE: +44 (0)1423 531127
FAX: +44 (0)1423 521325
EMAIL: admin@hgs.n-yorks.sch.uk
WEBSITE: www.hgs.n-yorks.sch.uk

Hastings College of Arts and Technology
Status State
Programme Diploma
Diploma Coordinator Chris Morrell
Gender Coeducational
Languages English
Boarding/day Mixed
Archery Road, St Leonards-on-Sea, East Sussex TN38 0HX, UK
TELEPHONE: +44 (0)1424 442 222
FAX: +44 (0)1424 721 763
EMAIL: studentadvisers@hastings.ac.uk
WEBSITE: www.hastings.ac.uk

Hautlieu School
Status State
Programme Diploma
Diploma Coordinator Paul Wallace-Sims
Gender Coeducational
Languages English
Boarding/day Day
Wellington Road, St Saviour, Jersey JE2 7TH
TELEPHONE: +44 (0) 1534 736 242
FAX: +44 (0) 1534 789 349
EMAIL: l.toms@hautlieu.sch.je
WEBSITE: www.hautlieu.net

Havering Sixth Form College
Status State
Programme Diploma
Diploma Coordinator Jessica Lawley
Wingletye Lane, Hornchurch, Essex RM11 3TB
TELEPHONE: +44 (0) 1708 514400
FAX: +44 (0) 1708 514488
EMAIL: mainoffice@havering-sfc.ac.uk
WEBSITE: www.havering-sfc.ac.uk

Henley College
Status State
Programme Diploma
Diploma Coordinator Bridie Hughes
Gender Coeducational
Languages English
Boarding/day Day
Deanfield Avenue, Henley-on-Thames, Oxfordshire RG9 1UH, UK
TELEPHONE: +44 (0)1491 579 988
FAX: +44 (0)1491 410 099
EMAIL: info@henleycol.ac.uk
WEBSITE: www.henleycol.ac.uk

Highlands School
Status State
Programme Diploma
Diploma Coordinator Karl Tuton
Gender Coeducational
Languages English
Boarding/day Day
148 Worlds End Lane, London N21 1QQ, UK
TELEPHONE: +44 (0)20 8370 1100
FAX: +44 (0)20 8370 1100
EMAIL: postbox@highlands.enfield.sch.uk
WEBSITE: www.highlands.enfield.sch.uk

Hockerill Anglo-European College
Status State
Programme Diploma
Diploma Coordinator Vicki Worsnop
Gender Coeducational
Languages English
Boarding/day Mixed
Dunmow Road, Bishops Stortford, Hertfordshire CM23 5HX, UK
TELEPHONE: +44 (0)1279 658451
FAX: +44 (0)1279 755918
EMAIL: admin@hockerill.herts.sch.uk
WEBSITE: www.hockerill.herts.sch.uk

Impington Village College
Status State
Programme Diploma
Diploma Coordinator Sandra Morton
Gender Coeducational
Languages English
Boarding/day Mixed
New Road, Impington, Cambridge, Cambridgeshire CB4 9LX, UK
TELEPHONE: +44 (0)1233 200 400
FAX: +44 (0)1223 200 418
EMAIL: office@ impingtonvc.cambs-schools.net
WEBSITE: www.impington.cambs.sch.uk

International Community School
Status Private
Programme PYP, MYP
MYP Coordinator Ean Orlando Alleyne
PYP Coordinator Lynne Horrobin
Gender Coeducational
Languages English
Boarding/day Day
4 York Terrace East, Regent's Park, London NW1 4PT, UK
TELEPHONE: +44 (0)20 7935 1206
FAX: +44 (0)20 7935 7915
EMAIL: admissions@ics.uk.net
WEBSITE: www.ics.uk.net

International School of Aberdeen
Status Private
Programme Diploma
Diploma Coordinator Mary Beth Kiley
Gender Coeducational
Languages English
Boarding/day Day
296 North Deeside Road, Milltimber, Aberdeen AB13 0AB, UK
TELEPHONE: +44 (0)1224 732267
FAX: +44 (0)1224 735648
EMAIL: admin@isa.aberdeen.sch.uk
WEBSITE: www.isa.aberdeen.sch.uk

INTERNATIONAL SCHOOL OF LONDON
Status Private
Programme PYP, MYP, Diploma
Diploma Coordinator Huw Davies
MYP Coordinator Paul Morris
PYP Coordinator Hala Fadda
Gender Coeducational
Languages English
Boarding/day Day
139 Gunnersbury Avenue, Acton, London W3 8LG, UK
TELEPHONE: +44 (0)20 8992 5823
FAX: +44 (0)20 8993 7012
EMAIL: mail@islondon.com
WEBSITE: www.islondon.com
see full details on page 100

Ivybridge Community College
Status State
Programme Diploma
Diploma Coordinator Sönke Beyer
Gender Coeducational
Languages English
Boarding/day Day
Harford Road, Ivybridge, Devon PL21 0JA, UK
TELEPHONE: +44 (0) 1752 691 000
FAX: +44 (0) 1752 691 247
EMAIL: grees@ivybridge.devon.sch.uk
WEBSITE: www.ivybridge.devon.sch.uk

KING EDWARD'S SCHOOL WITLEY
Status Private
Programme Diploma
Diploma Coordinator Christine Meharg
Gender Coeducational
Languages English
Boarding/day Mixed
Petworth Road, Wormley, Godalming, Surrey GU8 5SG, UK
TELEPHONE: +44 (0)1428 686768
FAX: +44 (0)1428 682850
EMAIL: admissions@kesw.surrey.sch.uk
WEBSITE: www.kesw.surrey.sch.uk
see full details on page 109

King Fahad Academy
Status Private
Programme Diploma
Diploma Coordinator Sue Austin
Gender Coeducational
Languages English
Boarding/day Day
Bromyard Avenue, Acton, London W3 7HD
TELEPHONE: +44 (0)20 8743 0131
FAX: +44 (0)20 8749 7085
EMAIL: academy@thekfa.org.uk
WEBSITE: www.thekfa.org.uk

KING WILLIAM'S COLLEGE
Status Private
Programme Diploma
Diploma Coordinator Dr Rene Filho
Gender Coeducational
Languages English
Boarding/day Mixed
Castletown, Isle of Man IM9 1TP, UK
TELEPHONE: +44 (0)1624 820428
FAX: +44 (0)1624 820401
EMAIL: Principal@kwc.sch.im
WEBSITE: www.kwc.im
see full details on page 110

KINGS COLLEGE FOR THE ARTS & TECHNOLOGY
Status State
Programme Diploma
Diploma Coordinator Nick Clay
Gender Coeducational
Languages English
Southway, Guildford, Surrey GU2 8DU, UK
TELEPHONE: +44 (0)1483 458 956
FAX: +44 (0)1483 458 957
EMAIL: info@kingscollegeguildford.com
WEBSITE: www.kingscollegeguildford.com
see full details on page 111

King's College School
Status Private
Programme Diploma
Diploma Coordinator Neil Tetley
Gender Male
Languages English
Boarding/day Day
Southside, Wimbledon Common, London SW19 4TT, UK
TELEPHONE: +44 (0)20 8255 5352
FAX: +44 (0)20 8255 5357
EMAIL: admissions@kcs.org.uk
WEBSITE: www.kcs.org.uk

Kings International College
Status State
Programme Diploma
Diploma Coordinator Anne Reynolds
Gender Coeducational
Languages English
Boarding/day Day
Watchetts Drive, Camberley, Surrey GU15 2PQ, UK
TELEPHONE: +44 (0)1276 683539
FAX: +44 (0)1276 709503
EMAIL: info@kings-international.co.uk

Lady Lumley's School
Status State
Programme Diploma
Diploma Coordinator Peter Howell
Gender Coeducational
Languages English
Boarding/day Day
Swainsea Lane, Pickering, North Yorkshire YO18 8NG, UK
TELEPHONE: +44 (0) 1751 472846
FAX: +44 (0) 1751 477259
EMAIL: admin@ladylumleys.freeserve.co.uk
WEBSITE: www.ladylumleys.org.uk

Lancaster & Morecambe College
Status State
Programme Diploma
Diploma Coordinator Tessa Jones
Languages English
Boarding/day Day
Morecambe Road, Lancaster, Lancashire LA1 2TY, UK
TELEPHONE: +44 (0)1524 66215
FAX: +44 (0)1524 843078
EMAIL: d.wood@lmc.ac.uk
WEBSITE: www.lmc.ac.uk

Liverpool College
Status Private
Programme Diploma
Diploma Coordinator Harry Lock
Gender Coeducational
Languages English
Boarding/day Day
Queen's Drive, Mossley Hill, Liverpool, Merseyside L18 8BG, UK
TELEPHONE: +44 (0)151 724 4000
FAX: +44 (0)151 729 0105
EMAIL: admin@liverpoolcollege.org.uk
WEBSITE: www.liverpoolcollege.org.uk

Luton Sixth Form College
Status State
Programme Diploma
Diploma Coordinator Colin Hall
Gender Coeducational
Languages English
Boarding/day Day
Bradgers Hill Road, Luton LU2 7EW, UK
TELEPHONE: +44 (0)1582 877500
FAX: +44 (0)1582 877501
EMAIL: college@lutonsfc.ac.uk
WEBSITE: www.lutonsfc.ac.uk

Maidstone Grammar School
Status State
Programme Diploma
Diploma Coordinator Keith Derrett
Gender Coeducational
Languages English
Boarding/day Day
Barton Road, Maidstone, Kent ME15 7BT, UK
TELEPHONE: +44 (0)1622 752101
FAX: +44 (0)1622 753680
EMAIL: school@mgs-kent.org.uk
WEBSITE: www.mgs.kent.sch.uk

Malvern College
Status Private
Programme Diploma
Diploma Coordinator John Knee
Gender Coeducational
Languages English
Boarding/day Mixed
College Road, Malvern, Worcestershire WR14 3DF, UK
TELEPHONE: +44 (0)1684 581500
FAX: +44 (0)1684 581617
EMAIL: registrar@malcol.org
WEBSITE: www.malcol.org

Manchester Grammar School
Status Private
Programme Diploma
Diploma Coordinator Chris Buckley
Gender Male
Languages English
Boarding/day Day
Old Hall Lane, Fallowfield, Manchester,
Greater Manchester M13 0XT, UK
TELEPHONE: +44 (0)161 224 7201
FAX: +44 (0)161 257 2446
EMAIL: enquiries@mgs.org
WEBSITE: www.mgs.org

MARYMOUNT INTERNATIONAL SCHOOL
Status Private
Programme MYP, Diploma
Diploma Coordinator Brian Johnson
MYP Coordinator Nicholas Marcou
Gender Female
Languages English
Boarding/day Both
George Road, Kingston upon Thames, Surrey
KT2 7PE, UK
TELEPHONE: +44 (0)20 8949 0571
FAX: +44 (0)20 8336 2485
EMAIL: admissions@marymountlondon.com
WEBSITE: www.marymountlondon.com
see full details on page 113

Newcastle Sixth Form College
Status State
Programme Diploma
Diploma Coordinator Lynda Evans
Gender Coeducational
Languages English
Boarding/day Day
Parsons Building, Rye Hill, Scotswood Road,
Newcastle upon Tyne, Tyne & Wear NE4 7SA
TELEPHONE: +44 (0) 191 200 4450
FAX: +44 (0) 191 200 4541
EMAIL: enquiries@ncl-coll.ac.uk
WEBSITE: www.ncl-coll.ac.uk

NORTH LONDON COLLEGIATE SCHOOL
Status Private
Programme Diploma
Diploma Coordinator Michael Burke
Gender Female
Languages English
Boarding/day Day
Canons, Canons Drive, Edgware, Middlesex
HA8 7RJ, UK
TELEPHONE: +44 (0)20 8952 0912
FAX: +44 (0)20 8951 1391
EMAIL: office@nlcs.org.uk
WEBSITE: www.nlcs.org.uk
see full details on page 121

Notre Dame High School
Status State
Programme Diploma
Diploma Coordinator Paul Short
Gender Coeducational
Languages English
Boarding/day Day
Surrey Street, Norwich, Norfolk NR1 3PB, UK
TELEPHONE: +44 (0) 1603 611431
FAX: +44 (0) 1603 763381
EMAIL:
office@notredamehigh.norfolk.sch.uk
WEBSITE: www.ndhs.org.uk

Oakham School
Status Private
Programme Diploma
Diploma Coordinator Simone Lorenz-Weir
Gender Coeducational
Languages English
Boarding/day Mixed
Chapel Close, Oakham, Rutland LE15 6DT, UK
TELEPHONE: +44 (0)1572 758758
FAX: +44 (0)1572 758595
EMAIL: admissions@oakham.rutland.sch.uk
WEBSITE: www.oakham.rutland.sch.uk

Overton Grange School
Status State
Programme Diploma
Diploma Coordinator Maria Cachia
Gender Coeducational
Languages English
Boarding/day Day
Stanley Road, Sutton, Surrey SM2 6TQ, UK
TELEPHONE: +44 (0) 20 8239 2383
FAX: +44 (0) 20 8239 2382
EMAIL: overtongrange@suttonlea.org
WEBSITE: www.overtongrange.sutton.sch.uk

Palmer's College
Status State
Programme Diploma
Diploma Coordinator John Death
Gender Coeducational
Languages English
Boarding/day Day
Chadwell Road, Grays, Essex RM17 5TD, UK
TELEPHONE: +44 (0) 1375 370121
FAX: +44 (0) 1375 385479
EMAIL: enquiries@palmers.ac.uk
WEBSITE: www.palmers.ac.uk

Queen Ethelburga's College
Status Private
Programme Diploma
Diploma Coordinator Denise Willis
Gender Coeducational
Languages English
Boarding/day Mixed
Thorpe Underwood Hall, Ouseburn, York
YO26 9SS, UK
TELEPHONE: +44 (0)1423 33 33 30
FAX: +44 (0)1423 33 14 44
EMAIL: enquiries@queenethelburgas.edu
WEBSITE: www.queenethelburgas.edu

Range High School
Status State
Programme Diploma
Diploma Coordinator Graham Aldridge
Gender Coeducational
Languages English
Boarding/day Day
Stapleton Road, Formby, Liverpool,
Merseyside L37 2YN, UK
TELEPHONE: +44 (0) 1704 879315
FAX: +44 (0) 1704 833470
EMAIL: contact@range.sefton.sch.uk
WEBSITE: www.range.sefton.sch.uk

RICHMOND UPON THAMES COLLEGE
Status State
Programme Diploma
Diploma Coordinator Stephen Winfield
Gender Coeducational
Languages English
Boarding/day Day
Egerton Road, Twickenham, Middlesex TW2
7SJ, UK
TELEPHONE: +44 (0)20 8607 8000/8294
FAX: +44 (0)20 8744 9738
EMAIL: swinfield@rutc.ac.uk
WEBSITE: www.rutc.ac.uk
see full details on page 128

ROSSALL SCHOOL
Status Private
Programme Diploma
Diploma Coordinator Dr Doris Dohmen
Gender Coeducational
Languages English
Boarding/day Mixed
Broadway, Fleetwood, Lancashire FY7 8JW, UK
TELEPHONE: +44 (0)1253 774260
FAX: +44 (0)1253 772052
EMAIL: enquiries@rossallcorporation.co.uk
WEBSITE: www.rossallschool.org.uk
see full details on page 129

RYDAL PENRHOS
Status Private
Programme Diploma
Diploma Coordinator Mr W Williams
Gender Coeducational
Languages English
Boarding/day Mixed
Pwllycrochan Avenue, Colwyn Bay, Conwy
LL29 7BT, UK
TELEPHONE: +44 (0)1492 530155
FAX: +44 (0)1492 531872
EMAIL: info@rydal-penrhos.com
WEBSITE: www.rydal-penrhos.com
see full details on page 130

SANDRINGHAM SCHOOL (BEAUSANDVER)
Status State
Programme Diploma
Diploma Coordinator Graeme Swann
Gender Coeducational
Languages English
Boarding/day Day
The Ridgeway, St Albans, Hertfordshire AL4 9NX, UK
TELEPHONE: +44 (0)1727 759 240
FAX: +44 (0)1727 759 242
EMAIL: graeme.swann@ sandringham.herts.sch.uk
WEBSITE: www.sandringham.herts.sch.uk
see full details on page 132

SCARBOROUGH COLLEGE
Status Private
Programme Diploma
Diploma Coordinator Amanda Evirgen
Gender Coeducational
Languages English
Boarding/day Mixed
Filey Road, Scarborough, North Yorkshire YO11 3BA, UK
TELEPHONE: +44 (0)1723 360620
FAX: +44 (0)1723 377265
EMAIL: admin@scarboroughcollege.co.uk
WEBSITE: www.scarboroughcollege.co.uk
see full details on page 134

SEVENOAKS SCHOOL
Status Private
Programme Diploma
Diploma Coordinator Nick Alchin
Gender Coeducational
Languages English
Boarding/day Mixed
Sevenoaks, Kent TN13 1HU, UK
TELEPHONE: +44 (0)1732 455133
FAX: +44 (0)1732 456143
EMAIL: nsa@sevenoaksschool.org
WEBSITE: www.sevenoaksschool.org
see full details on page 135

Sherborne School
Status Private
Programme Diploma
Diploma Coordinator Peter Such
Gender Male
Languages English
Boarding/day Boarding
Abbey Road, Sherborne, Dorset DT9 3AP, UK
TELEPHONE: +44 (0)1935 812249
FAX: +44 (0)1935 810423
EMAIL: enquiries@sherborne.org
WEBSITE: www.sherborne.org

Sherborne School for Girls
Status Private
Programme Diploma
Diploma Coordinator Penny Deacon
Gender Female
Languages English
Boarding/day Boarding
Sherborne, Dorset DT9 3QN, UK
TELEPHONE: +44 (0)1935 818287
FAX: +44 (0)1935 389445
EMAIL: enquiry@sherborne.com
WEBSITE: www.sherborne.com

Sidcot School
Status Private
Programme Diploma
Diploma Coordinator Philip Perkins
Gender Coeducational
Languages English
Boarding/day Mixed
Oakridge Lane, Winscombe, North Somerset BS25 1PD, UK
TELEPHONE: +44 (0)1934 843102
FAX: +44 (0)1934 844181
EMAIL: admissions@sidcot.org.uk
WEBSITE: www.sidcot.org.uk

Slough Grammar School
Status State
Programme Diploma
Diploma Coordinator Ruth Symons
Gender Coeducational
Languages English
Boarding/day Day
Lascelles Road, Slough SL3 7PR, UK
TELEPHONE: +44 (0)1753 522892
FAX: +44 (0)1753 538618
EMAIL: office@sloughgrammar.berks.sch.uk
WEBSITE: www.sloughgrammar.berks.sch.uk

South Wolds Community School
Status State
Programme Diploma
Diploma Coordinator Carole Hughes
Gender Coeducational
Languages English
Boarding/day Day
Church Drive, Keyworth, Nottingham, Nottinghamshire NG12 5FF, UK
TELEPHONE: +44 (0)115 937 3506
FAX: +44 (0)115 937 2905
EMAIL: ageorge@southwolds.notts.sch.uk
WEBSITE: www.southwolds.co.uk

Southbank International School – Hampstead
Status Private
Programme PYP
PYP Coordinator Charlotte Gregson
Gender Coeducational
Languages English
Boarding/day Day
16 Netherhall Gardens, London NW3 5TH, UK
TELEPHONE: +44 (0)20 7243 3803
FAX: +44 (0)20 7727 3290
EMAIL: admissions@southbank.org
WEBSITE: www.southbank.org

Southbank International School – Kensington
Status Private
Programme PYP
PYP Coordinator Mark Case
Gender Coeducational
Languages English
Boarding/day Day
36-38 Kensington Park Road, London W11 3BU, UK
TELEPHONE: +44 (0)20 7243 3803
FAX: +44 (0)20 7727 3290
EMAIL: admissions@southbank.org
WEBSITE: www.southbank.org

Southbank International School – Westminster
Status Private
Programme MYP, Diploma
Diploma Coordinator Paul Pickering
MYP Coordinator Lori Fritz
Gender Coeducational
Languages English
Boarding/day Day
63-65 Portland Place, London W1B 1QR, UK
TELEPHONE: +44 (0)20 7243 3803
FAX: +44 (0)20 7727 3290
EMAIL: admissions@southbank.org
WEBSITE: www.southbank.org

St Clare's, Oxford
Status Private
Programme Diploma
Diploma Coordinator Nick Lee
Gender Coeducational
Languages English
Boarding/day Mixed
139 Banbury Road, Oxford OX2 7AL
TELEPHONE: +44 (0)1865 552031
FAX: +44 (0)1865 513359
EMAIL: chris.osbourne@stclares.ac.uk
WEBSITE: www.stclares.ac.uk

St Columba's Catholic School
Status State
Programme PYP
PYP Coordinator Wendy Plevin
Gender Coeducational
Languages English
Boarding/day Day
Ripley Street, Bolton, Gtr Manchester BL2 3AR
TELEPHONE: +44 1204 333421
FAX: +44 1204 333420
EMAIL: collinsn@st-columbas.bolton.sch.uk
WEBSITE: www.stcolumba.ik.org

St Dunstan's College
Status Private
Programme Diploma
Diploma Coordinator Sue Algeo
Gender Coeducational
Languages English
Boarding/day Day
Stanstead Road, London SE6 4TY, UK
TELEPHONE: +44 (0)20 8516 7200
FAX: +44 (0)20 8516 7300
EMAIL: hm@sdmail.org.uk
WEBSITE: www.stdunstans.org.uk

ST EDWARD'S, OXFORD

Status Private
Programme Diploma
Diploma Coordinator Jesse Elzinga
Gender Coeducational
Languages English
Boarding/day Mixed
Woodstock Road, Oxford OX2 7NN, UK
TELEPHONE: +44 (0)1865 319323
FAX: +44 (0)1865 319242
EMAIL: registrar@stedwards.oxon.sch.uk
WEBSITE: www.stedwards.oxon.sch.uk
see full details on page 140

ST HELEN'S SCHOOL

Status Private
Programme Diploma
Diploma Coordinator Mary Bowman
Gender Female
Languages English
Boarding/day Day
Eastbury Road, Northwood, Middx HA6 3AS
TELEPHONE: +44 (0)1923 843210
FAX: +44 (0)1923 843211
EMAIL: enquiries@sthn.co.uk
WEBSITE: www.sthn.co.uk
see full details on page 143

St John's School & Community College

Status State
Programme Diploma
Diploma Coordinator Sue Round
Gender Coeducational
Languages English
Boarding/day Day
Orchard Road, Marlborough, Wilts SN8 4AX
TELEPHONE: +44 (0)1672 516156
FAX: +44 (0)1672 516664
EMAIL: phazlewood@stjohns.wilts.sch.uk
WEBSITE: www.stjohns.wilts.sch.uk

St Leonards School

Status Private
Programme Diploma
Diploma Coordinator Karen Wowk
Gender Coeducational
Languages English
Boarding/day Mixed
St Andrews, Fife KY16 9QJ, UK
TELEPHONE: +44 (0)1334 472126
FAX: +44 (0)1334 476152
EMAIL: info@stleonards-fife.org
WEBSITE: www.stleonards-fife.org

Stanborough School

Status Private
Programme Diploma
Diploma Coordinator Peter Martin
Gender Coeducational
Languages English
Boarding/day Mixed
Stanborough Park, Garston, Watford,
Hertfordshire WD25 9JT, UK
TELEPHONE: +44 (0)1923 673268
FAX: +44 (0)1923 893943
EMAIL: registrar@spsch.org
WEBSITE: www.spsch.org

Swansea College

Status State
Programme Diploma
Diploma Coordinator Sue Phillips
Gender Coeducational
Languages English
Boarding/day Day
Tycoch Road, Tycoch, Swansea SA2 9EB, UK
TELEPHONE: +44 (0)800 174 084
FAX: +44 (0)1792 284074

TASIS THE AMERICAN SCHOOL IN ENGLAND

Status Private
Programme Diploma
Diploma Coordinator Chantal Gordon
Gender Coeducational
Languages English
Boarding/day Mixed
Coldharbour Lane, Thorpe, Surrey TW20 8TE
TELEPHONE: +44 (0)1932 565252
FAX: +44 (0)1932 564644
EMAIL: ukadmissions@tasisengland.org
WEBSITE: www.tasis.com/England
see full details on page 145

Taunton School

Status Private
Programme Diploma
Diploma Coordinator Martin Bluemel
Gender Coeducational
Languages English
Boarding/day Mixed
Staplegrove Road, Taunton, Somerset TA2
6AD, UK
TELEPHONE: +44 (0)1823 349200
FAX: +44 (0)1823 349201
EMAIL: enquiries@tauntonschool.co.uk
WEBSITE: www.tauntonschool.co.uk

Taunton's College

Status State
Programme Diploma
Diploma Coordinator Catharine Yates
Gender Coeducational
Languages English
Boarding/day Day
Hill Lane, Southampton SO15 5RL, UK
TELEPHONE: +44 (0)23 8051 1811
FAX: +44 (0)23 8051 1991
EMAIL: email@tauntons.ac.uk
WEBSITE: www.tauntons.ac.uk

The Abbey School

Status Private
Programme Diploma
Diploma Coordinator Liz Robinson
Gender Female
Languages English
Boarding/day Day
Kendrick Road, Reading RG1 5DZ, UK
TELEPHONE: +44 (0)118 987 2256
FAX: +44 (0)118 987 1478
EMAIL: schooloffice@theabbey.co.uk
WEBSITE: www.theabbey.co.uk

The Bolitho School

Status Private
Programme Diploma
Diploma Coordinator Peter Trythall
Gender Coeducational
Languages English
Boarding/day Mixed
Polwithen, Penzance, Cornwall TR18 4JR, UK
TELEPHONE: +44 (0)1736 363271
FAX: +44 (0)1736 330960
EMAIL: enquiries@bolitho.cornwall.sch.uk
WEBSITE: www.bolitho.cornwall.sch.uk

The Cheltenham Ladies' College

Status Private
Programme Diploma
Diploma Coordinator Rebecca Revell
Bayshill Road, Cheltenham, Gloucestershire
GL50 3EP, UK
TELEPHONE: +44 (0)1242 520691
FAX: +44 (0)1242 227882
EMAIL: enquiries@cheltladiescollege.org
WEBSITE: www.cheltladiescollege.org

The Godolphin and Latymer School

Status Private
Programme Diploma
Diploma Coordinator Caroline Trimming
Gender Female
Languages English
Boarding/day Day
Iffley Road, Hammersmith, London W6 0PG
TELEPHONE: +44 (0)20 8741 1936
FAX: +44 (0)20 8735 9520
EMAIL: vcox@godolphinandlatymer.com
WEBSITE: www.godolphinandlatymer.com

The Grammar School at Leeds

Status Private
Programme Diploma
Diploma Coordinator Mark Humphries
Gender Coeducational
Languages English
Boarding/day Day
Alwoodley Gates, Harrogate Road, Leeds,
West Yorkshire LS17 8GS, UK
TELEPHONE: +44 (0)113 2291552
FAX: +44 (0)113 2285111
EMAIL: enquiries@gsal.org.uk
WEBSITE: www.gsal.org.uk

The Leigh City Technology College

Status State
Programme Diploma
Diploma Coordinator Colin Ankerson
Gender Coeducational
Languages English
Boarding/day Day
Green Street Green Road, Dartford, Kent DA1
1QE, UK
TELEPHONE: +44 (0)1322 620400
EMAIL: fgr@leighctc.kent.sch.uk
WEBSITE: www.leighctc.kent.sch.uk

THE NORTH LONDON INTERNATIONAL SCHOOL

Status Private
Programme PYP, MYP, Diploma
Diploma Coordinator Edith van der Linden
MYP Coordinator Yukesha Makhan
PYP Coordinator Theresa Heath
Gender Coeducational
Languages English
Boarding/day Day
Friern Barnet Lane, London N11 3LX, UK
TELEPHONE: +44 (0)20 8920 0600
FAX: +44 (0)20 8211 4605
EMAIL: admissions@nlis.org
WEBSITE: www.nlis.org
see full details on page 151

The Norton Knatchbull School

Status State
Programme Diploma
Diploma Coordinator Roger Baker
Gender Coeducational
Languages English
Boarding/day Day
Hythe Road, Ashford, Kent TN24 0QJ, UK
TELEPHONE: +44 (0)1233 620045
EMAIL: information@
norton-knatchbull.kent.sch.uk
WEBSITE:
www.norton-knatchbull.kent.sch.uk

The Ridings High School

Status State
Programme Diploma
Diploma Coordinator Laura Woodward
Gender Coeducational
Languages English
Boarding/day Day
High Street, Winterbourne, Bristol BS36 1JL
TELEPHONE: +44 (0)1454 252 041
EMAIL: rgibson@ridingshigh.org
WEBSITE: www.ridingshigh.org

The Rochester Grammar School

Status State
Programme Diploma
Diploma Coordinator Paul Saunders
Gender Coeducational
Languages English
Boarding/day Day
Maidstone Road, Rochester, Kent ME1 3BY
TELEPHONE: +44 (0)1634 843049
FAX: +44 (0)1634 818340
EMAIL: shepd004@medway.org.uk
WEBSITE:
www.rochestergrammar.medway.sch.uk

The Royal High School, Bath GDST

Status Private
Programme Diploma
Diploma Coordinator Ruth Sara
Gender Coeducational
Languages English
Boarding/day Day
Lansdown Road, Bath BA1 5SZ, UK
TELEPHONE: +44 (0)1225 313877
FAX: +44 (0)1225 465446
EMAIL: royalhigh@bat.gdst.net
WEBSITE: www.gdst.net/royalhighbath

The Sixth Form College, Colchester

Status State
Programme Diploma
Diploma Coordinator Jim Morrissey
Gender Coeducational
Languages English
Boarding/day Day
North Hill, Colchester, Essex CO1 1SN, UK
TELEPHONE: +44 (0)1206 500778
FAX: +44 (0)1206 500770
EMAIL: principal@colchsfc.ac.uk
WEBSITE: www.colchsfc.ac.uk

The Sixth Form College, Solihull

Status State
Programme Diploma
Diploma Coordinator Mike Padbury
Gender Coeducational
Languages English
Boarding/day Day
Widney Manor Road, Solihull, West Midlands
B91 3WR, UK
TELEPHONE: +44 (0)121 704 2581
FAX: +44 (0)121 711 1598
WEBSITE: www.solihullsfc.ac.uk

THE STEPHEN PERSE SIXTH FORM COLLEGE

Status Private
Programme Diploma
Diploma Coordinator Simon Armitage
Gender Coeducational
Languages English
Boarding/day Day
Shaftesbury Road, Cambridge,
Cambridgeshire CB2 8AA, UK
TELEPHONE: +44 (0)1223 488430
FAX: +44 (0)1223 467420
EMAIL: office@stephenperse.com
WEBSITE: www.stephenperse.com
see full details on page 152

Thomas Alleyne's High School

Status State
Programme Diploma
Diploma Coordinator Carole Dodd
Gender Coeducational
Languages English
Boarding/day Day
Dove Bank, Uttoxeter, Stafford, Staffordshire
ST14 8DU, UK
TELEPHONE: +44 (0) 1889 561820
FAX: +44 (0) 1889 561850
EMAIL: ib@tahs.net
WEBSITE: www.thomasalleynes.staffs.sch.uk

Thomas Deacon Academy

Status State
Programme Diploma
Diploma Coordinator Louise Moir
Gender Coeducational
Languages English
Boarding/day Day
Queen's Gardens, Peterborough PE1 2UW, UK
TELEPHONE: +44 (0)1733 426060
FAX: +44 (0)1733 426061
EMAIL: ib@thomasdeaconacademy.com
WEBSITE: www.thomasdeaconacademy.com

Thomas Hardye School

Status State
Programme Diploma
Diploma Coordinator Frances Anderson
Gender Coeducational
Languages English
Boarding/day Day
Queens Avenue, Dorchester, Dorset DT1 2ET
TELEPHONE: +44 (0)1305 266 064
EMAIL: iemelvin@
thomas-hardye.dorset.sch.uk
WEBSITE: www.thomas-hardye.dorset.sch.uk

TOLLBAR BUSINESS & ENTERPRISE COLLEGE

Status State
Programme Diploma
Diploma Coordinator Mrs D Shelton
Gender Coeducational
Languages English
Boarding/day Day
Station Road, New Waltham, Grimsby, North-
East Lincolnshire DN36 4RZ, UK
TELEPHONE: +44 (0)1472 500505
FAX: +44 (0)1472 500506
EMAIL: sixform@tollbarbec.co.uk
WEBSITE: www.tbecib.co.uk
see full details on page 155

Tonbridge Grammar School

Status State
Programme Diploma
Diploma Coordinator Marion Middleton
Gender Coeducational
Languages English
Boarding/day Day
Deakin Leas, Tonbridge, Kent TN9 2JR, UK
TELEPHONE: +44 (0)1732 365125
FAX: +44 (0)1732 359417
EMAIL: headteacher@tgs.kent.sch.uk
WEBSITE: www.tgs.kent.sch.uk

Top o 'th' Brow Community Primary School

Status State
Programme PYP
PYP Coordinator Janine Hopper
Gender Coeducational
Languages English
Boarding/day Day
Greenroyd Avenue, Breightmet, Bolton BL2
5DD, UK
TELEPHONE: +44 (0)1204 333 473
EMAIL: office@top-oth-brow.bolton.sch.uk
WEBSITE: www.top-oth-brow.bolton.sch.uk

Truro College

Status State
Programme Diploma
Diploma Coordinator Andy Wildin
Gender Coeducational
Languages English
Boarding/day Day
College Road, Truro, Cornwall TR1 3XX, UK
TELEPHONE: +44 (0)1872 267000
FAX: +44 (0)1872 267100
EMAIL: enquiry@trurocollege.ac.uk
WEBSITE: www.trurocollege.ac.uk

Tyne Metropolitan College

Status State
Programme Diploma
Diploma Coordinator Adrian Shepherd
Gender Coeducational
Languages English
Boarding/day Day
Embleton Avenue, Wallsend, Newcastle upon Tyne, Tyne & Wear NE28 9NJ, UK
TELEPHONE: +44 (0)191 229 5000
FAX: +44 (0)191 229 5301
EMAIL: enquiries@tynemet.ac.uk
WEBSITE: www.ntyneside.ac.uk

United World College of the Atlantic

Status Private
Programme Diploma
Diploma Coordinator Gareth Rees
Gender Coeducational
Languages English
Boarding/day Boarding
St Donat's Castle, Llantwit Major, Vale of Glamorgan CF61 1WF, UK
TELEPHONE: +44 (0)1446 799000
FAX: +44 (0)1446 799277
EMAIL: principal@uwcac.uwc.org
WEBSITE: www.atlanticcollege.org

Varndean College

Status State
Programme Diploma
Diploma Coordinator Sean McEvoy
Gender Coeducational
Languages English
Boarding/day Day
Surrenden Road, Brighton BN1 6WQ, UK
TELEPHONE: +44 (0)1273 508011
FAX: +44 (0)1273 542950
EMAIL: office@varndean.ac.uk
WEBSITE: www.varndean.ac.uk

VERULAM SCHOOL (BEAUSANDVER)

Status State
Programme Diploma
Diploma Coordinator Susan Turner
Gender Coeducational
Languages English
Boarding/day Day
Brampton Road, St Albans, Hertfordshire AL1 4PR, UK
TELEPHONE: +44 (0)1727 766 100
FAX: +44 (0)1727 766 256
EMAIL: sue.turner@verulam.herts.sch.uk
WEBSITE: www.verulamschool.net
see full details on page 158

Waingels College

Status State
Programme Diploma
Diploma Coordinator Jean Tillyard
Gender Coeducational
Languages English
Boarding/day Day
Denmark Avenue, Woodley, Reading RG5 4RF
TELEPHONE: +44 (0)118 969 0336
FAX: +44 (0)118 944 2843
EMAIL: grerg@waingels.wokingham.sch.uk
WEBSITE: www.waingels.wokingham.sch.uk

WARMINSTER SCHOOL

Status Private
Programme Diploma
Diploma Coordinator Olivia Bourne
Gender Coeducational
Languages English
Boarding/day Mixed
Church Street, Warminster, Wiltshire BA12 8PJ, UK
TELEPHONE: +44 (0)1985 210160
FAX: +44 (0)1985 210154
EMAIL: admin@warminsterschool.org.uk
WEBSITE: www.warminsterschool.org.uk
see full details on page 159

Warwickshire College

Status State
Programme Diploma
Diploma Coordinator Melvyn Colley
Gender Coeducational
Languages English
Boarding/day Day
Warwick New Road, Leamington Spa, Warwickshire CV32 5JE, UK
TELEPHONE: +44 (0)1926 318000
FAX: +44 (0)1926 318111
EMAIL: imorgan@warkscol.ac.uk
WEBSITE: www.warkscol.ac.uk

Wellington College

Status Private
Programme Diploma
Diploma Coordinator David James
Dukes Ride, Crowthorne, Wokingham RG45 7PU, UK
TELEPHONE: +44 (0)1344 444 000
FAX: +44 (0)1344 444 002
EMAIL: info@wellingtoncollege.org.uk
WEBSITE: www.wellingtoncollege.org.uk

Westbourne School

Status Private
Programme Diploma
Diploma Coordinator Gareth Jones
Gender Coeducational
Languages English
Boarding/day Day
4 Hickman Road, Penarth, Vale of Glamorgan CF6 2AJ, UK
TELEPHONE: +44 (0)29 2070 5705
FAX: +44 (0)29 2070 9988
EMAIL: enquiries@westbourneschool.com
WEBSITE: www.westbourneschool.com

Westminster Academy

Status State
Programme Diploma
Diploma Coordinator Oliver Wells
Gender Coeducational
Languages English
Boarding/day Day
The Naim Dangoor Centre, 255 Harrow Road, London W2 5EZ, UK
TELEPHONE: +44 (0)20 7121 0600
EMAIL: admin@westminsteracademy.biz
WEBSITE: www.westminsteracademy.biz

Whitchurch High School

Status State
Programme Diploma
Diploma Coordinator Jonathan Davies
Gender Coeducational
Languages English
Boarding/day Day
Penlline Road, Whitchurch, Cardiff CF4 2XJ
TELEPHONE: +44 (0)29 2062 9700
FAX: +44 (0)29 2062 9701
WEBSITE: www.whitchurchhs.com

WHITGIFT SCHOOL

Status Private
Programme Diploma
Diploma Coordinator Stewart Cook
Gender Male
Languages English
Boarding/day Day
Haling Park, South Croydon, Surrey CR2 6YT
TELEPHONE: +44 (0)20 8688 9222
FAX: +44 (0)20 8760 0682
EMAIL: office@whitgift.co.uk
WEBSITE: www.whitgift.co.uk
see full details on page 162

Windermere St Anne's School

Status Private
Programme Diploma
Diploma Coordinator Jenny Davey
Gender Coeducational
Languages English
Boarding/day Mixed
Patterdale Road, Windermere, Cumbria LA23 1NW, UK
TELEPHONE: +44 (0)15394 46164
FAX: +44 (0)15394 88414
EMAIL: admissions@wsaschool.com
WEBSITE: www.wsaschool.com

Worth School

Status Private
Programme Diploma
Diploma Coordinator Simon Smith
Gender Male (coed Sixth Form)
Languages English
Boarding/day Mixed
Paddockhurst Road, Turners Hill, Crawley, West Sussex RH10 4SD, UK
TELEPHONE: +44 (0)1342 710200
FAX: +44 (0)1342 710230
EMAIL: registry@worth.org.uk
WEBSITE: www.worthschool.co.uk

Wyggeston & Queen Elizabeth I College
Status State
Programme Diploma
Diploma Coordinator Helen Bull
Gender Coeducational
Languages English
Boarding/day Day
University Road, Leicester LE1 7RJ, UK
TELEPHONE: +44 (0)116 2231900
FAX: +44 (0)116 2231999
EMAIL: admissions@wqeic.ac.uk
WEBSITE: www.wqeic.ac.uk

UKRAINE

Kyiv International School
Status Private
Programme Diploma
Diploma Coordinator Sergey Berezhny
Gender Coeducational
Languages English
Boarding/day Day
3A Svyatoshinsky Provuluk, Kyiv 03115, Ukraine
TELEPHONE: +380 44 452 2793
FAX: +380 44 452 2998
EMAIL: kiev@qsi.org

Pechersk School International
Status Private
Programme PYP, MYP, Diploma
Diploma Coordinator Trevor Wilson
MYP Coordinator Katja Kolb
PYP Coordinator Tasha Cowdy
Gender Coeducational
Languages English
Boarding/day Day
7a Victora Zabily, Kyiv 3039, Ukraine
TELEPHONE: +380 44 455-95-85
FAX: +380 44 455-95-80
EMAIL: communication@psi.kiev.ua
WEBSITE: www.psi.kiev.ua

UNITED ARAB EMIRATES

Abu Dhabi International Private School WLL
Status Private
Programme Diploma
Diploma Coordinator Judith Hughes
Gender Coeducational
Languages English
Boarding/day Day
PO Box 25898, Al Karama Street, Al Rawda Sector, Abu Dhabi, United Arab Emirates
TELEPHONE: +971 2 4434433
EMAIL: aisem@emirates.net.ae
WEBSITE: www.aisuae.com

American Community School
Status Private
Programme Diploma
Diploma Coordinator Jennifer Wirth
Gender Coeducational
Languages English
Boarding/day Day
PO Box 42114, Abu Dhabi, UAE
TELEPHONE: +971 2 681 5115
EMAIL: george-robinson@acs.sch.ae
WEBSITE: http://acs.sch.ae

American International School in Abu Dhabi
Status Private
Programme Diploma
Diploma Coordinator Deborah Kelly
Gender Coeducational
Languages English
Boarding/day Day
PO Box 5992, Abu Dhabi, UAE
TELEPHONE: +971 2 4444 333
FAX: +971 2 444005
EMAIL: aisadirector@yahoo.com
WEBSITE: www.aisa.sch.ae

DEIRA INTERNATIONAL SCHOOL
Status Private
Programme Diploma
Diploma Coordinator Jenny Bastable
Gender Coeducational
Languages English
Boarding/day Day
PO Box 79043, Dubai, United Arab Emirates
TELEPHONE: +9714 2325552
FAX: +9714 2325151
EMAIL: jbastable@disdubai.ae
WEBSITE: www.disdubai.ae
see full details on page 74

Dubai American Academy
Status Private
Programme Diploma
Diploma Coordinator Dina Khalaf
Gender Coeducational
Languages English
Boarding/day Day
PO Box 32762, Dubai, United Arab Emirates
TELEPHONE: +971 4 347 9222
FAX: +971 4 347 6070
EMAIL: bmatthews@daa.sch.ae
WEBSITE: www.gemsaa-dubai.com

Dubai International Academy
Status Private
Programme PYP, MYP, Diploma
Diploma Coordinator Narendra Mehrotra
MYP Coordinator Marion Hawkins
PYP Coordinator Alison Besselaar
Gender Coeducational
Languages English, Arabic, French
Boarding/day Day/mixed
PO Box 118111, Dubai, United Arab Emirates
TELEPHONE: +971 4 368 4111
FAX: +971 4 324 8866
EMAIL: poonamb@diadubai.com
WEBSITE: www.diadubai.com

Emirates International School – Jumeirah
Status Private
Programme Diploma
Diploma Coordinator Patricia Sechusen
Gender Coeducational
Languages English
Boarding/day Day
PO Box 6446, Dubai, United Arab Emirates
TELEPHONE: +971 4 3489804
FAX: +971 4 3482 813
EMAIL: jkirwin@eischools.ae
WEBSITE: www.eischools.ae

Emirates International School – Meadows
Status Private
Programme Diploma
Diploma Coordinator Murray Lamshed
Gender Coeducational
Languages English
Boarding/day Day
PO Box 120118, Dubai, United Arab Emirates
TELEPHONE: +971 4 362 9009
FAX: +971 4 362 9229
EMAIL: marquandb@eischools.ae
WEBSITE: www.eischools.ae

Ras Al Khaimah English Speaking School
Status Private
Programme Diploma
Diploma Coordinator Ron Entwistle
Gender Coeducational
Languages English
Boarding/day Day
PO Box 975, Ras Al Khiamah, UAE
TELEPHONE: +971 7 236 2441
FAX: +971 7 236 2445
EMAIL: principal@rakess.net
WEBSITE: www.rakess.net

UNIVERSAL AMERICAN SCHOOL, DUBAI
Status Private
Programme Diploma
Diploma Coordinator Courtney Malone
Gender Coeducational
Languages English
Boarding/day Day
PO Box 79133, Dubai Festival City, UAE
TELEPHONE: +971 4 232 5222
FAX: +971 4 232 5545
EMAIL: rtaylor@uasdubai.ae
WEBSITE: www.uasdubai.ae
see full details on page 156

UNITED ARAB EMIRATES

Uptown School
Status Private
Programme PYP
PYP Coordinator Virginia Sutton
Gender Coeducational
Languages English
Boarding/day Day
PO Box 78181, Mirdif, Dubai, UAE
TELEPHONE: +971 4 288 6270
FAX: +971 4 288 6271
EMAIL: elizabethloadwick@hotmail.com
WEBSITE: www.uptownprimary.ae

UZBEKISTAN

Tashkent International School
Status Private
Programme Diploma
Diploma Coordinator Tim Getter
Gender Coeducational
Languages English
Boarding/day Day
38 Sarikulskaya Street, Tashkent 10005,
Uzbekistan
TELEPHONE: +998 71 291 1341
FAX: +998 71 120 6621
EMAIL: director@tashschool.org
WEBSITE: www.tashschool.org

ZAMBIA

American International School of Lusaka
Status Private
Programme PYP, MYP, Diploma
Diploma Coordinator Scott Genzer
MYP Coordinator Helen Jeffery
PYP Coordinator Sabrina Manhart
Gender Coeducational
Languages English
Boarding/day Day
PO Box 31617, Lusaka, Zambia
TELEPHONE: +260 1 260509/10
FAX: +260 1 260 538
EMAIL: twalters@aislusaka.org
WEBSITE: www.aislusaka.org

International School of Lusaka
Status Private
Programme PYP, Diploma
Diploma Coordinator Hugh King
PYP Coordinator Philip Bowen
Gender Coeducational
Languages English
Boarding/day Day
PO Box 50121, Lusaka, Zambia
TELEPHONE: +260 1 252291
FAX: +260 1 252865
EMAIL: int.school.lusaka@gmail.com
WEBSITE: www.ecis.org/lusaka

ZIMBABWE

Harare International School
Status Private
Programme PYP, Diploma
Diploma Coordinator David Crawford
PYP Coordinator Ivy Decker-Jones
Gender Coeducational
Languages English
Boarding/day Day
US Embassy, 172 Herbert Chitepo Avenue,
Harare, Zimbabwe
TELEPHONE: +263 4 870514
FAX: +263 4 883371
EMAIL: ppoore@his.ac.zw
WEBSITE: www.his-zim.com

St Johns College
Status State
Programme Diploma
Diploma Coordinator Diana Hale
Gender Coeducational
Languages English
Boarding/day Day
Po Box BW 600, Borrowdale, Harare,
Zimbabwe
TELEPHONE: +264-4-885102
FAX: +264-4-882779
EMAIL: andyv@stjohns.co.zw

IB
Asia Pacific

Asia Pacific

The IB Asia Pacific regional office, located in Singapore, provides services for the three IB programmes to schools in the following countries:

South-East Asia:	Brunei, Cambodia, Indonesia, Malaysia, Philippines, Singapore, Thailand, Vietnam, Laos
Australasia:	Australia, Fiji, New Zealand, Papua New Guinea
South Asia:	India, Bangladesh, Pakistan, Sri Lanka
East Asia:	Japan, Republic of Korea, Taiwan
Pacific Islands:	Guam
China:	China, Hong Kong (SAR), Mongolia

Some recent initiatives

In an effort to meet the professional development needs of schools and their teachers more effectively, the regional office is continuing to establish a wider range of Level 3 workshops. We have also conducted our first cross-programme workshop leader training in an effort to emphasize the links between the three IB programmes.

The 2008 Regional Conference in Beijing is seeking to provide a platform for discussion and feedback from teachers on pertinent education issues related to a vision on Sharing our Humanity and is targeting the issue of Educating for Social Responsibility.

The Asia Pacific office is continuing to promote IB recognition throughout the region, and has commissioned various research initiatives to further promote understanding about outcomes for students of IB programmes. A copy of the Australian Council for Educational Research report on Perceptions of the IB Diploma Programme amongst Australian and New Zealand Universities is downloadable from:

www.ibo.org/ibap/IBOPerceptionsReportFinal.pdf.pdf

Curriculum analysis studies comparing IB Diploma curriculums to state board curriculums in Australia and India will be available mid 2008.

The office continues to work on a range of fronts in its ongoing commitment to widen access and has consolidated its teacher training programmes to include Primary Teacher Training in Aceh and an Early Childhood Care and Development Teacher Training and Accreditation Pilot Programme in Sri Lanka as well as ongoing primary teacher training in Cambodia.

Some facts about this region

As at September 2008

IB Asia Pacific serves 338 IB World Schools located in 24 countries and offers 472 IB programmes in total.

DP programmes:	246
MYP programmes:	105
PYP programmes:	121
Schools offering all three programmes:	40
Schools offering DP and MYP:	17
Schools offering DP and PYP:	25
Schools offering MYP and PYP:	12
State school programmes:	72
Private school programmes:	400
State school programmes:	68
Private school programmes:	340

AUSTRALIA

American International School, Australia
Status Private
Programme Diploma
Diploma Coordinator Lyn Cheetham
Gender Coeducational
Locked Bag 204, Oatlands NSW 2117, Australia
TELEPHONE: +61 2 9890 3488
FAX: +61 2 9890 3499
EMAIL: lcheetham@ais.thin-ed.net
WEBSITE: www.amschool.com.au

Annesley College
Status Private
Programme PYP
PYP Coordinator Alison Hunt
Gender Female
Languages English
Boarding/day Mixed
89 Greenhill Road, Wayville SA 5034, Australia
TELEPHONE: +61 8 8422 2208
EMAIL: principal@annesley.sa.edu.au
WEBSITE: www.annesley.sa.edu.au

Auburn South Primary School
Status State
Programme PYP
PYP Coordinator Colleen Moore
Gender Coeducational
Languages English
Boarding/day Day
419 Tooronga Road, East Hawthorn, Melbourne VIC 3123, Australia
TELEPHONE: +61 3 9882 2140
FAX: +61 3 9813 1517
EMAIL: campbell.gary.gc@edumail.vic.gov.au
WEBSITE: www.auburnsthps.edu.au

AUSTRALIAN INTERNATIONAL ACADEMY
Status Private
Programme PYP, MYP, Diploma
Diploma Coordinator Mrs Maha Elsayegh
MYP Coordinator Mrs Gafiah Dickinson
PYP Coordinator Mrs Leyla Mohamoud
Gender Coeducational
Languages English
Boarding/day Day
56 Bakers Road, North Coburg VIC 3058, Australia
TELEPHONE: +61 3 9350 4533
FAX: +61 3 9354 4731
EMAIL: aia@aia.vic.edu.au
WEBSITE: www.aia.vic.edu.au
see full details on page 52

Australian International Academy – Sydney Campus
Status Private
Programme Diploma
Diploma Coordinator Wassim Zoabi
Gender Coeducational
Languages English
Boarding/day Day
420 Liverpool Road, Strathfield, Sydney NSW 2135, Australia
TELEPHONE: +61 2 9643 0104
FAX: +61 2 9642 0106
EMAIL: adminnsw@aia.nsw.edu.au
WEBSITE: www.aia.vic.edu.au

Belair Primary School
Status State
Programme MYP
MYP Coordinator Sonya Johinke
Gender Coeducational
Languages English
Boarding/day Day
45-83 Main Road, Belair SA 5052, Australia
TELEPHONE: +61 8 8370 3733
EMAIL: susan.copeland@belairschools.sa.edu.au
WEBSITE: www.belairschools.sa.edu.au

Bellevue Heights Primary School
Programme MYP
MYP Coordinator Sonya Johinke
Gender Coeducational
Languages English
Boarding/day Day
Vaucluse Cresent, Bellevue Heights SA 5050, Australia
TELEPHONE: +61 8 8278 7182
WEBSITE: www.bellevueps.sa.edu.au

Benton Junior College
Status State
Programme PYP
PYP Coordinator Patricia Wallace
261 Racecourse Road, Mornington VIC 3931, Australia
TELEPHONE: +61 5973 9100
EMAIL: irving.cheryl.cc@edumail.vic.gov.au
WEBSITE: www.benton.vic.edu.au

BLACKFRIARS PRIORY SCHOOL
Status Private
Programme PYP
PYP Coordinator John Niedzwiecki
Gender Male
Languages English
Boarding/day Day
17 Prospect Road, Prospect SA 5082, Australia
TELEPHONE: +61 (0) 8 8269 6333
FAX: +61 (0) 8 8269 7846
EMAIL: jniedzwiecki@bps.sa.edu.au
WEBSITE: www.bps.sa.edu.au
see full details on page 61

Blackwood High School
Status State
Programme MYP, Diploma
Diploma Coordinator Raphael Zadey
MYP Coordinator Christopher Rebbeck
Gender Coeducational
Languages English, French
Boarding/day Day
4 Seymour Street, Eden Hills SA 5050, Australia
TELEPHONE: +61 8 8278 0900
FAX: +61 8 8278 0999
EMAIL: susan.hyde@bhs.sa.edu.au
WEBSITE: www.bhs.sa.edu.au

Blackwood Primary School
Programme MYP
MYP Coordinator Sonya Johinke
Gender Coeducational
Boarding/day Boarding
4 Seymour Street, Eden Hills SA 5051, Australia
TELEPHONE: +61 2 8 8278 5355
EMAIL: swoollar@blackwoodps.sa.edu.au
WEBSITE: www.bhs.sa.edu.au

BRIGHTON PRIMARY SCHOOL
Status State
Programme PYP
PYP Coordinator Patrice Shadbolt
Gender Coeducational
Languages English
Boarding/day Day
Wilson Street, Brighton, VIC 3186, Australia
TELEPHONE: +61 39592 0177
FAX: +61 39593 1642
EMAIL: brighton.ps@brighton.vic.edu.au
WEBSITE: www.brighton.vic.edu.au
see full details on page 64

Cairns State High School
Status State
Programme Diploma
Diploma Coordinator Laura Mazzolini
Gender Coeducational
Languages English
Boarding/day Day
PO Box 5643, Cairns QLD 4870, Australia
TELEPHONE: +61 7 4050 3033
FAX: +61 7 4051 4972
EMAIL: tgord16@eq.edu.au
WEBSITE: www.cairnsshs.eq.edu.au

CAREY BAPTIST GRAMMAR SCHOOL
Status Private
Programme Diploma
Diploma Coordinator David Hamer
Gender Coeducational
Languages English
Boarding/day Day
349 Barkers Road, Kew VIC 3101, Australia
TELEPHONE: +61 39816 1222
FAX: +61 39816 1263
EMAIL: david.hamer@carey.com.au
WEBSITE: www.carey.com.au
see full details on page 70

Central Coast Grammar School
Status Private
Programme Diploma
Diploma Coordinator Janine Noy
Gender Coeducational
Languages English
Arundel Road, Erina Heights NSW 2260,
Australia
TELEPHONE: +61 02 4 367 6766
FAX: +61 02 4 365 1860
EMAIL: tburne@ccgs.nsw.edu.au
WEBSITE: www.ccgs.nsw.edu.au

Concordia College
Status Private
Programme MYP
MYP Coordinator Tony Shillitoe
Gender Coeducational
Languages English
Boarding/day Day
45 Cheltenham Street, Highgate SA 5063,
Australia
TELEPHONE: +61 8 8272 0444
FAX: +61 8 8272 1463
EMAIL:
lsaegenschnitter@concordia.sa.edu.au
WEBSITE: www.concordia.sa.edu.au

Coromandel Valley Primary School
Programme MYP
MYP Coordinator Liz Black
Gender Coeducational
Boarding/day Boarding
339 Main Road, Coromandel Valley SA 5051,
Australia
TELEPHONE: +61 8 8278 3693
EMAIL: info@coromands.sa.edu.au
WEBSITE: www.coromandps.sa.edu.au

Cowandilla Primary School
Status State
Programme MYP
MYP Coordinator Margaret Donovan
Gender Coeducational
Boarding/day Boarding
21 Jenkins Street, Cowandilla SA 5033,
Australia
TELEPHONE: +61 8 8443 7800
FAX: +61 8 8234 2445
EMAIL: info@cowandilla.sa.edu.au
WEBSITE: www.cowandilla.sa.edu.au

Direk Primary School
Programme MYP
MYP Coordinator Adrienne Gregory
Gender Coeducational
Boarding/day Day
17 Uraidla Avenue, Salisbury North SA 5108,
Australia
TELEPHONE: +61 08 8258 0666
EMAIL: robyn.ravalico@direkschs.sa.edu.au
WEBSITE: www.direkschs.sa.edu.au

Eden Hills Primary School
Programme MYP
MYP Coordinator Sonya Johinke
Gender Coeducational
Boarding/day Boarding
78 Wilpena Street, Eden Hills SA 5050,
Australia
TELEPHONE: +61 2 8 8278 2243
EMAIL: petero@edenhillps.sa.edu.au
WEBSITE: www.bhs.sa.edu.au

Fintona Junior School
Status Private
Programme PYP
PYP Coordinator Sally Clayton
Gender Female
Boarding/day Day
79 Balwyn Road, Balwyn VIC 3103, Australia
TELEPHONE: +61 3 9830 1388
FAX: +61 3 9888 5682
EMAIL: pcarder@fintona.vic.edu.au

Flinders Park Primary School
Programme MYP
MYP Coordinator Margaret Donovan
Gender Coeducational
Boarding/day Boarding
70 Holbrooks Road, Flinders Park SA 5025,
Australia
TELEPHONE: +61 (0) 8 8443 9356
EMAIL: info@flindspkps.sa.edu.au
WEBSITE: www.flindspkps.sa.edu.au

Geelong Grammar School
Status Private
Programme PYP, Diploma
Diploma Coordinator Mathew Alan White
PYP Coordinator Fiona Zinn
Gender Coeducational
Languages English
Boarding/day Mixed
50 Biddlecombe Avenue, Corio VIC 3214,
Australia
TELEPHONE: +61 3 5273 9200
FAX: +61 3 5274 1695
EMAIL: principal@ggs.vic.edu.au

German International School Sydney
Status Private
Programme Diploma
Diploma Coordinator Mark Corbett
Gender Coeducational
Languages English
Boarding/day Day
74 Belmore Street, Ryde NSW 2112, Australia
TELEPHONE: +61 (0) 2 94851900
FAX: +61 (0) 2 948551999
EMAIL:
klaus.steinmetz@germanschoolsydney.com
WEBSITE: www.germanschoolsydney.com

Gilles Street Primary School
Status State
Programme MYP
MYP Coordinator Alison Hicks
Gender Coeducational
Languages English
Boarding/day Day
91 Gilles Street, Adelaide SA 5000, Australia
TELEPHONE: +61 8 8223 5184
FAX: +61 8 8223 7114
EMAIL: admin@gillesstps.sa.edu.au
WEBSITE: www.gillesstps.sa.edu.au

Glen Osmond Primary School
Programme MYP
MYP Coordinator Steve Stylianou
Gender Coeducational
Boarding/day Boarding
5 Fisher Street, Myrtle Bank SA 5064, Australia
TELEPHONE: +61 8 8379 0500
EMAIL: kkavanag@glenosps.sa.edu.au

Glenunga International High School
Status State
Programme MYP, Diploma
Diploma Coordinator Mark Grantham Paul
MYP Coordinator Steve Stylianou
Gender Coeducational
Languages English
Boarding/day Day
L'Estrange Street, Glenunga SA 5064,
Australia
TELEPHONE: +61 88 379 5629
FAX: +61 88 338 2518
EMAIL: wendy.johnson@gihs.sa.edu.au

Haileybury
Status Private
Programme Diploma
Diploma Coordinator Scott Sweeney
Gender Coeducational
Languages English
Boarding/day Boarding
855-891 Springvale Road, Keysborough VIC
3173, Australia
TELEPHONE: +61 3 9213 2222
FAX: +61 3 9213 2295
EMAIL: rpargetter@haileybury.vic.edu.au
WEBSITE: www.haileybury.vic.edu.au

Hawthorndene Primary School
Programme MYP
MYP Coordinator Sonya Johinke
Gender Coeducational
Boarding/day Boarding
Suffolk Road, Hawthorndene SA 5051,
Australia
TELEPHONE: +61 8 8278 3551
FAX: +61 8 8370 2681
EMAIL: info@hthdeneps.sa.edu.au
WEBSITE: www.hthdeneps.sa.edu.au

Immanuel College
Status Private
Programme MYP
MYP Coordinator Louisa Mulligan
Gender Coeducational
Languages English
Boarding/day Mixed
32 Morphett Road, Novar Gardens SA 5040, Australia
TELEPHONE: +61 08 8294 3588
FAX: +61 08 8294 2658
EMAIL: krichardson@immanuel.sa.edu.au
WEBSITE: www.immanuel.sa.edu.au

Immanuel Primary School
Status Private
Programme PYP
PYP Coordinator Rebecca Clements
Gender Coeducational
Languages English
Boarding/day Day
Saratoga Drive, Novar Gardens SA 5040, Australia
TELEPHONE: +61 (0)8 8294 8422
EMAIL: principal@immanuelps.sa.edu.au
WEBSITE: www.immanuelps.sa.edu.au

Indooroopilly State High School
Status State
Programme Diploma
Diploma Coordinator Sylvia Moretto
Gender Coeducational
Languages English
Boarding/day Day
PO Box 61, Indooroopilly, Brisbane QLD 4068, Australia
TELEPHONE: +61 7 3327 8333
FAX: +61 7 3327 8300
EMAIL: info@indorooshs.eq.edu.au
WEBSITE: www.indorooshs.eq.edu.au

International School of Western Australia
Status Private
Programme Diploma
Diploma Coordinator Damien Kerrigan
Gender Coeducational
Languages English
Boarding/day Day
22 Kalinda Drive, City Beach WA 6015, Australia
TELEPHONE: +61 8 9285 1144
FAX: +61 8 9285 1188
EMAIL: ibayly@asie.wa.edu.au
WEBSITE: www.asie.wa.edu.au

Ivanhoe Grammar School
Status Private
Programme Diploma
Diploma Coordinator Nicholas de Dear
Gender Coeducational
Languages English
Boarding/day Day
The Ridgeway, Ivanhoe, Melbourne VIC 3079, Australia
TELEPHONE: +61 3 9490 1877
FAX: +61 3 9497 4368
EMAIL: rod.fraser@igs.vic.edu.au
WEBSITE: www.igs.vic.edu.au

Jervois Primary School
Programme MYP
MYP Coordinator Ivan Bronsert
Gender Coeducational
Boarding/day Day
Rayson Street , Jervois SA 5259, Australia
TELEPHONE: +61 0885 723 279
EMAIL: info@jervoisps.sa.edu.au

John Paul College
Status Private
Programme Diploma
Diploma Coordinator Tony Daley
Gender Coeducational
Languages English
Boarding/day Day
John Paul Drive, Daisy Hill, QLD 4127, Australia
TELEPHONE: +61 7 3826 3302
FAX: +61 7 3827 3434
EMAIL: mswann@jpc.qld.edu.au
WEBSITE: www.jpc.qld.edu.au

Kardinia International College
Status Private
Programme PYP, Diploma
Diploma Coordinator Jeanine Valmadre
PYP Coordinator Meredith Ferguson
Gender Coeducational
Languages English
Boarding/day Day
PO Box 17, Geelong VIC 3220, Australia
TELEPHONE: +61 3 52 789999
EMAIL: goodfellowj@kardinia.vic.edu.au
WEBSITE: www.kardinia.vic.edu.au

Kidman Park Primary School
Programme MYP
MYP Coordinator Margaret Donovan
Gender Coeducational
Boarding/day Boarding
Dean Ave, Kidman Park SA 5025, Australia

Kormilda College
Status Private
Programme Diploma
Diploma Coordinator Andrew Boukaseff
Gender Coeducational
Languages English
Boarding/day Mixed
PO Box 241, Berrimah NT 0828, Australia
TELEPHONE: +61 8 89 221611
FAX: +61 8 89 470792
EMAIL: malcolm.pritchard@kormilda.nt.edu.au
WEBSITE: www.kormilda.nt.edu.au

Korowa Anglican Girls' School
Status Private
Programme PYP
PYP Coordinator Elizabeth McLeod
Gender Female
Languages English
Boarding/day Day
Ranfurlie Crescent, Glen Iris VIC 3146, Australia
TELEPHONE: +61 3 9885 0336
FAX: +61 3 9886 0162
EMAIL: scarter@korowa.vic.edu.au
WEBSITE: www.korowa.vic.edu.au

LAURISTON GIRLS' SCHOOL
Status Private
Programme Diploma
Diploma Coordinator Eirwen Stevenson
Gender Female
Languages English
Boarding/day Day
38 Huntingtower Road, Armadale VIC 3143, Australia
TELEPHONE: +61 3 9864 7555
FAX: +61 3 9822 7950
EMAIL: admissions@lauriston.vic.edu.au
WEBSITE: www.lauriston.vic.edu.au
see full details on page 112

Linden Park Primary School
Status State
Programme PYP, MYP
MYP Coordinator Steve Stylianou
PYP Coordinator Marg Bartlett
Gender Coeducational
Languages English
Boarding/day Boarding/day
14 Hay Road, Linden Park, Adelaide SA 5065, Australia
TELEPHONE: +61 8 8379 2171

Littlehampton Primary School
Programme MYP
MYP Coordinator Roz Rose
Gender Coeducational
Boarding/day Day
16-30 Baker Street, Littlehampton SA 5250, Australia
TELEPHONE: +61 0883 911 194
EMAIL: john.hackett@littlehaps.sa.edu.au
WEBSITE: www.littlehaps.sa.edu.au

AUSTRALIA

Lloyd Street School
Status State
Programme PYP
PYP Coordinator Janet Williams
Gender Coeducational
Languages English
Boarding/day Day
Lloyd Street, East Malvern VIC 3145, Australia
TELEPHONE: +61 3 9571 0261
FAX: +61 3 9563 6721
EMAIL: smith.derida.j@edumail.voc.gov.au
WEBSITE: www.lloydstps.vic.edu.au

Lycée Condorcet – The French School of Sydney
Status Private
Programme Diploma
Diploma Coordinator Bernd Fichtner
Gender Coeducational
Boarding/day Day
758 Anzac Parade, Maroubra NSW 2035, Australia
TELEPHONE: +61 2 9344 8692
EMAIL: principal@condorcet.com.au
WEBSITE: http://condorcet.com.au

Macedon Grammar School
Status Private
Programme Diploma
Diploma Coordinator Irene O'Neill
Gender Coeducational
Languages English
Boarding/day Day
Po Box 176, Macedon VIC 3440, Australia
TELEPHONE: +61 3 5426 1751
FAX: +61 3 5426 3024
EMAIL: gillmgr@hotkey.net.au

Magill Primary School
Status State
Programme MYP
MYP Coordinator Gary Weiher
Gender Coeducational
Languages English
Boarding/day Day
Adelaide Street, Magill SA 5072, Australia
TELEPHONE: +61 8 8331 9422
EMAIL: helen.calvert@magillps.sa.edu.au
WEBSITE: www.magillps.sa.edu.au

Melba Copland Secondary School
Status State
Programme Diploma
Diploma Coordinator Mandy Trethowan
Gender Coeducational
Languages English
Copland Drive, Melba ACT 2615, Australia
TELEPHONE: +61 2 6205 7622
FAX: +61 2 6205 7629
EMAIL: bob.ross@coplandc.act.edu.au
WEBSITE: www.coplandc.act.edu.au

Mercedes College
Status Private
Programme PYP, MYP, Diploma
Diploma Coordinator Adrian Chiarolli
MYP Coordinator Ian de Boar
PYP Coordinator Shane Murphy
Gender Coeducational
Languages English
Boarding/day Day
540 Fullarton Road, Springfield SA 5062, Australia
TELEPHONE: +61 8 8372 3200
FAX: +61 8 8379 9540
EMAIL: pdaw@mercedes.adl.catholic.edu.au
WEBSITE: www.mercedes.adl.catholic.edu.au

Methodist Ladies' College
Status Private
Programme Diploma
Diploma Coordinator Merryn Dawborn-Gundlach
Gender Female
Languages English
Boarding/day Mixed
207 Barkers Road, Kew VIC 3101, Australia
TELEPHONE: +61 3 9274 6316
FAX: +61 3 9819 5143
EMAIL: admissions@mlc.vic.edu.au
WEBSITE: www.mlc.vic.edu.au

MLC School
Status Private
Programme Diploma
Diploma Coordinator Briony Morath
Gender Female
Languages English
Boarding/day Day
PO Box 643, Burwood NSW 1805, Australia
TELEPHONE: +61 2 9747 1266
FAX: +61 2 9745 3254
EMAIL: mtimmins@mlcysd.nsw.edu.au
WEBSITE: www.mlcsyd.nsw.edu.au

Monte Sant' Angelo Mercy College
Status Private
Programme Diploma
Diploma Coordinator Robyn Priestley
Gender Female
Languages English
Boarding/day Day
PO Box 1064, 128 Miller St, North Sydney NSW 2059, Australia
TELEPHONE: +61 2 9409 6200
EMAIL: calcock@monte.nsw.edu.au
WEBSITE: www.monte.nsw.edu.au

Mount Eliza North Primary School
Status State
Programme PYP
PYP Coordinator Victoria Vaughan
Gender Coeducational
Languages English
Boarding/day Day
Moseley Drive, PO Box 219, Mount Eliza VIC 3930, Australia
TELEPHONE: +61 3 9787 6611
FAX: +61 3 9787 6754
EMAIL: ingham.davdi.r@edumail.vic.gov.au
WEBSITE: www.menps.vic.edu.au

Mountain Creek State High School
Status State
Programme Diploma
Diploma Coordinator Kerri Davitt Barnard
Gender Coeducational
Languages English
Boarding/day Day
PO Box 827, Mooloolaba QLD 4557, Australia
TELEPHONE: +61 7 5477 8555
EMAIL: gpeac4@eq.edu.au
WEBSITE: http://mtncreekshs.qld.edu.au

Mowbray College
Status Private
Programme Diploma
Diploma Coordinator Kim Lanyon
Cnr Lake St & Caroline Springs College, Caroline Springs VIC 3023, Australia
TELEPHONE: +61 3 8361 2511
FAX: +61 3 9743 0035
EMAIL: osheajo@mowbray.vic.edu.au
WEBSITE: www.mowbray.vic.edu.au

Mowbray College
Status Private
Programme PYP, MYP
MYP Coordinator Scott Faulkner
PYP Coordinator Tammy-Jo Richter Walker
Gender Coeducational
Languages English
Boarding/day Day
PO Box 172, Melton VIC 3337, Australia
TELEPHONE: +61 3 8361 2511
FAX: +61 3 9743 0035
EMAIL: mowbray@mowbray.vic.edu.au
WEBSITE: www.mowbray.vic.edu.au

Mowbray College – Brookside Campus
Status Private
Programme PYP, MYP
MYP Coordinator Scott Faulkner
PYP Coordinator Tami-Jo Richter
Gender Coeducational
Languages English
Boarding/day Day
PO Box 172, Melton VIC 3337, Australia
TELEPHONE: +61 03 8361 2511
FAX: +61 03 9360 5166
EMAIL: mowbray@mowbray.vic.edu.au
WEBSITE: www.mowbray.vic.edu.au

Mt Zaagham International School
Status Private
Programme PYP
PYP Coordinator Susan Ledger
Languages English
Boarding/day Day
PO Box 616, Cairns QLD, Australia
TELEPHONE: +62 0901 43 4802
FAX: +62 901 43 4158
EMAIL: mel_soffe@fmi.com
WEBSITE: http://mzis.org

Murray Bridge High School
Status State
Programme MYP
MYP Coordinator Phil Fitzsimons
Gender Coeducational
Languages English
Boarding/day Day
Lohmann Street, Murray Bridge SA 5253,
Australia
TELEPHONE: +61 8 8532 1788
FAX: +61 8 8532 5335
EMAIL: mbhigh@murraybridgehs.sa.edu.au
WEBSITE: www.murraybridgehs.sa.edu.au

Murray Bridge North Primary School
Programme MYP
MYP Coordinator Ivan Bronsert
Gender Coeducational
Boarding/day Boarding
North Terrace, Murray Bridge SA 5253,
Australia
TELEPHONE: +61 0885 323 055
EMAIL: rwundke@mbnorthps.sa.edu.au

Mypolong Primary School
Programme MYP
MYP Coordinator Ivan Bronsert
Gender Coeducational
Languages German
Boarding/day Day
Williams Street, Mypolonga SA 5254,
Australia
TELEPHONE: +61 0885 354 191
EMAIL: principa@mypolongps.sa.edu.au
WEBSITE: www.mypolongps.sa.edu.au

Narrabundah College
Status State
Programme Diploma
Diploma Coordinator Sue Boettcher
Gender Coeducational
Languages English
Boarding/day Day
Jerrabomberra Avenue, Kingston ACT 2604,
Australia
TELEPHONE: +61 26 205 6999
FAX: +61 26 205 6969
EMAIL:
steve.kyburz@narrabundahc.act.edu.au
WEBSITE: www.narrabundahc.act.edu.au

Newington College
Status Private
Programme Diploma
Diploma Coordinator Greg Bell
Gender Male
Languages English, French
Boarding/day Mixed
200 Stanmore Road, Stanmore NSW 2048,
Australia
TELEPHONE: +61-2-9568-9333
FAX: +61-2-9569-0133
EMAIL:
d.scott@newingtoncollege.nsw.edu.au
WEBSITE: www.newingtoncollege.nsw.edu.au

Our Saviour Lutheran Primary School
Status Private
Programme MYP
MYP Coordinator Tony Shillitoe
Gender Coeducational
Languages English
Boarding/day Day
28 Taylors Road West, Aberfoyle Park SA 5159,
Australia
TELEPHONE: +61 8 8270 5488
FAX: +61 8 8270 5362
EMAIL: principal@osls.sa.edu.au
WEBSITE: www.osls.sa.edu.au

Pedare Christian College
Status Private
Programme MYP
MYP Coordinator David De Boer
Gender Coeducational
Languages English
Boarding/day Day
2-30 Surrey Farm Drive, Golden Grove SA
5125, Australia
TELEPHONE: +61 8 828 01700
EMAIL: amonceaux@pedarecc.sa.edu.au
WEBSITE: www.pedarecc.sa.edu.au

Pembroke School
Status Private
Programme PYP, Diploma
Diploma Coordinator Rosemary Abbott
PYP Coordinator Timothy Edmonds
Gender Coeducational
Languages English
Boarding/day Mixed
342 The Parade, Kensington Park SA 5068,
Australia
TELEPHONE: +61 8 8166 6225
FAX: +61 8 8366 6224
EMAIL: mlamb@pembroke.sa.edu.au
WEBSITE: www.pembroke.sa.edu.au

Penrith Anglican College
Status Private
Programme Diploma
Diploma Coordinator Els van Zwieten
Gender Coeducational
Languages English
Boarding/day Day
PO Box 636, Kingswood NSW 2747, Australia
TELEPHONE: +61 247 36 8100
FAX: +61 247 36 8300
EMAIL: headmaster@pac.nsw.edu.au
WEBSITE: www.pac.nsw.edu.au

Presbyterian Ladies College
Status Private
Programme Diploma
Diploma Coordinator Christine Bradbeer
Gender Female
Languages English
Boarding/day Mixed
141 Burwood Highway, Burwood VIC 3125,
Australia
TELEPHONE: +61 3 9808 5811
FAX: +61 3 9808 5998
EMAIL: cjerram@plc.vic.edu.au
WEBSITE: www.plc.vic.edu.au

Presbyterian Ladies' College – Perth
Status Private
Programme PYP, MYP
MYP Coordinator Kim Edwards
PYP Coordinator Alison Viney
Gender Female
Languages English
Boarding/day Mixed
PO Box 126, Cottesloe WA 6011, Australia
TELEPHONE: +61 8 9424 6428
FAX: +61 8 9424 6407
WEBSITE: www.plc.wa.edu.au

Prince Alfred College
Status Private
Programme PYP, Diploma
Diploma Coordinator Andrew Buxton
PYP Coordinator Neil Andary
Gender Male
Languages English
Boarding/day Mixed
PO Box 571, Kent Town SA 5071, Australia
TELEPHONE: +61 8 8334 1200
FAX: +61 8 8363 0702
EMAIL: ktutt@pac.edu.au
WEBSITE: www.pac.edu.au

**Queensland Academy – Science
Mathematics and Technology**
Status State
Programme Diploma
Diploma Coordinator Stewart Jones
Gender Coeducational
Languages English
Boarding/day Day
Strategy & Performance, Office of Education,
PO Box 15033, City East QLD 4002, Australia
TELEPHONE: +61 04-3407-9617
EMAIL: gpeac4@eq.edu.au
WEBSITE: www.qldacademies.eq.edu.au/

AUSTRALIA

Queensland Academy for Creative Industries
Status State
Programme Diploma
Diploma Coordinator Craig Hynes
Gender Coeducational
Languages English
Boarding/day Day
C/- Executive Assistant, Strategy and Preformance, Office of Education, City East QLD 4002, Australia
TELEPHONE: +61 04-3407-9617
EMAIL: gpeac4@eq.edu.au
WEBSITE: www.qldacademies.eq.edu.au/

Queensland Academy for Health Sciences
Status State
Programme Diploma
Diploma Coordinator Jane Sleeman
Gender Coeducational
Languages English
Boarding/day Boarding
Edmund Rice Drive, Southport 4215, PO Box 1115, Ashmore City QLD 4214, Australia
TELEPHONE: +61 7 5510 1100
FAX: +61 7 5510 1130
EMAIL: lnix03@eq.edu.au
WEBSITE: www.qldacademies.eq.edu.au

QUEENWOOD SCHOOL FOR GIRLS
Status Private
Programme Diploma
Diploma Coordinator Judy Tenzing
Gender Female
Languages English
Locked Bag 1, Mosman NSW 2088, Australia
TELEPHONE: +61 2 89687777
FAX: +61 2 89687778
EMAIL: q@queenwood.nsw.edu.au
WEBSITE: www.queenwood.nsw.edu.au
see full details on page 124

RAVENSWOOD
Status Private
Programme Diploma
Diploma Coordinator Robin Julian
Gender Female
Languages English
Boarding/day Mixed
1B Cecil Street, Gordon NSW 2072, Australia
TELEPHONE: +61 2 9498 9808
FAX: +61 2 9498 9999
EMAIL: enrol@ravenswood.nsw.edu.au
WEBSITE: www.ravenswood.nsw.edu.au
see full details on page 125

Red Hill School
Status State
Programme PYP
PYP Coordinator Judith Nash
Gender Coeducational
Languages English
Boarding/day Day
PO Box 22, Red Hill ACT 2603, Australia
TELEPHONE: +61 2 6205 7144
FAX: +61 2 6205 7145
EMAIL: chris.hamilton@ed.act.edu.au
WEBSITE: www.redhillps.act.edu.au

REDLANDS
Status Private
Programme Diploma
Diploma Coordinator Hugh King
Gender Coeducational
Languages English
Boarding/day Day
272 Military Road, Cremorne NSW 2090, Australia
TELEPHONE: +61 2 9908 6479
FAX: +61 2 9909 3228
EMAIL: hking@redlands.nsw.edu.au
registrar@redlands.nsw.edu.au
WEBSITE: www.redlands.nsw.edu.au
see full details on page 126

Ruthven Primary School
Status State
Programme PYP
PYP Coordinator Kent Silfo
Gender Coeducational
Languages English
Boarding/day Day
Glasgow Avenue, Reservoir 3073, Melbourne VIC 3073, Australia
TELEPHONE: +61 3 9460 1668
FAX: +61 3 9460 1858
EMAIL: ruthvenps@edumail.vic.gov.au
WEBSITE: www.ruthvenps.vic.edu.au

Sacred Heart College Geelong
Status Private
Programme MYP
MYP Coordinator Patricia Cosgriff
Gender Female
Languages English
Boarding/day Day
Retreat Road, Newtown VIC 3220, Australia
TELEPHONE: +61 3 52214211
FAX: +61 352213634
EMAIL: principal@shc.melb.catholic.edu.au
WEBSITE: www.shc.melb.catholic.edu.au

Salisbury High School
Status State
Programme MYP
MYP Coordinator Adrienne Gregory
Gender Coeducational
Languages English
Farley Grove, Salisbury North SA 5108, Australia
TELEPHONE: +61 08 8182 0200
EMAIL:
helen.paphitis@salisburyhigh.sa.edu.au
WEBSITE: www.salisburyhigh.sa.edu.au

Scotch College
Status Private
Programme PYP, MYP
MYP Coordinator Ben Beaton
PYP Coordinator Michael Rourke
Gender Coeducational
Languages English
Boarding/day Mixed
76 Shenton Road, Swanbourne, Perth WA 6025, Australia
TELEPHONE: +61 08 93841466
FAX: +61 08 93852286
EMAIL: apsyme@scotch.wa.edu.au
WEBSITE: www.scotch.wa.edu.au

Somerset College
Status Private
Programme PYP, MYP, Diploma
Diploma Coordinator Frederick Brohier
MYP Coordinator Michele Sauer
PYP Coordinator Brenda Millican
Gender Coeducational
Languages English
Boarding/day Day
Somerset Drive, Mudgeeraba QLD 4213, Australia
TELEPHONE: +61 0755 304100
FAX: +61 0755 303208
EMAIL: barnison@somerset.qld.edu.au
WEBSITE: www.somerset.qld.edu.au

St Andrew's Cathedral School
Status Private
Programme Diploma
Diploma Coordinator Sharon Munro
Gender Coeducational
Languages English
Boarding/day Day
Sydney Square, Sydney NSW 2000, Australia
TELEPHONE: +61 2 9286 9500
FAX: +61 2 9286 9550
EMAIL: pheath@sacs.nsw.edu.au
WEBSITE: www.sacs.nsw.edu.au

St Andrews Lutheran College
Status Private
Programme PYP
PYP Coordinator Jacqueline Faulkner
Gender Coeducational
Languages English
Boarding/day Day
PO Box 2142, Burleigh MDC QLD 4220, Australia
TELEPHONE: +61 7 5534 8522
FAX: +61 7 5534 8459
EMAIL: office@standrewslutheran.qld.edu.au
WEBSITE:
www.standrewslutheran.qld.edu.au

St Andrew's School

Status Private
Programme PYP, MYP
MYP Coordinator Steve Stylianou
PYP Coordinator Justine Lind
Gender Coeducational
Boarding/day Boarding/day
22 Smith Street, Walkerville SA 5081, Australia
TELEPHONE: +61 8 81685537
FAX: +61 8 8344 8670
EMAIL: dwoolnough@standrews.sa.edu.au
WEBSITE: www.standrews.sa.edu.au

St Catherine's School

Status Private
Programme PYP
PYP Coordinator Christine Gilliland
Gender Female
Languages English
Boarding/day Mixed
17 Heyington Place, Toorak VIC 3142, Australia
TELEPHONE: +61 3 9828 1285
FAX: +61 3 9828 7595
EMAIL: info@stcatherines.net.au
WEBSITE: www.stcatherines.net.au

St Hilda's School

Status Private
Programme MYP
MYP Coordinator Simone Sebban
Gender Female
Languages English
Boarding/day Day
PO Box 290, Southport, Gold Coast QLD 4215, Australia
TELEPHONE: +61 7 5532 4922
FAX: +61 7 5591 5352
EMAIL: principal@sthildas.qld.edu.au
WEBSITE: www.sthildas.qld.edu.au

St John's Lutheran Primary School, Highgate

Status Private
Programme MYP
MYP Coordinator Tony Shillitoe
Gender Coeducational
Languages English
Boarding/day Day
20 Highgate, St Highgate SA 5062, Australia
TELEPHONE: +61 8 8271 4299
EMAIL: admin@stjohnsls.sa.edu.au

St Leonard's College

Status Private
Programme PYP, Diploma
Diploma Coordinator Simon Vanderkelen
PYP Coordinator Carolyn Tudor
Gender Coeducational
Languages English
Boarding/day Day
163 South Road, Brighton East VIC 3187, Australia
TELEPHONE: +61 3 9909 9300
FAX: +61 3 9592 3439
EMAIL: roger.hayward@stleonards.vic.edu.au
WEBSITE: www.stleonards.vic.edu.au

St Leonard's College, Cornish Campus

Status Private
Programme PYP
PYP Coordinator Anne Beruldsen
Gender Coeducational
Languages English
63 Riverend Road, Bangholme VIC 3175, Australia
TELEPHONE: +61 03 9773 1011
EMAIL: roger.hayward@stleonards.vic.edu.au
WEBSITE: www.stleonards.vic.edu.au

St Michael's College

Status Private
Programme PYP
PYP Coordinator Ada D'Onofrio
Gender Male
Languages English
Boarding/day Day
78 East Avenue, Beverley SA 5009, Australia
TELEPHONE: +61 8 8346 6548
FAX: +61 8 8346 9449
EMAIL: smc@smc.catholic.schools.sa.edu.au
WEBSITE: www.smc.sa.edu.au

St Michael's Lutheran School

Status Private
Programme PYP
PYP Coordinator Victoria Weiss
Gender Coeducational
Languages English
Boarding/day Day
6 Balhannah Rd, Hahndorf SA 5250, Australia
TELEPHONE: +61 2883 887 228
EMAIL: principal@stmichaels.sa.edu.au
WEBSITE: www.stmichaels.sa.edu.au

St Paul's Grammar School

Status Private
Programme PYP, MYP, Diploma
Diploma Coordinator Antony Mayrhofer
MYP Coordinator Mary-Robyn Lane
PYP Coordinator Ruth Adams
Gender Coeducational
Languages English
Boarding/day Mixed
Locked Bag 16, Penrith NSW 2751, Australia
TELEPHONE: +61 2 4777 4888
FAX: +61 2 4777 4841
EMAIL: john.collier@stpauls.nsw.edu.au
WEBSITE: www.stpauls.nsw.edu.au

St Peter's College

Status Private
Programme Diploma
Diploma Coordinator Chris Taylor
Gender Male
Languages English
Boarding/day Mixed
Hackney Road, St Peters SA 5069, Australia
TELEPHONE: +61 8 8362 3451
FAX: +61 8 8363 2239
EMAIL: pgrutzner@stpeters.sa.edu.au

St Peters Lutheran College

Status Private
Programme Diploma
Diploma Coordinator Jennifer Winn
Gender Coeducational
Languages English
Boarding/day Mixed
66 Harts Road, Indooroopilly QLD 4068, Australia
TELEPHONE: +61 7-3377-6222
EMAIL: s.rudolph@stpeters.qld.edu.au
WEBSITE: www.stpeters.qld.edu.au

St Peter's Lutheran School Blackwood

Status Private
Programme PYP
PYP Coordinator Nicolle Jakube
Gender Coeducational
Languages English
Boarding/day Day
PO Box 1045, Blackwood SA 5051, Australia
TELEPHONE: +61 8 8278 9506
FAX: +61 8 8370 0414
EMAIL: admin@stpeterslutheran.sa.edu.au
WEBSITE: www.stpeterslutheran.sa.edu.au

Stradbroke Primary & Junior Primary School

Status State
Programme PYP, MYP
MYP Coordinator Gary Weiher
PYP Coordinator Emma Green
Gender Coeducational
Languages English
Boarding/day Day
Koonga Avenue, Rostrevor SA 5073, Australia
TELEPHONE: +61 8 8337 2861
EMAIL: catherine.wilson@stradsch.sa.edu.au
WEBSITE: www.stradsch.sa.edu.au

Tailem Bend Primary School

Programme MYP
MYP Coordinator Ivan Bronsert
Gender Coeducational
Boarding/day Day
1 Murray Street, Tailem Bend SA 5260, Australia
TELEPHONE: +61 0885 723 266
EMAIL: principa@tailembdps.sa.edu.au

Telopea Park High School

Status State
Programme MYP
MYP Coordinator Annie Termaat
Gender Coeducational
Languages English
New South Wales Crescent, Barton ACT 2600, Australia
TELEPHONE: +61 2 6205 5599
EMAIL: trish.wilks@telopea.act.edu.au
WEBSITE: www.telopea.act.edu.au

AUSTRALIA

The Canberra College
Status State
Programme Diploma
Diploma Coordinator Judy Talberg
Gender Coeducational
Languages English
Boarding/day Day
Woden Campus, Launceston Avenue, Phillip
ACT 2606, Australia
TELEPHONE: +61 44 2620 55777
FAX: +61 44 2620 55776
EMAIL: john.stenhouse@ed.act.edu.au
WEBSITE: www.canberrac.act.edu.au

The Friends' School
Status Private
Programme PYP, Diploma
Diploma Coordinator Tim Sprod
PYP Coordinator Lindsey Dobson
Gender Coeducational
Languages English
Boarding/day Mixed
PO Box 42, North Hobart TAS 7002, Australia
TELEPHONE: +61 3 6210 2200
FAX: +61 3 6234 8209
EMAIL: principal@friends.tas.edu.au
WEBSITE: www.friends.tas.edu.au

The Kilmore International School
Status Private
Programme Diploma
Diploma Coordinator Rod Mumford
Gender Coeducational
Languages English
Boarding/day Mixed
40 White Street, Kilmore VIC 3764, Australia
TELEPHONE: +61 3 5782 2211
FAX: +61 3 5782 2525
EMAIL: jsettle@kilmore.vic.edu.au
WEBSITE: www.kilmore.vic.edu.au

The Montessori School
Status Private
Programme Diploma
Diploma Coordinator Bobbie Beasley
Gender Coeducational
Languages English
Boarding/day Day
PO Box 194, Landsdale WA 6065, Australia
TELEPHONE: +61 89 409 9151
FAX: +61 89 409 1682
EMAIL: montessori_kingsley@yahoo.com
WEBSITE:
www.themontessorischool.wa.edu.au

The Norwood Morialta High School
Status State
Programme MYP
MYP Coordinator Gary Weiher
Gender Coeducational
Languages English
Boarding/day Day
Morialta Road West, Rostrevor SA 5073,
Australia
TELEPHONE: +61 8 83650455
FAX: +61 8 83378397
EMAIL: panayoula.parha@nmhs.sa.edu.au
WEBSITE: www.nmhs.sa.edu.au

The Pines Primary School
Programme MYP
MYP Coordinator Adrienne Gregory
Gender Coeducational
PO Box 576, Salisbury South SA 5106,
Australia
TELEPHONE: +61 08 8281 2199
EMAIL: erica.solowij@thepinesc7.sa.edu.au
WEBSITE: www.thepinesc7.sa.edu.au

Tintern Anglican Girls' Grammar School
Status Private
Programme Diploma
Diploma Coordinator Geoff Connor
Gender Coeducational
Languages English
Boarding/day Mixed
90 Alexandra Road, Ringwood East VIC 3135,
Australia
TELEPHONE: +61 3 9845 7802
FAX: +61 3 9845 7710
EMAIL: collije@tintern.vic.edu.au

Toorak College
Status Private
Programme PYP
PYP Coordinator Nicole Ginnane
Gender Coeducational
Languages English
Boarding/day Mixed
PO Box 150, Mount Eliza VIC 3930, Australia
TELEPHONE: +61 3 9788 7200
FAX: +61 3 9787 5888
EMAIL: noelt@toorak.vic.edu.au
WEBSITE: www.toorakc.vic.edu.au

Torrensville Primary School
Programme MYP
MYP Coordinator Margaret Donovan
Gender Coeducational
Boarding/day Boarding
35 Hayward Ave, Torrensville SA 5031,
Australia

Treetops Montessori School
Status Private
Programme Diploma
Diploma Coordinator Norman Megahey
Gender Coeducational
Languages English
Boarding/day Day
PO Box 59, Darlington WA 6076, Australia
TELEPHONE: +61 618 9299 6725
FAX: +14 618 9299 6724
EMAIL:
norman.megahey@treetops.wa.edu.au
WEBSITE: www.treetops.wa.edu.au

Trinity Grammar School, Sydney
Status Private
Programme Diploma
Diploma Coordinator Peter Goetze
Gender Male
Languages English
Boarding/day Boarding
PO Box 174, Summer Hill NSW 2130, Australia
TELEPHONE: +61 2 9581 6000
FAX: +61 2 9799 9449
EMAIL: mcujes@trinity.nsw.edu.au
WEBSITE: www.trinity.nsw.edu.au

Trinity Lutheran College
Status Private
Programme PYP, Diploma
Diploma Coordinator David Lyon
PYP Coordinator Lisa Kraft
Gender Coeducational
Languages English
Boarding/day Day
PO Box 322, Ashmore City QLD 4214,
Australia
TELEPHONE: +61 7 5556 8200
FAX: +61 7 5556 8215
EMAIL: ann.mitchell@tlc.qld.edu.au
WEBSITE: www.tlc.qld.edu.au

Underdale High School
Status State
Programme MYP
MYP Coordinator Melinda Boston
Gender Coeducational
Languages English
19 Garden Terrace, Underdale SA 5032,
Australia
TELEPHONE: +61 8 83018000
FAX: +61 8 234 2479
EMAIL: nigel.gill@underdale.sa.edu.au

Walford Anglican School for Girls
Status Private
Programme PYP, MYP, Diploma
Diploma Coordinator John Butler
MYP Coordinator Cathy Swain
PYP Coordinator Barbara Morrison
Gender Female
Languages English
Boarding/day Mixed
PO Box 430, Unley SA 5061, Australia
TELEPHONE: +61 8 8272 6555
FAX: +61 8 8272 0313
EMAIL: helen.trebilcock@walford.asn.au

Wesley College – Glen Waverley Campus
Status Private
Programme PYP
PYP Coordinator Kathy Saville
Gender Coeducational
Languages English
Boarding/day Day
620 High St Road, Glen Waverley VIC 3150,
Australia
TELEPHONE: +61 3 8102 6888
FAX: +61 3 9803 0851
EMAIL: chris.poulton@wesleycollege.net
WEBSITE: www.wesleycollege.net

Wesley College, Elsternwick Campus
Status Private
Programme PYP
PYP Coordinator Gabrielle Mullins
Gender Coeducational
Languages English
Boarding/day Day
5 Gladstone Parade, Elsternwick VIC 3185, Australia
TELEPHONE: +61 3 8102 6800
FAX: +61 3 9523 0562
WEBSITE: www.wesleycollege.net

WESLEY COLLEGE, MELBOURNE
Status Private
Programme PYP, Diploma
Diploma Coordinator Isaac Quist
PYP Coordinator Kathy Saville
Gender Coeducational
Languages English
Boarding/day Day
577 St Kilda Road, Melbourne VIC 3004, Australia
TELEPHONE: +61 3 8102 6888
FAX: +61 3 9510 6284
EMAIL: principal@wesleycollege.net
WEBSITE: www.wesleycollege.net
see full details on page 160

Woodcroft College
Status Private
Programme PYP, MYP, Diploma
Diploma Coordinator Richard Pope
MYP Coordinator Nicole Pilkington
PYP Coordinator Annette Mikulcic
Gender Coeducational
Languages English
Boarding/day Day
PO Box 48, Bains Road, Morphett Vale SA 5162, Australia
TELEPHONE: +61 8 8322 2333
FAX: +61 8 8322 6656
EMAIL: porter_m@woodcroft.sa.edu.au
WEBSITE: www.woodcroft.sa.edu.au

Xavier College
Status Private
Programme PYP
PYP Coordinator Timothy Bergin
Gender Coeducational
Languages English
Boarding/day Day
Barkers Road, Kew VIC 3101, Australia
TELEPHONE: +61 3 98 545411
FAX: +61 3 9855 4189
EMAIL: c.mccabe@xavier.vic.edu.gov.au
WEBSITE: www.xavier.vic.edu.au

BANGLADESH

American International School, Dhaka
Status Private
Programme Diploma
Diploma Coordinator Joyce Tromba
Gender Coeducational
Languages English
12 United Nations Road, Baridhara, Dhaka - 1212, Bangladesh
TELEPHONE: +880 2 882 2452/882 2860
FAX: +880-2-882-3175
EMAIL: info@ais-dhaka.net
WEBSITE: www.ais-dhaka.net

International School, Dhaka
Status Private
Programme PYP, MYP, Diploma
Diploma Coordinator Stephen Crane
MYP Coordinator Liz Carrick
PYP Coordinator Kate Grant
Gender Coeducational
Languages English
Boarding/day Day
c/o CIS, Dhaka Bag, 21a Lavant Street, Petersfield, Hampshire GU32 3EL, UK
TELEPHONE: +880 2 881 7101
FAX: +880 2 988 3622
EMAIL: john.sperandio@isdbd.org
WEBSITE: www.isdbd.org

BRUNEI DARUSSALAM

International School, Brunei
Status Private
Programme Diploma
Diploma Coordinator Paul Toomer
Gender Coeducational
Languages English
Boarding/day Day/boarding
Jalan Dato Haji Ahmad, Bandar Seri Begawan BB 1114, Brunei Darussalam
TELEPHONE: +673 233 6560
FAX: +673 233 7598
EMAIL: executive_principal@isb.edu.bn
WEBSITE: www.isb.edu.bn

CAMBODIA

International School of Phnom Penh
Status Private
Programme PYP, MYP, Diploma
Diploma Coordinator Tammy Rodabaugh
MYP Coordinator Brian Webster
PYP Coordinator Rosemary Wright
Gender Coeducational
Languages English
Boarding/day Day
PO Box 138, Phnom Penh, Cambodia
TELEPHONE: +855 23 213 103
FAX: +855 23 213104
EMAIL: robmockrish@ispp.edu.kh
WEBSITE: www.ispp.edu.kh

FIJI

International School Nadi
Status Private
Programme PYP, MYP, Diploma
Diploma Coordinator Joan Wilisoni
MYP Coordinator Joanne Semmens
PYP Coordinator Rosi Uluiviti
Gender Coeducational
Languages English
Boarding/day Day
Box 9686 Nadi Airport, Nadi, Fiji
TELEPHONE: +679 6702 060
EMAIL: jwilisoni@isn.school.fj
WEBSITE: www.isn.school.fj

International School Suva
Status Private
Programme PYP, MYP, Diploma
Diploma Coordinator Amy Lee
MYP Coordinator Mere Fong
PYP Coordinator Catriona Tuimaka
Gender Coeducational
Languages English
Boarding/day Day
PO Box 10828, Laucala Beach Estate, Suva, Fiji
TELEPHONE: +679 339 3300
FAX: +679 334 0017
EMAIL: dkorare@international.school.fj
WEBSITE: www.international.school.fj

GUAM

St John's School
Status Private
Programme Diploma
Diploma Coordinator J Robert Kelley
Gender Coeducational
Languages English
Boarding/day Day
911 Marine Drive, Tumon Bay 96913, Guam
TELEPHONE: +1 (671) 646 8080
FAX: +1 (671) 649 1055
EMAIL: jnelson@stjohnguam.com
WEBSITE: www.stjohnsguam.com

INDIA

Ahmedabad International School
Status Private
Programme PYP, Diploma
Diploma Coordinator Shivangi Panchal
PYP Coordinator Lakshmi Madhusoodanan
Gender Coeducational
Languages English
Boarding/day Day
Opp Rajpath Row Houses, Behind Kiran Motors, Judges Bungalow Road, Bodakdev Ahmedabad 380015, India
TELEPHONE: +91 79 2687 2459
EMAIL: ais_school2005@yahoo.com

American Embassy School
Status Private
Programme Diploma
Diploma Coordinator Iona Leriou
Gender Coeducational
Languages English
Boarding/day Day
Chandragupta Marg, Chanakyapuri, New Delhi 110021, India
TELEPHONE: +91 11 2 688 8854
FAX: +91 11 2 687 3320
EMAIL: bhetzel@aes.ac.in
WEBSITE: http://aes.ac.in

American International School – Chennai
Status Private
Programme Diploma
Diploma Coordinator Mark Robertson-Jones
Gender Coeducational
Languages English
Boarding/day Day
17 Murray's Gate Road, Alwarpet, Chennai (Madras) 600 018, India
TELEPHONE: +91 44 2254 9000
FAX: +91 44 2254 9001

AMERICAN SCHOOL OF BOMBAY
Status Private
Programme PYP, Diploma
Diploma Coordinator Dr Rob Allison
PYP Coordinator Khushnuma Ferzandi
Gender Coeducational
Languages English
Boarding/day Day
SF2, G-Block, Bandra Kurla Complex Road, Bandra East, Mumbai 400 098, India
TELEPHONE: +91 22 6772 7272
FAX: +91 22 2652 1234
EMAIL: asb@asbindia.org
WEBSITE: www.asbindia.org
see full details on page 47

Amity Global School
Status Private
Programme Diploma
Diploma Coordinator Jayshree Tripathi
Gender Coeducational
Languages English
Boarding/day Day
c/o Amity International School, Sector 46, Gurgaon, Harayana 122003, India
TELEPHONE: +91 98 1834 8935
FAX: +91 98 11 2433 9500
EMAIL: kaoshikneeti@gmail.com
WEBSITE: www.amity.edu
www.amityglobalschool.com

Bangalore International School
Status Private
Programme Diploma
Diploma Coordinator Susan Chrispal
Gender Coeducational
Languages English
Boarding/day Mixed
Geddalahalli, Hennur Bagalur Road, Kothanur Post, Bangalore 560077, India
TELEPHONE: +91 80 2846 5060/2844 5852
FAX: +91 80 2846 5059
EMAIL: principal@bisedu.co.in
WEBSITE: www.bangaloreinternationalschool.com

BD Somani International School
Status Private
Programme Diploma
Diploma Coordinator Sapna Srivastav
Gender Coeducational
Languages English
Boarding/day Day
625 GD Somani Marg, Cuffe Parade, Mumbai 400 005, India
TELEPHONE: +91-22-2218-7102
EMAIL: info@bdsint.com
WEBSITE: www.bdsint.com

Canadian International School, India
Status Private
Programme Diploma
Diploma Coordinator Craig Patterson
Gender Coeducational
Languages English
Boarding/day Day cum Boarding
Survey No 4 & 20, Manchenahalli, Yelahanka, Bangalore 560 064, India
TELEPHONE: +91 80 6451 4001/2/3/4/5/6/8
FAX: +91 80 2559 4557/2220 4083
EMAIL: admission@cisb.org.in
WEBSITE: www.cisb.org.in

Chinmaya International Residential School
Status Private
Programme Diploma
Diploma Coordinator E Venkatragavaraj
Gender Coeducational
Languages English
Boarding/day Boarding
Nallur Vayal Post, Siruvani Road, Coimbatore Tamil Nadu 641 114, India
TELEPHONE: +91 422 261 3300/3303
FAX: +91 422 261 5725
EMAIL: principal@cirschool.org
WEBSITE: www.cirschool.org

Choithram International
Status Private
Programme PYP, MYP
MYP Coordinator Manoj Parmar
PYP Coordinator Purti Singh
Gender Coeducational
Languages English
Boarding/day Mixed
5 Manik Bagh Road, Choithram Hospital Campus, Indore MP 452014, India
TELEPHONE: +91 0731 2360345/46
EMAIL: principalci@choithramschool.com
WEBSITE: http://global.choithramschool.com

DHIRUBHAI AMBANI INTERNATIONAL SCHOOL
Status Private
Programme Diploma
Diploma Coordinator Riad Rojoa
Gender Coeducational
Languages English
Boarding/day Day
Bandra-Kurla Complex, Bandra (East), Mumbai 400098, India
TELEPHONE: +91 22 40617000
FAX: +91 22 40617099
EMAIL: info@da-is.org
WEBSITE: www.da-is.org
see full details on page 75

DPS International, Saket
Status Private
Programme Diploma
Diploma Coordinator Varinder Puri
Gender Coeducational
Languages English
Boarding/day Day
P-37 MB Road, Sector VI, Pusph Vihar, Saket, India
TELEPHONE: +91 11 2956 1187
FAX: +91 11 2956 5903
EMAIL: dpsi@vsnl.net
WEBSITE: www.dpsi.ac.in

DRS International School
Status Private
Programme PYP
PYP Coordinator Seema Paul
Gender Coeducational
Languages English, French, Hindi, Spanish
Boarding/day Mixed
Survey No 523, Opposite Appael Park Gundla, Pochampally, Kampally, RR District Andhra Pradesh 0000, India
TELEPHONE: +91 4 23792123-27
FAX: +91 4 2379123-27
EMAIL: principal@drsinternational.com
WEBSITE: www.drsinternational.com

Ecole Mondiale World School
Status Private
Programme PYP, MYP, Diploma
Diploma Coordinator Helen Stanton
MYP Coordinator Ingur Shefalika
PYP Coordinator Trish Berry
Gender Coeducational
Languages English
Boarding/day Day
9th Cross Rd, Tilak Udyan, Gulmohar, Vile Parle West, Mumbai JPVD Scheme 400049, India
TELEPHONE: +91 22 5675 4185
WEBSITE: www.ecolemondiale.org

Fazlani L'Académie Globale
Status Private
Programme Diploma
Diploma Coordinator B Hosh
Gender Coeducational
Languages English
Boarding/day Day
PO Box 9992, Nirmal 21st Flr, Nariman Point, Mumbai 400021, India
TELEPHONE: +91 22 981 999 9394

G D Goenka World School
Status Private
Programme Diploma
Diploma Coordinator Bimla Gour
Gender Coeducational
Languages English
Boarding/day Mixed
Sohna-Gurgaon-Road, Sohna HR 122 103, India
TELEPHONE: +91 11 981 033 7236
EMAIL: worldschool@gdgoenka.com
WEBSITE: www.goenkaglobal.com

Good Shepherd International School
Status Private
Programme Diploma
Diploma Coordinator V Kalyan Ram
Gender Coeducational
Languages English
Boarding/day Boarding
Fernhill Post, Ootacamund 643004, The Nilgiris Tamil Nadu 643004, India
TELEPHONE: +91 423 2550071
FAX: +91 423 2550386
EMAIL: info@gsis.ac.in
WEBSITE: www.gsis.ac.in

HFS International
Status Private
Programme Diploma
Diploma Coordinator Kalyani Patnaik
Gender Coeducational
Languages English
Boarding/day Boarding
Hiranandani Complex, Powai, Mumbai 400076, India
TELEPHONE: +91 22 2570 0045
FAX: +91 22 2570 0148
EMAIL: iyerdrkrishnan1@rediffmail.com
WEBSITE: www.hiranandanischools.edu.in

IILM Early College
Status Private
Programme Diploma
Diploma Coordinator Kakoli Sen
Gender Coeducational
Languages English
Boarding/day Day
3 Institutional Area, Lodhi Road, New Delhi 110003, India
TELEPHONE: +91 11 4355 9300
FAX: +91 4355 9339
EMAIL: kakoli.sen@iilm.edu

Indus International School
Status Private
Programme PYP, Diploma
Diploma Coordinator Antony D'Souza
PYP Coordinator Monita Sen
Gender Coeducational
Languages English
Boarding/day Mixed
Billapura Cross, Sarjapur, Bangalore 562125, India
TELEPHONE: +91 80 782 3888
FAX: +91 80 782 3850
EMAIL: sarojini.rao@indusschool.com
WEBSITE: www.indusschool.com

International School Aamby
Status Private
Programme Diploma
Diploma Coordinator Anne Thomson
Gender Coeducational
Languages English
Boarding/day Boarding
Aamby Valley City, Vill-Ambavene, Tal-Mulshi, Maharashtra Pune 410401, India
TELEPHONE: +91 20 3910 2500
EMAIL: ibcoordinatorisa@gmail.com
WEBSITE: www.internationalschoolaamby.com

International School of Hyderabad
Status Private
Programme Diploma
Diploma Coordinator Vasundara Bhalla
Gender Coeducational
Languages English
Boarding/day Day
6-3-346 Road #1, Banjara Hills, Hyderabad Andhra Pradesh 500034, India
TELEPHONE: +91 40 23351110
FAX: +91 040 23395065
EMAIL: ish@ishhyd.com
WEBSITE: www.ishhyd.com

Jamnabai Narsee School
Status Private
Programme Diploma
Diploma Coordinator Sarojini Duggal
Gender Coeducational
Languages English
Boarding/day Day
Narsee Monjee Bhavan, NS Road #7, JVPD Scheme, Vile Parle (W), Mumbai Maharashtra 400 049, India
TELEPHONE: +91 22 2614 6262
FAX: +91 22 2614 6262
EMAIL: principal@jns.ac.in
WEBSITE: www.jjns.ac.in/ib

Jankidevi Public School
Status Private
Programme Diploma
Diploma Coordinator Veena Verma
Gender Coeducational
Languages English
Boarding/day Boarding
Jankidevi School Road, Mhada Layout, Andheri (W), Mumbai 53, India
TELEPHONE: +91 22 2636 9845
FAX: +91 22 2639 0329
EMAIL: jankidevieducationaltrust@hotmail.com
WEBSITE: www.jankidevipublicschool-m.com

Johnson Grammar School ICSE
Status Private
Programme Diploma
Diploma Coordinator Saraswathi Rao
Gender Coeducational
Languages English
Boarding/day Day
Street No 3, Kakatiya Nagar, Habsiguda, Hyderabad Andhra Pradesh 500007, India
TELEPHONE: +91 40 2715 0555
FAX: +91 40 2717 1683
EMAIL: jgschooliso@yahoo.com
WEBSITE: www.jgschool.org

Kodaikanal International School
Status Private
Programme MYP, Diploma
Diploma Coordinator Kaisar Dopaishi
MYP Coordinator Mary Philip
Gender Coeducational
Languages English
Boarding/day Boarding
PO Box 25, Kodaikanal, Tamil Nadu 624 101, India
TELEPHONE: +91 4542 247 200
FAX: +91 4542 241 109
EMAIL: principal@kis.in
WEBSITE: www.kis.in

Mahatma Gandhi International School
Status Private
Programme MYP, Diploma
Diploma Coordinator Ravinder Kaur
MYP Coordinator Minoo Joshi
Gender Coeducational
Languages English
Boarding/day Boarding
Sheth Hirabhai Motilal Bhavan, Mithakali, Ahmedabad, Gujarat, India
TELEPHONE: +91 79 646 3888
EMAIL: anjoupascal@yahoo.com
WEBSITE: www.idealfoundation.com

Mahindra United World College of India
Status Private
Programme Diploma
Diploma Coordinator Susan Tham
Gender Coeducational
Languages English
Boarding/day Boarding
PO Paud, Taluka Mulshi, District Pune 412108, India
TELEPHONE: +91 20 22943262
FAX: +91 20 22943260
EMAIL: dwilkinson@muwci.net
WEBSITE: www.muwci.net

Mercedes Benz International School
Status Private
Programme PYP, MYP, Diploma
Diploma Coordinator Mrs Avalokita Nanda
MYP Coordinator Monica Drego
PYP Coordinator Sujata Mallic Kumar
Gender Coeducational
Languages English
Boarding/day Mixed
Plot No P-26, Rajeev Ganhi Infotech Park, Hinjewadi, Pune 411057, India
TELEPHONE: +91 20 229 344 01
FAX: +91 20 293 2762
EMAIL: michael.thompson@mbis.org
WEBSITE: www.mbis.org

Navrachana International School
Status Private
Programme PYP, MYP, Diploma
Diploma Coordinator Manju Gupta
MYP Coordinator Usha Singh
PYP Coordinator Anjalika Sharma
Gender Coeducational
Languages English
Boarding/day Mixed
Bhayali, Vadodara 391410, India
TELEPHONE: +91 265 645 3401
EMAIL: principal@navrachana.ac.in
WEBSITE: www.navrachana.ac.in

NSS Hill Spring International School
Status Private
Programme PYP
PYP Coordinator Nisha Vahi
Gender Coeducational
Languages English
Boarding/day Day
C Wing, NSS Educational Complex, MP Mill Compound, Tardeo, Mumbai 400 034, India
TELEPHONE: +91 22 3295 3775
FAX: +91 22 2351 3163
EMAIL: principalhsi@nsseducation.org
WEBSITE: www.nsseducation.org

Oakridge International School
Status State/private
Programme PYP, Diploma
Diploma Coordinator Janajit Ray
PYP Coordinator C Adilakshmi
Gender Coeducational
Languages English
Boarding/day Day
Khajaguda, Nanakramguda Road, Cyberabad, Hyderabad 500008, India
TELEPHONE: +91-40-2300-6436/7/8/9
EMAIL: janajit@oakridgeschools.net
WEBSITE: www.oakridgeinternational.com

Pathways World School
Status Private
Programme Diploma
Diploma Coordinator Grace Mangar
Gender Coeducational
Languages English
Boarding/day Mixed
Aravali Retreat, Off Gurgaon Sohna Road, Gurgaon Haryana 122102, India
TELEPHONE: +91 124 2318881
FAX: +91 124 2318880
EMAIL: schooldir@pathways.ac.in
WEBSITE: www.pathways.ac.in

Podar International School
Status Private
Programme PYP, Diploma
Diploma Coordinator Mr K X George
PYP Coordinator Shahina Momin
Gender Coeducational
Languages English
Boarding/day Day
Above Ramniranjan Podar Hall, Saraswati Road, Santacruz (West), Mumbai, Maharashtra 400054, India
TELEPHONE: +91 22 6711 1111
FAX: +91 22 2648 6692
EMAIL: lulla_vandana@hotmail.com
WEBSITE:
www.podarinternationalschool.com

Pranjali International School
Status Private
Programme Diploma
Diploma Coordinator D Prakash
Gender Coeducational
Languages English
Boarding/day Day
155-157 A.K. Marg, Next to St Stephen Church, Kemps Corner, Mumbai 400036, India
TELEPHONE: +91-22-2363-9166
FAX: +91-22-2369-5235
EMAIL: smita@pranjaliworldschool.com
WEBSITE: www.pranjaliworldschool.com

RBK International Academy
Status Private
Programme Diploma
Diploma Coordinator Ulrich Nikolai
Gender Coeducational
Languages English
Boarding/day Day
349 Business Point, 5th Floor, Western Express Highway, Andheri East, Mumbai 400 069, India
TELEPHONE: +91 22 693 7777
FAX: +91 22 6593 5252
EMAIL: principal@rbkia.org
WEBSITE: www.rbkia.org

SelaQui World School
Status Private
Programme Diploma
Diploma Coordinator Rohit Pathak
Gender Coeducational
Languages English
Boarding/day Boarding
PO Sela Kui, Chakrata Road, Dehra Dun 248197, India
TELEPHONE: +91 135 2698 700
EMAIL: headmaster@selaqui.org
WEBSITE: www.schoolselaqui.org

Sharad Pawar International School, Pune
Status Private
Programme Diploma
Diploma Coordinator Jayshree Tripathi
Gender Coeducational
Languages English
Boarding/day Mixed
Charoli Budruk, Taluka Haveli, Maharashtra Pune 411012, India
TELEPHONE: +91 203 061 2708
FAX: +91 203 061 2718
EMAIL: principal@internationalschool.in
WEBSITE: www.internationalschool.in

Singapore International School

Status Private
Programme Diploma
Diploma Coordinator Sharonee Mullick
Gender Coeducational
Languages English
Boarding/day Mixed
United Educare Foundation, 6th Floor
Shashmira Centre, 176 CST Road, Kalina,
Mumbai 400098, India
TELEPHONE: +91 22 2665 2052
FAX: +91 22 2665 2361
EMAIL: headmaster@sisindia.net
WEBSITE: www.sisindia.net

Step by Step High School

Status Private
Programme Diploma
Diploma Coordinator Manisha Razdan
Gender Coeducational
Languages English
Boarding/day Day
3 Chitrakoot Scheme, Adjoining Stadium,
Ajmer Road, Jaipur, Rajasthan 302021, India
TELEPHONE: +91-141-5175-222
EMAIL: rperiwal@gmail.com
WEBSITE: www.stepbystephigh.com

SVKM International School

Status Private
Programme Diploma
Diploma Coordinator Leena Pimpley
Dadabhai Road, Vile Parle West, Mumbai
400056, India
TELEPHONE: +91 22 2617 1169/70
FAX: +91 22 2613 3400
EMAIL: lata.munjal@gmail.com
WEBSITE: http://svkmdp.ac.in

Symbiosis International School

Status Private
Programme PYP, Diploma
Diploma Coordinator Swapna Nimbalkar
PYP Coordinator Lakshmi Santosh
Gender Coeducational
Languages English
Boarding/day Mixed
Survey #231 , HISSA 3A & 4, Symbiosis Viman
Nagar Campus, Viman Nagar Pune 411014,
India
TELEPHONE: +91-20-2663-4550
EMAIL: principalsis@symbiosis.ac.in
WEBSITE: www.symbiosis.ac.in

The Banyan Tree School

Status Private
Programme Diploma
Diploma Coordinator Meenakshi Roy
Gender Coeducational
Languages English
Boarding/day Day
Plot No: 70, Sector 53, Gurgaon, NCR Delhi
122003, India
TELEPHONE: +91 124 4559 300
FAX: +91 124 4559 390
EMAIL: arai@iilm.edu
WEBSITE: www.iilm.ws

The British School

Status Private
Programme Diploma
Diploma Coordinator Kristina Mowat
Gender Coeducational
Languages English
Boarding/day Day
Dr Jose Rizal Marg, Chanakyapuri, New Delhi
110021, India
TELEPHONE: +91 11 2467 8524
FAX: +91 11 2611 2363
EMAIL: i.bayly@british-school.org
WEBSITE: www.british-school.org

The Doon School

Status Private
Programme Diploma
Diploma Coordinator Sumit Dargan
Gender Male
Languages English
Boarding/day Boarding
Mall Road, Dehradun, Uttaranchal 248001,
India
TELEPHONE: +91 135 2526 600
FAX: +91 135 2757 275
EMAIL: hmdosco@sancharnet.in
WEBSITE: www.doonschool.com

The International School Bangalore

Status Private
Programme Diploma
Diploma Coordinator Azra Begum
Gender Coeducational
Languages English
Boarding/day Mixed
Whitefield-Sarjapur Road, Near
Dommasandra Circle, Bangalore Karnataka
562125, India
TELEPHONE: +91 8 0 7822550
FAX: +91 80 7822553
EMAIL: admission@tisb.ac.in
WEBSITE: www.tisb.org

The Shri Ram School

Status Private
Programme Diploma
Diploma Coordinator Manisha Malhotra
Gender Coeducational
Languages English
Boarding/day Day
Moulsari Avenue DLF Phase-3, Gurgaon
Haryana 122002, India
TELEPHONE: +91 124 235 2173
EMAIL: sarita.mathur@tsrsnet.org
WEBSITE: www.tsrs.org/ib

Victorious Kidss Educares

Status Private
Programme PYP
PYP Coordinator Anuja Lunkad
Gender Coeducational
Languages English
Boarding/day Day
Bunglow Shukrana Survey, No 64/3/2 Kawade
Mala Behind Empress Garden, Pune 411001,
India
TELEPHONE: +91 2026718099
FAX: +91 2026878333
EMAIL: kakanchan@yahoo.com
WEBSITE: www.vkidss.org

Vishwashanti Gurukul

Status Private
Programme Diploma
Diploma Coordinator Satyajit Banerjee
Gender Coeducational
Languages English
Boarding/day Boarding
Rajbaug, off Pune-Solapur Highway, Loni,
Pune Maharashtra 412201, India
TELEPHONE: +91 20 39210101
EMAIL: sunilkarad@mitpune.com
WEBSITE: www.mitgurukul.com

INDONESIA

Bali International School

Status Private
Programme PYP, MYP, Diploma
Diploma Coordinator Russell McGrath
MYP Coordinator Curtis Beaverford
PYP Coordinator Clarence Coombs
Gender Coeducational
Languages English
Boarding/day Day
PO Box 3259, Denpasar, Bali, Indonesia
TELEPHONE: +62 361 288 770
FAX: +62361 285 103
EMAIL: russell@baliis.net
WEBSITE: www.baliinternationalschool.com

Bandung International School

Status Private
Programme PYP, Diploma
Diploma Coordinator Henri Bemelmans
PYP Coordinator Ken Buchanan
Gender Coeducational
Languages English
Boarding/day Day
PO Box 1167, Bandung West Java 40011,
Indonesia
TELEPHONE: +62 22 201 4995
FAX: +62 22 201 2688
EMAIL: head@bisdragons.com
WEBSITE: www.bisdragons.com

Bina Tunas Bangsa School

Status Private
Programme Diploma
Diploma Coordinator Ron Verburgt
Gender Coeducational
Languages English
Boarding/day Day
Jl Pluit Timur, Blok MM, Laguna Apartments,
Jakarta 15224, Indonesia
TELEPHONE: +62 21 3003 1300
EMAIL: ardikho@binatunasbangsa.com
WEBSITE: www.binatunasbangsa.com

BINUS SCHOOL SIMPRUG

Status Private
Programme PYP, MYP, Diploma
Diploma Coordinator Erdolfo L Lardizabal
MYP Coordinator Tommy Mangoendaan
PYP Coordinator Richel Langit-Dursin
Gender Coeducational
Languages English
Boarding/day Day
Jl Sultan Iskandar, Muda Kav G-8, Simprug,
Jakarta Selatan 12220, Indonesia
TELEPHONE: +62-21-724-3663
FAX: +62-21-7278-3939
EMAIL: psaidi@binus.edu
WEBSITE: www.binus-school.net
see full details on page 60

British International School, Jakarta

Status Private
Programme Diploma
Diploma Coordinator Ian Davies
Gender Coeducational
Languages English
Boarding/day Day
Bintaro Jaya Sektor IX, JL Raya Jombane
Cileduk, Pondok Aren Tangerang 15227,
Indonesia
TELEPHONE: +62 21 745 1670
FAX: +62 21 745 1671
EMAIL: admissions@bis.or.id
WEBSITE: www.bis.or.id

Cita Hati Christian Senior School

Status Private
Programme Diploma
Diploma Coordinator Erlangga Pramudya
Dharma
Gender Coeducational
Languages English
Boarding/day Day
JL Kejawan Putih Barat 28-30, Pakuwon City
Surabaya 60112, Indonesia
TELEPHONE: +62 31 591 5774
FAX: +62 31 591 4582
EMAIL: julie-anne@citahati.org
WEBSITE: www.citahati.org

Gandhi Memorial International School

Status Private
Programme PYP, MYP, Diploma
Diploma Coordinator Rowena Macaraig
MYP Coordinator Vinu Cyrus
PYP Coordinator Danilo Villanueva
Gender Coeducational
Languages English
Boarding/day Day
Jalan Landas Pacu Timur, Kota Baru Bandar,
Kemayoran, Jakarta Utara 14410, Indonesia
TELEPHONE: +62 21 658 656 85
FAX: +62 21 658 656 77
EMAIL: headmaster@gandhijkt.org
WEBSITE: www.gandhijkt.org

Jakarta International School

Status Private
Programme Diploma
Diploma Coordinator Roger Brumby
Gender Coeducational
Languages English
Boarding/day Day
Administration, PO Box 1078 JKS, Jakarta
12010, Indonesia
TELEPHONE: +62 21 769 2555
FAX: +62 21 750 3644
EMAIL: dcramer@jisedu.or.id
WEBSITE: www.jisedu.org

Medan International School

Status Private
Programme PYP, MYP
MYP Coordinator Viki Rudez
PYP Coordinator Julie Forman
Gender Coeducational
Languages English
Boarding/day Day
PO Box 1190, Medan North Sumatra 20111,
Indonesia
TELEPHONE: +62 61 836 1894
FAX: +62 61 836 1894
EMAIL: mismedanprincipal@
mis-medanintschool.com
WEBSITE: www.mis-medanintschool.com

Sekolah Ciputra, Surabaya

Status Private
Programme PYP, MYP, Diploma
Diploma Coordinator Hasto Pidekso
MYP Coordinator Stuart Chisholm
PYP Coordinator Frida Dwiyanti
Gender Coeducational
Languages English
Boarding/day Day
Kawasan Puri Widya Kencana, Citra Raya
Surabaya East Java 60213, Indonesia
TELEPHONE: +62 31-741-5018
EMAIL: director@ciputra-sby.sch.id
WEBSITE: www.ciputra-sby.sch.id

Sekolah Global Jaya

Status Private
Programme PYP, MYP, Diploma
Diploma Coordinator Kevin McRae
MYP Coordinator Eva Sidabutar
PYP Coordinator Allison Stekelenburg
Gender Coeducational
Languages English
Boarding/day Day
Jl Raya Jombang, Bintaro Jaya Sektor IX,
Pondok Aren, Tangerang 15224, Indonesia
TELEPHONE: +62 21-745-7562
FAX: +62 21-745-7561
EMAIL: richard@globaljaya.com
WEBSITE: www.globaljaya.com

Sekolah Mentari Junior High

Status Private
Programme MYP
MYP Coordinator Albert Racho
Gender Coeducational
Languages English, Indonesian
Boarding/day Day
Jalan Haji Jian No 6-A, Cipete Utara, Jakarta
Sealatan, Jakarta 12150, Indonesia
TELEPHONE: +62 21 727 95288
FAX: +62 21 727 94870
EMAIL: clarissa53@yahoo.com
WEBSITE: www.sekolahmentari.org

Sekolah Mutiara Nusantara

Status Private
Programme Diploma
Diploma Coordinator Pravin M Dongardive
Gender Coeducational
Languages English
Boarding/day Day
Kompleks Graha Puspa, Sersan Bajuri,
Setiabuidhi, Bandung 40154, Indonesia
TELEPHONE: +1 62 22 278 8558
FAX: +1 62 22 278 8597
EMAIL: wjohnson7@hotmail.com
WEBSITE: www.mutiaranusantara.com

Sekolah Pelita Harapan

Status Private
Programme PYP, MYP, Diploma
Diploma Coordinator John Evans
MYP Coordinator Rebecca Metcalfe
PYP Coordinator Ester Hastuti
Gender Coeducational
Languages English
Boarding/day Day
Senior school, 2500 Bulevar Palem Raya,
Lippo Karawaci, Tangerang Banten 15811,
Indonesia
TELEPHONE: +62 21 546 0234
FAX: +62 21 546 0246
EMAIL: cox.brian@sph.ac.id
WEBSITE: www.sph.edu

Sekolah Pelita Harapan Lippo Cikarang
Status State/private
Programme PYP, Diploma
Diploma Coordinator Andrew Paterson
PYP Coordinator Ratna Setyowati Putri
Gender Coeducational
Languages English
Boarding/day Day
Jl Dago Pemai No 1, Komplek Dago Villas,
Lippo Cikarang, Bekasi 17550, Indonesia
TELEPHONE: +62 21 897 2786
FAX: +62 21 897 2795
EMAIL: eric@sphlc.sch.id
WEBSITE: www.sph.edu

Sekolah Pelita Harapan-Sentul
Status Private/state
Programme PYP, MYP, Diploma
Diploma Coordinator Yulvita Hadi Yarti
MYP Coordinator Jan-Mark Seewald
PYP Coordinator Murray Scoble
Gender Coeducational
Languages English
Boarding/day Mixed
Academic, Jl Babakan Madang, Bukit Sentul,
Bogor Jawa Barat 16810, Indonesia
TELEPHONE: +62 21 879 60135
WEBSITE: www.sph.edu

Sekolah Tunas Bangsa
Status Private
Programme PYP
PYP Coordinator Ronald Sahat Tua Simbolon
Gender Coeducational
Languages English
Boarding/day Day
Jalan Arteri Supadio, (Achmad Yani II) Km 2,
Pontianak West Kalimantan 78391, Indonesia
TELEPHONE: +62 561 725555
FAX: +62 561 723333
EMAIL: tunasbangsa@ptk.centrin.net.id
WEBSITE: www.tunasbangsa.sch.id

Sekolah Tunas Muda
Status State/private
Programme MYP, Diploma
Diploma Coordinator Nigel Leonard Robson
MYP Coordinator Averne Loos
Gender Coeducational
Languages English
Boarding/day Day
Jl Meruya Utara Raya, No 71 Kembangan,
Jakarta Barat 11620, Indonesia
TELEPHONE: +62 21 587 0329
EMAIL: cservice@sekolahtunasmuda.com
WEBSITE: www.sekolahtunasmuda.com

Sekolah Tunas Muda (Kedoya)
Status Private
Programme PYP
PYP Coordinator Eka Patinama
Gender Coeducational
Languages English, Indonesian
Boarding/day Day
Jl Angsana Raya D8/2, Taman Kedoya Baru,
Jakarta Barat 11520, Indonesia
TELEPHONE: +62 21 5818766
EMAIL: ossc@indo.net.id
WEBSITE: www.sekolahtunasmuda.com

Sekolah Victory Plus
Status Private
Programme PYP
PYP Coordinator Isti Handayani
Gender Coeducational
Languages English
Boarding/day Day
Jl Kemang Pratama Raya, AN 2-3 Kemang
Pratama , Bekasi, Jawa Barat 17116, Indonesia
TELEPHONE: +62 21 8240 3878
FAX: +62 21 8242 6326
EMAIL: mm_isti2003@yahoo.com
WEBSITE: http://sekolahvictoryplus.com

STB-ACS (International) Jakarta
Status Private
Programme PYP, Diploma
Diploma Coordinator Richard Sidharta
PYP Coordinator Gaynor Davis
Gender Coeducational
Languages English, Indonesian
Boarding/day Mixed
Jl Batar Jati, Kelurahan Setu, Jakarta Timur,
Indonesia
TELEPHONE: +62 21 8459 7175
FAX: +62 21 8459 7180
EMAIL: dforde@stbangsa.org
WEBSITE: www.stbangsa.org

Stella Maris School
Status Private
Programme Diploma
Diploma Coordinator Henky Sasmita
Gender Coeducational
Languages English
Boarding/day Day
Artha Kencana Kav, C-1 no 1, Kencana Loka,
BSD Sector 12, Tangerang 15318, Indonesia
TELEPHONE: +62 21-7-566 566 (ext302/304)
FAX: +62 21-7-566-562
EMAIL: theo_kurniadi@yahoo.com
WEBSITE: www.stellamarisschool.com

The International School of Bogor
Status Private
Programme PYP
PYP Coordinator Lizette Turnbull
Boarding/day Day
Jalan Papandayan No 7, Bogor 16151,
Indonesia
TELEPHONE: +62 251 324360
FAX: +62 251 328512
EMAIL: isb@isbogor.org

JAPAN

Canadian Academy
Status Private
Programme Diploma
Diploma Coordinator Melanie Vrba
Gender Coeducational
Languages English
Boarding/day Mixed
4-1 Koyo-Cho Naka, Higashinada-ku Kobe
658-0032, Japan
TELEPHONE: +81 78 857 0100
FAX: +81 78 857 3250
EMAIL: fwesson@mail.canacad.ac.jp
WEBSITE: www.canacad.ac.jp

European School - Kobe
Status Private
Programme PYP
PYP Coordinator Alexander Inman
Gender Coeducational
Languages English
Boarding/day Day
1-3-22 Sowa-cho, Nada-ku, Kobe 657-0063,
Japan
TELEPHONE: +81 078 851 6414
EMAIL: schulleiter@dskobe.org
WEBSITE: www.dskobe.org

Fukuoka International School
Status Private
Programme Diploma
Diploma Coordinator James Hatch
Gender Coeducational
Languages English
Boarding/day Day
Momochi 3-chome 18-50, Sawara-ku,
Fukuoka-shi 814, Japan
TELEPHONE: +81 92 841 7601
FAX: +81 92 841 7602
EMAIL: administration@fis.ed.jp
WEBSITE: www.fis.ed.jp

Hiroshima International School
Status Private
Programme PYP, Diploma
Diploma Coordinator Charles Hearsum
PYP Coordinator Brett MacKenzie
Gender Coeducational
Languages English
Boarding/day Day
3-49-1 Kurakake, Asakita-Ku, Hiroshima 739-
1743, Japan
TELEPHONE: +81 82 843 4111
FAX: +81 82 843 6399
EMAIL: pmackenzie@hiroshima-is.ac.jp
WEBSITE: www.hiroshima-is.ac.jp

K. International School Tokyo
Status Private
Programme PYP, MYP, Diploma
Diploma Coordinator Mark Cowe
MYP Coordinator Ashish Trivedi
PYP Coordinator Paul Longtree
Gender Coeducational
Languages English
Boarding/day Day
1-5-15 Shirakawa, Kiyosumi Shirakawa,
Koto-ku, Tokyo, Japan
TELEPHONE: +81 3 3642 9993
FAX: +81 3 3642 9994
EMAIL: info@kist.ed.jp
WEBSITE: www.kist.ed.jp

Katoh Gakuen Gyoshu Senior High School
Status Private
Programme MYP, Diploma
Diploma Coordinator Allan Hamer
MYP Coordinator Darryl Mann
Gender Coeducational
Languages English
Boarding/day Day
1361-1 Nakamiyo Okanomiya, Shizuoka
4100011, Japan
TELEPHONE: +81 55 924 3322
FAX: +81 55 924 3352
WEBSITE: www.katoh-net.ac.jp/GyoshuHS/

Kyoto International School
Status Private
Programme PYP
PYP Coordinator Annette Levy
Gender Coeducational
Languages English
Boarding/day Day
317 Kitatawara-cho, Nakadachiuri-sagaru,
Yoshiyamachi-dori, Kamigyo-ku, Kyoto 602-
8247, Japan
TELEPHONE: +81 75 451 1022
FAX: +81 75 451 1023
EMAIL: kisadmin@kyoto-is.org

Nagoya International School
Status Private
Programme Diploma
Diploma Coordinator Paul Moody
2686 Minamihara, Nakashidami,
Moriyama-ku, Nagoya 463-0002, Japan
TELEPHONE: +81 52 736 2025
FAX: +81 052 736 3883
EMAIL: rrisch@nis.ac.jp
WEBSITE: www.nis.ac.jp

Osaka International School
Status Private
Programme PYP, MYP, Diploma
Diploma Coordinator Peter Heimer
MYP Coordinator Gwyn Underwood
PYP Coordinator Clarence Coombs
Gender Coeducational
Languages English
Boarding/day Day
Onohara-Nishi 4-4-16, Minoh City Osaka
562-0032, Japan
TELEPHONE: +81 727 27 5050
FAX: +81 72 727 5055
EMAIL: kcaffin@senri.ed.jp
WEBSITE: www.senri.ed.jp

Saint Maur International School
Status Private
Programme Diploma
Diploma Coordinator Timothy Matsumoto
Gender Coeducational
Languages English
Boarding/day Day
83 Yamate-cho, Naka-ku, Yokohama
231-8654, Japan
TELEPHONE: +81 45 641 5751
FAX: +81 45 641 6688
EMAIL: office@stmaur.ac.jp
WEBSITE: www.stmaur.ac.jp

Seisen International School
Status Private
Programme PYP, Diploma
Diploma Coordinator Robert Stern
PYP Coordinator Sandra Mulligan
Gender Female
Languages English
Boarding/day Day
1-12-15 Yoga, Setagaya-ku, Tokyo 158-0097,
Japan
TELEPHONE: +81 3 3704 2661
FAX: +81 3 3701 1033
EMAIL: sishead@seisen.com
WEBSITE: www.seisen.com

St Mary's International School
Status Private
Programme Diploma
Diploma Coordinator Peter Hauet
Gender Male
Languages English
Boarding/day Day
1-6-19 Seta, Setagaya Ku, Tokyo 158-8668,
Japan
TELEPHONE: +81 3 3709 3411
FAX: +81 3 3707 1950
EMAIL: jutrasm@smis.ac.jp

Tokyo International School
Status Private
Programme PYP, MYP
MYP Coordinator Andrew Hancock
PYP Coordinator Inese Zvirgzdins
Gender Coeducational
Languages English
Boarding/day Day
3-4-22 Mita, Minato-Ku, Tokyo 108-0073,
Japan
TELEPHONE: +81 3 5484 1160
FAX: +81 3 5484 1139
EMAIL: darren@tokyois.jp
WEBSITE: www.tokyois.com

Yokohama International School
Status Private
Programme PYP, Diploma
Diploma Coordinator Stephen McIlroy
PYP Coordinator Toni Bell
Gender Coeducational
Languages English
Boarding/day Day
258 Yamate-cho, Naka-ku, Yokohama
231-0862, Japan
TELEPHONE: +81 45 622 0084
FAX: +81 45 621 0379
EMAIL: yis@yis.ac.jp
WEBSITE: www.yis.ac.jp

LAOS

Vientiane International School
Status Private
Programme Diploma
Diploma Coordinator Don Tingley
Gender Coeducational
Languages English, French
Boarding/day Day
PO Box 3180, Sapanthong Tai Road,
Vientiane, Laos
TELEPHONE: +856 21 313 606
FAX: +856 21 313 008
EMAIL: alexandersteve@hotmail.com
WEBSITE: www.vis.laopdr.com

MALAYSIA

International School of Kuala Lumpur
Status Private
Programme Diploma
Diploma Coordinator Gary Piech
Gender Coeducational
Languages English
Boarding/day Day
PO Box 12645, Kuala Lumpur 50784, Malaysia
TELEPHONE: +60 3 4259 5620
FAX: +60 3 4257 9044
EMAIL: Bill_Powell@iskl.edu.my

KDU SMART SCHOOL SDN BHD (SEKOLAH SRI KDU®)
Status Private
Programme Diploma
Diploma Coordinator Jonathon Shaw
Gender Coeducational
Languages English
Boarding/day Day
No 5 & 7, Jalan Teknologi 2/1, Kota Damansara, 47800 Daerah Petaling Selangor, Malaysia
TELEPHONE: +60 03 6157 8123/6145 3888
FAX: +60 03 6156 9011/6145 3838
EMAIL: info@srikdu.edu.my
WEBSITE: www.srikdu.edu.my
see full details on page 108

MARA College Banting
Status State
Programme Diploma
Diploma Coordinator Noraini Ab Rahman
Gender Coeducational
Languages English
Boarding/day Boarding
Bukit Changgang, Banting Selangor 42700, Malaysia
TELEPHONE: +60 3 3149 1318
FAX: +60 3 3149 1061
EMAIL: abdullahar@mara.gov.my

Mara College Seremban
Status State
Programme Diploma
Diploma Coordinator Rohana Bt Abd Halim
Gender Coeducational
Languages English
Boarding/day Boarding
Jalan Aminuddin Baki, Seremban 70100, Malaysia
TELEPHONE: +606 7622 372 / 373
EMAIL: padzilah@mara.gov.my
WEBSITE: www.mrsmkm.edu.my/seremban

Mont'Kiara International School
Status Private
Programme Diploma
Diploma Coordinator Michael Daly
Gender Coeducational
Languages English
Boarding/day Day
22 Jalan Kiara, Off Jalan Bukit Kiara, Kuala Lumpur 50480, Malaysia
TELEPHONE: +60 3 2093 8604
FAX: +60 3 2093 6045
EMAIL: wcmorris@mkis.edu.my
WEBSITE: www.mkis.edu.my

THE INTERNATIONAL SCHOOL OF PENANG (UPLANDS)
Status Private
Programme PYP, Diploma
Diploma Coordinator Isabel Henriques Davis
PYP Coordinator Ali Nicholson
Gender Coeducational
Languages English
Boarding/day Mixed
Jalan Sungai Satu, Batu Feringgi, 11100 Penang, Malaysia
TELEPHONE: +604 8819 777
FAX: +604 8819 778
EMAIL: info@uplands.org
WEBSITE: www.uplands.org
see full details on page 150

MONGOLIA

International School of Ulaanbaatar
Status Private
Programme PYP, MYP, Diploma
Diploma Coordinator Andy Rossberg
MYP Coordinator Paul Starr
PYP Coordinator Dr Darren Arbour
Gender Coeducational
Languages English
Boarding/day Day
PO Box 49/564, Ulaanbaatar, Mongolia
TELEPHONE: +976 11 452 839
FAX: +976 11 450340
EMAIL: int.school.ub@gmail.com
WEBSITE: www.isumongolia.edu.mn

NEW ZEALAND

Auckland International College
Status Private
Programme Diploma
Diploma Coordinator Garry Thorpe Lewis
Gender Coeducational
Languages English
Boarding/day Mixed
85 Airedale Street, Auckland 1010, New Zealand
TELEPHONE: +64 9 309 4480
FAX: +64 9 309 4484
EMAIL: awillmann@aic.ac.nz
WEBSITE: www.aic.ac.nz

Diocesan School for Girls
Status Private
Programme Diploma
Diploma Coordinator Christine Buist
Gender Female
Languages English
Boarding/day Boarding
Clyde Street, Epsom, Auckland, New Zealand
TELEPHONE: +64 9 520 0221
FAX: +64 9 520 9376
EMAIL: amildenhall@diocesan.school.nz
WEBSITE: www.diocesan.school.nz

Glendowie Primary School
Status State
Programme PYP
PYP Coordinator Christine Matos
Gender Coeducational
Languages English
Boarding/day Day
217 Riddell Road, Glendowie, Auckland 1071, New Zealand
TELEPHONE: +64 9 575 7374
FAX: +64 9 575 7374
EMAIL: annemarieb@glendowieprimary.school.nz
WEBSITE: www.glendowieprimary.school.nz

John McGlashan College
Status State
Programme Diploma
Diploma Coordinator Chris Knopp
Gender Male
Languages English
Boarding/day Mixed
2 Pilkington Street, Maori Hill, Dunedin 9001, New Zealand
TELEPHONE: +64 3 4676620
FAX: +64 3 4676622
EMAIL: admin@mcglashan.school.nz
WEBSITE: www.mcglashan.school.nz

Kristin School
Status Private
Programme PYP, Diploma
Diploma Coordinator Debbie Dwyer
PYP Coordinator Robert Hutton
Gender Coeducational
Languages English
Boarding/day Day
PO Box 300-087, Albany, Auckland, New Zealand
TELEPHONE: +64 9 415 9566
FAX: +64 9 415 8495
EMAIL: pclague@kristin.school.nz
WEBSITE: www.kristin.school.nz

Saint Kentigern College
Status Private
Programme Diploma
Diploma Coordinator John Andrews
Gender Coeducational
Languages English
Boarding/day Mixed
PO Box 51060, Pakuranga Manukau 2010, New Zealand
TELEPHONE: +64 9 576 9019
FAX: +64 9 576 1700
EMAIL: peatw@skc.school.nz
WEBSITE: www.saintkentigern.com

Selwyn House School
Status Private
Programme PYP
PYP Coordinator Rachel Huggins
Gender Coeducational
Languages English
Boarding/day Day
122 Merivale Lane, 8104, Christchurch, New Zealand
TELEPHONE: +64 3 3557299
FAX: +64 3 3554339
EMAIL: jlapthorne@selwynhouse.school.nz
WEBSITE: www.selwynhouse.school.nz

St George's Preparatory School
Status Private
Programme PYP
PYP Coordinator Pauline Donaldson
Gender Coeducational
Languages English
Boarding/day Day
Grey Street, Wanganui, New Zealand
TELEPHONE: +64 6 3490298
FAX: +64 6 3490299
EMAIL: kmcleay@stgeorge.school.nz
WEBSITE: www.stgeorge.school.nz

St Margaret's College
Status Private
Programme Diploma
Diploma Coordinator Marilyn Copland
Gender Female
Languages English
Boarding/day Mixed
PO Box 25094, Winchester Street, Christchurch, Canterbury, New Zealand
TELEPHONE: +64 3 379 2000
FAX: +64 3 365 5748
EMAIL: admin@stmargarets.school.nz
WEBSITE: www.stmargarets.school.nz

St Peter's School, Cambridge
Status Private
Programme Diploma
Diploma Coordinator Julie Earl
Gender Coeducational
Languages English
Boarding/day Day
Private Bag 884, Cambridge 3450, New Zealand
TELEPHONE: +64 7 827 9899
FAX: +64 7 827 9812
EMAIL: stever@stpeters.school.nz
WEBSITE: www.stpeters.school.nz

Wellington Diocesan School For Girls – Nga Tawa
Status State
Programme Diploma
Diploma Coordinator Christine Michalski
Gender Female
Languages English
Boarding/day Boarding
Marton 5460, New Zealand
TELEPHONE: +64 6 3276429
FAX: +64 6 3277954
EMAIL: nga.tawa.school@xtra.co.nz

PAKISTAN

The International School
Status Private
Programme MYP, Diploma
Diploma Coordinator Iris Lazarus
MYP Coordinator David Joseph Ford
Gender Coeducational
Languages English
Boarding/day Day
Executive, 51-c Old Clifton, Near Mohatta Palace, Karachi, Sind, Pakistan
TELEPHONE: +92 21 5835805-6
FAX: +92 21 5832755
EMAIL: taymur@tis.edu.pk
WEBSITE: www.tis.edu.pk

PAPUA NEW GUINEA

Port Moresby International School
Status Private
Programme Diploma
Diploma Coordinator Steven Rowley
Gender Coeducational
Languages English
Boarding/day Day
PO Box 276, Boroko, Papua New Guinea
TELEPHONE: +675 325 3166
FAX: +675 325 4439
EMAIL: jsloan@pmis.iea.ac.pg

PHILIPPINES

Brent International School – Baguio
Status Private
Programme Diploma
Diploma Coordinator Les Pickett
Gender Coeducational
Languages English
Boarding/day Mixed
Brent Road, Baguio City 2600, Philippines
TELEPHONE: +63 74 442 2260
FAX: +63 74 442 3638
EMAIL: brent@brentschoolbaguio.com
WEBSITE: www.brentschoolbaguio.com

Brent International School – Manila
Status Private
Programme Diploma
Diploma Coordinator Maria Cristina Pozon
Gender Coeducational
Languages English
Boarding/day Day
Brentville Subdivision, Mamplasan, Biñan Laguna 4024, Philippines
TELEPHONE: +63 2 6001-0300/9
FAX: +63 49 511-4356
EMAIL: drobbins@brent.edu.ph
WEBSITE: www.brent.edu.ph

Cebu International School
Status Private
Programme Diploma
Diploma Coordinator Jennifer Basa
Gender Coeducational
Languages English
Boarding/day Day
PO Box 735, Pit-os, Cebu City 6000, Philippines
TELEPHONE: +63 32 417 6327
FAX: +63 32 417 6394
EMAIL: superintendent@cis.edu.ph
WEBSITE: www.cis.edu.ph

Eurocampus – (European International School) Manila
Status State
Programme Diploma
Diploma Coordinator Philippe Durant
Gender Coeducational
Languages English
Boarding/day Day
75 Swaziland Street, Better Living Subd, Paranaque, Metro Manila, Philippines
TELEPHONE: +63 2 776 1000
FAX: +63 2 824 1517
EMAIL: Wkollecker@eis-manila.org
WEBSITE: www.eis-manila.org

INTERNATIONAL SCHOOL MANILA
Status Private
Programme Diploma
Diploma Coordinator Sandy Van Nooten
Gender Coeducational
Languages English
Boarding/day Day
University Parkway, Fort Bonifacio, Global City, Taguig, PO Box 1526 MCPO, 1255, Makati City, Philippines
TELEPHONE: +63 2 8488440
FAX: +63 2 8408489
EMAIL: tozed@ismanila.org
WEBSITE: www.ismanila.org
see full details on page 96

Southville International School & Colleges
Status Private
Programme Diploma
Diploma Coordinator Anthony Calado
Gender Coeducational
Languages English
Boarding/day Day
1281 Tropical Avenue Corner, Luxembourg Street, BF Homes International, Las Pinas City, Philippines
TELEPHONE: +63-2-820-8702
EMAIL: gene@sville.edu.ph
WEBSITE: www.sville.edu.ph

The Beacon School
Status Private
Programme PYP, MYP
MYP Coordinator Mariles Matias
PYP Coordinator Georgianna de Vera
Gender Coeducational
Languages English
Boarding/day Day
PCPD Building, 2332 Chino Roces Extn, Taguig, Metro Manila, Philippines
TELEPHONE: +632 840 5040
EMAIL: headmaster@beaconschool.ph
WEBSITE: www.beaconschool.ph

The British School, Manila
Status Private
Programme Diploma
Diploma Coordinator Carl Piaf
Gender Coeducational
Languages English
Boarding/day Day
PO Box 2079 MCPO 1260, Makati, Metro Manila, Philippines
TELEPHONE: +63 2 840 1570
FAX: +63 2 840 1520
EMAIL: head@britishschoolmanila.org
WEBSITE: www.britishschoolmanila.org

PR CHINA

American International School of Guangzhou
Status Private
Programme PYP, Diploma
Diploma Coordinator Jason Crook
PYP Coordinator Rick Elya
Gender Coeducational
Languages English
Boarding/day Day/boarding
No 3 Yan Yu Street South, Er Sha Island, Yuexiu District, Guangzhou 510105, PR China
TELEPHONE: +86 20 8735 3392/3393
FAX: +86 20 8735 3339
EMAIL: jstucker@aisgz.edu.cn
WEBSITE: www.aisgz.edu.cn

Australian International School Hong Kong
Status Private
Programme Diploma
Diploma Coordinator Mr Chris McCorkell
Gender Coeducational
Languages English
Boarding/day Day
3A Norfolk Road, Kowloon Tong, Hong Kong, SAR, PR China
TELEPHONE: +852 2304 6078
FAX: +852 2304 6077
EMAIL: info@aishk.edu.hk
WEBSITE: www.aishk.edu.hk

Beijing BISS International School
Status Private
Programme PYP, MYP, Diploma
Diploma Coordinator Lennox Meldrum
MYP Coordinator Ross Brown
PYP Coordinator Clare Demnar
Gender Coeducational
Languages English
Boarding/day Day
No 17, Area 4, An Zhen Xi Li, Chaoyang District, Beijing 100029, PR China
TELEPHONE: +86 10 64 433155
FAX: +86 10 64 433156
EMAIL: afowles@biss.com.cn
WEBSITE: www.biss.com.cn

Beijing City International School
Status Private
Programme PYP, MYP, Diploma
Diploma Coordinator Frank Davis
MYP Coordinator Lotty Cole
PYP Coordinator Alan Cox
Gender Coeducational
Languages English, Mandarin
Boarding/day Day
77 Baiziwan Nan Er Lu, Chaoyang, Beijing 100022, PR China
TELEPHONE: +86 10 8771 7171
FAX: +86 10 8771 778
EMAIL: mark.bretherton@bcis.cn
WEBSITE: www.bcis.cn

Beijing Huijia Private School
Status Private
Programme Diploma
Diploma Coordinator Victor Tian
Gender Coeducational
Languages English
Boarding/day Boarding
PO Box 1010, Changping, Beijing 102200, PR China
TELEPHONE: +86 10 607 85798
FAX: +86 10 607 85886
EMAIL: xz8101@hj2000.net.cn
WEBSITE: www.huijia2000.com

Beijing No 55 High School
Status State
Programme MYP, Diploma
Diploma Coordinator Wu Ying Ying
MYP Coordinator Wu Ying Ying
Gender Coeducational
Languages English, Chinese
Boarding/day Day/mixed
12# Xin Zhong Jie Street, Dong Cheng District, Beijing 100027, PR China
TELEPHONE: +86 10 64162247
EMAIL: rushanchen2003@yahoo.com.cn

Beijing World Youth Academy
Status Private
Programme Diploma
Diploma Coordinator David Heath
Gender Coeducational
Languages English
Boarding/day Mixed
40# Liang Ma Qiao Road, Chao Yang District, Beijing 100016, PR China
TELEPHONE: +86 10 8454 3478/6461 7787
FAX: +86 10 6461 7717
EMAIL: admissions@ibwya.net
WEBSITE: www.ibwya.net

Canadian International School of Hong Kong
Status Private
Programme Diploma
Diploma Coordinator Anita George
Gender Coeducational
Languages English
Boarding/day Day
36 Nam Long Shan Road, Aberdeen, Hong Kong, SAR, PR China
TELEPHONE: +852 2525 7088
FAX: +852 2525 7579
EMAIL: info@cdnis.edu.hk
WEBSITE: www.cdnis.edu.hk

Changchun American International School
Status Private
Programme Diploma
Diploma Coordinator Edward Kwan
2899 Dong Nan Hu Road, Changchun, Jilin Province 130033, PR China
TELEPHONE: +86 431 8458 1234
FAX: +86 431 8458 2345
EMAIL: muerkvitz@ccischina.org
WEBSITE: www.ccischina.org

Chinese International School
Status Private
Programme MYP, Diploma
Diploma Coordinator Craig Boyce
MYP Coordinator Maninder Kalsi
Gender Coeducational
Languages English
Boarding/day Day
1 Hau Yuen Path, Braemar Hill, Hong Kong, SAR, PR China
TELEPHONE: +852 2 510 7288
FAX: +852 2 510 7378
EMAIL: rmb@cis.edu.hk
WEBSITE: www.cis.edu.hk

DULWICH COLLEGE BEIJING

Status Private
Programme Diploma
Diploma Coordinator Kevin Huntley
Gender Coeducational
Languages English
Boarding/day Day
89 Capital Airport Road, Shunyi District,
Beijing 101300, PR China
TELEPHONE: +86 10 6454 9000
FAX: +86 10 6454 9001
EMAIL: info@dulwich-beijing.cn
WEBSITE: www.dulwich-beijing.cn
see full details on page 76

DULWICH COLLEGE SHANGHAI

Status Private
Programme Diploma
Diploma Coordinator Michelle Brinn
Gender Coeducational
Languages English
Boarding/day Day
266 Lan An Road, JinQiao, Pu Dong, Shanghai
201206, PR China
TELEPHONE: +8621 5899 9910
FAX: +8621 5899 9810
EMAIL: info@dulwich-shanghai.cn
WEBSITE: www.dulwich-shanghai.cn
see full details on page 77

EtonHouse International School, Suzhou

Status Private
Programme PYP
PYP Coordinator Jacqui Patrick
Gender Coeducational
Languages English
Boarding/day Mixed
70 Jin Shan Lu, New District, Suzhou Jiang Su
215011, PR China
TELEPHONE: +86 0512 6825 5666
FAX: +86 0512 6825 5939
EMAIL: enquiry@etonhouse-sz.com
WEBSITE: www.etonhouse-sz.com

French International School

Status Private
Programme Diploma
Diploma Coordinator Mary Lawton
Gender Coeducational
Languages English
Boarding/day Day
165 Blue Pool Road, Happy Valley, Hong
Kong, SAR, PR China
TELEPHONE: +852 2 577 6217
FAX: +852 2 577 9658
EMAIL: fis@lfis.edu.hk

Guang Ya School

Status Private
Programme MYP, Diploma
Diploma Coordinator Janice Hew
MYP Coordinator Li Li
Gender Coeducational
Languages Chinese, English
Boarding/day Boarding
Dujiangya, Sichuan 611833, PR China
TELEPHONE: +86 28 8722 4909
EMAIL: qguangya@sohu.com
WEBSITE: www.guangyaschool.com

Guangdong Country Garden School

Status Private
Programme MYP, Diploma
Diploma Coordinator Huo Jianhua
MYP Coordinator Jianghui Peng
Gender Coeducational
Languages English
Boarding/day Boarding
ShundeCountry Gardens, Beijiao Town,
Shunde District, Foshan City, Guangdong
Province 528312, PR China
TELEPHONE: +86 757 26677 947
FAX: +86 757 26635 118
EMAIL: hjh@bgymail.gd.cn
WEBSITE: www.bgy.gd.cn

HIGH SCHOOL AFFILIATED TO NANJING NORMAL UNIVERSITY

Status State
Programme Diploma
Diploma Coordinator Gong Yan
Gender Coeducational
Languages English
Boarding/day Mixed
37 Chahaer Road, Jiangsu Province, Nanjing
210003, PR China
TELEPHONE: +86 25 8346 9052
FAX: +86 25 8346 9052
EMAIL: wzb@nsfz.net
WEBSITE: www.nsfz.net
see full details on page 90

Hong Kong Academy Primary School

Status Private
Programme PYP
PYP Coordinator Kassandra Boyd
Gender Coeducational
Languages English
Boarding/day Day
15 Stubbs Road, 4/F Chung On Hall, Wanchai
Hong Kong, SAR, PR China
TELEPHONE: +852 2575 8282
FAX: +852 2891 4460
EMAIL: andy.pagesmith@hkacademy.edu.hk
WEBSITE: www.hkacademy.edu.hk

International School of Beijing – Shunyi

Status Private
Programme Diploma
Diploma Coordinator Sharon Boyle-Woods
Gender Coeducational
Languages English
Boarding/day Day
No 10 An Hua Street, Shunyi District, Beijing
101318, PR China
TELEPHONE: +86 10 8149 2345 ext 1001
FAX: +86 10 8045 2001
EMAIL: thawkins@isb.bj.edu.cn
WEBSITE: www.isb.bj.edu.cn

INTERNATIONAL SCHOOL OF TIANJIN

Status Private
Programme PYP, MYP, Diploma
Diploma Coordinator Susan Hall
MYP Coordinator Barbara Wrightson
PYP Coordinator Josianne Fitzgerald
Gender Coeducational
Languages English
Boarding/day Day
Weishan Road, Shuanggang, Jinnan District,
Tianjin 300350, PR China
TELEPHONE: +86 22 2859 2001
FAX: +86 22 2859 2007
EMAIL: info@istianjin.net
WEBSITE: www.istianjin.org
see full details on page 102

Island School

Status Private
Programme Diploma
Diploma Coordinator Daniel Trump
Gender Coeducational
Languages English
Boarding/day Day
20 Borrett Road, Hong Kong, SAR, PR China
TELEPHONE: +852 2524 7135
FAX: +852 2840 1673
EMAIL: school@mail.island.edu.hk
WEBSITE: www.island.edu.hk

Japanese International School

Status Private
Programme PYP
PYP Coordinator Claire Forbes
Gender Coeducational
Languages English
Boarding/day Day
4663 Tai Po Road, Tai Po, New Territories
Hong Kong, SAR, PR China
TELEPHONE: +852 2834 3531
FAX: +852 2652 2166
EMAIL: mistruzzi@jis.edu.hk
WEBSITE: www.jis.edu.hk

Kiangsu-Chekiang College, International Section
Status Private
Programme Diploma
Diploma Coordinator John Beattie
Gender Coeducational
Languages English
Boarding/day Day
20 Braemar Hill Road, North Point, Hong Kong, SAR, PR China
TELEPHONE: +852 2570 1281
FAX: +852 2570 3281
EMAIL: jdaniel@kcis.edu.hk
WEBSITE: www.kcis.edu.hk

King George V School
Status Private
Programme Diploma
Diploma Coordinator Arnett Edwards
Gender Coeducational
Languages English
Boarding/day Day
2 Tin Kwong Road, Homantin, Kowloon, Hong Kong, SAR, PR China
TELEPHONE: +852 2711 3029
FAX: +852 2760 7116
EMAIL: office@kgv.edu.hk
WEBSITE: www.kgv.edu.hk

Kingston International Kindergarten
Status Private
Programme PYP
PYP Coordinator Nerida Ashton
Gender Coeducational
Boarding/day Day
12-14 Cumberland Road, Kowloon Tong, Hong Kong, SAR, PR China
TELEPHONE: +852 2337 9049
FAX: +852 2337 7382
EMAIL: enquiry@kingston.edu.hk
WEBSITE: www.kingston.edu.hk

Kingston International School
Status Private
Programme PYP
PYP Coordinator John Harper
Gender Coeducational
Boarding/day Day
113 Waterloo Road, Kowloon Tong, Hong Kong, SAR, PR China
TELEPHONE: +852 2337 9031
FAX: +852 2337 9970
EMAIL: kispc@kingston.edu.hk

Li Po Chun United World College of Hong Kong
Status Private
Programme Diploma
Diploma Coordinator Martin Gough
Gender Coeducational
Languages English
Boarding/day Boarding
10 Lok Wo Sha Lane, off Sai Sha Road, Ma On Shan, Hong Kong, SAR, PR China
TELEPHONE: +852 2640 0424
FAX: +8522643 4088
EMAIL: office@lpcuwc.edu.hk
WEBSITE: www.lpcuwc.edu.hk

Manila Xiamen International School
Status Private
Programme Diploma
Diploma Coordinator E D A Africa-Coronel
Gender Coeducational
Languages English
Boarding/day Mixed
No. 735 Long Hu San Lu, Zeng Cou An, Si Ming District, Xiamen 361005, PR China
TELEPHONE: +86 592 2516373
FAX: +86 592 2516370
EMAIL: mxis@public.xm.fj.cn
WEBSITE: www.mxis-cn.com

Nanjing International School
Status Private
Programme PYP, MYP, Diploma
Diploma Coordinator Jemma de Smidt
MYP Coordinator Denise Walsh
PYP Coordinator Felicity Hewett
Gender Coeducational
Languages English
Boarding/day Day
Xian Lin College and, University Town, Qi Xia District, Nanjing 210046, PR China
TELEPHONE: +86 25 85899111
FAX: +86 25 85899222
EMAIL: enquires@nanjing-school.com
WEBSITE: www.nanjing-school.com

Oriental English College, Shenzhen
Status Private
Programme Diploma
Diploma Coordinator C K Kung
Gender Coeducational
Languages English
Boarding/day Mixed
Baoan Education City, National Highway 107, Shenzhen, Guangdong 518218, PR China
TELEPHONE: +86 755 27516124
FAX: +86 755 27516898
EMAIL: highschoole@szoec.com.cn
WEBSITE: www.szoec.com.cn

RENAISSANCE COLLEGE HONG KONG
Status Private
Programme PYP, MYP, Diploma
Diploma Coordinator Ms Carol Larkin
MYP Coordinator Mr Grant Rogers
PYP Coordinator Ms Rosario Colet
Gender Coeducational
Languages English
Boarding/day Day
5 Hang Ming Street, Ma On Shan, New Territories Hong Kong, SAR, PR China
TELEPHONE: +852 3556 3556
FAX: +852 3556 3446
EMAIL: info@renaissance.edu.hk
WEBSITE: www.renaissance.edu.hk
see full details on page 127

Sha Tin College
Status Private
Programme Diploma
Diploma Coordinator Neil Hodgson
Gender Coeducational
Languages English
Boarding/day Day
3 Lai Wo Lane, Fo Tan, Sha Tin, New Territories, Hong Kong, SAR, PR China
TELEPHONE: +852 2699 1811
FAX: +852 2695 0592
EMAIL: info@shatincollege.edu.hk
WEBSITE: www.shatincollege.edu.hk

Shanghai American School
Status Private
Programme Diploma
Diploma Coordinator James Leung
Gender Coeducational
Languages English
Boarding/day Mixed
50 Ji Di Lu, Zhudi Town, Shanghai, Minhang District 201107, PR China
TELEPHONE: +86 21 6221 1445
FAX: +86 21 6224 1269
EMAIL: james.leung@saschina.org
WEBSITE: www.saschina.org

Shanghai American School (Pudong Campus)
Status Private
Programme Diploma
Diploma Coordinator Michael Chao
Gender Coeducational
Languages English
Boarding/day Day
Shanghai Links Executive Community, 1600 Ling Bai Hwy, San Jia Gang, Shanghai, Pudong New Area 201201, PR China
TELEPHONE: +86 21 6221 1445 x3000
EMAIL: dennis.larkin@saschina.org
WEBSITE: www.saschina.org

Shanghai Community International Schools – Hongqiao Campus
Status Private
Programme Diploma
Diploma Coordinator Jeff Stubbs
1161 HongQiao Road, Shanghai 200051, PR China
TELEPHONE: +86 21 6261 3668
FAX: +86 21 6261 4639
EMAIL: bparker@scischina.org
WEBSITE: www.scischina.org

Shanghai High School
Status State
Programme Diploma
Diploma Coordinator Zhu Zhenyi
Gender Coeducational
Languages English
Boarding/day Boarding
400 ShangZhong Road, Shanghai 200231, PR China
TELEPHONE: +86 21 64768691
FAX: +86 21 64765510
EMAIL: shms@public.sta.net.cn
WEBSITE: www.shsid.org

Shanghai Jin Cai High School
Status State
Programme MYP
MYP Coordinator Sally Zhang
Gender Coeducational
Languages Chinese
Boarding/day Mixed
2788 Mid-Yanggao Road, Pudong New Area,
Shanghai 200135, PR China
TELEPHONE: +86 21-6854-3533
WEBSITE: www.jincai.sh.cn

Shanghai Pinghe School
Status Private
Programme Diploma
Diploma Coordinator Cao Lei
Gender Coeducational
Languages English
Boarding/day Mixed
261 Huang Yang Road, Pudong, Shanghai, PR
China
TELEPHONE: +86 21 5031 9151
FAX: +86 21 5031 9151
EMAIL: mir@shphschool.com
WEBSITE: www.shphschool.com

Shanghai Singapore International School
Status Private
Programme MYP, Diploma
Diploma Coordinator Wei Min Ng
MYP Coordinator Joel Sze Hon Seow
Gender Coeducational
Languages English
Boarding/day Day
301 Zhu Jian Road, Hua Cao Town, Shanghai,
Minhang District 201107, PR China
TELEPHONE: +86 21 6221 9288
FAX: +86 21 6221 9188
EMAIL: lcchong@ssis.cn
WEBSITE: www.ssis.cn

Shanghai Victoria Wah Kwong Kindergarten
Status Private
Programme PYP
PYP Coordinator Gong Yang
Gender Coeducational
Languages English
Boarding/day Day
No 81 Lane 3297, Hong Mei Road, Shanghai
201103, PR China
TELEPHONE: +86 21 6405 6668
FAX: +86 21 6405 5941
EMAIL: mkoong@victoria.edu.hk
WEBSITE: www.victoria.sh.cn

Shanghai World Foreign Language Middle School
Status Private
Programme MYP
MYP Coordinator Wang Si-jiao
Gender Coeducational
Languages Chinese
Boarding/day Mixed
380 Pu Bei Road, Xu Hui District, Shanghai
200233, PR China
TELEPHONE: +86 21 5419 0068
EMAIL: Jason_xu1968@hotmail.com
WEBSITE: www.wflms.com

Shanghai World Foreign Language Primary School
Status Private
Programme PYP
PYP Coordinator Halina Werchiwski
Gender Coeducational
Languages English
Boarding/day Day
No 35 Lane 239, Gui Ling East Street, Xu Hui
District, Shanghai 200233, PR China
TELEPHONE: +86 21 6436 3556
FAX: +86 21 5479 5704
WEBSITE: www.wflps.com

South Island School
Status Private
Programme Diploma
Diploma Coordinator Danny O'Connor
Gender Coeducational
Languages English
Boarding/day Day
50 Nam Fung Road, Aberdeen, Hong Kong,
SAR, PR China
TELEPHONE: +852 2555 9313
FAX: +852 2553 8811
EMAIL: sis@mail.sis.edu.hk
WEBSITE: www.sis.edu.hk

Suzhou Singapore International School
Status Private
Programme MYP, Diploma
Diploma Coordinator Jozef Fryckowski
MYP Coordinator Werner Paetzold
Gender Coeducational
Languages English
Boarding/day Day
208 Zhong Nan Street, Suzhou Industrial
Park, Suzhou Jiangsu 215021, PR China
TELEPHONE: +86 512 6258 0388
EMAIL: jonlane@ssis-suzhou.com.cn
WEBSITE: www.ssis-suzhou.com

The British International School of Shanghai (Puxi Campus)
Status Private
Programme Diploma
Diploma Coordinator Simon Scott
Gender Coeducational
Languages English
Boarding/day Day
111 Jinguang Road, Huacao Town, Minhang
District, Puxi, Shanghai 201107, PR China
TELEPHONE: +86-21-5226-3211
FAX: +86-21-5226-3212
EMAIL: s-scott@bisspuxi.com
WEBSITE: www.bisspuxi.com

The British International School, Shanghai
Status Private
Programme Diploma
Diploma Coordinator Trevor Gale
Gender Coeducational
Languages English
Boarding/day Day
600 Cambridge Forest New Town, 2729
Hunan Road, Pudong, Shanghai 201315, PR
China
TELEPHONE: +86-21-5812-7455
EMAIL: principal-pudong@bisschina.com
WEBSITE: www.bisshanghai.com

Tianjin Experimental High School
Status State
Programme MYP, Diploma
Diploma Coordinator Xiping Wang
MYP Coordinator Xiulan Wang
Gender Coeducational
Languages Chinese, English
Boarding/day Mixed
No 1 Pingshan Road, Hexi District, Tianjin
300074, PR China
TELEPHONE: +86 22 2335 8689
EMAIL: zhanghong@syzx.tj.edu.cn
WEBSITE: www.tjsyzx.cn

UTAHLOY INTERNATIONAL SCHOOL GUANGZHOU
Status Private
Programme MYP, Diploma
Diploma Coordinator Urs Jungo
MYP Coordinator Jacqui Cussen
Gender Coeducational
Languages English
Boarding/day Day
6km Sha Tai Highway, JinBao Gong, Tong He,
Guangzhou, Guangdong 510515, PR China
TELEPHONE: +8620 87202019
FAX: +8620 87044296
EMAIL: uis@utahloy.com
WEBSITE: www.utahloy.com
see full details on page 157

Utahloy International School Zeng Cheng
Status Private
Programme Diploma
Diploma Coordinator Robert King
Gender Coeducational
Languages English
Boarding/day Mixed
San Jiang Town, Zeng Cheng City, Guangdong Province 511325, PR China
TELEPHONE: +86 20 8291 3201
EMAIL: shanekells@utahloy.com
WEBSITE: www.utahloy.com/zc/

Victoria Belcher Kindergarten
Status Private
Programme PYP
PYP Coordinator Jason Doucette
Gender Coeducational
Languages English
Boarding/day Day
Portion of Level 3 (Kindergarten Area), The Westwood, 8 Belchers Street, Hong Kong, SAR, PR China
TELEPHONE: +852 2542 7001
EMAIL: mkoong@victoria.edu.hk
WEBSITE: www.victoria.edu.hk

Victoria Shanghai Academy
Status Private
Programme PYP, MYP, Diploma
Diploma Coordinator Rick Spadafora
MYP Coordinator Margareth Harris
PYP Coordinator Dawn Crouse
Gender Coeducational
Languages English
Boarding/day Day
19 Shum Wan Road, Aberdeen, Hong Kong, SAR, PR China
TELEPHONE: +852 3402 1200
FAX: +852 3402 1299
EMAIL: lhshiu@victoria.edu.hk
WEBSITE: www.victoria.edu.hk

West Island School
Status Private
Programme Diploma
Diploma Coordinator Craig Davis
Gender Coeducational
Languages English
Boarding/day Day
250 Victoria Road, Pokfulam, Hong Kong, SAR, PR China
TELEPHONE: +852 2819 1962
FAX: +852 2816 7257
EMAIL: wis@wis.edu.hk
WEBSITE: www.wis.edu.hk

Western Academy Of Beijing
Status Private
Programme PYP, MYP, Diploma
Diploma Coordinator Robin Klymow
MYP Coordinator Rebecca Butterworth
PYP Coordinator Sarah Harris
Gender Coeducational
Languages English
Boarding/day Day
PO Box 8547, 10 Lai Guang Ying Dong Lu, Chao Yang District, Beijing 100103, PR China
TELEPHONE: +86 10 8456 4155
FAX: +86 10 6432 2440
EMAIL: wabinfo@wab.edu
WEBSITE: www.wab.edu

Xiamen International School
Status Private
Programme PYP, MYP, Diploma
Diploma Coordinator Mrs Kirsty Wilkinson
MYP Coordinator Dr David Freeman
PYP Coordinator Michael Vieira
Gender Coeducational
Languages English
Boarding/day Day
262 Xing Bei San Lu, Xinglin, Jimei District, Xiamen 361022, PR China
TELEPHONE: +86 592 625 6581
FAX: +86 592 625 6584
EMAIL: john.godwin@xischina.com
WEBSITE: www.xischina.com

Yew Chung International School – Hong Kong
Status Private
Programme Diploma
Diploma Coordinator Iyad Matuk
Gender Coeducational
Languages English
Boarding/day Day
Administration, 6 Caldecott Road, Pipers Hill, Kowloon, Hong Kong, SAR, PR China
TELEPHONE: +852 2336 3443
FAX: +852 2337 5370
EMAIL: katheriney@ycef.com
WEBSITE: www.ycef.com

Yew Chung International School of Beijing
Status Private
Programme Diploma
Diploma Coordinator Bruce Michael
Gender Coeducational
Languages English, Chinese
Boarding/day Day
Honglingjin Park, No: 5 Houbalizhuang, Chao Yang District, Beijing 100025, PR China
TELEPHONE: +86 10 8583 3731
FAX: +86 10 8583 2734
EMAIL: nickc@bj.ycef.com
WEBSITE: www.ycef.com

Yew Chung International School Shanghai
Status Private
Programme Diploma
Diploma Coordinator Sarah Lee
Gender Coeducational
Languages English
Boarding/day Day
11 Shui Cheng Road, Shanghai 200336, PR China
TELEPHONE: +86 21 62195910
FAX: +86 21 62190675
EMAIL: jamesf@sis.ycef.com
WEBSITE: www.ycef.com

Zhengzhou Middle School
Status State
Programme MYP
MYP Coordinator Sun Guiling
Gender Coeducational
Languages Chinese
Boarding/day Boarding
2# Yinghua Street, Hi-Tech Development Zone, Zhengzhou, Henan 450001, PR China
TELEPHONE: +86 (0)371 63262310
EMAIL: gaozhengqi2005@yahoo.com.cn
WEBSITE: www.zzms.com

REPUBLIC OF KOREA

International School of Busan
Status Private
Programme Diploma
Diploma Coordinator Dennis Robinson
Gender Coeducational
Languages English
Boarding/day Day
1492-12 Jung-2-Dong, Haeundae-Gu, Busan 612849, Republic of Korea
TELEPHONE: +82 51 742 3332
FAX: +82 51 742 3375
EMAIL: ispusan@ispusan.co.kr
WEBSITE: www.isbusan.org

Seoul Foreign School
Status Private
Programme Diploma
Diploma Coordinator Linda Cameron
Gender Coeducational
Languages English
Boarding/day Day
55 Yonhi Dong, Seoul 120-113, Republic of Korea
TELEPHONE: +82 2 330 3100
FAX: +82 2 335 1857
EMAIL: admissions@seoulforeign.org
WEBSITE: www.seoulforeign.org

TAEJON CHRISTIAN INTERNATIONAL SCHOOL
Status Private
Programme PYP, Diploma
Diploma Coordinator Ken Gunther
PYP Coordinator Liz Harder
Gender Coeducational
Languages English
Boarding/day Mixed
201-1 O-Jung Dong, Daedeok-Gu, Daejeon
306-819, Republic of Korea
TELEPHONE: +82 042 633 3663
FAX: +82 042 631 5732
EMAIL: hdmst@tcis.or.kr
WEBSITE: www.tcis.or.kr
see full details on page 144

SINGAPORE

ACS (INTERNATIONAL), SINGAPORE
Status Private
Programme Diploma
Diploma Coordinator Daniel Toyne
Gender Coeducational
Languages English
Boarding/day Mixed
61 Jalan Hitam Manis, Singapore 278475
TELEPHONE: +65 6472 1477
FAX: +65 6472 0477
EMAIL:
john.barrett@acsinternational.com.sg
WEBSITE: www.acsinternational.com.sg
see full details on page 39

Anglo-Chinese School (Independent)
Status Private
Programme Diploma
Diploma Coordinator Siew Hwa Chock
Gender Coeducational
Boarding/day Both
121 Dover Road, Singapore 139650
TELEPHONE: +65 6773 1633
EMAIL: ongtc@acsindep.edu.sg
WEBSITE: www.acs.sch.edu.sg/acs_indep

Australian International School, Singapore
Status Private
Programme PYP, MYP
MYP Coordinator Angela Gravina
PYP Coordinator Ardene Mandziy
Gender Coeducational
Languages English
Boarding/day Day
1 Loring Chuan, Singapore 556818
TELEPHONE: +65 6883 5155
FAX: +65 6285 5255
EMAIL: enquiries@ais.com.sg
WEBSITE: www.ais.com.sg

Canadian International School
Status Private
Programme PYP, MYP, Diploma
Diploma Coordinator Metty Antony
MYP Coordinator Miles Beasley
PYP Coordinator Keri-Lee Beasley
Gender Coeducational
Languages English
Boarding/day Day
71 Bukit Tinggi Road, Singapore 289759
TELEPHONE: +65 6 875 1519
FAX: +65 6 875 1516
EMAIL: jdalziel@cis.edu.sg
WEBSITE: www.cis.edu.sg

Chatsworth International School
Status Private
Programme Diploma
Diploma Coordinator Caroline Hutchison
Gender Coeducational
Languages English
Boarding/day Day
37 Emerald Hill Road, Singapore 229313
TELEPHONE: +65 6737 5955
FAX: +65 6737 5655
EMAIL: jgchswth@singnet.com.sg
WEBSITE: www.chatsworth-international.com

Chinese International School
Status Private
Programme Diploma
Diploma Coordinator Robert Powers
Gender Coeducational
Languages English
Boarding/day Mixed
60-62 Dunearn Road, Singapore 309434
TELEPHONE: +65 6254 0200
FAX: +65 6252 5120
EMAIL: admin@cnis.edu.sg
WEBSITE: www.cnis.edu.sg

Emaar International School
Status Private
Programme Diploma
Diploma Coordinator David Banham
Gender Coeducational
Languages English
Boarding/day Day
201 Ulu Pandan Road, Singapore 596468
TELEPHONE: +65 6536 6566
FAX: +65 6536 6866
EMAIL: enquiries@eis.edu.sg
WEBSITE: www.eis.edu.sg

EtonHouse International School
Status Private
Programme PYP
PYP Coordinator Ellen Fielder
Gender Coeducational
Languages English
Boarding/day Day
51 Broadrick Road, Singapore 439501
TELEPHONE: +65 6346 6922
FAX: +65 6346 6522
EMAIL: johncooley@etonhouse.com.sg
WEBSITE: www.etonhouse.com.sg

German European School, Singapore
Status Private
Programme MYP, Diploma
Diploma Coordinator Iain Fish
MYP Coordinator Wayne Burnett
Gender Coeducational
Languages English
Boarding/day Mixed
72 Bukit Tinggi Road, Singapore 289760
TELEPHONE: +65 6469 1131
FAX: +65 6469 0308
EMAIL: guenter.boos@gess.sg
WEBSITE: www.gess.sg

Global Indian International School
Status Private
Programme Diploma
Diploma Coordinator Omkar Joshi
Gender Coeducational
Languages English
Boarding/day Mixed
1 Mei Chin Road, Singapore 149253
TELEPHONE: +65 6479 1511
FAX: +65 6479 1248
EMAIL:
admissions@sg.globalindianschool.org
WEBSITE: www.globalindianschool.org

Hwa Chong International School
Status Private
Programme Diploma
Diploma Coordinator Shiueh Ling Mok
Gender Coeducational
Languages English
Boarding/day Day
663 Bukit Timah Road, Singapore 269783
TELEPHONE: +65 6464 7077
FAX: +65 6464 7060
EMAIL: yeongsc@hcis.edu.sg
WEBSITE: www.hcis.edu.sg

ISS INTERNATIONAL SCHOOL SINGAPORE
Status Private
Programme PYP, MYP, Diploma
Diploma Coordinator Stuart Jones
MYP Coordinator Elizabeth Carrick
PYP Coordinator George Piacentini
Gender Coeducational
Languages English
Boarding/day Day
21 Preston Road, Singapore 109355
TELEPHONE: +65 6475 4188
FAX: +65 6273 7065
EMAIL: admissions@iss.edu.sg
WEBSITE: www.iss.edu.sg
see full details on page 104

Overseas Family School
Status Private
Programme PYP, MYP, Diploma
Diploma Coordinator Keith McDonnell
MYP Coordinator Suzanne Bentin
PYP Coordinator Da-Khue Ng
Gender Coeducational
Languages English
Boarding/day Day
25F Paterson Road, Singapore 238515
TELEPHONE: +65 673 802 11
FAX: +65 6 733 8825
EMAIL: david_perry@ofs.edu.sg
WEBSITE: www.ofs.edu.sg/

St Joseph's Institution International
Status Private
Programme Diploma
Diploma Coordinator Pamela Carter
Gender Coeducational
Languages English
Boarding/day Boarding
490/500 Thomson Road, Singapore 298191
TELEPHONE: +65 6353 9383
FAX: +65 6354 3103
EMAIL: andrew.bennett
@sji-international.com.sg
WEBSITE: www.sji-international.com.sg

United World College of South East Asia
Status Private
Programme PYP, Diploma
Diploma Coordinator Geraint Jones
PYP Coordinator Geraldine Brogden
Gender Coeducational
Languages English
Boarding/day Mixed
Pasir Panjang, PO Box 15, Singapore 911121
TELEPHONE: +65 6 775 5344
FAX: +65 6 778 5846
EMAIL: info@uwcsea.edu.sg
WEBSITE: www.uwcsea.edu.sg

SRI LANKA

Overseas School of Colombo
Status Private
Programme PYP, MYP, Diploma
Diploma Coordinator Ray Lewis
MYP Coordinator Paulenne Hosegood
PYP Coordinator Geraldine Rasiah
Gender Coeducational
Languages English
Boarding/day Day
PO Box 9, Pelawatte, Battaramulla 10120, Sri Lanka
TELEPHONE: +94 11 2784 920-2
FAX: +94 11 2784 999
EMAIL: admin@osc.lk
WEBSITE: www.osc.lk

The British School in Colombo
Status Private
Programme Diploma
Diploma Coordinator Jayaweera Pilimatalawwe
Gender Coeducational
Languages English
Boarding/day Day
63 Elvitigala Mawatha, Mawatha, Colombo 08, Sri Lanka

TAIWAN

Taipei American School
Status Private
Programme Diploma
Diploma Coordinator Joseph Earley
Gender Coeducational
Languages English
Boarding/day Day
800 Chung Shan North Road, Sec 6, Taipei, Taiwan
TELEPHONE: +886 22 873 9900
FAX: +886 22 873 1641
EMAIL: hannac@tas.edu.tw

Taipei European School
Status Private
Programme Diploma
Diploma Coordinator Stewart James Redden
Gender Coeducational
Languages English
Boarding/day Day
Swire European Campus, 31 Chien Yeh Road, Yang Ming Shan, Shihlin, Taipei 111, Taiwan
TELEPHONE: +886 2 2862 2920
FAX: +886 2 2862 1458
EMAIL: ceo-nixon@tes.tp.edu.tw
WEBSITE: www.taipeieuropeanschool.com

THAILAND

Bangkok Patana School
Status Private
Programme Diploma
Diploma Coordinator Darren Taylor
Gender Coeducational
Languages English
Boarding/day Day
2/38 Soi Lasalle, Sukhumvit 105, Bangkok 10260, Thailand
TELEPHONE: +66 2 398 0200
FAX: +66 2 399 3179
EMAIL: mami@patana.ac.th
WEBSITE: www.patana.ac.th

BRITISH INTERNATIONAL SCHOOL, PHUKET
Status Private
Programme Diploma
Diploma Coordinator Nico van de Casteele
Gender Coeducational
Languages English
Boarding/day Mixed
59 Moo 2, Thepkrasattri Road, Tambon Koh Kaew, Amphur Muang, Phuket 83000, Thailand
TELEPHONE: +66 (0)76238711
FAX: +66 (0)76238750
EMAIL: info@bcis.ac.th
WEBSITE: www.bcis.ac.th
see full details on page 66

Concordian International School
Status Private
Programme PYP, MYP, Diploma
Diploma Coordinator James Leung
MYP Coordinator Greg Mellor
PYP Coordinator Julie Watts
Gender Coeducational
Languages English
Boarding/day Day
918 Moo 8, Bangna-Trad Highway Km 7, near the new airport, Bangkaew, Banglplee Samutprakarn 10540, Thailand
TELEPHONE: +662 706 9000
FAX: +662 706 9001
EMAIL: enquiries@concordian.ac.th
WEBSITE: www.concordian.ac.th

Garden International School
Status Private
Programme Diploma
Diploma Coordinator Sue Burke
Gender Coeducational
Languages English
Boarding/day Mixed
188/24 Pala-Ban Chang Road, Tambol Pala, Amphur Ban Chang, Rayong 21130, Thailand
TELEPHONE: +66 38 880 360
FAX: +66 38 630735
EMAIL: gisrayon@loxinfo.co.th

International School Bangkok
Status Private
Programme Diploma
Diploma Coordinator Jayne Lund
Gender Coeducational
Languages English
Boarding/day Day
39/7 Soi Nichada Thani, Ha Yaek Pakkret, Nonthaburi 11120, Thailand
TELEPHONE: +66 2 963-5800
FAX: +66 2 583-5432
EMAIL: billg@isb.ac.th
WEBSITE: www.isb.ac.th

International School Eastern Seaboard
Status State
Programme Diploma
Diploma Coordinator Catherine Evans
Gender Coeducational
Languages English
Boarding/day Day
PO Box 6, Banglamung, Chonburi 20150, Thailand
TELEPHONE: +66 (0) 38 372 591
FAX: +66 (0) 38 345 156
EMAIL: rschultz@ise.ac.th
WEBSITE: www.ise.ac.th

KIS International School
Status Private
Programme PYP, MYP, Diploma
Diploma Coordinator Neil MacDonald
MYP Coordinator Michael Hirsch
PYP Coordinator June Van Den Bos
Gender Coeducational
Languages English
Boarding/day Day
999/124 Kesineeville, Pracha Utit Road, Hway Kwang, Bangkok 10320, Thailand
TELEPHONE: +66 2 274 3444
FAX: +66 02 274 3452
EMAIL: sally@kis.ac.th
WEBSITE: www.kis.ac.th

NEW INTERNATIONAL SCHOOL OF THAILAND
Status Private
Programme PYP, MYP, Diploma
Diploma Coordinator Helen Stanton
MYP Coordinator Pia Bergqvist
PYP Coordinator Kate Grant
Gender Coeducational
Languages English
Boarding/day Day
36 Soi 15 Sukhumvit Road, Wattana, Bangkok 10110, Thailand
TELEPHONE: +66 2 651 2065
FAX: +66 2 253 3800
EMAIL: nist@nist.ac.th
WEBSITE: www.nist.ac.th
see full details on page 120

Prem Tinsulanonda International School
Status Private
Programme PYP, MYP, Diploma
Diploma Coordinator Dr Alison Dangerfield
MYP Coordinator Robert Service
PYP Coordinator Catherine Nicol
Gender Coeducational
Languages English
Boarding/day Both
PO Box 1, Mae Rim, Chiangmai 50180, Thailand
TELEPHONE: +66 53 301500
FAX: +66 53 301507
EMAIL: daviba@premcenter.org
WEBSITE: www.premcenter.org

Ruamrudee International School
Status Private
Programme Diploma
Diploma Coordinator Joe McMillan
Gender Coeducational
Languages English
Boarding/day Day
42 Moo 4, Ramkamhaeng 184, Minburi, Bangkok 10510, Thailand
TELEPHONE: +662 5180320 29
FAX: +662 5180334
EMAIL: wirach@rism.ac.th
WEBSITE: www.rism.ac.th

St Andrews International School
Status Private
Programme Diploma
Diploma Coordinator Rob King
PO Box 54, Banchang, Rayong 21130, Thailand
TELEPHONE: +66 38 8937168
FAX: +66 38 893720
EMAIL: aharrison@standrews-schools.com
WEBSITE: www.standrews-schools.com

St Andrew's International School Bangkok
Status Private
Programme Diploma
Diploma Coordinator Simon Lawrence
Gender Coeducational
Languages English
Boarding/day Day
9 Predee Panumyong, Sukhumvit Soi 71, Bangkok 10110, Thailand
TELEPHONE: +66 2 381 2387
FAX: +66 2 391 5227
EMAIL: pschofield@standrews.ac.th
WEBSITE: www.standrews.ac.th

The Regent's School (Pattaya & Bangkok)
Status Private
Programme Diploma
Diploma Coordinator Pam Carter
Gender Coeducational
Languages English
Boarding/day Mixed
Pattaya, PO Box 33 Naklua, Banglamung, Chonburi 20150, Thailand
TELEPHONE: +66 38 734 777
FAX: +66 38 734 778
EMAIL: headsec-pty@regents.ac.th

The Regent's School, Bangkok
Status Private
Programme Diploma
Diploma Coordinator Derek Barham
Gender Coeducational
Languages English
Boarding/day Mixed
592 Pracha-Uthit Road, Huai Kwang, Bangkok 10310, Thailand
TELEPHONE: +66 2 690 3777
FAX: +66 2 390 3778
EMAIL: head-bkk@regents.ac.th
WEBSITE: www.regents.ac.th

VIETNAM

British International School, Vietnam
Status Private
Programme Diploma
Diploma Coordinator Emma Tully
Gender Coeducational
Languages English
Boarding/day Day
246 Nguyen Van Huong, Thao Dien Ward, District 2, Ho Chi Minh City, Vietnam
TELEPHONE: +84 8 744 2335
FAX: +84 8 744 2334
EMAIL: shaunwilliams@bisvietnam.com
WEBSITE: www.bisvietnam.com

Hanoi International School
Status Private
Programme Diploma
Diploma Coordinator Shane Shedden
Gender Coeducational
Languages English
Boarding/day Day
48 Lieu Giai Street, Ba Dinh District, Hanoi, Vietnam
TELEPHONE: +84 4 832 8140
FAX: +84 4 8327 535
EMAIL: gmundy@hisvietnam.com
WEBSITE: www.hisvietnam.com

International School, Ho Chi Minh City
Status Private
Programme PYP, MYP, Diploma
Diploma Coordinator Simon Thom
MYP Coordinator Linda Kay-Peni
PYP Coordinator Wayne Derrick
Gender Coeducational
Languages English
Boarding/day Day
649A Vo Truong Toan St, An Phu, District 2, Ho Chi Minh City, Vietnam
TELEPHONE: +84 8 89 89 100
FAX: +84 8 88 74 022
EMAIL: admission@ishcmc.edu.vn
WEBSITE: www.ishcmc.com

United Nations International School of Hanoi
Status Private
Programme PYP, MYP, Diploma
Diploma Coordinator Jeremy Thompson
MYP Coordinator Jane Altemen
PYP Coordinator Peter Westwood
Gender Coeducational
Languages English
Boarding/day Day
GPO PO Box 313, Hanoi, Vietnam
TELEPHONE: +84 4758 1551
FAX: +84 4758 1542
EMAIL: info@unishanoi.org
WEBSITE: www.unishanoi.org

IB
Latin America

Latin America

Located in Buenos Aires, the Latin America office provides services to authorized, candidate and interested IB World Schools in the following countries:

Argentina	Ecuador	Panama
Bolivia	El Salvador	Paraguay
Brazil	Guatemala	Peru
Chile	Honduras	Uruguay
Colombia	Mexico	Venezuela
Costa Rica	Nicaragua	

Some recent initiatives

Ecuador project

With the support of Ecuador education authorities and the commitment of local IB World Schools, a project aimed at implementing the Diploma Programme in one state school in every province has been initiated. As from October 2008, five of these schools have been welcomed as IB World Schools: Colegio Experimental Capitan Edmundo Chiriboga, Unidad Educativa Experimental Manuela Cañizares, Colegio Nacional Luis Cordero, Colegio Fiscomisional San José, and Colegio Nacional Experimental Ambato. The remaining schools are at different stages of the authorization process.

IB Latin America regional conference

The IB Latin America regional conference was held in San Jose, Costa Rica, from June 5 to 8, 2008. Over the years this conference has become a place of gathering, reflection and learning for members of the IB community in the Latin American region, and this year was no exception. Presentations were given by representatives from IB World Schools and these focused on the conference theme 'Building a Better World' and highlighted the successful experiences taking place in the schools. 215 participants from 12 Latin American countries attended the conference.

A highlight of the conference was the opening address from the vice president of Costa Rica, Laura Chinchilla, who inspired the participants with a speech written by president Oscar Arias entitled 'Latin America is a Blank Canvas'. She referred to Costa Rica as a "land of teachers" where ideas are valued more highly than weapons.

First IB Latin America meeting of Associations and Networks of IB World Schools

In all countries, IB World Schools have developed strong links among them. In some cases these links evolved into a formal association, in others the network exists informally. In order to share their experiences and to discuss new documents produced by the IB, a meeting with representatives of associations and networks took place in Chile in the first week of October. This was a very fruitful gathering that stressed the importance of the associations and networks in promoting and supporting the IB programmes as well as strengthening their communication and professional contributions.

Some facts about this region

As at September 2008

IB Latin America serves 240 schools in 17 countries and offers 312 IB programmes in total.

DP programmes:	209
MYP programmes:	46
PYP programmes:	57
Schools offering all three programmes:	18
Schools offering DP and MYP:	13
Schools offering DP and PYP:	13
Schools offering MYP and PYP:	10
State school programmes:	15
Private school programmes:	297

ARGENTINA

Asociación Cultural Pestalozzi
Status Private
Programme Diploma
Diploma Coordinator Norma P Zanelli
Gender Coeducational
Languages Spanish, German
Boarding/day Day
R Freire 1882, C1428CYB Ciudad de Buenos Aires, Argentina
TELEPHONE: +54 11 4555 3688
FAX: +54 11 4554 1157
EMAIL: rectoria@pestalozzi.edu.ar
WEBSITE: www.pestalozzi.edu.ar

Asociación Escuelas Lincoln
Status Private
Programme Diploma
Diploma Coordinator K J Glittenberg
Gender Coeducational
Languages English
Boarding/day Day
Andres Ferreyra 4073, B1637 AOS La Lucila, Buenos Aires, Argentina
TELEPHONE: +54 11 4794 9400
FAX: +54 11 4790 2117
EMAIL: pacha_c@lincoln.edu.ar
WEBSITE: www.lincoln.edu.ar

Colegio De La Salle
Status Private
Programme Diploma
Diploma Coordinator Carlos Villegas
Gender Coeducational
Languages Spanish
Boarding/day Day
Riobamba 650, Buenos Aires 1025, Argentina
TELEPHONE: +54 011 4374 0657
FAX: +54 011 4373 2760
EMAIL: dirgral@delasalle.esc.edu.ar
WEBSITE: www.delasalle.esc.edu.ar

Colegio de Todos Los Santos
Status Private
Programme Diploma
Diploma Coordinator Pedro Pablo Koller
Gender Coeducational
Languages Spanish, English
Boarding/day Day
Thames 798, Villa Adelina, 1607 Buenos Aires,
TELEPHONE: +54 114 766 3878
FAX: +54 114 766 3878
EMAIL: mtmayochi@cdtls.com.ar
WEBSITE: www.detodoslosantos.edu.ar

Colegio Franco Argentino
Status Private
Programme Diploma
Diploma Coordinator Maria Virginia Petrella
Gender Coeducational
Languages Spanish
Boarding/day Day
Lavalle 1067, Acassuso, San Isidro, Buenos Aires B1641ALU, Argentina
TELEPHONE: +54 11 4793 4432
FAX: +54 11 4793 1556
EMAIL: pchama@cfam.edu.ar
WEBSITE: www.cfam.edu.ar

Colegio Lincoln
Status Private
Programme Diploma
Diploma Coordinator M S Cordoba de Piaggi
Gender Coeducational
Languages Spanish, English
Boarding/day Day
Olleros 2283, Buenos Aires 1426, Argentina
TELEPHONE: +54 11 4778 1997
FAX: +54 11 4772 1167
EMAIL: bach@lincoln.esc.edu.ar
WEBSITE: www.lincoln.esc.edu.ar

Colegio Mark Twain
Status Private
Programme Diploma
Diploma Coordinator R E Oviedo
Gender Coeducational
Languages Spanish
Boarding/day Boarding
José Roque Funes 1525, Córdoba 5009, Argentina
TELEPHONE: +543 514 815 874
FAX: +543 514 812 104
EMAIL: pfrench@british-school.com.ar
WEBSITE: www.marktwaincba.com.ar

Colegio Padre Luis Maria Etcheverry Boneo
Status Private
Programme Diploma
Diploma Coordinator María Alejandra Rayneli
Gender Female
Languages Spanish
Boarding/day Day
Juncal 2131, Buenos Aires 1125, Argentina
TELEPHONE: +54 11 4822 3687
FAX: +54 11 4806 8663

Colegio Palermo Chico A-871
Status Private
Programme Diploma
Diploma Coordinator Graciela Lopez
Gender Coeducational
Languages Spanish
Boarding/day Day
Thames 2041/37, Buenos Aires 1425, Argentina
TELEPHONE: +54 114 774 3975
FAX: +54 114 7740224
EMAIL: palchico@impsat1.com.ar

Colegio San Ignacio
Status Private
Programme Diploma
Diploma Coordinator Alicia Lodeserto
Gender Coeducational
Languages Spanish
Boarding/day Day
Guardias Nacionales, Rio Cuarto, Cordoba 1400-5800, Argentina
TELEPHONE: +54 (358) 464 8484
FAX: +54 (358) 464 8484
EMAIL: alodeserto@stignatiuscollege.com.ar
WEBSITE: www.stignatiuscollege.com.ar

Colegio San Marcos
Status Private
Programme Diploma
Diploma Coordinator G Alvarez de Martin
Gender Coeducational
Languages Spanish
Boarding/day Day
Secundaria, Mariano Alegre 334, Monte Grande, Buenos Aires 1842, Argentina
TELEPHONE: +54 114 296 4215
FAX: +54 114 290 1261
EMAIL: gabrielajalvarez@hotmail.com

Colegio San Martin de Tours (Mujeres)
Status Private
Programme Diploma
Diploma Coordinator Juan José Delaney
Gender Female
Languages Spanish
Boarding/day Day
Ortiz de Ocampo 2840, C1425DSQ, Buenos Aires, Argentina
TELEPHONE: +54 11 4807 1212
FAX: +54 11 4807 3077
EMAIL: info@smt.edu.ar
WEBSITE: http://smt.edu.ar

Colegio San Patricio
Status Private
Programme Diploma
Diploma Coordinator Diana Parrau de Pindar
Gender Coeducational
Languages Spanish
Boarding/day Day
Moreno y Camino a las Higueritas, Yerba Buena, Tucumán 4107, Argentina
TELEPHONE: +54 381 4250 708
FAX: +54 381 4250 708

Colegio San Pedro Apostol
Status Private
Programme Diploma
Diploma Coordinator M C Otaño de Caminoa
Gender Coeducational
Languages Spanish
Boarding/day Day
Av del Piamonte esq Nazca, Cordoba 5003, Argentina
TELEPHONE: +54 3 51 4846584
FAX: +54 3 51 4849684
EMAIL: sanpedro@sanpedroapostol.com
WEBSITE: www.sanpedroapostol.com

Colegio Santa María
Status Private
Programme Diploma
Diploma Coordinator Julio Nakhlé
Gender Coeducational
Languages Spanish
Boarding/day Day
Coronel Suárez 453, Salta 4400, Argentina
TELEPHONE: +54 387 4213127
EMAIL: abdo@arnet.com.ar

Colegio Tarbut
Status Private
Programme Diploma
Diploma Coordinator Cristina Hidalgo
Gender Coeducational
Languages Spanish
Boarding/day Day
Rosales 3019, Olivos, Buenos Aires 1636, Argentina
TELEPHONE: +54 11 4794 3444
FAX: +54 11 4790 0423
EMAIL: dvoskin@tarbut.esc.edu.ar
WEBSITE: www.tarbut.net

Escuela de Educación Media No 6
Status State
Programme Diploma
Diploma Coordinator T Papa Rua de Quiroga
Gender Coeducational
Languages Spanish
Agustín Alvarez 1431, Vicente López, Buenos Aires 1638, Argentina
TELEPHONE: +54 114 795 8889
FAX: +54 114 701 6608
EMAIL: anpega@sinetics.com.ar

Escuela Goethe Rosario – 8222
Status Private
Programme Diploma
Diploma Coordinator Alicia Cristina Unrein
Gender Coeducational
Languages Spanish
Boarding/day Day
Ayacucho 2205 4° A, España 430, Rosario, Santa Fe 2000, Argentina
TELEPHONE: +54 3 414 263024
FAX: +54 3 414263024
EMAIL: goethe@citynet.net.ar

Escuela Normal Superior en LV 'Sofia Broquen de Spangenberg'
Status State
Programme Diploma
Diploma Coordinator A de Lellis de Cattaneo
Gender Coeducational
Languages Spanish
Boarding/day Day
Juncal 3251, Buenos Aires 1425, Argentina
TELEPHONE: +54 114 807 2967/2966
FAX: +54 114 821 4035
EMAIL: postmaster@mbenke.edu.ar

HOLY TRINITY COLLEGE
Status Private
Programme Diploma
Diploma Coordinator V Tommasi de Ruival
Gender Coeducational
Languages English
Boarding/day Day
Gascón 544, Mar del Plata 7600, Argentina
TELEPHONE: +54 223 451 0168
FAX: +54 223 451 0168
EMAIL: trinity@trinity.esc.edu.ar
WEBSITE: www.trinity.esc.edu.ar
see full details on page 91

Instituto Ballester
Status Private
Programme Diploma
Diploma Coordinator Laura Amorós
Gender Coeducational
Languages Spanish
Boarding/day Day
San Martin 444, (1653) Villa Ballester, Buenos Aires 1653, Argentina
TELEPHONE: +54 1 11 4768 0760
FAX: +54 1 11 4738 3512
EMAIL: dir@iballester.edu.ar
WEBSITE: www.iballester.esc.edu.ar

Instituto San Jorge
Status Private
Programme Diploma
Diploma Coordinator L Perello de Miranda
Gender Coeducational
Languages Spanish
Boarding/day Day
Godoy Cruz, Pedro J Godoy 1191, Mendoza 5547, Argentina
TELEPHONE: +54 2 614 287 247
FAX: +54 2 614 240 830
EMAIL: rectoria@colegiosanjorge.com
WEBSITE: www.colegiosanjorge.com

Instituto San Patricio
Status Private
Programme Diploma
Diploma Coordinator Mónica Fernández
Gender Coeducational
Languages Spanish
Boarding/day Day
Provincia de Buenos Aires, Tucuman y Gaona sin/número, Luján, Buenos Aires 6700, Argentina
TELEPHONE: +54 02323 437998
FAX: +54 02323 437998
EMAIL: monicaf1@s6.coopenet.com.ar

Instituto Santa Brigida
Status Private
Programme Diploma
Diploma Coordinator María Graciela Alippe
Gender Coeducational
Languages Spanish
Boarding/day Day
Av Gaona 2068, C 1416DRV, Buenos Aires 1416DRV, Argentina
TELEPHONE: +54 1 145 811 268
FAX: +54 114 584 2531
EMAIL: rectoria@santabrigida.esc.edu.ar

Islands International School
Status Private
Programme Diploma
Diploma Coordinator Peter Stoyle
Gender Coeducational
Languages Spanish
Boarding/day Day
Amenábar 1840, Buenos Aires 1428, Argentina
TELEPHONE: +54 11 4787 2294
FAX: +54 11 4786 9904
EMAIL: direccion@intschools.org

New Model International School
Status Private
Programme Diploma
Diploma Coordinator Renato Pinto
Gender Coeducational
Languages Spanish
Boarding/day Day
El Salvador 3952/58, Buenos Aires 1175, Argentina
TELEPHONE: +54 11 4825 2900
FAX: +54 11 4 826 3937
EMAIL: carlostonelli@newmodel.com.ar

Northern International School
Status Private
Programme Diploma
Diploma Coordinator Peter Stoyle
Gender Coeducational
Languages Spanish
Boarding/day Day
Ruta 8km 61.5, Fátima, Pilar, Buenos Aires 1633, Argentina
TELEPHONE: +54 2322 49 1208
FAX: +54 2322 49 1208
EMAIL: info@intschools.org

Northlands
Status Private
Programme PYP, Diploma
Diploma Coordinator Marcela Scarone
PYP Coordinator Adriana Garcia Posadas
Gender Female
Languages English
Boarding/day Day
Roma 1248, Olivos, Buenos Aires 1636, Argentina
TELEPHONE: +54 11 4711 8400
FAX: +54 11 4711 8401
EMAIL: info@northlands.org.ar

Northlands ACB
Status Private
Programme PYP
PYP Coordinator Verónica Leonardi
Gender Coeducational
Languages Spanish, French, English
Boarding/day Day
Avda de los Colegios 680, Pcia Buenos Aires B1670NNN, Argentina
TELEPHONE: +54 11 4871 2668/9
FAX: +54 11 4871 2667
EMAIL: smagenta@northlands.org.ar
WEBSITE: www.northlands.org.ar

Quilmes High School
Status Private
Programme Diploma
Diploma Coordinator Daniel Pauni
Gender Coeducational
Languages Spanish
Boarding/day Day
Rivadavia 460, Quilmes, Buenos Aires 1878, Argentina
TELEPHONE: +54 11 4253 0123
FAX: +54 11 4253 2142
EMAIL: info@qhs.com.ar
WEBSITE: www.qhs.com.ar

Saint Mary of the Hills School
Status Private
Programme Diploma
Diploma Coordinator G C de Ojea Quintana
Gender Coeducational
Languages Spanish
Boarding/day Day
Xul Solar 6650, San Fernando, Buenos Aires 1646, Argentina
TELEPHONE: +54 11 4714 0330
FAX: +54 11 4714 0330
EMAIL: rrpp@stmary.esc.edu.ar
WEBSITE: www.stmary.esc.edu.ar

Saint Mary of the Hills Sede Pilar
Status Private
Programme Diploma
Diploma Coordinator Mariana Xanthopoulos
Gender Coeducational
Languages Spanish
Boarding/day Boarding
Ruta 25 y Caamaño, Pilar, Buenos Aires 1644
TELEPHONE: +54 2322 458181
EMAIL: gbx@stmary.edu.ar
WEBSITE: www.stmary.edu.ar

Southern International School
Status Private
Programme Diploma
Diploma Coordinator Peter Stoyle
Gender Coeducational
Languages Spanish
Boarding/day Day
Autopista BS As-La, Plata km 30.5, Hudson, Berazategui, Provincia de Buenos Aires 1884
TELEPHONE: +54 11 4215 3636
FAX: +54 11 4215 0707
EMAIL: southern@datamarkets.com.ar
WEBSITE: www.intschools.org/eng_ubicacion.htm

St Andrew's Scots School
Status Private
Programme Diploma
Diploma Coordinator Guillermo Rodriguez
Gender Coeducational
Languages English
Boarding/day Day
Roque Saenz Peña 601, Olivos, Buenos Aires 1636, Argentina
TELEPHONE: +54 114 790 8032/3
FAX: +54 114 799/8318
WEBSITE: www.sanandres.esc.edu.ar

St Catherine's Moorlands Belgrano
Status Private
Programme PYP, MYP, Diploma
Diploma Coordinator Agustina Boucau
MYP Coordinator Mabel Mary Manzitti
PYP Coordinator Rosanne Little De Urquiola
Gender Coeducational
Languages English, Spanish
Boarding/day Day
Carbajal 3250, Buenos Aires 1426, Argentina
TELEPHONE: +54 11 4552 4353
FAX: +54 11 4554 4113
EMAIL: colegio@stcatherine-m.com.ar
WEBSITE: www.scms.edu.ar

St Catherine's Moorlands Tortuguitas
Status Private
Programme PYP
PYP Coordinator Nuria Solé
Gender Coeducational
Boarding/day Day
Ruta Panamericana Km 38 Ramal Pilar, Buenos Aires, Argentina
TELEPHONE: +54 3488 639000
EMAIL: scmoorlands@equal.com.ar

ST GEORGE'S COLLEGE
Status Private
Programme PYP, Diploma
Diploma Coordinator Chris Gregory
PYP Coordinator Mabel Orlando
Gender Coeducational
Languages English, Spanish
Boarding/day Mixed
Guido 800, B1878WAA Quilmes, Buenos Aires
TELEPHONE: +54 11 4257 3472 ext 146
FAX: +54 11 4253 0030
EMAIL: info@stgeorge.com.ar
WEBSITE: www.stgeorge.com.ar
see full details on page 142

St George's College North
Status Private
Programme PYP, MYP, Diploma
Diploma Coordinator Miriam Bertone
MYP Coordinator Susana Arienti
PYP Coordinator Veronica Day
Gender Coeducational
Languages English, Spanish
Boarding/day Day
Casilla de Correo No 2, Los Polvorines, Buenos Aires 1613, Argentina
TELEPHONE: +54 114 663 2494
FAX: +54 114 663 2494
EMAIL: iant@stgeorgen.org.ar
WEBSITE: www.stgeorge.com.ar

St John's School, Beccar
Status Private
Programme Diploma
Diploma Coordinator Ricardo Wydler
Gender Coeducational
Languages Spanish
Boarding/day Day
España 348/370, Beccar, Buenos Aires 1643
TELEPHONE: +54 11 4513 4400
EMAIL: secretariabeccar@stjohnsschool.edu.ar
WEBSITE: www.stjohnsschool.edu.ar

St John's School, Pilar
Status Private
Programme Diploma
Diploma Coordinator Diego Bertotto
Gender Coeducational
Languages English
Boarding/day Day
Panamericana, ramal Pilar Km 48.8, Pilar, Buenos Aires B1629MYA, Argentina
TELEPHONE: +54 2322 667 667
EMAIL: admisionespilar@stjohnsschool.edu.ar
WEBSITE: www.stjohnsschool.edu.ar

St Mary's International College
Status Private
Programme MYP, Diploma
Diploma Coordinator Gloria María Morchio
MYP Coordinator Maria Laura Raffo
Gender Coeducational
Languages English, Spanish
Boarding/day Day
Martin Garcia 1435/1236, Ezeiza, Buenos Aires 1804, Argentina
TELEPHONE: +54 11 4295 2896
FAX: +54 11 4295 2896
EMAIL: colsantamariaba@ciudad.com.ar

St Xavier's College
Status Private
Programme MYP, Diploma
Diploma Coordinator Gabriel Solari
MYP Coordinator Gabriel Solari
Gender Coeducational
Languages English
Boarding/day Day
José Antonio Cabrera 5901, Buenos Aires 1414
TELEPHONE: +54 114 777 5011/14
FAX: +54 114777 5011/14
EMAIL: informes@colegiosanjavier.com.ar
WEBSITE: www.colegiosanjavier.com.ar

Sunrise School
Status Private
Programme Diploma
Diploma Coordinator Susan Cortés
Gender Coeducational
Languages Spanish
Boarding/day Day
Rio Negro, Casilla de Correo 79 (8324) Cipolletti, Río Negro, Argentina
TELEPHONE: +54 299 4786590
FAX: +54 299 4786590
EMAIL: alyons@sunrisepatagonia.org

Villa Devoto School
Status Private
Programme Diploma
Diploma Coordinator Virginia Petrella
Gender Coeducational
Languages English
Boarding/day Day
Pedro Morán 4441, Buenos Aires 1419
TELEPHONE: +54 114 501 9419
FAX: +54 114 503 5166
EMAIL: dirgral@vdevoto.esc.edu.ar

Washington School
Status Private
Programme PYP, MYP, Diploma
Diploma Coordinator Victoria Carrera Pereyra
MYP Coordinator Roxana Custo
PYP Coordinator Ma Celia Méndez Casariego
Gender Coeducational
Languages Spanish
Boarding/day Day
Buenos Aires, Argentina, Avenida Federico Lacroze 2012, Buenos Aires 1426, Argentina
TELEPHONE: +54 114 7728131
FAX: +54 114 7783433
EMAIL: rectoria@washington.esc.edu.ar
WEBSITE: www.washington.esc.edu.ar

BOLIVIA

American International School of Bolivia
Status Private
Programme Diploma
Diploma Coordinator Kathleen Asbún
Gender Coeducational
Languages English
Boarding/day Day
Casilla 5309, Cochabamba, Bolivia
TELEPHONE: +591 4 428 8577
FAX: +591 4-428-8576
EMAIL: kathieasbun@hotmail.com

Colegio Alemán Santa Cruz
Status Private
Programme Diploma
Diploma Coordinator Christiane Beuvink
Gender Coeducational
Languages Spanish
Boarding/day Day
Casilla 624, Av San Martin s/n, Santa Cruz, Bolivia
TELEPHONE: +591 3 3326820
FAX: +591 3 3351282
EMAIL: direccion@
colegioaleman-santacruz.edu.bo
WEBSITE:
www.colegioaleman-santacruz.edu.bo

BRAZIL

Associação Escola Graduada De São Paulo
Status Private
Programme Diploma
Diploma Coordinator Sherry McClelland
Gender Coeducational
Languages English
Boarding/day Day
Administration, Caixa Postal 1976, São Paulo 01059-970, Brazil
TELEPHONE: +55 11 3747 4800
FAX: +55 11 3742 9358
EMAIL: drandall@graded.br
WEBSITE: www.graded.br

Centro Internacional de Educaçào Integrada
Status Private
Programme PYP, Diploma
Diploma Coordinator Claudia Stadelmann
PYP Coordinator Claudia Stadelmann
Gender Coeducational
Languages English
Boarding/day Day
Estrada do Pontal 2093, Recreio dos Bandeirantes, 22.785-560 Rio de Janeiro 22785, Brazil
TELEPHONE: +55 21 2490 1673
FAX: +55 21 2490 1673
EMAIL: info@ciei.ch

Colégio Suíço-Brasileiro de Curitiba
Status Private
Programme Diploma
Diploma Coordinator Raquel Oisiovici Borge
Gender Coeducational
Languages English
Boarding/day Day
Rua Wanda dos Santos Mallmann, 537, Jardim Pinhais, Pinhais, Paraná 83323-400
TELEPHONE: +55 41 667 3321
FAX: +55 41 667 3321
EMAIL: wstooss@chpr.com.br
WEBSITE: www.chpr.com.br

Escola Americana de Belo Horizonte
Status Private
Programme PYP
PYP Coordinator Catarina Song Chen
Gender Coeducational
Languages Portuguese
Boarding/day Day
Av Deputado Cristovan Chiaradia 120, Bairro Buritis, Belo Horizonte, Minas Gerias 30575
TELEPHONE: +55 31 3378 6700
FAX: +55 31 3378 6868
EMAIL: tomtunny@eabh.com.br
WEBSITE: www.eabh.com.br

Escola Americana do Rio de Janeiro
Status Private
Programme Diploma
Diploma Coordinator Joe Santos
Gender Coeducational
Languages English
Boarding/day Day
Estrada da Gávea Nº132, Rio de Janeiro 22451-260, Brazil
TELEPHONE: +55 21 2512 9830
FAX: +55 21 2259 6720
EMAIL: peter.cooper@earj.com.br
WEBSITE: www.earj.com.br

Escola Maria Imaculada
Status Private
Programme Diploma
Diploma Coordinator Howard Murphy
Gender Coeducational
Languages English
Boarding/day Day
Rua Vigário João de Pontes, 537, Chácara Flora, São Paulo, SP CEP 04748-000, Brazil
TELEPHONE: +55 11 2101 7400
FAX: +55 11 5521 7763
EMAIL: ciallelo@chapelschool.com
WEBSITE: www.chapelschool.com

Escola Suíço-Brasileira de São Paulo
Status Private
Programme Diploma
Diploma Coordinator Heitor J S França
Gender Coeducational
Languages German, Portuguese
Boarding/day Day
R Visconde de Porto Seguro 391, Alto da Boa Vista, São Paulo 04642-000, Brazil
TELEPHONE: +55 11 5682 2140
EMAIL: director@esbsp.com.br
WEBSITE: www.esbsp.com.br

International School of Curitiba
Status Private
Programme Diploma
Diploma Coordinator W Livingston Pessoa
Gender Coeducational
Languages English
Boarding/day Day
Av Dr Eugenio Bertolli, 3900, Santa Felicidade, Curitiba, Paraná 82410-530
TELEPHONE: +55 41 3364 7400
FAX: +55 41 3364 9663
EMAIL: bill.pearson@iscbrazil.com
WEBSITE: www.iscbrazil.com

Pan American School of Porto Alegre
Status Private
Programme PYP
PYP Coordinator Cassie Koscianski Varella
Gender Coeducational
Languages English, Portuguese
Boarding/day Day
Avenida João Obino 110, Barrio Petropolis, Porto Alegre 90470, Brazil
TELEPHONE: +55 513 334 5866
FAX: +55 513 334 5866
EMAIL: murrayvosper@panamerican.com.br
WEBSITE: www.panamerican.com.br

ST FRANCIS COLLEGE
Status Private
Programme PYP, MYP, Diploma
Diploma Coordinator Luis Prado
MYP Coordinator Sean Quinn
PYP Coordinator Agustin Onsari
Gender Coeducational
Languages English, Portuguese
Boarding/day Day
Rua Bélgica 399, Jardim Europa, São Paulo 01448-030 SP, Brazil
TELEPHONE: +55 11 3082 7640
FAX: +55 11 3898 2891
EMAIL: office@stfrancis.com.br
WEBSITE: www.stfrancis.com.br
see full details on page 141

St Nicholas School
Status Private
Programme PYP, Diploma
Diploma Coordinator George McCombe
PYP Coordinator Elena Valavicius
Gender Coeducational
Languages English
Boarding/day Day
School, Av Eusébio Matoso 333, Pinheiros, São Paulo CEP 05423-180, Brazil
TELEPHONE: +55 11 3814 1355
FAX: +55 11 30316608
EMAIL: school@stnicholas.com.br
WEBSITE: www.stnicholas.com.br

St Paul's School
Status Private
Programme Diploma
Diploma Coordinator Joe Thomas
Gender Coeducational
Languages English
Boarding/day Day
Rua Juquiá 166, Jardim Paulistano, São Paulo
SP 01440-903, Brazil
TELEPHONE: +55 11 3085-3399
FAX: +55 11 3085-3708
EMAIL: spshead@stpauls.br
WEBSITE: www.stpauls.br

THE BRITISH SCHOOL, RIO DE JANEIRO
Status Private
Programme Diploma
Diploma Coordinator Ralph Jennings
Gender Coeducational
Languages English
Boarding/day Day
Rua Real Grandeza 87, Botafogo, Rio de
Janeiro-RJ 22281-030, Brazil
TELEPHONE: +55 21 2539 2717
FAX: +55 21 2244 5591
EMAIL: edu@britishschool.g12.br
admissions@britishschool.g12.br
WEBSITE: www.britishschool.g12.br
see full details on page 147

CHILE

Colegio Alemán de San Felipe de Aconcagua
Status Private
Programme Diploma
Diploma Coordinator Lorena Loyola Goich
Gender Coeducational
Languages Spanish
Boarding/day Day
Casilla de Correo 110, San Felipe, Chile
TELEPHONE: +56 34 59 11 71
FAX: +56 34 59 12 22
EMAIL: rector@dssanfelipe.cl
WEBSITE: www.dssanfelipe.cl

Colegio Craighouse
Status Private
Programme MYP, Diploma
Diploma Coordinator Jamie Concha
MYP Coordinator Andrés Molina
Gender Coeducational
Languages Spanish, English
Boarding/day Day
Casilla 20 007, Correo 20, Santiago, Chile
TELEPHONE: +56 2 7560218
FAX: +56 2 216 9139
EMAIL: headmaster@craighouse.cl
WEBSITE: www.craighouse.cl

Colegio de los Sagrados Corazones – Padres Franceses
Status Private
Programme PYP
PYP Coordinator Carlos Agustín Ogno Cortez
Gender Coeducational
Languages Spanish
Boarding/day Day
Independencia 2086, Valparaiso, Chile
TELEPHONE: +56 32 381 196
EMAIL: nrivera@colegiosscc.cl
WEBSITE: www.colegiosscc.cl

Colegio de los Sagrados Corazones Valparaíso
Status Private
Programme PYP
PYP Coordinator Carlos Agustín Ogno Cortez
Gender Coeducational
Languages Spanish
Boarding/day Day
Independencia 2086, Valparaíso, Chile
TELEPHONE: +56 32 387 413
EMAIL: nrivera@colegiosscc.cl
WEBSITE: www.colegiosscc.cl

Colegio Internacional SEK-Chile
Status Private
Programme Diploma
Diploma Coordinator Marcela Gangas
Gender Coeducational
Languages Spanish
Boarding/day Day
Los Militares 6640, Las Condes, Santiago, Chile
TELEPHONE: +56 2 212 7116
FAX: +56 2 211 4471
EMAIL: sekdir@sekmail.com
WEBSITE: www.sek.net

Colegio 'La Maisonette'
Status Private
Programme PYP, Diploma
Diploma Coordinator Patricia Larrain
PYP Coordinator Constanza Hutt Hesse
Gender Female
Languages Spanish
Boarding/day Day
History, Avda Luis Pasteur 6076, Vitacura, Santiago, Chile
TELEPHONE: +56 2 2185779
FAX: +56 2 218 5431
EMAIL: pmeryd@lamaisonnette.cl
WEBSITE: www.lamaisonnette.cl

Dunalastair
Status Private
Programme Diploma
Diploma Coordinator Alvaro Fuentealba
Gender Coeducational
Languages Spanish
Boarding/day Day
Av Las Condes 11931, Las Condes, Santiago de Chile, Chile
TELEPHONE: +562 495 6610
FAX: +562 495 6652
EMAIL: rector@dunalastair.cl
WEBSITE: www.dunalastair.cl

International School
Status Private
Programme Diploma
Diploma Coordinator Claudia Rose
Gender Coeducational
Languages English
Boarding/day Day
Casilla 27020, Correo 27, Santiago, Chile
TELEPHONE: +56 2 216 6842
EMAIL: dbergman@nido.cl
WEBSITE: www.nido.cl

Liceo A 43 'Liceo Siete'
Status State
Programme Diploma
Diploma Coordinator Gabriela Parra
Gender Female
Languages Spanish
Boarding/day Day
Monseñor Sótero Sanz 060, Santiago, Chile
TELEPHONE: +56 2 2357155
EMAIL: sartigas@cdsprovidencia.cl

Mackay School
Status Private
Programme Diploma
Diploma Coordinator Sócrates Aguilera
Gender Male
Languages English
Boarding/day Day
Casilla 558, Viña del Mar, Chile
TELEPHONE: +56 32 835|121
FAX: +56 32 831539
EMAIL: saguilera@mackay.cl

Redland School
Status Private
Programme MYP, Diploma
Diploma Coordinator Robert Franklin
MYP Coordinator Eugenia Sepulveda
Gender Coeducational
Languages Spanish
Boarding/day Day
Camino El Alba 11357, Las Condes, Santiago 6780082, Chile
TELEPHONE: +56 2 247 5410
FAX: +56 2 247 5407
EMAIL: headmaster@redland.cl

SANTIAGO COLLEGE
Status Private
Programme PYP, MYP, Diploma
Diploma Coordinator Luz Maria Garcelón
MYP Coordinator Andrea Strauszer
PYP Coordinator Jessica Allen
Gender Coeducational
Languages Spanish, English
Boarding/day Day
Lota 2465, Providencia, Santiago, Chile
TELEPHONE: +56 2 7513800
FAX: +56 2 7513802
EMAIL: master@scollege.cl
WEBSITE: www.scollege.cl
see full details on page 133

St Gabriel's School
Status Private
Programme Diploma
Diploma Coordinator Vera Rojic Stancic
Gender Coeducational
Languages Spanish
Boarding/day Day
Av Bilbao 3070, Casilla 16095, Santiago, Chile
TELEPHONE: +56 2 462 5400
FAX: +56 2 225 2136
EMAIL: sgabriel@sg.tie.cl.

St John's School
Status Private
Programme Diploma
Diploma Coordinator Marisol Heijboer
Gender Coeducational
Languages English
Boarding/day Day
Pedro de Valdivia 1711, Casilla 284,
Concepción, Chile
TELEPHONE: +56 41 331 044
FAX: +56) 41 340 809
EMAIL: rector@stjohns.cl

St Margaret's British School For Girls
Status Private
Programme MYP, Diploma
Diploma Coordinator Carolyn Pettersen
MYP Coordinator Nancy Cohen
Gender Female
Languages Spanish
Boarding/day Day
Casilla 392, Viña del Mar, Quinta Región,
Chile
TELEPHONE: +56 32 451703
FAX: +56 32 451720
EMAIL: csm.5@ctcinternet.cl

The British School – Punta Arenas
Status Private
Programme Diploma
Diploma Coordinator Rodrigo Siron
Gender Coeducational
Languages Spanish
Boarding/day Day
Waldo Seguel 454, Punta Arenas, Chile
TELEPHONE: +56 61 22 33 81
FAX: +56 61 22 33 81
EMAIL: rector@britishschool.cl
WEBSITE: www.britishschool.cl

The Mayflower School
Status Private
Programme Diploma
Diploma Coordinator Anamaria Figueroa
Gender Coeducational
Languages Spanish
Boarding/day Day
Avda Las Condes 12 167, Las Condes, Santiago
668 2347, Chile
TELEPHONE: +56 2 2151738
FAX: +56 2 217 1037
EMAIL: gtonini@mayflower.cl

Wenlock School
Status Private
Programme Diploma
Diploma Coordinator John Bell
Gender Coeducational
Languages Spanish
Boarding/day Day
Casilla 27169, Correo 27, Santiago, Chile
TELEPHONE: +56 2 212 8982
FAX: +56 2 212 9226
EMAIL: cwenlock@wenlock.cl

COLOMBIA

Aspaen Gimnasio Iragua
Status Private
Programme Diploma
Diploma Coordinator M H Jiménez de Flórez
Gender Female
Languages Spanish
Boarding/day Boarding
c/o Sra Ma Helena Jiménez, Coordinadora BI,
Diagonal 170 # 66-51, Bogotá, Colombia
TELEPHONE: +57 1 667 9500
FAX: +57 1 670 9570
EMAIL: academicas@iragua.edu.co

Buckingham School
Status Private
Programme Diploma
Diploma Coordinator Ximena Castro
Gender Coeducational
Languages English
Cra 52 No 214 - 55, Bogotá, Colombia
TELEPHONE: +57 1 6760812
FAX: +57 1 6760884
EMAIL: buckingham@interratnet.com
WEBSITE: www.colegiobuckingham.com

Centro Integral de Educación Individualizada CIEDI
Status Private
Programme PYP, MYP, Diploma
Diploma Coordinator Jermaine McDougald
MYP Coordinator Felipe Palacios
PYP Coordinator Rocio Aranzáles
Gender Coeducational
Languages Spanish
Boarding/day Day
Km 3 vía Suba-Cota, Bogotá, Colombia
TELEPHONE: +57 1 683 0604
FAX: +57 1 681 5391
EMAIL: info@mail.colegiociedi.edu.co
WEBSITE: www.colegiociedi.edu.co

Colegio Alemán
Status Private
Programme Diploma
Diploma Coordinator Brigitte Kuhlmann
Gender Coeducational
Languages Spanish
Apartado Áereo 50101, Autopista al Mar Cra
49 pst 89, Baranquilla, Colombia
TELEPHONE: +57 5359 8520
FAX: +57 5359 9924
EMAIL: hkohl@colegioaleman.edu.co

Colegio Anglo-Colombiano
Status Private
Programme PYP, MYP, Diploma
Diploma Coordinator Maria Clara Janer
MYP Coordinator Marion McAusland
PYP Coordinator Sarah Osborne
Gender Coeducational
Languages Spanish, English
Boarding/day Day
Apartado Aéreo 253393, Avenida 19 Nº, Santa
Fé de Bogotá 15248, Colombia
TELEPHONE: +57 1 259 57 00
FAX: +57 1 216 0571
EMAIL: rector@anglocolombiano.edu.co
WEBSITE: www.anglocol.edu.co

Colegio Británico de Cartagena
Status Private
Programme MYP
MYP Coordinator Adriana Torres
Gender Coeducational
Languages Spanish, English
Boarding/day Day
Bocagrande, Calle 7 No. 2-71, Cartegena,
Colombia
TELEPHONE: +57 5 673 5059
WEBSITE: www.colbritanico.com

Colegio Britanico Internacional
Status Private
Programme Diploma
Diploma Coordinator Leonard Mabe
Gender Coeducational
Languages English
Boarding/day Mixed
Apartado Aéreo 4368, Barranquilla, Colombia
TELEPHONE: +57 5 359 9243
FAX: +57 5 359 9320
EMAIL: lhmabe@hotmail.com

Colegio Colombo Britanico
Status Private
Programme Diploma
Diploma Coordinator Miguel Díaz
Gender Coeducational
Languages English, Spanish
Boarding/day Day
Avenida La Maria #69 Pance, Cali, Colombia
TELEPHONE: +57 2 555 5385
FAX: +57 2 555 1191
EMAIL: info@colombobritanico.edu.co
WEBSITE: www.colombobritanico.edu.co

Colegio Gran Bretaña
Status Private
Programme Diploma
Diploma Coordinator Sandra Diaz Rojas
Gender Coeducational
Languages Spanish
Boarding/day Day
Carrera 51 No 215-20, Bogota, Colombia
TELEPHONE: +57 1 676 0391
FAX: +57 1 676 0426
EMAIL: director@cgb.edu.co
WEBSITE: www.cgb.edu.co

Colegio Internacional de Bogota

Status Private
Programme Diploma
Diploma Coordinator Germán A Gallo
Gender Coeducational
Languages English
Boarding/day Day
Carrera 49 no 202-85, Apartado Aereo 103314,
Bogotá, Colombia
TELEPHONE: +57 1 676 2200
FAX: +57 1 676 1305
EMAIL: rectoria@cib.edu.co

Colegio Los Tréboles

Status Private
Programme Diploma
Diploma Coordinator C V Vargas
Gender Coeducational
Languages English
Boarding/day Day
Vereda Cerca de Piedra, Chía, Cundinamarca,
Colombia
TELEPHONE: +57 1 862 4830
FAX: +57 1 862 3536
EMAIL: cristinadevalenzuela@hotmail.com
WEBSITE: www.colegiolostreboles.edu.co

Deutsche Schule – Cali/Kolumbien

Status Private
Programme Diploma
Diploma Coordinator Leonor Anzola Ospina
Gender Coeducational
Languages Spanish
Avenida Gualí Nº 31, Barrio Ciudad Jardín,
Cali, Colombia
TELEPHONE: +57 2 6858900
EMAIL: direccion@dscali.edu.co
WEBSITE: www.dasan.de/cali

Fundacion Colegio de Inglaterra – The English School

Status Private
Programme PYP, Diploma
Diploma Coordinator M Fleming de Pérez
PYP Coordinator Ángela Botero
Gender Coeducational
Languages English, Spanish
Boarding/day Day
Calle 170 No 15-68, Bogotá, Colombia
TELEPHONE: +57 1 676 7700
FAX: +57 1 671 1318
EMAIL: headmaster@englishschool.edu.co
WEBSITE: www.englishschool.edu.co

Fundación Nuevo Marymount

Status Private
Programme Diploma
Diploma Coordinator Liliana Manzanera
Gender Female
Languages Spanish
Boarding/day Day
Calle 169B, No 74A-02, Bogotá DC, Colombia
TELEPHONE: +57 1 669 9077
EMAIL: rectoria@marymountschool.edu.co
WEBSITE: www.marymountschool.edu.co

Gimnasio Campestre San Rafael

Status Private
Programme Diploma
Diploma Coordinator C Parra de Calderón
Gender Coeducational
Languages Spanish
Boarding/day Day
Km 6 Via Siberia – Tenjo, Cundinamarca,
Colombia
TELEPHONE: +571 8646966
FAX: +571 4343990
EMAIL: colproyectos@minutodedios.org
WEBSITE: www.colegios.minutodedios.org

Gimnasio de Los Cerros

Status Private
Programme Diploma
Diploma Coordinator E Manrique Andrade
Gender Male
Languages Spanish
Boarding/day Day
Calle 119 Nº 0-68, Usaquén, Santafé de
Bogotá DC, Cundinamarca, Colombia
TELEPHONE: +57 1 215 0111
EMAIL: rector@loscerros.edu.co
WEBSITE: www.loscerros.edu.co

Gimnasio Del Norte

Status Private
Programme Diploma
Diploma Coordinator José Contreras
Gender Coeducational
Languages Spanish
Boarding/day Day
Calle 207 Nº 70-50, Bogotá, DC Sur América
57, Colombia
TELEPHONE: +57 1 6762577
FAX: +57 1 676 1999
EMAIL: bgomez@gimnorte.com
WEBSITE: www.gimnorte.com

Gimnasio Femenino

Status Private
Programme Diploma
Diploma Coordinator L P Gómez Murillo
Gender Female
Languages Spanish
Boarding/day Day
Cr # 128-40, Bella Suiza, Bogotá, Colombia
TELEPHONE: +571 657 8420
FAX: +571 657 8445
EMAIL: trudy.md@gimnasiofemenino.edu.co
WEBSITE: www.gimnasiofemenino.edu.co

Gimnasio Los Alcazares

Status Private
Programme Diploma
Diploma Coordinator J H Rodriguez Arias
Gender Male
Languages Spanish
Boarding/day Day
Antioquia, Apartado Aéreo 50996 Medellín,
Antioquia, Colombia
TELEPHONE: +57 4 288 4000
FAX: +57 4 288 0184
EMAIL: alcazares@alcazares.edu.co

The Victoria School

Status Private
Programme PYP, Diploma
Diploma Coordinator Jonah Blake Sims
PYP Coordinator María Isabel Aguer
Gender Coeducational
Languages English, Spanish
Boarding/day Day
Calle 215 Nº 50-60, Bogotá, Colombia
TELEPHONE: +57 1 676 3435
FAX: +57 1 676 2029
EMAIL: director@tvs.edu.co
WEBSITE: www.tvs.edu.co

COSTA RICA

European School

Status Private
Programme Diploma
Diploma Coordinator Karen A Bye
Gender Coeducational
Languages English
Boarding/day Day
PO Box 177, Heredia 3000, Costa Rica
TELEPHONE: +50 6 261 0717
FAX: +50 6 263 5793
EMAIL: annearonson@europeanschool.com
WEBSITE: www.europeanschool.com

Liceo de Costa Rica

Status State
Programme Diploma
Diploma Coordinator A V Chacón Abarca
Gender Male
Languages Spanish
Boarding/day Day
Calle 9, Avenida 18 y 20, San José, Costa Rica
TELEPHONE: +506 221 3792
FAX: +506 221 3792
EMAIL: jaarva@costarricense.cr

Liceo Experimental Bilingue de Palmare

Status State
Programme Diploma
Diploma Coordinator D Gutiérrez Morales
Gender Coeducational
Languages Spanish
Boarding/day Day
50 Metros sur Banco Popular, Palmares,
Alajuela 215-4300, Costa Rica
TELEPHONE: +506 452 0157
FAX: +506 452 0157
EMAIL: jcalvoq@gmail.com

Lincoln School

Status Private
Programme Diploma
Diploma Coordinator Daniel Walker
Gender Coeducational
Languages English
Boarding/day Day
PO Box 1919, San Jose, Costa Rica
TELEPHONE: +1 506 247 6623
FAX: +1 506 247 6700
EMAIL: director@lincoln.ed.cr
WEBSITE: www.lincoln.ed.cr

The Blue Valley School
Status Private
Programme Diploma
Diploma Coordinator Erika Quiñones
Gender Coeducational
Languages English
Boarding/day Day
Escazú, Costa Rica
TELEPHONE: +50 6 215 2204
FAX: +50 6 215 2205
EMAIL: bvschool@racsa.co.cr
WEBSITE: www.bluevalley.ed.cr

The British School of Costa Rica
Status Private
Programme Diploma
Diploma Coordinator Clive Walker
Gender Coeducational
Languages English
Boarding/day Day
PO Box 8184, San José 1000, Costa Rica
TELEPHONE: +50 6 200 131
FAX: +50 6 2 327 833
EMAIL: trevordavies_cr@yahoo.ie
WEBSITE: www.infoweb.co.cr/britsch

United World College Costa Rica/Colegio del Mundo Unido CR
Status Private
Programme Diploma
Diploma Coordinator Pilar Orellana
Gender Coeducational
Languages Spanish
Boarding/day Day
Santa Ana, 100M Este y100 Norte, Supermercado Pali, Santa Ana, San José 678-6150, Costa Rica
TELEPHONE: +50 6 282 1538
FAX: +50 6 282 1540
EMAIL: mauricio.viales@soskdi.or.cr
WEBSITE: www.uwccr.com

ECUADOR

Academia Cotopaxi American International School
Status Private
Programme PYP, Diploma
Diploma Coordinator Joseph Clay
PYP Coordinator Prescilla Riofrio
Gender Coeducational
Languages English
Boarding/day Day
PO Box 17-11-6510, Quito, Ecuador
TELEPHONE: +593 2 246 7411
FAX: +593 2 2445 195
EMAIL: bjohnston@cotopaxi.k12.ec
WEBSITE: www.cotopaxi.k12.ec

Centro Educativo Bilingue Internacional
Status Private
Programme Diploma
Diploma Coordinator Francisco López
Languages Spanish
Boarding/day Day
Calle Alfredo Sevilla y Av Pedro Vásconez, Parroquia Izamba, Ambato, Ecuador
TELEPHONE: +593 3285 4400
FAX: +593 3285 4165
EMAIL: vero.ll@hotmail.com
WEBSITE: www.cebi.edu.ec

Colegio Alemán Humboldt de Guayaquil
Status Private
Programme Diploma
Diploma Coordinator Mrs Leticia del Hierro
Gender Coeducational
Languages Spanish
Boarding/day Day
Dirección general, Dr Héctor Romero #216, Los Ceibos, Guayaquil, Guayas 09-01-4760
TELEPHONE: +593 428 50260
FAX: +593 428 54139
EMAIL: secret_general@aleman.k12.ec
WEBSITE: www.aleman.k12.ec

Colegio Americano De Guayaquil
Status Private
Programme Diploma
Diploma Coordinator Maria Laura Armijo
Gender Coeducational
Languages Spanish
Boarding/day Day
Direccion General, Casilla 3304, Guayaquil
TELEPHONE: +593 4 2255 503
FAX: +593 4 2250 453
EMAIL: keithjdmiller@hotmail.com

Colegio Americano de Quito
Status Private
Programme MYP, Diploma
Diploma Coordinator Betty Weiser
MYP Coordinator Leah Yepez
Gender Coeducational
Languages English
Boarding/day Day
Casilla 17-01-157, Pichincha Province, Quito, Ecuador
TELEPHONE: +593 2 2472 974
FAX: +593 2 2472 972
EMAIL: sbarba@fcaq.k12.ec
WEBSITE: www.fcaq.k12.ec

Colegio Balandra Cruz del Sur
Status Private
Programme Diploma
Diploma Coordinator M Guillén Jiménez
Gender Coeducational
Languages Spanish
Boarding/day Day
PO Box 10 206, Guayaquil, Ecuador
TELEPHONE: +593 4 285 0020
EMAIL: mafioravanti@hotmail.com
WEBSITE: www.balandra-cruzdelsur.com

Colegio Experimental Alberto Einstein
Status Private
Programme Diploma
Diploma Coordinator Zuleika Cruz
Gender Coeducational
Languages Spanish
Boarding/day Day
Casilla 17-11-5018, Quito, Pichincha 5018, Ecuador
TELEPHONE: +593 2 88 4515
FAX: +593 2 470-144
EMAIL: banano59@einstein.k12.ec
WEBSITE: www.einstein.k12.ec

Colegio Experimental Luis Cordero
Status State
Programme Diploma
Diploma Coordinator Liliana Arias Gutiérrez
Gender Coeducational
Languages Spanish
Boarding/day Day
Ingapirca y Rafael Maria Garcia, Azoguez Cañar, Ecuador
TELEPHONE: +593 7224 0067
FAX: +593 7224 0067
EMAIL: colegioluiscordero@ipcluiscordero.org

Colegio Fiscomisional 'San José'
Status State
Programme Diploma
Diploma Coordinator Edwin Gonzalo Canseco Guerrero
Gender Coeducational
Languages Spanish
Boarding/day Day
Calle Juan Montalvo y Misión Josefina, Tena Napo, Ecuador
TELEPHONE: +593 06 288 6241
FAX: +593 06 288 6241
EMAIL: chavezruben2007@hotmail.com

Colegio Internacional Rudolf Steiner
Status Private
Programme Diploma
Diploma Coordinator Fernando Rojas
Languages Spanish
Boarding/day Day
Calle Francisco Montalvo Nro 212, y Av Mariscal Sucre, (Av Occidental), Sector Cochabampa, Quito, Ecuador
TELEPHONE: +593 2244 3315
FAX: +593 2244 7402
EMAIL: katbelo@punto.net.ec

Colegio Internacional SEK-Ecuador
Status Private
Programme Diploma
Diploma Coordinator Cinthia Chiluiza
Gender Coeducational
Languages Spanish
Boarding/day Boarding
PO Box 09-04-0878-Policentro, Guayaquil Guayas 11373, Ecuador
TELEPHONE: +593 4 2 738066
FAX: +593 4 2 738 068
EMAIL: rc@sekmail.com

Colegio Internacional SEK-Ecuador, Quito

Status Private
Programme Diploma
Diploma Coordinator Patricio Novoa
Gender Coeducational
Languages Spanish
Boarding/day Day
Carmen Olmo Mancebo y Carlos, Arcos Franco s/n, Quito, Pichincha 17-17-422
TELEPHONE: +593 2 408 909
FAX: +593 2 408 824
EMAIL: graham.hurrell@sekmail.com
WEBSITE: www.sekmail.com

Colegio Intisana

Status Private
Programme Diploma
Diploma Coordinator D J Astudillo Cervantes
Gender Male
Languages Spanish
Boarding/day Mixed
Pichincha, Avenida Occidental 5329, Quito
TELEPHONE: +593 2 2440 128
FAX: +593 2 2431 610
EMAIL: jeperezg@hotmail.com
WEBSITE: www.intisana.com

Colegio Los Pinos

Status Private
Programme Diploma
Diploma Coordinator Mariela Bernal de Lugo
Gender Female
Languages Spanish
Boarding/day Day
Calle Agustín Zambrano s/n , Ciudadela Mexterior, Quito, PO Box 8720, Ecuador
TELEPHONE: +593 2 2434 046
FAX: +593 2 2434 021
EMAIL: rectorado@colegiolospinos.k12.ec

Colegio Municipal Experimental 'Sebastián de Benalcázar'

Status State
Programme Diploma
Diploma Coordinator Patricio Montúfar
Gender Coeducational
Languages Spanish
Boarding/day Day
Rectorado, Av 6 Diciembre e Irlanda, Apartado Postal 17-01-25, Quito, Pichincha
TELEPHONE: +593 2 243 5313
FAX: +593 2 243 5312
EMAIL: benalcazar2@bellsouthmail.com

Colegio Nacional Experimental Ambato

Status State
Programme Diploma
Diploma Coordinator L E Muñoz Hugo
Gender Coeducational
Languages Spanish
Boarding/day Day
Ave Humberto Albornoz, S/N y Vargas Torres, 18001 Ambato, Tungurahu, Ecuador
TELEPHONE: +59 03 282 1776
FAX: +59 03 242 0474
EMAIL: raulrodro@yahoo.com

Colegio Nacional Experimental 'Capitán Edmundo Chiriboga'

Status Private
Programme Diploma
Diploma Coordinator C G García Ramírez
Gender Coeducational
Languages Spanish
Boarding/day Day
Av 9 de Octubre y Garcia Moreno, Chimborazo, Riobamba, Ecuador
TELEPHONE: +593 03 295 3406
FAX: +593 03 296 1688
EMAIL: colegiochiriboga@andinanat.net
WEBSITE: www.colegiochiriboga.edu.ec

Colegio Politécnico

Status Private
Programme Diploma
Diploma Coordinator Luis García Alvarado
Languages Spanish
Apartado 09-01-5863, Guayaquil, Guayas, Ecuador
TELEPHONE: +593 4 269 651
FAX: +593 4 269 650
EMAIL: maluces@hotmail.com

ISM International Academy

Status Private
Programme Diploma
Diploma Coordinator Aurora Gargurevich
Gender Coeducational
Languages English, Spanish
Boarding/day Day
Calle Unión 886 y Ave Geovanny Calle, Sector Calderon, Quito, Ecuador
TELEPHONE: +593 2 282 0549
FAX: +593 2 203 6001
EMAIL: ism@interactive.net.ec
WEBSITE: www.ism.edu.ec

Ludoteca Elementary & High School, Padre Victor Grados

Status Private
Programme MYP
MYP Coordinator Mario Carillo Cruz
Gender Coeducational
Languages English, Spanish
Boarding/day Day
Av Simón Bolívar y Camino de los Incas # 5-6, Nueva Vía Oriental, Quito, Ecuador
TELEPHONE: +593 2 268 8142
FAX: +593 2 273 4621
EMAIL: nancy_al@uio.satnet.net
WEBSITE: http://ludoteca.edu.ec

The British School Quito

Status Private
Programme Diploma
Diploma Coordinator Karen Simpson
Gender Coeducational
Languages English
Boarding/day Day
Casilla 17-21-52, Quito, Ecuador
TELEPHONE: +593 2 2 374 649
FAX: +593 2 2 374 650
EMAIL: director@bsq.edu.ec

Unidad Educativa Experimental 'Manuala Cañizares'

Status State
Programme Diploma
Diploma Coordinator R E de la Cadena Mejía
Gender Coeducational
Languages Spanish
Boarding/day Day
Av 6 de diciembre N24-176, Quito, Ecuador
TELEPHONE: +593 02 223 0271
FAX: +593 02 252 0642
EMAIL: recadenam@yahoo.com

Unidad Educativa Letort

Status Private
Programme Diploma
Diploma Coordinator Nancy Carrillo Sánchez
Gender Coeducational
Languages Spanish
Boarding/day Day
Los Guayabos Nro E 13-05 y Farsalias, San Isidro del Inca, Quito, Ecuador
TELEPHONE: +593 2 326 0202
FAX: +593 2 326 0222
EMAIL: fermuvi@gmail.com
WEBSITE: www.colegioletort.edu.ec

EL SALVADOR

Academia Britanica Cuscatleca

Status Private
Programme Diploma
Diploma Coordinator Marc Starr
Gender Coeducational
Languages English
Boarding/day Day
Apartado Postal 121, Santa Tecla, El Salvador
TELEPHONE: +503 2241 4400
FAX: +503 2228 2956
EMAIL: headmaster@abc.edu.sv
WEBSITE: www.abc.edu.sv

Colegio La Floresta

Status Private
Programme Diploma
Diploma Coordinator Laura de Calderón
Gender Female
Languages Spanish
Boarding/day Day
Kilómetro 13 1/2 Carretera al, Puerto de La Libertad, Call La Floresta, La Libertad, El Salvador
TELEPHONE: +503 2229 5336/2246 3600
FAX: +503 2229 5345
EMAIL: emilia.guerrero@lafloresta.edu.sv
WEBSITE: www.lafloresta.edu.sv

EL SALVADOR

Deutsche Schule – Escuela Alemana San Salvador
Status Private
Programme Diploma
Diploma Coordinator J de Schönenberg
Gender Coeducational
Languages Spanish
Boarding/day Day
Apartado Postal 01-183, San Salvador CA, El Salvador
TELEPHONE: +503 243 2279
FAX: +503 243 2129
EMAIL: ulrich.lehmann@ds.edu.sv
WEBSITE: www.ds.edu.sv

GUATEMALA

Centro Escolar Campoalegre
Status Private
Programme Diploma
Diploma Coordinator Sheryl Marie Gomez
Gender Female
Languages Spanish
35 Calle and 12 Av Final, Zona 11, Código 01011, Guatemala
TELEPHONE: +502 2485 9494
FAX: +502 442 2468
EMAIL: mcmarroquin@campoalegre.edu.gt
WEBSITE: www.campoalegre.edu.gt

Centro Escolar 'El Roble'
Status Private
Programme MYP, Diploma
Diploma Coordinator L E Gonzalez Diaz
MYP Coordinator Iván Cisneros
Gender Male
Languages Spanish, English
Boarding/day Day
11 Avenida Sur Final Las Charcas, Zona 11, Guatemala City 01011, Guatemala
TELEPHONE: +502 2476 2973
FAX: +502 2442 2288
EMAIL: jrasturias@ceroble.edu.gt
WEBSITE: www.ceroble.edu.gt

Centro Escolar Entrevalles
Status Private
Programme Diploma
Diploma Coordinator D Ruano de Torres
Gender Coeducational
Languages Spanish
Boarding/day Day
Km 16.8 carretera a El Salvador, Guatemala
TELEPHONE: +502 6685 3232
EMAIL: mbonilla@entrevalles.edu.gt
WEBSITE: www.entrevalles.com

Centro Escolar Solalto
Status Private
Programme Diploma
Diploma Coordinator J E Aguirre Rodríguez
Gender Coeducational
Languages English, Spanish
Boarding/day Day
Km 22.5, Carretera a Fraijanes, Guatemala
TELEPHONE: +502 6634 9260
EMAIL: mvasquez@apde.edu.gt
WEBSITE: www.solalto.edu.gt

HONDURAS

The American School of Tegucigalpa
Status Private
Programme Diploma
Diploma Coordinator Maria Motz
Gender Coeducational
Languages English
c/o I M C TGU Dept, #227, PO Box 025320, Miami FL 33102 -5320, USA
TELEPHONE: +1 504 239 3333
EMAIL: ljenkins@amschool.org

MEXICO

BACHILLERATO ALEXANDER BAIN SC
Status Private
Programme MYP, Diploma
Diploma Coordinator J F Uribe Gaudry
MYP Coordinator Gloria E Prian Arroyo
Gender Coeducational
Languages Spanish, English
Boarding/day Day
Las Flores 497, Tlacopac, Mexico
TELEPHONE: +52 55 5683 2911
FAX: +52 55 5683 3529
EMAIL: jose.uribe@alexander-bain.edu.mx
WEBSITE: www.alexander-bain.edu.mx
see full details on page 53

Centro de Ensenanza Media de la Universidad Autonoma
Status State
Programme Diploma
Diploma Coordinator Leticia Ramirez de León
Gender Coeducational
Languages Spanish
Boarding/day Day
Av de la Convencion Esq, Av Independencia, Aguascalientes CP 20020, Mexico
TELEPHONE: +52 49 14 71 74
FAX: +52 49 14 77 08
EMAIL: eleon@correo.uaa.mx

Centro de Ensenanza Tecnica y Superior
Status Private
Programme Diploma
Diploma Coordinator Alberto Alvarez Noriega
Gender Coeducational
Languages Spanish
Boarding/day Day
Apartado Postal 4012, Zona Centro, Tijuana Baja California 22550, Mexico
TELEPHONE: +52 9031800
FAX: +52 664- 625 39 51
EMAIL: alberto@tij.cetys.mx
WEBSITE: www.tij.cetys.mx

Centro de Investigación y Desarrollo de Educación Bilingüe
Status State
Programme Diploma
Diploma Coordinator Celina Garza
Gender Coeducational
Languages Spanish, English
Boarding/day Day
Lázaro Cárdenas Al Ote, Sin Número, Unidad Mederos, Monterrey 64930, Mexico
TELEPHONE: +52 818 3294180
EMAIL: socorro_gg@hotmail.com
WEBSITE: www.uanl.mx/org/cideb/index.html

Centro Educativo CRECER AC
Status Private
Programme PYP
PYP Coordinator Martha Clara López Jáuregui
Calle del Vecino No 3, Atlihuetzia, Yahuquehmecan, Tlaxcala 90459, Mexico
TELEPHONE: +52 124 646 13 148
FAX: +52 124 646 12 148
EMAIL: martha@crecer.edu.mx
WEBSITE: www.crecer.edu.mx

CENTRO ESCOLAR INSTITUTO LA PAZ, SC
Status Private
Programme PYP, MYP
MYP Coordinator José Luis García Ramírez
PYP Coordinator Liliana Muñoz López
Gender Coeducational
Languages English, Spanish
Boarding/day Day
Av Plan de San Luis 445, Col Nueva Santa María, México City 02800, Mexico
TELEPHONE: +52 55 55 56 66 46
FAX: +52 55 55 56 66 46
EMAIL: institutolapaz@infosel.net.mx
WEBSITE: www.institutolapaz.edu.mx
see full details on page 72

Colegio Álamos
Status Private
Programme Diploma
Diploma Coordinator Albert Wynder Walsh
Gender Male
Languages Spanish
Boarding/day Day
Acceso al Aeropuerto Nro 1000, Colonia Arboledas, Santiago de Querétaro 76940
TELEPHONE: +52 442 182 0222
EMAIL: pjbellog@colegioalamos.edu.mx
WEBSITE: www.colegioalamos.edu.mx

Colegio Alemán de Guadalajara
Status Private
Programme Diploma
Diploma Coordinator Frank Walter
Gender Coeducational
Languages Spanish, German
Boarding/day Day
Av Bosques de los Cedros Nº32, Las Cañadas, Zapopan Jalisco 45132, Mexico
TELEPHONE: +52 33 3685 00 60
EMAIL: quennet@prodigy.net.mx
WEBSITE:
www.colegioalemanguadalajara.edu.mx

COLEGIO ALEXANDER BAIN S.C.o
Status Private
Programme PYP, MYP
MYP Coordinator Gloria Estela Prian Arroyo
PYP Coordinator Teresa Yánez Clavel
Gender Coeducational
Languages Spanish
Barranca de Pilares 29, Tlacopac 01760, Mexico
TELEPHONE: +52 55 5595 0499
EMAIL: ana.palacios@alexander-bain.edu.mx
WEBSITE: www.alexander-bain.edu.mx
see full details on page 53

Colegio Arji
Status Private
Programme Diploma
Diploma Coordinator Pablo Martinez Alvarez
Gender Coeducational
Languages Spanish
Boarding/day Day
Tabasco, Avenida México No 2, Colonia del Bosque, Villahermosa Tabasco 86160, Mexico
TELEPHONE: +52 993 3 510 250
FAX: +52 993 3 510 324
EMAIL: marianel@arji.edu.mx
WEBSITE: www.arji.edu.mx

Colegio Atid AC
Status Private
Programme PYP, Diploma
Diploma Coordinator Emanuel Jinich
PYP Coordinator Manuel Rojano Herrera
Gender Coeducational
Languages Spanish, English
Boarding/day Day
Carlos Echánove 224, Colonia Lomas de Vista Hermosa, Del Cuajimalpa, Mexico DF 05100, Mexico
TELEPHONE: +52 55 5814 0800
FAX: +52 55 5292 5805
EMAIL: spodgaetz@atid.edu.mx
WEBSITE: www.atid.edu.mx

Colegio Bilingüe Carson de Ciudad Delicias
Status Private
Programme PYP
PYP Coordinator Guadalupe Sánchez
Gender Coeducational
Ave 8va sur 801, Delicias, Chihuahua 33000, Mexico
TELEPHONE: +52 (639) 472 9340
EMAIL: cterraza@webtelmex.net.mx

Colegio Bilingüe Madison
Status Private
Programme PYP
PYP Coordinator Claudia Terrazas Gracia
Gender Coeducational
Boarding/day Day
Fuente De Trevi No 7001, Frac Puerta de Hierro, Chihuahua Chih Mexico 31250
TELEPHONE: +52 614 430 1464
FAX: +52 614 430 1464
EMAIL: cterraza@webtelmex.net.mx

Colegio Bilingüe Madison de Monterrey
Status Private
Programme PYP, MYP
MYP Coordinator Sergio Joaquin Reyes Ruiz
PYP Coordinator Nelly Mendiola
Gender Coeducational
Languages English, Spanish
Boarding/day Day
Prolongación Marsella 3055, Col Alta Vista, Monterrey Nuevo León 64840, Mexico
TELEPHONE: +52 81 835 90627
FAX: +52 81 835 95166
EMAIL: edmay@prodigy.net.mx
WEBSITE: www.colegiosmadison.edu.mx

Colegio Celta Internacional
Status Private
Programme PYP
PYP Coordinator Alejandro Galindo de MyC
Gender Coeducational
Languages English, Spanish
Boarding/day Day
Libramiento Sur-Poniente Km 4+200, Colonia Los Olvera, Villa Corregidora, Querétaro 76902, Mexico
TELEPHONE: +52 442 227 3628
EMAIL: elisa.penela@celtic.edu.mx
WEBSITE: www.celtic.edu.mx

Colegio Ciudad de México
Status Private
Programme PYP, MYP, Diploma
Diploma Coordinator Elynn Vázquez
MYP Coordinator Georgina Diaz
PYP Coordinator Yolanda Prian
Gender Coeducational
Languages Spanish
Boarding/day Day
Campos Elíseos # 139, Col Polanco, Mexico DF 11560, Mexico
TELEPHONE: +52 55 5203 7894
FAX: +52 55 525 440 53
EMAIL: amparolapiedra@espcm.edu.mx
WEBSITE: www.espcm.edu.mx

Colegio Ciudad de Mexico – Plantel Contadero
Status Private
Programme PYP
PYP Coordinator Maricela Flores Barrera
Gender Coeducational
Calle de la Bolsa 456, El Contadero, Cuajimalpa CP 05500, Mexico
TELEPHONE: +52 58 12 06 10
FAX: +52 (58) 12 27 39 (70)
EMAIL: dianabackal@espcm.edu.mx

Colegio del Valle de Culiacán, AC
Status Private
Programme PYP, MYP
MYP Coordinator José Alberto Tostado Flores
PYP Coordinator Loreto Barraza Lobo
Gender Coeducational
Languages English, Spanish
Boarding/day Day
Avenida Monte Azul 612 pte, Balcones de San Miguel, Culiacán Sinaloa 80224, Mexico
TELEPHONE: +52 667 713 9089
FAX: +52 667 712 7794
EMAIL: dir_general@cvalle.edu.mx
WEBSITE: www.cvalle.edu.mx

Colegio Hebreo Maguen David
Status Private
Programme PYP, MYP, Diploma
Diploma Coordinator Maria del Carmen Fernandez Mejia
MYP Coordinator Lina López Valls
PYP Coordinator Rivka Tzuk
Gender Coeducational
Languages Spanish, English
Boarding/day Day
Antiguo Camino a Tecamachalco, #370 Col Vista Hermosa, Cuajimalpa, Mexico, DF, CP 05100, Mexico
TELEPHONE: +52 55 52 55531614
FAX: +52 55531617
EMAIL: mcfernandez@chmd.edu.mx
WEBSITE: www.chmd.edu.mx

Colegio Hebreo Tarbut
Status Private
Programme PYP
PYP Coordinator Ada Blanck
Gender Coeducational
Languages English, Spanish
Boarding/day Day
Loma del Parque 216, Colonia Vista Hermosa, Delegación Cuajimalpa C.P., México D. F. 05100, Mexico
TELEPHONE: +52 55 55814 0500
FAX: +52 55 55814 0521
EMAIL: direccion@tarbut.edu.mx
WEBSITE: www.tarbut.edu.mx

Colegio Internacional Tlalpan
Status Private
Programme Diploma
Diploma Coordinator Moisés J Castillo Rojas
Gender Coeducational
Languages Spanish
Boarding/day Mixed
Carretera Libre a Cuernavaca, 6867 Km 24, San Andrés Totoltepec Tlalpan 14400, Mexico
TELEPHONE: +52 58 491884
FAX: +52 (58) 492354
EMAIL: pgaldames@peterson.edu.mx
WEBSITE: www.peterson.edu.mx

Colegio Laureles IAP
Status Private
Programme Diploma
Diploma Coordinator J D Gómez Rodríguez
Gender Coeducational
Languages English, Spanish
Boarding/day Day
Inzancanac s/n esq Jugueteros y Canteros,
Barrio Tlatel Xochitenco, Chimalhuacan
56330, Mexico
TELEPHONE: +525 5852 9002
FAX: +525 5852 6158
EMAIL: laurafh@prodigy.net.mx
WEBSITE: www.colegiolaureles.com

Colegio Maria Montessori de Monclova
Status Private
Programme Diploma
Diploma Coordinator A L Ramos Esquivel
Blvd Harold R Pape Nro 2002, Col Jardines del
Valle, Monclova, Coah 25730, Mexico
TELEPHONE: +52 866 633 2993
FAX: +52 866 633 2993
EMAIL: aurora@montessorimonclova.com
WEBSITE: www.montessorimonclova.com

Colegio Springfield, SC
Status Private
Programme Diploma
Diploma Coordinator C A Garcia González
Gender Coeducational
Languages Spanish
Boarding/day Day
Isidro Fabela Nte 1061, Col Tres Caminos,
Toluca 50020, Mexico
TELEPHONE: +52 722 237 1317
EMAIL: alejandrazam@hotmail.com
WEBSITE: www.springfield.edu.mx

Colegio Vista Hermosa
Status Private
Programme MYP, Diploma
Diploma Coordinator Maria Antonieta Molina
MYP Coordinator Ramon Garcia Govea
Gender Coeducational
Languages Spanish
Boarding/day Day
Bachillerato, Av Loma de Vista Hermosa 221,
Cuajimalpa, Mexico City DF 05100, Mexico
TELEPHONE: +52 55 50914630
FAX: +52 55 50914640
EMAIL: ariasgj@cvh.edu.mx
WEBSITE: www.cvh.edu.mx

Colegio Williams
Status Private
Programme Diploma
Diploma Coordinator Mayte de Lassé Cañas
Gender Coeducational
Languages Spanish
Boarding/day Day
Empresa 8, Col Mixcoac, Del Benito Juárez,
México DF 03910, Mexico
TELEPHONE: +52 55 1087 9797
FAX: +52 55 1087 9797
EMAIL: jwm@colegiowilliams.edu.mx
WEBSITE: www.colegiowilliams.edu.mx

Colegio Williams de Cuernavaca
Status Private
Programme PYP, MYP
MYP Coordinator Martha A Nocetti Vilchis
PYP Coordinator Patricia Martinez
Gender Coeducational
Languages English, Spanish
Boarding/day Day
Luna #32, Jardines de Cuernavaca,
Cuernavaca Morelos 62360, Mexico
TELEPHONE: +52 (777) 3223640
EMAIL: alfonsog@
williams-cuernavaca.edu.mx
WEBSITE: www.williams-cuernavaca.edu.mx

El Colegio Británico (Edron Academy)
Status Private
Programme Diploma
Diploma Coordinator Andrés Suárez
Gender Coeducational
Languages English
Boarding/day Day
Cal. al Desierto de los, Leones 5578, Col
Olivar de los Padres, Mexico DF 01740, Mexico
TELEPHONE: +52 558 51920
FAX: +52 5 585 28 46
EMAIL: edronoffice1@mexis.com
WEBSITE: www.edron.edu.mx

ESCUELA ALEXANDER BAIN SCo
Status Private
Programme PYP, MYP
MYP Coordinator Gloria Estela Prian Arroyo
PYP Coordinator Teresa Yáñez Clavel
Gender Coeducational
Barranca de Pilares 4, Tlacopac 01040, Mexico
TELEPHONE: +52 56 833 255
EMAIL: laburto@avantel.net
WEBSITE: www.alexander-bain.edu.mx
see full details on page 53

Escuela Ameyalli SC
Status Private
Programme PYP, MYP
MYP Coordinator María C Morales Hernández
PYP Coordinator Claudia A Badin Cherit
Gender Coeducational
Languages Spanish
Boarding/day Day
Calzada de las Águilas 1972, Col Axomiatla,
Álvaro Obregón DF 01820, Mexico
TELEPHONE: +52 55 12 85 70 20 x 204
EMAIL: olgapatricia@ameyalli.edu.mx
WEBSITE: www.ameyalli.edu.mx

Escuela Bancaria y Comercial, SC
Status Private
Programme Diploma
Diploma Coordinator Galo M H Soledad
Gender Coeducational
Languages Spanish
Boarding/day Day
Mexico, DF, Liverpool, 54, Col Juárez, Mexico
DF 06600, Mexico
TELEPHONE: +52 (55) 91 49 20 56
FAX: +52 (55) 91 49 2070
EMAIL: rodore@hotmail.com
WEBSITE: www.ebc.mx

Escuela John F Kennedy
Status Private
Programme Diploma
Diploma Coordinator Adrian Leece
Gender Coeducational
Languages Spanish
Boarding/day Day
Av Sabinos 272, Jurica, Querétaro 76100
TELEPHONE: +52 442 218 0075
FAX: +52 442 218 1784
EMAIL: mstappung@jfk.edu.mx
WEBSITE: www.jfk.edu.mx

Escuela Lomas Atlas S.C.
Status Private
Programme PYP
PYP Coordinator Isela Consuegra
Gender Coeducational
Languages Spanish, English
Boarding/day Day
Montañas Calizas #305, Lomas de
Chapultepec, Mexico DF 11000, Mexico
TELEPHONE: +52 55 552 053 75
EMAIL: lomasaltas@compuserve.com.mx
WEBSITE: www.lomasaltas.com.mx

Escuela Preparatoria Federal 'Lázaro Cárdenas'
Status State
Programme Diploma
Diploma Coordinator Oscar J S Zamora
Gender Coeducational
Languages Spanish
Boarding/day Day
c/o 416 W San Ysidro Blvd, STE-L-(008), San
Ysidro CA 92073, USA
TELEPHONE: +1 52 664 686 12 97
EMAIL: cruzhol@hotmail.com.mx

Eton Santa Fe
Status Private
Programme MYP, Diploma
Diploma Coordinator C Ll Balawender
MYP Coordinator R Díaz-Vélez Aguirre
Gender Coeducational
Languages Spanish
Boarding/day Day
Santa Lucia 220, Prados de la Montaña,
Cujaimalpa de Morelos, México, DF 05619
TELEPHONE: +52 92 22 94 (al 97)
EMAIL: etonschoolmx@yahoo.com.mx
WEBSITE: www.eton.edu.mx

FUNDACIÓN COLEGIO AMERICANO DE PUEBLA
Status Private
Programme PYP, MYP, Diploma
Diploma Coordinator Erika Würfl Marx
MYP Coordinator Sofía Dolega Zakrzewski
PYP Coordinator Rosario Pérez Lozano
Gender Coeducational
Languages Spanish, English
Boarding/day Day
9 Poniente 2709, Puebla 72160, Mexico
TELEPHONE: +52 222 30 30 400
EMAIL: info@cap.edu.mx
WEBSITE: www.cap.edu.mx
see full details on page 81

Greengates School

Status Private
Programme PYP, Diploma
Diploma Coordinator Graham Maclure
PYP Coordinator Cindy Blanes
Gender Coeducational
Languages English
Boarding/day Day
Apartado Postal 10-1112, CP 11002, Mexico
11002, Mexico
TELEPHONE: +52 52 55 5373 0088
FAX: +52 55 5373 0765
EMAIL: sarav@greengates.edu.mx
WEBSITE: www.greengates.edu.mx

INSTITUTO ALEXANDER BAIN SCo

Status Private
Programme PYP, MYP
MYP Coordinator Gloria Estela Prian Arroyo
PYP Coordinator Teresa Yáñez Clavel
Gender Coeducational
Cascada 320, Jardines del Pedregal, Mexico
TELEPHONE: +52 55 5595 6579
WEBSITE: www.alexander-bain.edu.mx
see full details on page 53

Instituto Anglo Británico AC

Status Private
Programme PYP, MYP
MYP Coordinator Benjamín Arriola Casasús
PYP Coordinator Gabriela May de Brull
Gender Coeducational
Languages English, Spanish
Boarding/day Day
Ave Isidoro Sepúlveda 555, Col La
Encarnación, Apodaca, Nuevo León 66633,
Mexico
TELEPHONE: +52 81 8321 5000
FAX: +52 81 8321 5032
EMAIL: gmay@iab.edu.mx
WEBSITE: www.iab.edu.mx/index.htm

Instituto D'Amicis, AC

Status Private
Programme PYP, MYP, Diploma
Diploma Coordinator Rosalino Pérez Ramirez
MYP Coordinator Lucila Sotomayor
PYP Coordinator Angélica Matute Casillas
Gender Coeducational
Languages Spanish
Boarding/day Day
Camino a Morillotla s/n, Colonia Bello
Horizonte, Puebla 72170, Mexico
TELEPHONE: +52 222 303 2618
FAX: +52 222 303 2603
EMAIL: laura.montesdeoca@damicis.edu.mx
WEBSITE: www.institutodamicis.edu.mx

INSTITUTO EDUCATIVO OLINCA

Status Private
Programme PYP, MYP, Diploma
Diploma Coordinator María C S de García
MYP Coordinator María C B Aguerrebere
PYP Coordinator Claudio Ghigliazza
Gender Coeducational
Languages Spanish, English, French
Boarding/day Day
Periférico Sur 5170, Col Pedregal de Carrasco,
Delegación Coyoacán, 04700 México DF
TELEPHONE: +52 5 55 606 3113
FAX: +52 5 55 665 7613
EMAIL: buzon@olinca.edu.mx
WEBSITE: www.olinca.edu.mx
see full details on page 94

Instituto Educativo Olinca Plantel Cuernavaca

Status Private
Programme PYP
PYP Coordinator Teresa Corona López
Gender Coeducational
Boarding/day Day
Paseo de Atzingo No 515, Colonia Lomas de
Atzingo, Cuernavaca, Morelos 62180, Mexico
TELEPHONE: +52 777 313 1232
EMAIL: dircuernavaca@olinca.edu.mx
WEBSITE: www.olinca.edu.mx

Instituto Jefferson de Morelia

Status Private
Programme Diploma
Diploma Coordinator Erendira Loza Contreras
Gender Coeducational
Languages Spanish
Boulevard Jefferson No 666, Carretera a Sta,
Maria Jesús del Monte 58080, Mexico
TELEPHONE: +34 3 324 3636
EMAIL: carlos_sandovalcuellar@yahoo.com
WEBSITE: www.jeffersondemorelia.com

Instituto Piaget

Status Private
Programme PYP
PYP Coordinator Ángel René López Mestiza
Gender Coeducational
Languages English, Spanish
Boarding/day Day
Nubes 413, Col Jardines del Pedregal, México
D. F. 01900, Mexico
TELEPHONE: +52 55 55 68 71 28
FAX: +52 55 56 52 65 94
EMAIL: institutopiaget1@prodigy.net.mx
WEBSITE: www.institutopiaget.com.mx

Instituto Senda del Río, AC

Status Private
Programme PYP
PYP Coordinator Dionisia Pappatheodoru
Gender Coeducational
Boarding/day Day
Av Eldorado 1405, Oeste Colonia Las Quintas,
Culiacán Sinaloa 80600, Mexico
TELEPHONE: +52 667 715 43 11
EMAIL: ncampos@senda.edu.mx
WEBSITE: www.senda.edu.mx

Instituto Tecnologico y De Estudios Superiores De Monterrey

Status Private
Programme Diploma
Diploma Coordinator David Lee
Gender Coeducational
Languages Spanish
Campus Toluca, Eduardo Monroy Cardenas
No 200, Toluca Edo de Mexi, Toluca Estado De
México 50110, Mexico
TELEPHONE: +52 7 279 9990
EMAIL: sortiz@itesm.mx

International School Querétaro S. C.

Status Private
Programme PYP
PYP Coordinator Tania Martínez Berlanga
Gender Coeducational
Languages English
Boarding/day Day
Paseo del Mesón 77, Jurica CP, Querétaro
76100, Mexico
TELEPHONE: +52 442 234 3042
FAX: +52 442 234 3043
EMAIL: biglesias@isq.edu
WEBSITE: www.isq.edu.mx

ITESM (Campus Ciudad de México)

Status Private
Programme Diploma
Diploma Coordinator Francisco I Nájera
Gender Coeducational
Languages Spanish
Campus Ciudad de Mexico, Calle del Puente
222, Ejidos de Huipulco Tlalpan DF 14380,
Mexico
TELEPHONE: +52 55 5483 2110
EMAIL: jespitia@itesm.mx

ITESM Campus Cumbres

Status Private
Programme Diploma
Diploma Coordinator Myrna Valadez
Gender Coeducational
Languages Spanish
Boarding/day Day
Prol Alejandro de Rodas S/N, Col Cumbres
Elite, Monterrey NL 64349, Mexico
TELEPHONE: +52 (81) 8158 4600
EMAIL: mmaqueo@itesm.mx
WEBSITE: www.prepatec.mty.itesm.mx

ITESM Campus Eugenio Garza Lagüera

Status Private
Programme Diploma
Diploma Coordinator Angeles Carranza
Gender Coeducational
Languages Spanish
Boarding/day Day
Topolobampo #4603, Valle de las Brisas,
Monterrey NL 64790, Mexico
TELEPHONE: +52 (81) 8155 4445
FAX: +52 (81) 8155 4506
EMAIL: apena@itesm.mx
WEBSITE: www.prepatec.mty.itesm.mx

ITESM Campus Eugenio Garza Sada

Status Private
Programme Diploma
Diploma Coordinator Mónica Otalora
Gender Coeducational
Languages Spanish
Boarding/day Day
Dinamarca # 451, Col del Carmen, Monterrey Nuevo León 64710, Mexico
TELEPHONE: +52 (81) 8151 4253
EMAIL: masaenz@itesm.mx
WEBSITE: www.prepatec.mty.itesm.mx

ITESM Campus Santa Catarina

Status Private
Programme Diploma
Diploma Coordinator Martha Camacho
Gender Coeducational
Languages Spanish
Boarding/day Day
Morones Prieto No 290 Pte, Col Jesús M Garza, Santa Catarina Nuevo León 66180, Mexico
TELEPHONE: +52 (81) 8153 4132
EMAIL: rabrego@itesm.mx
WEBSITE: www.prepatec.mty.itesm.mx

Liceo de Monterrey

Status Private
Programme Diploma
Diploma Coordinator C M García Bernal
Gender Coeducational
Languages Spanish
Col Valle Ote, Garza Garcia 66220, Mexico
TELEPHONE: +52 818363 2710
FAX: +52 8187484147
EMAIL: aejasso@liceodemonterrey.edu.mx

Liceo de Monterrey – Centro Educativo

Status Private
Programme Diploma
Diploma Coordinator José Portillo Ponce
Gender Male
Languages Spanish
Boarding/day Day
Col Sendero San Jeronimo, Monterrey, Nuevo Leon 64659, Mexico
TELEPHONE: +1 8122 8900
EMAIL: jmroqueni@mail.liceo.edu.mx

Liceo Federico Froebel de Oaxaca SC

Status Private
Programme Diploma
Diploma Coordinator Gerardo Pascal Cervantes Rodríguez
Gender Coeducational
Languages English, Spanish, French
Boarding/day Day
Ajusco Nro 100, Colonia Volcanes, Oaxaca 68020, Mexico
TELEPHONE: +52 951 5200 675
FAX: +52 951 5200 675
EMAIL: info@federicofroebel.org
WEBSITE: www.federicofroebel.org

Peterson Lomas Preparatoria SC

Status Private
Programme Diploma
Diploma Coordinator Javier Piña Altamirano
Gender Coeducational
Languages Spanish
Huizachito No 80 Col, Lomas de Vista Hermosa, Del Cuajimalpa de Morelos 05720, Mexico
TELEPHONE: +52 55 58130114
FAX: +52 55 58133435
EMAIL: kpeterson@peterson.edu.mx
WEBSITE: www.peterso.ed.mx

Tecnológico de Monterrey – Campus Estado de México

Status Private
Programme Diploma
Diploma Coordinator Mariana Martinez
Gender Coeducational
Languages Spanish
Boarding/day Day
Carretera Lago de Guadalupe, km 3.5 col Margarita Maza de, Juárez Atizapán De Zaragoza 52916, Mexico
TELEPHONE: +52 (55) 5864 57 00
FAX: +52 (55) 5864 57 01
EMAIL: vmendoza@itesm.mx
WEBSITE: www.cem.itesm.mx

Tecnológico de Monterrey – Campus Puebla

Status Private
Programme Diploma
Diploma Coordinator R P Martínez Lozano
Gender Coeducational
Languages Spanish
Boarding/day Day
Vía Atlixcáyotl 2301, San Andrés Cholula, Puebla 72800, Mexico
TELEPHONE: +52 222 303 2096
FAX: +52 222 303 2097
EMAIL: roberto.martinez@itesm.mx
WEBSITE: www.pue.itesm.mx

Tecnológico de Monterrey – Campus Querétaro

Status Private
Programme Diploma
Diploma Coordinator Eugenia Olivera
Gender Coeducational
Languages Spanish
Boarding/day Mixed
Av Epigmenio González #500, Fracc San Pablo, Santiago de Querétaro 76130, Mexico
TELEPHONE: +52 442 2383208
FAX: +52 442 2173887
EMAIL: cmmartin@itesm.mx
WEBSITE: www.qro.itesm.mx

Tecnológico de Monterrey – Campus Santa Fe

Status Private
Programme Diploma
Diploma Coordinator R D Cooksey Fernández
Gender Coeducational
Languages Spanish, English
Boarding/day Day
Av Carlos Lazo #100, Santa Fe, Delegación Alvaro Obregón CP 01389, Mexico
TELEPHONE: +52 55 9177 8000 x8131
EMAIL: elazarin@itesm.mx
WEBSITE: www.csf.itesm.mx

Tecnológico de Monterrey – Campus Valle Alto

Status Private
Programme Diploma
Diploma Coordinator Ángeles Carranza
Gender Coeducational
Languages Spanish
Boarding/day Day
Carretera Nacional Km 927, Monterrey Nuevo León 64790, Mexico
TELEPHONE: +52 (81) 8155 4445
WEBSITE: www.prepatec.mty.itesm.mx

Tecnológico de Monterrey – Campus Metepec

Status Private
Programme Diploma
Diploma Coordinator David Lee
Gender Coeducational
Languages French
Boarding/day Day
Avda Las Torres s/n casi esqu Avda Tecnológico, San Salvador Tizatlalli, Metepec Estado De México 52172, Mexico
TELEPHONE: +52 722 271 5977
FAX: +52 722 271 5977
EMAIL: gsuarez@itesm.mx
WEBSITE: www.tol.itesm.mx

The American School Foundation, A.C.

Status Private
Programme PYP, MYP, Diploma
Diploma Coordinator Amy Gallie
MYP Coordinator Veronika Saldana
PYP Coordinator Cindy Berry
Gender Coeducational
Languages English
Boarding/day Day
Calle Sur 136-135, Colonia Las Americas, Mexico DF 01120, Mexico
TELEPHONE: +52 555 227 4900
FAX: +52 555 2274928
EMAIL: cortesd@asf.edu.mx
WEBSITE: www.asf.edu.mx

The Churchill School
Status Private
Programme PYP, MYP
MYP Coordinator José A Zepeda Navarrete
PYP Coordinator Armando Andrade
Gender Coeducational
Languages English
Boarding/day Day
Felipe Villanueva 52, Col Guadalupe Inn, Mexico 01020, Mexico
TELEPHONE: +52 55 93 74 98
FAX: + 52 55 93 79 83
EMAIL: mcardena@tcs.org.mx
WEBSITE: www.tcs.org.mx

The Lancaster School
Status Private
Programme PYP, Diploma
Diploma Coordinator M S García Ramírez
PYP Coordinator Jacqueline Harmer
Gender Coeducational
Languages English, Spanish
Boarding/day Boarding/day
Av Insurgentes sur 3838, Col. Tlalpan CP 14000, Mexico
TELEPHONE: +52 5556 6697 96
FAX: +52 5556 6697 96
EMAIL: alan@lancaster.edu.mx
WEBSITE: www.lancaster.edu.mx

Universidad de Monterrey
Status Private
Programme Diploma
Diploma Coordinator J H Cárdenas Vidaurri
Gender Coeducational
Languages Spanish
Boarding/day Day
Ave.Morones Prieto 4500 Pte, San Pedro Garza Garcia NL 66238, Mexico

Universidad de Monterrey Unidad Valle Alto
Status Private
Programme Diploma
Diploma Coordinator Jair J Aguilar Batista
Gender Coeducational
Languages English
Boarding/day Day
Carretera Nacionala Salida Valle Alto Km1, Colonia Valle Alto, Monterrey NL 64989, Mexico

NICARAGUA

Colegio Alemán Nicaragüense
Status Private
Programme Diploma
Diploma Coordinator Arnold Cabrera
Gender Coeducational
Languages Spanish
Boarding/day Day
Apartado 1636, Managua, Nicaragua
TELEPHONE: +505 265 8449
FAX: +505 265 8117
EMAIL: coalnic@ibw.com.ni
WEBSITE: www.dasan.de/ds_managua

Notre Dame School
Status Private
Programme Diploma
Diploma Coordinator Silvia Vallecillo
Gender Coeducational
Languages English
Boarding/day Day
Apartado 6092, Managua, Nicaragua
TELEPHONE: +505 2 760353
FAX: +505 2 760416
EMAIL: dirnd@notredame.edu.ni

PANAMA

International School of Panama
Status Private
Programme Diploma
Diploma Coordinator Salah Altaji
Gender Coeducational
Languages English
Boarding/day Day
Apartado 0819-02588, Panama
TELEPHONE: +507 266 7862/9532
FAX: +507 266 7808
EMAIL: director@isp.edu.pa
WEBSITE: www.isp.edu.pa

PARAGUAY

St Anne's School
Status Private
Programme MYP, Diploma
Diploma Coordinator Mirko Zayas
MYP Coordinator Mirko Zayas
Gender Coeducational
Languages English
Boarding/day Day
Boggiani 5881 c/Bélgica, Asunción, Paraguay
TELEPHONE: +595 21 603 366
FAX: +595 21 606 830
EMAIL: jestimson@yahoo.com
WEBSITE: www.sas.edu.py

PERU

Asociacion Educacional Williamson Newton College
Status Private
Programme PYP, Diploma
Diploma Coordinator David Bruggers
PYP Coordinator Geoffrey Brown
Gender Coeducational
Languages English
Boarding/day Day
Apartado 12-137, La Molina, Lima, Peru
TELEPHONE: +51 1479 0460
FAX: +51 1479 0430
EMAIL: acino@newton.edu.pe
WEBSITE: www.newton.edu.pe

Casuarinas College
Status Private
Programme PYP, MYP, Diploma
Diploma Coordinator Kathleen Gallagher
MYP Coordinator Vilma López de La Torre
PYP Coordinator Marisa Odria
Gender Coeducational
Languages Spanish, English
Boarding/day Day
Av Jacarandá 421, Cuadra 4, Valle Hermoso, Monterrico, Lima 33, Peru
TELEPHONE: +51 1 4366 949
FAX: +51 1 344 1133
EMAIL: ccollege@casuarinas.edu.pe

CEP Altair SAC
Status Private
Programme PYP, MYP, Diploma
Diploma Coordinator Mónica Cilloniz
MYP Coordinator Jimena La Rosa
PYP Coordinator Pilar Cervantes
Gender Coeducational
Languages Spanish, English
Boarding/day Day
Avenida La Arboleda 385, La Molina, Lima, Peru
TELEPHONE: +511 365 0298
EMAIL: direccion@altair.edu.pe
WEBSITE: www.altair.edu.pe

CEP Mixto Reina del Mundo
Status Private
Programme Diploma
Diploma Coordinator Luis E Gutiérrez López
Gender Coeducational
Languages Spanish
Boarding/day Day
Aveinda Rinconada del Lago 675, La Molina , Lima 12, Peru
TELEPHONE: +51 1 368 0496
FAX: +51 1 368 0497
EMAIL: reina-schule@rdm.edu.pe
WEBSITE: www.rdm.edu.pe

CEP San Ignacio de Recalde
Status Private
Programme Diploma
Diploma Coordinator María Luisa Salleres
Gender Coeducational
Languages English
Boarding/day Boarding
Calle Géminis 251, Urb Las Begonias, San Borja, Lima, Peru
TELEPHONE: +51 1 211 9430
FAX: +51 1 475 8480
EMAIL: efarje@sir.edu.pe
WEBSITE: www.sir.edu.pe

Colegio Euroamericano

Status Private
Programme Diploma
Diploma Coordinator Sonia Palicio
Gender Coeducational
Languages Spanish, English
Boarding/day Day
Parcela 183-187 Mz C, Fundo Casablanca,
Pachacámac, Peru
TELEPHONE: +51 1 231 1617
FAX: +51 1 231 1698
EMAIL: rmatthews@euroamericano.edu.pe
WEBSITE: www.euroamericano.edu.pe

Colegio Franklin Delano Roosevelt

Status Private
Programme PYP, MYP, Diploma
Diploma Coordinator Jeffrey Smith
MYP Coordinator Kirsten Welbes
PYP Coordinator Jon Schatzky
Gender Coeducational
Languages English, Spanish
Boarding/day Day
Apartado 18-0977, Lima 18, Peru
TELEPHONE: +51 1 702 4511
FAX: +51 1 702 4500
EMAIL: fwesson@amersol.edu.pe
WEBSITE: www.amersol.edu.pe/index.asp

Colegio Magister

Status Private
Programme Diploma
Diploma Coordinator Giancarlo Belloni
Gender Coeducational
Languages Spanish
Boarding/day Day
Francisco de Cuéllar #686, Surco, Lima 33,
Peru
TELEPHONE: +51 1 437 9029
FAX: +51 1 437 3911
EMAIL: magister@terra.com.pe
WEBSITE: www.magister.edu.pe

Colegio Peruano Británico

Status Private
Programme Diploma
Diploma Coordinator Geoff Lewis
Gender Coeducational
Languages English, Spanish
Boarding/day Day
Colegio Peruano Británico, Av Via Lactea 445,
Surco, Lima 33, Peru
TELEPHONE: +51 1 436 0151
FAX: +51 1 436-1006
EMAIL: epascoe@britishschool.edu.pe
WEBSITE: www.britishschool.edu.pe

Colegio Peruano Norteamericano Abraham Lincoln

Status Private
Programme MYP, Diploma
Diploma Coordinator Humberto Lara Ceroni
MYP Coordinator Roxana Calderón
Gender Coeducational
Languages Spanish, English
Boarding/day Day
Calle José Antonio 475, Urb Parque de
Monterrico, La Molina Lima 12, Peru
TELEPHONE: +51 1 6127000
EMAIL: jmigone@abrahamlincoln.edu.pe
WEBSITE: www.abrahamlincoln.edu.pe

Colegio Pestalozzi

Status Private
Programme Diploma
Diploma Coordinator Ramiro Febres Tapia
Gender Coeducational
Languages Spanish
Boarding/day Day
Casilla 18-1027, Aurora-Miraflores, Lima 18,
Peru
TELEPHONE: +51 1 241 4218
FAX: +51 1 446 4007
EMAIL: ursus@pestalozzi.edu.pe
WEBSITE: www.pestalozzi.edu.pe

Colegio Sagrados Corazones 'Recoleta'

Status Private
Programme Diploma
Diploma Coordinator Maria Ines Prado
Vargas-Machuca
Languages Spanish
Boarding/day Day
Av El Golf de los Incas 368, La Molina, Lima,
Peru
TELEPHONE: +51 435 2991
FAX: +51 435 2991
EMAIL: brunoeh@recoleta.edu.pe
WEBSITE: www.recoleta.edu.pe

Davy College

Status Private
Programme MYP, Diploma
Diploma Coordinator Williams Amaya Pelaez
MYP Coordinator Francisco Vargas
Gender Coeducational
Languages Spanish
Boarding/day Day
Avenida Hoyos Rubio 2684, Cajamarca,
Casilla 1, Peru
TELEPHONE: +51 76 827 501
FAX: +51 76 827 502
EMAIL: jiminport99@hotmail.com
WEBSITE: www.davycollege.edu.pe

Hiram Bingham, The British International School of Lima

Status Private
Programme PYP, MYP, Diploma
Diploma Coordinator Jim Norbury
MYP Coordinator Ana-Belen Horruitiner
PYP Coordinator Rocio Tello
Gender Coeducational
Languages English, Spanish
Boarding/day Day
Paseo de la Castellana 919, Surco, Lima 33,
Peru
TELEPHONE: +51 1 271 9880
FAX: +51 1 448 6260
EMAIL: informes@hirambingham.edu.pe
WEBSITE: www.hirambingham.edu.pe

Liceo Naval 'Almirante Guise'

Status State
Programme Diploma
Diploma Coordinator Mónica Harm
Fernández-Dávila
Gender Coeducational
Languages Spanish
Boarding/day Day
Calle Monti 350, San Borja, Lima 41, Peru
TELEPHONE: +51 1 475 8055
FAX: +51 1 475 8040
EMAIL: rforlin@lnag.edu.pe
WEBSITE: www.lnag.edu.pe

Markham College

Status Private
Programme Diploma
Diploma Coordinator Colin Bibby
Gender Coeducational
Languages English
Boarding/day Day
Apartado 18-1048, Miraflores, Lima, Peru
TELEPHONE: +51 1 241 7677
FAX: +51 1 241 7678
EMAIL: dowdles@markham.edu.pe

San Silvestre School

Status Private
Programme Diploma
Diploma Coordinator Richard Holt
Gender Female
Languages English
Boarding/day Day
Apartado 18-0492, Miraflores, Lima 18, Peru
TELEPHONE: +51 1 2413334
FAX: +51 14 455 075
EMAIL: rbayly@sansilvestre.edu.pe
WEBSITE: www.sansil.edu.pe

URUGUAY

British Schools
Status Private
Programme Diploma
Diploma Coordinator David Rennie
Gender Coeducational
Languages English
Boarding/day Day
Máximo Tajes 6400, esq Havre, Montevideo 11500, Uruguay
TELEPHONE: +598 2 600 8958
FAX: +598 2 601 6338
EMAIL: ggisby@british.edu.uy
WEBSITE: www.british.edu.uy

Colegio Stella Maris
Status Private
Programme Diploma
Diploma Coordinator Rubén C Basanta
Gender Coeducational
Languages Spanish
Boarding/day Day
Máximo Tajes 7357/7359, CP 11500 Montevideo 11500, Uruguay
TELEPHONE: +598 2 600 0702
FAX: +598 2 600 0702 x31
EMAIL: info@stellamaris.edu.uy
WEBSITE: www.stellamaris.edu.uy

Escuela Integral Hebreo Uruguaya
Status Private
Programme Diploma
Diploma Coordinator Isabel Burstein de Kohn
Gender Coeducational
Languages Spanish
Boarding/day Day
Jose Benito Lamas 2835, Montevideo 11300, Uruguay
TELEPHONE: +598 2 708 1712
FAX: +598 2 708 4450
EMAIL: ssoloducho@escuelaintegral.edu.uy

St Brendan's School
Status Private
Programme PYP, MYP, Diploma
Diploma Coordinator Rosario Rodriguez
MYP Coordinator Jorge Nández Britos
PYP Coordinator Jimena Taboada
Gender Coeducational
Languages Spanish
Boarding/day Day
Av Rivera 2314, Montevideo CP 11100, Uruguay
TELEPHONE: +598 2 409 4939
EMAIL: rpmorgan@stbrendan.edu.uy
WEBSITE: www.stbrendan.edu.uy

St Clare's College
Status Private
Programme Diploma
Diploma Coordinator Daniel Reta
Gender Coeducational
Languages Spanish
Boarding/day Day
California y los Médanos, Punta del Este, San Rafael 20000, Uruguay
TELEPHONE: +598 42 490200
EMAIL: sports@stclares.edu.uy
WEBSITE: www.stclares.edu.uy

St Patrick's College
Status Private
Programme MYP
MYP Coordinator Mary Evans
Gender Coeducational
Languages Spanish
Boarding/day Day
Camino Gigantes 2735, Montevideo 12100, Uruguay
TELEPHONE: +598 2 601 3474
FAX: +598 2 601 6538
EMAIL: spc@stpatrick.edu.uy
WEBSITE: www.stpatrick.edu.uy

Woodlands School
Status Private
Programme MYP
MYP Coordinator Sandra Senz
Gender Coeducational
Languages Spanish
Boarding/day Day
Avenida Cooper 2271, Montevideo 11500, Uruguay
TELEPHONE: +5982 600 3443
EMAIL: direccionliceo@woodlands.edu.uy

VENEZUELA

Colegio Bellas Artes
Status Private
Programme Diploma
Diploma Coordinator E Rodríguez de Petzold
Gender Coeducational
Languages Spanish
Boarding/day Day
Zulia, Av 3F, con calle 71, Maracaibo, Zulia 4002, Venezuela
TELEPHONE: +58 0261 7911 175
FAX: +58 0261 7923 055
EMAIL: colbellasartes@telcel.net.ve

Colegio Internacional de Caracas
Status Private
Programme MYP, Diploma
Diploma Coordinator Clive Russell
MYP Coordinator Larry Wilson
Gender Coeducational
Languages English
Boarding/day Day
c/o Pakmail 6030, PO Box 02 5304, Miami FL 33102-5304, USA
TELEPHONE: +58 212 945 0444
EMAIL: wsargent@ciccaracas.com.ve
WEBSITE: www.cic-caracas.org

Colegio Los Campitos
Status Private
Programme Diploma
Diploma Coordinator Vivian Quintero de Lira
Gender Female
Languages Spanish
Boarding/day Day
Ruta C, Urbanización Los Campitos, Prados del Este, Miranda, Venezuela
TELEPHONE: +58 212 977 1768
FAX: +58 212 976 4694
EMAIL: iboclc@colegioloscampitos.com

Colegio Los Robles
Status Private
Programme MYP
MYP Coordinator Militza Hernández
Gender Coeducational
Languages English, Spanish
Boarding/day Day
Callejón Mañongo (al lado del Parque Dunas), Valencia Estado Carabobo, Venezuela
TELEPHONE: +58 241 842 7385
FAX: +58 241 842 0137
EMAIL: ceog04@cantv.net
WEBSITE: www.colegiolosrobles.e12.ve

Escuela Bella Vista
Status Private
Programme Diploma
Diploma Coordinator Padmini Sankaran
Gender Coeducational
Languages English
Boarding/day Day
c/o Buzoom C-Mar-P-1815, PO Box 02-8537, Miami FL 33102, USA
TELEPHONE: +1 582 61 791 1674
EMAIL: sibleys@ebv.org.ve
WEBSITE: www.ebv.org.ve

Escuela Campo Alegre
Status Private
Programme Diploma
Diploma Coordinator Winfield Lowman
Gender Coeducational
Languages English
Boarding/day Day
c/o 8424 NW 56th Street, Suite CCS 00007, Miami FL 33166, USA
TELEPHONE: +1 58 212 993 3922
FAX: +1 582 12 993 0219
EMAIL: jean_vahey@eca.com.ve
WEBSITE: www.eca.com.ve

Instituto De Educacion Activa
Status Private
Programme Diploma
Diploma Coordinator Silvia Roque
Gender Coeducational
Languages Spanish
Boarding/day Day
Avenida Bolívar de Naguanagua, Frente al Fuerte Paramacay, Valencia, Estado Carabobo 2002, Venezuela
TELEPHONE: +58 241 8685 801
FAX: +58 241 8680 834
EMAIL: idea@telcel.net.ve
WEBSITE: www.miacademia.com/idea

Instituto Educacional Juan XXIII
Status Private
Programme PYP, Diploma
Diploma Coordinator Jorge Luis Bolívar
Manzano
PYP Coordinator María Inés Mayaudon
Gender Coeducational
Languages Spanish
Boarding/day Day
Calle San Enrique No 85-70, Trigal Centro,
Valencia, Estado Carabobo 2002, Venezuela
TELEPHONE: +58 241 8425732
FAX: +58 241 8425570
EMAIL: virginia@juanxxiii.e12.ve
WEBSITE: www.juanxxiii.e12.ve

Liceo Los Robles
Status Private
Programme Diploma
Diploma Coordinator Ramón Rincón
Gonzalez
Gender Male
Languages Spanish
Boarding/day Day
Urbanización el Doral Norte, Calle 34 esquina
con Avenida, Fuerzas Armadas, Mar, Estado
Zulia 4002, Venezuela
TELEPHONE: +58 0261 7421833
FAX: +58 0261 7432444
EMAIL: lrobles@telcel.net.ve

Unidad Educativa Academia Washington
Status Private
Programme Diploma
Diploma Coordinator Jose Ruggiero
Gender Coeducational
Languages Spanish
Boarding/day Day
Coordinacion BI, Calle 'C', Colina de Valle
Arriba, Caracas, Estado Miranda 1080,
Venezuela
TELEPHONE: +58 0212 9757077
FAX: +58 0212 9757340
EMAIL: jruggieror@yahoo.com

IB

North America | Caribbean

North America and the Caribbean

The IB North America and the Caribbean office provides support services to applicant and authorized IB World Schools in:

The Bahamas	Cuba
Barbados	Dominican Republic
Bermuda	Jamaica
British Virgin Islands	Netherlands Antilles
Canada	USA
Cayman Islands	

Some Recent Initiatives

In Canada

In the last year, the number of IB World Schools in Canada has increased from 211 to 265. Policy developments include waiving provincial requirements for all IB Diploma Programme students in Nova Scotia and British Columbia as well as the availability of provincial scholarships based on IB coursework for British Columbia students.

In Nova Scotia, the province continued with its commitment to ultimately provide access to the IB Diploma Programme to 90% of its high school student population. As a result of the province's strong commitment and efforts, what began as two public and two private schools offering the IB Diploma Programme in Nova Scotia has now grown to an additional 11 public schools as of September 2008. Additionally, the province of Prince Edward Island has one candidate school in Charlottetown undergoing the IB authorization process.

With regards to university recognition, Nova Scotia universities offer a variety of incentives for IB Diploma graduates based on their anticipated IB grades submitted before March 15 of their final year and consider IB graduates with a score of 35 points or better for all major scholarships.

In the United States

In 2008, the IB was granted a $450,000 grant from the Bill and Melinda Gates Foundation to undertake a comprehensive analysis of the Diploma Gap – the gap between the numbers of high school students who could be reached by the IB's rigorous Diploma Programme and those who currently are. The IB has already undertaken several projects to address the Diploma Gap, including a multi-year project with the US Department of Education to develop support structures for Title I eligible high schools.

Support from the Gates Foundation will allow the IB to engage consultants with the skills and experience necessary to address the complex educational and business issues of the Diploma Gap. The IB is committed to this project at the highest levels, including the Board of Governors, the director general, and the academic director.

The three-year Advanced Placement Initiative (API) Grant, awarded to IB North America in 2006 in the amount of $1.08 million, has continued to move forward, establishing partnerships to carry out the core activities for the project as well as developing services and support structures such as coaching models and resource guides. Over the next 12 months, we plan to publish a set of resource materials for Title I eligible high schools, continue to pilot a coaching model, finalize an annual programme evaluation tool for schools, and offer backward mapping workshops for Diploma Programme and Middle Years Programme teachers.

Some facts about this region

As of September 2008

IB North America serves 1194 authorized IB World Schools in nine countries and offers 1334 IB programmes in total.

DP programmes:	748
MYP programmes:	401
PYP programmes:	185
Schools offering all three programmes:	11
Schools offering DP and MYP:	97
Schools offering DP and PYP:	10
Schools offering MYP and PYP:	12
State school programmes:	1171
Private school programmes:	163

BAHAMAS

Lucaya International School
Status Private
Programme PYP, Diploma
Diploma Coordinator Ray Lee
PYP Coordinator Rachel-Ceri MacKinnon
Gender Coeducational
Languages English
Boarding/day Day
Chesapeake Drive, PO Box F-44066, Freeport
Grand Bahamas Island, Bahamas
TELEPHONE: +1 242 373 4004
FAX: +1 242 373 6510
EMAIL: lisdirector@coralwave.com
WEBSITE: www.lucaya-is.org

Lyford Cay International School
Status Private
Programme MYP, Diploma
Diploma Coordinator Kirti Joshi
MYP Coordinator Jenny Richardson
Gender Coeducational
Languages English
Boarding/day Day
PO Box N-7776, Nassau NB, Bahamas
TELEPHONE: +1 242 362 4774 ext 223
FAX: +1 242 362 5198
EMAIL: ecollier-bain@lyfordcayschool.net
WEBSITE: www.lyfordcayschool.net

St Andrew's School, The International School of the Bahamas
Status Private
Programme PYP, Diploma
Diploma Coordinator Carey Christensen
PYP Coordinator Nicole Procacci
Gender Coeducational
Languages English
Boarding/day Boarding/day
PO Box EE 17340, Nassau, NP EE 17340, Bahamas
TELEPHONE: +1 242 324 2621
FAX: +1 242 324 0816
EMAIL: dmackinnon@st-andrews.com
WEBSITE: www.st-andrews.com

BARBADOS

The Codrington School
Status Private
Programme PYP
PYP Coordinator Eliana Marcenaro
Gender Coeducational
Languages English
Boarding/day Day
St John BB 20008, Barbados
TELEPHONE: +1246 423 2570
FAX: +1246 423 3653
EMAIL: administration@codrington.edu.bb
WEBSITE: www.codrington.edu.bb

BERMUDA

Bermuda High School
Status Private
Programme Diploma
Diploma Coordinator Kate Ross
Gender Coeducational
Languages English
Boarding/day Day
19 Richmond Road, Pembroke HM08, Bermuda
TELEPHONE: +1 441 295 6153
FAX: +1 441 295 2754
EMAIL: head.school@bhs.bm
WEBSITE: www.bhs.bm

Somersfield Academy
Status Private
Programme MYP
MYP Coordinator Jeneba O'Connor
Gender Coeducational
Languages English
Boarding/day Day
107 Middle Road, Devonshire DV 06, Bermuda
TELEPHONE: +1 441 236 9797
EMAIL: head@somersfield.bm
WEBSITE: www.somersfield.bm

Warwick Academy
Status Private
Programme Diploma
Diploma Coordinator Adela Ruberry
Gender Coeducational
Languages English
Boarding/day Day
117 Middle Road, Warwick (Parish) PG 01, Bermuda
TELEPHONE: +1 441 236 1917
FAX: +1 441 236 9995
EMAIL: head@warwickacad.bm
WEBSITE: www.warwickacad.bm

CANADA
Alberta

Archbishop Macdonald High School
Status State
Programme MYP, Diploma
Diploma Coordinator Edward Jean
MYP Coordinator Cindy Dallaire
Gender Coeducational
Languages English
Boarding/day Day
10810-142 Street, Edmonton AB, T5N 2P7, Canada
TELEPHONE: +1 780 451 1470
FAX: +1 780 455 5571
EMAIL: maleckid@ecsd.net
WEBSITE:
www.archbishopmacdonald.ecsd.net

Bellerose Composite High School
Status State
Programme Diploma
Diploma Coordinator Jyoti Mangat
Gender Coeducational
Languages English
Boarding/day Day
49 Giroux Road, St Albert AB, T8N 6N4, Canada
TELEPHONE: +1 780 460 8490 ext 125
FAX: +1 780 459 0798
EMAIL: mentzg@spschools.org
WEBSITE: http://bchs.spschools.org

Bishop O'Byrne High School
Status State
Programme Diploma
Diploma Coordinator David Paraschuk
Gender Coeducational
Languages English
Boarding/day Day
333 Shawville Blvd SE, Suite 500, Calgary AB, T2Y 4H3, Canada
TELEPHONE: +1 403-252-4320
FAX: +1 403-201-4228
EMAIL: michael.ross@cssd.ab.ca
WEBSITE: http://bishopobyrne.ca

Coronation School
Programme MYP
MYP Coordinator Kelly Davis Chernishenko
Gender Coeducational
Boarding/day Boarding
10925-139 Street, Edmonton AB, T5M 1P8, Canada
TELEPHONE: +1 780 455 2008

Father Lacombe High School
Status State
Programme Diploma
Diploma Coordinator Brendan Bulger
Gender Coeducational
Languages English
Boarding/day Day
3615 Radcliffe Drive SE, Calgary AB, T2A 6B4, Canada
TELEPHONE: +1 403 248 9559
FAX: +1 403 235 1270
EMAIL: maria.dellarocchette@cssd.ab.ca
WEBSITE: www.fatherlacombe.calgary.ab.ca/

Glenora School
Programme MYP
MYP Coordinator Kelly Davis Chernishenko
Gender Coeducational
Boarding/day Boarding
13520-102 Avenue, Edmonton AB, T5N 0N7, Canada
TELEPHONE: +1 780 452 4740

Harry Ainlay High School
Status State
Programme Diploma
Diploma Coordinator Diane Fischer
Gender Coeducational
Languages English
Boarding/day Day
Harry Ainlay, 4350-111 Street, Edmonton AB,
T6J 1E8, Canada
TELEPHONE: +1 780 413 2700
FAX: +1 780 438 1465
EMAIL: mliguori@epsb.ca
WEBSITE: www.ainlay.ca/

Henry Wise Wood High School
Status State
Programme Diploma
Diploma Coordinator Francois Fortin
Gender Coeducational
Languages English
Boarding/day Day
910-75th Avenue SW, Calgary AB, T2V OS6,
Canada
TELEPHONE: +1 403 253 2261
FAX: +1 403 777 7929
EMAIL: jlangley@cbe.ab.ca
WEBSITE: www.cbe.ab.ca/b836

Holy Trinity Academy
Status State
Programme Diploma
Diploma Coordinator Scott Royce
Languages English
53 Cimarron Drive, Okotoks AB, T0L 1T5,
Canada
TELEPHONE: +1 403 938 4600
FAX: +1 403 938 5324
EMAIL: smorrison@redeemer.ab.ca

Holy Trinity High School
Status State
Programme MYP, Diploma
Diploma Coordinator Brent McDonough
MYP Coordinator Brent McDonough
Gender Coeducational
Languages English
Boarding/day Day
7007-28th Avenue, Edmonton AB, T6K 4A5,
Canada
TELEPHONE: +1 780 462 5777
FAX: +1 780 462 5820
EMAIL: radyob@ecsd.net
WEBSITE: www.holytrinity.ecsd.net

J Percy Page High School
Status State
Programme Diploma
Diploma Coordinator Janet Jorgensen
Gender Coeducational
Languages English
Boarding/day Day
2707 Millwoods Road NW, Edmonton AB, T6K
3Z3, Canada
TELEPHONE: +1 780-462-3322
FAX: +1 780-462-7803
EMAIL: jean.stiles@epsb.ca
WEBSITE: www.jpercypage.com

Jasper Place High School
Status State
Programme Diploma
Diploma Coordinator Lynne Burns
Gender Coeducational
Languages English
8950-163 Street, Edmonton AB, T5R 2P2,
Canada
TELEPHONE: +1 780-408-9000
FAX: +1 780 486-1984
EMAIL: bcoggles@epsb.ca
WEBSITE: http://jp.epsb.net

John G Diefenbaker High School
Status State
Programme Diploma
Diploma Coordinator Jack Cohen
Gender Coeducational
Languages English
Boarding/day Day
6620-4th Street NW, Calgary AB, T2K 1C2,
Canada
TELEPHONE: +1 403 274 2240
FAX: +1 403 777 7669
EMAIL: rtink@cbe.ab.ca
WEBSITE: www.cbe.ab.ca/b860

Lester B Pearson High School
Status State
Programme Diploma
Diploma Coordinator Brent Benard
Languages English
Boarding/day Day
3020-52nd Street NE, Calgary AB, T1Y 5P4,
Canada
TELEPHONE: +1 403-244-2278
EMAIL: blbenard@cbe.ab.ca
WEBSITE: www.schools.cbe.ab.ca

Lindsay Thurber Comprehensive High School
Status State
Programme Diploma
Diploma Coordinator David Smith
Gender Coeducational
Languages English
Boarding/day Day
4204-58th Street, Red Deer AB, T4N 2L6,
Canada
TELEPHONE: +1 403 347 1171
FAX: +1 403 340 1676
EMAIL: gunterschultz@rdpsd.ab.ca
WEBSITE: http://rdpsd.ab.ca/ltchs

Louis St Laurent
Status State
Programme Diploma
Diploma Coordinator Marlene McDonald
Gender Coeducational
Languages English
Boarding/day Day
11230-43 Avenue, Edmonton AB, T6J 0X3,
Canada
TELEPHONE: +1 780 435 3964
FAX: +1 780 437 7228
EMAIL: tourangeauk@ecsd.net
WEBSITE: www.louisstlaurent.ecsd.net

Lynnwood School
Programme MYP
MYP Coordinator Kelly Davis Chernishenko
Gender Coeducational
Boarding/day Boarding
15451-84 Avenue, Edmonton AB, T5R 3Y1,
Canada
TELEPHONE: +1 780 489 4500

M E La Zerte High School
Status State
Programme Diploma
Diploma Coordinator Trina Empson
Gender Coeducational
Languages English
Boarding/day Day
6804-144 Avenue, Edmonton AB, T5C 3C7,
Canada
TELEPHONE: +1 780 408 9800
FAX: +1 780 472 0058
EMAIL: sburghar@epsb.ca
WEBSITE: http://melazerte.com

McNally School
Status State
Programme Diploma
Diploma Coordinator Laurel Usher
Gender Coeducational
Languages English
Boarding/day Day
8440-105 Avenue, Edmonton AB, T6A 1B6,
Canada
TELEPHONE: +1 780 469 0442
FAX: +1 780 465 5958
EMAIL: grice@epsb.ca

Old Scona Academic High School
Status State
Programme Diploma
Diploma Coordinator Lorne Pascoe
Gender Coeducational
Languages English
Boarding/day Day
10523-84th Avenue, Edmonton AB, T6E 2H5,
Canada
TELEPHONE: +1 780 433 0627
FAX: +1 780 433 4994
EMAIL: lyaniw@epsb.ca

Ross Sheppard Composite High School
Status State
Programme Diploma
Diploma Coordinator B. Jane Taylor
Gender Coeducational
Languages English
Boarding/day Day
13546-111th Avenue, Edmonton AB, T5M 2P2,
Canada
TELEPHONE: +1 780 448-5000
FAX: +1 780 452 7563
EMAIL: marilyn.cross@epsb.ca
WEBSITE: www.shep.net

Salisbury Composite High School
Status State
Programme Diploma
Diploma Coordinator Hugh Ross
Gender Coeducational
Languages English
Boarding/day Day
#20 Festival Way, Sherwood Park AB, T8A 4Y1,
Canada
TELEPHONE: +1 403 467 8816
EMAIL: dianna.sacha@ei.educ.ab.ca

**Sir Winston Churchill High School,
Calgary**
Status State
Programme Diploma
Diploma Coordinator Cody Antonuk
Gender Coeducational
Languages English
Boarding/day Day
5220 Northland Drive NW, Calgary AB,
T2L 2J6, Canada
TELEPHONE: +1 403 289 9241
FAX: +1 403 777-7309
EMAIL: jhunt@cbe.ab.ca

St Albert Catholic High School
Status State
Programme Diploma
Diploma Coordinator Cindy Madill
Languages English
33 Malmo Drive, St Albert AB, T8N 1L5,
Canada
TELEPHONE: +1 780 459 7781
FAX: +1 780 458 7912
EMAIL: podea@sachs.gsacrd.ab.ca

**St Clement Catholic Elementary/Junior
High School**
Status State
Programme PYP, MYP
MYP Coordinator Brent McDonough
PYP Coordinator Rosanne Boutin
Gender Coeducational
Boarding/day Boarding
7620 Mill Woods Road South, Edmonton AB,
T6K 2P7, Canada
TELEPHONE: +1 780 462 3806
EMAIL: tourangeauk@ecsd.net
WEBSITE: www.stclement.ecsd.net

St Edmund Elementary School
Programme MYP
MYP Coordinator Daniel Forest
Gender Coeducational
Boarding/day Boarding
10810-142 Street, Edmonton AB, T5N 2P7,
Canada
TELEPHONE: +1 780 451 1470
EMAIL: myskiww@ecsd.net

St Edmund Junior High School
Status State
Programme PYP
PYP Coordinator Dana Hutton
Gender Coeducational
11712-130th Avenue, Edmonton AB, T5E 0V2,
Canada
TELEPHONE: +1 780-453-1596
EMAIL: rankinl@ecsd.net
WEBSITE: http://stedmund.ecsd.net

St Mary's High School
Status State
Programme Diploma
Diploma Coordinator Janet Herrem
Gender Coeducational
Languages English
Boarding/day Day
111-18th Avenue SW, Calgary Catholic,
Calgary AB, T2S 0B8, Canada
TELEPHONE: +1 403 228 5810
FAX: +1 403 229 9280
EMAIL: simone.gratton@cssd.ab.ca
WEBSITE: http://stmaryshs.calgary.ab.ca

**St Thomas More Catholic Junior High
School**
Programme MYP
MYP Coordinator John Fiacco
Gender Coeducational
Boarding/day Boarding
9610-165 Street, Edmonton AB, T5P 3S6,
Canada
TELEPHONE: +1 101 780 484 2434
EMAIL: myskiww@ecsd.net

Strathcona Tweedsmuir School
Status Private
Programme PYP, Diploma
Diploma Coordinator Bob Shaw
PYP Coordinator Peggy Bumanis
Gender Coeducational
Languages English
Boarding/day Day
RR #2, Okotoks AB, T1S 1A2, Canada
TELEPHONE: +1 403 938 8302
FAX: +1 403 938 8319
EMAIL: raaflac@sts.ab.ca
WEBSITE: www.sts.ab.ca

**Victoria School of Performing and
Visual Arts**
Status State
Programme PYP, MYP, Diploma
Diploma Coordinator Bill Howe
MYP Coordinator Kelly Davis Chernishenko
PYP Coordinator Cheryl Weighill
Gender Coeducational
Languages English
Boarding/day Day
10210-108 Avenue, Edmonton AB, T5H 1A8,
Canada
TELEPHONE: +1 780 426 3010
EMAIL: ingrid.neitsch@epsb.ca
WEBSITE: http://victoria.epsb.net

**Vincent J Maloney Catholic Junior High
School**
Status State
Programme MYP
MYP Coordinator Adrian Joosten
Gender Coeducational
Languages English
Boarding/day Day
20 Mont Clare Place, St Albert AB, T8N 1K9,
Canada
TELEPHONE: +1 780 458 1113
FAX: +1 780 458 6261
EMAIL: scimino@gsacrd.ab.ca
WEBSITE: www.vjm.gsacrd.ab.ca

Western Canada High School
Status State
Programme Diploma
Diploma Coordinator David Kelly
Gender Coeducational
Languages English
Boarding/day Day
641-17th Avenue South West, Calgary AB,
T2S 0B5, Canada
TELEPHONE: +1 403 228 5363
FAX: +1 403 777 7089

Westglen School
Programme MYP
MYP Coordinator Kelly Davis Chernishenko
Gender Coeducational
Boarding/day Boarding
10950-127 Street, Edmonton AB, T5M 0S7,
Canada
TELEPHONE: +1 780 454 3449

Westminster School
Programme MYP
MYP Coordinator Kelly Davis Chernishenko
Gender Coeducational
Boarding/day Boarding
13712-102 Avenue, Edmonton AB, T5N 0W4,
Canada
TELEPHONE: +1 780 452 4343

Winston Churchill High School
Status State
Programme Diploma
Diploma Coordinator Carey Rowntree
Gender Coeducational
Languages English
Boarding/day Day
1605-15th Avenue North, Lethbridge AB,
T1H 1W4, Canada
TELEPHONE: +1 403 328 4723
FAX: +1 403 329 4572
EMAIL: clark.bosch@lethsd.ab.ca
WEBSITE: www.wchs.lethsd.ab.ca

British Columbia

Abbotsford Collegiate
Status State
Programme Diploma
Diploma Coordinator Karen Saenger
Gender Coeducational
Languages English
Boarding/day Day
2329 Crescent Way, Abbotsford BC, V2S 3M1,
Canada
TELEPHONE: +1 604-853-3367
FAX: +1 604-853-3045

Aspengrove School
Status Private
Programme PYP, MYP
MYP Coordinator Sarah Marshall
PYP Coordinator Sofia LaBounty
Gender Coeducational
Languages English
Boarding/day Day
7660 Clark Drive, RR2, Lantzville BC,
V0R 2H0, Canada
TELEPHONE: +1 250 390 2201
FAX: +1 250 390 2281
EMAIL: zfitzgerald@aspengroveschool.ca
WEBSITE: http://aspengroveschool.ca

Britannia Secondary School
Status State
Programme Diploma
Diploma Coordinator Leo Boissy
Gender Coeducational
Languages English
Boarding/day Day
1001 Cotton Drive, Vancouver BC, V5L 3T4,
Canada
TELEPHONE: +1 604 713 8266
FAX: +1 604 713 8265
EMAIL: rclark@vsb.bc.ca
WEBSITE: http://britannia.vsb.bc.ca

Brockton Preparatory School
Status Private
Programme PYP
PYP Coordinator Sandy Brun
Gender Coeducational
Languages English
Boarding/day Day
3467 Duval Road, North Vancouver BC,
V7J 3E8, Canada
TELEPHONE: +1 604 929 9201
FAX: +1 604 929 9501
EMAIL: rhinnell@brocktonschool.com
WEBSITE: www.brocktonschool.com

G W Graham Middle-Secondary School
Status State
Programme MYP
MYP Coordinator Terry Jensen
45955 Thomas Road, Chilliwack BC, V2R 0B5,
Canada
TELEPHONE: +1 604 847 0772
FAX: +1 604 824 0711
EMAIL: diego_testa@sd33.bc.ca
WEBSITE: www.gwgraham.ca

Garibaldi Secondary School
Status State
Programme Diploma
Diploma Coordinator Steve Moore
Gender Coeducational
Languages English
Boarding/day Day
24789 Dewdney Trunk Road, Maple Ridge BC,
V4R 1X2, Canada
TELEPHONE: +1 604 463 6287
FAX: +1 604 463 0896
EMAIL: sderinzy@sd42.ca
WEBSITE: http://gss.sd42.ca

Glenlyon Norfolk School
Status Private
Programme PYP, MYP, Diploma
Diploma Coordinator Jane Hicks
MYP Coordinator Heather Lapper
PYP Coordinator Tanya de Hoog
Gender Coeducational
Languages English
Boarding/day Day
801 Bank Street, Victoria BC, V8S 4A8,
Canada
TELEPHONE: +1 250 370-6802
FAX: +1 250 370-6811
EMAIL: head@glenlyonnorfolk.bc.ca
WEBSITE: www.glenlyonnorfolk.bc.ca

King George Secondary
Status State
Programme MYP
MYP Coordinator Fernanda Pires
Gender Coeducational
Languages English
Boarding/day Day
1755 Barclay Street, Vancouver BC, V6G 1K6,
Canada
TELEPHONE: +1 604 713 8999
FAX: +1 604 713 8998
EMAIL: thowe@vsb.bc.ca
WEBSITE: http://kgdragons.com

Lester B Pearson/UWC of the Pacific
Status Private
Programme Diploma
Diploma Coordinator Laura Fulton
Gender Coeducational
Languages English
Boarding/day Boarding
650 Pearson College Drive, Victoria BC,
V9C 4H7, Canada
TELEPHONE: +1 250 391 2411
FAX: +1 250 391 2412
EMAIL: admin@pearsoncollege.ca
WEBSITE: www.pearsoncollege.ca

Lord Roberts Elementary School
Status State
Programme MYP
MYP Coordinator Grant Miller
Gender Coeducational
Languages English
Boarding/day Day
1100 Bidwell Street, Vancouver BC, V6G 2K4,
Canada
TELEPHONE: +1 604 713 5055
FAX: +1 604 713 5057
EMAIL: vcoopersmith@vsb.bc.ca
WEBSITE: http://lordroberts.vsb.bc.ca

MEADOWRIDGE SCHOOL
Status Independent
Programme PYP, MYP
MYP Coordinator Ms Kuldeep Thendal
PYP Coordinator Mr Terry Donaldson
Gender Coeducational
Languages English
Boarding/day Day
12224-240th Street, Maple Ridge BC,
V4R 1N1, Canada
TELEPHONE: +1 604 467 4444
FAX: +1 604 467 4989
EMAIL: info@meadowridge.bc.ca
WEBSITE: www.meadowridge.bc.ca
see full details on page 114

Mountain Secondary School
Status State
Programme Diploma
Diploma Coordinator Lynn Gibson
Gender Coeducational
Languages English
Boarding/day Day
7755-202 A Street, Langley BC, V2Y 1W4,
Canada
TELEPHONE: +1 604 888 3033
FAX: +1 604 888 2873
EMAIL: dmichel@sd35.bc.ca
WEBSITE: www.msssd35.bc.ca

MULGRAVE INDEPENDENT SCHOOL
Status Private
Programme PYP, Diploma
Diploma Coordinator Isobel Willard
PYP Coordinator Patricia Jolley
Gender Coeducational
Languages English
Boarding/day Day
2330 Cypress Lane, West Vancouver BC,
V7S 3H9, Canada
TELEPHONE: +1 604 922 3223
FAX: +1 604 922 3328
EMAIL: tmacoun@mulgrave.com
WEBSITE: www.mulgrave.com
see full details on page 118

New Westminster Secondary School
Status State
Programme Diploma
Diploma Coordinator Jim Janz
Gender Coeducational
Languages English
Boarding/day Day
835 Eighth Street, New Westminster BC,
V3M 3S9, Canada
TELEPHONE: +1 604 517 6220
FAX: +1 604 517 6204
EMAIL: jsahli@sd40.bc.ca

Pacific Academy
Status Private
Programme Diploma
Diploma Coordinator Brad Smith
Gender Coeducational
Languages English
Boarding/day Day
10238-168th Street, Surrey BC, V4N 1Z4,
Canada
TELEPHONE: +1 604 581 5353
FAX: +1 604 581 0087
EMAIL: tkooy@papcs.com
WEBSITE: www.pacificacademy.net

Port Moody Secondary School
Status State
Programme Diploma
Diploma Coordinator Laurie Saucier
Gender Coeducational
Languages English
Boarding/day Day
300 Albert Street, Port Moody BC, V3H 2M5,
Canada
TELEPHONE: +1 604 939 6656
FAX: +1 604 939 5833
EMAIL: kjensen@sd43.bc.ca
WEBSITE: http://pmssblues.net

Richmond Senior Secondary School
Status State
Programme Diploma
Diploma Coordinator Remigio Vicente
Gender Coeducational
Languages English
Boarding/day Day
7171 Minoru Boulevard, Richmond BC,
V6Y 1Z3, Canada
TELEPHONE: +1 604 668 6400
FAX: +1 604 668 6405
EMAIL: dmacklam@richmond.sd38.bc.ca

Semiahmoo Secondary School
Status State
Programme Diploma
Diploma Coordinator David Baldasso
Gender Coeducational
Languages English
Boarding/day Day
1785-148th Street, Surrey BC, V4A 4M6,
Canada
TELEPHONE: +1 604 536 6174
FAX: +1 604 536 4970
EMAIL: clarke_s@fc.sd36.bc.ca
WEBSITE: www.semi.sd36.bc.ca/ibdept

Sir Winston Churchill Secondary School, Vancouver
Status State
Programme Diploma
Diploma Coordinator Isobel Willard
Gender Coeducational
Languages English
Boarding/day Day
7055 Heather Street, Vancouver BC, V6P 3P7,
Canada
TELEPHONE: +1 604 713 8189
FAX: +1 604 713 8188
EMAIL: akrawczyk@vsb.bc.ca

Southridge Junior School
Status Private
Programme PYP
PYP Coordinator Shanaz Ramji
Gender Coeducational
Languages English
Boarding/day Day
2656-160th Street, Surrey BC, V3S 0B7,
Canada
TELEPHONE: +1 604 535 5056
FAX: +1 604 542 2343
EMAIL: dstephen@southridge.bc.ca
WEBSITE: www.southridge.bc.ca

Stratford Hall
Status Private
Programme PYP, Diploma
Diploma Coordinator Matthew Allen
PYP Coordinator Rama Ramswamy
Gender Coeducational
Languages English
Boarding/day Day
3000 Commercial Drive, Vancouver BC,
V5N 4E2, Canada
TELEPHONE: +1 604 436 0608
EMAIL: jmcconnell@stratfordhall.bc.ca
WEBSITE: www.stratfordhall.bc.ca

West Bay Elementary
Status State
Programme PYP
PYP Coordinator Misty Paterson
Gender Coeducational
Languages English
Boarding/day Day
3175 Thompson Place, West Vancouver BC,
V7V 3E3, Canada
TELEPHONE: +1 604 981 1260
FAX: +1 604 981 1261
EMAIL: mlaudien@sd45.bc.ca
WEBSITE: http://sd45.bc.ca

West Vancouver Secondary School
Status State
Programme Diploma
Diploma Coordinator Hilary Matts
Gender Coeducational
Languages English
Boarding/day Mixed
1750 Mathers Avenue, West Vancouver BC,
V7V 2G7, Canada
TELEPHONE: +1 604 981 1100
FAX: +1 604 981 1101
EMAIL: swareing@sd45.bc.ca
WEBSITE: www.sd45.bc.ca

Manitoba

Balmoral Hall School
Status State
Programme PYP
PYP Coordinator Jackie Copp
Gender Female
Languages English
Boarding/day Mixed
630 Westminster Ave, Winnipeg MB, R3C 3S1,
Canada
TELEPHONE: +1 204 784 1600
FAX: +1 204 774 5534
EMAIL: csumerlus@balmoralhall.com
WEBSITE: www.balmoralhall.com

Collège Louis-Riel
Status State
Programme Diploma
Diploma Coordinator Claudine Lupien
Gender Coeducational
Boarding/day Day
585 rue Saint-Jean-Baptiste, Winnipeg MB,
R2H 2Y2, Canada
TELEPHONE: +1 204 237 8927
EMAIL: mmatte@atrium.ca
WEBSITE: www.louis-riel.mb.ca

Collège Sturgeon Heights Collegiate
Status State
Programme Diploma
Diploma Coordinator Ivano Buccini
Gender Coeducational
Languages English
Boarding/day Day
350 Lodge Avenue, Winnipeg MB, R3J 0S4,
Canada
TELEPHONE: +1 204 837 1321
FAX: +1 204 889 9997
EMAIL: rpelletier@sjsd.net

Kelvin High School
Status State
Programme Diploma
Diploma Coordinator Melani Decelles
Gender Coeducational
Languages English
Boarding/day Day
155 Kingsway, Winnipeg MB, R3M 0G3,
Canada
TELEPHONE: +1 204 474 1492
FAX: +1 204 453 2116
EMAIL: jhornsby@wsd1.org

Miles MacDonell Collegiate
Status State
Programme Diploma
Diploma Coordinator John Syvitski
Gender Coeducational
Languages English
Boarding/day Day
757 Roch Street, Winnipeg MB, R2K 2R1,
Canada
TELEPHONE: +1 204 667 1103
FAX: +1 204 654 3803
EMAIL: gbowles@retsd.mb.ca

Neelin High School
Status State
Programme Diploma
Diploma Coordinator Tannis MacDonald
Gender Coeducational
Languages English
Boarding/day Day
1020 Brandon Ave, Brandon MB, R7A 1K6,
Canada
TELEPHONE: +1 204 729 3180
FAX: +1 204 726 5813
EMAIL: malazdrewicz.greg@
portal.brandonsd.mb.ca
WEBSITE: www.brandonsd.mb.ca/neelin

Westwood Collegiate
Status State
Programme Diploma
Diploma Coordinator Al Allison
Gender Coeducational
Languages English
Boarding/day Day
360 Rouge Road, Winnipeg MB, R3K 1K3,
Canada
TELEPHONE: +1 204 888 7650
FAX: +1 204 889 0802
EMAIL: slockhart@sjsd.net

New Brunswick

Ecole Mathieu-Martin
Status State
Programme Diploma
Diploma Coordinator Ronald LeBlanc
Gender Coeducational
Languages French
Boarding/day Day
511 rue Champlain, Dieppe NB, E1A 1P2,
Canada
TELEPHONE: +1 506 856-2791
FAX: +1 506 856-2779
EMAIL: melansyl@nbed.nb.ca

Rothesay Netherwood School
Status Private
Programme Diploma
Diploma Coordinator Tammy Earle
Gender Coeducational
Languages English
Boarding/day Mixed
40 College Hill Road, Rothesay NB, E2E 5H1,
Canada
TELEPHONE: +1 506 847 8224
FAX: +1 506 848 0851
EMAIL: kitchnep@rns.cc
WEBSITE: www.rns.cc

St John High School
Status State
Programme Diploma
Diploma Coordinator Ann Perry
Gender Coeducational
Languages English
Boarding/day Day
170-200 Prince William Street, #8,
Saint John NB, E2L 2B7, Canada
TELEPHONE: +1 506 658 5358
FAX: +1 506 658 3745
EMAIL: barry.harbinson@nbed.nb.ca
WEBSITE: www.sjhigh.ca

Newfoundland & Labrador

Holy Heart of Mary High School
Status State
Programme Diploma
Diploma Coordinator Colleen Field
Gender Coeducational
Languages English
Boarding/day Day
55 Bonaventure Avenue, Torbay NL, A1C 3Z3,
Canada
TELEPHONE: +1 709 754 1600
FAX: +1 709 754 0855
EMAIL: dcooper@stemnet.ca
WEBSITE: www.hhm.k12.nf.ca

Nova Scotia

Avon View High School
Status State
Programme Diploma
Diploma Coordinator Claire Surette
Gender Coeducational
Languages English
Boarding/day Day
PO Box 700, Windsor NS, B0N 2T0, Canada
TELEPHONE: +1 902 792 6740
FAX: +1 902 792 6762
EMAIL: larry.frenette@avrsb.ednet.ns.ca
WEBSITE: www.avhs.ednet.ns.ca

Charles P Allen High School
Status State
Programme Diploma
Diploma Coordinator Jennifer Williams
Gender Coeducational
Languages English
Boarding/day Day
196 Rocky Lake Drive, Bedford NS, B4A 2T6,
Canada
TELEPHONE: +1 902 832 8964
FAX: +1 902 832 8981
EMAIL: lewis@staff.ednet.ns.ca
WEBSITE: www.cpa.ednet.ns.ca

Cobequid Educational Centre
Status State
Programme Diploma
Diploma Coordinator Terry Thorsen
Gender Coeducational
Languages English
Boarding/day Day
34 Lorne Street, Truro NS, B2N 3K3, Canada
TELEPHONE: +1 902 896 5700
FAX: +1 902 896 5707
EMAIL: cecprincipal@ccrsb.ednet.ns.ca
WEBSITE:
http://schools.ccrsb.ednet.ns.ca/cec

Cole Harbour District High School
Status State
Programme Diploma
Diploma Coordinator Mark Sweetapple
Gender Coeducational
Languages English
Boarding/day Day
2 Chameau Cresent, Dartmouth NS,
B2W 4X4, Canada
TELEPHONE: +1 902 464 5220
FAX: +1 902 464 5241
WEBSITE: www.coleharbourhigh.ednet.ns.ca

Dr John Hugh Gills Regional High School
Status State
Programme Diploma
Diploma Coordinator Mary MacDonald
Gender Coeducational
Languages English
Boarding/day Day
105 Braemore Avenue, Antigonish NS,
B2G 1L3, Canada
TELEPHONE: +1 902 863 1620
FAX: +1 902 863 8284
EMAIL: arnie.farrell@strait.ednet.ns.ca
WEBSITE: www.drjohngillis.ednet.ns.ca

École du Carrefour
Status State
Programme Diploma
Diploma Coordinator Sophie Pedneault
201A Avenue du Portage, Dartmouth NS,
B2X 3T4, Canada
TELEPHONE: +1 902 433 7000
FAX: +1 902 433 7020
EMAIL: eartha.monard@csap.ednet.ns.ca
WEBSITE: http://carrefour.ednet.ns.ca

Halifax Grammar School
Status Private
Programme Diploma
Diploma Coordinator Laura Brock
Gender Coeducational
Languages English
Boarding/day Day
5750 Atlantic Street, Halifax NS, B3H 1G9,
Canada
TELEPHONE: +1 902 422 6497
FAX: +1 902 422 4884
EMAIL: headmaster@hgs.ns.ca
WEBSITE: www.hgs.ns.ca

Halifax West High School
Status State
Programme Diploma
Diploma Coordinator Joanne Des Roches
Gender Coeducational
Languages English
Boarding/day Day
283 Thomas Raddall Drive, Halifax NS,
B3S 1R1, Canada
TELEPHONE: +1 902 457 8900
FAX: +1 902 457 8980
EMAIL: walker@hrsb.ns.ca
WEBSITE: www.hwhs.ednet.ns.ca

King's-Edgehill School
Status Private
Programme Diploma
Diploma Coordinator Debra Medina
Gender Coeducational
Languages English
Boarding/day Mixed
33 King's-Edgehill Lane, Windsor NS,
B0N 2T0, Canada
TELEPHONE: +1 902 798 2278
FAX: +1 902 798 2105
EMAIL: jseagram@kes.ns.ca
WEBSITE: www.kes.ns.ca

**Northumberland Regional High
School**
Status State
Programme Diploma
Diploma Coordinator Jeffery Green
Gender Coeducational
Languages English, French
Boarding/day Day
104 Alma Road, RR #3, Westville NS,
B0K 2A0, Canada
TELEPHONE: +1 902 396 2750
FAX: +1 902 396 2755
EMAIL: nrhsprincipal@ccrsb.ednet.ns.ca
WEBSITE: http://schools.ccrsb.ednet.ns.ca/
nrhs/home1.htm

Park View Education Centre
Status State
Programme Diploma
Diploma Coordinator Charlotte Brooks
Gender Coeducational
Languages English
Boarding/day Day
1485 King Street, Bridgewater NS, B4V 1C4,
Canada
TELEPHONE: +1 902 541 8200
FAX: +1 902 541 8210
EMAIL: precprincipal@ssrsb.ca
WEBSITE: www.pvec.ednet.ns.ca

Prince Andrew High School
Status State
Programme Diploma
Diploma Coordinator Debra Roberts-Regan
Gender Coeducational
Languages English
Boarding/day Day
37 Woodlawn Road, Dartmouth NS, B2W 2R7,
Canada
TELEPHONE: +1 902 435 8452
FAX: +1 902 435 8398
EMAIL: dmackenzie@hrsb.ns.ca
WEBSITE: www.pahs.ednet.ns.ca

Queen Elizabeth High School
Status State
Programme Diploma
Diploma Coordinator Ian Morrison
Gender Coeducational
Languages English
Boarding/day Day
1929 Robie Street, Halifax NS, B3H 3G1,
Canada
TELEPHONE: +1 902 421 6804
FAX: +1 902 421 2523
EMAIL: qeh@staff.ednet.ns.ca
WEBSITE: www.qeh.ednet.ns.ca

Sydney Academy
Status State
Programme Diploma
Diploma Coordinator Janet Beaton
Languages English
Boarding/day Day
49 Terrace Street, Sydney NS, B1P 2L4, Canada
TELEPHONE: +1 902 562 5464
FAX: +1 902 564 4472
EMAIL: bdwyer@sacademy.cbv.ns.ca

**Yarmouth Consolidated Memorial
High School**
Status State
Programme Diploma
Diploma Coordinator Michael Drew
Gender Coeducational
Languages English
Boarding/day Day
52 Parade Street, Yarmouth NS, B5A 3A9,
Canada
TELEPHONE: +1 902 749 2810
FAX: +1 902 749 2811
EMAIL: bjamieson@tcrsb.ca
WEBSITE: www.ycmhs.com

Ontario

Académie de la Capitale
Status Private
Programme PYP
PYP Coordinator Linda Halberstadt
Gender Coeducational
Languages French, English
Boarding/day Day
1010 Morrison Dr Suite 200, Ottawa ON,
K2H 8K7, Canada
TELEPHONE: +1 613 721 3872
EMAIL: info@acadecap.org
WEBSITE: www.acadecap.org

**Académie Ste Cécile International
School**
Status Private
Programme Diploma
Diploma Coordinator Ron Kingham
Gender Coeducational
Languages English
Boarding/day Mixed
925 Cousineau Road, Windsor ON, N9G 1V8,
Canada
TELEPHONE: +1 519 969 1291
FAX: +1 519 969 7953
EMAIL: stececil@uwindsor.ca
WEBSITE: www.stececile.ca

Arlington Middle School
Programme MYP
MYP Coordinator Kathy Botham
Gender Coeducational
Boarding/day Day
501 Arlington Avenue, Toronto ON, M6C 3A4,
Canada
TELEPHONE: +1 416 394 2200

Ashbury College
Status Private
Programme Diploma
Diploma Coordinator Marilynne Sinclair
Gender Coeducational
Languages English
Boarding/day Mixed
362 Mariposa Avenue, Ottawa ON, K1M 0T3,
Canada
TELEPHONE: +1 613 749 5954
FAX: +1 613 749 9724
EMAIL: tmatthews@ashbury.on.ca
WEBSITE: www.ashbury.ca

**Assumption College Catholic High
School**
Status State
Programme Diploma
Diploma Coordinator Genevieve Cano
Gender Coeducational
Languages English
Boarding/day Day
1100 Huron Church Road, Windsor ON,
N9C 2K7, Canada
TELEPHONE: +1 519-256-7801 ext 278
FAX: +1 519-256-0417
EMAIL: marymargaret_parent@wecdsb.on.ca
WEBSITE: www.wecdsb.on.ca

Bayview Hill Elementary School
Status State
Programme PYP
PYP Coordinator Rita Angellotti
Gender Coeducational
Languages English
Boarding/day Day
81 Strathearn Avenue, Richmond Hill ON,
L4B 2J5, Canada
TELEPHONE: +1 905 508 0806
FAX: +1 905 508 6119
EMAIL: david.honsberger@yrdsb.edu.on.ca
WEBSITE:
www.cfbisd.edu/schools/goo/index.htm

Bayview Secondary School
Status State
Programme Diploma
Diploma Coordinator Gerry Trefler
Gender Coeducational
Languages English
Boarding/day Day
10077 Bayview Avenue, Richmond Hill ON,
L4C 2L4, Canada
TELEPHONE: +1 905 884 4453
FAX: +1 905 770 3580
EMAIL: peter.tse@yrdsb.edu.on.ca
WEBSITE: www.bayview.ss.yrdsb.edu.on.ca

BRANKSOME HALL
Status Independent
Programme PYP, MYP, Diploma
Diploma Coordinator David Mindorff
MYP Coordinator Heather Friesen
PYP Coordinator Anne Beveridge
Gender Female
Languages English
Boarding/day Mixed
10 Elm Avenue, Toronto ON, M4W 1N4,
Canada
TELEPHONE: +1 416 920 9741
FAX: +1 416 920 5390
EMAIL: kmurton@branksome.on.ca
WEBSITE: www.branksome.on.ca
see full details on page 63

Brockville Collegiate Institute
Status State
Programme Diploma
Diploma Coordinator Philip Wells
Gender Coeducational
Languages English
Boarding/day Day
90 Pearl Street East, Brockville ON, K6V1P8,
Canada
TELEPHONE: +1 613-345-5641
FAX: +1 613-498-2563
EMAIL: david.coombs@ucdsb.on.ca
WEBSITE: www.bcirams.ca

Cameron Heights Collegiate Institute
Status State
Programme Diploma
Diploma Coordinator Roger Roth
Gender Coeducational
Languages English
301 Charles Street East, Kitchener ON,
N2G 2P8, Canada
TELEPHONE: +1 519 578 8330
FAX: +1 519 578 1376
EMAIL: kelly_kempel@wrdsb.on.ca

Catholic Central High School
Status State
Programme Diploma
Diploma Coordinator Maurice Blanchard
Gender Coeducational
Languages English
Boarding/day Day
450 Dundas Street, London ON, N6B 3K3,
Canada
TELEPHONE: +1 519 675 4431
FAX: +1 519 433 1934
EMAIL: d.hammond@ldcsb.on.ca
WEBSITE: www.ldcsb.on.ca

Cobourg District Collegiate Institute East
Status State
Programme Diploma
Diploma Coordinator Bruce LePage
Gender Coeducational
Languages English
Boarding/day Day
335 King Street East, Cobourg ON, K9A 1M2,
Canada
TELEPHONE: +1 905 372 2271
FAX: +1 905 372 5343
EMAIL: charlotte_majic@kprdsb.ca
WEBSITE: www.cobourgeast.ca

Collège Catholique Franco-Ouest
Status State
Programme MYP, Diploma
Diploma Coordinator Nathalie Kayser
MYP Coordinator Kim Brisebois
Gender Coeducational
Languages French
Boarding/day Day
411 promenade Seyton, Nepean ON, K2H 8X1,
Canada
TELEPHONE: +1 613 820 2920
FAX: +1 613 820 7593
EMAIL: poulif@ceclf.edu.on.ca
WEBSITE: www.ceclf.edu.on.ca/fou

Colonel By Secondary School
Status State
Programme Diploma
Diploma Coordinator Michel Bélanger
Gender Coeducational
Languages English
Boarding/day Day
2381 Ogilvie Road, Ottawa ON, K1J 7N4,
Canada
TELEPHONE: +1 613 745 9411
FAX: +1 613 745 4680
EMAIL: france_thibault@ocdsb.edu.on.ca
WEBSITE: www.colonelby.com

École secondaire catholique Père-René-de-Galinée
Status State
Programme MYP
MYP Coordinator Hélène-Pascale Lemieux
450 chemin Maple Grove, Cambridge ON,
N3H 4R7, Canada
TELEPHONE: +1 519 650 9444
FAX: +1 519 650 9313
EMAIL: cwilson@csdccs.edu.on.ca
WEBSITE: http://prdg.csdccs.edu.on.ca

École secondaire catholique Sainte-Famille
Status State
Programme MYP, Diploma
Diploma Coordinator Nathalie Bédard
MYP Coordinator Alain Lalonde
Gender Coeducational
Languages French
Boarding/day Day
1780 Boulevard Meadowvale,
Mississauga ON, L5N 7K8, Canada
TELEPHONE: +11 905 814 0318
FAX: +11 905 814 8480
EMAIL: drouselle@csdccs.edu.on.ca
WEBSITE: www.ste-famille.com

École secondaire Jeunes sans frontières
Status State
Programme Diploma
Diploma Coordinator Dr Irène Leroy-Syed
Gender Coeducational
Languages French
Boarding/day Day
1445 Promenade Lewisham, Mississauga ON,
L5J 3R2, Canada
TELEPHONE: +1 905 823 4424
EMAIL: lambertx@csdcso.on.ca
WEBSITE:
www.jeunessansfrontieres.csdcso.on.ca

École Secondaire Publique Deslauriers
Status State
Programme MYP, Diploma
Diploma Coordinator Claude Ethier
MYP Coordinator Iftin Osman
Gender Coeducational
Languages French
Boarding/day Day
159 Chesterton, Ottawa ON, K2E 7E6, Canada
TELEPHONE: +1 613 820 0992
FAX: +1 613 820 9012
EMAIL: lucie.archambault@cepeo.on.ca
WEBSITE: www.deslauriers.cepeo.on.ca

Elmwood School
Status Private
Programme PYP, MYP, Diploma
Diploma Coordinator Gretta Bradley
MYP Coordinator Gretta Bradley
PYP Coordinator Kate Angell
Gender Female
Languages English
Boarding/day Day
261 Buena Vista Road, Ottawa ON, K1M 0V9,
Canada
TELEPHONE: +1 613 749 6761
FAX: +1 613 741 8210
EMAIL: cboughton@elmwood.on.ca
WEBSITE: www.elmwood.on.ca

Georgetown District High School
Status State
Programme Diploma
Diploma Coordinator James Ha
Gender Coeducational
Languages English
Boarding/day Day
70 Guelph Street, Georgetown ON, L7G 3Z5,
Canada
TELEPHONE: +1 905 877 6966
FAX: +1 905 873 9689
EMAIL: millers@hdsb.ca
WEBSITE:
www.georgetowndistricthighschool.com/ib

Glenforest Secondary School
Status State
Programme Diploma
Diploma Coordinator Grace Dittrich
Gender Coeducational
Languages English
3575 Fieldgate Drive, Mississauga ON,
L4X 2J6, Canada
TELEPHONE: +1 905 625 7731
EMAIL: bryonie.baxter@peelsb.co
WEBSITE: www.glenforestlibrary.com

Grey Gables International School of Niagara
Status Private
Programme MYP
Gender Coeducational
Languages English
Boarding/day Day
1 Dexter Street, St Catharines ON, L2S 2L4,
Canada
TELEPHONE: +1 905 685 4577
FAX: +1 905 685 5102
EMAIL:
kathleenmiller@greygablesschool.com
WEBSITE: www.greygablesschool.com

Harrison Public Elementary School
Status State
Programme PYP
PYP Coordinator Cathy Shore
Gender Coeducational
Boarding/day Day
81 Harrison Road, Toronto ON, M2L 1V9,
Canada
TELEPHONE: +1 416 395 2530
EMAIL: paul.woods@tdsb.on.ca

I E Weldon Secondary School
Status State
Programme Diploma
Diploma Coordinator Marilyn Thayer
Gender Coeducational
Languages English
Boarding/day Boarding
24 Weldon Road, Lindsay ON, K9V 4R6,
Canada
TELEPHONE: +1 705 324 3585
FAX: +1 705 878 3685
EMAIL: richard.evans@tldsb.on.ca
WEBSITE: www.tldsb.on.ca/schools/iewss

Kenner Collegiate Vocational Institute & Intermediate School
Status State
Programme Diploma
Diploma Coordinator Ellen Bond
Gender Coeducational
Languages English
Boarding/day Day
633 Monaghan Road South,
Peterborough ON, K9J 5J2, Canada
TELEPHONE: +1 705 743 2181
FAX: +1 705 749 6238
EMAIL: john_ringereide@kprdsb.ca
WEBSITE: www.kenner.kprdsb.ca

Kingston Collegiate & Vocational Institute
Status State
Programme Diploma
Diploma Coordinator David Stocks
Gender Coeducational
Languages English
235 Frontenac Street, Kingston ON, K7L3S7,
Canada
TELEPHONE: +1 613 544 4811
FAX: +1 613 544 8795
EMAIL: kicvi@limestone.on.ca

Korah Collegiate and Vocational School
Status State
Programme Diploma
Diploma Coordinator Paul Caldbick
Gender Coeducational
Languages English
636 Goulais Avenue, Sault Ste Marie ON,
P6C 5A7, Canada
TELEPHONE: +1 705 945 7180
EMAIL: wicketh@adsb.on.ca

Le Collège Français
Status State
Programme Diploma
Diploma Coordinator Bruce Bartlett
Gender Coeducational
Languages French
Boarding/day Day
100 rue Carlton, Toronto ON, M5B 1M3,
Canada
TELEPHONE: +1 416 393 0175
FAX: +1 416 393 0884
EMAIL: durandj@csdcso.on.ca

Lo-Ellen Park Secondary School
Status State
Programme Diploma
Diploma Coordinator Alison Gomm
Gender Coeducational
Languages English
275 Loach's Road, Sudbury ON, P3E 2P8,
Canada
TELEPHONE: +1 705 522 2320
FAX: +1 705 522 8178
EMAIL: mckibbj@rainbowschools.ca

Michael Power – St Joseph High School
Status State
Programme Diploma
Diploma Coordinator Adrienne Murphy
Languages English
105 Eringate Drive, Toronto ON, M9C 3Z7,
Canada
TELEPHONE: +1 416 393 5529
FAX: +1 416 393 5742
EMAIL: rory.mcguckin@tcdsb.org

Milne Valley Middle School
Status State
Programme MYP
MYP Coordinator Marlene Reynolds
Gender Coeducational
Languages English
Boarding/day Day
100 Underhill Drive, Toronto ON, M3A 2J9,
Canada
TELEPHONE: +1 416 395 2700
FAX: +1 416 395 3958
EMAIL: ruth.bell-libera@tdsb.on.ca

Moira Secondary School
Status State
Programme Diploma
Diploma Coordinator Peter Nagler
Gender Coeducational
Languages English
Boarding/day Mixed
275 Farley Avenue, Belleville ON, K8N 4M2,
Canada
TELEPHONE: +1 613 962 8668
FAX: +1 613 962 4866
EMAIL: lvincent@hpedsb.on.ca

Monarch Park Collegiate
Status State
Programme Diploma
Diploma Coordinator John Au
Gender Coeducational
Languages English
Boarding/day Day
1 Hanson Street, Toronto ON, M4J 1G6,
Canada
TELEPHONE: +1 416 393 0190
FAX: +1 416 393 0834
EMAIL: Rob.MacKinnon@tdsb.on.ca
WEBSITE:
http://schools.tdsb.on.ca/monarch/

Nicholson Catholic College
Status State
Programme Diploma
Diploma Coordinator John Kavanaugh
Gender Coeducational
Languages English
Boarding/day Boarding
301 Church Street, Belleville ON, K8N 3C7, Canada
TELEPHONE: +1 613 967-0404
FAX: +1 613 967-1963
EMAIL: macdonjo@alcdsb
WEBSITE: www.nccschool.org

Notre Dame Secondary School
Status State
Programme Diploma
Diploma Coordinator Josie Comella
Gender Coeducational
Languages English
Boarding/day Day
2 Notre Dame Avenue, Brampton ON, L6Z 4L5, Canada
TELEPHONE: +1 905 840 2802
FAX: +1 905 846 2625
EMAIL: frank.scarcelli@dpcdsb.org

Parkdale Collegiate Institute
Status State
Programme Diploma
Diploma Coordinator Tina Cerven-Shaw
Gender Coeducational
Languages English
Boarding/day Day
209 Jameson Avenue, Toronto ON, M6K 2Y3, Canada
TELEPHONE: +1 416 393 9000
FAX: +1 416 393 8160
EMAIL: david.freedman@tdsb.on.ca
WEBSITE: http://schools.tdsb.on.ca/parkdale

Pope John Paul II Catholic Secondary School
Status State
Programme Diploma
Diploma Coordinator Tracey Robertson & Clare Ann Greco
Gender Coeducational
Languages English
685 Military Trail, Toronto ON, M1E 4P6, Canada
TELEPHONE: +1 416 393 5531
FAX: +1 416 393 5735
EMAIL: paul.mcalpine@tcdsb.org
WEBSITE: www.pjpii.com

Regiopolis-Notre Dame Catholic High School
Status State
Programme Diploma
Diploma Coordinator Len Whalen
Gender Coeducational
Languages English
Boarding/day Day
130 Russell Street, Kingston ON, K7K 2E9, Canada
TELEPHONE: +1 613 545 1902
FAX: +1 613 548 4024
EMAIL: whalen@alcdsb.on.ca

Robert Bateman High School
Status State
Programme Diploma
Diploma Coordinator Alexander Skene
Gender Coeducational
Languages English
Boarding/day Day
5151 New Street, Burlington ON, L7L 1V3, Canada
TELEPHONE: +1 905 632 5151
FAX: +1 905 333 5841
EMAIL: dick-westerbymj@hdsb.ca
WEBSITE: www.rbh.hdsb.ca

Sir Wilfrid Laurier Collegiate Institute
Status State
Programme Diploma
Diploma Coordinator Inna Belozorovich
Gender Coeducational
Languages English
Boarding/day Day
145 Guildwood Parkway, Scarborough ON, M1E 1P5, Canada
TELEPHONE: +1 416 396 6820
FAX: +1 416 396 6872
EMAIL: paul.ambrose@tdsb.on.ca
WEBSITE: http://schools.tdsb.on.ca/laurier

Sir Winston Churchill Collegiate and Vocational Institute
Status State
Programme Diploma
Diploma Coordinator Noel Jones
Gender Coeducational
Languages English
Boarding/day Day
130 W Churchill Drive, Thunder Bay ON, P7C 1V5, Canada
TELEPHONE: +1 807 473 8100
FAX: +1 807 475 4732
EMAIL: awarwick@lhbe.edu.on.ca
WEBSITE: http://swc.lhbe.edu.on.ca

St Francis Xavier Secondary School
Status State
Programme Diploma
Diploma Coordinator Subash Rego
Gender Coeducational
Languages English
Boarding/day Day
50 Bristol Road West, Mississauga ON, L5R 3K3, Canada
TELEPHONE: +1 905 507 6666
FAX: +1 905 568 1026
EMAIL: subash.rego@dpcdsb.org

St John's – Kilmarnock School
Status State
Programme PYP
PYP Coordinator Mary Perrett
Gender Coeducational
Boarding/day Day
2201 Shantz Station Road, Box 179, Breslau ON, N0B 1M0, Canada
TELEPHONE: +1 519 648 2183
EMAIL: glukachko@sjkschool.org
WEBSITE: www.sjkschool.org

St Robert Catholic High School
Status State
Programme Diploma
Diploma Coordinator Bernie Smith
Gender Coeducational
Languages English
Boarding/day Day
8101 Leslie Street, Thornhill ON, L3T 7P4, Canada
TELEPHONE: +1 905 889 4982
FAX: +1 905 889 8083
EMAIL: pinellt@ycdsb.edu.on.ca

Sunnybrook School
Status Private
Programme PYP
PYP Coordinator Micheal Ruffolo
Boarding/day Day
469 Merton Street, Toronto ON, M4S 1B4, Canada
TELEPHONE: +1 416 487 5308
EMAIL: idavy@sunnybrookschool.com

THE YORK SCHOOL
Status Private
Programme PYP, MYP, Diploma
Diploma Coordinator David Hanna
MYP Coordinator Eric Robertson
PYP Coordinator Patricia Jerred
Gender Coeducational
Languages English
Boarding/day Day
1320 Yonge Street, Toronto ON, M4T 1X2, Canada
TELEPHONE: +1 416-646-5275 (Admissions)
+1 416-926-1325 (Main switchboard)
FAX: +1 416-926-9592
EMAIL: ezio_crescenzi@tys.on.ca
WEBSITE: www.yorkschool.com
see full details on page 154

Toronto French School
Status Private
Programme Diploma
Diploma Coordinator Michael Bales
Gender Coeducational
Languages English
Boarding/day Day
318 Lawrence Avenue East, Toronto ON,
M4N 1T7, Canada
TELEPHONE: +1 416 484 6533
FAX: +1 416 488 2928
EMAIL: jgodfrey@tfs.ca
WEBSITE: http://tfs.on.ca

Toronto Montessori Academy
Status Private
Programme MYP
MYP Coordinator Vanessa Wonnacott
Gender Coeducational
Languages English
Boarding/day Day
8569 Bayview Avenue, Richmond Hill ON,
L4B 3M7, Canada
TELEPHONE: +1 905 889 6882
FAX: +1 905 886 6516
EMAIL: gzederayko@torontomontessori.ca
WEBSITE: www.torontomontessori.ca

Turner Fenton Campus
Status State
Programme MYP, Diploma
Diploma Coordinator Lee Roe-Etter
MYP Coordinator Lee Roe-Etter
Gender Coeducational
Languages English
Boarding/day Day
7935 Kennedy Road South, Brampton ON,
L6V 3N2, Canada
TELEPHONE: +1 905 453 9220
FAX: +1 905 453 9692
EMAIL: minibear@sympatico.ca
WEBSITE: www.turnerfenton.com

Upper Canada College
Status Private
Programme PYP, Diploma
Diploma Coordinator Steve Griffin
PYP Coordinator Dianne Jojic
Gender Male
Languages English
Boarding/day Mixed
200 Lonsdale Road, Toronto ON, M4V 1W6,
Canada
TELEPHONE: +1 416 484 8636
FAX: +1 416 484 8657
EMAIL: jpower@ucc.on.ca

Vaughan Road Academy
Status State
Programme MYP, Diploma
Diploma Coordinator Anthony Masciello
MYP Coordinator Kathy Botham
Gender Coeducational
Languages English
Boarding/day Day/boarding
529 Vaughan Road, Toronto ON, M6C 2R1,
Canada
TELEPHONE: +1 416 394 3222
FAX: +1 416 394 4478
EMAIL: suzana.greenaway@tdsb.on.ca

Victoria Park Collegiate Institute
Status State
Programme Diploma
Diploma Coordinator Sheldon Usprech
Gender Coeducational
Languages English
Boarding/day Day
15 Wallingford Road, North York ON,
M3A 2V1, Canada
TELEPHONE: +1 416 395 3310
FAX: +1 416 395 4208

Westdale Secondary School
Status State
Programme Diploma
Diploma Coordinator Paul Smith
Gender Coeducational
Languages English
Boarding/day Day
700 Main Street West, Hamilton ON, L8S 1A5,
Canada
TELEPHONE: +1 905 522 1387
FAX: +1 905 521 0542
EMAIL: westdale@hwdsb.on.ca
WEBSITE: www.hwdsb.on.ca/westdale

Weston Collegiate Institute
Status State
Programme Diploma
Diploma Coordinator Gary Hophan
Gender Coeducational
Languages English
Boarding/day Day
100 Pine Street, Toronto ON, M9N 2Y9,
Canada
TELEPHONE: +1 416 394 3250
FAX: +1 416 394 4429
EMAIL: angela.petitti@tdsb.on.ca

White Oaks Secondary School
Status State
Programme Diploma
Diploma Coordinator Michelle Lemaire
Gender Coeducational
Languages English
Boarding/day Day
1330 Montclair Drive, Oakville ON, L6K 1Z5,
Canada
TELEPHONE: +1 905 845 5200
FAX: +1 905 845 9136
EMAIL: stievaj@hdsb.ca
WEBSITE: www.wossweb.com

William Grenville Davis Senior Public School
Programme MYP
MYP Coordinator Lee Roe-Etter
Gender Coeducational
Boarding/day Day
491 Bartley Bull Parkway, Brampton ON,
L6W 2M7, Canada
TELEPHONE: +1 905-459-3661
EMAIL: paul.fiorini@peelsb.com
WEBSITE: www.wgdavis.com

Windfields Junior High School
Status State
Programme MYP
MYP Coordinator Sita Dubeau
375 Banbury Road, North York ON, M2L 2V2,
Canada
TELEPHONE: +11 1 416 395 3100
FAX: +11 1 416 395 3105
EMAIL: windfields@tdsb.on.ca
WEBSITE:
http://schools.tdsb.on.ca/windfieldsjhs

Quebec

Académie Antoine-Manseau
Status Private
Programme MYP
MYP Coordinator Martine Paré
Gender Coeducational
Languages French
Boarding/day Day
20 rue St Charles Borromée Sud, CP 410,
Joliette PQ, J6E 3Z9, Canada
TELEPHONE: +1 450 753 4271
FAX: +1 450 753 3661
EMAIL: courrier@amanseau.qc.ca

Académie François-Labelle
Status Private
Programme PYP
PYP Coordinator Stéphane Vallée
Gender Coeducational
1227 rue Notre Dame, Repentigny PQ,
J5Y 3H2, Canada
TELEPHONE: +1 450 582-2020
EMAIL: afl@classomption.qc.ca

Académie Lafontaine
Status Private
Programme MYP
MYP Coordinator Louise d'Aragon
Gender Coeducational
Languages French
Boarding/day Day
2171 boulevard Maurice, Saint-Jérôme,
Québec PQ, J7Z 4M7, Canada
TELEPHONE: +1 450-431-3733
FAX: +1 450-431-7390
EMAIL: potvinc@academielafontaine.qc.ca
WEBSITE: http://academielafontaine.qc.ca

Beurling Academy
Status State
Programme MYP
MYP Coordinator Sara Marquis
Gender Coeducational
Boarding/day Day
6100 Boulevard Champlain, Verdun, Montreal PQ, H4H 1A5, Canada
TELEPHONE: +1 514 766 2357
FAX: +1 514 768 9207
EMAIL: aandrews@lbpsb.qc.ca
WEBSITE: http://beurling.lbpsb.qc.ca

Chambly Academy
Status State
Programme MYP
MYP Coordinator Sue Duquette
Gender Coeducational
Languages English
Boarding/day Day
675 Green Street, St Lambert PQ, J4P 1V9, Canada
TELEPHONE: +1 450 671 5534
FAX: +1 450 671 3564
EMAIL: anardozza@rsb.qc.ca
WEBSITE: www.chamblyacademy.rsb.qc.ca

Champlain Regional College
Status State
Programme Diploma
Diploma Coordinator Steve R Hreha
Gender Coeducational
Languages English
Boarding/day Day
900 Riverside Drive, St Lambert PQ, J4P 3P2, Canada
TELEPHONE: +1 450 672 7360
FAX: +1 450 672 9299
EMAIL: shewan@champlaincollege.qc.ca

Children's World Academy
Status State
Programme PYP
PYP Coordinator Tania D'Alessandro
Gender Coeducational
Boarding/day Day
2241 rue Ménard, Lasalle PQ, H8N 1J4, Canada
TELEPHONE: +1 514 595 2043
EMAIL: dmeloche@lbpsb.qc.ca
WEBSITE: www.lbpsb.qc.ca

Collège André-Laurendeau
Status State
Programme Diploma
Diploma Coordinator Guy Décarie
Gender Coeducational
Languages French
Boarding/day Day
1111 rue Lapierre, Lasalle PQ, H8N 2J4, Canada
TELEPHONE: +1 514 364 3320 ext 160
FAX: +1 514 364 7130
EMAIL: dg@claurendeau.qc.ca
WEBSITE: www.claurendau.qc.ca

Collège Charlemagne
Status Private
Programme MYP
MYP Coordinator Isabelle Lussier
Gender Coeducational
Languages French
Boarding/day Day
5000 rue Pilon, Pierrefonds, Québec PQ, H9K 1G4, Canada
TELEPHONE: +1 514 626 7060
FAX: +1 514 626 1806
EMAIL: laudy@collegecharlemagne.com

College de L'Assomption
Status Private
Programme MYP
MYP Coordinator Ginette Dalpé
Gender Coeducational
Languages English
Boarding/day Day
270 boul l'Ange-Gardien, L'Assomption, Québec PQ, J5W 1R7, Canada
TELEPHONE: +1 450 589 5621
FAX: +1 450 589 2910
EMAIL: dirgen@classomption.qc.ca
WEBSITE: www.classomption.qc.ca

Collège de Lévis
Status Private
Programme MYP
MYP Coordinator Stuart Lopez
Gender Coeducational
Languages French
Boarding/day Boarding
9 rue Mgr Gosselin, Lévis PQ, G6V 5K1, Canada
TELEPHONE: +1 418 833 1249
FAX: +1 418 833 1974
EMAIL: dlehoux@collegedelevis.qc.ca

Collège Esther-Blondin
Status Private
Programme MYP
MYP Coordinator Etienne Pellerin
Gender Coeducational
Languages French
Boarding/day Day
101 rue Sainte-Anne, Saint-Jacques, Québec PQ, J0K 2R0, Canada
TELEPHONE: +1 450 839 3672
FAX: +1 450 839 3951
EMAIL: jpothier@collegeblondin.qc.ca
WEBSITE: http://collegeblondin.qc.ca

College François-Xavier-Garneau
Status State
Programme Diploma
Diploma Coordinator Pierre Vachon
Gender Coeducational
Languages French
Boarding/day Day
1660 boulevard de l'Entente, Québec PQ, G1S 4S3, Canada
TELEPHONE: +1 418 688 8310#2296
FAX: +1 418 688 1539
EMAIL: yblouin@cegep-fxg.qc.ca
WEBSITE: www.cegep-fxg.qc.ca/bi

Collège Jean-de-Brebeuf
Status Private
Programme Diploma
Diploma Coordinator Bernard Dugas
Gender Coeducational
Languages French
Boarding/day Mixed
3200 chemin Sainte-Catherine, Montréal PQ, H3T 1C1, Canada
TELEPHONE: +1 514 342 9342 (5224)
FAX: +1 514 342 0693
EMAIL: jcgaudet@brebeuf.qc.ca
WEBSITE: www.brebeuf.qc.ca

Collège Jésus-Marie de Sillery
Status Private
Programme MYP
MYP Coordinator Céline B Tremblay
Gender Female
Languages French
Boarding/day Mixed
2047 chemin Saint-Louis, Québec PQ, G1T 1P3, Canada
TELEPHONE: +1 418 687 9250
FAX: +1 418 687 9847
EMAIL: dir.gen@cjmds.qc.ca
WEBSITE: www.cjmds.qc.ca

Collège Laflèche
Status Private
Programme Diploma
Diploma Coordinator Josée Bélanger
Gender Coeducational
Languages French
Boarding/day Day
1687 boulevard du Carmel, Trois-Rivières PQ, G8Z 3R8, Canada
TELEPHONE: +1 819 375 7346
FAX: +1 819 375 7347
EMAIL: jean.morin@clafleche.qc.ca
WEBSITE: www.clafleche.qc.ca

Collège Mont Notre-Dame de Sherbrooke
Status Private
Programme MYP
MYP Coordinator Chérif Milky
Gender Female
Languages French
Boarding/day Day
114 rue Cathédrale, Sherbrooke, Québec PQ, J1H 4M1, Canada
TELEPHONE: +1 819 563 4104
FAX: +1 819 563 8689
EMAIL: mrobert@mont-notre-dame.qc.ca
WEBSITE: www.mont-notre-dame.qc.ca

Collège Notre-Dame-de-l'Assomption

Status Private
Programme MYP
MYP Coordinator Eric Milette
Gender Coeducational
Languages French
Boarding/day Mixed
225 rue Saint-Jean-Baptiste, Nicolet, Québec PQ, J3T 0A2, Canada
TELEPHONE: +1 819 293 4500
FAX: + 819 293 2099
EMAIL: rcyr@cnda.qc.ca
WEBSITE: http://cnda.qc.ca

Collège Notre-Dame-de-Lourdes

Status Private
Programme MYP
MYP Coordinator Lucie D'Amour
Gender Coeducational
Languages French
Boarding/day Day
845 chemin Tiffin, Longueuil, Québec PQ, J4P 3G5, Canada
TELEPHONE: +1 450 670 4740
FAX: +1 450 670 2800
EMAIL: ldamour@ndl.qc.ca

Collège Saint-Louis

Status State
Programme MYP
MYP Coordinator Charles Vien
Gender Coeducational
Languages French
Boarding/day Day
9343 Rue Jean-Milot, Lasalle PQ, H8R 1Y7, Canada
TELEPHONE: +1 514 595 2045
FAX: +1 514 595 2131
EMAIL: charles.vien@csmb.qc.ca

Collège Saint-Maurice

Status Private
Programme MYP
MYP Coordinator Hélène Leblanc
Gender Female
Languages French
Boarding/day Day
630 rue Girouard Ouest, Saint-Hyacinthe PQ, J2S 2Y3, Canada
TELEPHONE: +1 450 773-7478 #222
FAX: +1 450 773-1413
EMAIL: jpjeannotte@csm.qc.ca
WEBSITE: www.csm.qc.ca

Collège Saint-Paul

Status Private
Programme MYP
MYP Coordinator Martine Roy
Gender Coeducational
Languages French
Boarding/day Day
235 rue Ste-Anne, Varenne, Québec PQ, J3X 1P9, Canada
TELEPHONE: +1 450 652 2941
FAX: +1 450 652 4461
EMAIL: alangevin@college-st-paul.qc.ca
WEBSITE: www.college-st-paul.qc.ca

Collège Ville-Marie

Status Private
Programme MYP
MYP Coordinator Denis Robillard
Gender Coeducational
Languages French
Boarding/day Day
2850 rue Sherbrooke Est, Montréal, Québec PQ, H2K 1H3, Canada
TELEPHONE: +1 514 525 2516
FAX: +1 514 525 7675
EMAIL: helene.sirois@cvmarie.qc.ca
WEBSITE: www.cvmarie.qc.ca

École Bois-Joli Sacré-Coeur

Status State
Programme PYP
PYP Coordinator Élise Perreault
Gender Coeducational
Languages English
Boarding/day Day
775 rue Sacré Coeur Ouest, Ste-Hyacinthe PQ, J2S 1V2, Canada
TELEPHONE: +1 450 774-0412
FAX: +1 450 774-0412
EMAIL: catherine.bassaler@prologue.qc.ca; nancy.brodeur@prologue.qc.ca
WEBSITE: http://bj.cssh.qc.ca/index.html

École Chabot et du Châtelet

Status State
Programme PYP
PYP Coordinator Edith Morency
1659 rue Lozère, Charlesbourg PQ, G1G 3L4, Canada
TELEPHONE: +1 418 624 3752
EMAIL: chabot@csdps.qc.ca

École de la Baie-Saint-François

Status State
Programme MYP
MYP Coordinator Jean Lemay
Gender Coeducational
Languages French
Boarding/day Day
70 rue Louis VI Major, Salaberry-de-Valleyfield PQ, J6T 3G2, Canada
TELEPHONE: +1 450 371 2004
EMAIL: bsf@csvt.qc.ca

École de la Magdeleine

Status State
Programme MYP
MYP Coordinator Lise Charland
Gender Coeducational
Languages French
Boarding/day Day
1100 boulevard Taschereau, La Prairie PQ, J5R 1W8, Canada
TELEPHONE: +1 514 380 8899
EMAIL: tremblay.maryse@csdgs.qc.ca
WEBSITE: www.lamagdeleine

École d'éducation internationale

Status State
Programme MYP
MYP Coordinator Marie Van de Moortele
Gender Coeducational
Languages French
Boarding/day Day
720 rue Morin, McMasterville PQ, J3G 1H1, Canada
TELEPHONE: +1 450 467 4222
EMAIL: marie-rose.vandemoortele@csp.qc.ca
WEBSITE: http://eei.csp.qc.ca

École D'Youville Lambert

Status State
Programme PYP
PYP Coordinator Julie Bourque
Gender Coeducational
Languages English
Boarding/day Day
155 rue Ste-Christine, Saint-Joseph-de-Beauce PQ, G0S 2V0, Canada
TELEPHONE: +1 418 397 6845
FAX: +1 418 397 6325
EMAIL: louis.audet@csbe.qc.ca

École Edgar-Hebert

Programme MYP
MYP Coordinator Jean Lemay
Gender Coeducational
Boarding/day Boarding
161 rue Saint Thomas, Salaberry-de-Valleyfield PQ, J6T 4K1, Canada
TELEPHONE: +1 450 371 2008
EMAIL: edgar-hebert@csvt.qc.ca

Ecole Filteau Saint-Mathieu

Status State
Programme PYP
PYP Coordinator Madeleine Pichette
Gender Coeducational
Languages French
Boarding/day Day
830 rue de Saurel, Sainte Foy PQ, G1X 3P6, Canada
TELEPHONE: +1 418 652 2152
FAX: +1 418 652 2305
EMAIL: louise.gascon@csdecou.qc.ca
WEBSITE: www.csdecou.qc.ca/filteau

École Guy-Drummond

Status State
Programme PYP
PYP Coordinator Sylvie Denizon
Gender Coeducational
Languages English
Boarding/day Day
1475 avenue La Joie, Outremont PQ, H2V 1P9, Canada
TELEPHONE: +1 514 270 4866
FAX: +1 514 270 7165
EMAIL: francine.trudel@csmb.qc.ca

École Hubert Maisoneuve
Programme MYP
MYP Coordinator Sylvaine Tremblay
Gender Coeducational
Boarding/day Boarding
364 Rue Académie, Rosemère PQ, J7A 1ZA, Canada
TELEPHONE: +1 514 621 2003 ext.1
WEBSITE: http://cssmi.qc.ca

École internationale de Laval
Status State
Programme MYP
MYP Coordinator Danielle Langlois
Gender Coeducational
Languages French
Boarding/day Day
125 Boul Des Prairies, Laval PQ, H7N 2T6, Canada
TELEPHONE: +1 450 662 7000 4300
EMAIL: lbelisle@cslaval.qc.ca

École internationale de Montréal
Status State
Programme PYP, MYP
MYP Coordinator Gauthier Sandra
PYP Coordinator Pierre Desforges
Gender Coeducational
Languages French
Boarding/day Day
11 chemin Côte St-Antoine, Westmount PQ, H3Y 2H7, Canada
TELEPHONE: +1 514 596 7240
EMAIL: cormierg@csdm.qc.ca
WEBSITE: http://eim.csdm.qc.ca

École internationale primaire de Greenfield Park
Status State
Programme PYP
PYP Coordinator Anna Pamel
776 Cambell, Greenfield Park PQ, J4V 1YZ, Canada
TELEPHONE: +1 450 672 0042
EMAIL: gpis@rsb.qc.ca

École internationale St-Edmond
Status State
Programme MYP
MYP Coordinator Louise Perreault
Gender Coeducational
Languages French
Boarding/day Day
346 rue Hubert, Greenfield Park PQ, J4V 1S2, Canada
TELEPHONE: +1 450 671 6339
EMAIL: saint_edmond@csmv.qc.ca

École Joseph François Perrault
Status State
Programme MYP
MYP Coordinator Stéphane Lance
Gender Coeducational
Languages French
7540 rue François Perrault, Montréal PQ, H2A 1L9, Canada
TELEPHONE: +1 514 596 4620
EMAIL: jfperrault@csdm.qc.ca

École La Vérendrye
Status State
Programme PYP
PYP Coordinator Line Demers
Gender Coeducational
Languages French
3055 Mousseau, Montréal PQ, H1L 4W1, Canada
TELEPHONE: +1 514 596 4845
EMAIL: gallichandl@csdm.qc.ca
WEBSITE: www.csdm.qc.ca/laverendrye

École Le tandem
Programme MYP
MYP Coordinator Aline Martin
Gender Coeducational
Boarding/day Boarding
605 rue Notre-dame Ouest, Victoriaville PQ, G6P 6Y9, Canada
TELEPHONE: +1 819 758 1534

École Marie-Clarac
Status Private
Programme MYP
MYP Coordinator Diane Rinaldis
Gender Coeducational
Languages French
3530 Boul Gouin Est, Montréal-Nord PQ, H1H 1B7, Canada
TELEPHONE: +1 514 322 1160
EMAIL: md'amours@marie-clarac.qc.ca

École Paul-Hubert
Status State
Programme MYP
MYP Coordinator Michel Genest
Gender Coeducational
Languages French
Boarding/day Day
250 Boul Arthur Buies Ouest, Rimouski PQ, G5L 7A7, Canada
TELEPHONE: +1 418 724 3458
EMAIL: fdoucet@csphares.qc.ca
WEBSITE: http://ph.csphares.qc.ca/

École Plein Soleil
Status Private
Programme PYP
PYP Coordinator Natalie Pouliot
Gender Coeducational
Languages French
Boarding/day Day
300, rue de Montréal, Sherbrooke PQ, J1H 1E5, Canada
TELEPHONE: +1 819 569 8359
FAX: +1 819 569 3979
EMAIL: mjmayrand@pleinsoleil.qc.ca
WEBSITE: www.pleinsoleil.qc.ca

École Pointe-Lévy
Status State
Programme MYP
MYP Coordinator Pierre Blanchet
Gender Coeducational
Languages French
Boarding/day Day
55 Rue des Commandeurs, Levis PQ, G6V 1P5, Canada
TELEPHONE: +1 418 838 8401
FAX: +1 418 838 8480
EMAIL: jean.bruneau@csnavigateurs.qc.ca
WEBSITE: www.pointe-levy.qc.ca

École Polyvalente Le boisé
Status State
Programme MYP
MYP Coordinator Aline Martin
Gender Coeducational
Languages French
Boarding/day Boarding
605 rue Notre-dame Est, Victoriaville PQ, G6P 6Y9, Canada
TELEPHONE: +1 819 758 1534

École Polyvalente Le Carrefour
Status State
Programme MYP
MYP Coordinator Louise Sylvestre
Gender Coeducational
Languages French
Boarding/day Boarding
125 Rue Self, Val d'Òr, Québec PQ, J9P 3N2, Canada
TELEPHONE: +1 819 825 4670
EMAIL: carrier.jean@csob.qc.ca

École Saint-Jean
Programme MYP
MYP Coordinator Michel Genest
Gender Coeducational
Boarding/day Boarding
245 2e Rue Ouest, Rimouski PQ, G5L 4Y1, Canada
TELEPHONE: +1 418 724 3381
EMAIL: st-jean@csphares.qc.ca
WEBSITE: http://ph.csphares.qc.ca/

École Saint-Louis-de-Gonzague
Status Private
Programme PYP
PYP Coordinator Josée Brousseau
Gender Male
Languages French
Boarding/day Day
980 rue Richelieu, Quebec City PQ, G1R 1L5, Canada
TELEPHONE: +1 418 692 1072
EMAIL: dirgen@eslg.qc.ca
WEBSITE: www.eslg.qc.ca

École Saint-Pierre et des Sentiers

Status State
Programme MYP
MYP Coordinator Isabelle Girard
Gender Coeducational
Languages French
Boarding/day Day
1090 Château Bigot, Charlesbourg PQ,
G2L 1G1, Canada
TELEPHONE: +1 418 624 3757 #0226
EMAIL: carl.ouellet@csdps.qc.ca
WEBSITE: www.csdps.qc.ca

École secondaire André-Laurendeau

Status State
Programme MYP
MYP Coordinator Didier Mendes
Gender Coeducational
Languages French
Boarding/day Day
7450 boulevard Cousineau, St-Hubert PQ,
J3Y 3L4, Canada
TELEPHONE: +1 450 678 2080
EMAIL: daniel_ouimet@csmv.qc.ca
WEBSITE:
http://educ.csmv.qc.ca/andre_laurendeau

École secondaire Antoine-Brossard

Status State
Programme MYP
MYP Coordinator Lise Lalonde Gaucher
Gender Coeducational
Languages French
3055 boulevard Rome, Brossard PQ, J4Y 1S9,
Canada
TELEPHONE: +1 450 443 0010
EMAIL: sylvain_caron@csmv.qc.ca

Ecole secondaire Armand-Corbeil

Status State
Programme MYP
MYP Coordinator Josee Gaboury
Gender Coeducational
Languages French
795 JF Kennedy Ouest, Terrebonne PQ,
J6W 1X2, Canada
TELEPHONE: +1 450 492 3619 #1112
FAX: +1 450 492 3417
EMAIL:
raymond.durocher@eco.csaffluents.qc.ca

École secondaire Arthur Pigeon

Status State
Programme MYP
MYP Coordinator André Miville-Deschènes
Gender Coeducational
1 rue Arthur-Pigeon, Huntingdon PQ, J0S 1H0,
Canada
TELEPHONE: +1 450 264 5374
EMAIL: raymondn@csvt.qc.ca

École secondaire de l'Île

Status State
Programme MYP
MYP Coordinator Pierre Marinier
Gender Coeducational
Languages French
Boarding/day Day
255 rue Saint-Rédempteur, Gatineau PQ,
J8X 2T4, Canada
TELEPHONE: +1 819 771 6126
EMAIL: bastienre@cspo.qc.ca

École secondaire De Mortagne

Status State
Programme MYP
MYP Coordinator Yanick St-Onge
Gender Coeducational
Languages French
Boarding/day Day
955 Boulevard De Montarville,
Boucherville PQ, J4B 1Z6, Canada
TELEPHONE: +1 450 655 7311
FAX: +1 450 655 2932
EMAIL: michel.langis@csp.qc.ca
WEBSITE:
www.csp.qc.ca/ecolesweb/ecs117.htm

École secondaire de Neufchâtel

Status State
Programme MYP
MYP Coordinator Francois Pouliot
Gender Coeducational
Languages French
3600 avenue Chauveau, Neufchâtel PQ,
G2C 1A1, Canada
TELEPHONE: +1 418 847 7300
EMAIL: genest.nadine@cscapitale.qc.ca
WEBSITE: www.cscapitale.qc.ca/neufchatel

École secondaire de Rivière-du-Loup

Status State
Programme MYP
MYP Coordinator Sonia Julien
Gender Coeducational
Languages French
Boarding/day Day
320 Rue Saint-Pierre, Rivière du Loup PQ,
G5R 3V3, Canada
TELEPHONE: +1 418 868 2233
EMAIL: juliens@cskamloup.qc.ca
WEBSITE: www.cskamloup.qc.ca

École secondaire de Rochebelle

Status State
Programme MYP
MYP Coordinator Louise Gascon
Gender Coeducational
Languages French
Boarding/day Day
1095 de Rochebelle, Sainte-Foy PQ, G1V 4P8,
Canada
TELEPHONE: +1 418 652 2167
EMAIL: guy.dumais@csdecou.qc.ca
WEBSITE: www.derochebelle.qc.ca

École secondaire des Chutes

Status State
Programme MYP
MYP Coordinator Yamilé Bournival
Gender Coeducational
Languages French
Boarding/day Day
5285 avenue Albert-Tessier, CP 190,
Shawinigan PQ, G9N 6T9, Canada
TELEPHONE: +1 819 539 2285
EMAIL: deschutes@csenergie.qc.ca

École secondaire des Patriotes-de-Beauharnois

Status State
Programme MYP
MYP Coordinator Marie-Claude Desrosiers
Gender Coeducational
Languages French
Boarding/day Boarding
250 rue Gagnon, Beauharnois PQ, J6N 2W8,
Canada
TELEPHONE: +1 450 225 2260
EMAIL: byetter@csvt.qc.ca

École secondaire des Pionniers

Status State
Programme MYP
MYP Coordinator Pierre Blanchette
Gender Coeducational
Languages French
Boarding/day Day
3750 rue Jean-Bourdon, Trois-Rivières PQ,
G8Y 2A5, Canada
TELEPHONE: +1 819 379 5822
EMAIL: dls.dir@csduroy.qc.ca
WEBSITE: http://csduroy.qc.ca/DesPionniers

École secondaire des Sources

Status State
Programme MYP
MYP Coordinator Lyne Harvey
Gender Coeducational
Languages French
Boarding/day Day
2900 chemin Lake, Dollard-des-Ormeaux PQ,
H9B 2P1, Canada
TELEPHONE: +1 514 683-5595
EMAIL: direction.des_sources@csmb.qc.ca

École secondaire d'Oka

Status State
Programme MYP
MYP Coordinator Chantal Bourdon
Gender Coeducational
Languages French
Boarding/day Boarding
1700 Chemin Oka, Oka PQ, J0N 1E0, Canada

École secondaire Dorval Jean XXIII
Status State
Programme MYP
MYP Coordinator Suzanne Daoust
Gender Coeducational
Languages French
Boarding/day Day
1301 avenue Dawson, Dorval PQ, H9S 1Y3,
Canada
TELEPHONE: +1 514 636 1711
EMAIL: direction.jean_xxiii@csmb.q.c.c2

École secondaire du Phare
Status State
Programme MYP
MYP Coordinator Donald Landry
Gender Coeducational
Languages French
Boarding/day Day
405 rue Sara, Ascot PQ, J1H 5S6, Canada
TELEPHONE: +1 819 822 5455 x227
EMAIL: lamarchea@csrs.qc.ca
WEBSITE: http://phare.csrs.qc.ca/

École secondaire Gérard-Filion
Status State
Programme MYP
MYP Coordinator Jean-Yves Datey
Gender Coeducational
Boarding/day Boarding
1330 boulevard Curé-Poirier, Longueuil PQ,
J4K 2G8, Canada
TELEPHONE: +1 450 679-9100
EMAIL: jeanyves_datey@csmv.qc.ca

École secondaire Grande-Rivière
Status State
Programme MYP
MYP Coordinator Annie Lavigne
Gender Coeducational
Languages French
Boarding/day Day
100 rue Broad, Gatineau PQ, J9H 6A9, Canada
TELEPHONE: +1 819 682 8222 274
EMAIL: corneaun@cspo.qc.ca
WEBSITE: www.cspo.qc.ca

École secondaire Guillaume-Couture
Status State
Programme MYP
MYP Coordinator Pierre Blanchet
Gender Coeducational
Languages French
Boarding/day Day
70 Rue Philippe-Boucher, Levis PQ, G6V 1M5,
Canada
TELEPHONE: +1 418 838 8550
FAX: +1 418 838 8544
EMAIL: luc.levesque@csnavigateurs.qc.ca
WEBSITE: www.guillaumecouture.qc.ca

École secondaire Henri-Bourassa
Status State
Programme MYP
MYP Coordinator Francesca Bojanowski
Gender Coeducational
Languages French
Boarding/day Day
6051 boul Maurice-Duplessis,
Montréal-Nord PQ, H1G 1Y6, Canada
TELEPHONE: +1 514 328 3200 #3210
EMAIL: emilio-panetta@cspi.qc.ca

École secondaire Hormisdas-Gamelin
Status State
Programme MYP
MYP Coordinator Julie Fleurant
Gender Coeducational
Languages French
Boarding/day Day
580 rue Maclaren Est, Gatineau PQ, J8L 2W2,
Canada
TELEPHONE: +1 819 986 8511
EMAIL: marleau.leo@cscv.qc.ca
WEBSITE: www.cscv.qc.ca

École secondaire Jacques-Rousseau
Status State
Programme MYP
MYP Coordinator Linda Delorme
Gender Coeducational
Languages French
444 rue Gentilly est, Longueuil PQ, J4H 3X7,
Canada
TELEPHONE: +1 450 651 6800x467
EMAIL: martine_roy@csmv.qc.ca

École secondaire Jean-Baptiste-Meilleur
Status State
Programme MYP
MYP Coordinator Ginette Tessier
Gender Coeducational
Languages French
Boarding/day Day
777 boul d`Iberville, Repentigny PQ, J5Y 1A2,
Canada
TELEPHONE: +1 450 492-3777
EMAIL:
jacques.menard@eco.csaffluents.qc.ca
WEBSITE: www.csaffluents.qc.ca/wjbm

École secondaire Jean-Jacques-Bertrand
Status State
Programme MYP
MYP Coordinator Daniel Lussier
Gender Coeducational
Languages French
255 rue Saint-André Sud, Farnham PQ,
J2N 2B8, Canada
TELEPHONE: +1 450 293 3181#223

École secondaire Jeanne-Mance
Programme MYP
MYP Coordinator Line Lacroix
Gender Coeducational
Boarding/day Boarding
45 avenue des Freres, Drummondville PQ,
J2B 6A2, Canada
TELEPHONE: +1 819 474 0753
EMAIL: jeanne.mance@csdeschenes.qc.ca

École secondaire Joseph-François-Perrault
Status State
Programme MYP
MYP Coordinator Miriam Rodriguez
Gender Coeducational
Languages French
Boarding/day Day
140 chemin Ste-Foy, Québec PQ, G1R 1T2,
Canada
TELEPHONE: +1 418 525-8169
EMAIL: genestn@cscapitale.qc.ca
WEBSITE: www.cscapitale.qc.ca/jfperrault

École secondaire Joseph-Hermas-Leclerc
Status State
Programme MYP
MYP Coordinator Normand Gagnon
Gender Coeducational
Languages French
Boarding/day Day
1111 rue Simonds Sud, Granby PQ, J2G 9H7,
Canada
TELEPHONE: +1 450 378 9981
EMAIL: bechardl@csvdc.qc.ca
WEBSITE: www.jhleclerc.com

École secondaire Kénogami
Status State
Programme MYP
MYP Coordinator Yves Larouche
Languages French
1954 Boulevard des Etudiants, Jonquière,
Québec PQ, G7X 4B1, Canada

École secondaire La Courvilloise
Status State
Programme MYP
MYP Coordinator Louise Savard
Gender Coeducational
Languages French
Boarding/day Day
2265 avenue Larue, Beauport PQ, G1C 1J9,
Canada
TELEPHONE: +1 418 821 4220
EMAIL: eslc@csdps.qc.ca
WEBSITE: www.csdps.qc.ca

École secondaire L'Envolée
Programme MYP
MYP Coordinator Normand Gagnon
Gender Coeducational
Boarding/day Day
549 rue Fournier, Granby PQ, J2J 2K5, Canada
TELEPHONE: +1 450 777 7536
EMAIL: chicoiner@csvdc.qc.ca
WEBSITE: www.envolee.csvdc.qc.ca

École secondaire Lionel-Groulx
Status State
Programme MYP
MYP Coordinator Martine Lepage
Gender Coeducational
Languages French
Boarding/day Day
400 avenue St Charles, Vaudreuil-Dorion PQ,
J7V 6B1, Canada
TELEPHONE: +1 514 455 9311
EMAIL: rbeauchamp@cstrois-lacs.qc.ca
WEBSITE: www.cstrois-lacs.qc.ca

École secondaire Louis-Philippe-Paré
Status State
Programme MYP
MYP Coordinator Michelle Laplante
Gender Coeducational
Languages French
Boarding/day Boarding
235 boulevard Brisebois, Châtaeuguay PQ,
J6K 3X4, Canada
TELEPHONE: +1 450 692 8261
EMAIL: berube.nathalie@csdgs.qc.ca

École secondaire Mont Saint-Sacrement
Status State
Programme MYP
MYP Coordinator Jean Drolet
Gender Coeducational
Languages French
Boarding/day Day
200 boulevard Saint-Sacrement, Saint-
Gabriel-de-Valcartier PQ, GoA 4S0, Canada
TELEPHONE: +1 418 844-3771 P35
EMAIL: pierre.lantier@mss.qc.ca
WEBSITE: www.mss.qc.ca

École secondaire Mont-Royal
Status State
Programme MYP
MYP Coordinator Marcel Gargour
Gender Coeducational
Languages French
Boarding/day Day
50 avenue Montgomery, Ville Mont-Royal PQ,
H3R 2B3, Canada
TELEPHONE: +1 514 731 2761
EMAIL: direction.mont-royal@csmb.qc.ca
WEBSITE: www.ecolemont-royal.com

École secondaire Ozias-Leduc
Status State
Programme MYP
MYP Coordinator Denise Gauvreau
Gender Coeducational
Languages French
Boarding/day Day
525 rue Jolliet, Mont-Saint-Hilaire PQ,
J3H 3N2, Canada
TELEPHONE: +1 450 467 0261

École secondaire Rive-Nord
Status State
Programme MYP
MYP Coordinator Sylvaine Tremblay
Gender Coeducational
Languages French
Boarding/day Day
400 rue Joseph-Paquette, Bois des Filions PQ,
J6Z 4P7, Canada
TELEPHONE: +1 450 621 3686
WEBSITE: http://cssmi.qc.ca

École secondaire Roger-Comtois
Status State
Programme MYP
MYP Coordinator Pierre Lapointe
Gender Coeducational
Languages French
158 boulevard des Étudiants, Loretteville PQ,
G2A 1N8, Canada
TELEPHONE: +1 418 847 7201
EMAIL: ecole.rcomtois@cscapitale.qc.ca

École secondaire Saint-Joseph de Saint-Hyacinthe
Status Private
Programme MYP
MYP Coordinator Simone LeBlanc
Gender Coeducational
Languages French
Boarding/day Day
2875 Bourdages Nord, Saint-Hyacinthe PQ,
J2S 5S3, Canada
TELEPHONE: +1 450 774 3775
EMAIL: direction@essj.qc.ca

École secondaire Serge-Bouchard
Status State
Programme MYP
MYP Coordinator Diane Boivin
Gender Coeducational
Languages French
Boarding/day Day
640 boulevard Blanche, Baie-Comeau PQ,
G5C 2B3, Canada
TELEPHONE: +1 418 589 1301 poste 3306
EMAIL: lucie.bherer@csestuaire.qc.ca
WEBSITE: http://essb.ca.tc

École secondaire Soulanges
Status State
Programme MYP
MYP Coordinator Lorraine Clairoux
Gender Coeducational
Languages French
Boarding/day Day
137 Sainte-Catherine, St Polycarpe PQ,
J0P 1X0, Canada
TELEPHONE: +1 450 265 3232
EMAIL: luc.gervais@cstrois-lacs.qc.ca

École secondaire St-Gabriel
Programme MYP
MYP Coordinator Sylvaine Tremblay
Gender Coeducational
Boarding/day Boarding
8 Rue Tassé, Ste Thérèse PQ, J7E 1V3, Canada
TELEPHONE: +1 514 433 5445 ext.238
EMAIL: violaine.grandbois@cssmi.qc.ca
WEBSITE: http://cssmi.qc.ca

École secondaire Vaudreuil
Programme MYP
MYP Coordinator Martine Lepage
Gender Coeducational
Boarding/day Boarding
400 avenue St Charles, Pavillon H, Vaudreuil-
Dorion PQ, J7V 6B1, Canada
TELEPHONE: +1 450 455 9311
WEBSITE: www.cstrois-lacs.qc.ca

École Ste-Thérèse-de-l'Enfant-Jésus
Status State
Programme PYP
PYP Coordinator Carole Goudreau
Gender Coeducational
Languages French
Boarding/day Day
700 9e rue, Saint Jérôme PQ, J7Z 2Z5, Canada
TELEPHONE: +1 450 438 8828
WEBSITE: www.csrdn.qc.ca/ste-therese

École Wilfrid-Pelletier
Status State
Programme PYP
PYP Coordinator Marie-France Duchesneau
Gender Coeducational
Languages French
Boarding/day Day
8301 boulevard Wilfrid-Pelletier, Montréal
(Anjou) PQ, H1K 1M2, Canada
TELEPHONE: +1 514 352 7300
EMAIL: celine-gadoury@cspi.qc.ca
WEBSITE: www.cspi.qc.ca/wp/

Heritage Regional High School
Status State
Programme MYP
MYP Coordinator Lisa Rae
Gender Coeducational
7445 Chambly Road, St Hubert PQ, J3Y 3S3,
Canada
TELEPHONE: +1 450 678 1070
EMAIL: kscott@rsb.qc.ca

JOHN PAUL I HIGH SCHOOL
Status State
Programme MYP
MYP Coordinator Anne-Marie Delisle
Gender Coeducational
Languages English (56%), French (44%)
Boarding/day Day
8455 Pre-Laurin, St Leonard PQ, H1R 3P3,
Canada
TELEPHONE: +1 514 328 7171
FAX: +1 514 328 7804
EMAIL: amdelisle@emsb.qc.ca
WEBSITE: www.emsb.qc.ca/johnpauli
see full details on page 106

Lakeside Academy
Status State
Programme MYP
MYP Coordinator Alain Rodrigue
Gender Coeducational
Languages English
Boarding/day Day
5050 Sherbrooke, Lachine PQ, H8T 1H8, Canada
TELEPHONE: +1 514 637 2505
FAX: +1 514 637-9452
EMAIL: jwallach@lbpsb.qc.ca
WEBSITE: http://lakesideacademy.lbpsb.qc.ca

LaSalle Community Comprehensive High School
Status State
Programme MYP
MYP Coordinator Jason Thivierge
Gender Coeducational
Languages English
140-9th Avenue, LaSalle PQ, H8P 2N9, Canada
TELEPHONE: +1 514 595 2050
EMAIL: ppedroso@lbpsb.qc.ca
WEBSITE: www.lcchs.lbpsb.qc.ca

LAURIER MACDONALD HIGH SCHOOL
Status State
Programme MYP
MYP Coordinator Anne-Marie Delisle
Gender Coeducational
Languages English (77%), French (23%)
Boarding/day Day
7355 Boulevard Viau, St Leonard PQ, H1S 3C2, Canada
TELEPHONE: +1 514 374 6000
FAX: +1 514 374 7220
EMAIL: amdelisle@emsb.qc.ca
WEBSITE: www.lauriermacdonald.ca
see full details on page 107

Le Collège Saint-Bernard
Status Private
Programme MYP
MYP Coordinator Guylaine Taillon
Gender Coeducational
Languages French
25 avenue des Frères, Drummondville PQ, J2B 6A2, Canada
TELEPHONE: +1 819 478 3330
FAX: +1 819 478 2582
EMAIL: acusson@csb.qc.ca

Le Petit Seminaire De Quebec
Status Private
Programme MYP
MYP Coordinator Guy Langlois
Gender Coeducational
Languages French
Boarding/day Day
6 rue de la Vieille-Université, Québec PQ, G1R 5X8, Canada
TELEPHONE: +1 418 694 1020
EMAIL: rlemay@psq.qc.ca
WEBSITE: www.psq.qc.ca

Le Petit Séminaire de Québec (Hull)
Status Private
Programme Diploma
Diploma Coordinator Patrick Milot
Gender Coeducational
Languages French
Boarding/day Day
6 rue de l'Université, Québec PQ, G1R 5X8, Canada
TELEPHONE: +1 418.694.1020
EMAIL: cforget@psq.qc.ca
WEBSITE: www.multicollege.qc.ca

L'École des Ursulines de Québec
Status Private
Programme PYP
PYP Coordinator Josée Martineau
Gender Female
4 rue du Parloir, CP 820, Haute-Ville, Québec PQ, G1R 4S7, Canada
TELEPHONE: +1 418 692 2612
FAX: +1 418) 692 1240
EMAIL: dia7par@ursulinesquebec.com

L'Externat Saint-Jean-Eudes
Status State
Programme MYP
MYP Coordinator Sébastien Lavoie
Gender Coeducational
Languages French
Boarding/day Day
650 avenue du Bourg-Royal, Charlesbourg, Québec PQ, G2L 1M8, Canada
TELEPHONE: +1 418 627 1550
FAX: +1 418 627 0770
EMAIL: malenfante@sje.qc.ca
WEBSITE: www.sje.qc.ca

Marymount Academy
Status State
Programme MYP
MYP Coordinator John Wright
Gender Coeducational
Languages English
5100 Côte St-Luc Road, Montréal PQ, H3W 2G9, Canada
TELEPHONE: +1 514 488 8144
FAX: +1 514 488 8183
EMAIL: pminiaci@emsb.qc.ca

Pavillon Saint-Pierre
Programme MYP
MYP Coordinator Chantal Boiteau
Gender Coeducational
Boarding/day Boarding
5250 des Sauges, Charlesbourg PQ, G1G 3V6, Canada
TELEPHONE: +1 418 624 3760
EMAIL: stpierre@csdps.qc.ca
WEBSITE: www.csdps.qc.ca

Pensionnat du Saint-Nom-de-Marie
Status Private
Programme MYP
MYP Coordinator Danielle Perras
Gender Female
Languages French
Boarding/day Mixed
628 chemin de la Côte, St Catherine, Outremont PQ, H2V 2C5, Canada
TELEPHONE: +1 514 735 5261
EMAIL: k.caissy@psnm.qc.ca
WEBSITE: www.psnm.qc.ca

Pierrefonds Comprehensive High School
Status State
Programme MYP
MYP Coordinator Melanie Rousseau
Gender Coeducational
Languages English
Boarding/day Day
13800 Pierrefonds Boulevard, Pierrefonds PQ, H9A 1A7, Canada
TELEPHONE: +1 514 626 9610
EMAIL: chumphries@lbpsb.qc.ca

Polyvalente Chanoine-Armand-Racicot
Status State
Programme MYP
MYP Coordinator Rene Chamberland
Gender Coeducational
Languages French
Boarding/day Day
940 boulevard de Normandie, St-Jean-sur-Richelieu, Québec PQ, J3A 1A7, Canada
TELEPHONE: +1 450-348-6134
EMAIL: montpetitr@csdhr.qc.ca

Polyvalente de Thetford Mines
Status State
Programme MYP
MYP Coordinator Alain Fournier
Gender Coeducational
Languages French
Boarding/day Day
561 rue St-Patrick, Thetford Mines, Québec PQ, G6G 5W1, Canada
TELEPHONE: +1 418 338 7832 x1514
FAX: +1 418 338 7881
EMAIL: polytm@csappalaches.qc.ca

Polyvalente des Quatre-Vents
Status State
Programme MYP
MYP Coordinator Carl Bouchard
Gender Coeducational
Languages French
Boarding/day Day
1099 boul Hamel, St-Félicien, Québec PQ, G8K 2R4, Canada
TELEPHONE: +1 418 275 4585
FAX: +1 418 679 8765
EMAIL: boivinp@cspaysbleuets.qc.ca
WEBSITE: www.cspaysbleuets.qc.ca/pvq

Polyvalente Deux-Montagnes
Status State
Programme MYP
MYP Coordinator Xavier Le Moëligou
Gender Coeducational
Languages French
500 chemin des Anciens, Deux-Montagnes
PQ, J7R 6A7, Canada
TELEPHONE: +1 450 472 3070
EMAIL: luc.desilets@cssmi.qc.ca

Polyvalente Hyacinthe-Delorme
Status State
Programme MYP
MYP Coordinator Jocelyne Perrot
Gender Coeducational
Languages French
Boarding/day Day
2700 Avenue T D Bouchard, Saint-Hyacinthe
PQ, J2S 7G2, Canada
TELEPHONE: +1 450 773 8401
EMAIL: gilles.charest@phd.cssh.qc.ca

Polyvalente Le Carrefour
Status State
Programme MYP
MYP Coordinator Sandra Beauchamp
Gender Male
Languages French
Boarding/day Day
50 chemin de la Savane, Gatineau PQ,
J8T 3N2, Canada
TELEPHONE: +1 819 568 9012
EMAIL: gcote@csdraveurs.qc.ca

Polyvalente Saint-François
Status State
Programme MYP
MYP Coordinator Nicole Poulin
Gender Coeducational
Languages French
Boarding/day Day
228 Avenue Lambert, Beauceville PQ,
G5X 3N9, Canada
TELEPHONE: +1 418 774 3391
EMAIL: germain.ouellet@csbe.qc.ca
WEBSITE: http://polyst-francois.qc.ca

Polyvalente Saint-Jérôme
Status State
Programme MYP
MYP Coordinator Rémi Simard
Gender Coeducational
Languages French
Boarding/day Day
535 rue Filion, Saint-Jérôme PQ, J7Z 1J6,
Canada
TELEPHONE: +1 450 436 4330
EMAIL: labellen@csrdn.qc.ca
WEBSITE: www.psj.csrdn.qc.ca

Séminaire Sainte-Marie de Shawinigan
Status Private
Programme MYP
MYP Coordinator Yves Davidson
Gender Coeducational
Languages French
Boarding/day Day
5655 boulevard des Hêtres, Shawinigan PQ,
G9N 4V9, Canada
TELEPHONE: +1 819 539 5493
EMAIL: rejeanlemay@ssm1950.qc.ca
WEBSITE: http://ssm1950.qc.ca

St Thomas High School
Status State
Programme MYP
MYP Coordinator David Weber
Gender Coeducational
Languages English
Boarding/day Day
120 Ambassador, Pointe-Claire PQ, H9R 1S8,
Canada
TELEPHONE: +1 514 694 3770
FAX: +1 514 694 3378
EMAIL: cmerilees@lbpsb.qc.ca

Vanier College
Status State
Programme Diploma
Diploma Coordinator Julie Plante
Gender Coeducational
Languages English
Boarding/day Day
821 Avenue Ste-Croix, St Laurent PQ, H4L 3X9,
Canada
TELEPHONE: +1 514 744 7025
FAX: +1 514 744 7952
EMAIL: dg@vaniercollege.qc.ca
WEBSITE: www.vaniercollege.qc.ca

Saskatchewan

Campbell Collegiate
Status State
Programme Diploma
Diploma Coordinator Brian Ransom
Gender Coeducational
Languages English
Boarding/day Day
102 Massey Road, Regina SK, S4S 4M9,
Canada
TELEPHONE: +1 306 791 8380
FAX: +1 306 584 5995
EMAIL: hjesse@rbe.sk.ca
WEBSITE: http://campbellcollegiate.rbe.sk.ca

Luther College
Status Private
Programme Diploma
Diploma Coordinator Clint Uhrich
Gender Coeducational
Languages English
Boarding/day Mixed
1500 Royal Street, Regina SK, S4T 5A5 Canada
TELEPHONE: +1 306 791 9150
FAX: +1 306 359 6962
EMAIL: berbel.knoll@dlcwest.com
WEBSITE: www.luthercollege.edu

North Battleford Comprehensive High School
Status State
Programme Diploma
Diploma Coordinator Allison Hawwyliw
Gender Coeducational
Languages English
Boarding/day Day
1791-110th Street, North Battleford SK,
S9A 2Y2, Canada
TELEPHONE: +1 306 445 6101
FAX: +1 306 445 6878
EMAIL: agabert@isksd.ca
WEBSITE: www.nbchs.north-battleford.sk.ca

Thom Collegiate
Status State
Programme Diploma
Diploma Coordinator Don Ready
Gender Coeducational
Languages English
Boarding/day Day
265 North Argyle Street, Regina SK, S4R 4C7,
Canada
TELEPHONE: +1 306 791 8425
FAX: +1 306 791 8672
EMAIL: bill.derosier@rbe.sk.ca
WEBSITE: www.thomcollegiate.rbe.sk.ca

CAYMAN ISLANDS

Cayman International School
Status Private
Programme Diploma
Diploma Coordinator Jodi McDonald
Gender Coeducational
Languages English
Boarding/day Day
PO Box 31364, KY1-1206, Grand Cayman,
Cayman Islands
TELEPHONE: +345 945 4664
FAX: +345 945 4650
EMAIL: jcaskey_cis@iss.edu
WEBSITE:
www.caymaninternationalschool.org

CUBA

International School of Havana
Status Private
Programme Diploma
Diploma Coordinator Osmery Martinez
Gender Coeducational
Languages English
Boarding/day Day
Calle 18 #315 Miramar, esq 5ta Ave, Playa,
Miramar, La Habana, Cuba
TELEPHONE: +53 7 204 2540
FAX: +53 7 204 2723
EMAIL: office@ish.co.cu
WEBSITE: www.ishav.org

DOMINICAN REPUBLIC

Saint George School, Santo Domingo
Status Private
Programme Diploma
Diploma Coordinator Lourdes Sánchez
Gender Coeducational
Languages Spanish
Boarding/day Day
c/o 1733 NW 79 Avenue, CPS #404,
Miami FL 33126, USA
TELEPHONE: +809 562 5262
EMAIL: mtejeda@stgeorge.edu.do
WEBSITE: www.stgeorge.edu.do

JAMAICA

Hillel Academy
Status Private
Programme Diploma
Diploma Coordinator Lloyd Holmes
Gender Coeducational
Languages English
Boarding/day Day
PO Box 2687, 51 Upper Mark Way, Kingston 8,
Jamaica
TELEPHONE: +876 925 1980
FAX: +876 925 1834
EMAIL: hilleldirector@cwjamaica.com
WEBSITE: www.hilleljm.com

NETHERLANDS ANTILLES

INTERNATIONAL SCHOOL OF CURAÇAO
Status Private
Programme Diploma
Diploma Coordinator Suhasini M Iyengar
Gender Coeducational
Languages English
Boarding/day Day
PO Box 3090, Koninginnelaan z/n, Curaçao,
Netherlands Antilles
TELEPHONE: +599 9 737 3633
FAX: +599 9 737 3142
EMAIL: muralis@isc.an
WEBSITE: www.isc.an
see full details on page 99

USA
Alaska

Palmer High School
Status State
Programme Diploma
Diploma Coordinator Wolfgang Winter
Gender Coeducational
Languages English
Boarding/day Day
1170 West Arctic Avenue, Ma-Su Borough
School District, Palmer AK 99645, USA
TELEPHONE: +1 907 746 8408
FAX: +1 907 746 0569
EMAIL: wolfgang.winter@matsuk12.us

West Anchorage High School
Status State
Programme Diploma
Diploma Coordinator Ted Stuff
Gender Coeducational
Languages English
Boarding/day Day
1700 Hillcrest Drive, Anchorage AK 99517,
USA
TELEPHONE: +1 907 742 2610
FAX: +1 907 742 2525
EMAIL: stuffted@asdk12.org
WEBSITE:
www.asdk12.org/schools/west/pages

Alabama

Auburn High School
Status State
Programme Diploma
Diploma Coordinator Sherel Perry
Gender Coeducational
Languages English
Boarding/day Day
405 South Dean Road, Auburn AL 36830, USA
TELEPHONE: +1 334 887 4970
FAX: +1 334 887 4177
EMAIL: clong@auburnschools.org
WEBSITE: www.auburnschools.org

Austin High School
Status State
Programme MYP, Diploma
Diploma Coordinator Susan Giguere
MYP Coordinator Susan Giguere
Gender Coeducational
Languages English
Boarding/day Day
1625 Danville Rd SW, Decatur AL 35601, USA
TELEPHONE: +1 256 552 3060
FAX: +1 256 350 7802
EMAIL: dsnow@dcs.edu
WEBSITE:
www.ptc.dcs.edu/schools/hs/ahs/ahs.html

Benjamin Davis Elementary School
Status State
Programme PYP
PYP Coordinator Caroline Weems
Gender Coeducational
Languages English
Boarding/day Day
417 Monroe Drive NW, Decatur AL 35601, USA
TELEPHONE: +1 256 552 3025
FAX: +1 256 552 4698
EMAIL: david.kross@dcs.edu
WEBSITE: www.ptc.dcs.edu/schools/
elem/bd/start.html

Brookhaven Middle School
Status State
Programme MYP
MYP Coordinator Susan Giguere
1302 5th Avenue SW, Decatur AL 35601, USA
TELEPHONE: +1 256 552 3045
FAX: +1 256 552 3047
EMAIL: lcollier@bms.dcs.edu
WEBSITE: www.ptc.dcs.edu/schools/
ms/bhms/bms.html

Cedar Ridge Middle School
Status State
Programme MYP
MYP Coordinator Susan Giguere
2715 Danville Road SW, Decatur AL 35603,
USA
TELEPHONE: +1 256 552 4622
FAX: +1 256 552 4623
EMAIL: beth.weinbaum@dcs.edu
WEBSITE: www.ptc.dcs.edu/schools/
ms/crms/crms.html

Central High School, Tuscaloosa
Status State
Programme Diploma
Diploma Coordinator David Truhett
Gender Coeducational
Languages English
Boarding/day Mixed
1715 MLK Jr Blvd, Tuscaloosa AL 35401, USA
TELEPHONE: +1 205-759-3720
FAX: +1 205 759 3756
EMAIL: hragsdal@chs.tusc.k12.al.us

Columbia High School
Status State
Programme Diploma
Diploma Coordinator Carol Nixon
Gender Coeducational
Languages English
Boarding/day Day
300 Explorer Boulevard, Huntsville AL 35806,
USA
TELEPHONE: +1 256 428 7576
FAX: +1 256 428 7579
EMAIL: jgarrett@hsv.k12.al.us
WEBSITE: www.hsv.k12.al.us/schools/
high/chs/index.htm

Daphne High School
Status State
Programme Diploma
Diploma Coordinator Joe Roh
Gender Coeducational
Languages English
Boarding/day Day
9300 Lawson Road, Daphne AL 36526, USA
TELEPHONE: +1 251 626 8787
FAX: +1 251 626 3024
EMAIL: dblanchard@bcbe.org
WEBSITE: www.daphnehs.com

Decatur High School
Status State
Programme MYP, Diploma
Diploma Coordinator Kim Qualls
MYP Coordinator Kim Qualls
Gender Coeducational
Languages English
Boarding/day Day
1011 Prospect Drive SE, Decatur AL 35601, USA
TELEPHONE: +1 256 552 3011
FAX: +1 256 208 2535
EMAIL: mike.ward@dhs.dcs.edu
WEBSITE: www.dcs.edu

Fairhope High School
Status State
Programme Diploma
Diploma Coordinator Melinda Oliver
Gender Coeducational
Languages English
Boarding/day Day
One Pirate Drive, Fairhope AL 36532, USA
TELEPHONE: +1 251 928 8309
FAX: +1 251 990 2053
EMAIL: bthomas1@bcbe.org
WEBSITE: www.fairhopehs.com

Hoover High School
Status State
Programme Diploma
Diploma Coordinator Melody Greene
Gender Coeducational
Languages English
Boarding/day Day
1000 Buccaneer Drive, Hoover AL 35244, USA
TELEPHONE: +1 205 439 1200
FAX: +1 205 439 1201
EMAIL: sspivey@hoover.k12.al.us

Jefferson County IB School
Status State
Programme Diploma
Diploma Coordinator Linda Jones
Gender Coeducational
Languages English
Boarding/day Day
6100 Old Leeds Road, Birmingham AL 35210, USA
TELEPHONE: +1 205 379 5356
FAX: +1 205 951 1372
EMAIL: bobjones@prodigy.net

Leon Sheffield Magnet School
Status State
Programme PYP
PYP Coordinator Nancy Brewer
Gender Coeducational
Languages English
Boarding/day Day
801 Wilson Street NW, Decatur AL 35601, USA
TELEPHONE: +1 256 552 3056
FAX: +1 256 552 4690
WEBSITE: www.ptc.dcs.edu/schools/
elem/gb/gb.html

Murphy High School
Status State
Programme Diploma
Diploma Coordinator Reenie Aldes
Gender Coeducational
Languages English
Boarding/day Day
100 South Carlen Street, Mobile AL 36606, USA
TELEPHONE: +1 251 221 3186
FAX: +1 251 221 3196
EMAIL: destle@mcpss.com
WEBSITE:
www.murphy.mcs.schoolinsites.com

Oak Park Middle School
Status State
Programme MYP
MYP Coordinator Kim Qualls
1218 16th Avenue, Decatur AL 35640, USA
TELEPHONE: +1 256 552 3035
FAX: +1 256 552 3082
EMAIL: dwight.satterfield@dcs.edu
WEBSITE: www.dcs.edu

W P Davidson High School
Status State
Programme Diploma
Diploma Coordinator Lydia Edmonds
Gender Coeducational
Languages English
Boarding/day Day
3900 Pleasant Valley Road, Mobile AL 36609, USA
TELEPHONE: +1 251 221 3084
FAX: +1 251 221 3083
EMAIL: copeland@mcpss.com
WEBSITE:
http://davidson.mcs.schoolinsites.com

Arkansas

Barry Goldwater High School
Status State
Programme Diploma
Diploma Coordinator Speranta Klees
Gender Coeducational
Languages English
Boarding/day Day
2820 West Rose Garden Lane, Deer Valley
United School Dist, Phoenix AR 85027, USA
TELEPHONE: +1 623 445-3004
FAX: +1 623 445-3081
EMAIL: ib@bg.dvusd.org
WEBSITE: www.dvusd.org

Bentonville High School
Status State
Programme Diploma
Diploma Coordinator Jeff Hagers
Gender Coeducational
Languages English
Boarding/day Day
1901 S.E. 'J' Street, Bentonville AR 72712, USA
TELEPHONE: +1 479 254 5100
FAX: +1 479 271 1180
EMAIL: sjacoby@bentonville.k12.ar.us
WEBSITE:
http://users.bentonville.k12.ar.us/bhssite

College Hill Elementary School
Status State
Programme PYP
PYP Coordinator Wanda Roberts
Gender Coeducational
Languages English
Boarding/day Day
200 Artesian, Texarkana AR 71854, USA
TELEPHONE: +1 870 774 9111
FAX: +1 870 773 0643
EMAIL: dhuman@txk.k12.ar.us
WEBSITE: www.txk.k12.ar.us

Hall High School
Status State
Programme Diploma
Diploma Coordinator Mary Katharine Sanders
Gender Coeducational
Languages English
Boarding/day Day
6700 'H' Street, Little Rock AR 72205, USA
TELEPHONE: +1 501 447 1900
FAX: +1 501 447 1901
EMAIL: john.bacon@lrsd.org
WEBSITE: www.lrsd.org/hall

Hot Springs High School
Status State
Programme MYP, Diploma
Diploma Coordinator Paula Redding
MYP Coordinator Jule Grant
Gender Coeducational
Languages English
Boarding/day Day
701 Emory Street, Hot Springs AR 71913, USA
TELEPHONE: +1 501 624-5286
FAX: +1 501 620-7840
EMAIL: laribea@hssd.net
WEBSITE: www.hsprings.dsc.k12.ar.us

Hot Springs Middle School
Programme MYP
MYP Coordinator Jule Grant
Gender Coeducational
Boarding/day Boarding
701 Main Street, Hot Springs AR 71913, USA
TELEPHONE: +1 501 624 5228

Mount Saint Mary Academy
Status Private
Programme Diploma
Diploma Coordinator Kelly O'Rourke
Gender Girls
Languages English
Boarding/day Day
3224 Kavanaugh Blvd, Little Rock AR 72205, USA
TELEPHONE: +1 501 664 8006
FAX: +1 501 666 4382
EMAIL: srcward@mtstmary.edu
WEBSITE: www.mtstmary.edu

North Little Rock High School West Campus
Status State
Programme Diploma
Diploma Coordinator Mary Hicks
Languages English
101 West 22nd Street, North Little Rock AR 72114, USA
TELEPHONE: +1 501 771 8100
FAX: +1 501 771 8123
EMAIL: maryehicks@cs.com

Park International Magnet School
Status State
Programme PYP
PYP Coordinator Becky Rosburg
Gender Coeducational
Boarding/day Day
220 Tom Ellsworth Drive, Hot Springs
AR 71901, USA
TELEPHONE: +1 501 623 5661
FAX: +1 501 620 7835
EMAIL: beards@hssd.net
WEBSITE: www.hssd.net

Springdale High School
Status State
Programme Diploma
Diploma Coordinator Carol Turley
Gender Coeducational
Boarding/day Day
1103 West Emma Avenue, Springdale
AR 72764, USA
TELEPHONE: +1 479 750 8832
EMAIL: dkellogg@sdale.org
WEBSITE: www.shs.springdaleschools.org

Westwood Elementary School
Status State
Programme PYP
PYP Coordinator Nandra Campbell
Gender Coeducational
Languages English
Boarding/day Day
1850 McRay, Springdale AR 72762, USA
TELEPHONE: +1 479 750 8871
FAX: +1 479 750 8873
EMAIL: jrogers@sdale.org
WEBSITE:
http://westwood.springdaleschools.org

Arizona

Cactus Shadows High School
Status State
Programme Diploma
Diploma Coordinator Monica Barrett
Gender Coeducational
Languages English
Boarding/day Day
PO Box 426, Cave Creek AZ 85327-0426, USA
TELEPHONE: +1 480-575-2400
FAX: +1 480-488-6701
EMAIL: sbailey@ccusd93.org
WEBSITE: www.cshsweb.com

Chandler High School
Status State
Programme Diploma
Diploma Coordinator Sherry Gore
Gender Coeducational
Languages English
Boarding/day Day
350 North Arizona Avenue, Chandler
AZ 85225, USA
TELEPHONE: +1 480 812 7700
FAX: +1 480 812 7720
EMAIL: wilsont@chandler.k12.az.us

Cholla High Magnet School
Status State
Programme Diploma
Diploma Coordinator Joyce E Meyer
Gender Coeducational
Languages English
Boarding/day Day
2001 W Starr Boulevard, Tucson AZ 85713,
USA
TELEPHONE: +1 520 225 4004
FAX: +1 520 225 4001
WEBSITE: http://edweb.tusd1.org/Cholla

Desert Mountain High School
Status State
Programme Diploma
Diploma Coordinator Laura Kamka
Gender Coeducational
Languages English
Boarding/day Day
12575 E Via Linda, Scottsdale Unified,
Scottsdale AZ 85259, USA
TELEPHONE: +1 480 484-7009
FAX: +1 480 484-7001
EMAIL: gmilbrandt@susd.org
WEBSITE:
www.susd.org/schools/high/Desertmtn/

Grand Canyon Elementary School
Status State
Programme PYP, MYP
MYP Coordinator Becky Crumbo
PYP Coordinator Deb Goepfrich
Gender Coeducational
Languages English
Boarding/day Day
1 Boulder Street, PO Box 519, Grand Canyon
AZ 86023, USA
TELEPHONE: +1 928 638 2461
EMAIL: sheila@grandcanyonschool.org
WEBSITE: www.grandcanyonschool.org/

Grand Canyon Unified School District #4
Status State
Programme MYP
MYP Coordinator Becky Crumbo
Gender Coeducational
Languages English
Boarding/day Day
PO Box 519, Grand Canyon AZ 86023, USA
TELEPHONE: +1 928 638 2461 x200
EMAIL: bobk@grandcanyonschool.org
WEBSITE: www.grandcanyonschool.org

Ironwood High School
Status State
Programme Diploma
Diploma Coordinator Nancy Lewis
Gender Coeducational
Languages English
Boarding/day Day
6051 West Sweetwater Avenue, Glendale
AZ 85304, USA
TELEPHONE: +1 623 486 6400
EMAIL: mmatheso@peoriaud.k12.az.us
WEBSITE:
http://ironwoodhigh.peoriaud.k12.az.us

Nogales High School
Status State
Programme Diploma
Diploma Coordinator Karen Ralston
Gender Coeducational
Languages English
Boarding/day Day
1905 North Apache Boulevard, Nogales
AZ 85621, USA
TELEPHONE: +1 602 287 0900
FAX: +1 520 281 4448
EMAIL: mvalenzuela@nusd.k12.az.us

North Canyon High School
Status State
Programme Diploma
Diploma Coordinator Catherine Flesner
Gender Coeducational
Languages English
Boarding/day Day
1700 East Union Hills Drive, Phoenix
AZ 85024, USA
TELEPHONE: +1 623 780 4200
FAX: +1 623 780 4304
EMAIL: cpollack@pvusd.k12.az.us
WEBSITE: www.pvschools.net

North High School
Status State
Programme Diploma
Diploma Coordinator Julie Pallissard
Gender Coeducational
Languages English
Boarding/day Day
1101 East Thomas Road, Phoenix AZ 85014,
USA
TELEPHONE: +1 602 764- 6511
FAX: +1 602 271 2765
EMAIL: pletenik@phxhs.k12.az.us
WEBSITE: www.globalc.org/puhsd/north

Verde Valley School
Status Private
Programme Diploma
Diploma Coordinator Paul Stein
Gender Coeducational
Languages English
Boarding/day Mixed
3511 Verde Valley School Road, Sedona
AZ 86351, USA
TELEPHONE: +1 928 284 2274
FAX: +1 928 284 0432
EMAIL: pauld@verdevalleyschool.org
WEBSITE: www.vvsaz.org

Westwood High School
Status State
Programme Diploma
Diploma Coordinator Gregg Good
Gender Coeducational
Boarding/day Day
945 West 8th Street, Mesa AZ 85201-3999,
USA
TELEPHONE: +1 480 472 4400
EMAIL: hdriddle@mpsaz.org
WEBSITE: www.mpsaz.org/westwood

Willow Canyon High School
Status State
Programme Diploma
Diploma Coordinator Amy Hartjen
Gender Coeducational
Languages English
Boarding/day Day
17901 West Lundberg St, Surprise AZ 85388, USA
TELEPHONE: +1 623-523-8000
FAX: +1 623-523-8011
EMAIL: kvogt@dysart.org
WEBSITE: www.dysart.org

California

Albert Einstein Academy Charter School
Status State
Programme PYP
PYP Coordinator Libby Krueger
Gender Coeducational
Languages English
Boarding/day Day
3035 Ash Street, San Diego CA 92102, USA
TELEPHONE: +1 619 795 1190
FAX: +1 619 795 1180
EMAIL: lfowers@aeacs.org
WEBSITE: www.alberteinsteinacademy.org

Amelia Earhart Elementary
Status State
Programme PYP
PYP Coordinator Joy Bugg
Gender Coeducational
Boarding/day Day
45-250 Dune Palms Road, Indio CA 92201, USA
TELEPHONE: +1 760 200 3720

Andrew P Hill High School
Status State
Programme Diploma
Diploma Coordinator Michael Winsatt
Gender Coeducational
Languages English
3200 Senter Road, San Jose CA 95111-1399, USA
TELEPHONE: +1 408 347 4100
FAX: +1 408 347 4115
EMAIL: rileyd@esuhsd.org

Anna Borba Fundamental Elementary School
Status State
Programme PYP
PYP Coordinator Loretta Nance
Gender Coeducational
Languages English
Boarding/day Day
12970 Third Street, Chino CA 91710, USA
TELEPHONE: +1 909 627 9613
FAX: +1 909 590 1650
EMAIL: kathy_hemlock@chino.k12.ca.us
WEBSITE: http://borba.chino.k12.ca.us

Armijo High School
Status State
Programme Diploma
Diploma Coordinator Ashley Parks
Gender Coeducational
Languages English
824 Washington Street, Fairfield CA 94533, USA
TELEPHONE: +1 707 438 3366
FAX: +1 707 422 3390
EMAIL: rickv@fsusd.k12.ca.us
WEBSITE: www.fsusd.k12.ca.us.armijo/armijo/htm

Arroyo Valley High School
Status State
Programme Diploma
Diploma Coordinator Robert Grande
Gender Coeducational
Languages English
Boarding/day Day
1881 W Base Line, San Bernardino CA 92411, USA
TELEPHONE: +1 909 381 4295
FAX: +1 909 386 2577
EMAIL: karen.craig@sbcusd.k12.ca.us
WEBSITE: www.arroyovalleyhighschool.org

Berkeley High School
Status State
Programme Diploma
Diploma Coordinator Rory Bled
Gender Coeducational
Languages English
Boarding/day Day
1980 Allston Way, Berkeley CA 94704, USA
TELEPHONE: +1 510 644 6120
FAX: +1 510 548 4221
EMAIL: jslemp@berkeley.k12.ca.us
WEBSITE: www.bhs.berkeley.k12.ca.us

Bishop Amat Memorial High School
Status State
Programme Diploma
Diploma Coordinator Raphael Domingo
Gender Coeducational
Languages English
Boarding/day Day
14301 Fairgrove, La Puente CA 91746, USA
TELEPHONE: +1 626 962 2495
EMAIL: mhemenway@bishopamat.org
WEBSITE: www.bishopamat.org

Blair High School
Status State
Programme MYP, Diploma
Diploma Coordinator Elizabeth Klinger
MYP Coordinator Elizabeth Klinger
Gender Coeducational
Boarding/day Day
1201 S Marengo Avenue, Pasadena CA 91106, USA
TELEPHONE: +1 626 441 2201
FAX: +1 626 441 6148
EMAIL: rboccia@pusd.us
WEBSITE: www.blairibmagnet.org

Bonita Vista High School
Status State
Programme Diploma
Diploma Coordinator Janice Anderson
Gender Coeducational
Languages English
Boarding/day Day
751 Otay Lakes Road, Chula Vista CA 91913, USA
TELEPHONE: +1 619 216 5000
FAX: +1 619 656 1203
EMAIL: bettina.batista@suhsd.k12.ca.us
WEBSITE: www.suhsd.k12.ca.us/bvh/

Burnett Academy
Programme MYP
MYP Coordinator Diane Shearer
Gender Coeducational
Boarding/day Mixed
850 North Second Street, San Jose CA 95112, USA
TELEPHONE: +1 408 535 6267
EMAIL: diane_shearer@sjusd.org

Cajon High School
Status State
Programme Diploma
Diploma Coordinator Steven Flitsch
Gender Coeducational
Languages English
Boarding/day Day
1200 Hill Drive, San Bernardino CA 92407, USA
TELEPHONE: +1 909 881 8120
FAX: +1 909 881 8141
EMAIL: brett.killeen@sbcusd.k12.ca.us

Canyon High School
Status State
Programme Diploma
Diploma Coordinator Brenna Heid
Gender Coeducational
Languages English
Boarding/day Day
220 S Imperial Highway, Anaheim CA 92807, USA
TELEPHONE: +1 714 532 8000
FAX: +1 714 532 8065
EMAIL: relhinn@aol.com

Capistrano Valley High School
Status State
Programme Diploma
Diploma Coordinator William Redding
Gender Coeducational
Languages English
Boarding/day Day
26301 Via Escolar, Mission Viejo CA 92692, USA
TELEPHONE: +1 949 364 6100
EMAIL: tressler@capousd.org
WEBSITE: www.cvhs.com/

Capuchino High School
Status State
Programme Diploma
Diploma Coordinator Naomi Tuite
Gender Coeducational
Languages English
Boarding/day Day
1501 Magnolia Avenue, San Bruno CA 94066, USA
TELEPHONE: +1 650 558-2700
FAX: +1 650 558 2759
EMAIL: kvillalobos@smuhsd.org
WEBSITE: www.chs.smuhsd.org

Castle Park High School
Status State
Programme Diploma
Diploma Coordinator Ileana Rodriguez
Gender Coeducational
Languages English
Boarding/day Day
1395 Hilltop Drive, SUHSD, Chula Vista CA 91911, USA
TELEPHONE: +1 619 691 5600
FAX: +1 619 427 5967
EMAIL: maria.castilleja@suhsd.k12.ca.us

Castle Rock Elementary School
Status State
Programme PYP
PYP Coordinator Peggy Vera
Gender Coeducational
Languages English
Boarding/day Day
2975 Castle Rock Road, Diamond Bar CA 91765, USA
TELEPHONE: +1 909 598 5006
FAX: +1 909 598 5960
EMAIL: mchavez@walnutvalley.k12.ca.us
WEBSITE: www.walnutvalley.k12.ca.us/castlerock/

Centennial High School
Status State
Programme MYP, Diploma
Diploma Coordinator Linda Linville
MYP Coordinator Linda Linville
Gender Coeducational
Languages English
Boarding/day Day
1820 Rimpau Avenue, Corona CA 92881-7405, USA
TELEPHONE: +1 909 739 5670
FAX: +1 909 739 5683
EMAIL: sbuenrostro@cnusd.k12.ca.us

Charter Oak High School
Status State
Programme Diploma
Diploma Coordinator Pat Nixon
Gender Coeducational
Languages English
Boarding/day Day
PO Box 9, Covina CA 91723, USA
TELEPHONE: +1 626 915 5841
FAX: +1 626 915 3398
EMAIL: dsauvageau@cousd.k12.ca.us

Corona Fundamental Intermediate
Programme MYP
MYP Coordinator Linda Linville
Gender Coeducational
Boarding/day Boarding
1230 South Main Street, Corona CA 92882, USA
TELEPHONE: +1 909 736 3321

Coronado High School
Status State
Programme Diploma
Diploma Coordinator Jennifer Moore
Gender Coeducational
Languages English
Boarding/day Day
650 D Avenue, Coronado CA 92118, USA
TELEPHONE: +1 619 522 8907
FAX: +1 619 437 0236
EMAIL: ebennett@coronado.k12.ca.us
WEBSITE: www.chs.coronado.k12.ca.us

Cyrus J Morris Elementary School
Status State
Programme PYP
PYP Coordinator Diva Abel
Gender Coeducational
Languages English
Boarding/day Day
91785 E Calle Baja, Walnut CA 91789, USA
TELEPHONE: +1 909 594 0053
FAX: +1 909 595 9438
EMAIL: sarzola@walnutvalley.k12.ca.us
WEBSITE: www.walnutvalley.k12.ca.us

David Starr Jordan High School
Status State
Programme Diploma
Diploma Coordinator Steve Rockenbach
Gender Coeducational
Languages English
Boarding/day Day
6500 Atlantic Avenue, Long Beach Unified School Dist, Long Beach CA 90805, USA
TELEPHONE: +1 562 423 1471
FAX: +1 562 422 9091
EMAIL: khurley@lbusd.k12.ca.us

Diamond Bar High School
Status State
Programme Diploma
Diploma Coordinator Dena Lordi
Gender Coeducational
Languages English
Boarding/day Day
21400 East Pathfinder Rd, Diamond Bar CA 91765, USA
TELEPHONE: +1 909 594 1405
FAX: +1 909 595 8301
EMAIL: denisrpaul@aol.com
WEBSITE: www.walnutvalley.k12.ca.us/dbhs

Dos Pueblos High School
Status State
Programme Diploma
Diploma Coordinator Karen Beckstead
Languages English
7266 Alameda Avenue, Goleta CA 93117, USA
TELEPHONE: +1 805 968 2541
FAX: +1 805 968 7681
EMAIL: qpanek@dphs.org

El Toro High School
Status State
Programme Diploma
Diploma Coordinator David Skidmore
Gender Coeducational
Languages English
25255 Toledo Way, Lake Forest CA 92630, USA
TELEPHONE: +1 949 586 6333
FAX: +1 949 380 9874
EMAIL: skidmored@svusd.ca.us

Elizabeth Hudson School
Status State
Programme PYP
PYP Coordinator Lori DeWitt
Gender Coeducational
Languages English
Boarding/day Day
2335 Webster Avenue, Long Beach CA 90810, USA
TELEPHONE: +1 562 426 0470
FAX: +1 562 595 4120
EMAIL: wclaflin@lbusd.k12.ca.ua
WEBSITE: www.lbusd.k12.ca.us/hudson/hudson.htm

Fairmont Preparatory Academy
Status Private
Programme Diploma
Diploma Coordinator Steven Georgiades
Gender Coeducational
Languages English
Boarding/day Day
2200 West Sequoia Avenue, Anaheim CA 92801, USA
TELEPHONE: +1 714 999 5055
FAX: +1 714 999 0150
EMAIL: ugemba@fairmontschools.com
WEBSITE: www.fairmontschools.com

Foothill High School
Status State
Programme Diploma
Diploma Coordinator Victoria Owens
Gender Coeducational
Languages English
Boarding/day Day
19251 Dodge Avenue, Santa Ana CA 92705, USA
TELEPHONE: +1 714 730 7464
EMAIL: amarzilli@.tustin.k12.ca.us
WEBSITE: www.tustin.k12.ca.us/foothill

Foothill High School
Status State
Programme Diploma
Diploma Coordinator Rebecca Farley
Gender Coeducational
Languages English
Boarding/day Day
501 Park Drive, Bakersfield CA 93306, USA
TELEPHONE: +1 661 366 4491
EMAIL: mrichardson@khsd.k12.ca.us
WEBSITE: www.khsd.k12.ca.us/foothill

Frances E Willard Elementary Magnet School
Status State
Programme PYP
PYP Coordinator Linda Wittry
Gender Coeducational
Boarding/day Day
301 South Madre Street, Pasadena CA 91107, USA
TELEPHONE: +1 626 793 6163
EMAIL: konoye@pusd.us
WEBSITE: www.pusd.us

Franklin High School
Status State
Programme Diploma
Diploma Coordinator Erin Thiele
Gender Coeducational
Languages English
Boarding/day Day
300 North Gertrude Avenue, Stockton Unified, Stockton CA 95215, USA
TELEPHONE: +1 209 953 4373
FAX: +1 209 464 4708
EMAIL: sluhn@stockton.k12.ca.us
WEBSITE: www.franklinib.org

Fresno High School
Status State
Programme Diploma
Diploma Coordinator Laura Spongberg
Languages English
1839 N Echo Avenue, Fresno CA 93704, USA
TELEPHONE: +1 559 457 2793
FAX: +1 559 457 2801
EMAIL: rxreyes@fresno.k12.ca.us

Fullerton Union High School
Status State
Programme Diploma
Diploma Coordinator Mark Henderson
Gender Coeducational
Languages English
Boarding/day Day
201 East Chapman Avenue, Fullerton CA 92832-1925, USA
TELEPHONE: +1 714 626-3802
FAX: +1 714 626-3839
EMAIL: cgach@fjuhsd.k12.ca.us

German American International School
Status Private
Programme PYP
PYP Coordinator Maike Silver
Gender Coeducational
Languages German, English
Boarding/day Day
275 Elliott Drive, Menlo Park CA 94025, USA
TELEPHONE: +1 650 324 8617
FAX: +1 650 324 9548
EMAIL: info@germanamericanschool.org
WEBSITE: www.germanamericanschool.org/

Glen A Wilson High School
Status State
Programme Diploma
Diploma Coordinator Patricia Tsuneyoshi
Gender Coeducational
Languages English
Boarding/day Day
16455 East Wedgeworth Drive, Hacienda Heights CA 91745, USA
TELEPHONE: +1 626 934-4401
FAX: +1 626 855 3792
EMAIL: aclegg@hlpusd.k12.ca.us

Granite Bay High School
Status State
Programme Diploma
Diploma Coordinator Sharry Colnar
Gender Coeducational
Languages English
Boarding/day Day
1 Grizzly Way, Granite Bay CA 95746, USA
TELEPHONE: +1 916 786 8676
FAX: +1 916 786 0766
EMAIL: scolnar@rjuhsd.k12.ca.us
WEBSITE: http://granitebayhigh.org

Granite Hills High School
Status State
Programme Diploma
Diploma Coordinator Patricia Gage
Gender Coeducational
Languages English
1719 East Madison Avenue, El Cajon CA 92021, USA
TELEPHONE: +1 619 593-5500
FAX: +1 619 588 9389
EMAIL: gtorres@guhsd.net

Great Oak High School
Status State
Programme Diploma
Diploma Coordinator January King
Gender Coeducational
Languages English
Boarding/day Day
32555 Deer Hollow Road, Temecula CA 92592, USA
TELEPHONE: +1 951-294-6450
FAX: +1 951-294-6477
EMAIL: tritter@tvusd.k12.ca.us
WEBSITE: http://gohs.tvusd.k12.ca.us/

Guajome Park Academy
Status State
Programme MYP, Diploma
Diploma Coordinator Gayle Garcia
MYP Coordinator Gayle Garcia
Gender Coeducational
Languages English
Boarding/day Day
2000 North Santa Fe Avenue, Vista Unified School District, Vista CA 92083, USA
TELEPHONE: +1 760- 631-5000
FAX: +1 760 940-0393
EMAIL: harrisonpe@guajome.com
WEBSITE: www.guajome.net

Highland High School
Status State
Programme Diploma
Diploma Coordinator Glen Horst
Languages English
39055 25th Street West, Palmdale CA 93551, USA
TELEPHONE: +1 661 538 0304
FAX: +1 661 538 0405
EMAIL: sbryant@avhsd.org

International High School of F.A.I.S
Status Private
Programme Diploma
Diploma Coordinator Richard Ulffers
Gender Coeducational
Languages English
Boarding/day Day
150 Oak Street, San Francisco CA 94102-6124, USA
TELEPHONE: +1 415 558 2022
FAX: +1 415 626 8551
EMAIL: janec@fais-ihs.org
WEBSITE: www.fais-ihs.org

John F Kennedy High School
Status State
Programme MYP, Diploma
Diploma Coordinator Cam Peterson
MYP Coordinator Joanna Meyer
Gender Coeducational
Languages English
Boarding/day Day
8281 Walker Street, La Palma CA 90623, USA
TELEPHONE: +1 714 220 4118
FAX: +1 714 995 1833
EMAIL: wilson_k@auhsd.k12.ca.us

John Glenn Middle School
Status State
Programme MYP
MYP Coordinator Patricia Deragisch
Gender Coeducational
Boarding/day Day
79-655 Miles Avenue, DSUSD, Indio CA 92201, USA
TELEPHONE: +1 760 200 3700
EMAIL: marcus.wood@dsusd.us
WEBSITE:
www.dsusd.k12.ca.us/schools/JGMS

John Wesley North High School
Status State
Programme Diploma
Diploma Coordinator Christine Schive
Gender Coeducational
Languages English
Boarding/day Day
1550 Third Street, Riverside CA 92507, USA
TELEPHONE: +1 951 788 7311
FAX: +1 951 276 2075
EMAIL: dkinnear@north.rusd.k12.ca.us

La Mirada High School
Status State
Programme Diploma
Diploma Coordinator Guy Roberts
Gender Coeducational
Languages English
Boarding/day Day
13520 Adelfa Drive, La Mirada CA 90638, USA
TELEPHONE: +1 562 868 0431 x3101
EMAIL: jones_don@nlmusd.k12.ca.us
WEBSITE: www.lamiradahighschool.com/

La Quinta High School
Status State
Programme MYP, Diploma
Diploma Coordinator Diana Cinatl
MYP Coordinator Deborah Dolan
Gender Coeducational
Languages English
Boarding/day Day
79-255 Westward Ho Drive, La Quinta
CA 92253, USA
TELEPHONE: +1 760 772 4150
FAX: +1 760 772 4166
EMAIL: donna.salazar@dsvsd.us
WEBSITE:
www.dsusd.k12.ca.us/schools/LQHS/

La Quinta Middle School
Status State
Programme MYP
MYP Coordinator Deborah Dolan
Gender Coeducational
Languages English
Boarding/day Day
78-900 Avenue 50, La Quinta CA 92253, USA
TELEPHONE: +1 760 777 4220
FAX: +1 760 777 4216
EMAIL: janet.seto@dsusd.us
WEBSITE: www.dsusd.us

Laguna Hills High School
Status State
Programme Diploma
Diploma Coordinator Barbee Martin
Gender Coeducational
Languages English
Boarding/day Day
25401 Paseo de Valencia, Saddleback Unified,
Laguna Hills CA 92653, USA
TELEPHONE: +1 949 770 5447
FAX: +1 949 830 0295
EMAIL: adams@svusd.k12.ca.us

Letha Raney Intermediate
Programme MYP
MYP Coordinator Linda Linville
Gender Coeducational
Boarding/day Boarding
1010 West Citron Street, Corona CA 92882,
USA
TELEPHONE: +1 909 736 3221

Lexington Elementary School
Status State
Programme PYP
PYP Coordinator Gayle Gordon
Gender Coeducational
Languages English
Boarding/day Day
19700 Old Santa Cruz Highway, Los Gatos
CA 95033, USA
TELEPHONE: +1 408 335 2150
FAX: +1 408 354 2014
EMAIL: dfreed@lgusd.k12.ca.us
WEBSITE: www.lex.lgusd.k12.ca.us

Loara High School
Status State
Programme Diploma
Diploma Coordinator Lyle Higger
Gender Coeducational
Languages English
Boarding/day Day
1765 W Cerritos Avenue, Anaheim CA 92804,
USA
TELEPHONE: +1 714 999-3677
FAX: +1 714-999-3703
EMAIL: krey_p@auhsd.k12.ca.us
WEBSITE: www.loaraib.net

Luther Burbank High School
Status State
Programme Diploma
Diploma Coordinator Chris Coey
Gender Coeducational
Languages English
Boarding/day Day
3500 Florin Road, Sacramento CA 95823, USA
FAX: +1 916 433-5199
EMAIL: chriscoey@mindspring.com
WEBSITE: www.lutherburbankhs.com

Lycee International de Los Angeles
Status Private
Programme Diploma
Diploma Coordinator Alexander McGregor
Gender Coeducational
Languages English
Boarding/day Day
4155 Russell Avenue, Los Angeles CA 90027,
USA
TELEPHONE: +1 323 665 4526
FAX: +1 323 665 2607
EMAIL: elizabeth.chaponot@lilaschool.com
WEBSITE: www.lilaschool.com

Marco Antonio Firebaugh High School
Status State
Programme Diploma
Diploma Coordinator Sarah Mott
Gender Coeducational
Languages English
Boarding/day Day
5246 Martin Luther King Jr Blvd, Lynwood
CA 90262, USA
TELEPHONE: +1 310 886 5200
FAX: +1 310 637 8041
EMAIL: jsilverio@lynwoodusd.org
WEBSITE: http://fhs.lynwoodusd.org

McKinleyville High School
Status State
Programme Diploma
Diploma Coordinator Jack Bareilles
Gender Coeducational
Languages English
Boarding/day Day
1300 Murray Road, McKinleyville CA 95519,
USA
TELEPHONE: +1 707 839 6400
FAX: +1 707 839 6407
EMAIL: dlonn@nohum.k12.ca.us
WEBSITE: www.nohum.k12.ca.us/mhs/

Mira Loma High School
Status State
Programme MYP, Diploma
Diploma Coordinator David Mathews
MYP Coordinator Guy Roberts
Gender Coeducational
Languages English
Boarding/day Day
4000 Edison Avenue, San Juan Unified,
Sacramento CA 95821, USA
TELEPHONE: +1 916 971 7973
FAX: +1 916 971 7483
EMAIL: choffman@sanjuan.edu
WEBSITE:
www.sanjuan.edu/schools/miraloma.htm

Mission Bay High School
Status State
Programme Diploma
Diploma Coordinator Melissa Romero
Gender Coeducational
Languages English
Boarding/day Day
2475 Grand Ave, San Diego CA 92109, USA
TELEPHONE: +1 858 273 1313
FAX: +1 858 270 8294
EMAIL: cseelos@sandi.net
WEBSITE: www.sandi.net/missionbayhigh

Mission Viejo High School
Status State
Programme Diploma
Diploma Coordinator Jerry Chris
Gender Coeducational
Languages English
Boarding/day Day
25025 Chrisanta Drive, Mission Viejo
CA 9269, USA
TELEPHONE: +1 949 837 7722
FAX: +1 949 830 0782
EMAIL: mcdowell@svusd.k12.ca.us

Modesto High School
Status State
Programme Diploma
Diploma Coordinator Susan Elliott
Gender Coeducational
Languages English
Boarding/day Day
First & H Street, Modesto City Schools,
Modesto CA 95351, USA
TELEPHONE: +1 209 576-4404
FAX: +1 209 576 4434
EMAIL: byers.m@monet.k12.ca.us

Montgomery High School
Status State
Programme Diploma
Diploma Coordinator Dorothy Battenfeld
Gender Coeducational
Languages English
Boarding/day Day
1250 Hahman Drive, Santa Rosa CA 95405,
USA
TELEPHONE: +1 707 528 5512
FAX: +1 707 528 5056
EMAIL: lfong@srcs.k12.ca.us
WEBSITE: www.montgomeryhighschool.com

Newbury Park High School
Status State
Programme Diploma
Diploma Coordinator Marcine Solarez
Gender Coeducational
Languages English
Boarding/day Day
456 Reino Road, Newbury Park CA 91320,
USA
TELEPHONE: +1 805 498 3676
EMAIL: mbeaman@conejo.k12.ca.us
WEBSITE: http://nphs.conejo.k12.ca.us

Nogales High School
Status State
Programme Diploma
Diploma Coordinator Robert Cook
Gender Coeducational
Languages English
Boarding/day Day
401 Nogales Street, Rowland Unified School
Distric, La Puente CA 91744, USA
TELEPHONE: +1 626 965 3437
EMAIL: kcoggins@mail.rowland.k12.ca.us

Norte Vista High School
Status State
Programme Diploma
Diploma Coordinator Shawn Marshall
Gender Coeducational
Languages English
Boarding/day Day
6585 Crest Avenue, Riverside CA 92503, USA
TELEPHONE: +1 951 351 9316
FAX: +1 951 351 9249
EMAIL: scampos@alvord.k12.ca.us
WEBSITE: www.alvord.k12.ca.us/nortevista

Northcoast Preparatory and Performing Arts Academy
Status State
Programme Diploma
Diploma Coordinator Amy Miller-Bazemore
Gender Coeducational
Languages English
Boarding/day Boarding
PO Box 865, Trinidad CA 95570, USA
TELEPHONE: +1 707 677-3737
EMAIL: am_bazemore@hotmail.com

Oakmont High School
Status State
Programme Diploma
Diploma Coordinator Michelle Mahoney
Gender Coeducational
Languages English
Boarding/day Day
1710 Cirby Way, Roseville CA 95661, USA
TELEPHONE: +1 916 782 3781
FAX: +1 916 782 4943
EMAIL: ksirovy@rjuhsd.us
WEBSITE: http://ohs.rjuhsd.us

Ocean View High School
Status State
Programme Diploma
Diploma Coordinator James Burch
Gender Coeducational
Languages English
Boarding/day Day
17071 Gothard Street, Huntington Beach
CA 92647, USA
TELEPHONE: +1 714-848-0656
FAX: +1 714-843-0541
EMAIL: kgilden@ovhs.info

Pacific Beach Middle School
Status State
Programme MYP
MYP Coordinator Jennifer Sims
Gender Coeducational
Languages English
Boarding/day Day
4676 Ingraham Street, San Diego CA 92109,
USA
TELEPHONE: +1 858 273 9070
FAX: +1 858 270 8063
EMAIL: mirwin1@sandi.net
WEBSITE: www.pbmiddle.sandi.net

Pleasant Valley High School
Status State
Programme Diploma
Diploma Coordinator Dan Beadle
Gender Coeducational
Languages English
Boarding/day Day
1475 East Avenue, Chico CA 95926, USA
TELEPHONE: +1 530 879 5102
FAX: +1 530 879 5263
EMAIL: mrupp@pvchico.org

Quartz Hill High School
Status State
Programme Diploma
Diploma Coordinator Kathleen Parks
Languages English
6040 West Avenue L, Quartz Hill CA 93536,
USA
TELEPHONE: +1 661 718 3100
FAX: +1 661 943 8203
EMAIL: mbryant@avhsd.org

Rancho Buena Vista High School
Status State
Programme Diploma
Diploma Coordinator Eileen Hermansen
Gender Coeducational
Languages English
Boarding/day Day
1601 Longhorn Drive, Vista CA 92083, USA
TELEPHONE: +1 760 727 7284
EMAIL: ralderso@vusd.k12.ca.us

Rio Mesa High School
Status State
Programme Diploma
Diploma Coordinator Lori A Wrout
Gender Coeducational
Languages English
Boarding/day Day
545 Central Avenue, Oxnard CA 93030, USA
TELEPHONE: +1 805 278 5500
EMAIL: rrickard@ouhsd.k12.ca.us
WEBSITE: www.ouhsd.k12.ca.us

Roosevelt Middle School
Programme MYP
MYP Coordinator Nirit Cohen-Vardi
Gender Coeducational
Boarding/day Day
3366 Park Blvd, San Diego CA 92103, USA
TELEPHONE: +1 619-293-4450
EMAIL: jmartel@sandi.net
WEBSITE: http://roosevelt.sandi.net

Rowland High School
Status State
Programme Diploma
Diploma Coordinator Donnette Waters
Gender Coeducational
Languages English
Boarding/day Day
2000 S Otterbein Avenue, Rowland Heights
CA 91748, USA
TELEPHONE: +1 626 965 3448
EMAIL: rrobinson@mail.rowland.k12.ca.ua
WEBSITE: www.rhs.rowland.k12.ca.us

Saint Helena High School
Status State
Programme Diploma
Diploma Coordinator Cynthia Brown
Gender Coeducational
Languages English
Boarding/day Day
1401 Grayson Avenue, Saint Helena CA 94574, USA
TELEPHONE: +1 707 967 2740
FAX: +1 707 967 2735
EMAIL: jzoll@sthelena.k12.ca.us
WEBSITE: www.sthelena.k12.ca.us

San Clemente High School
Status State
Programme Diploma
Diploma Coordinator Kathleen Sigafoos
Gender Coeducational
Languages English
Boarding/day Day
700 Avenida Pico, San Clemente CA 92673, USA
TELEPHONE: +1 949 492 4165
FAX: +1 949 361 5175
EMAIL: cdhinman@capousd.org

San Diego High School
Status State
Programme MYP, Diploma
Diploma Coordinator Karen de Laurier
MYP Coordinator Nirit Cohen-Vardi
Gender Coeducational
Languages English
Boarding/day Day
1405 Park Boulevard, San Diego Unified, San Diego CA 92101 4799, USA
TELEPHONE: +1 619 525 7455
EMAIL: kwroblew@mail.sandi.net
WEBSITE: www.sdhs.sandi.net/

San Jose High Academy
Status State
Programme MYP, Diploma
Diploma Coordinator Nancy Pereira
MYP Coordinator Liz Seabury
Gender Coeducational
Languages English
Boarding/day Day
275 North 24th Street, San Jose CA 95116, USA
TELEPHONE: +1 408 535 6320
FAX: +1 408 535 2355
EMAIL: betsy_doss@sjusd.org
WEBSITE: www.sjha.ca.campusgrid.net/home

Santa Margarita Catholic High School
Status Private
Programme Diploma
Diploma Coordinator Lyn Alexander
Gender Coeducational
Languages English
Boarding/day Day
22062 Antonio Parkway, Rancho Santa Margarita CA 92688, USA
TELEPHONE: +1 949 766 6000
FAX: +1 949 766 6005
EMAIL: monroel@smhs.org
WEBSITE: www.smhs.org

Santa Rosa Charter School
Status State
Programme PYP
PYP Coordinator Cyndi Chapman
Gender Coeducational
Languages English
Boarding/day Day
1835a West Steele Lane, Santa Rosa CA 95403, USA
TELEPHONE: +1 707 547 2480
FAX: +1 707 547 2482
EMAIL: charterschool@mac.com
WEBSITE: www.charterschool.mac.com/charterschool

Santa Ynez Valley Union High School
Status State
Programme Diploma
Diploma Coordinator Chris Avery
Gender Coeducational
Languages English
Boarding/day Day
PO Box 398, Santa Ynez CA 93460, USA
TELEPHONE: +1 805 688 6487
FAX: +1 805 686 3577
EMAIL: nclevenger@sbceo.og
WEBSITE: www.syvuhsd.org

Scotts Valley High School
Status State
Programme Diploma
Diploma Coordinator David Crawford
Gender Coeducational
Languages English
Principal, 555 Glenwood Drive, Scotts Valley CA 95066, USA
TELEPHONE: +1 831 439 9555
FAX: +1 831 439 9501
EMAIL: ggunkel@santacruz.k12.ca.us

Selby Lane School
Status State
Programme MYP
MYP Coordinator Vicki Lawlor
Gender Coeducational
Languages English
Boarding/day Day
170 Selby Lane, Atherton CA 94027, USA
TELEPHONE: +1 650 368 3996
FAX: +1 650 367 4366
EMAIL: cwilliams@rcsd.k12.ca.us
WEBSITE: http://selbylane.rcsd.k12.ca.us

Sequoia High School
Status State
Programme Diploma
Diploma Coordinator Marlyn Bussey
Gender Coeducational
Languages English
Boarding/day Day
1201 Brewster Avenue, Redwood City CA 94062, USA
TELEPHONE: +1 650 369 1411
FAX: +1 650 368 5180
EMAIL: mmarchba@seq.org
WEBSITE: www.sequoiahs.org

Sonora High School
Status State
Programme Diploma
Diploma Coordinator Robin Oliver
Gender Coeducational
Languages English
Boarding/day Day
401 South Palm Street, Fullerton Joint Union, La Habra CA 90631, USA
TELEPHONE: +1 562 266-2013
FAX: +1 562 266 2040
EMAIL: robinloliver@hotmail.com

St Mary & All Angels School
Status Private
Programme PYP, MYP
MYP Coordinator Sharon Taylor
PYP Coordinator Sharon Taylor
Gender Coeducational
Languages French
Boarding/day Day
7 Pursuit, Aliso Viejo CA 92656, USA
TELEPHONE: +1 949 448 9027
FAX: +1 949 448 0605
EMAIL: diane.dicorpo-fuller@smaa.org
WEBSITE: www.smaa.org

Sunny Hills High Schools
Status State
Programme Diploma
Diploma Coordinator Jeffrey Nelson
Gender Coeducational
Languages English
Boarding/day Day
1801 Warburton Way, Fullerton CA 92833, USA
TELEPHONE: +1 714 626 4213
FAX: +1 714 738 3728
EMAIL: iknelson36@earthlink.net

Sunnybrae Elementary School
Status State
Programme PYP
PYP Coordinator Wynne Hegarty
Gender Coeducational
Languages English
Boarding/day Day
1031 South Delaware Street, San Mateo CA 94402, USA
TELEPHONE: +1 650 312 7599
FAX: +1 650 312 7596
EMAIL: gjohnson@smfc.k12.ca.us
WEBSITE: www.smfc.k12.ca.us/sunnybrae

Trabuco Hills High School
Status State
Programme Diploma
Diploma Coordinator Susan Gordon
Languages English
27501 Mustang Run, Mission Viejo CA 92691, USA
TELEPHONE: +1 949 768 1934
FAX: +1 949 588 0763
EMAIL: sullivand@svusd.k12.ca.us

Tracy Joint Union High School

Status State
Programme Diploma
Diploma Coordinator Terri Sorgent
Gender Coeducational
Languages English
Boarding/day Day
315 East 11th Street, Tracy Public Schools, Tracy CA 95376, USA
TELEPHONE: +1 209 8315100 X2001
FAX: +1 209 831 5123
EMAIL: glindquist@tusd.net

Troy High School

Status State
Programme Diploma
Diploma Coordinator Priscilla Cheney
Gender Coeducational
Languages English
Boarding/day Day
2200 East Dorothy Lane, Fullerton CA 92831, USA
TELEPHONE: +1 714 626-4401
FAX: +1 714 626-4437
EMAIL: cmaruca@fjuhsd.k12.ca.us
WEBSITE: www.troyhigh.com

Valencia High School

Status State
Programme Diploma
Diploma Coordinator Fred Jenkins
Languages English
500 N Bradford Avenue, Placentia CA 92870, USA
TELEPHONE: +1 714 996 4970
FAX: +1 714 993 6124
EMAIL: bcline@pylusd.k12.ca.us

Vista High School

Status State
Programme Diploma
Diploma Coordinator Doreen Robinson
Gender Coeducational
Languages English
Boarding/day Day
1 Panther Way, Vista CA 92084, USA
TELEPHONE: +1 760 726 5611
FAX: +1 760 630 9738
EMAIL: lwhite@vusd.k12.ca.us

Walker Junior High School

Programme MYP
MYP Coordinator Joanna Meyer
Gender Coeducational
Boarding/day Boarding
8132 Walker Street, La Palma CA 90632, USA
TELEPHONE: +1 714 220 4051
EMAIL: fox_k@auhsd.k12.ca.us

Walnut High School

Status State
Programme Diploma
Diploma Coordinator Donna Crisci
Languages English
400 N Pierre Rd, Walnut CA 91789, USA
TELEPHONE: +1 909 594 1333
FAX: +1 909 594 7853
EMAIL: rlee-sung@walnutvalley.k12.ca.us

Wawona Middle School

Status State
Programme MYP
MYP Coordinator Geraldine Yamasaki
Gender Coeducational
Languages English
Boarding/day Day
4524 North Thorne Avenue, Fresno CA 93704, USA
TELEPHONE: +1 559 248 7310
WEBSITE:
www.fresno.k12.ca.us/schools/s079/

Wilmer Amina Carter High School

Status State
Programme Diploma
Diploma Coordinator Robin Pearce
Gender Coeducational
Languages English
Boarding/day Day
2630 North Linden Avenue, Rialto CA 92377, USA
TELEPHONE: +1 909 854 4100
FAX: +1 909 562 0232
EMAIL: vsmith@rialto.k12.ca.us
WEBSITE: www.rialto.k12.ca.us

Wilson Middle School

Status State
Programme MYP
MYP Coordinator Diane Tellefsen
Gender Coeducational
Languages English
Boarding/day Day
300 S Madre Street, Pasadena CA 91107, USA
TELEPHONE: +1 626 449 7390
EMAIL:
mabrahamson.pusdpost.pusdgw@pusd.us

Winston Churchill Middle School

Programme MYP
MYP Coordinator Guy Roberts
Gender Coeducational
Boarding/day Boarding
4900 Whitney Avenue, Carmicheal CA 95608, USA
TELEPHONE: +1 916 971 7324

Yosemite Union High School

Status State
Programme Diploma
Diploma Coordinator Randy Hyatt
Gender Coeducational
Languages English
Boarding/day Day
50200 Road 427, Oakhurst CA 93644, USA
TELEPHONE: +1 559 683 4667
FAX: +1 559 683 4160
EMAIL: sraupp@yosemiteuhsd.com

Colorado

Alpine Elementary School

Status State
Programme PYP
PYP Coordinator Amy Herrman
Gender Coeducational
Languages English
Boarding/day Day
2005 Alpine Street, Longmont CO 80501, USA
TELEPHONE: +1 720 652 8140
FAX: +1 720 652 8141
EMAIL: gordon_paige@stvrain.k12.co.us
WEBSITE: http://aes.stvrain.k12.co.us

Alsup Elementary School

Status State
Programme PYP
PYP Coordinator Mary Williams
Gender Coeducational
Languages English
Boarding/day Day
7101 Birch Street, Commerce City CO 80022, USA
TELEPHONE: +1 303 288 6865
FAX: +1 303 288 6866
EMAIL: lheintzman@acsd14.k12.co.us
WEBSITE: www.acsd14.k12.co.us

Antelope Trails Elementary

Status State
Programme PYP
PYP Coordinator Nageeba Davis
Gender Coeducational
Languages English
Boarding/day Day
15280 Jessie Drive, Colorado Springs CO 80921, USA
TELEPHONE: +1 719 234 4100
FAX: +1 719 234 4199
EMAIL: rgetche@d20.co.edu
WEBSITE:
http://academy.d20.co.edu/aate/index.html

Aspen High School

Status State
Programme Diploma
Diploma Coordinator Karen Jaworski
Gender Coeducational
Languages English
Boarding/day Day
235 High School Road, Aspen CO 81611, USA
TELEPHONE: +1 970 925 3760
FAX: +1 970 925 1205
EMAIL: canastas@aspenk12.net
WEBSITE: www.aspenk12.net

Aurora Hills Middle School

Programme MYP
MYP Coordinator Mary Perron
Gender Coeducational
Boarding/day Day
1009 S Uvalda, Aurora CO 80012, USA
TELEPHONE: +1 303 341 7450
EMAIL: jchaberer@aps-k12.co.us

Bennett Elementary School
Status State
Programme PYP, MYP
MYP Coordinator Karen Hammann
PYP Coordinator Michael Schooler
Gender Coeducational
Languages English
Boarding/day Boarding/day
1125 Bennett School Road, Fort Collins
CO 80521, USA
TELEPHONE: +1 970 484 6125
EMAIL: sreid@psdschools.org

Boulder Country Day School
Status Private
Programme MYP
MYP Coordinator Scott Alexander
Gender Coeducational
Languages English
Boarding/day Day
4820 Nautilus Court North, Boulder
CO 80301, USA
TELEPHONE: +1 303 527-4931
FAX: +1 303 527-4944
EMAIL: info@bouldercountryday.org
WEBSITE: www.bouldercountryday.org

Breckenridge Elementary School
Status State
Programme PYP
PYP Coordinator Debbie Griffith
Gender Coeducational
Languages English
Boarding/day Day
312 Harris Street, PO Box 1213, Breckenridge
CO 80424, USA
TELEPHONE: +1 970 453 2845
FAX: +1 07- 453 0156
EMAIL: hbates@summit.m12.co.us
WEBSITE: http://summit.k12.co.us/schools/
schools.htm

Centaurus High School
Status State
Programme Diploma
Diploma Coordinator Susie Mitzelfeld
Gender Coeducational
Languages English
Boarding/day Day
10300 E South Boulder Road, Lafayette
CO 80026, USA
TELEPHONE: +1 303-665-9211
FAX: +1 303-447-5368
EMAIL: deirdre.gibson@bvsd.org
WEBSITE: www.bvsd.org

Century Middle School
Status State
Programme MYP
MYP Coordinator Jennifer Viers
Gender Coeducational
Boarding/day Boarding
13000 Lafayette Street, Thornton CO 80241,
USA
TELEPHONE: +1 720 972 5240
WEBSITE: www.century.adams12.org

Challenge School
Status State
Programme PYP
PYP Coordinator Edie Alvarez
Boarding/day Day
9659 East Mississippi Avenue, Denver
CO 80247, USA
TELEPHONE: +1 720 747 2103

Cherokee Trail High School
Status State
Programme Diploma
Diploma Coordinator Diane Davison
Gender Coeducational
Languages English
Boarding/day Day
25901 E Arapahoe Road, Aurora CO 80016,
USA
TELEPHONE: +1 720 886 1900
EMAIL: mjarvis@cherrycreekschools.org
WEBSITE: www.cths.ccsd.k12.co.us

Clear Lake Middle School
Status State
Programme MYP
MYP Coordinator Colin Lee
Gender Coeducational
Languages English
Boarding/day Day
2401 West 80th Avenue, Denver CO 80221,
USA
TELEPHONE: +1 303 428 7503
FAX: +1 303 657 3943
EMAIL: cpeters@adams50.org
WEBSITE:
http://hodg.adams50.org/home.asp

Dillon Valley Elementary School
Status State
Programme PYP
PYP Coordinator Deborah Griffith
Gender Coeducational
Languages English
Boarding/day Day
PO Box 4788, Dillon CO 80435, USA
TELEPHONE: +1 970 468 9026
FAX: +1 970 468 9026
EMAIL: gjones@summit.k12.co.us
WEBSITE: http://summit.k12.co.us/schools/
dvelem/dve/dvehomep.htm

Discovery Canyon Campus
Status State
Programme MYP
MYP Coordinator Genevieve Price
Gender Coeducational
Languages English
Boarding/day Day
1810 Northgate Boulevard, Colorado Springs
CO 80921, USA
TELEPHONE: +1 719 234 1800
FAX: +1 719 234 1898
EMAIL: gbatsel@asd20.org
WEBSITE: http://school.asd20.org/DCC

Douglas County High School
Status State
Programme Diploma
Diploma Coordinator Steven Fleet
Gender Coeducational
Languages English
Boarding/day Day
2842 Front Street, Castle Rock CO 80104, USA
TELEPHONE: +1 303 814 4598
FAX: +1 303 387 1001
EMAIL: edna.doherty@dcsdk12.org
WEBSITE: www.dcsdk12.org

Dunn Elementary School
Status State
Programme PYP, MYP
MYP Coordinator Karen Hammann
PYP Coordinator Jan Borman
Gender Coeducational
Languages English
Boarding/day Boarding
501 South Washington, Fort Collins CO 80521,
USA
TELEPHONE: +1 970 482 0450
FAX: +1 970 212 0303
EMAIL: jkborman@psd.k12.co.us

Eugene Field Elementary School
Status State
Programme PYP
PYP Coordinator Martha Hussain
Gender Coeducational
Languages English
Boarding/day Day
5402 South Sherman Way, Littleton CO 80121,
USA
TELEPHONE: +1 303 347 4475
EMAIL: mmontgomery@lps.k12.co.us
WEBSITE:
www.field.littletonpublicschools.net

Fairview High School
Status State
Programme Diploma
Diploma Coordinator Susan Wei
Gender Coeducational
Languages English
Boarding/day Day
1515 Greenbriar Boulevard, Boulder
CO 80305, USA
TELEPHONE: +1 303 447 7600
FAX: +1 303 447 5353
EMAIL:
donald.stensrud@admin.bvsd.k12.co.us
WEBSITE:
http://flatirons.org/courses/ib.index.shtml

George Washington High School
Status State
Programme Diploma
Diploma Coordinator Suzanne Geimer
Gender Coeducational
Languages English
Boarding/day Day
655 South Monaco Street, Denver CO 80224, USA
TELEPHONE: +1 303 394 8620
FAX: +1 720 423 8614
EMAIL: mario_williams@dpsk12.org

Greeley West High School
Status State
Programme Diploma
Diploma Coordinator Daniel Augenstein
Gender Coeducational
Languages English
Boarding/day Day
2401 35th Avenue, Greeley CO 80634, USA
TELEPHONE: +1 970 348-5489
FAX: +1 970 348-5432
EMAIL: bobh@greeleyschools.org
WEBSITE: www.greeleywest.org

Heritage Middle School
Status State
Programme MYP
MYP Coordinator Jennifer Simms
233 East Mountain View Avenue, Longmont CO 80501, USA
TELEPHONE: +1 303 772 7900
FAX: +1 303 776 4376
EMAIL: borski_karolyn@stvrain.k12.co.us
WEBSITE: http://hms.stvrain.k12.co.us

Hinkley High School
Status State
Programme MYP, Diploma
Diploma Coordinator Jan Lotter
MYP Coordinator Jan Lotter
Gender Coeducational
Languages English
Boarding/day Day
1250 Chambers Road, Aurora, Arapahoe CO 80011, USA
TELEPHONE: +1 303 340 1500
FAX: +1 303 326 1274
EMAIL: jerryc@hinkley.aps.k12.co.us

Iver C Ranum High School
Status State
Programme MYP, Diploma
Diploma Coordinator Katie Ryan
MYP Coordinator Katie Ryan
Gender Coeducational
Languages English
Boarding/day Day
2401 W 80th Avenue, Denver CO 80221, USA
TELEPHONE: +1 303 428 9577
FAX: +1 303 657 3952
EMAIL: kryan@adams50.k12.co.us

John F Kennedy High School
Status State
Programme MYP, Diploma
Diploma Coordinator Matt Brown
MYP Coordinator Don Marsh
Gender Coeducational
Languages English
Boarding/day Day
2855 South Lamar Street, Denver CO 80227, USA
TELEPHONE: +1 720 423 4300
FAX: +1 720 423 4309
EMAIL: jeannie_peppel@dpsk12.org
WEBSITE: http://kennedy.dpsk12.org

Lake Middle School
Status State
Programme MYP
MYP Coordinator Kristy Briggs
Gender Coeducational
Languages English
Boarding/day Day
1820 Lowell Blvd, Denver CO 80204, USA
TELEPHONE: +1 720 424 0261
FAX: +1 720 424 0380
EMAIL: hans_kayser@dpsk12.org
WEBSITE: www.dpslake.org

Lakewood High School
Status State
Programme Diploma
Diploma Coordinator Dorsee Johnson-Tucker
Languages English
Boarding/day Day
9700 West 8th Avenue, Jefferson County - R1, Lakewood CO 80215, USA
TELEPHONE: +1 303 982-7085
FAX: +1 303 982 7098
EMAIL: rcastagn@jeffco.k12.co.us

Lesher Junior High School
Programme MYP
MYP Coordinator Karen Hammann
Gender Coeducational
Boarding/day Boarding
1600 Lancer Drive, Fort Collins CO 80521, USA
TELEPHONE: +1 970 484 3073
EMAIL: eginty@psdschools.org

Lincoln Junior High School
Status State
Programme MYP
MYP Coordinator Bobby Young
Gender Coeducational
Languages English
Boarding/day Day
1600 Lancer Drive, Fort Collins CO 80521, USA
TELEPHONE: +1 970 488 5700
EMAIL: lmarches@psdschools.org
WEBSITE: www.mylincolnonline.com

Littleton High School
Status State
Programme Diploma
Diploma Coordinator Claudia Anderson
Gender Coeducational
Languages English
Boarding/day Day
199 East Littleton Boulevard, Littleton CO 80121, USA
TELEPHONE: +1 303 347-7700
FAX: +1 303 347-7750
EMAIL: twesterberg@lps.k12.co.us

Loveland High School
Status State
Programme Diploma
Diploma Coordinator Glenda Nachtrieb
Languages English
Boarding/day Day
920 W 29th Street, Loveland CO 80538, USA
TELEPHONE: +1 970 613 5222
FAX: +1 970 613 7191
EMAIL: deasond@thompson.k12.co.us
WEBSITE: www.thompson.k12.co.us

Mackintosh Academy
Status Private
Programme PYP
PYP Coordinator Sharon Muench
Gender Coeducational
Languages English
Boarding/day Day
7018 S Prince Street, Littleton CO 80120, USA
TELEPHONE: +1 303 794 6222
FAX: +1 303 794 2286
EMAIL: renu@mail.mackintoshacademy.com
WEBSITE: www.mackintoshacademy.com

McGraw Elementary School
Status State
Programme PYP, MYP
MYP Coordinator Karen Hammann
PYP Coordinator Paul Schkade
Gender Coeducational
Boarding/day Boarding
4800 Hinsdale drive, Fort Collins CO 80526, USA
TELEPHONE: +1 970 223 0137
FAX: +1 970 223 0306
EMAIL: jpease@psd.k12.co.us

Midland International Elementary School
Status State
Programme PYP
PYP Coordinator Christina Allem
Gender Coeducational
Boarding/day Day
2110 W Broadway, Colorado Springs CO 80904, USA
TELEPHONE: +1 719 328 4500
EMAIL: bishobk@d11.org
WEBSITE: www.cssd11.k12.co.us/midland

Mountain Ridge Middle School
Programme MYP
MYP Coordinator Susan Bierman
Gender Coeducational
Boarding/day Boarding
8250 Lexington Drive, Academy D-20,
Colorado Springs CO 80920, USA
TELEPHONE: +1 719 594 9292
WEBSITE: http://ns2.d20.co.edu/mrms/

Niwot High School
Status State
Programme Diploma
Diploma Coordinator Nancy Lee
Gender Coeducational
Languages English
Boarding/day Day
8989 E Niwot Road, Niwot CO 80503, USA
TELEPHONE: +1 303 652 2550
FAX: +1 303 652 2003
EMAIL: daly_dennis@stvrain.k12.co.us
WEBSITE: http://nhs.stvrain.k12.co.us

North Middle School
Programme MYP
MYP Coordinator Carolyn Derr
Gender Coeducational
Boarding/day Boarding
301 North Nevada Avenue, Colorado Springs
CO 80903, USA
TELEPHONE: +1 719 328 5078

Palisade High School
Status State
Programme Diploma
Diploma Coordinator Tracy Hornsby
Gender Coeducational
Languages English
Boarding/day Day
3679 G Road, Palisade CO 81526, USA
TELEPHONE: +1 970 464 5937
FAX: +1 970 464 5102
EMAIL: mdiers@mesa.k12.co.us
WEBSITE: www.phs.mesa.k12.co.us/

Patterson Elementary School
Status State
Programme PYP
PYP Coordinator Chris Curtis
Gender Coeducational
Languages English
Boarding/day Day
1263 S Dudley Street, Lakewood CO 80232,
USA
TELEPHONE: +1 303 982 8470
FAX: +1 303 982 8467
EMAIL: sdamanti@jeffco.k12.co.us
WEBSITE: http://scjeffco.k12.co.us/patterson

Poudre High School
Status State
Programme MYP, Diploma
Diploma Coordinator Christine Hays
MYP Coordinator Karen Hammann
Gender Coeducational
Languages English
Boarding/day Day
201 Impala Drive, Fort Collins CO 80521, USA
TELEPHONE: +1 970 416 6034
FAX: +1 970 416 6207
EMAIL: slundt@psdschools.org
WEBSITE:
http://oldwww.psd.k12.co.us/schools/phs

Pueblo East High School
Status State
Programme Diploma
Diploma Coordinator Lori Quigley
Gender Coeducational
Languages English
Boarding/day Day
9 MacNeil Road, Pueblo CO 81001, USA
TELEPHONE: +1 719 549 7222
FAX: +1 719 545 0389
EMAIL: anelms@pueblo60.k12.co.us

Rampart High School
Status State
Programme MYP, Diploma
Diploma Coordinator Bill Thompson
MYP Coordinator Susan Bierman
Gender Coeducational
Languages English
Boarding/day Day
Rampart HS Administration, 8250 Lexington
Drive, Colorado Springs CO 80920, USA
TELEPHONE: +1 719 234 2010
FAX: +1 719 234 2199
EMAIL: gbierma@d20.co.edu
WEBSITE:
http://academy.d20.co.edu/rhs/ib/ib.html

Rockrimmon Elementary School
Status State
Programme PYP
PYP Coordinator Maureen Lang
Gender Coeducational
Boarding/day Boarding
194 W Mikado Drive, Colorado Springs
CO 80919, USA
TELEPHONE: +1 719 598 7045
FAX: +1 719 598 9661
EMAIL: ashikle@d20.co.edu

S Arthur Henry Middle School
Status State
Programme MYP
MYP Coordinator Don Marsh
Gender Coeducational
Languages English
Boarding/day Day
3005 South Golden Way, Denver CO 80227,
USA
TELEPHONE: +1 720 423 9560
FAX: +1 720 423 9585
EMAIL: wendy_lanier@dpsk12.org
WEBSITE: http://henry.dpsk12.org

Smoky Hill High School
Status State
Programme Diploma
Diploma Coordinator Patricia Wetmore
Gender Coeducational
Languages English
Boarding/day Day
16100 East Smoky Hill Road, Aurora
CO 80015, USA
TELEPHONE: +1 720-886-5403
FAX: +1 720-886-5408
EMAIL: jbrown@cherrycreekschools.org

Summit High School
Status State
Programme MYP, Diploma
Diploma Coordinator Nanci Morse
MYP Coordinator Nanci Morse
Gender Coeducational
Languages English
Boarding/day Day
PO Box 7, Frisco CO 80443, USA
TELEPHONE: +1 970 547 9311
FAX: +1 970 547 1061
EMAIL: jhesse@summit.k12.co.us
WEBSITE:
www.summit.k12.co.us/schools/Shs

Summit High School
Programme MYP
MYP Coordinator Nanci Morse
Gender Coeducational
PO Box 7, Frisco CO 80443, USA
TELEPHONE: +1 970 547 9311
FAX: +1 970 547 1061

The Academy International Elementary School
Status State
Programme PYP
PYP Coordinator Ms Diane Jensen
Gender Coeducational
Languages English
Boarding/day Day
8550 Charity Drive, Colorado Springs
CO 80920, USA
TELEPHONE: +1 719 282-3402
FAX: +1 719 282-9530
EMAIL: acanham@asd20.org
WEBSITE: www.academy.d20.co.edu/aie/

Thornton High School
Status State
Programme MYP, Diploma
Diploma Coordinator Roger Dowd
MYP Coordinator Anne Frazier
Gender Coeducational
Languages English
Boarding/day Day
9351 North Washington Street, Thornton
CO 80229, USA
TELEPHONE: +1 720 972 4803
FAX: +1 720 972 4999
EMAIL: janette.walters@adams12.org
WEBSITE: www.ad12.k12.co.us

Whittier Elementary School
Status State
Programme PYP
PYP Coordinator Cindy Bigelow
Gender Coeducational
Boarding/day Day
2008 Pine Street, Boulder CO 80302, USA
TELEPHONE: +1 303 442 2282
FAX: +1 303 442 2296
EMAIL: lauren.hoyt@bvsd.org
WEBSITE:
www.bvsd.k12.co.us/schools/whittier/

William J Palmer High School
Status State
Programme MYP, Diploma
Diploma Coordinator Steve Kern
MYP Coordinator Carolyn Derr
Gender Coeducational
Languages English
Boarding/day Day
301 North Nevada Avenue, Colorado Springs
CO 80903, USA
TELEPHONE: +1 719 328 5042
EMAIL: reynoka@d11.org

Woodmen-Roberts Elementary
Status State
Programme PYP
PYP Coordinator Jeanna Gamber-Bivin
Gender Coeducational
Languages English
Boarding/day Day
8365 Orchard Path Road, Colorado Springs
CO 80919, USA
TELEPHONE: +1 719 234 5300
EMAIL: tirawle@d20.co.edu
WEBSITE:
http://academy.d20.co.edu/wre/index.html

Connecticut

East Hartford High School
Status State
Programme Diploma
Diploma Coordinator Michael Abelon
Gender Coeducational
Languages English
Boarding/day Day
869 Forbes Street, East Hartford CT 06118,
USA
TELEPHONE: +1 860 622 5203
EMAIL: cjordan@easthartford.org
WEBSITE: www.cibanet.org

International School at Rogers Magnet
Status State
Programme PYP
PYP Coordinator Virginia Maher
Gender Coeducational
Languages English
83 Lockwood Avenue, Stamford CT 06902,
USA
TELEPHONE: +1 203 977 4562
EMAIL: ccummings@ci.stamford.ct.us
WEBSITE: www.rogersmagnetschool.org

King/Robinson Inter-District Magnet School
Status State
Programme PYP, MYP
MYP Coordinator Patricia Brittingham
PYP Coordinator Cheryl Merritt
Gender Coeducational
Languages English
Boarding/day Day
150 Fournier Street, New Haven CT 06511, USA
TELEPHONE: +1 203 691 2700
FAX: +1 203 691 2786
EMAIL: iline.tracey@new-haven.ct.k12.us

Robert E Fitch Senior High School
Status State
Programme Diploma
Diploma Coordinator Amy Frayne
Gender Coeducational
Languages English
Boarding/day Day
101 Groton Long Point Road, Groton
CT 06340, USA
TELEPHONE: +1 860 449 7215
FAX: +1 860 449 7255
EMAIL: jluciano@groton.k12.ct.us
WEBSITE: www.groton.k12.ct.us

The International School at Dundee
Status State
Programme PYP
PYP Coordinator Angela Schmidt
Gender Coeducational
55 Florence Road, Riverside CT 06878, USA
TELEPHONE: +1 203 637 3800
FAX: +1 203 637 5423
EMAIL: terry_ricci@greenwich.k12.ct.us
WEBSITE: www.greenwichschools.org/isd

Warren Harding High School
Status State
Programme Diploma
Diploma Coordinator Mariel Bowker
Languages English
1743 Central Avenue, Fairfield County,
Bridgeport CT 06610, USA
TELEPHONE: +1 203 576 7330
FAX: +1 203 576 7762
EMAIL: hsanchez@bridgeportedu

Washington DC

Benjamin A Banneker Academic High School
Status State
Programme Diploma
Diploma Coordinator Nancy Gorden
Gender Coeducational
Languages English
Boarding/day Day
800 Euclid Street NW, Washington DC 20001,
USA
TELEPHONE: +1 202 673 7325
FAX: +1 202 673 2231
EMAIL: anita.berger@k12.dc.us
WEBSITE: www.benjaminbanneker.org

BRITISH SCHOOL OF WASHINGTON
Status Private
Programme Diploma
Diploma Coordinator Scott Hussey
Gender Coeducational
Languages English
Boarding/day Day
2001 Wisconsin Ave NW, Washington
DC 20007, USA
TELEPHONE: +1 202 829 3700
FAX: +1 202 829 6522
EMAIL: headbsw@britishschool.org
WEBSITE: www.britishschool.org
see full details on page 67

Mariner High School – ICAT Academy
Status State
Programme MYP
MYP Coordinator DeAnne Findlay
Gender Coeducational
Boarding/day Day
200 120th St SW, Everett WA 98204, USA
TELEPHONE: +1 425 356 1700
FAX: +1 425 356 1717
EMAIL: klinebt@mukilteo.wednet.edu
WEBSITE:
http://schools.mukilteo.wednet.edu

Washington International School
Status Private
Programme PYP, MYP, Diploma
Diploma Coordinator David Merkel
MYP Coordinator Rita Adhikari
PYP Coordinator Dawn Darling
Gender Coeducational
Languages English, French, Spanish, Dutch
Boarding/day Day
3100 Macomb Street North West, Washington
DC 20008, USA
TELEPHONE: +1 202 243 1800
FAX: +1 202 243 1802
EMAIL: bennett@wis.edu
WEBSITE: www.wis.edu

Delaware

Mount Pleasant High School
Status State
Programme MYP, Diploma
Diploma Coordinator Lynn Wright
MYP Coordinator Leslie Carlson
Gender Coeducational
Languages English
Boarding/day Day
5201 Washington St Extension, Wilmington
DE 19809, USA
TELEPHONE: +1 302 762 7054
FAX: +1 302 762 7042
EMAIL: gregg.robinson@bsd.k12.de.us
WEBSITE: www.k12.de.us/mtpleasanths

Talley Middle School
Programme MYP
MYP Coordinator Leslie Carlson
Gender Coeducational
Boarding/day Day
1110 Cypress Road, Wilmington DE 19810, USA
TELEPHONE: +1 840 302 475 3976
EMAIL: barbara.starkey@bsd.k12.de.us
WEBSITE: www.k12.de.us/talley/

Wilmington Friends School
Status Private
Programme Diploma
Diploma Coordinator Richard Grier-Reynolds
Gender Coeducational
Languages English
Boarding/day Boarding
101 School Road, Wilmington DE 19803, USA
TELEPHONE: +1 302 576 2900
FAX: +1 302 576 2939
EMAIL:
rgrierreynolds@friends.wilmington.de.us
WEBSITE: www.wilmingtonfriends.org

Florida

Ada Merritt Elementary School
Status State
Programme PYP
PYP Coordinator Jackeline Sanchez-Jimenez
Gender Coeducational
Languages English
Boarding/day Day
660 SW 3 Street, Miami FL 33130, USA
TELEPHONE: +1 305 326 0791
FAX: +1 305 326 0749
WEBSITE: www.adamerritt.dadeschools.net/

Allen D Nease High School
Status State
Programme Diploma
Diploma Coordinator Aletha Dresback
Gender Coeducational
Languages English
Boarding/day Day
10550 Ray Road, St Augustine FL 32095, USA
TELEPHONE: +1 904 824 7275
FAX: +1 904 824 5281
EMAIL: thomasl@stjohns.k12.fl.us

American International School of Kingston
Status Private
Programme Diploma
Diploma Coordinator Abby Wynter
Gender Coeducational
Languages English
Boarding/day Day
7979 NW 21st Street, KIN 1399, Doral
FL 33122-1616, USA
TELEPHONE: +1 876 755 2635-7
FAX: +1 876 925 4749
EMAIL: office@aisk.com
WEBSITE: www.aisk.com

Atlantic Community High School
Status State
Programme MYP, Diploma
Diploma Coordinator David A Youngman
MYP Coordinator Lorraine Fitz
Gender Coeducational
Languages English
Boarding/day Day
2455 West Atlantic Ave, Palm Beach County, Delray Beach FL 33445, USA
TELEPHONE: +1 561 243 1502
FAX: +1 561 243 1532
EMAIL: weigelk@palmbeach.k12.fl.us
WEBSITE: www.atlantichs.org

Boyd Anderson High School
Status State
Programme MYP, Diploma
Diploma Coordinator Joyce Harrington
MYP Coordinator Hallie Hopper
Gender Coeducational
Languages English
Boarding/day Day
3050 North West 41st Street, Broward County, Lauderdale Lakes FL 33309, USA
TELEPHONE: +1 954 497 3800
FAX: +1 954 497 3819
EMAIL: jebianca@aol.com

Brookside Middle School
Status State
Programme MYP
MYP Coordinator Joan Cardinale
Gender Coeducational
Languages English
Boarding/day Day
3636 South Shade Avenue, Sarasota FL 34239, USA
TELEPHONE: +1 941 361 6472
FAX: +1 941 361 6508
EMAIL: karen_rose@sarasota.k12.fl.us
WEBSITE: www.sarasota.k12.fl.us/brookside

C Leon King High School
Status State
Programme Diploma
Diploma Coordinator Mathew Romano
Gender Coeducational
Languages English
Boarding/day Day
6815 North 56th Street, Tampa FL 33610, USA
TELEPHONE: +1 813 744 8333
FAX: +1 813 744 8434
EMAIL: carla.bruning@sdhc.k12.fl.us
WEBSITE: www.sdhc.k12.fl.us/ffiking.high/

Cape Coral High School
Status State
Programme Diploma
Diploma Coordinator Keith Lindahl
Gender Coeducational
Languages English
Boarding/day Day
2300 Santa Barbara Blvd, Cape Coral
FL 33991, USA
TELEPHONE: +1 239 574 6766
EMAIL: ericjmc@leeschools.net
WEBSITE: www.leeschools.net/schools/cch

Cardinal Newman High School
Status Private
Programme Diploma
Diploma Coordinator Theresa Fretterd
Gender Coeducational
Languages English
Boarding/day Day
512 Spencer Drive, West Palm Beach FL 33409, USA
TELEPHONE: +1 561 683 6266
EMAIL: david.carr@worldnet.att.net
WEBSITE: www.cardinalnewman.com

Carrollton School of the Sacred Heart
Status Private
Programme Diploma
Diploma Coordinator Lillian Solis-Silva
Gender Female
Languages English
Boarding/day Day
3747 Main Highway, Miami FL 33133, USA
TELEPHONE: +1 305 446 5673
EMAIL: scooke@carrollton.org
WEBSITE: www.carrollton.org

Carrollwood Day School
Status Private
Programme PYP, MYP, Diploma
Diploma Coordinator Stephen W Orbison
MYP Coordinator Jennifer Dosher
PYP Coordinator Sabrina McCartney
Gender Coeducational
Languages English
Boarding/day Day
1515 W Bearss Avenue, Tampa FL 33613, USA
TELEPHONE: +1 813 920 2288
EMAIL: mlk4309@aol.com
WEBSITE: www.carrollwooddayschool.org

Carver Middle School
Programme MYP
MYP Coordinator Barbara Dilthey
Gender Coeducational
Boarding/day Day
101 Barwick Road, Delray Beach FL 33445, USA
TELEPHONE: +1 561 638 2100
EMAIL: dilthey@palmbeach.k12.fl.us
WEBSITE: www.edline.net/pages/
carver_middle_school

Carver Middle School
Status State
Programme MYP
MYP Coordinator Cassandra Perez
4500 W Columbia Street, Orlando FL 32811, USA
TELEPHONE: +1 407 296 5110
FAX: +1 407 296 6407
EMAIL: evand@ocps.net
WEBSITE: www.carvermiddle.ocps.net

Choctawhatchee High School

Status State
Programme Diploma
Diploma Coordinator Judy Kane
Gender Coeducational
Languages English
Boarding/day Day
110 Racetrack Road, Fort Walton Beach
FL 32547, USA
TELEPHONE: +1 904 833 3614
FAX: +1 904 833 3410
EMAIL: massarellic@mail.okaloosa.k12.fl.us
WEBSITE: www.okaloosa.k12.fl.us/choctaw/

Clearwater Central Catholic High School

Status Private
Programme Diploma
Diploma Coordinator Margaret Carrington
Gender Coeducational
Languages English
Boarding/day Day
2750 Haines Bayshore Road, Clearwater
FL 33760, USA
TELEPHONE: +1 727 531 1449
FAX: +1 727 451 0101
EMAIL: jventurella@ccchs.org
WEBSITE: www.ccchs.org

Cocoa Beach High School

Status State
Programme MYP, Diploma
Diploma Coordinator Lori Masterson
MYP Coordinator Connie Pisani
Gender Coeducational
Languages English
Boarding/day Day
1500 Minutemen Causeway, Cocoa Beach
FL 32931, USA
TELEPHONE: +1 321 783 1776
FAX: +1 321 868 6602
EMAIL: coolt@brevard.k12.fl.us

Coral Gables Senior High School

Status State
Programme Diploma
Diploma Coordinator Nicki Brisson
Gender Coeducational
Languages English
Boarding/day Day
450 Bird Road, Coral Gables FL 33146, USA
TELEPHONE: +1 305 443 4871
FAX: +1 305 441 8094
EMAIL: amartinez@cghs.dadeschools.net
WEBSITE: www.cghs.dade.k12.fl.us

Coral Reef High School

Status State
Programme Diploma
Diploma Coordinator Michele Patterson
Gender Coeducational
Languages English
Boarding/day Day
10101 SW 152 Street, Miami FL 33157, USA
TELEPHONE: +1 305 232 2044
FAX: +1 305 252 3454
EMAIL: leal@coralreef.dadeschools.net
WEBSITE: http://coralreef.dadeschools.net

Cypress Creek High School

Status State
Programme Diploma
Diploma Coordinator Barbara Breidt
Gender Coeducational
Languages English
Boarding/day Day
1101 Bear Crossing Drive, Orange County,
Orlando FL 32824, USA
TELEPHONE: +1 407 852 3400
FAX: +1 407 850 5160
EMAIL: storchs@ocps.net

Deerfield Beach High School

Status State
Programme MYP, Diploma
Diploma Coordinator Judith Olivero
MYP Coordinator MJ Caputo
Gender Coeducational
Languages English
Boarding/day Day
910 Southwest 15 Street, School Board of
Broward County, Deerfield Beach FL 33441-
6299, USA
TELEPHONE: +1 754 322 0656
FAX: +1 754 322 0780
EMAIL:
kathleen.martinez@browardschools.com

Deerfield Beach Middle School

Status State
Programme MYP
MYP Coordinator Regino del Pino
Gender Coeducational
Boarding/day Day
701 SE 6th Avenue, Deerfield Beach FL 33441,
USA
TELEPHONE: +1 754 322 3300
EMAIL: gdelpino@aol.com
WEBSITE: www.deerfieldbeachmiddle.com

Deland High School

Status State
Programme Diploma
Diploma Coordinator Johnnie Ebbert
Gender Coeducational
Languages English
Boarding/day Day
800 North Hill Avenue, Volusia, Deland
FL 32724, USA
TELEPHONE: +1 386 822 6909
FAX: +1 386 822 6556
EMAIL: mmoyer@volusia.k12.fl.us
WEBSITE:
www.volusia.k12.fl.us/schools/delandhigh/

Eastside High School

Status State
Programme Diploma
Diploma Coordinator Ann Marie Heller
Gender Coeducational
Languages English
Boarding/day Day
1201 South East 43rd Street, Gainesville
FL 32641-7698, USA
TELEPHONE: +1 352 955 6704
EMAIL: charbojl@sbac.edu
WEBSITE: www.ehs.sbac.edu

Evans High School

Status State
Programme MYP
MYP Coordinator Jennifer Bohn
Gender Coeducational
Languages English
Boarding/day Day
4949 Silver Star Road, Orlando FL 32808, USA
TELEPHONE: +1 407 522 3400
FAX: +1 407 522 6048
EMAIL: wilsonk@ocps.net
WEBSITE: http://evanshs.ocps.net

Flagler Palm Coast High School

Status State
Programme Diploma
Diploma Coordinator Terry Smith
Gender Coeducational
Languages English
Boarding/day Day
PO Box 488, Bunnell FL 32110, USA
TELEPHONE: +1 386 437 7540
EMAIL: delbruggeb@flagler.k12.fl.us
WEBSITE: www.flagler.k12.fl.us

Forest Hill Community High School

Status State
Programme Diploma
Diploma Coordinator Dr John E Romeo
Gender Coeducational
Languages English
Boarding/day Day
6901 Parker Avenue, West Palm Beach
FL 33405, USA
TELEPHONE: +1 561 540 2400
FAX: +1 561 540 2440
EMAIL: stafform@mail.palmbeach.k12.fl.us

Fort Myers High School

Status State
Programme Diploma
Diploma Coordinator Rose Browning
Gender Coeducational
Languages English
Boarding/day Day
2635 Cortez Boulevard, Fort Myers FL 33901,
USA
TELEPHONE: +1 239 334 2167
FAX: +1 239 334 2177
EMAIL: davidpl@leeschools.net
WEBSITE:
www.lee.k12.fl.us/schools/fmh/home.asp

Frank C Martin Elementary School

Status State
Programme PYP, MYP
MYP Coordinator Sharon Humphrey
PYP Coordinator Elyse Waronker
Gender Coeducational
Languages English
Boarding/day Day
14250 Boggs Drive, Miami FL 33176, USA
TELEPHONE: +1 305 238 3688
FAX: +1 305 232 4068
EMAIL: pbrown@dadeschools.net
WEBSITE: www.fcmartin.dadeschools.net

Freedom 7 Elementary School of International Studies
Status State
Programme PYP
PYP Coordinator Mary Helen King
Gender Coeducational
Languages English
Boarding/day Day
400 4th Street South, Cocoa Beach FL 32931, USA
TELEPHONE: +1 321 868 6610
EMAIL: zimmermand@brevard.k12.fl.us
WEBSITE: www.freedom.es.brevard.k12.fl.us

Gateway High School
Status State
Programme Diploma
Diploma Coordinator Daniel Farmer
Gender Coeducational
Languages English
Boarding/day Day
93 Panther Paws Trail, Osceola School District, Kissimmee FL 34744, USA
TELEPHONE: +1 407 935 3600
FAX: +1 407 935 3609
EMAIL: andrewst@osceola.k12.fl.us

Glenridge Middle School
Status State
Programme MYP
MYP Coordinator Judy Lister
Gender Coeducational
Languages English
2900 Upper Park Road, Orlando FL 32814, USA
TELEPHONE: +1 407 623 1415
EMAIL: ericksm2@ocps.net
WEBSITE: www.ibatwphs.org

Gulf High School
Status State
Programme Diploma
Diploma Coordinator Deborah Lepley
Gender Coeducational
Languages English
Boarding/day Day
5355 School Road, New Port Richey FL 34652, USA
TELEPHONE: +1 727 774 3300
FAX: +1 727 774 3391
EMAIL: timerson@pasco.k12.fl.us
WEBSITE: www.gulfhigh.org

Gulliver Preparatory School
Status Private
Programme Diploma
Diploma Coordinator Jan Patterson
Gender Coeducational
Languages English
Boarding/day Day
6575 North Kendall Drive, Miami FL 33156, USA
TELEPHONE: +1 305 666-7937
FAX: +1 305 665 3791
EMAIL: patj@gulliverschools.org
WEBSITE: www.gulliverschools.org

Haines City High School
Status State
Programme Diploma
Diploma Coordinator Sue Braiman
Gender Coeducational
Languages English
Boarding/day Day
2800 Hornet Drive, Haines City FL 33844, USA
TELEPHONE: +1 863 419 3371
FAX: +1 863 419 3373
EMAIL: duane.collins@polk-fl.net
WEBSITE: www.hainescityhighschool.com

Henry D Perry Middle School
Status State
Programme MYP
MYP Coordinator Christopher Simmons
Gender Coeducational
Languages English
Boarding/day Day
3400 Wildcat Way, Miramar FL 33023, USA
TELEPHONE: +1 754 323 3900
FAX: +1 754 323 3985
EMAIL: steve.frazier@browardschools.com
WEBSITE: www.perrymiddle.com

Herbert A Ammons Middle School
Status State
Programme MYP
MYP Coordinator Ken Clark
Gender Coeducational
Languages English
Boarding/day Day
17990 SW 142 Avenue, Miami FL 33177, USA
TELEPHONE: +1 305 971 0158
FAX: +1 305 971 0179
EMAIL: adleri@ammons.dadeschools.net
WEBSITE: http://ammons.dadeschools.net

Hillsborough High School
Status State
Programme Diploma
Diploma Coordinator Donna Scheirer
Gender Coeducational
Languages English
Boarding/day Day
5000 Central Avenue, Tampa FL 33603, USA
TELEPHONE: +1 813 276 5620
FAX: +1 813 276 2400
EMAIL: williamorr@sdhc.k12.fl.us
WEBSITE: www.sdhc.k12.fl.us

Independent Day School – Corbett Campus
Status Private
Programme MYP
MYP Coordinator Betty George
Gender Coeducational
Languages English
Boarding/day Day
12015 Orange Grove Drive, Tampa FL 33618, USA
TELEPHONE: +1 813 961 3087
FAX: +1 813 963 0846
EMAIL: jswarzman@idsyes.com
WEBSITE: www.idsyes.com

International Baccalaureate School at Bartow High School
Status State
Programme Diploma
Diploma Coordinator Edwin Vetter
Gender Coeducational
Languages English
Boarding/day Day
1270 South Broadway Avenue, Bartow FL 33830, USA
TELEPHONE: +1 863 534-0194
FAX: +1 863 534-0077
EMAIL: ibatpcs@gate.net

James B Sanderlin Elementary
Status State
Programme PYP
PYP Coordinator Joyce Reichle
Gender Coeducational
Languages English
Boarding/day Day
2350 22nd Avenue South, St Petersburg FL 33712, USA
TELEPHONE: +1 727 552 1700
FAX: +1 727 552 1701
EMAIL: denise_miller@places.pcsb.org
WEBSITE: www.sanderlin-es.pinellas.k12.fl.us

James S Rickards High School
Status State
Programme Diploma
Diploma Coordinator Betty Newman
Gender Coeducational
Languages English
Boarding/day Day
3013 Jim Lee Road, Leon District Schools, Tallahassee FL 32301-7057, USA
TELEPHONE: +1 850 488 1783
FAX: +1 850 922 7104
EMAIL: hightowerp2@mail.rickards.leon.k12.fl.us

Jean Ribault High School
Status State
Programme Diploma
Diploma Coordinator Lashanda Allen
Gender Coeducational
Languages English
Boarding/day Day
3701 Winton Drive, Jacksonville FL 32208, USA
TELEPHONE: +1 904 924 3092
FAX: +1 904 924 3101
EMAIL: turnerr@educationcentral.org
WEBSITE: www.educationcentral.org/rhs/

John A Ferguson Senior High School
Status State
Programme Diploma
Diploma Coordinator Susan Rodriguez
Gender Coeducational
Boarding/day Day
15900 SW 56th Street, Miami FL 33185, USA
TELEPHONE: +1 305 408 2700
EMAIL: jgarraux@dadeschools.net
WEBSITE: http://ferguson.dadeschools.net

Jones High School

Status State
Programme MYP
MYP Coordinator Ansley Hammond
801 South Rio Grande Avenue, Orlando
FL 32805, USA
TELEPHONE: +1 407 835 2300
FAX: +1 407 245 2765
EMAIL: williab@ocps.net
WEBSITE: www.jones.ocps.net

Lamar Louise Curry Middle School

Status State
Programme MYP
MYP Coordinator Eric Wright
Gender Coeducational
Languages English
Boarding/day Day
15750 SW 47th Street, Miami FL 33185, USA
TELEPHONE: +1 305 222 2775
FAX: +1 305 229 1521
EMAIL: cmontano@dadeschools.net

Land O'Lakes High School

Status State
Programme Diploma
Diploma Coordinator Caryn McDermott
Gender Coeducational
Languages English
Boarding/day Day
20325 Gator Lane, Land O'Lakes FL 34639,
USA
TELEPHONE: +1 813 794 9400
FAX: +1 813 794 9491
EMAIL: rbonti@pasco.k12.fl.us

Lauderdale Lakes Middle School

Programme MYP
MYP Coordinator Hallie Hopper
Gender Coeducational
Boarding/day Day
3911 Northwest 30 th Avenue, Lauderdale
Lakes FL 33309, USA
TELEPHONE: +1 954 497 3900
EMAIL: jezdimir_stephanie@
bcpsgw.broward.k12.fl.us

Lee Middle School

Status State
Programme MYP
MYP Coordinator J Tyler Bumsted
Gender Coeducational
Languages English
Boarding/day Day
1333 Marsh Avenue, Fort Myers FL 33905, USA
TELEPHONE: +1 239 337 1333
FAX: +1 239 334 4144
EMAIL: vivianms@leeschools.net

Liberty Magnet Elementary School

Status State
Programme PYP
PYP Coordinator Theresa Wagner
Gender Coeducational
Languages English
Boarding/day Day
6850 81st Street, Vero Beach FL 32967, USA
TELEPHONE: +1 772 564 5300
EMAIL: dale.klaus@indian-river.k12.fl.us
WEBSITE: www.indian-river.K12.fl.us

Lincoln Park Academy

Status State
Programme MYP, Diploma
Diploma Coordinator Claudia Trew
MYP Coordinator Claudia Trew
Gender Coeducational
Languages English
Boarding/day Day
1806 Avenue I, St Lucie County, Fort Pierce
FL 34950, USA
TELEPHONE: +1 772 468 5474
FAX: +1 772 585 3294
EMAIL: andersonp@stucie.k12.fl.us
WEBSITE: www.stlucie.k12.fl.us/LPA

Macfarlane Park Elementary Magnet School

Status State
Programme PYP
PYP Coordinator Lynn Beer
Gender Coeducational
Languages English
Boarding/day Day
1721 North MacDill Avenue, Tampa FL 33607,
USA
TELEPHONE: +1 813 356 1760
FAX: +1 813 356 1764
EMAIL: denyse.riverio@sdhc.k12.fl.us
WEBSITE: http://macfarlanepark.mysdhc.org

Melbourne High School

Status State
Programme Diploma
Diploma Coordinator Michele Canose
Gender Coeducational
Languages English
Boarding/day Day
74 Bulldog Boulevard, Melbourne FL 32901,
USA
TELEPHONE: +1 321 952 5880
FAX: +1 321 952 5898
EMAIL: willcoxonj@brevard.k12.fl.us
WEBSITE:
http://melbourne.hs.brevard.k12.fl.us

Memorial Middle School

Status State
Programme MYP
MYP Coordinator Ansley Hammond
2220 W 29th Street, Orlando FL 32805, USA
TELEPHONE: +1 407 245 1810
EMAIL: burkeg@acps.net
WEBSITE: www.memorial.ocps.net

Miramar High School

Status State
Programme MYP, Diploma
Diploma Coordinator John Lamb
MYP Coordinator Christopher Simmons
Gender Coeducational
Languages English
Boarding/day Day
3601 SW 89th Avenue, Miramar FL 33025, USA
TELEPHONE: +1 754 323 1350
FAX: +1 754 323 1480
EMAIL: deborah.davey@browardschools.com
WEBSITE:
www.broward.k12.fl.us/miramarhigh

Morikami Park Elementary School

Status State
Programme PYP
PYP Coordinator Diane Schreiber
Gender Coeducational
6201 Morikami Park Road, Delray Beach
FL 33484, USA
TELEPHONE: +1 561 865-3960
FAX: +1 561 865-3965
EMAIL: kennede@palmbeach.k12.fl.us

North Broward Preparatory School

Status Private
Programme Diploma
Diploma Coordinator Bill Parsons
Gender Coeducational
Languages English
Boarding/day Mixed
7600 Lyons Road, Coconut Creek FL 33073,
USA
TELEPHONE: +1 954 247 0011
FAX: +1 954 247 0012
EMAIL: tuchmand@nbps.org
WEBSITE: www.nbps.org

North Miami Senior High School

Status State
Programme Diploma
Diploma Coordinator Lawrence Jurrist
Gender Coeducational
Languages English
Boarding/day Day
800 North East 137 Street, North Miami
FL 33161, USA
TELEPHONE: +1 305 891 6590
FAX: +1 305 895 1788
EMAIL: cawhite@dadeschools.net
WEBSITE: www.dadeschools.net

Pahokee Middle Senior High School

Status State
Programme MYP, Diploma
Diploma Coordinator Shelley Stone Kelley
MYP Coordinator Randal Oddi
Gender Coeducational
900 Larrimore Road, Pahokee FL 33476, USA
TELEPHONE: +1 561 924 6400
FAX: +1 561 924 6457
EMAIL: bainr@palmbeach.k12.fl.us
WEBSITE: www.palmbeach.k12.fl.us/
pahokeemiddlesrhigh

Palm Harbor University High School
Status State
Programme Diploma
Diploma Coordinator Christine O Lowry
Gender Coeducational
Languages English
Boarding/day Day
1900 Omaha Street, Palm Harbor FL 34683, USA
TELEPHONE: +1 727 669 1131
FAX: +1 727 725 7936
EMAIL: brownh@pcsb.org
WEBSITE: www.phuhs.pinellas.k12.fl.us

Paxon Middle School
Status State
Programme MYP
MYP Coordinator Marla D Almon
3276 Norman Thargard Boulevard, Jackonsville FL 32254, USA
TELEPHONE: +1 904 693 7600
FAX: +1 904 693 7661
WEBSITE: www.dreamsbeginhere.org/school/92

Paxon School for Advanced Studies
Status State
Programme Diploma
Diploma Coordinator Mary Breitenbach
Gender Coeducational
Languages English
Boarding/day Day
3239 Norman E Thagard Blvd, Jacksonville FL 32254, USA
TELEPHONE: +1 904 693 7583
FAX: +1 904 693 7597
EMAIL: danielsc@dreamsbeginhere.org
WEBSITE: www.dreamsbeginhere.org/psas

Pensacola High School
Status State
Programme Diploma
Diploma Coordinator Colleen Boyett
Gender Coeducational
Languages English
Boarding/day Day
A and Maxwell Streets, Pensacola FL 32501, USA
TELEPHONE: +1 850-5951500
FAX: +1 850-595-1516
EMAIL: salewis@escambia.k12.fl.us
WEBSITE: www.phstigers.org

Phillippi Shores Elementary School
Status State
Programme PYP
PYP Coordinator Cynthia McGrail
Gender Coeducational
Languages English
Boarding/day Day
4747 South Tamiami Trail, Sarasota FL 34231, USA
TELEPHONE: +1 941 361 6424
FAX: +1 941 361 6814
EMAIL: candace_dearing@sarasota.k12.fl.us
WEBSITE: www.sarasota.k12.fl.us/pse

Ponce de Leon Middle Community School
Status State
Programme MYP
MYP Coordinator Marlene Ramos
5801 Augusto Street, Coral Gables FL 33146, USA
TELEPHONE: +1 305 661 1611 X2212
FAX: +1 305 666 3140
EMAIL: annarodriguez@dadeschools.net
WEBSITE: http://ponce.dadeschools.net

Port St Lucie High School
Status State
Programme Diploma
Diploma Coordinator Kareem Rodriguez
Gender Coeducational
Languages English
Boarding/day Day
1201 S E Jaguar Lane, Port St Lucie FL 34952, USA
TELEPHONE: +1 772 337 6770
FAX: +1 772 337 6039
EMAIL: davidster@stlucie.k12.fl.us
WEBSITE: www.stlucie.k12.fl.us/pslh

Richard L Brown Elementary School
Status State
Programme PYP
PYP Coordinator Maysha Shelton
Gender Coeducational
Languages English
Boarding/day Day
1535 Milnor Street, Jacksonville FL 32205, USA
TELEPHONE: +1 904 630 6570
FAX: +1 904 630 6576
WEBSITE: www.duvalschools.org/rlbrown

Ridgeview High School Academy for Advanced Studies
Status State
Programme Diploma
Diploma Coordinator Vickie Bandy
Gender Coeducational
Languages English
Boarding/day Day
466 Madison Avenue, Clay County, Orange Park FL 32065, USA
TELEPHONE: +1 904 213 5203
FAX: +1 904 213 3033
EMAIL: jwestmoreland@mail.clay.k12.fl.us
WEBSITE: www.clay.k12.fl.us/rhs

Riverdale High School
Status State
Programme Diploma
Diploma Coordinator Michael Cavanaugh
Gender Coeducational
Languages English
Boarding/day Day
2600 Buckingham Road, Fort Myers FL 33905, USA
TELEPHONE: +1 239 694 4141
FAX: +1 239 694 3527
EMAIL: geraldbd@leeschools.net
WEBSITE: www.lee.k12.fl.us/schools/rdh

Riverview High School
Status State
Programme Diploma
Diploma Coordinator Paul Gallagher
Gender Coeducational
Languages English
Boarding/day Day
One Ram Way, Sarasota FL 34231, USA
TELEPHONE: +1 941 923 1484
FAX: +1 941 361 6175
EMAIL: linda_nook@sarasota.k12.fl.us
WEBSITE: www.riverviewib.com

Robert E Lee Middle School
Status State
Programme MYP
MYP Coordinator Doris Keeler
Gender Coeducational
Languages English
Boarding/day Day
1201 Maury Road, Orlando FL 32804, USA
TELEPHONE: +1 407 245 1800
FAX: +1 407 245 1809
EMAIL: pylantw@ocps.net
WEBSITE: www.lee.ocps.net

Robinswood Middle School
Status State
Programme MYP
MYP Coordinator Jennifer Bohn
6305 Balboa Drive, Orlando FL 32818, USA
TELEPHONE: +1 407 296 5140
FAX: +1 407 296 5148
EMAIL: petersh@ocps.net
WEBSITE: http://robinswood.ocps.net

Rutherford High School
Status State
Programme Diploma
Diploma Coordinator Karen Brown
Gender Coeducational
Languages English
Boarding/day Day
1000 School Avenue, Panama City FL 32401, USA
TELEPHONE: +1 850 872 4500
FAX: +1 850 747 5439
EMAIL: kennemr@bay.k12.fl.us

Sebastian River High School
Status State
Programme MYP, Diploma
Diploma Coordinator Catherine Ziegler
MYP Coordinator Roxanne Decker
Gender Coeducational
Languages English
9001 90th Avenue, Indian River, Sebastian FL 32958, USA
TELEPHONE: +1 772 564 4170
FAX: +1 772 564 4182
EMAIL: peggy.jones@indian-river.k12.fl.us
WEBSITE: www.indian-river.k12.us/srhs/main.html

Sebastian River Middle School
Programme MYP
MYP Coordinator Mike Hall
Gender Coeducational
9400 State Road 512, Sebastian FL 32958, USA
TELEPHONE: +1 772 564 5111
EMAIL: eileen.shirah@indian-river.k12.fl.us
WEBSITE: www.indian-river.k12.fl.us/srms

Seminole High School
Status State
Programme Diploma
Diploma Coordinator Mary Neal
Gender Coeducational
Languages English
Boarding/day Day
2701 Ridgewood Avenue, Seminole, Sanford
FL 32773-4916, USA
TELEPHONE: +1 407 320 5100
FAX: +1 407 320 5024
EMAIL: walt_griffin@scps.k12.fl.us
WEBSITE: www.seminolehs.scps.k12.fl.us

South Fork High School
Status State
Programme Diploma
Diploma Coordinator Kelly George
Gender Coeducational
Languages English
Boarding/day Day
10205 SW Pratt & Whitney Road, Martin
County, Stuart FL 34997, USA
TELEPHONE: +1 772-219-1840
FAX: +1 772- 219 1860
EMAIL: schmoyp@martin.k12.fl.us

Southeast High School
Status State
Programme Diploma
Diploma Coordinator Brenda O'Connor
Gender Coeducational
Languages English
Boarding/day Day
1200 37th Avenue East, Bradenton FL 34208,
USA
TELEPHONE: +1 941 741 3366
FAX: +1 941 741 3372
EMAIL: hornem@fc.manatee.k12.fl.us

Spruce Creek High School
Status State
Programme Diploma
Diploma Coordinator Vicki Murphy
Gender Coeducational
Languages English
Boarding/day Day
801 Taylor Road, Port Orange FL 32127, USA
TELEPHONE: +1 386 322 6272
FAX: +1 386 756 7270
EMAIL: tegnor@mail.volusia.k12.fl.us

St Petersburg High School
Status State
Programme Diploma
Diploma Coordinator Susan Farias
Gender Coeducational
Languages English
Boarding/day Day
2501 Fifth Avenue North, St Petersburg FL
33713, USA
TELEPHONE: +1 813 893 1842
FAX: +1 813 893 1852
EMAIL: JanssenJ@pcsb.org
WEBSITE: www.stpetehigh.com

Stanton College Preparatory School
Status State
Programme Diploma
Diploma Coordinator Kimbely Borree
Gender Coeducational
Languages English
Boarding/day Day
1149 West 13th Street, Jacksonville FL 32209,
USA
TELEPHONE: +1 904 630 6760
FAX: +1 904 630 6758
EMAIL: lynchd@educationcentral.org
WEBSITE: www.stantoncollegeprep.org

Stonewall Jackson Middle School
Status State
Programme MYP
MYP Coordinator Jhunu Mohapatra
6000 Stonewall Jackson Road, Orlando FL
32807, USA
TELEPHONE: +1 407 249 6430
FAX: +1 407 249 6438
EMAIL: millerj10@ocps.net
WEBSITE: www.stonewalljackson.ocps.net

Suncoast Community High School
Status State
Programme Diploma
Diploma Coordinator Craig Howard
Gender Coeducational
Languages English
Boarding/day Day
600 West 28th Street, Riviera Beach FL 33404,
USA
TELEPHONE: +1 561 882 3418
FAX: +1 407 882 3443
EMAIL:
gloriacrutchfieldphd@palmbeach.k12.fl.us
WEBSITE: www.palmbeach.fl.us/suncoasths

T R Robinson High School
Status State
Programme Diploma
Diploma Coordinator Kellie M Norton
Gender Coeducational
Languages English
Boarding/day Day
6311 S Lois Avenue, Tampa FL 33616-1617, USA
TELEPHONE: +1 813 272 3006
FAX: +1 813 272 2169
EMAIL: laura.zavatkay@sdhc.k12.fl.us
WEBSITE: www.robinsonhs.mysdhc.org

University High School
Status State
Programme Diploma
Diploma Coordinator Julia Cording
Gender Coeducational
Languages English
Boarding/day Day
11501 Eastwood Drive, Orange County,
Orlando FL 32817, USA
TELEPHONE: +1 407 482 8700
FAX: +1 407 737 1455
EMAIL: christd@ocps.net

Vanguard High School
Status State
Programme Diploma
Diploma Coordinator Sara Dassance
Gender Coeducational
Languages English
Boarding/day Day
7 NW 28th Street, Ocala FL 34475, USA
TELEPHONE: +1 352-671-4900
EMAIL: david.ellers@marion.k12.fl.us

Wakeland Elementary School of International Studies
Status State
Programme PYP
PYP Coordinator Michelle Compton
Gender Coeducational
Languages English
Boarding/day Day
1812 27th Street East, Bradenton FL 34208,
USA
TELEPHONE: +1 941 741 3358
FAX: +1 941 741 3549
EMAIL: fradleyc@fc.manatee.k12.fl.us
WEBSITE: www.manatee.k12.fl.us

Westward Elementary
Status State
Programme PYP
PYP Coordinator Traci Boysaw
Gender Coeducational
1101 Golf Avenue, Palm Beach, West Palm
Beach FL 33401, USA
TELEPHONE: +1 561 802 2130
FAX: +1 561 802 2135
EMAIL: penderm@palmbeach.k12.fl.us

Williams Middle Magnet School for International Studies
Status State
Programme MYP
MYP Coordinator Jody Locke
Gender Coeducational
Languages English
Boarding/day Day
5020 N 47th Street, Tampa FL 33610, USA
TELEPHONE: +1 813 744 8600
EMAIL: patricia.harrell@sdhc.k12.fl.us
WEBSITE: www.williams.mysdhc.org/

Wilton Manors Elementary School
Status State
Programme PYP
PYP Coordinator Lori Goldsmith
Gender Coeducational
Languages English
Boarding/day Day
2401 NE 3rd Avenue, Wilton Manors FL 33305, USA
TELEPHONE: +1 754 322-8950
FAX: +1 754 322-8990
EMAIL: mark.narkier@browardschools.com
WEBSITE: www.broward.k12.fl.us/wiltonmanorselem

Winter Park High School
Status State
Programme Diploma
Diploma Coordinator Robert Bass
Gender Coeducational
Languages English
Boarding/day Day
2100 Summerfield Road, Winter Park FL 32792, USA
TELEPHONE: +1 407 622 3212
EMAIL: bassr@ocps.k12.fl.us

Winter Park High School
Programme MYP
MYP Coordinator Judy Lister
Gender Coeducational
2100 Summerfield Road, Winter Park FL 32789, USA
TELEPHONE: +1 407 622 3212
EMAIL: gordonw@ocps.net
WEBSITE: http://ibatwphs.org

Georgia

Academy of Richmond County
Status State
Programme Diploma
Diploma Coordinator Charlie Tudor III
Languages English
910 Russell Street, Augusta GA 30904, USA
TELEPHONE: +1 706 737 7152
FAX: +1 706 737 7155
EMAIL: robbida@boe.richmond.k12.ga.us

Atlanta International School
Status Private
Programme PYP, Diploma
Diploma Coordinator Rachel Hovington
PYP Coordinator Leonie Ley-Mitchell
Gender Coeducational
Languages English, French, Spanish, German
Boarding/day Day
2890 North Fulton Drive, Atlanta GA 30305, USA
TELEPHONE: +1 404 841 3840
FAX: +1 404 841 3873
EMAIL: info@aischool.org
WEBSITE: www.aischool.org

Avondale Elementary School
Status State
Programme PYP
PYP Coordinator Melissa McMillan
Gender Coeducational
Languages English
Boarding/day Day
10 Lakeshore Drive, Avondale Estates GA 30052, USA
TELEPHONE: +1 678 676 5202
FAX: +1 678 676 5210
EMAIL: rosemary_e_malone@dekalb.k12.ga.us
WEBSITE: http://schools.dekalb.k12.ga.us/avondale

Benjamin H Hardaway High School
Status State
Programme Diploma
Diploma Coordinator Ethelyn Riley
Languages English
2901 College Drive, Columbus GA 31906, USA
TELEPHONE: +1 706 649 0748
FAX: +1 706 649 0886
EMAIL: hardaway@mscd-gd.net

Calhoun High School
Status State
Programme Diploma
Diploma Coordinator Kathryn Sproull
Gender Coeducational
Languages English
Boarding/day Day
315 South River Street, Calhoun GA 30701, USA
TELEPHONE: +1 706 629 9213
FAX: +1 706 602 6652
EMAIL: westmorelandw@calhounschools.org
WEBSITE: www.calhounschools.org

Campbell High School
Status State
Programme Diploma
Diploma Coordinator Judy Romanchuk
Gender Coeducational
Languages English
Boarding/day Day
5265 Ward Street, Cobb County, Smyrna GA 30080, USA
TELEPHONE: +1 678 842 6850
FAX: +1 678 842 6852
EMAIL: kehl.arnson@cobbk12.org

Central High School, Macon
Status State
Programme Diploma
Diploma Coordinator Chris Kirby
Gender Coeducational
Languages English
Boarding/day Day
2155 Napier Avenue, Macon GA 31204, USA
TELEPHONE: +1 478 751 6770
FAX: +1 478 751 6834
EMAIL: eweaver.central@bibb.k12.ga.us

Clubview Elementary School
Status State
Programme PYP
PYP Coordinator Angie Shehane
Gender Coeducational
Languages English
2836 Edgewood Road, Columbus GA 31906, USA
TELEPHONE: +1 706 565 3017
EMAIL: alindsey@mcsdga.net
WEBSITE: www.clubviewelementaryschool.com

Dalton High School
Status State
Programme Diploma
Diploma Coordinator Mona Howell
Gender Coeducational
Languages English
Boarding/day Day
1500 Manly Street, Dalton GA 30720, USA
TELEPHONE: +1 706 278 8757
FAX: +1 706 226 2430
EMAIL: pbrown@dalton.k12.ga.us
WEBSITE: www.dalton.k12.ga.us/dhs/

Douglas County High School
Status State
Programme Diploma
Diploma Coordinator Corrine Barnes
Gender Coeducational
Languages English
Boarding/day Day
8705 Campbellton Street, Douglasville GA 30134, USA
TELEPHONE: +1 770 651 6500
FAX: +1 770 651 6504
EMAIL: randy_dye@douglas.k12.ga.us
WEBSITE: http://web.douglas.k12.ga.us/web/schools/dchs/index.htm

Druid Hills High School
Status State
Programme Diploma
Diploma Coordinator Martha Donovan
Languages English
Boarding/day Day
1798 Haygood Drive NE, Atlanta GA 30307, USA
TELEPHONE: +1 678 874 6300
FAX: +1 678 874 6310
EMAIL: martha_k_donovan@fc.dekalb.k12.ga.us
WEBSITE: www.dekalb.k12.ga.us/ffidruidhills/

E Rivers Elementary School
Status State
Programme PYP
PYP Coordinator Mary Katherine Peele
Gender Coeducational
Languages English
Boarding/day Day
8 Peachtree Battle Avenue, Atlanta GA 30305, USA
TELEPHONE: +1 404 350 2150
EMAIL: rwoese@atlanta.k12.ga.us
WEBSITE: www.erivers-elem.org

Fair Street Elementary School

Status State
Programme PYP
PYP Coordinator Carol Brinson
Gender Coeducational
Languages English
Boarding/day Day
695 Fair Street, Gainsville GA 30501, USA
TELEPHONE: +1 770 536 5295
FAX: +1 770 287 2016
EMAIL: merrianne.dyer@gcssk12.net
WEBSITE:
www.gcssk12.net/fsweb/default.htm

Fernbank Elementary School

Status State
Programme PYP
PYP Coordinator Sandra Thibodeaux
Gender Coeducational
Languages English
Boarding/day Day
157 Heaton Park Drive NE, Atlanta GA 30307, USA
TELEPHONE: +1 678 874 9302
FAX: +1 678 874 9311
EMAIL: jason_marshall@fc.dekalb.k12.ga.us
WEBSITE: www.dekalb.k12.ga.us/ffifernbank

Garden Hills Elementary School

Status State
Programme PYP
PYP Coordinator Stephanie J Kastner
Gender Coeducational
Languages English
Boarding/day Day
285 Sheridan Drive, Atlanta GA 30305, USA
TELEPHONE: +1 404 842 3103
EMAIL: amwilson@atlanta.k12.ga.us
WEBSITE: www.gardenhillselementary.com

Groves High School

Status State
Programme Diploma
Diploma Coordinator Andrea Mobley
Gender Coeducational
Languages English
Boarding/day Day
100 Wheathill Road, Garden City GA 31408, USA
TELEPHONE: +1 912 965 2520
FAX: +1 912 965 2564
EMAIL:
lucille.philip@savannah.chatham.k12.ga.us

High Meadows School

Status Private
Programme PYP
PYP Coordinator Stephanie Dempsey
Gender Coeducational
Languages English
Boarding/day Day
1055 Willeo Road, Roswell GA 30075, USA
TELEPHONE: +1 770 993 2940
FAX: +1 770 993 8331
EMAIL: egembecki@highmeadows.org
WEBSITE: www.highmeadows.org

International Community School

Status State
Programme PYP
PYP Coordinator Laurent Ditmann
Gender Coeducational
Languages English
Boarding/day Day
3260 Covington Highway, Decatur GA 30032, USA
TELEPHONE: +1 404 499 8969
FAX: +1 404 499 8968
EMAIL: bmoon@intcomschool.org
WEBSITE: www.intcomschool.org

International Studies Elementary Magnet

Status State
Programme PYP
PYP Coordinator Laytona Stephenson
Gender Coeducational
Languages English
Boarding/day Day
2237 Cutts Drive, Albany GA 31705, USA
TELEPHONE: +1 229 431 3384
FAX: +1 229 431 3381
EMAIL: wmallard@docoschools.org

Johnson High School

Status State
Programme Diploma
Diploma Coordinator Amanda Griffin
Gender Coeducational
Languages English
Boarding/day Day
3305 Poplar Springs Road, Gainesville GA 30507, USA
TELEPHONE: +1 770 536 2394
FAX: +1 770 531 3046
WEBSITE: www.hallco.org/johnsonhs

Lovejoy High School

Programme Diploma
Diploma Coordinator Nelle M Ivey
Gender Coeducational
Languages English
Boarding/day Day
1587 McDonough Road, Hampton GA 30228, USA
TELEPHONE: +1 770-473-2920
FAX: +1 770-473-2928
EMAIL: sjackson@clayton.k12.ga.us
WEBSITE:
www.clayton.k12.ga.us/schools/006

Marietta High School

Status State
Programme MYP, Diploma
Diploma Coordinator Debbie Woolard
MYP Coordinator Debbie Woolard
Gender Coeducational
Languages English
Boarding/day Day
1171 Whitlock Avenue, Marietta GA 30064, USA
TELEPHONE: +1 770 428 2631
FAX: +1 770 429 3151
EMAIL: lcolburn@marietta-city.k12.ga.us
WEBSITE: www.marietta-city.k12.ga.us/mhs

Marietta Middle School

Status State
Programme MYP
MYP Coordinator Debbie Woolard
121 Winn Street, Marietta GA 30064, USA
TELEPHONE: +1 770 422 0311
EMAIL: tjones@marietta-city.k12.ga.us
WEBSITE: www.marietta-city.k12.ga.us/mms

Marietta Sixth Grade Academy

Status State
Programme MYP
MYP Coordinator Debbie Woolard
340 Aviation Road, Marietta GA 30060, USA
TELEPHONE: +1 770 429 3115
EMAIL: mcesaretti@marietta-city.k12.ga.us
WEBSITE: www.marietta-city.k12.ga.us

Marshpoint Elementary School

Status State
Programme PYP
PYP Coordinator Sylvia Shealy
Gender Coeducational
Languages English
Boarding/day Day
135 Whitemarsh Island Road, Savannah GA 31410, USA
TELEPHONE: +1 912 898-4000
FAX: +1 912 898 4001
EMAIL:
cindi.kobleur@savannah.chatham.k12.ga.us
WEBSITE: www.savannah.chatham.k12.ga.us/marshpoint

Martin Luther King Jr High School

Status State
Programme Diploma
Diploma Coordinator Frances Dale
Gender Coeducational
Languages English
Boarding/day Day
3991 Snapfinger Road, Lithonia GA 30038, USA
TELEPHONE: +1 678 874 5402
FAX: +1 678 874 5403
EMAIL:
sylvester_nelloms@fc.dekalb.k12.ga.us
WEBSITE: www.dekalb.ga.us/ffimlking/

Midvale Elementary School

Status State
Programme PYP
PYP Coordinator Susan W Levy
Gender Coeducational
Languages English
Boarding/day Day
3836 Midvale Road, Tucker GA 30084, USA
TELEPHONE: +1 678 874 3402
FAX: +1 678 874 3410
EMAIL: susan_c_wilson@fc.dekalb.k12.ga.us
WEBSITE: www.dekalb.k12.ga.us/ffimidvale

Morgan County High School
Status State
Programme Diploma
Diploma Coordinator Denise Frost
Gender Coeducational
Languages English
Boarding/day Day
1231 College Drive, Madison GA 30650, USA
TELEPHONE: +1 706 342 2336
FAX: +1 706 342 5046
EMAIL: pleming@morgan.k12.ga.us
WEBSITE: www.morgan.k12.ga.us/mchs

Morris Brandon Elementary School
Programme PYP
PYP Coordinator Theresa Bowen
Gender Coeducational
Languages English
Boarding/day Day
2741 Howell Mill Road, Atlanta GA 30327, USA
TELEPHONE: +1 770 350 2153
FAX: +1 404 350 2826
EMAIL: kmevans@atlanta.k12.ga.us
WEBSITE: www.morrisbrandon.com

Norcross High School
Status State
Programme MYP, Diploma
Diploma Coordinator Maria Chininis
MYP Coordinator Pat Greeson
Gender Coeducational
Languages English
Boarding/day Day
5041 Staverly Lane, Norcross GA 30092, USA
TELEPHONE: +1 770 448 3674
FAX: +1 770 447 2664
EMAIL: jonathan_patterson@gwinnett.k12.ga.us
WEBSITE: www.norcrosshigh.org

North Atlanta High School
Status State
Programme MYP, Diploma
Diploma Coordinator Doug Frutiger
MYP Coordinator Ramon Reeves
Gender Coeducational
Languages English
Boarding/day Day
2875 Northside Drive, Atlanta GA 30303, USA
TELEPHONE: +1 404 3510 895
FAX: +1 404 802 4799
EMAIL: jdenine@atlanta.k12.ga.us
WEBSITE: www.northatlantahigh.org

North Clayton High School
Status State
Programme Diploma
Diploma Coordinator Charlton Norah
Gender Coeducational
Languages English
Boarding/day Day
1525 Norman Drive, College Park GA 30349, USA
TELEPHONE: +1 770-994-4035
EMAIL: rayh@clayton.k12.ga.us
WEBSITE: www.clayton.k12.ga.us/schools/004/

North Hall High School
Status State
Programme Diploma
Diploma Coordinator Anita Cox
Gender Coeducational
Languages English
Boarding/day Day
4885 Mt Vernon Road, Gainesville GA 30506, USA
TELEPHONE: +1 770 983 7331
FAX: +1 770 983 7941
EMAIL: joe.gheesling@hallco.org
WEBSITE: www.hallco.org/nhhs

Pinckneyville Middle School
Status State
Programme MYP
MYP Coordinator Pat Greeson
5440 West Jones Bridge Road, Norcross GA 30092, USA
TELEPHONE: +1 770 263 0860
FAX: +1 770 447 2617
EMAIL: nancy_martin@gwinnett.k12.ga.us
WEBSITE: www.pinckneyvillemiddle.org

Richards Middle School
Status State
Programme MYP
MYP Coordinator Kathryn A Hesler
Gender Coeducational
Languages English
Boarding/day Day
2892 Edgewood Road, Columbus GA 31906, USA
TELEPHONE: +1 706 569 3697
FAX: +1 706 569 3704
EMAIL: mikejohnson@mcsdga.net
WEBSITE: www.Richards

Riverwood High School
Status State
Programme Diploma
Diploma Coordinator Jonathan Bradley
Gender Coeducational
Languages English
Boarding/day Day
5900 Heards Drive NW, Atlanta GA 30328, USA
TELEPHONE: +1 404 847 1980
FAX: +1 404 255 8709
EMAIL: echols@fulton.k12.ga.us
WEBSITE: www.riverwoodhs.org

Sarah Smith Elementary School
Status State
Programme PYP
PYP Coordinator Amanda Ashworth
Gender Coeducational
Languages English
Boarding/day Day
370 Old Ivy Road, Atlanta GA 30342, USA
TELEPHONE: +1 404 842-3120
FAX: +1 404 842 3046
EMAIL: sbaker@atlanta.k12.ga.us
WEBSITE: www.atlanta.k12.ga.us

Sawyer Road Elementary School
Programme PYP
PYP Coordinator Susan Grigg
Gender Coeducational
Languages English
Boarding/day Day
840 Sawyer Road, Marietta GA 30062, USA
TELEPHONE: +1 770 429 9923
FAX: +1 770 429 9936
EMAIL: jsims@marietta-city.k12.ga us
WEBSITE: www.marietta-city.k12.ga.us/sawyerroad

Shamrock Middle School
Status State
Programme MYP
MYP Coordinator Lisa Slappey
Gender Coeducational
Languages English
Boarding/day Day
3100 Mount Olive Drive, Decatur GA 30033, USA
TELEPHONE: +1 678 874 7747
FAX: +1 678 874 7610
EMAIL: robert_b_thorpe@mail.fc.dekalb.k12.ga.us
WEBSITE: www.dekalb.k12.ga.us/ffishamrock

Sol C Johnson High School
Status State
Programme Diploma
Diploma Coordinator Jason Buelterman
Languages English
3012 Sunset Blvd, Savannah GA 31404, USA
TELEPHONE: +1 912 303-6400
FAX: +1 912 303-6418
EMAIL: gary.lackey@savannah.chatham.k12.ga.us

South Forsyth High School
Status State
Programme Diploma
Diploma Coordinator Carrie Jean Paulson
Gender Coeducational
Languages English
Boarding/day Day
585 Peachtree Parkway, Forsyth County, Cumming GA 30041, USA
TELEPHONE: +1 770 781 2264
FAX: +1 770 888 0203
EMAIL: rgill@forsyth.k12.ga.us
WEBSITE: www.forsyth.k12.ga.us

St Andrew's School
Status Private
Programme Diploma
Diploma Coordinator Kelley Waldron
Gender Coeducational
Languages English
Boarding/day Day
PO Box 30639, Savannah GA 31410, USA
TELEPHONE: +1 912 897 4941
FAX: +1 912 897 4943
EMAIL: hubbarde@saintschool.com
WEBSITE: www.saintschool.com

Summerour Middle School
Status State
Programme MYP
MYP Coordinator Pat Greeson
585 Mitchell Road, Norcross GA 30071, USA
TELEPHONE: +1 770 448 3045
FAX: +1 770 417 2476
EMAIL: dana_pugh@gwinnett.k12.ga.us
WEBSITE:
www.gwinnett.k12.ga.us/summerourms

Tucker High School
Status State
Programme Diploma
Diploma Coordinator Robert McCormick
Gender Coeducational
Languages English
Boarding/day Day
5036 Lavista Road, Tucker GA 30084, USA
TELEPHONE: +1 678 874-3702
EMAIL:
robert_c_mccormick@fc.dekalb.k12.ga.us
WEBSITE: www.dekalb.k12.ga.us/ffitucker/

Warren T Jackson Elementary School
Programme PYP
PYP Coordinator Lauren Owen
Gender Coeducational
Languages English
Boarding/day Day
1325 Mt. Paran Road, Atlanta GA 30327, USA
TELEPHONE: +1 404 842 3100
FAX: +1 404 842 1177
EMAIL: lreich@atlanta.k12.ga.us
WEBSITE: www.wtjackson.org

West Hall High School
Status State
Programme Diploma
Diploma Coordinator Laurie Ecke
Gender Coeducational
Languages English
Boarding/day Day
5500 McEver Road, Oakwood GA 30566, USA
TELEPHONE: +1 770 967 9826
FAX: +1 770 967 4864
EMAIL: jackie@hallco.org
WEBSITE: www.hallco.org/whhs

Willis H Sutton Middle School
Status State
Programme MYP
MYP Coordinator Ramon Reeves
Gender Coeducational
Languages English
Boarding/day Day
4360 Powers Ferry Road, Atlanta GA 30327,
USA
TELEPHONE: +1 404 256 6920
FAX: +1 404 802 5698
EMAIL: mmygrant@atlanta.k12.ga.us
WEBSITE: http://suttonmiddleschool.org

Woodland School
Status State
Programme Diploma
Diploma Coordinator Jennilyn Hawn
Gender Coeducational
Languages English
Boarding/day Day
800 Old Alabama Road, Bartow County,
Cartersville GA 30120, USA
TELEPHONE: +1 770 606 5870
FAX: +1 770 606 2080
EMAIL: nholt@bartow.k12.ga.us
WEBSITE: www.bartow.k12.ga.us/whs/

Hawaii

James Campbell High School
Status State
Programme Diploma
Diploma Coordinator Julie L Do
Gender Coeducational
Languages English
Boarding/day Day
91-980 North Road, Ewa Beach HI 96706, USA
TELEPHONE: +1 808 689 1200
FAX: +1 808 689 1242
EMAIL: gail_awakuni@notes.k12.hi.us
WEBSITE: www.campbell.k12.hi.us

Mid-Pacific Institute
Status Private
Programme Diploma
Diploma Coordinator Gareth Russell
Languages English
Boarding/day Mixed
2445 Kaala Street, Honolulu HI 96822, USA
TELEPHONE: +1 808 973 5020
FAX: +1 808 973 5137
EMAIL: rschaffer@midpac.edu
WEBSITE: www.midpac.edu

Iowa

Des Moines Public Schools: Central Academy
Status State
Programme Diploma
Diploma Coordinator Tamara Pfantz
Gender Coeducational
Languages English
Boarding/day Day
1800 Grand Avenue, Des Moines IA 50309,
USA
TELEPHONE: +1 515 235 4618
EMAIL: dennis.johnson@dmps.k12.ia.us
WEBSITE: www.dmhec.com

Idaho

Coeur d'Alene High School
Status State
Programme Diploma
Diploma Coordinator Michael Nelson
Gender Coeducational
Languages English
Boarding/day Day
5530 N 4th St, Coeur d'Alene ID 83815, USA
TELEPHONE: +1 208 667 4507
EMAIL: rrussell@cdaschools.org
WEBSITE: www.cdaschools.org/chs

Lake City High School
Status State
Programme Diploma
Diploma Coordinator Deanne Clifford
Gender Coeducational
Languages English
Boarding/day Day
6101 N Ramsey Rd, Coeur d'Alene ID 83815,
USA
TELEPHONE: +1 208 769 0769
FAX: +1 208 769 2969
EMAIL: jbrumley@sd271.k12.id.us
WEBSITE: www.cdaschools.org

Riverstone Community School
Status Private
Programme Diploma
Diploma Coordinator Joseph Kennedy
Gender Coeducational
Languages English
Boarding/day Day
5493 Warm Springs Avenue, Boise ID 83716,
USA
TELEPHONE: +1 208 424 5000
FAX: +1 208 424 0033
EMAIL: headofschool@riverstonecs.org
WEBSITE: www.riverstonecs.org

Illinois

Alice L Barnard Computer, Math and Science Center
Programme MYP
MYP Coordinator Gail Tennial
Gender Coeducational
Boarding/day Boarding
10354 South Charles, Chicago IL 60643, USA

Andrew Carnegie Elementary School
Status State
Programme MYP
MYP Coordinator Juanita Stem
Gender Coeducational
1414 East 61st Place, Chicago IL 60637, USA
TELEPHONE: +1 773 535 0882

Austin Community Academy High School
Status State
Programme Diploma
Diploma Coordinator Carrie Murphy-Kelso
Gender Coeducational
Languages English
231 North Pine Avenue #299, Chicago IL
60644, USA
TELEPHONE: +1 773 534 6300
FAX: +1 773 534 6046
EMAIL: clmurphy@cps.k12.il.us

Coretta Scott King Magnet School
Status State
Programme PYP
PYP Coordinator Gail Bohnenstiehl
Gender Coeducational
Languages English
Boarding/day Day
1009 Blackhawk Drive, University Park IL 60466, USA
TELEPHONE: +1 708 672 2651
FAX: +1 708 672 2653
EMAIL: debartoe@cm201u.org
WEBSITE: www.cm201u.org/csk

Curie Metropolitan High School
Status State
Programme MYP, Diploma
Diploma Coordinator Sharyl Barnes
MYP Coordinator Dorothy Carroll
Gender Coeducational
Languages English
Boarding/day Day
4959 South Archer Avenue, Chicago IL 60632, USA
TELEPHONE: +1 773 535 2100
FAX: +1 773 535 2049
EMAIL: jerryelyn.l.jones@cps.k12.il.us
WEBSITE: www.curiehs.com

Douglass Junior High School
Programme MYP
MYP Coordinator Judy Knox Carter
Gender Coeducational
Boarding/day Boarding
543 N Waller Avenue, Chicago IL 60644, USA
TELEPHONE: +1 733 534 6716
EMAIL: ddcrump@cps.k12.il.us

Elizabeth Sutherland Elementary School
Programme MYP
MYP Coordinator Gail Tennial
Gender Coeducational
Boarding/day Boarding
10015 South Leavitt Avenue, Chicago IL 60643, USA
TELEPHONE: +1 773 535 2580

Esmond Elementary School
Programme MYP
MYP Coordinator Gail Tennial
Gender Coeducational
Boarding/day Boarding
1865 W Montvale Avenue, Chicago IL 60643, USA

Francisco I Madero Middle School
Programme MYP
MYP Coordinator Dorothy Carroll
Gender Coeducational
3202 West 28th Street, Chicago IL 60623, USA
TELEPHONE: +1 773 535 4466
EMAIL: drosa98@hotmail

George Washington High School
Status State
Programme MYP, Diploma
Diploma Coordinator Beverly Matushek
MYP Coordinator Teddy Allen
Gender Coeducational
Languages English
Boarding/day Day
3535 East 114th Street, Chicago IL 60617, USA
TELEPHONE: +1 773 535 6430
FAX: +1 773 535 5038
EMAIL: juana.rivera-vidal@cps.k12.il.us

Henry R Clissold School
Programme MYP
MYP Coordinator Nicole Aquino
Gender Coeducational
Languages English
Boarding/day Day
2350 West 110th Place, Chicago IL 60643, USA
TELEPHONE: +1 773 535 2560
WEBSITE: www.clissoldschool.org

Hubbard High School
Status State
Programme Diploma
Diploma Coordinator Charmayne Posey
Gender Coeducational
Languages English
6200 South Hamlin Avenue, Chicago IL 60629, USA
TELEPHONE: +1 773 535 2403
FAX: +1 773 535 0175
EMAIL: sealed@prodigy.net

Hyde Park Academy
Status State
Programme MYP, Diploma
Diploma Coordinator Marilyn Rogawski
MYP Coordinator Patricia Smith
Gender Coeducational
Languages English
Boarding/day Boarding
6220 South Stoney Island Ave, Chicago IL 60637, USA
TELEPHONE: +1 773 535 0882
FAX: +1 773 535 0633
EMAIL: sdmcjunkins@cps.k12.il.us

James B McPherson Elementary School
Programme MYP
MYP Coordinator Tanya Baxter
Gender Coeducational
Boarding/day Boarding
4728 N Wolcott, Chicago IL 60640, USA
TELEPHONE: +1 773 534 2625
EMAIL: carmen.a.gianfortone@cps.k12.il.us

John L Marsh Elementary School
Programme MYP
MYP Coordinator Teddy Allen
Gender Coeducational
Boarding/day Boarding
9810 South Exchange Avenue, Chicago IL 60617, USA
TELEPHONE: +1 773 535 6430

John M Smyth Magnet School
Status State
Programme MYP
MYP Coordinator Kimberly Lebovitz
Gender Coeducational
Languages English
Boarding/day Day
1059 West 13th Street, Chicago IL 60608, USA
TELEPHONE: +1 773 534 7180
FAX: +1 773 534 7127
EMAIL: rwhitmore@cps.k12.il.us
WEBSITE: www.smythelementary.org

Kate Starr Kellogg Electronic Research Academy
Programme MYP
MYP Coordinator Gail Tennial
Gender Coeducational
Boarding/day Boarding
9241 S Leavitt Street, Chicago IL 60620, USA
TELEPHONE: +1 773 535 2590

Lincoln Park High School
Status State
Programme Diploma
Diploma Coordinator Mary Enda Tookey
Gender Coeducational
Languages English
Boarding/day Day
2001 North Orchard Street Mall, Chicago IL 60614, USA
TELEPHONE: +1 773 534 8149
FAX: +1 773 534 8214
EMAIL: lpibprogram@aol.com
WEBSITE: http://lincolnparkhs.org/

Locke Elementary School
Programme MYP
MYP Coordinator Deborah O'Brien
Gender Female
Boarding/day Day
2828 North Oak Park Avenue, Chicago IL 60634, USA
TELEPHONE: +1 773 534 3300
EMAIL: gortega@cps.k12.il.us

Marquette Elementary School
Programme MYP
MYP Coordinator Meg Venckus
Gender Coeducational
3939 West 79th Street, Chicago IL 60652, USA
TELEPHONE: +1 773 535 2174
EMAIL: rcmiller@cps.k12.il.us

Michele Clark Academic Preparatory Magnet High School
Status State
Programme MYP, Diploma
Diploma Coordinator Steve Waryjas
MYP Coordinator Eileen O'Toole
Gender Coeducational
Languages English
Boarding/day Day
5101 West Harrison Street, Chicago IL 60644, USA
TELEPHONE: +1 773 534 6250
EMAIL: agurley@cps.k12.il.us

Morgan Park High School
Status State
Programme MYP, Diploma
Diploma Coordinator Edna Brown
MYP Coordinator Gail Tennial
Gender Coeducational
Languages English
Boarding/day Day
1744 West Pryor, Chicago IL 60643, USA
TELEPHONE: +1 773-535-2550
FAX: +1 773-535-2506
EMAIL: ebmpib@hotmail.com
WEBSITE: www.cs.iit.edu/ffimorganpk

Nicholas Senn High School
Status State
Programme Diploma
Diploma Coordinator Mary Pat McKenna
Gender Coeducational
Languages English
Boarding/day Day
5900 Glenwood Avenue, Chicago IL 60660, USA
TELEPHONE: +1 773 534 2365
FAX: +1 773 534 2369
EMAIL: rsnorman@cps.k12.il.us

Prosser Career Academy
Status State
Programme Diploma
Diploma Coordinator Mark Wollschlaeger
Gender Coeducational
Languages English
Boarding/day Day
2148 North Long Avenue, Chicago IL 60639, USA
TELEPHONE: +1 773 534 3200
FAX: +1 773 534 3293
EMAIL: ken.hunter@cps.k12.il.us

Richard Edwards School
Programme MYP
MYP Coordinator Michael Rassel
Gender Coeducational
Boarding/day Day
4815 S Karlov Avenue, Chicago IL 60632, USA
TELEPHONE: +1 773 535 4878
EMAIL: dinwiddie@cps.k12.il.us
WEBSITE: edwardsschool.cps.k12.il.us

Richwoods High School
Status State
Programme Diploma
Diploma Coordinator Ron Kaufman
Gender Coeducational
Languages English
6301 North University, Peoria IL 61614, USA
TELEPHONE: +1 309 693 4400
FAX: +1 309 693 4414
EMAIL: john.meisinger@psd150.org

Roald Amundsen High School
Status State
Programme MYP, Diploma
Diploma Coordinator Minh Nguyen
MYP Coordinator Tanya Baxter
Gender Coeducational
Languages English
Boarding/day Day
5110 N Damen Avenue, Chicago IL 60625, USA
TELEPHONE: +1 773 534 2320
FAX: +1 773 534 2330
EMAIL: cmunoz@cps.k12.il.us

St Scholastica Academy
Status Private
Programme Diploma
Diploma Coordinator Judith Zonsius
Gender Female
Languages English
Boarding/day Day
7416 North Ridge Boulevard, Chicago IL 60645-1903, USA
TELEPHONE: +1 773 764 5715
FAX: +1 773 764 0304
EMAIL: amatz@scholastica.us
WEBSITE: www.scholastica.us

Steinmetz Academic Centre
Status State
Programme MYP, Diploma
Diploma Coordinator Ms Nancyanne Ferrarini
MYP Coordinator Ms Carol Mittleman
Gender Coeducational
Languages English
Boarding/day Day
3030 North Mobile Avenue, Chicago IL 60634, USA
TELEPHONE: +1 773 534 3030/2911
FAX: +1 773 534 3151
EMAIL: emadon@cps.edu
WEBSITE: www.steinmetzac.com

Thomas Kelly High School
Status State
Programme Diploma
Diploma Coordinator Raymond Buniak
Gender Coeducational
Languages English
Boarding/day Day
4136 South California Avenue, Chicago IL 60632, USA
TELEPHONE: +1 773 535 4915
FAX: +1 773 535 4841
EMAIL: acpretkelis@cps.k12.il.us
WEBSITE: www.schools.cps.k12.il.us/kelly/

Trinity College Preparatory High School
Status Private
Programme Diploma
Diploma Coordinator Rose Crnkovich
Gender Female
Languages English
Boarding/day Day
7574 West Division Street, River Forest IL 60305, USA
TELEPHONE: +1 708 771 8383
FAX: +1 708 488 2014
EMAIL: mwhitehead@trinityhs.org
WEBSITE: www.trinityhs.org

Wildwood Elementary School
Programme MYP
MYP Coordinator Annette Dluger
Gender Coeducational
6950 N Hiawatha, Chicago IL 60646, USA
TELEPHONE: +1 773 534 1187
EMAIL: esavoy@wildwood.cps.k12.il.us

William Howard Taft High School
Status State
Programme Diploma
Diploma Coordinator John Mullins
Gender Coeducational
Languages English
6530 West Bryn Mawr Avenue, Region 1 Area 19, Chicago IL 60631, USA
TELEPHONE: +1 773 534 1000
FAX: +1 773 534 1027
EMAIL: antarvardian@cps.k12.il.us

William J Bogan Computer Technical High
Status State
Programme MYP, Diploma
Diploma Coordinator Diane Williams
MYP Coordinator Meg Venckus
Gender Coeducational
Languages English
Boarding/day Day/boarding
3939 West 79th Street, Chicago IL 60652, USA
TELEPHONE: +1 773 535 2238
FAX: +1 773 535 0227

Indiana

Ben Davis High School
Status State
Programme Diploma
Diploma Coordinator Bridgette Joseph
Gender Coeducational
Languages English
Boarding/day Day
1200 N Girls School Road, Indianapolis IN 46214, USA
TELEPHONE: +1 317 244 7691
FAX: +1 317 243 5506
EMAIL: joel.mckinney@wayne.k12.in.us
WEBSITE: www.wayne.k12.in.us

Benjamin Bosse High School
Status State
Programme Diploma
Diploma Coordinator Amy Bonenberger
Gender Coeducational
Languages English
Boarding/day Day
1300 Washington Avenue, Evansville IN 47714, USA
TELEPHONE: +1 812-477-1661
FAX: +1 812-474-6976
EMAIL: wtrober@evsc.k12.in.us
WEBSITE: www.evsc.k12.in.us/schoolzone/schools/bossehs/bhs.htm

Carmel High School
Status State
Programme Diploma
Diploma Coordinator Kerry Hoffman
Gender Coeducational
Languages English
Boarding/day Day
520 East Main Street, Carmel IN 46032, USA
TELEPHONE: +1 317-846-7721
FAX: +1 317-571-4066
EMAIL: jwilliam@ccs.k12.in.us
WEBSITE: http://carmelhighschool.net

Cathedral High School
Status Private
Programme Diploma
Diploma Coordinator Kenneth Steeb
Gender Coeducational
Languages English
Boarding/day Day
5225 E 56th Street, Indianapolis IN 46226, USA
TELEPHONE: +1 317 968 7306
FAX: +1 317 543 5050
EMAIL: dworland@cathedral-irish.org
WEBSITE: www.cathedral-irish.org

Center for Inquiry
Status State
Programme PYP, MYP
MYP Coordinator Carrie Gaffney
PYP Coordinator Beth Young
Gender Coeducational
Languages English
Boarding/day Day
25 N New Jersey Street, Indianapolis IN 46202, USA
TELEPHONE: +1 317 226 4202
FAX: +1 317 226 3740
EMAIL: collierc@ips.k12.in.us
WEBSITE: www.302.ips.k12.in.us

Chesterton High School
Status State
Programme Diploma
Diploma Coordinator Becky Gierke
Gender Coeducational
Languages English
Boarding/day Day
2125 S 11th Street, Chesterton IN 46304, USA
TELEPHONE: +1 219 983 3730
EMAIL: jim.goetz@duneland.k12.in.us
WEBSITE: www.duneland.k12.in.us/chs

Fishers High School
Status State
Programme Diploma
Diploma Coordinator Valerie Piehl
Gender Coeducational
Languages English
Boarding/day Day
13000 Promise Road, Fishers IN 46038, USA
TELEPHONE: +1 317 915 4290
FAX: +1 317 915 4299
EMAIL: ssyverson@hse.k12.in.us
WEBSITE: http://hse.k12.in.us/fhs/

Goshen High School
Status State
Programme Diploma
Diploma Coordinator RaShella Wilfong
Gender Coeducational
Languages English
Boarding/day Day
401 Lincolnway East, Goshen IN 46526, USA
TELEPHONE: +1 574 533 8651
FAX: +1 574 534 1567
EMAIL: jkirkton@goshenschools.org
WEBSITE: http://ghs.goshenschools.org

International School of Indiana
Status Private
Programme Diploma
Diploma Coordinator Mitch Chabraja
Gender Coeducational
Languages English, French, Spanish
Boarding/day Day
4330 North Michigan Road, Indianapolis IN 46208, USA
TELEPHONE: +1 317 923 1951
FAX: +1 317 255 1910
EMAIL: dgarner@isind.org
WEBSITE: www.isind.org

John Adams High School
Status State
Programme Diploma
Diploma Coordinator Rosemary Hess
Gender Coeducational
Languages English
Boarding/day Day
808 South Twyckenham Blvd, South Bend IN 46615, USA
TELEPHONE: +1 574 283 7700
FAX: +1 574 283 7704
EMAIL: twiedemann@sbcsc.k12.in.us
WEBSITE: www.sbcsc.k12.in.us

Lawrence Central High School
Status State
Programme Diploma
Diploma Coordinator Pamela Brandley
Languages English
7300 East 56th Street, Indianapolis IN 46226, USA
TELEPHONE: +1 317 454 5301
FAX: +1 317 543 3348
EMAIL: pamelabrandley@msdlt.k12.in.us

Lawrence North High School
Status State
Programme Diploma
Diploma Coordinator Jennifer Oliver
Languages English
7601 East 56th Street, Indianapolis IN 45226, USA
TELEPHONE: +1 317 849 9455
FAX: +1 317 576 6406
EMAIL: williamellery@msdlt.k12.in.us

North Central High School
Status State
Programme Diploma
Diploma Coordinator Judith Libby
Gender Coeducational
Languages English
Boarding/day Day
1801 East 86th Street, Indianapolis IN 46240, USA
TELEPHONE: +1 317 259 5345
FAX: +1 317 259 5369
EMAIL: cequandt@msdwt.k12.in.us

Northwest High School
Status State
Programme Diploma
Diploma Coordinator Zoretta Ward-Holloway
Gender Coeducational
Languages English
Boarding/day Day
5525 W 34th St, Indianapolis IN 46224, USA
TELEPHONE: +1 317 693 5600
FAX: +1 317 226 3409
EMAIL: simpsore@ips.k12.in.us
WEBSITE: www.723.ips.k12.in.us

Pike High School
Status State
Programme Diploma
Diploma Coordinator Donna Cracraft
Gender Coeducational
Languages English
Boarding/day Day
5401 West 71th street, Indianapolis IN 46268, USA
TELEPHONE: +1 317387 2600
FAX: +1 317 328 7239
EMAIL: djacobs@pike.k12.in.us
WEBSITE: www.pike.k12.in.us

Saint Theodore Guerin High School
Status Private
Programme Diploma
Diploma Coordinator Kelly Hamilton
Gender Coeducational
Languages English
Boarding/day Day
15300 Gray Road, Noblesville IN 46062, USA
TELEPHONE: +1 317-582-0120
FAX: +1 317-582-0140
EMAIL: rwagner@guerincatholic.org
WEBSITE: www.guerincatholic.org

Signature School, Inc.
Status State
Programme Diploma
Diploma Coordinator Susie Kuhlenschmidt
Gender Coeducational
Languages English
Boarding/day Day
610 Main Street, Evansville IN 47708, USA
TELEPHONE: +1 812-421-1820
FAX: +1 812-421-9189
EMAIL: vicki.snyder@signature.edu
WEBSITE: www.signature.edu

South Side High School, Fort Wayne
Status State
Programme Diploma
Diploma Coordinator Nancy Vojtash Moore
Gender Coeducational
Languages English
Boarding/day Day
3601 South Calhoun Street, Fort Wayne
IN 46807, USA
TELEPHONE: +1 260 425 7620
FAX: +1 260 425 7649
EMAIL: thomas.smith@fwcs.k12.in.us

Valparaiso High School
Status State
Programme Diploma
Diploma Coordinator Debbie Fray
Gender Coeducational
Languages English
Boarding/day Day
2727 North Campbell Street, Valparaiso
IN 46383, USA
TELEPHONE: +1 219 531 3070
FAX: +1 219 531 3076
EMAIL: kbrist@mail.valpo.k12.in.us

Kansas

Hutchinson High School
Status State
Programme Diploma
Diploma Coordinator Todd Ray
Gender Coeducational
Languages English
Boarding/day Day
1401 North Severance, Hutchinson KS 67501,
USA
TELEPHONE: +1 620 665-4500
FAX: +1 620 665-4580
EMAIL: roehmr@usd308.com
WEBSITE: http://hhs.usd308.com

Hyman Brand Hebrew Academy
Status Private
Programme PYP, MYP
MYP Coordinator Clayton Lucas
PYP Coordinator Laura Hewitt
Gender Coeducational
Languages English
Boarding/day Day
5801 West 115th Street, Overland Park
KS 66211, USA
TELEPHONE: +1 913 327 8150
EMAIL: hhaas@hbha.edu
WEBSITE: www.hbha.edu

Shawnee Mission East High School
Status State
Programme Diploma
Diploma Coordinator Rebecca Murphy
Gender Coeducational
Languages English
Boarding/day Day
7500 Mission Road, Shawnee Mission
KS 66208-4298, USA
TELEPHONE: +1 913 993 6600
FAX: +1 913 993 6899
EMAIL: eacocoli@smsd.org

**Shawnee Mission Northwest High
School**
Status State
Programme Diploma
Diploma Coordinator Bill Sanderson
Gender Coeducational
Languages English
Boarding/day Day
12701 West 67th Street, Shawnee KS 66216,
USA
TELEPHONE: +1 913 993 7200
FAX: +1 913 993 7499
EMAIL: billharrington
WEBSITE: www.smsd.org

Sumner Academy of Arts and Science
Status State
Programme Diploma
Diploma Coordinator Sylvia Parra
Gender Coeducational
Languages English
Boarding/day Day
1610 N 8th Street, Kansas City KS 66101, USA
TELEPHONE: +1 913 627 7200
FAX: +1 913 627 7205
EMAIL: maviver@kckps.org

Wichita High School East
Status State
Programme Diploma
Diploma Coordinator Steven Shook
Gender Coeducational
Languages English
Boarding/day Day
2301 East Douglas, Wichita KS 67211, USA
TELEPHONE: +1 316 973 7289
FAX: +1 316 973 7209
EMAIL: kthiessen@usd259.net
WEBSITE: www.east.usd259.org/

Kentucky

Apollo High School
Status State
Programme Diploma
Diploma Coordinator Rachel Rosales
Gender Coeducational
Languages English
2280 Tamarack Road, Owensboro KY 42301,
USA
TELEPHONE: +1 270 852 7100
FAX: +1 270 852 7110
EMAIL: tpurcell@daviess.k12.ky.us

Atherton High School
Status State
Programme Diploma
Diploma Coordinator Pam Mechetner
Gender Coeducational
Languages English
Boarding/day Day
3000 Dundee Road, Louisville KY 40205, USA
TELEPHONE: +1 502 485 8202
FAX: +1 502 485 8985
EMAIL: jhudson1@jefferson.k12.ky.us

Holmes High School
Status State
Programme Diploma
Diploma Coordinator William Grein
Gender Coeducational
Languages English
Boarding/day Day
25th and Madison Avenue, Covington
Independent Schools, Covington KY 41014,
USA
TELEPHONE: +1 859 655 9545
FAX: +1 859 581 7259
EMAIL: rfinke@covington.k12.ky.us

Sacred Heart Academy
Status Private
Programme Diploma
Diploma Coordinator Carol Sherman
Gender Female
Languages English
Boarding/day Day
3175 Lexington Road, Louisville KY 40206,
USA
TELEPHONE: +1 502 897 6097
FAX: +1 502 893 0120
EMAIL: bmcauliffe@sacredheartacad.com
WEBSITE: www.sacredheartacad.com

Tates Creek High School
Status State
Programme Diploma
Diploma Coordinator Teri Harper
Gender Coeducational
Languages English
Boarding/day Day
1111 Centre Parkway, Lexington KY 40517, USA
TELEPHONE: +1 859 381 3620
FAX: +1 859 381 3635
EMAIL: sam.meaux@fayette.kyschools.us
WEBSITE: www.tchs.fcps.net

Louisiana

John Ehret High School
Status State
Programme Diploma
Diploma Coordinator Donna Donahoe
Gender Coeducational
Languages English
Boarding/day Day
4300 Patriot Street, Marrero LA 70072, USA
TELEPHONE: +1 504-340-7651
FAX: +1 504-340-7295
EMAIL: clothilde.cobert@jppss.k12.la.us
WEBSITE: http://ehret.jppss.k12.la.us

Louisiana State University Laboratory School
Status State
Programme PYP, MYP, Diploma
Diploma Coordinator Steve Delacroix
MYP Coordinator Emily Turner
PYP Coordinator Christelle Thompson
Gender Coeducational
Languages English
Boarding/day Day
45 Dalrymple Drive, Baton Rouge
LA 70803-0501, USA
TELEPHONE: +1 225 578 9147
EMAIL: acambu1@lsu.edu
WEBSITE: www.uhigh.lsu.edu

Riverdale High School
Status State
Programme Diploma
Diploma Coordinator Holly Howat
Gender Coeducational
Languages English
Boarding/day Day
240 Riverdale Drive, Jefferson LA 70121, USA
TELEPHONE: +1 504-833-7288
EMAIL: connie.tiliakos@jppss.k12.la.us
WEBSITE: http://riverdalehigh.jppss.k12.la.us

Riverdale Middle School
Status State
Programme MYP
MYP Coordinator Amy Schayot
Gender Coeducational
Languages English
Boarding/day Day
3900 Jefferson Hwy, Jefferson LA 70121, USA
TELEPHONE: +1 504 828 2706
FAX: +1 504 833 5125
EMAIL: randybennett@jppss.k12.la.us
WEBSITE:
www.riverdalemiddle.jppss.k12.la.us

Massachusetts

British School of Boston
Status Private
Programme Diploma
Diploma Coordinator Ruth Williams
Gender Coeducational
Languages English
Boarding/day Day
416 Pond Street, Boston MA 02130, USA
TELEPHONE: +1 617 522 2261
WEBSITE: www.britishschool.org/boston

Brockton High School
Status State
Programme Diploma
Diploma Coordinator Maria Lefort
Gender Coeducational
Languages English
Boarding/day Day
470 Forest Ave, Brockton MA 02301, USA
TELEPHONE: +1 508 580 7633
EMAIL: susanszachowicz@
brocktonpublicschools.com
WEBSITE: http://brocktonpublicschools.com

High School of Commerce
Status State
Programme Diploma
Diploma Coordinator John G Piponidis
Gender Coeducational
Languages English
Boarding/day Day
415 State Street, Springfield Public Schools,
Springfield MA 01105, USA
TELEPHONE: +1 413 787 7220
FAX: +1 413 787 7041
EMAIL: stennetta@sps.springfield.ma.us

International School of Boston
Status Private
Programme Diploma
Diploma Coordinator Tracey Wood
Gender Coeducational
Languages English
Boarding/day Day
45 Matignon Road, Cambridge MA 02140,
USA
TELEPHONE: +1 617 499 1451
FAX: +1 617 499 1454
EMAIL: jlarner@isbos.org
WEBSITE: www.isbos.org

Kensington Avenue Magnet School
Status State
Programme PYP
PYP Coordinator Gail Manuel
Gender Coeducational
Languages English
Boarding/day Day
31 Kensington Avenue, Springfield MA 01108,
USA
TELEPHONE: +1 413 787 7522
FAX: +1 413 787 7374
EMAIL: thompsonm@sps.springfield.ma.us
WEBSITE:
www.sps.springfield.ma.us/magnet

Mystic Valley Regional Charter School
Status State
Programme Diploma
Diploma Coordinator Gordon Bradford
Gender Coeducational
Languages English
Boarding/day Day
770 Salem Street, Malden MA 02148, USA
TELEPHONE: +1 781 953 5485
WEBSITE: www.mvrcs.com

Sturgis Charter School
Status State
Programme Diploma
Diploma Coordinator Arthur Pontes
Gender Coeducational
Languages English
Boarding/day Day
Administration, 427 Main Street, Hyannis
MA 02601, USA
TELEPHONE: +1 508 778 1782
FAX: +1 508 771 6785
EMAIL: ehieser@yahoo.com
WEBSITE: www.sturgischarterschool.com

Maryland

Albert Einstein High School
Status State
Programme Diploma
Diploma Coordinator Malissa McCormick
Languages English
11135 Newport Mill Road, Kensington
MD 20895, USA
TELEPHONE: +1 301 929 2200
FAX: +1 301 962 1016
EMAIL:
malissa_mccormick@fc.mcps.k12.md.us

Annapolis High School
Status State
Programme Diploma
Diploma Coordinator Fawn Mete
Gender Coeducational
Languages English
Boarding/day Day
2700 Riva Road, Annapolis MD 21401, USA
TELEPHONE: +1 410 266 5240
EMAIL: dlilley@aacps.org
WEBSITE: www.aacps.org

Baltimore City College
Status State
Programme Diploma
Diploma Coordinator Cindy Harcum
Gender Coeducational
Languages English
Boarding/day Day
3220 The Alameda, Baltimore MD 21218, USA
TELEPHONE: +1 410 396 6557
FAX: +1 410 243 0669
EMAIL: tdawson@bcps.k12.md.us

Bethesda-Chevy Chase High School
Status State
Programme MYP, Diploma
Diploma Coordinator Beth Groeneman
MYP Coordinator Martha Cohen-Tomlinson
Gender Coeducational
Languages English
Boarding/day Day
4301 East West Highway, Bethesda MD 20814,
USA
TELEPHONE: +1 240 497 6300
FAX: +1 240 497 6326
EMAIL: sean_w_bulson@mcpsmd.org
WEBSITE: www.montgomeryschoolsmd.org

Central High School, Capitol Heights
Status State
Programme Diploma
Diploma Coordinator Jay Friedenberg
Gender Coeducational
Languages English
Boarding/day Day
200 Cabin Branch Road, Capitol Heights
MD 20743, USA
TELEPHONE: +1 301 499 7080
FAX: +1 301 499 7087
EMAIL: jay.friedenberg@pgcps.org

Chevy Chase Elementary School
Programme MYP
MYP Coordinator Marjorie Lope
Gender Coeducational
Boarding/day Day
4015 Rosemary Street, Chevy Chase
MD 20815, USA
EMAIL: marjorie_d_lope@fc.mcps.k12.md.us

College Gardens Elementary School
Status State
Programme PYP
PYP Coordinator Elizabeth Rogovoy
Gender Coeducational
Languages English
Boarding/day Day
1700 Yale Place, Rockville MD 20850, USA
TELEPHONE: +1 301 279 8470
FAX: +1 301 279 8473
EMAIL: albert_dupont@mcpsmd.org
WEBSITE: www.mcps.k12.md.us/schools/
collegegardenses

Julius West Middle School
Status State
Programme MYP
MYP Coordinator Gail Fribush
Gender Coeducational
Languages English
Boarding/day Day
651 Great Falls Road, Rockville MD 20850,
USA
TELEPHONE: +1 301 279 3979
WEBSITE: www.montgomeryschoolsmd.org

Kenwood High School
Status State
Programme Diploma
Diploma Coordinator Brenda DeGori
Gender Coeducational
Languages English
Boarding/day Day
501 Stemmers Run Road, Baltimore County,
Baltimore MD 21221, USA
TELEPHONE: +1 410 887 0153
FAX: +1 410 887 6382
EMAIL: pmartin2@bcps.org

Laurel High School
Status State
Programme Diploma
Diploma Coordinator Patricia Bocock
Gender Coeducational
Languages English
Boarding/day Day
8000 Cherry Lane, Laurel MD 20707, USA
TELEPHONE: +1 301 497 2050
FAX: +1 301 497 2066
EMAIL: dwayne.jones@pgcps.org
WEBSITE: www.pgcps.org/ffilaurel

Meade Senior High School
Status State
Programme Diploma
Diploma Coordinator Jennifer Quinn
Gender Coeducational
Languages English
Boarding/day Day
1100 Clark Road, Ft Meade MD 20755, USA
TELEPHONE: +1 410 674 7710
FAX: +1 410 674 8750
EMAIL: dekennedy@aacps.org
WEBSITE: www.meadesenior.org

Milford Mill Academy High School
Status State
Programme Diploma
Diploma Coordinator Barbara Birt
Gender Coeducational
Languages English
Boarding/day Day
3800 Washington Avenue, Baltimore
MD 21244-3799, USA
TELEPHONE: +1 410 887 0660
FAX: +1 410 887 0681
EMAIL: ngibson@bcps.org

Newport Mill Middle School
Status State
Programme MYP
MYP Coordinator Laura Marion
Gender Coeducational
Languages English
Boarding/day Day
11311 Newport Mill Road, Kensington
MD 20895, USA
TELEPHONE: +1 301 929 2244
FAX: +1 301 929 2274
EMAIL: nelson_mcleod@mcpsmd.org
WEBSITE: www.mcps.k12.md.us/schools/
newportmillms

**North Chevy Chase Elementary
School**
Programme MYP
MYP Coordinator Marjorie Lope
Gender Coeducational
Boarding/day Day
3700 Jones Bridge Road, Chevy Chase
MD 20815, USA
EMAIL: marjorie_d_lope@fc.mcps.k12.md.us

North Hagerstown High School
Status State
Programme Diploma
Diploma Coordinator Kevin G Jackson
Gender Coeducational
Languages English
Boarding/day Day
1200 Pennsylvania Ave, Hagerstown
MD 21742, USA
TELEPHONE: +1 301-766-8238
FAX: +1 301-733-3158
EMAIL: novakval@wcboe.k12.md.us
WEBSITE: www.wcboe.kqw.md.us

Old Mill High School
Status State
Programme Diploma
Diploma Coordinator Elizabeth Mitchell
Gender Coeducational
Boarding/day Day
600 Patriot Lane, Millersville MD 21108, USA
TELEPHONE: +1 410 969 9010
EMAIL: aliverman@aacps.org
WEBSITE: www.aacps.org

**Our Lady of Good Counsel High
School**
Status Private
Programme Diploma
Diploma Coordinator Thomas Campbell
Gender Coeducational
Languages English
Boarding/day Day
11601 Georgia Avenue, Wheaton MD 20902,
USA
TELEPHONE: +1 301 942 1155
FAX: +1 301 942 3656
EMAIL: graham@olgchs.org
WEBSITE: http://olgchs.cor

Parkdale High School
Status State
Programme Diploma
Diploma Coordinator Carol Terry
Gender Coeducational
Languages English
Boarding/day Day
6001 Good Luck Road, Riverdale MD 20737,
USA
TELEPHONE: +1 301 513 5700
FAX: +1 301 486-3728
EMAIL: horrigan@pgcps.org

Richard Montgomery High School
Status State
Programme MYP, Diploma
Diploma Coordinator Jennifer Hoover
MYP Coordinator Parfait Awono
Gender Coeducational
Languages English
Boarding/day Day
250 Richard Montgomery Drive, Rockville
MD 20852, USA
TELEPHONE: +1 301 279 8400
EMAIL: moreno_e_carrasco@mcpsmd.org
WEBSITE: http://montgomeryschoolsmd.org/
schools/rmhs

Rockville High School
Status State
Programme Diploma
Diploma Coordinator Deborah Wilchek
Gender Coeducational
Languages English
Boarding/day Day
2100 Baltimore Road, Rockville MD 21805,
USA
TELEPHONE: +1 301 517 8105
EMAIL: debra_s_munk@mcpsmd.org
WEBSITE: www.montgomeryschoolsmd.org/
schools/rockvillehs

Silver Spring International Middle School
Status State
Programme MYP
MYP Coordinator Elisabeth Williams-Caison
Gender Coeducational
Languages English
Boarding/day Day
313 Wayne Avenue, Silver Spring MD, USA
TELEPHONE: +1 301 650 6544
FAX: +1 301 652 5244
EMAIL: lily_v_lake-parcan@mcpsmd.org
WEBSITE:
http://mcps.k12.md.us/schools/ssims/

Springbrooke High School
Status State
Programme Diploma
Diploma Coordinator John Day
Gender Coeducational
Languages English
Boarding/day Day
201 Valley Brook Drive, Silver Spring
MD 20904, USA
TELEPHONE: +1 301 989 5700
FAX: +1 301 622 1875
EMAIL: michael_a_durso@mcpsmd.org
WEBSITE: www.mcps.k12.md.us/schools/
springbrookhs/

St Timothy's School
Status Private
Programme Diploma
Diploma Coordinator Adam Man
Gender Female
Languages English
Boarding/day Mixed
8400 Greenspring Ave, Stevenson MD 21153,
USA
TELEPHONE: +1-410-486-7400
FAX: +1-410-484-5910
EMAIL: rstevens@sttims-school.org
WEBSITE: www.sttims-school.org

Suitland High School
Status State
Programme Diploma
Diploma Coordinator Myrtle Brijbasi
Gender Coeducational
Languages English
Boarding/day Day
5200 Silver Hill Road, Forestville MD 20747,
USA
TELEPHONE: +1 301 817 0500
FAX: +1 301 817 7946
EMAIL: gallen@pgcps.org

The Boys' School of St Paul's Parish
Status Private
Programme Diploma
Diploma Coordinator John Thorpe
Gender Male
Languages English
Boarding/day Day
PO Box 8100, Brooklandville MD 21022-8100,
USA
TELEPHONE: +1 410 825 4400
EMAIL: treid@stpaulsschool.org
WEBSITE: www.stpaulsschool.org

Thomas Jefferson Elementary
Status State
Programme PYP
PYP Coordinator Sara Huppert
Gender Coeducational
Languages English
Boarding/day Day
605 Dryden Drive, Baltimore MD 21229, USA
TELEPHONE: +1 410 396 0534
FAX: +1 410 545 7830
EMAIL: wleishear@bcps.k12.md.us

Urbana High School
Status State
Programme Diploma
Diploma Coordinator Helen Golibart
Languages English
3471 Campus Drive, Ijamsville MD 21754, USA
TELEPHONE: +1 240 236 7600
FAX: +1 240 236 7601
EMAIL: george.seaton@fcps.org

Watkins Mill High School
Status State
Programme Diploma
Diploma Coordinator Lisa Ingram
Languages English
10301 Apple Ridge Road, Gaithersburg
MD 20879, USA
TELEPHONE: +1 301 840 3959
FAX: +1 301 840 3980
EMAIL: peter_j_cahall@fc.mcps.k12.md.us

Westland Middle School
Programme MYP
MYP Coordinator Marjorie Lope
Gender Coeducational
Boarding/day Day
5511 Massachusetts Avenue, Bethedsa
MD 20816, USA
TELEPHONE: +1 301 320 6515
EMAIL: marjorie_d_lope@fc.mcps.k12.md.us

Maine

Kennebunk High School
Status State
Programme Diploma
Diploma Coordinator Susan Cressey
Gender Coeducational
Languages English
Boarding/day Day
89 Fletcher Street, Kennebunk ME 04043, USA
TELEPHONE: +1 207 985 1110
EMAIL: pdawson@msad71.net
WEBSITE: http://khs.msad71.net

Michigan

Andover High School
Status State
Programme MYP
MYP Coordinator Jason Rubel
Gender Coeducational
Languages English
Boarding/day Day
4200 Andover Road, Bloomfield Hills
MI 48302, USA
TELEPHONE: +1 248 341 5500
FAX: +1 248 341 5699
EMAIL: hkattula@bloomfield.org
WEBSITE: http://andover.bloomfield.org

Detroit Country Day School
Status Private
Programme Diploma
Diploma Coordinator Charles Fremuth
Gender Coeducational
Languages English
Boarding/day Mixed
22305 West 13 Mile Road, Beverly Hills
MI 48025-4435, USA
TELEPHONE: +1 248 646 7717
FAX: +1 248 646 2458
EMAIL: jerryhansen@dcds.edu
WEBSITE: www.dcds.edu

Herbert Henry Dow High School
Status State
Programme Diploma
Diploma Coordinator Amy Ochander
Gender Coeducational
Languages English
Boarding/day Day
3901 North Saginaw Road, Midland MI 48640,
USA
TELEPHONE: +1 989 923 5382
FAX: +1 989 923 5301
EMAIL: goodalljk@mps.k12.mi.us
WEBSITE: www.dhs.mps.k12.mi.us

Heritage High School
Status State
Programme Diploma
Diploma Coordinator Sandra Terbrack
Gender Coeducational
Languages English
Boarding/day Day
3465 N Center, Saginaw MI 48603, USA
TELEPHONE: +1 989 799 5790
FAX: +1 989 799 5159
EMAIL: msnewman@stcs.org
WEBSITE: www.stcs.org

International Academy
Status State
Programme Diploma
Diploma Coordinator Patricia Steeby
Gender Coeducational
Languages English
Boarding/day Day
1020 East Square Lake Road, Bloomfield Hills
MI 48304, USA
TELEPHONE: +1 248 341 5900
EMAIL: bokma@bloomfield.org
WEBSITE: www.iatoday.org

Lansing Eastern High School
Status State
Programme Diploma
Diploma Coordinator Mary Witherspoon
Gender Coeducational
Languages English
Boarding/day Day
220 North Pennsylvania Ave, Lansing
MI 48912, USA
TELEPHONE: +1 517-325-6500
FAX: +1 517-325-7341
EMAIL: pkdiggs@lsd.k12.mi.us
WEBSITE: www.lsd.k12.mi.us

Lone Pine Elementary
Status State
Programme PYP
PYP Coordinator Jean Ramseyer
Gender Coeducational
Languages English
Boarding/day Day
3100 Lone Pine Road, Orchard Lake MI 48323,
USA
TELEPHONE: +1 248 341 7300
FAX: +1 248 341 7399
EMAIL: mmccuen@bloomfield.org
WEBSITE: http://lonepine.bloomfield.org

Midland High School
Status State
Programme Diploma
Diploma Coordinator Amy Hutchinson
Gender Coeducational
Languages English
Boarding/day Day
1301 Eastlawn Drive, Midland MI 48642, USA
TELEPHONE: +1 989 923 5181
FAX: +1 989 923 5100
EMAIL: frazeemr@mps.k12.mi.us
WEBSITE: www.mhs.mps.k12.mi.us

Notre Dame Preparatory School & Marist Academy
Status Private
Programme Diploma
Diploma Coordinator Sharon Derico
Gender Coeducational
Languages English
Boarding/day Day
1300 Giddings Road, Pontiac MI 48340, USA
TELEPHONE: +1 248 373 5300
FAX: +1 248 373 8024
EMAIL: lolszamowski@ndpma.org
WEBSITE: www.ndpma.org

Portage Central High School
Status State
Programme Diploma
Diploma Coordinator Nancy Pederson
Gender Coeducational
Languages English
Boarding/day Day
8135 South Westnedge Avenue, Portage
MI 49002, USA
TELEPHONE: +1 269 323 5255
FAX: +1 269 323 5290
EMAIL: ealburtus@portageps.org
WEBSITE: www.portageps.org

Portage Northern High School
Status State
Programme Diploma
Diploma Coordinator Linda Trepanier
Gender Coeducational
Languages English
Boarding/day Day
1000 Idaho Avenue, Portage MI 49024-1233,
USA
TELEPHONE: +1 269-323-5455
FAX: +1 269-323-5490
EMAIL: klathwell@portageps.org
WEBSITE:
www.portageps.org/high_schools/Northern

West Hills Middle School
Status State
Programme MYP
MYP Coordinator Jason Rubel
Gender Coeducational
Languages English
Boarding/day Day
2601 Lone Pine Road, West Bloomfield
MI 28323, USA
TELEPHONE: +1 248 341 6100
FAX: +1 248 341 6199
EMAIL: ebretzlaff@bloomfield.org
WEBSITE: http://westhills.bloomfield.org

Minnesota

Benjamin E Mays Magnet School
Status State
Programme PYP
PYP Coordinator Nancy Hall
Gender Coeducational
Languages English
Boarding/day Day
560 Concordia Avenue, St Paul MN 55103,
USA
TELEPHONE: +1 651 325 2400
FAX: +1 651 325 2401
EMAIL: graneze.fretwell@spps.org
WEBSITE: www.maysmagnet.spps.org

Carl Sandburg Middle School
Status State
Programme MYP
MYP Coordinator Lauren Hildebrand
Gender Coeducational
2400 Sandburg Lane, Golden Valley
MN 55427, USA
TELEPHONE: +1 763 504 8201
EMAIL: tom_henderlite@rdale.k12.mn.us
WEBSITE: www.rdale.k12.mn.us/sms

Central High School, St Paul
Status State
Programme Diploma
Diploma Coordinator Leslie Warner Tonyan
Gender Coeducational
Languages English
Boarding/day Day
275 North Lexington Parkway, Independent
School #625, St Paul MN 55104, USA
TELEPHONE: +1 651 632 6000
FAX: +1 651 293-5433
EMAIL: mary.mackbee@spps.org

Champlin Park High School
Status State
Programme Diploma
Diploma Coordinator JeanMarie Burtness
Gender Coeducational
Languages English
Boarding/day Day
6025 109th Avenue North, Champlin
MN 55316, USA
TELEPHONE: +1 763-506-6800
EMAIL: rhoda.mhiripiri@anoka.k12.mn.us
WEBSITE: www.anoka.k12.mn.us/cphs

Crosswinds East Metro Arts & Science School
Programme MYP
MYP Coordinator Christine Silvis
Gender Coeducational
Languages English
Boarding/day Day
600 Weir Drive, Woodbury MN 55125, USA
TELEPHONE: +1 651 379 2600
EMAIL: anne.andersen@emid6067.net
WEBSITE: www.emid6067.net

Earle Brown Elementary
Status State
Programme PYP
PYP Coordinator Nichole Rens
Gender Coeducational
Languages English
Boarding/day Day
1500 59th Avenue North, Brooklyn Center
MN 55430, USA
TELEPHONE: +1 763 561 4480
EMAIL: rkoch@brookcntr.k12.mn.us
WEBSITE: www.brookcntr.k12.mn.us

Elizabeth Hall International Elementary School
Status State
Programme PYP
PYP Coordinator Kristi Bostad
Gender Coeducational
Languages English
Boarding/day Day
1601 Aldrich Avenue North, Minneapolis
MN 55411, USA
TELEPHONE: +1 612 668 2650
EMAIL: bennicey@mpls.k12.mn.us
WEBSITE: http://hall.mpls.k12.mn.us

Evergreen Park World Studies Elementary School
Status State
Programme PYP
PYP Coordinator Jodi Baker
Gender Coeducational
Languages English
Boarding/day Day
7020 Dupont Avenue North, Brooklyn Center
MN 55430, USA
TELEPHONE: +1 763 506 2500
EMAIL: jill.griffith-mcraith@
anoka.k12.mn.us
WEBSITE:
www.anoka.k12.mn.us/evergreenpark

Fairmont High School
Status State
Programme Diploma
Diploma Coordinator Carol Nasby
Gender Coeducational
Languages English
Boarding/day Day
900 Johnson Street, Fairmont MN 56031, USA
TELEPHONE: +1 507 238 4411
FAX: +1 507 235 4130
EMAIL: cbusch@fairmont.k12.mn.us

Fridley High School
Status State
Programme MYP
MYP Coordinator Renee Van Gorp
Gender Coeducational
Languages English
Boarding/day Day
6000 West Moore Lake Drive, Fridley
MN 55432, USA
TELEPHONE: +1 763 502-5600
FAX: +1 763- 502-5640
EMAIL: dave.webb@fridley.k2.mn.us
WEBSITE: www.fridley.k12.mn.us

Fridley Middle School
Status State
Programme MYP
MYP Coordinator Renee Van Gorp
Gender Coeducational
Languages English
Boarding/day Day
6100 West Moore Lake Drive, Fridley
MN 55432, USA
TELEPHONE: +1 763 502-5400
FAX: +1 763- 502-5440
EMAIL: margaret.leibfried@fridley.k12.mn.us
WEBSITE: www.fridley.k12.mn.us

Grand Rapids Senior High School
Status State
Programme Diploma
Diploma Coordinator Beth Waskosky
Gender Coeducational
Languages English
Boarding/day Day
800 Conifer Drive, Grand Rapids MN 55744,
USA
TELEPHONE: +1 218 327-5760
FAX: +1 218 327-5761
EMAIL: jsmokrovich@isd318.org
WEBSITE: www.isd318.org

Great River School
Status State
Programme Diploma
Diploma Coordinator Angela van der Puije
Gender Coeducational
Languages English
Boarding/day Day
1326 Energy Park Drive, St Paul MN 55108,
USA
TELEPHONE: +1 651 305 2780
FAX: +1 651 305 2781
EMAIL: adrevlow@greatriverschool.org
WEBSITE: www.greatriverschool.org

Harding High School
Status State
Programme Diploma
Diploma Coordinator Robert Bergstrom
Gender Coeducational
Languages English
Boarding/day Day
1540 East Sixth Street, St Paul MN 55106, USA
TELEPHONE: +1 651 793 4700
FAX: +1 651 293 8912
EMAIL: todd.hochman@spps.org

Highland Park Elementary School
Status State
Programme PYP
PYP Coordinator Diane Zanter
Gender Coeducational
Languages English
Boarding/day Day
1700 Saunders Avenue, St Paul MN 55116,
USA
TELEPHONE: +1 651 293 8770
FAX: +1 651 293 8983
EMAIL: teresa.ciccarelli@spps.org
WEBSITE: www.highlandel.spps.org

Highland Park Senior High School
Status State
Programme Diploma
Diploma Coordinator Charlotte Landreau
Gender Coeducational
Languages English
1015 South Snelling Avenue, Saint Paul
MN 55116, USA
TELEPHONE: +1 651 293 8940
FAX: +1 651 293 8939
EMAIL: omoyefe.agbamu@spps.org

Minnetonka High School
Status State
Programme Diploma
Diploma Coordinator Ann Swanson
Gender Coeducational
Languages English
Boarding/day Day
18301 Highway 7, Minnetonka MN 55345,
USA
TELEPHONE: +1 952 401 5703
FAX: +1 952 401 5814
WEBSITE: www.minnetonka.k12.mn.us/mhs

North View Junior High School
Status State
Programme MYP
MYP Coordinator Jon Peterson
Gender Coeducational
Languages English
Boarding/day Day
5869 69th Avenue North, Brooklyn Park
MN 55429, USA
TELEPHONE: +1 763 585 7200
FAX: +1 763 585 7210
EMAIL: vickermanp@district279.org
WEBSITE: www.district279.org/sec/nvjh

Northeast Middle School
Status State
Programme MYP
MYP Coordinator Laurie Lamberty
2955 Hayes Street North East, Minneapolis
MN 55418, USA
TELEPHONE: +1 612 668 1500
FAX: +1 612 668 1510
EMAIL: padmini.udupa@mpls.k12.mn.us
WEBSITE: www.northeast.mpls.k12.mn.us

Park Center Senior High School
Status State
Programme MYP
MYP Coordinator Jon Peterson
Gender Coeducational
Languages English
Boarding/day Day
7300 Brooklyn Boulevard, Brooklyn Park
MN 55443, USA
TELEPHONE: +1 763 569 7600
FAX: +1 763 569 7606
EMAIL: parpartk@district279.org
WEBSITE: www.district279.org/sec/pcsh

Patrick Henry Senior High School
Status State
Programme Diploma
Diploma Coordinator Jane Kostik
Gender Coeducational
Languages English
Boarding/day Day
4320 Newton Ave N, Minneapolis MN 55412,
USA
TELEPHONE: +1 612 668 2000
FAX: +1 612 668 1993
EMAIL: gary.kociemba@mpls.k12.mn.us

Robbinsdale Cooper High School
Status State
Programme MYP, Diploma
Diploma Coordinator Holly Lewis
MYP Coordinator Lauren Hildebrand
Gender Coeducational
Languages English
Boarding/day Day
8230-47th Avenue North, New Hope
MN 55428, USA
TELEPHONE: +1 763 504 8501
FAX: +1 753 504 8531
EMAIL: jeff_mcgonigal@rdale.k12.mn.us
WEBSITE: www.rdale.k12.mn.us/chs/ib/

South St Paul High School
Status State
Programme MYP, Diploma
Diploma Coordinator Katherine Fleming
MYP Coordinator Melissa Miller
Gender Coeducational
Languages English
Boarding/day Day
700 Second St North, South St Paul
MN 55075, USA
TELEPHONE: +1 651 457 9454
FAX: +1 651 457 9455
EMAIL: tjohnson@sspps.org
WEBSITE: http://sspps.govoffice.com

Southwest High School

Status State
Programme Diploma
Diploma Coordinator Richard Schwartz
Gender Coeducational
Languages English
Boarding/day Day
3414 West 47th Street, Minneapolis
MN 55410, USA
TELEPHONE: +1 612 668 3030
FAX: +1 612 668 3080
EMAIL: bsmith@mpls.k12.mn.us

St Louis Park Senior High School

Status State
Programme Diploma
Diploma Coordinator Bruce McLean
Gender Coeducational
Languages English
Boarding/day Day
6425 W 33nd Street, St Louis Park MN 55426,
USA
TELEPHONE: +1 952 928 6107
FAX: +1 952 928 6113
EMAIL: laney.bob@slpschools.org

Whittier International Elementary School

Status State
Programme PYP
PYP Coordinator Melissa Anderson-Rossini
Gender Coeducational
Languages English
Boarding/day Day
315 West 26th Street, Minneapolis MN 55404,
USA
TELEPHONE: +1 612 668 4170
FAX: +1 612 668 4180
EMAIL: armando.camacho@mpls.k12.mn.us
WEBSITE: http://whittier.mpls.k12.mn.us

Missouri

Camdenton High School

Status State
Programme Diploma
Diploma Coordinator Paula Brown
Gender Coeducational
Languages English
Boarding/day Day
119 Service Road, Camdenton MO 65020, USA
TELEPHONE: +1 573 346 6336
FAX: +1 573 346 0674
EMAIL: bhenry@mail.camdenton.k12.mo.us
WEBSITE: http://camdenton.k12.mo.us

Central High School, Springfield

Status State
Programme Diploma
Diploma Coordinator Vicki Johnson
Gender Coeducational
Languages English
Boarding/day Day
423 East Central, Springfield MO 65802, USA
TELEPHONE: +1 417 523-9602
FAX: +1 417 523-9695
EMAIL: eisaacs@spsmail.org

Lee's Summit High School

Status State
Programme Diploma
Diploma Coordinator Christopher Bobal
Gender Coeducational
Languages English
Boarding/day Day
400 Blue Parkway, Lee's Summit MO 64063,
USA
TELEPHONE: +1 816 986 2000
FAX: +1 816 986 2095
EMAIL:
john.faulkenberry@leesummit.k12.mo.us
WEBSITE: www.leesummit.k12.mo.us

Lee's Summit North High School

Status State
Programme Diploma
Diploma Coordinator Jeremy Plowman
Gender Coeducational
Languages English
Boarding/day Day
901 NE Douglas, Lee's Summit MO 64086,
USA
TELEPHONE: +1 816 986 3005
FAX: +1 816 986 3170
EMAIL: david.ulrich@leesummit.k12.mo.us
WEBSITE: www.leesummit.k12.mo.us/lsnhs/

Lee's Summit West High School

Status State
Programme Diploma
Diploma Coordinator Tricia Lawrence
Gender Coeducational
Languages English
2600 SW Ward Road, Lee's Summit
MO 64082, USA
TELEPHONE: +1 816-986-4000
EMAIL: lswhs@leesummit.k12.mo.us

Lincoln College Preparatory Academy

Status State
Programme MYP, Diploma
Diploma Coordinator Sharon Showalter
MYP Coordinator Debby Haynes
Gender Coeducational
Languages English
Boarding/day Day
2111 Woodland Avenue, Kansas City
MO 64108, USA
TELEPHONE: +1 816 418 3000
FAX: +1 816 418 3015

Lindbergh High School

Status State
Programme Diploma
Diploma Coordinator Irv Mueller
Gender Coeducational
Languages English
Boarding/day Day
4900 South Lindbergh, St Louis MO 63126,
USA
TELEPHONE: +1 314 729 2410
FAX: +1 314 729 2412
EMAIL: imueller@lindberghschools.ws

Metro Academic & Classical High School

Status State
Programme Diploma
Diploma Coordinator Georgia Schoeffel
Gender Coeducational
Languages English
Boarding/day Day
4015 McPherson Avenue, St Louis MO 63108,
USA
TELEPHONE: +1 314 534 3894
FAX: +1 314 531 4894
EMAIL: wilfred.moore@slps.org

North Kansas City High School

Status State
Programme Diploma
Diploma Coordinator Jane Reed
Gender Coeducational
Languages English
Boarding/day Day
620 East 23rd Avenue, North Kansas City
MO 64116, USA
TELEPHONE: +1 816 413 5900
FAX: +1 816 413 5905
EMAIL: dwartick@nkcsd.k12.mo.us
WEBSITE: www.nkcsd.k12.mo.us

Mississippi

Davis Magnet School

Status State
Programme PYP
PYP Coordinator Juliet Frate
Gender Coeducational
Boarding/day Day
750 North Congress Street, Jackson
MS 39202, USA
TELEPHONE: +1 601 960 5333
EMAIL: cmwilliams@jackson.k12.ms.us
WEBSITE: www.jackson.k12.ms.us

Hayes Cooper Center

Status State
Programme PYP
PYP Coordinator Debra Fioranelli
Gender Coeducational
Languages English
Boarding/day Day
500 North Martin Luther King, Merigold
MS 37859, USA
TELEPHONE: +1 662 748 2734
FAX: +1 662 748 2735
EMAIL: hccprinbh@yahoo.com
WEBSITE: http://hayescc.dixie-net.com

Jim Hill High School

Status State
Programme MYP, Diploma
Diploma Coordinator Barbara Hilliard
MYP Coordinator Linda Smith
Gender Coeducational
Languages English
Boarding/day Day
2185 Fortune Street, Jackson Public Schools,
Jackson MS 39204, USA
TELEPHONE: +1 601 960 5354
FAX: +1 601 360 2625
EMAIL: lhaynes@jackson.k12.ms.us

Northwest Middle School
Programme MYP
MYP Coordinator Linda Smith
Gender Coeducational
Boarding/day Boarding
7020 Highway 49N, Jackson MS 39213, USA

Siwell Middle School
Programme MYP
MYP Coordinator Linda Smith
Gender Coeducational
Boarding/day Boarding
1983 North Siwell Road, Jackson MS 39209, USA
TELEPHONE: +1 601 923 2550
EMAIL: gterry@jackson.k12.ms.us

Montana

Flathead High School
Status State
Programme Diploma
Diploma Coordinator John York
Gender Coeducational
Languages English
644 4th Avenue West, Kalispell Public Schools, Kalispell MT 59901, USA
TELEPHONE: +1 406 751 3462
FAX: +1 406 751 3505
EMAIL: langohrc@sd5.k12.mt.us
WEBSITE: www.sd5.k12.mt.us

North Carolina

Albemarle Road Middle School
Status State
Programme MYP
MYP Coordinator Heather LaJoie
Gender Coeducational
Languages English
Boarding/day Day
6900 Democracy Drive, Charlotte NC 28212, USA
TELEPHONE: +1 980 343 6420
EMAIL: thomas.lamb@cms.k12.nc.us

Ashley Elementary Magnet School
Status State
Programme PYP
PYP Coordinator Brenda Coles
Gender Coeducational
Languages English
1647 Ashley School Circle, Winston-Salem NC 27105, USA
TELEPHONE: +1 336 727 2343
EMAIL: bbutler@wsfcs.k12.nc.us
WEBSITE: www.web2k.wsfcs.k12.nc.us/ashleyes/

Beddingfield High School
Status State
Programme Diploma
Diploma Coordinator Marsha Irvin
Gender Coeducational
Languages English
Boarding/day Day
4510 Old Stantonsburg Road, Wilson NC 27893, USA
TELEPHONE: +1 252 399 7880
EMAIL: robert.pope@mail.wilson.k12.nc.us

Ben L Smith High School
Status State
Programme Diploma
Diploma Coordinator Gayle Nelson
Gender Coeducational
Languages English
Boarding/day Day
2407 South Holden Road, Greensboro NC 27407, USA
TELEPHONE: +1 336 294 7300
FAX: +1 336 294 7313
EMAIL: rogersn2@gcsnc.com
WEBSITE: www.schools.guilford.k12.nc.us

Burton Geo-World Elementary Magnet
Status State
Programme PYP
PYP Coordinator Nancy Cheek
Gender Coeducational
Languages English
Boarding/day Day
1500 Mathison Street, Durham NC 27701, USA
TELEPHONE: +1 919 560 3908
FAX: +1 919 560 2087
EMAIL: phil.holmes@dpsnc.net
WEBSITE: www.burton.dpsnc.net

Cedar Ridge High School
Status State
Programme Diploma
Diploma Coordinator Paul Causey
Gender Coeducational
Languages English
Boarding/day Day
1125 New Grady Brown School Road, Hillsborough NC 27278, USA
TELEPHONE: +1 919 245-4000
FAX: +1 919 245-4010
WEBSITE: www.orange.k12.nc.us/crhs

Charlotte Country Day School
Status Private
Programme PYP, Diploma
Diploma Coordinator Jane Politte
PYP Coordinator Sally Wilkins
Gender Coeducational
Languages English
Boarding/day Day
1440 Carmel Road, Charlotte NC 28226, USA
TELEPHONE: +1 704 9434521
FAX: +1 704 9434525
EMAIL: margaret.gragg@charlottecountryday.org
WEBSITE: www.charlottecountryday.org

Daniels Middle School
Programme MYP
MYP Coordinator Kirsten Justice
Gender Coeducational
Boarding/day Boarding
2816 Oberlin Road, Raleigh NC 27608, USA
TELEPHONE: +1 919 881 4860

Davidson Middle School
Programme MYP
MYP Coordinator Patricia Watson
Gender Coeducational
Boarding/day Day
PO Box 369, Davidson NC 28036-0369, USA
TELEPHONE: +1 980 343 5185
EMAIL: jo.karney@cms.k12.nc.us
WEBSITE: www.cms.k12.nc.us/davidsonib

East Garner Magnet Middle School
Status State
Programme MYP
MYP Coordinator Katie McMahon
Gender Coeducational
Languages English
Boarding/day Day
6301 Jones Sausage Road, Garner NC 27529, USA
TELEPHONE: +1 919 662 2339
FAX: +1 919 662 2352
WEBSITE: http://eastgarnerms.wcpss.net

East Mecklenburg High School
Status State
Programme MYP, Diploma
Diploma Coordinator Heather LaJoie
MYP Coordinator Heather LaJoie
Gender Coeducational
Languages English
Boarding/day Day
6800 Monroe Road, Charlotte NC 28212, USA
TELEPHONE: +1 980 343 6430
FAX: +1 980 343 6437
EMAIL: m.nixon@cms.k12.nc.us

East Millbrook Magnet Middle School
Programme MYP
MYP Coordinator Kirsten Justice
Gender Coeducational
Boarding/day Boarding
3801 Spring Forest Road, Raleigh NC 27616, USA
TELEPHONE: +1 919 850 8755

Farmington Woods Elementary School
Status State
Programme PYP
PYP Coordinator Sarah Balkcum
Boarding/day Day
1413 Hampton Valley Road, Cary NC 27511, USA
TELEPHONE: +1 919 460 3469
FAX: +1 919 460 3423
EMAIL: fvenezia@wcpss.net

Garner Senior High School
Status State
Programme MYP, Diploma
Diploma Coordinator Cheryl Biconish
MYP Coordinator Katie McMahon
Gender Coeducational
Languages English
Boarding/day Day
2101 Spring Drive, Garner NC 27529, USA
TELEPHONE: +1 919 662 2379
EMAIL: iholton@wcpss.net
WEBSITE: http://garnerhs.wcpss.net

Grimsley High School
Status State
Programme Diploma
Diploma Coordinator Clyde Bud Harrelson
Gender Coeducational
Languages English
Boarding/day Day
801 Westover Terrace, Greensboro NC 27408, USA
TELEPHONE: +1 336 370 8184
FAX: +1 336 370 8194
EMAIL: gasparr@guilford.k12.nc.us

Harding University High School
Status State
Programme MYP, Diploma
Diploma Coordinator Deborah McRae
MYP Coordinator Deborah McRae
Gender Coeducational
Languages English
Boarding/day Day
2001 Alleghany Street, Charlotte NC 28208, USA
TELEPHONE: +1 980 343 6007
FAX: +1 980 343 6015
EMAIL: curtis.carroll@cms.k12.nc.us
WEBSITE: www.cms.k12.nc.us

Hickory Day School
Status Private
Programme PYP
PYP Coordinator Janice Dollar
Gender Coeducational
Languages English
Boarding/day Day
2535 21st Ave NE, Hickory NC 28601, USA
TELEPHONE: +1 828 256 9492
EMAIL: jdollar@hickoryday.org
WEBSITE: www.hickoryday.org

Hickory High School
Status State
Programme Diploma
Diploma Coordinator Mercia Barringer
Gender Coeducational
Languages English
Boarding/day Day
1234 3rd Street NE, Hickory NC 28601, USA
TELEPHONE: +1 828 322 5860
FAX: +1 828 326 7101
EMAIL: mattoxki@hickory.k12.nc.us
WEBSITE: http://hickory.k12.nc.us/HHS/Home.htm

High Point Central High School
Status State
Programme Diploma
Diploma Coordinator Sharon Haynes
Gender Coeducational
Languages English
Boarding/day Day
801 Ferndale Boulevard, High Point NC 27262, USA
TELEPHONE: +1 336 819 2825
FAX: +1 336 819 2991
EMAIL: hayness@guilford.k12.nc.us

Hillside High School
Status State
Programme MYP, Diploma
Diploma Coordinator Brandi Jones
MYP Coordinator Robert Hunter
Gender Coeducational
Languages English
Boarding/day Day
3727 Fayetteville Street, Durham NC 27707, USA
TELEPHONE: +1 919) 560 3925
FAX: +1 919) 560 3945
EMAIL: eunice.sanders@dpsnc.net

Hunt High School
Status State
Programme Diploma
Diploma Coordinator Marsha Irvin
Gender Male
Languages English
Boarding/day Day
4559 Lamm Road, Wilson NC 27893, USA
TELEPHONE: +1 252 399 7930
FAX: +1 252 399 7897
EMAIL: bill.williamson@mail.wilson.k12.nc.us

Hunter Huss High School
Status State
Programme MYP, Diploma
Diploma Coordinator Sarah Drennan
MYP Coordinator Sarah Drennan
Gender Coeducational
Languages English
Boarding/day Day
1518 Edgefield Avenue, Gastonia NC 28052, USA
TELEPHONE: +1 704 866 6610
FAX: +1 704 866 6613
EMAIL: kgwaltney@gaston.k12.nc.us
WEBSITE: www.gaston.k12.nc.us

Huntingtowne Farms Elementary School
Status State
Programme PYP
PYP Coordinator Valerie Dixon
Gender Coeducational
Languages English
Boarding/day Day
2520 Huntingtowne Farms Lane, Charlotte NC 28210, USA
TELEPHONE: +1 980 343-3625
FAX: +1 980 343-3731
EMAIL: Pamela.Frederick@cms.k12.nc.us
WEBSITE: www.cms.k12.nc.us/allschools/huntingtownefarms/

J Y Joyner Center for Spanish Language
Status State
Programme PYP
PYP Coordinator Denise Smith
Gender Coeducational
Languages English, Spanish
Boarding/day Day
2300 Noble Road, Raleigh NC 27608, USA
TELEPHONE: +1 919 856 7650
FAX: +1 919 856 7661
EMAIL: cknott3@wcpss.net
WEBSITE: http://joyneres.wcpss.net

Jacksonville High School
Status State
Programme Diploma
Diploma Coordinator Laura Rumbley
Gender Coeducational
Languages English
Boarding/day Day
1021 Henderson Drive, Jackonsville NC 28540, USA
TELEPHONE: +1 910 989 2048
FAX: +1 910 989 2046
EMAIL: susie.barrett@onslow.k12.nc.us
WEBSITE: www.onslow.k12.nc.us/jhs

Kinston High School
Status State
Programme Diploma
Diploma Coordinator Ron Owens
Gender Coeducational
Languages English
Boarding/day Day
2601 North Queen Street, Kinston NC 28501, USA
TELEPHONE: +1 252 527 8067
FAX: +1 252 527 4090
EMAIL: chill@lenoir.k12.nc.us

Millbrook Elementary Magnet School
Status State
Programme PYP
PYP Coordinator Terri Walker
Gender Coeducational
Boarding/day Day
1520 East Millbrook Road, Raleigh NC 27609, USA
TELEPHONE: +1 919 850 8700
EMAIL: ptrantham@wcpss.net
WEBSITE: http://millbrookes.wcpss.net

Morganton Day School
Status Private
Programme PYP
PYP Coordinator Susan Searcy
Gender Coeducational
Languages English
Boarding/day Day
305 West Concord Street, Morganton NC 28655, USA
TELEPHONE: +1 828 437 6782
FAX: +1 828 437 8840
EMAIL: dbain@morgantondayschool.com
WEBSITE: www.morgantondayschool.com

Myers Park High School

Status State
Programme MYP, Diploma
Diploma Coordinator Ron Thomas
MYP Coordinator Ron Thomas
Gender Coeducational
Languages English
Boarding/day Day
2400 Colony Road, Charlotte NC 28209, USA
TELEPHONE: +1 704 343 5800
FAX: +1 704 343 5803
EMAIL: r.thomas@cms.k12.nc.us
WEBSITE: www.tolerancematters.org

Needham B Broughton High School

Status State
Programme MYP, Diploma
Diploma Coordinator Wynn Cherry
MYP Coordinator Myra Smith
Gender Coeducational
Languages English
723 St Mary's Street, Raleigh NC 27605, USA
TELEPHONE: +1 919 856 7810
FAX: +1 919 856 7822
EMAIL: lteel@wcpss.net
WEBSITE: http://broughton.wcpss.net

North Mecklenburg High School

Status State
Programme MYP, Diploma
Diploma Coordinator Jane Royal
MYP Coordinator Patricia Watson
Gender Coeducational
Languages English
Boarding/day Day
11201 Old Statesville Road, Huntersville
NC 28078, USA
TELEPHONE: +1 980 343 3840
FAX: +1 980 343 3845
EMAIL: joey.burch@cms.k12.nc.us

Paisley Magnet School

Status State
Programme MYP
MYP Coordinator Donald Lail
Gender Coeducational
Languages English
1400 Grant Street, Winston-Salem NC 27105,
USA
TELEPHONE: +1 336-727-2775
EMAIL: gccone@wsfcs.k12.nc.us

Parkland High School

Status State
Programme Diploma
Diploma Coordinator Michael Bourke
Gender Coeducational
Languages English
Boarding/day Day
1600 Brewer Road, Winston-Salem NC 27127,
USA
TELEPHONE: +1 336 771 4700
EMAIL: tlee@wsfcs.k12.nc.us
WEBSITE: www.parklandmagneths.com

Piedmont Open Middle School

Status State
Programme MYP
MYP Coordinator Dawn Johnston
Gender Coeducational
Languages English
Boarding/day Day
1241 East 10th Street, Charlotte NC 28204,
USA
TELEPHONE: +1 980 343 5435
FAX: +1 980 343 5557
EMAIL: d.gardner@cms.k12.nc.us
WEBSITE: www.cms.k12.nc.us/allschools/
piedmont/index.htm

Pinecrest High School

Status State
Programme Diploma
Diploma Coordinator Lorna Martin
Gender Coeducational
Languages English
250 Voit Gilmore Lane, Southern Pines
NC 28387, USA
TELEPHONE: +1 910 692 6554
FAX: +1 910 692 0606
EMAIL: jcounty@mcs.k12.nc.us
WEBSITE: www.pinecresthighschool.org

Ralph L Fike High School

Status State
Programme Diploma
Diploma Coordinator Jeannette Etheridge
Languages English
500 Harrison Drive, Wilson NC 27893, USA
TELEPHONE: +1 252 399 7905
FAX: +1 252 399 7893
EMAIL:
jimmy.tillman@mail.wilson.k12.nc.us

Randolph Middle School

Programme MYP
MYP Coordinator Ron Thomas
Gender Coeducational
Boarding/day Day
4400 Water Oak Road, Charlotte NC 28211,
USA
TELEPHONE: +1 980 343 6700
EMAIL: jackie.menser@cms.k12.nc.us
WEBSITE:
www.cms.k12.nc.us/allschools/randolph

Reidsville High School

Status State
Programme Diploma
Diploma Coordinator Mary Ellen Guzy
Gender Coeducational
Languages English
Boarding/day Day
1901 South Park Drive, Reidsville NC 27320,
USA
TELEPHONE: +1 336 349 6361
FAX: +1 336 349 3205
EMAIL: jking@rock.k12.nc.us

Rocky Mount Senior High School

Status State
Programme Diploma
Diploma Coordinator Bonnie Kane
Gender Coeducational
Languages English
308 South Tillery Street, Rocky Mount
NC 27804, USA
TELEPHONE: +1 252 977 3085
FAX: +1 252 985 4321
EMAIL: jbradshaw@nrms.k12.nc.us

Shepard Magnet Middle School

Status State
Programme MYP
MYP Coordinator Robert Hunter
Gender Coeducational
Languages English
Boarding/day Day
2401 Dakota Street, Durham NC 27707, USA
TELEPHONE: +1 919 560 3938
EMAIL: kenneth.barnes@dpsnc.net
WEBSITE: www.dpsnc.net/shepard

South View High School

Status State
Programme Diploma
Diploma Coordinator Steven Barbour
Gender Coeducational
Languages English
Boarding/day Day
4184 Elk Road, Cumberland County, Hope
Mills NC 28348, USA
TELEPHONE: +1 910 425 8181
FAX: +1 910 425 2962
EMAIL: stevenbarbour@ccs.k12.nc.us

Southern Middle School

Status State
Programme MYP
MYP Coordinator Julia Webster
Gender Coeducational
Languages English
Boarding/day Day
717 Johnson Street, Aberdeen NC 28315, USA
TELEPHONE: +1 910 693 1550
FAX: +1 910 693 1544
EMAIL: dwarren@mcs.k12.nc.us
WEBSITE: http://schoolcenter.mcs.k12.nc.us/
education/school/school.php?sectionid=16

Statesville Road Elementary

Status State
Programme PYP
PYP Coordinator Mona Maruca
Gender Coeducational
Languages English
Boarding/day Day
3855 Milhaven Road, Charlotte NC 28269,
USA
TELEPHONE: +1 980 343 6815
FAX: +1 980 343 6794
EMAIL: ronnie.scott@cms.k12.nc.us
WEBSITE:
www.cms.k12.nc.us/allschools/statesvillerd

W G Enloe High School
Status State
Programme Diploma
Diploma Coordinator Susan Mastro
Gender Coeducational
Languages English
Boarding/day Day
128 Clarendon Crescent, Wake County Public Schools, Raleigh NC 27610, USA
TELEPHONE: +1 919 856 7918
FAX: +1 919 856 7917
EMAIL: bcochran@wcpss.net
WEBSITE: http://www1.enloe.wake.k12.nc.us

Waldo C Falkener Elementary School
Status State
Programme PYP
PYP Coordinator Randy Morgan
Gender Coeducational
Languages English
Boarding/day Day
3931 Naco Road, Greensboro NC 27401, USA
TELEPHONE: +1 339 370 8150
FAX: +1 336 370 8025
EMAIL: holcombea@gcsnc.com
WEBSITE: www.guilford.k12.nc.us

Walter Hines Page High School
Status State
Programme Diploma
Diploma Coordinator John Meyer
Gender Coeducational
Languages English
Boarding/day Day
201 Alma Pinnix Drive, Greensboro NC 27405, USA
TELEPHONE: +1 336 370 8200
FAX: +1 336 370 8219
EMAIL: worrelt@gcsnc.com
WEBSITE: www.gcsnc.com/page

West Charlotte High School
Status State
Programme Diploma
Diploma Coordinator Evelyn Allison
Gender Coeducational
Boarding/day Day
2219 Senior Drive, Charlotte NC 28216, USA
TELEPHONE: +1 980 343 6060
EMAIL: d.lee@cms.k12.nc.us
WEBSITE: www.cms.k12.nc.us/allschools/westchar

York Chester Middle School
Status State
Programme MYP
MYP Coordinator Sarah Drennan
Gender Coeducational
Languages English
Boarding/day Day
601 S Clay Street, Gastonia NC 28052, USA
TELEPHONE: +1 704 866 6298
FAX: +1 704 866 6319
EMAIL: cwhite@gaston.k12.nc.us
WEBSITE: www.gaston.k12.nc.us/schools/yorkchester

Nebraska

Bess Streeter Aldrich Elementary
Status State
Programme PYP
PYP Coordinator Sharon Epstein
Gender Coeducational
Languages English
Boarding/day Day
506 N 162nd Street, Omaha NE 68118, USA
TELEPHONE: +1 402 715 2020
FAX: +1 402 715 2035
EMAIL: srmelliger@mpsomaha.org
WEBSITE: www.mpsomah.org/aldrich

Lincoln High School
Status State
Programme Diploma
Diploma Coordinator John Heineman
Gender Coeducational
Languages English
Boarding/day Day
2229 J Street, Lincoln NE 68510, USA
TELEPHONE: +1 402 436 1301
FAX: +1 402 436 1540
EMAIL: mwortman@lps.org
WEBSITE: http://lhs.lps.org

Millard North High School
Status State
Programme MYP, Diploma
Diploma Coordinator William Daughtridge
MYP Coordinator Maureen Preble
Gender Coeducational
Languages English
Boarding/day Day
1010 S 144th Street, Millard Public Schools, Omaha NE 68154, USA
TELEPHONE: +1 402 715 1363
FAX: +1 402 715 1253
EMAIL: rmwerkheiser@mpsomaha.org
WEBSITE: www.millard.esu3.org/mnhs

Millard North Middle School
Status State
Programme MYP
MYP Coordinator Susan Marlatt
Gender Coeducational
Languages English
Boarding/day Day
2828 South 139th Plaza, Omaha NE 68144, USA
TELEPHONE: +1 402 691 1280
FAX: +1 402 691 1275
EMAIL: gbarta@mpsomaha.org
WEBSITE: www.mpsohama.org/nms/home.htm

New Hampshire

Bedford High School
Status State
Programme Diploma
Diploma Coordinator Bob Jozokos
Gender Coeducational
Languages English
Boarding/day Day
47 Nashua Road, Bedford NH 03110, USA
TELEPHONE: +1 603 310 9423
FAX: +1 603 472 2754
EMAIL: edwardsg@sau25.net
WEBSITE: www.sau25.net/highschool/BHShome.htm

New Jersey

Bergen County Academies
Status State
Programme Diploma
Diploma Coordinator Victor Truscelli
Gender Coeducational
Languages English
Boarding/day Day
200 Hackensack Avenue, Hackensack NJ 07601, USA
TELEPHONE: +1 201 343 6000 #3385
FAX: +1 201 343 8884
EMAIL: patcos@bergen.org
WEBSITE: www.bergen.org

Bernards High School
Status State
Programme Diploma
Diploma Coordinator Richard Charwin
Gender Coeducational
Languages English
25 Olcott Avenue, Bernardsville NJ 07924, USA
TELEPHONE: +1 908 630 3000
FAX: +1 908 953 0453
EMAIL: csoriano@shsd.org

Biotechnology High School
Status State
Programme Diploma
Diploma Coordinator William Hercek
Gender Coeducational
Languages English
Boarding/day Day
5000 Kozloski Road, Freehold NJ 07728, USA
TELEPHONE: +1 732 431 7208
FAX: +1 732 431 7943
EMAIL: linda_eno@mcvsd.org
WEBSITE: www.bths.mcvsd.org

Bret Harte Elementary School
Status State
Programme PYP
PYP Coordinator Hope Jenkins
Gender Coeducational
Languages English
1909 Queen Anne Road, Cherry Hill NJ 08003, USA
TELEPHONE: +1 856 795 0515
EMAIL: jcafagna@chclc.org
WEBSITE: www.harte.cherryhill.k12.nj.us

Cherry Hill High School West
Status State
Programme MYP, Diploma
Diploma Coordinator Walter Brown
MYP Coordinator Carole Roskoph
Gender Coeducational
Languages English
Boarding/day Day
2101 Chapel Avenue, Cherry Hill NJ 08002,
USA
TELEPHONE: +1 856 663 8006 330
FAX: +1 856 665 5683
EMAIL: mgrayson@chclc.org
WEBSITE: http://west.cherryhill.k12.nj.us/ib

Henry C Beck Middle School
Programme MYP
MYP Coordinator Carole Roskoph
Gender Coeducational
Boarding/day Boarding
950 Cropwell Road, Cherry Hill NJ 08003, USA
TELEPHONE: +1 856 424 8602
EMAIL: gdouglas@chclc.org

Hoboken High School
Status State
Programme Diploma
Diploma Coordinator Fiona Duncanson
Gender Coeducational
Languages English
Boarding/day Day
9th & Clinton Streets, Hoboken, Hudson
County NJ 07030, USA
TELEPHONE: +1 201 356 3717
FAX: +1 201 356 3704
EMAIL: FPechello@Hoboken.K12.NJ.US

J F Cooper Elementary School
Status State
Programme PYP
PYP Coordinator Hope Jenkins
Gender Coeducational
Languages English
Boarding/day Day
1960 Greentree Road, Cherry Hill NJ 08003,
USA
TELEPHONE: +1 856 424 4554
FAX: +1 856 751 0954
EMAIL: mkline@chclc.org
WEBSITE: http://cooper.cherryhill.k12.nj.us

Joseph D Sharp Elementary School
Status State
Programme PYP
PYP Coordinator Hope Jenkins
Gender Coeducational
Languages English
Boarding/day Day
300 Old Orchard Road, Cherry Hill NJ 08003,
USA
TELEPHONE: +1 856 424 1550
FAX: +1 856 424 6577
EMAIL: rhomer@chclc.org
WEBSITE: http://sharp.cherryhill.k12.nj.us

Linden High School
Status State
Programme Diploma
Diploma Coordinator Bernadette Bottino
Gender Coeducational
Languages English
121 W St Georges Avenue, Georges Avenue,
Linden NJ 07036, USA
TELEPHONE: +1 908 486 5432
FAX: +1 908 486 3242
EMAIL: baguero@comcast.net

Newark Academy
Status Private
Programme Diploma
Diploma Coordinator Neil Stourton
Gender Coeducational
Languages English
Boarding/day Day
91 South Orange Avenue, Livingston
NJ 07039, USA
TELEPHONE: +1 973 992 7000
FAX: +1 973 992 8962
EMAIL: daustin@newarka.edu

Rosa International Middle School
Programme MYP
MYP Coordinator Carole Roskoph
Gender Coeducational
Boarding/day Boarding
485 Browning Lane, Cherry Hill NJ 08003,
USA
TELEPHONE: +1 856 616 8787

Shore Regional High School
Status State
Programme Diploma
Diploma Coordinator Tracy Handerhan
Gender Coeducational
Languages English
Boarding/day Day
132 Monmouth Park Highway, West Long
Branch NJ 07764, USA
TELEPHONE: +1 732 222 9300 ext 210
FAX: +1 732 222 8849
EMAIL: lschnappauf@shoreregional.org
WEBSITE: www.shoreregional.org

St Dominic Academy
Status Private
Programme Diploma
Diploma Coordinator Cathy Jo Lombardi
Gender Female
Languages English
Boarding/day Day
2572 Kennedy Boulevard, Jersey City
NJ 07304, USA
TELEPHONE: +1 201 434 5938
FAX: +1 201 434 2603
EMAIL: degan@stdominicacad.com
WEBSITE: http://stdominicacad.com

Thomas Paine Elementary School
Status State
Programme PYP
PYP Coordinator Mary Ellen Sigman
Gender Coeducational
Boarding/day Day
4001 Church Road, Cherry Hill NJ 08034, USA
TELEPHONE: +1 856 667 1350
FAX: +1 856 755 1491
EMAIL: jedi76@hotmail.com

West Morris Central High School
Status State
Programme Diploma
Diploma Coordinator Joan Grant
Gender Coeducational
Languages English
Boarding/day Day
259 Bartley Road, Chester NJ 07930, USA
TELEPHONE: +1 908 879 6212
FAX: +1 908 879 2741
EMAIL: ibgrant@wmchs.org

West Morris Mendham High School
Status State
Programme Diploma
Diploma Coordinator Kathleen Kremins
Gender Coeducational
Languages English
Boarding/day Day
East Main Street, Mendham NJ 07945, USA
TELEPHONE: +1 973 543 2501
FAX: +1 201 543 6739
EMAIL: mmatyas@wmmhs.org
WEBSITE: http://wmmhs.org

New Mexico

Desert Academy at Santa Fe
Status Private
Programme Diploma
Diploma Coordinator Colin Pierce
Gender Coeducational
Languages English
Boarding/day Day
313 Camino Alire, Santa Fe NM 87501, USA
TELEPHONE: +1 505 992 8284
FAX: +1 505 992 8270
EMAIL: tpassalacqua@desertacademy.org
WEBSITE: www.desertacademy.org

United World College – USA
Status Private
Programme Diploma
Diploma Coordinator Adriana Botero
Gender Coeducational
Languages English
Boarding/day Boarding
PO Box 248, Route 65, Montezuma
NM 87731, USA
TELEPHONE: +1 505 454 4247
FAX: +1 505 454 4275
EMAIL: lisa.darling@uwc-usa.org
WEBSITE: www.uwc-usa.org

Nevada

Earl Wooster High School
Status State
Programme Diploma
Diploma Coordinator Daryl DiBitonto
Gender Coeducational
Languages English
Boarding/day Day
1331 East Plumb Lane, Reno NV 89502, USA
TELEPHONE: +1 775 333 5100
FAX: +1 775 333 5108
EMAIL: jecastillo@washoe.k12.nv.us
WEBSITE: www.washoe.k12.nv.us/wooster

Green Valley High School
Status State
Programme Diploma
Diploma Coordinator Jeri Roberts
Gender Coeducational
Languages English
Boarding/day Day
460 Arroyo Grande Boulevard, Clark County,
Henderson NV 89014, USA
TELEPHONE: +1 702 799 0950
FAX: +1 702 799 0975
EMAIL: jmhorn@interact.ccsd.net

Roy Martin Middle School
Status State
Programme MYP
MYP Coordinator Sherrie Nelson
Gender Coeducational
Languages English, French, Spanish
Boarding/day Day
2800 East Stewart Avenue, Las Vegas
NV 89101, USA
TELEPHONE: +1 702 799 7922
EMAIL: reginajadams@interact.ccsd.net
WEBSITE: www.ccsd.net/schools/roymartin

Sandy Searles Miller Academy for International Studies
Status State
Programme PYP
PYP Coordinator Joseph Barazza
Gender Coeducational
Languages English
Boarding/day Day
4851 East Lake Mead Boulevard, Las Vegas
NV 89115, USA
TELEPHONE: +1 702 799-8830
FAX: +1 702- 799-3259
EMAIL: amg304@interact.ccsd.net
WEBSITE: www.ccsd.net/schools/sandymiller

Valley High School
Status State
Programme MYP, Diploma
Diploma Coordinator Anthony Gebbia
MYP Coordinator Andrea Brosche
Gender Coeducational
Languages English
Boarding/day Day
2839 South Burnham Avenue, Las Vegas
NV 89109, USA
TELEPHONE: +1 702 799 5450
EMAIL: aegebbia@hotmail.com
WEBSITE: www.ccsd.net/schools/valley

New York

Albany High School
Status State
Programme Diploma
Diploma Coordinator Thomas McGurn
Gender Coeducational
Languages English
Boarding/day Day
700 Washington Avenue, Albany NY 12203,
USA
TELEPHONE: +1 518 454 3987 x920
EMAIL: mcioffi@albany.k12.ny.us

Baccalaureate School for Global Education
Status State
Programme MYP, Diploma
Diploma Coordinator Jennifer Dikes
MYP Coordinator Yvette Rivera
Gender Coeducational
Languages English
Boarding/day Day
34-12 36th Avenue, Astoria NY 11106, USA
TELEPHONE: +1 718 361 5275
FAX: +1 718 361 5395
EMAIL: kjohns02@schools.nyc.gov
WEBSITE: www.bsge.org

Binghamton High School
Status State
Programme Diploma
Diploma Coordinator Patricia Gazda-Grace
Gender Coeducational
Languages English
Boarding/day Day
31 Main Street, Binghamton NY 13905, USA
TELEPHONE: +1 607 762 8239
FAX: +1 607 762 8399
EMAIL: pennaa@bcsdgw.stier.org
WEBSITE: www.bcsd.stier.org

Bloomfield High School
Status State
Programme Diploma
Diploma Coordinator Kathryn Taylor
Gender Coeducational
Languages English
Boarding/day Day
PO Box 250, Oakmount Avenue, East
Bloomfield NY 14469, USA
TELEPHONE: +1 585-657-6121
FAX: +1 585-657-6060
EMAIL: mreho@bloomfieldcsd.org
WEBSITE: www.bloomfieldcsd.org

Brooklyn Friends School
Status Private
Programme Diploma
Diploma Coordinator Trefor Davies
Gender Coeducational
Languages English
Boarding/day Day
375 Pearl Street, Brooklyn, New York
NY 11201, USA
TELEPHONE: +1 718 852 1029
FAX: +1 718 643 4869
EMAIL: mnill@brooklynfriends.org
WEBSITE: www.brooklynfriends.org

Buckman Heights School of Inquiry
Status State
Programme PYP
PYP Coordinator Janet Clarke-Hazlett
Gender Coeducational
Languages English
Boarding/day Day
550 Buckman Road, Rochester NY 14615, USA
TELEPHONE: +1 585 966 5900
FAX: +1 585 966 5939
EMAIL: vburke@greece.k12.ny.us
WEBSITE: www.greece.k12.ny.us

Canandaigua Academy
Status State
Programme Diploma
Diploma Coordinator Daniel Richardson
Languages English
1 Academy Circle, Canandaigua NY 14424,
USA
TELEPHONE: +1 585 396 3802
FAX: +1 585 396 3806
EMAIL: erdlel@canandaiguaschools.org

Casimir Pulaski School
Status State
Programme PYP
PYP Coordinator Jelia Honeywell
Gender Coeducational
Languages English
Boarding/day Day
150 Kings Cross, Scarsdale NY 10583, USA
TELEPHONE: +1 914 376 8575
FAX: +1 914 722 7692
EMAIL: smurphy@yonkerspublicschools.org
WEBSITE: http://pulaski.ypschools.org

City Honors School
Status State
Programme MYP, Diploma
Diploma Coordinator Elissa Morganti Banas
MYP Coordinator Erin Comerford
Gender Coeducational
Languages English
Boarding/day Day
186 E North Street, Buffalo NY 14204, USA
TELEPHONE: +1 716 816 4230
FAX: +1 716 888 7145
EMAIL: wkresse@buffaloschools.org
WEBSITE: www.cityhonors.org

Clarkstown High School North
Status State
Programme Diploma
Diploma Coordinator Annie Streiff
Gender Coeducational
Languages English
Boarding/day Day
151 Congers Road, New City NY 10956-6272,
USA
TELEPHONE: +1 845 639 6500
FAX: +1 845 639 9665
EMAIL: hleonard@ccsd.edu
WEBSITE: www.ccsd.edu/north

Clarkstown Senior High School South

Status State
Programme Diploma
Diploma Coordinator Thomas Jeffery
Gender Coeducational
Languages English
Boarding/day Day
31 Demarest Mill Road, West Nyack NY 10994, USA
TELEPHONE: +1 845 624 3400
EMAIL: jvitale@ccsd.edu
WEBSITE: www.ccsd.edu/south

Commack High School

Status State
Programme Diploma
Diploma Coordinator Theresa Napp
Gender Coeducational
Languages English
Boarding/day Day
1 Scholar Lane, Commack NY 11725-1297, USA
TELEPHONE: +1 631-912-2106
FAX: +1 631 266 2408
EMAIL: rvale@commack.k12.ny.us
WEBSITE: www.commack.k12.ny.us/chs

Corning East High School

Status State
Programme MYP, Diploma
Diploma Coordinator Carol Casbeer
MYP Coordinator Eileen Bowen
Gender Coeducational
Languages English
Boarding/day Day
201 Cantigny Street, Corning NY 14830, USA
TELEPHONE: +1 607 936 3746
EMAIL: jtobia@cppmail.com
WEBSITE: www.corningareaschools.com/east

Corning Free Academy

Programme MYP
MYP Coordinator Eileen Bowen
Gender Coeducational
Boarding/day Day
West Third Street, Corning NY 14830, USA
TELEPHONE: +1 607 936 3788
EMAIL: rkimble@cppmail.com
WEBSITE:
www.corningareaschools.com/cfa.asp

Corning West High School

Status State
Programme MYP, Diploma
Diploma Coordinator Cathy Honness
MYP Coordinator Eileen Bowen
Gender Coeducational
Languages English
Boarding/day Day
Victory Highway, Painted Post NY 14870, USA
TELEPHONE: +1 607 936-3794
EMAIL: jwood@cppmail.com
WEBSITE: www.corningareaschools.com/west

Curtis High School

Status State
Programme Diploma
Diploma Coordinator Margarita Fernandez
Gender Coeducational
Languages English
Boarding/day Day
105 Hamilton Avenue, Staten Island NY 10301, USA
TELEPHONE: +1 718 390 1800
FAX: +1 718 556 4800
EMAIL: acurtis@schools.nyc.gov
WEBSITE: http://curtishs.net

Dobbs Ferry High School

Status State
Programme Diploma
Diploma Coordinator Constance Addabbo
Gender Coeducational
Languages English
Boarding/day Day
505 Broadway, Dobbs Ferry NY 10522, USA
TELEPHONE: +1 914 693 7645
FAX: +1 914 693 5227
EMAIL: yik@dfsd.org

East High School

Status State
Programme MYP
MYP Coordinator Lynne Giglia-Hawthorne
Gender Coeducational
Languages English
Boarding/day Day
1801 E Main Street, Rochester NY 14609, USA
TELEPHONE: +1 585 288 3130

Eastridge High School

Status State
Programme Diploma
Diploma Coordinator John Edwards
Gender Coeducational
Languages English
Boarding/day Day
2350 East Ridge Road, Rochester NY 14622, USA
TELEPHONE: +1 585 339 1450
FAX: +1 585 339 1459
EMAIL: thomas_cox@eastiron.monroe.edu
WEBSITE: www.eicsd.k12.ny.us

Fairport High School

Status State
Programme Diploma
Diploma Coordinator Patricia Impson
Languages English
1358 Ayrault Road, Fairport NY 14450, USA
TELEPHONE: +1 585 421 2100
FAX: +1 585 421 4645
EMAIL: dave_paddock@fairport.monroe.edu

Greece Odyssey High School

Status State
Programme Diploma
Diploma Coordinator Lisa Chapman
Gender Coeducational
Languages English
133 Hoover Drive, Rochester NY 14615, USA
TELEPHONE: +1 585 966 5500
FAX: +1 585 966 5539
EMAIL: lisa.chapman@greece.k12.ny.us

Hilton High School

Status State
Programme Diploma
Diploma Coordinator Tim Ackroyd
Gender Coeducational
Languages English
400 East Avenue, Hilton NY 14468, USA
TELEPHONE: +1 716 392 1000
FAX: +1 716 392 1052
EMAIL: bbartalo@hilton.k12.ny.us

Holmes Road School of Inquiry

Status State
Programme PYP
PYP Coordinator Janet Clarke-Hazlett
Gender Coeducational
Languages English
Boarding/day Day
300 Holmes Road, Rochester NY 14626, USA
TELEPHONE: +1 585 966 4900
FAX: +1 585 966 4939
EMAIL: charlene.frye@greece.k12.ny.us
WEBSITE: www.greece.k12.ny.us

James A Beneway High School

Status State
Programme Diploma
Diploma Coordinator Mark MacMillan
Gender Coeducational
Languages English
Boarding/day Day
6200 Ontario Center Road, Ontario Center NY 14520, USA
TELEPHONE: +1 315 524 1050
FAX: +1 315 524 1079
EMAIL: jsiracuse@wayne.k12.ny.us
WEBSITE: www.wayne.k12.ny.us

James Madison School of Exellence

Programme MYP
MYP Coordinator Lynne Giglia-Hawthorne
Gender Coeducational
Boarding/day Boarding
200 Genesse Street, Rochester NY 14611, USA
TELEPHONE: +1 585 436 4100

Locust Valley High School

Status State
Programme Diploma
Diploma Coordinator Robert Buonaspina
Gender Coeducational
Languages English
Boarding/day Day
99 Horse Hollow Road, Locust Valley NY 11560, USA
TELEPHONE: +1 516 674 6300
EMAIL: sfeeney@lvcsd.k12.ny.us
WEBSITE: www.lvcsd.k12.ny.us

Manchester-Shortsville High School
Status State
Programme Diploma
Diploma Coordinator Rosemary Fry
Gender Coeducational
Languages English
1506 Route 21, Shortsville NY 14548, USA
TELEPHONE: +1 716 289 3964
FAX: +1 716 289 6660
EMAIL: tbenjamin@redjacket.org

Massena Central High School
Status State
Programme Diploma
Diploma Coordinator Susan Bellor
Gender Coeducational
Languages English
Boarding/day Day
84 Nightengale Avenue, Massena NY 13662, USA
TELEPHONE: +1 315 764 3710
FAX: +1 315 764 3719
EMAIL: cmcdevitt@mcs.k12.ny.us
WEBSITE: http://mcs.k12.ny.us

Mott Hall Bronx High School
Status State
Programme Diploma
Diploma Coordinator Mary FitzMaurice
Gender Coeducational
Languages English
Boarding/day Day
450 St Paul's Place, Bronx NY 10456, USA
TELEPHONE: +1 718 588 0918
FAX: +1 718 588 0328
EMAIL: dtinagero@nycboe.net

Northport High School
Status State
Programme Diploma
Diploma Coordinator David Storch
Gender Coeducational
Languages English
Boarding/day Day
154 Laurel Hill Road, Northport/East Northport, Northport NY 11768, USA
TELEPHONE: +1 631 262 6652
FAX: +1 631 262 6736
EMAIL: imcloughlin@northport.k12.ny.us
WEBSITE: www.northport.k12.ny.us

Northside-Blodgett Middle School
Programme MYP
MYP Coordinator Eileen Bowen
Gender Coeducational
Boarding/day Day
143 Princeton Avenue, Corning NY 14830, USA
TELEPHONE: +1 607 936 3791
EMAIL: rrossi@cppmail.com
WEBSITE: www.corningareaschools.com/northside.cfm

Palmyra-Macedon High School
Status State
Programme Diploma
Diploma Coordinator Lisa Cardillo
Languages English
151 Hyde Parkway, Palmyra NY 14454, USA
TELEPHONE: +1 315 597 3420
FAX: +1 315 597 3438
EMAIL: bpersia@palmac.k12.ny.us

Pine Bush High School
Status State
Programme Diploma
Diploma Coordinator Mark Cartisano
Languages English
PO Box 670, Pine Bush NY 12566, USA
TELEPHONE: +1 845 744 2031
FAX: +1 845 744 3488
EMAIL: jgreene@pb.ouboces.org

Quest Elementary School
Status State
Programme PYP
PYP Coordinator Karen Spillman
Gender Coeducational
Languages English
Boarding/day Day
225 West Ave, Hilton NY 14468, USA
TELEPHONE: +1 585 392-1000 ext 6100
FAX: +1 585 392-1065
EMAIL: lmccabe@hilton.k12.ny.us
WEBSITE: www.hilton.k12.ny.us/QE.htm

Red Hook Central High School
Status State
Programme Diploma
Diploma Coordinator Patricia Mayo
Gender Coeducational
Languages English
Boarding/day Day
103 West Market Street, Red Hook NY 12571, USA
TELEPHONE: +1 845 758 2241 ext3247
FAX: +1 845 758 0482
EMAIL: rpaisley@rhcsd.dcboces.org
WEBSITE: www.redhookcentralschools.org

Rosemarie Ann Siragusa School
Status State
Programme PYP
PYP Coordinator Marlene Feder
Gender Coeducational
Languages English
Boarding/day Day
60 Crescent Place, Yonkers NY 10701, USA
TELEPHONE: +1 914 376 8570
EMAIL: apetrone1@yonkerspublicschools.org

SAINT EDMUND PREPARATORY HIGH SCHOOL
Status Private
Programme Diploma
Diploma Coordinator Raffaele Malafronte
Gender Coeducational
Languages English
Boarding/day Day
2474 Ocean Avenue, Brooklyn, New York NY 11229, USA
TELEPHONE: +1 718 743 6100
FAX: +1 718 743 5243
EMAIL: rmalafronte@stedmundprep.org
WEBSITE: www.stedmundprep.org
see full details on page 131

Schenectady High School
Status State
Programme Diploma
Diploma Coordinator Rosaline Horowitz
Languages English
1445 The Plaza, Schenectady NY 12308, USA
TELEPHONE: +1 518 370 8190
FAX: +1 518 881 3790
EMAIL: spadaforaa@schenectady.k12.ny.us

South Side High School
Status State
Programme Diploma
Diploma Coordinator John Murphy
Gender Coeducational
Languages English
Boarding/day Day
140 Shepherd Street, Rockville Centre NY 11570, USA
TELEPHONE: +1 516 255 8834
FAX: +1 516 255 8848
EMAIL: cburris@rvcschools.org

THE DWIGHT SCHOOL
Status Private
Programme PYP, MYP, Diploma
Diploma Coordinator Anthony Foster
MYP Coordinator Dianne Drew
PYP Coordinator Elaine Natalicchi
Gender Coeducational
Languages English
Boarding/day Day/mixed
291 Central Park West, New York NY 10024, USA
TELEPHONE: +1 212 724 6360
FAX: +1 212 874 4232
WEBSITE: www.dwight.edu
see full details on page 148

Thomas J Corcoran High School
Status State
Programme Diploma
Diploma Coordinator Leo Cosgrove
Gender Coeducational
Languages English
Boarding/day Day
919 Glenwood Avenue, Syracuse NY 13207, USA
TELEPHONE: +1 315 435 4321
FAX: +1 315 435 4024
EMAIL: lcosgrove2002@yahoo.com
WEBSITE: www.syracusecityschools.com

Thurgood Marshall Academy for Learning and Social Change
Status State
Programme MYP
MYP Coordinator Sandra Loyd Blackman
Gender Coeducational
Languages English
Boarding/day Day
200-214 West 135th Street, New York
NY 10030, USA
TELEPHONE: +1 212 283 8055 x3152
FAX: +1 212 690 2918
EMAIL: sjohns03@schools.nyc.gov
WEBSITE: www.adcorp.org/tma.html

United Nations International School
Status Private
Programme Diploma
Diploma Coordinator P Atkinson/Ms L Gross
Gender Coeducational
Languages English
Boarding/day Day
24-50 Franklin D Roosevelt Drive, New York
NY 10010, USA
TELEPHONE: +1 212 684 7400
FAX: +1 212 889 8959
EMAIL: kwrye@unis.org
WEBSITE: www.unis.org/

Vestal Senior High School
Status State
Programme Diploma
Diploma Coordinator Sally Lowenstein
Gender Coeducational
Languages English
Boarding/day Day
205 Woodlawn Drive, Vestal NY 13850, USA
TELEPHONE: +1 607 757 2281
FAX: +1 607 757 2301
EMAIL: chepler@vcs.stier.org

Victor Central High School
Status State
Programme Diploma
Diploma Coordinator Dawn Santiago-Marullo
Gender Coeducational
Languages English
Boarding/day Day
953 High Street, Victor NY 14564, USA
TELEPHONE: +1 585 924 3252
FAX: +1 585-924-9536
EMAIL: o'sheay@victorschools.org
WEBSITE: www.victorschools.org

Washington Irving High School
Status State
Programme Diploma
Diploma Coordinator Stephanie Baker
Gender Coeducational
Languages English
Boarding/day Day
40 Irving Palace, New York NY 10003, USA
TELEPHONE: +1 212 674 5000
FAX: +1 212 673 9569
EMAIL: denisedicarlo@msn.com

Wilson Magnet High School
Status State
Programme Diploma
Diploma Coordinator Christopher Connell
Gender Coeducational
Languages English
Boarding/day Day
501 Genesee Street, Rochester NY 14611, USA
TELEPHONE: +1 585 328 3440
FAX: +1 585 464 6153
EMAIL: J1989@aol.com

Woodlands Middle School
Status State
Programme MYP
MYP Coordinator Patricia Simone
Gender Coeducational
Languages English
Boarding/day Day
475 West Hartsdale Avenue, Hartsdale
NY 10570, USA
TELEPHONE: +1 914 761 6052
FAX: +1 914 686 0445
EMAIL: mchambless@greenburgh7.com
WEBSITE: www.greenburgh.k12.ny.us

Xaverian High School
Status Private
Programme Diploma
Diploma Coordinator Nancy Heiles
Gender Male
Languages English
Boarding/day Day
7100 Shore Road, Brooklyn NY 11209, USA
TELEPHONE: +1 718 836 7100
FAX: +1 718 836 7114
EMAIL: jmarino@xaverian.org
WEBSITE: www.xaverian.org

Yonkers Middle/High School
Status State
Programme MYP, Diploma
Diploma Coordinator Marcella Lentine
MYP Coordinator Candy Debiak
Gender Coeducational
Languages English
150 Rockland Avenue, Yonkers NY 10705, USA
TELEPHONE: +1 914 376 8200
FAX: +1 914 376 8245
EMAIL: rvigliotti@yonkers.ypschools.org
WEBSITE: http://yonkers.ypschools.org

Ohio

Amelia High School
Status State
Programme Diploma
Diploma Coordinator Stacey Novak
Gender Coeducational
Languages English
Boarding/day Day
1351 Clough Pike, Batavia OH 45103, USA
TELEPHONE: +1 513 753 5120
FAX: +1 513 753 2419
EMAIL: campbell_g@hccanet.org
WEBSITE: www.westcler.org

Aurora High School
Status State
Programme Diploma
Diploma Coordinator Nancy Dowling
Gender Coeducational
Languages English
Boarding/day Day
109 West Pioneer Trail, Aurora OH 44202, USA
TELEPHONE: +1 330 562 3501
FAX: +1 330 562 3588
EMAIL: rbailey@aurora-schools.org
WEBSITE: www.aurora-schools.org

Bexley Middle School
Status State
Programme MYP
MYP Coordinator Janice Meckley
Gender Coeducational
Languages English
Boarding/day Day
300 South Cassingham Road, Bexley
OH 43209, USA
TELEPHONE: +1 614 237-4277
FAX: +1 614 338-2090
EMAIL: hwiliams@bexley.k12.oh.us
WEBSITE: www.bexley.k12.oh.us

Cassingham Elementary School
Status State
Programme PYP
PYP Coordinator Sonja Hutchison
Gender Coeducational
Languages English
Boarding/day Day
250 South Cassingham Road, Bexley
OH 43209, USA
TELEPHONE: +1 614 237 4266
FAX: +1 614 338 2092
EMAIL: bheisel@bexley.k12.oh.us
WEBSITE: www.bexley.k12.oh.us

Columbus Alternative High School
Status State
Programme Diploma
Diploma Coordinator David Fawcett
Gender Coeducational
Languages English
Boarding/day Day
2632 McGuffey Road, Columbus OH 43211,
USA
TELEPHONE: +1 614 365 6006
FAX: +1 614 365 6300
EMAIL: sbadger@columbus.k12.oh.us
WEBSITE: www.columbus.k12.oh.us

Dublin Coffman High School
Status State
Programme Diploma
Diploma Coordinator Bryan Stork
Gender Coeducational
Languages English
Boarding/day Day
6780 Coffman Road, Dublin OH 43107-1099,
USA
TELEPHONE: +1 614 764 5900
FAX: +1 614 764 5925
EMAIL: miller_tracey@mail.dublin.k12.oh.us
WEBSITE: www.dublincoffman.com

Dublin Jerome High School
Status State
Programme Diploma
Diploma Coordinator Mike Uretsky
Gender Coeducational
Languages English
Boarding/day Day
8300 Hyland-Croy Road, Dublin OH 43016, USA
TELEPHONE: +1 614 873 7377
FAX: +1 614 873 1937
EMAIL: sankey_cathy@mail.dublin.k12.oh.us
WEBSITE: www.dublinjerome.net

Dublin Scioto High School
Status State
Programme Diploma
Diploma Coordinator Jayne Sulser
Gender Coeducational
Languages English
Boarding/day Day
400 Hard Road, Dublin OH 43016-8349, USA
TELEPHONE: +1 614 718 8300
FAX: +1 614 717 2484
EMAIL: davis_marina@mail.dublin.k12.oh.us
WEBSITE: http://scioto.dublin.k12.oh.us

Fairmont High School
Status State
Programme Diploma
Diploma Coordinator Jan Wagoner
Gender Coeducational
Languages English
Boarding/day Day
3301 Shroyer Road, Kettering OH 45429, USA
TELEPHONE: +1 937 499 1601
FAX: +1 927 499 1661
EMAIL: jim.schoenlein@kettering.k12.oh.us
WEBSITE: www.kettering.k12.oh.us

Firestone High School
Status State
Programme Diploma
Diploma Coordinator Barbara Crucs
Gender Coeducational
Languages English
Boarding/day Day
333 Rampart Avenue, Akron OH 44313, USA
TELEPHONE: +1 330 873 3315
FAX: +1 330 873 3318
EMAIL: lhumphre@akron.k12.oh.us
WEBSITE: www.akron.k12.oh.us

Meadowdale High School
Status State
Programme Diploma
Diploma Coordinator Kathy Borneman
Gender Coeducational
Languages English
4417 Williamson Drive, Dayton OH 45416, USA
TELEPHONE: +1 937 542 7030
FAX: +1 937 542 7031
EMAIL: dcarson@dps.k12.oh.us

Princeton High School
Status State
Programme Diploma
Diploma Coordinator Tim Dugan
Gender Coeducational
Languages English
Boarding/day Day
11080 Chester Road, Princeton City Schools, Cincinnati OH 45246, USA
TELEPHONE: +1 513 552 8200
FAX: +1 513 552 8224
EMAIL: rspicher@princeton.k12.oh.us
WEBSITE: www.phs.princeton.k12.oh.us

Springfield North High School
Status State
Programme Diploma
Diploma Coordinator Linda Bodey
Gender Coeducational
Languages English
Boarding/day Day
701 East Home Road, Springfield OH 45504, USA
TELEPHONE: +1 937 342 4100
EMAIL: lnickels@spr.k12.oh.us
WEBSITE: www.spr.k12.oh.us/

Springfield South High School
Status State
Programme Diploma
Diploma Coordinator Benjamin Feinstein
Gender Coeducational
Boarding/day Day
700 South Limestone Street, Springfield OH 45505, USA
TELEPHONE: +1 937 328 2027
EMAIL: swanp@spr.k12.oh.us
WEBSITE: www.spr.k12.oh.us

Tri-County International Academy
Status State
Programme Diploma
Diploma Coordinator Jack Ehrmantraut
Gender Coeducational
Languages English
Boarding/day Day
c/o Wooster H.S., 515 Oldman Road, Wooster OH 44691, USA
TELEPHONE: +1 330 345 4000
FAX: +1 330 345 3501
EMAIL: bauer.ma@wooster.k12.oh.us
WEBSITE: www.youresc.k12.oh.us

Upper Arlington High School
Status State
Programme Diploma
Diploma Coordinator Cynthia Ballheim
Gender Coeducational
Languages English
Boarding/day Day
1650 Ridgeview Road, Upper Arlington OH 43221, USA
TELEPHONE: +1 614 487 5200
FAX: +1 614 487 5238
EMAIL: kgreenhill@uaschools.org
WEBSITE: www.uaschools.org

Warren G Harding High School
Status State
Programme Diploma
Diploma Coordinator Lisa Bennett
Gender Coeducational
Languages English
Boarding/day Day
860 Elm Road North East, Warren, Trumbull County OH 44483, USA
TELEPHONE: +1 330 841 2316
FAX: +1 330 841 2289
EMAIL: wem2@aol.com

Westerville South High School
Status State
Programme Diploma
Diploma Coordinator Phyllis Magold
Gender Coeducational
Languages English
Boarding/day Day
303 South Otterbein Avenue, Westerville OH 43081, USA
TELEPHONE: +1 614 797 6000
FAX: +1 614 797 6001
WEBSITE: www.wcsoh.org/south

Withrow International High School
Status State
Programme Diploma
Diploma Coordinator Mary O'Donnell-Good
Gender Coeducational
Languages English
Boarding/day Day
2488 Madison Road, Cincinnati Public Schools, Cincinnati OH 45208, USA
TELEPHONE: +1 513 363-9090
FAX: +1 513 363-9020
EMAIL: clevelc@cpsboe.k12.oh.us

Oklahoma

Booker T Washington High School
Status State
Programme MYP, Diploma
Diploma Coordinator Sharon Lazdins
MYP Coordinator Brenda Casper
Gender Coeducational
Languages English
Boarding/day Day
1514 East Zion Street, Tulsa OK 74106, USA
TELEPHONE: +1 918 428 6000
FAX: +1 918 428 6001
EMAIL: boylede@tulsaschools.org

Classen School of Advanced Studies
Status State
Programme Diploma
Diploma Coordinator Valerie Harris
Gender Coeducational
Languages English
Boarding/day Day
1901 North Elison Street, Oklahoma City OK 73106, USA
TELEPHONE: +1 405 556 5070
FAX: +1 405 556 5080
EMAIL: vhcsas@aol.com

George Washington Carver Magnet Middle School
Programme MYP
MYP Coordinator Brenda Casper
Gender Coeducational
Boarding/day Boarding
624 E Oklahoma Place, Tulsa OK 74106, USA
TELEPHONE: +1 918 595 2939
EMAIL: drivecl@tulsaschools.org

Wilson Middle School
Programme MYP
MYP Coordinator Brenda Casper
Gender Coeducational
Boarding/day Boarding
1127 S Columbia Avenue, Tulsa OK 74104, USA
TELEPHONE: +1 918 833 9340
EMAIL: wettspa@tulsaschools.org

Oregon

Beaverton High School
Status State
Programme Diploma
Diploma Coordinator Kim Barrett
Gender Coeducational
Languages English
Boarding/day Day
13000 SW Second Street, Beaverton
OR 97005-2615, USA
TELEPHONE: +1 503 259 5000
FAX: +1 503 259 4990
EMAIL: janice_adams@beavton.k12.or.us
WEBSITE:
www.beaverton.k12.or.us/beaverton/

Cleveland High School
Status State
Programme Diploma
Diploma Coordinator Jennifer Wiandt
Languages English
3400 SE 26 Ave, Portland OR 97202, USA
TELEPHONE: +1 503-916-5120
FAX: +1 503-916-2692
EMAIL: pcook@pps.k12.or.us

Eugene International High School
Status State
Programme Diploma
Diploma Coordinator Melodee Soczek
Gender Coeducational
Languages English
Boarding/day Day
400 East 19th Avenue, Eugene OR 97401, USA
TELEPHONE: +1 541 687 3196
FAX: +1 541 687 3685
EMAIL: curtis_m@4j.lane.edu

Gresham High School
Status State
Programme Diploma
Diploma Coordinator Patricia Gray
Gender Coeducational
Languages English
Boarding/day Day
1200 North Main Street, Gresham
OR 97030-3899, USA
TELEPHONE: +1 503 674 5500
FAX: +1 503 674 5549
EMAIL:
carol_daiberl@gbsd.gresham.k12.or.us
WEBSITE: www.ghs.gresham.k12.or.us

Hillsboro High School
Status State
Programme Diploma
Diploma Coordinator Todd McKee
Gender Coeducational
Languages English
3285 SE Rood Bridge Road, Hillsboro
OR 97123-4108, USA
TELEPHONE: +1 503 844 1980
FAX: +1 503 693 0645
EMAIL: bertelld@hsd.k12.or.us

International School of Beaverton
Status State
Programme MYP, Diploma
Diploma Coordinator Ross Duran
MYP Coordinator Ross Duran
Gender Coeducational
Languages English
Boarding/day Day
17770 SW Blanton Street, Beaverton
OR 97007, USA
TELEPHONE: +1 503 259 3800
FAX: +1 503 259 3803
EMAIL:
sheila_baumgerdner@beavton.k12.or.us
WEBSITE: www.beaverton.k12.or.us/isb

International School of the Cascades
Status State
Programme MYP, Diploma
Diploma Coordinator Denise Roberts
MYP Coordinator Renee Hamilton
Gender Coeducational
Languages English, French
Boarding/day Day
Hartman Annex, 2105 W Antler, Redmond
OR 97756, USA
TELEPHONE: +1 541 923 4840
FAX: +1 541 923 4846
EMAIL: shay.mikalson@redmond.k12.or.us
WEBSITE: www.redmond.k12.or.us/isc/

Lincoln High School
Status State
Programme Diploma
Diploma Coordinator Kathryn Humes
Gender Coeducational
Languages English
Boarding/day Day
1600 South West Salmon Street, Portland
OR 97205, USA
TELEPHONE: +1 503 916-5200
FAX: +1 503 916 2700
EMAIL: hamilton@pps.k12.or.us

North International High School
Status State
Programme Diploma
Diploma Coordinator Katherine Schimmer
Gender Coeducational
Languages English
Boarding/day Day
200 Silver Lane, Eugene OR 97404, USA
TELEPHONE: +1 541 687 3261
FAX: +1 541 687 3683
EMAIL: henry_l@4j.lane.edu
WEBSITE: www.nehs.lane.edu

Obsidian Middle School
Status State
Programme MYP
MYP Coordinator Renee Hamilton
Gender Coeducational
Languages English
Boarding/day Day
1335 Obsidian Avenue, Redmond OR 97756, USA
TELEPHONE: +1 541 923 4900
FAX: +1 541 923 6509
EMAIL: joe.beck@redmond.k12.or.us
WEBSITE:
www.redmond.k12.or.us/ObsidianInfo.htm

Rex Putnam High School
Status State
Programme Diploma
Diploma Coordinator Traci Phillis
Gender Coeducational
Languages English
Boarding/day Day
4950 SE Roethe Road, Milwaukie OR 97267, USA
TELEPHONE: +1 503 353 5860
FAX: +1 503 353 5875
EMAIL: quintanillac@nclack.k12.or.us
WEBSITE: http://putnam.nclack.k12.or.us

South Salem High School
Status State
Programme Diploma
Diploma Coordinator Charles Chamberlain
Gender Coeducational
Languages English
Boarding/day Day
1910 Church Street SE, Salem OR 97302, USA
TELEPHONE: +1 503 399 3252
FAX: +1 503 375 7805
EMAIL: caldarazzo_guido@salkeiz.k12.or.us
WEBSITE: http://south.salkeiz.k12.or.us

Southridge High School
Status State
Programme Diploma
Diploma Coordinator Celeste Colasurdo
Gender Coeducational
Languages English
Boarding/day Day
9625 SW 125th Street, Beaverton OR 97008, USA
TELEPHONE: +1 503 259 5400
FAX: +1 503 259 5425
EMAIL: amy_gordon@beavton.k12.or.us
WEBSITE: www.beavton.k12.or.us/southridge

Sunset High School
Status State
Programme Diploma
Diploma Coordinator Matt Hiefield
Languages English
13840 NW Cornell Road, Portland OR 97229, USA
TELEPHONE: +1 503 259 5050
FAX: +1 503 259 5066
EMAIL: carl_mead@beavton.k12.or.us

Tigard High School
Status State
Programme Diploma
Diploma Coordinator Ken Teschner
Gender Coeducational
Languages English
Boarding/day Day
9000 SW Durham Road, Tigard OR 97224, USA
TELEPHONE: +1 503 431 5400
FAX: +1 503 431 5410
EMAIL: phenslee@ttsd.k12.or.us

Tualatin High School
Status State
Programme Diploma
Diploma Coordinator Heidi Kropp
Gender Coeducational
Languages English
Boarding/day Day
22300 South West Ferry Road, Boones Ferry Road, Tualatin OR 97062, USA
TELEPHONE: +1 503 431 5600
FAX: +1 503 431 5610
EMAIL: jsmith@ttsd.k12.or.us

Willamette High School
Status State
Programme Diploma
Diploma Coordinator Jade Starr
Gender Coeducational
Boarding/day Day
1801 Echo Hollow Road, Eugene OR 97402, USA
TELEPHONE: +1 541 689 0731
EMAIL: jjamieson@bethel.k12.or.us
WEBSITE: www.bethel.k12.or.us/schools/whs

Woodburn High School
Status State
Programme Diploma
Diploma Coordinator Lynn King
Gender Coeducational
Languages English
1785 N Front Street, Woodburn OR 97071, USA
TELEPHONE: +1 503-981-2600
FAX: +1 503-981-2675
EMAIL: llanka@woodburn.k12.or.us

Pennsylvania

Boyce Middle School
Programme MYP
MYP Coordinator Clark Remington
Gender Coeducational
Boarding/day Boarding
1500 Boyce Road, Upper St Clair PA 15241, USA
TELEPHONE: +1 412 833 1600
EMAIL: kbrown@uscsd.k12.pa.us

Central High School
Status State
Programme Diploma
Diploma Coordinator Dena Kaplan
Gender Coeducational
Languages English
Boarding/day Day
Ogontz and Olney Avenues, Philadelphia PA 19141, USA
TELEPHONE: +1 215 276 5262
EMAIL: spavel@phila.k12.pa.us
WEBSITE: www.centralhigh.net

Fort Couch Middle School
Programme MYP
MYP Coordinator Clark Remington
Gender Coeducational
Boarding/day Boarding
515 Ft Couch Road, Upper St Clair PA 15241, USA
TELEPHONE: +1 412 833 1600
EMAIL: jdemar@uscsd.k12.pa.us

George School
Status Private
Programme Diploma
Diploma Coordinator Ralph Lelii
Gender Coeducational
Languages English
Boarding/day Boarding
PO Box 4000, Newtown PA 18940, USA
TELEPHONE: +1 215 579 6703
FAX: +1 215 579 6604
EMAIL: nancy_starmer@georgeschool.org
WEBSITE: www.georgeschool.org

George Washington High School
Status State
Programme Diploma
Diploma Coordinator Yury Belyavsky
Gender Coeducational
Languages English
Boarding/day Day
10175 Bustleton Avenue, Philadelphia PA 19116, USA
TELEPHONE: +1 215 961 2001
EMAIL: aliebowitz@phila.k12.pa.us
WEBSITE: www.gwhs.phila.k12.pa.us

Harriton High School
Status State
Programme Diploma
Diploma Coordinator Thomas O'Brien
Gender Coeducational
Languages English
Boarding/day Day
600 North Ithan Avenue, Rosemont PA 19010, USA
TELEPHONE: +1 610 658-3970
FAX: +1 610 525 6771
WEBSITE: www.lmsd.org

J P McCaskey High School
Status State
Programme Diploma
Diploma Coordinator Jane Krepp
Gender Coeducational
Languages English
Boarding/day Day
445 North Reservoir St, Lancaster PA 17602, USA
TELEPHONE: +1 717 291 6211
FAX: +1 717 390 - 2567
EMAIL: thaley@lancaster.k12.pa.us
WEBSITE: www.lancaster.k12.pa.us

Lehigh Valley Academy Regional Charter School
Status State/private
Programme PYP, Diploma
Diploma Coordinator Andrew Hall
PYP Coordinator Terri D Walter
Gender Coeducational
Languages English
Boarding/day Day
1560 Valley Center Parkway, Suite 200, Bethlehem PA 18017, USA
TELEPHONE: +1 610 866 9660
FAX: +1 610 849 7854
EMAIL: linds@lvacademy.org
WEBSITE: www.lvacademy.org

Mercyhurst Preparatory School
Status Private
Programme Diploma
Diploma Coordinator Kathryn Donovan
Gender Coeducational
Languages English
Boarding/day Day
538 East Grandview Boulevard, Erie PA 16504, USA
TELEPHONE: +1 814 824 2323
EMAIL: maste@mpslakers.com
WEBSITE: www.mpslakers.com

Northeast High School
Status State
Programme Diploma
Diploma Coordinator Marcella Weisberg
Gender Coeducational
Languages English
Boarding/day Day
Cottman & Algon Avenues, Philadelphia
PA 19111, USA
TELEPHONE: +1 215 728 5018
EMAIL: kbarton@phila.k12.pa.us
WEBSITE: http://nehs.phila.k12.pa.us/

Philadelphia High School for Girls
Status State
Programme Diploma
Diploma Coordinator Sandra Johnson
Gender Female
Languages English
Boarding/day Day
1400 West Olney Avenue, Philadelphia
PA 19141-2398, USA
TELEPHONE: +1 215 276 5258
EMAIL: gmyles@phila.k12.pa.us
WEBSITE:
www.phila.k12.pa.us/schools/girlshigh

Quaker Valley Senior High School
Status State
Programme MYP
MYP Coordinator Linda Conlon
Gender Coeducational
Languages English
Boarding/day Day
625 Beaver St, Quaker Valley, Leetsdale
PA 15056, USA
TELEPHONE: +1 412 749 6000
EMAIL: ondekh@qvsd.org
WEBSITE: www.qvsd.org

Quaker Valley Senior High School
Programme MYP
MYP Coordinator Linda Conlon
Gender Coeducational
Boarding/day Day
203 Graham Street, Sewickley PA 15143, USA
TELEPHONE: +1 412 749 5079
WEBSITE: www.qvsd.org

Schenley High School Teacher Center
Status State
Programme Diploma
Diploma Coordinator Oscar Alan Huber
Gender Coeducational
Languages English
Boarding/day Day
4101 Bigelow Boulevard, Pittsburgh PA 15213,
USA
TELEPHONE: +1 412 622 8200
FAX: +1 412 622 8238
EMAIL: hbullard1@pghboe.net
WEBSITE: www.schenleyhs.pghboe.net

The Harrisburg Academy
Status Private
Programme Diploma
Diploma Coordinator Susan Roller
Gender Coeducational
Languages English
Boarding/day Day
10 Erford Road, Wormleysburg PA 17043, USA
TELEPHONE: +1 717 763 7811
FAX: +1 717 975 0894
EMAIL: tbanks@harrisburgacademy.org
WEBSITE: www.harrisburgacademy.org

Upper St Clair High School
Status State
Programme MYP, Diploma
Diploma Coordinator Clark Remington
MYP Coordinator Barbara Andrews
Gender Coeducational
Languages English
Boarding/day Day
1825 McLaughlin Run Road, Upper St Clair
PA 15241, USA
TELEPHONE: +1 412 833 1600
FAX: +1 412 833 4889
EMAIL: tsteinhauer@uscsd.k12.pa.us
WEBSITE: http://uscsd.k12.pa.us

Upper St Clair International School
Status State
Programme PYP
PYP Coordinator Nancy Trau
Boarding/day Day
1560 Ashlawn Avenue, Upper St Clair
PA 15241, USA
TELEPHONE: +1 412 833 1600
EMAIL: bkrill@uscsd.k12.pa.us

Vincentian Academy-Duquesne University
Status Private
Programme Diploma
Diploma Coordinator Robert Caler
Gender Coeducational
Languages English
Boarding/day Day
Peebles and McKnight Roads, Pittsburgh
PA 15237, USA
TELEPHONE: +1 412 364 1616
FAX: +1 412 367 5722
EMAIL: rusnakt@duq.edu
WEBSITE: www.vaduq.edu

William W Bodine High School for International Affairs
Status State
Programme Diploma
Diploma Coordinator Charles Young
Gender Coeducational
Languages English
Boarding/day Day
1101 North 4th Street, Philadelphia PA 19123,
USA
TELEPHONE: +1 215 351 7332
EMAIL: khill@phila.k12.pa.us
WEBSITE:
www.phila.k12.pa.us/schools/bodine

Rhode Island

Prout School
Status Private
Programme Diploma
Diploma Coordinator Louise Pearson
Gender Coeducational
Languages English
Boarding/day Day
4640 Tower Hill Road, Wakefield RI 02879,
USA
TELEPHONE: +1 401 789 9262
FAX: +1 401 782 2262
EMAIL: eprecourt@theproutschool.org

South Carolina

A C Flora High School
Status State
Programme MYP, Diploma
Diploma Coordinator Roberta Scott
MYP Coordinator Louisa Tiller
Gender Coeducational
Languages English
Boarding/day Day
1 Falcon Drive, Columbia SC 29204, USA
TELEPHONE: +1 803 738 7300
FAX: +1 803 738 7300
EMAIL: kgreer@richlandone.org
WEBSITE: http://richlandone.org/acflora

A R Rucker Midde School
Status State
Programme MYP
MYP Coordinator Sarah Deason
Gender Coeducational
Languages English
Boarding/day Day
422 Old Dixie Road, Lancaster SC 29720, USA
TELEPHONE: +1 803 416 8555
FAX: +1 803 285 1534
EMAIL: rucker@lcsd.k12.sc.us
WEBSITE: http://rms.lancasterscschools.org/
home.aspx

Aiken High School
Status State
Programme Diploma
Diploma Coordinator James Sheehan
Languages English
449 Rutland Drive, Aiken SC 29801, USA
TELEPHONE: +1 803 641 2500
FAX: +1 803 641 2501
EMAIL: jpadget@aiken.k12.sc.us

Aynor High School
Status State
Programme Diploma
Diploma Coordinator Michelle Altman
Gender Coeducational
Languages English
Boarding/day Day
PO Box 128, Aynor SC 29511, USA
TELEPHONE: +1 843-358-6261
FAX: +1 843-358-7401
EMAIL: mshaw@ah.hcs.k12.sc.us

Battery Creek High School
Status State
Programme Diploma
Diploma Coordinator Betsy Calhoon
Gender Coeducational
Languages English
Boarding/day Day
1 Blue Dolphin Drive, Beaufort SC 29906, USA
TELEPHONE: +1 843 322-5546
FAX: +1 843 322-5609
EMAIL: rj2481@beaufort.k12.sc.us

Beaufort High School
Status State
Programme Diploma
Diploma Coordinator Bill Damude
Gender Coeducational
Languages English
Boarding/day Day
84 Sea Island Parkway, BCSD, Beaufort SC 29902, USA
TELEPHONE: +1 843-322-2110
FAX: +1-843-322-2158
EMAIL: dhd3495@beaufort.k12.sc.us

Beck Academy of Languages
Programme MYP
MYP Coordinator Dee Davies
Gender Coeducational
Boarding/day Boarding
302 McAlister Road, Greenville SC 29607, USA
TELEPHONE: +1 864 241 3268

Broad River Elementary School
Status State
Programme PYP
PYP Coordinator Donna Haram-Deines
Gender Coeducational
Boarding/day Day
474 Broad River Boulevard, Beaufort SC 29906, USA
TELEPHONE: +1 843 322-8400
FAX: +1 843 525 4307
EMAIL: gail.wages@beaufort.k12.sc.us
WEBSITE: www.beaufort.k12.sc.us

Buist Academy for Advanced Studies
Status State
Programme PYP
PYP Coordinator Nicole Barrett
Gender Coeducational
Languages English
Boarding/day Day
103 Calhoun Street, Charleston SC 29401, USA
TELEPHONE: +1 843 724 7750
FAX: +1 843 724 1493
EMAIL: sallie_ballard@charleston.k12.sc.us
WEBSITE: http://buist.ccsdschools.com

Chandler Creek Elementary School
Status State
Programme PYP
PYP Coordinator Angela Gossett
Gender Coeducational
Languages English
301 Chandler Road, Greer SC 29651, USA
TELEPHONE: +1 864 355 2400
EMAIL: kbayne@greenville.k12.sc.us
WEBSITE: www.greenville.k12.sc.us/ccreek/

Christ Church Episcopal School
Status Private
Programme PYP, MYP, Diploma
Diploma Coordinator Nancy White
MYP Coordinator Kathy Adamee
PYP Coordinator Terri Garvin
Gender Coeducational
Languages English
Boarding/day Day
567 Wenwood Road, Greenville SC 29607, USA
TELEPHONE: +1 864 299 1522
FAX: +1 864 277-0785
EMAIL: coxl@cces.org

Crayton Middle School
Programme MYP
MYP Coordinator Louisa Tiller
Gender Coeducational
Boarding/day Day
5000 Clemson Avenue, Columbia SC 29206, USA
TELEPHONE: +1 803 738 7224
EMAIL: vlacy@richlandone.org

Fork Shoals Elementary School
Status State
Programme PYP
PYP Coordinator Amy Wall
Gender Coeducational
Boarding/day Day
916 McKelvey Road, Pelzer SC 29669, USA
TELEPHONE: +1 864 243 5680
EMAIL: djohnsto@greenville.k12.sc.us
WEBSITE: www.greenville.k12.sc.us/forksh

Fort Dorchester High School
Status State
Programme Diploma
Diploma Coordinator Lisa Shaffer
Languages English
8500 Patriot Boulevard, North Charleston SC 29420, USA
TELEPHONE: +1 843 760 4450
FAX: +1 843 760 4852
EMAIL: tpayne@dorchester2.k12.sc.us

Greer High School
Status State
Programme MYP, Diploma
Diploma Coordinator Marian Coggins
MYP Coordinator Chris Elliott
Gender Coeducational
Languages English
Boarding/day Day
3032 East Gap Creek Road, Greer SC 29651, USA
TELEPHONE: +1 864 355 5819
FAX: +1 864 355 9500
EMAIL: celliott@greenville.k12.sc.us
WEBSITE: www.greenville.k12.sc.us/greerhs

Greer Middle School
Status State
Programme MYP
MYP Coordinator Chris Elliott
Gender Coeducational
Languages English
Boarding/day Day
3032 East Gap Creek Road, Greer SC 29651, USA
TELEPHONE: +1 864 355 5800
EMAIL: srhymer@greenville.k12.sc.us
WEBSITE: www.greenville.k12.sc.us/greerms

Hartsville High School
Status State
Programme Diploma
Diploma Coordinator John L Andrews Jr
Gender Coeducational
Languages English
Boarding/day Day
701 Lewellyn Avenue, Hartsville SC 29550, USA
TELEPHONE: +1 843 857 3700
FAX: +1 843 857 3715
EMAIL: charlieb@darlington.k12.sc.us
WEBSITE: http://hhs.dcsdschools.org

Heritage Elementary School
Status State
Programme PYP
PYP Coordinator Brett DeLoach
Gender Coeducational
Languages English
Boarding/day Day
1592 Geer Highway, Traveler's Rest SC 29690, USA
TELEPHONE: +1 864 834 6424
EMAIL: mkinard@greenville.k12.sc.us

Hilton Head Elementary School
Status State
Programme PYP
PYP Coordinator Maxine Bone
Gender Coeducational
Boarding/day Day
30 School Road, Hilton Head Island, Hilton Head SC 29926, USA
TELEPHONE: +1 843 342 5218
EMAIL: marymbriggs@yahoo.com

Hilton Head High School
Status State
Programme Diploma
Diploma Coordinator Patricia Whyte
Gender Coeducational
Languages English
Boarding/day Day
70 Wilborn Road, Beaufort, Hilton Head Island SC 29926, USA
TELEPHONE: +1 843-689-4801
FAX: +1 843-689-4947
EMAIL: hr8681@beaufort.k12.sc.us
WEBSITE: www.beaufort.k12.sc.us

Irmo High School
Status State
Programme MYP, Diploma
Diploma Coordinator Nora T Whitley
MYP Coordinator Scot Hockman
Gender Coeducational
Languages English
Boarding/day Day
6671 St Andrews Road, Columbia SC 29212, USA
TELEPHONE: +1 803 732-8100
FAX: +1 803 732-8074
EMAIL: ewalker@lex5.k12.sc.us
WEBSITE: www.lex5.k12.sc.us/ihs/

James Island High School
Status State
Programme Diploma
Diploma Coordinator Deborah Farrell
Gender Coeducational
Languages English
1000 Fort Johnson Road, Charleston SC 29412, USA
TELEPHONE: +1 843 762 2754
FAX: +1 843 762 2791
EMAIL: robert_bohnstengel@charleston.k12.sc.us

Lexington High School
Status State
Programme Diploma
Diploma Coordinator Sherry Walters
Gender Coeducational
Languages English
Boarding/day Day
2463 Augusta Highway, Lexington SC 29072, USA
TELEPHONE: +1 803 359 5565
FAX: +1 803 359 8726
EMAIL: ctyler@lexington1.net
WEBSITE: www.lexington1.net/lhs/index.htm

Lower Richland High School
Status State
Programme Diploma
Diploma Coordinator Joya Gregg
Gender Coeducational
Languages English
Boarding/day Day
2615 Lower Richland Blvd, Hopkins SC 29061, USA
TELEPHONE: +1 803 695 3000
EMAIL: lmalloy@richlandone.org
WEBSITE: www.lowerrichland.com

North Augusta High School
Status State
Programme Diploma
Diploma Coordinator Galan Potter
Gender Coeducational
Languages English
2000 Knobcone Avenue, Aiken County, North Augusta SC 29841, USA
TELEPHONE: +1 803 442 6100
FAX: +1 803 442 6127
EMAIL: ksmith@aiken.k12.sc.us

Northwest Middle School
Programme MYP
MYP Coordinator Lori Mason
Gender Coeducational
Boarding/day Day
1606 Geer Hwy, Travelers Rest SC 29690, USA
TELEPHONE: +1 864 834 6807
EMAIL: lgivins@greenville.k12.sc.us
WEBSITE: www.northwestmiddle.com

Northwestern High School
Status State
Programme Diploma
Diploma Coordinator Martha Hamric
Gender Coeducational
Languages English
Boarding/day Day
2503 West Main Street, Rock Hill SC 29732, USA
TELEPHONE: +1 803 981 1200
FAX: +1 803 981 1250
EMAIL: jblake@rock-hill.k12.sc.us

Orangeburg-Wilkinson High School
Status State
Programme Diploma
Diploma Coordinator Alexander Tryciecky
Gender Coeducational
Languages English
Boarding/day Day
601 Bruin Parkway, Orangeburg SC 29115, USA
TELEPHONE: +1 803 534 6180, 6823
FAX: +1 803 533 6310
EMAIL: swbrowne99@yahoo.com

Port Royal Elementary School
Status State
Programme PYP
PYP Coordinator Kim Jones
Gender Coeducational
Boarding/day Day
1214 Paris Avenue, Beaufort SC 29935, USA
TELEPHONE: +1 843 322 0820
FAX: +1 843 525 4238
EMAIL: kimjones_99@yahoo.com

Rock Hill High School
Status State
Programme Diploma
Diploma Coordinator Patricia Sanford
Gender Coeducational
Languages English
Boarding/day Day
320 West Springdale Road, Rock Hill SC 29730, USA
TELEPHONE: +1 803 981 1300
FAX: +1 803 981 1343
EMAIL: jmobley@rock-hill.k12.sc.us
WEBSITE: www.rock-hill.k12.sc.us/schools/high/rhhs/default.htm

Rosewood Elementary
Status State
Programme PYP
PYP Coordinator Anna Hodge
Gender Coeducational
Boarding/day Day
2240 Rosewood Drive, Rock Hill SC 29730, USA
TELEPHONE: +1 803 981 1540
EMAIL: sward@rock-hill.k12.sc.us

Saluda Trail Middle School
Status State
Programme MYP
MYP Coordinator Carolyn Moore
2300 Saluda Road, Rock Hill SC 29730, USA
TELEPHONE: +1 803 981 1800
FAX: +1 803 981 1819
EMAIL: bdcampb@rock-hill.k12.sc.us
WEBSITE: www.rock-hill.k12.sc.us/schools/middle/stms/main.htm

Sara Collins Elementary School
Status State
Programme PYP
PYP Coordinator Alice Arrington
Gender Coeducational
Boarding/day Day
101 E Butler Road, Mauldin SC 29662, USA
TELEPHONE: +1 864 299 8343
EMAIL: znabers@greenville.k12.sc.us

Socastee High School
Status State
Programme Diploma
Diploma Coordinator Danny Wilson
Gender Coeducational
Languages English
Boarding/day Day
4900 Socastee Boulevard, Myrtle Beach SC 29588, USA
TELEPHONE: +1 843 293 2513
FAX: +1 843 293 3393
EMAIL: pbrowni@sh.hcs.k12.sc.us
WEBSITE: www.hcs.k12.sc.us/high/sh/

South Pointe High School
Programme Diploma
Diploma Coordinator Stephanie DiStasio
Gender Coeducational
Languages English
Boarding/day Day
806 Neely Road, Rock Hill SC 29730, USA
TELEPHONE: +1 803-984-3558
FAX: +1 803-981-1094
EMAIL: aleonard@rock-hill.k12.sc.us
WEBSITE: http://rock-hill.k12.sc.us/schools/high/sphs/

Southside High School
Status State
Programme MYP, Diploma
Diploma Coordinator Jan Janarella
MYP Coordinator Dee Davies
Gender Coeducational
Languages English
Boarding/day Day
100 Blassingame Road, Greenville SC 29605, USA
TELEPHONE: +1 864 299 8393
FAX: +1 864 299 8395
EMAIL: ppayne@greenville.k12.sc.us

Spartanburg Day School
Status Private
Programme PYP, MYP
MYP Coordinator Mary Kay Deese
PYP Coordinator Mary Kay Deese
Gender Coeducational
Languages English
Boarding/day Day
1701 Skylyn Drive, Spartanburg SC 29307, USA
TELEPHONE: +1 864 582 8380
FAX: +1 864 948 0026
EMAIL: chris.dorrance@sdsgriffin.org
WEBSITE: www.spartanburgdayschool.org

Sullivan Middle School
Status State
Programme MYP
MYP Coordinator Christine Senbertrand-McLean
1825 Eden Terrace, Rock Hill SC 29730, USA
TELEPHONE: +1 803 981 1450
FAX: +1 803 981 1456
EMAIL: rheath@rock-hill.k12.sc.us
WEBSITE: www.rock-hill.k12.sc.us/schools/middle/slms/default.htm

Sumter High School
Status State
Programme Diploma
Diploma Coordinator Bonnie de M Boland
Gender Coeducational
Languages English
2580 McCray's Mill Road, School District 17, Sumter SC 29154-6098, USA
TELEPHONE: +1 803 481 4480
FAX: +1 803 481 4021
EMAIL: rut@sumter17.k12.sc.us
WEBSITE: www.district.sumter17.k12.sc.us

Travelers Rest High School
Status State
Programme MYP, Diploma
Diploma Coordinator Lori Mason
MYP Coordinator Lori Mason
Gender Coeducational
Languages English
Boarding/day Day
301 North Main Street, Travelers Rest SC 29690, USA
TELEPHONE: +1 864 355 0000
EMAIL: llavely@greenville.k12.sc.us
WEBSITE: www.greenville.k12.sc.us/trest

Waccamaw High School
Status State
Programme Diploma
Diploma Coordinator Patricia Canada
Gender Coeducational
Languages English
Boarding/day Day
2412 Kings River Road, Pawleys Island SC 29585, USA
TELEPHONE: +1 843 237 9899
FAX: +1 843 237 9883
EMAIL: rbrown@wh.gcsd.k12.sc.us
WEBSITE: www.gcsd.k12.sc.us

Williams Middle School
Programme MYP
MYP Coordinator Marsha Burch
Gender Coeducational
Boarding/day Boarding
1119 North Irby Street, Florence SC 29501, USA
TELEPHONE: +1 843 664 8162
EMAIL: hsharper@fsd1.org

Wilson High School
Status State
Programme MYP, Diploma
Diploma Coordinator Marsha Burch
MYP Coordinator Marsha Burch
Gender Coeducational
Languages English
Boarding/day Day
1411 Old Marion Highway, Florence SC 29506, USA
TELEPHONE: +1 843 664 8440
FAX: +1 843 664 8176
EMAIL: gedwards@fsd1.org

Woodmont High School
Status State
Programme MYP, Diploma
Diploma Coordinator Christopher Chapman
MYP Coordinator Brenda Elmore
Gender Coeducational
Languages English
150 Woodmont School Road, Greenville County, Piedmont SC 29673, USA
TELEPHONE: +1 864 299 8300
FAX: +1 864 299 8422
EMAIL: bgriffit@greenville.k12.sc.us

Woodmont Middle School
Programme MYP
MYP Coordinator Brenda Elmore
Gender Coeducational
325 North Flat Rock Road, Piedmont SC 29673, USA
TELEPHONE: +1 864 299 8373
EMAIL: bcampbel@greenville.k12.sc.us
WEBSITE: www.greenville.k12.sc.us/wdmontm

Tennesse

Bellevue Middle School
Status State
Programme MYP
MYP Coordinator Cathye Hancock
Gender Coeducational
Languages English
Boarding/day Day
655 Colice-Jeanne Road, Nashville TN 37221, USA
TELEPHONE: +1 615 662-3000
FAX: +1 615 662-5728
EMAIL: john.duckworth@mnps.org
WEBSITE: www.bellevuems.mnps.org

Brick Church Middle School
Programme MYP
MYP Coordinator Bethany Peach
Gender Coeducational
Languages English
Boarding/day Day
2835 Brick Church Pike, Nashville TN 37207, USA
TELEPHONE: +1 615 262 6665
FAX: +1 615 262 6966

Cookeville High School
Status State
Programme Diploma
Diploma Coordinator Aliene Click
Gender Coeducational
Languages English
Boarding/day Day
2335 North Washington Avenue, Cookeville TN 38501, USA
TELEPHONE: +1 931 520 2287
FAX: +1 931 520 2268
EMAIL: shanksw@k12tn.net
WEBSITE: www.cookevillecavaliers.com

Franklin High School
Status State
Programme Diploma
Diploma Coordinator Ken Curtis
Gender Coeducational
Languages English
Boarding/day Day
810 Hillsboro Road, Franklin TN 37064, USA
TELEPHONE: +1 615 472 4468
FAX: +1 615 790 0686
EMAIL: willied@wcs.edu
WEBSITE: www.wcs.edu/fhs

Germantown High School

Status State
Programme Diploma
Diploma Coordinator Melinda Keller
Gender Coeducational
Languages English
Boarding/day Day
7653 Old Poplar Pike, Germantown TN 38138, USA
TELEPHONE: +1 901 756 2350
FAX: +1 901 756 2356
EMAIL: germantown.hs.scsk12.org
WEBSITE: www.scsk12.org/SCS/high/Germantwon/index.htm

Goodlettsville Middle School

Status State
Programme MYP
MYP Coordinator Bethany Peach
Gender Coeducational
Languages English
Boarding/day Day
300 South Main Street, Goodlettsville TN 37072, USA
TELEPHONE: +1 615 859 8956
FAX: +1 615 859 8961
EMAIL: sarah.moore@mnps.org
WEBSITE: www.mnps.org

Hillsboro Comprehensive High School

Status State
Programme Diploma
Diploma Coordinator Mary C Bradshaw
Gender Coeducational
Languages English
Boarding/day Day
3812 Hillsboro Road, Nashville TN 37215, USA
TELEPHONE: +1 615 298 8400
FAX: +1 615 298 8402
EMAIL: robert.lawson@mnps.org

Hillwood High School

Status State
Programme Diploma
Diploma Coordinator Donna Harper
Gender Coeducational
Languages English
Boarding/day Day
400 Davidson Road, Nashville TN 37205, USA
TELEPHONE: +1 615 353 2029
FAX: +1 615 353 2027
WEBSITE: www.hillwood.k12tn.net

Hunters Lane Comprehensive High School

Status State
Programme MYP, Diploma
Diploma Coordinator Sharon Chaney
MYP Coordinator Bethany Peach
Gender Coeducational
Languages English
Boarding/day Boarding/day
1150 Hunters Lane, Nashville TN 37207, USA
TELEPHONE: +1 615 860 1401
FAX: +1 615 860 7541
EMAIL: robert.myers@mnps.org
WEBSITE: www.hunterslane.org

J T Moore Middle School

Status State
Programme MYP
MYP Coordinator Amy Cate
Gender Coeducational
Languages English
Boarding/day Day
4425 Granny White Pike, Nashville TN 37204, USA
TELEPHONE: +1 615 298 8095
FAX: +1 615 298 8452
EMAIL: jill.pittman@mnps.org
WEBSITE: www.jtmoore.org

Neely's Bend Middle School

Status State
Programme MYP
MYP Coordinator Bethany Peach
Gender Coeducational
Languages English
Boarding/day Day
1251 Neely's Bend Road, Madison TN 37115, USA
TELEPHONE: +1 615 860 1477
FAX: +1 615 612 3669
EMAIL: ralph.tagg@mnps.org

Oakland High School

Status State
Programme Diploma
Diploma Coordinator Sandra Eaton
Gender Coeducational
Languages English
Boarding/day Day
2225 Patriot Drive, Murfreesboro TN 37130, USA
TELEPHONE: +1 615 904 3780
FAX: +1 615 904 3781
EMAIL: vaughnb@rcs.k12.tn.us
WEBSITE: www.ohs.rcs.k12.tn.us

Science Hill High School

Status State
Programme Diploma
Diploma Coordinator Selene Hardin
Gender Coeducational
Languages English
Boarding/day Day
1509 John Exum Parkway, Johnson City TN 37604, USA
TELEPHONE: +1 423 232 2190
FAX: +1 423 232 2172
WEBSITE: www.jcschools.org

Texas

Aldine Academy

Status State
Programme PYP
PYP Coordinator Kim Corrick
Gender Coeducational
Languages English
Boarding/day Day
7007 Fallbrook, Houston TX 77086, USA
TELEPHONE: +1 281 878 1530
FAX: +1 281 878 1536
EMAIL: dmhagood@aldine.k12.tx.us
WEBSITE: www.aldine.k12.tx.us

Allen High School

Status State
Programme Diploma
Diploma Coordinator Alicia Maphies
Gender Coeducational
Languages English
Boarding/day Day
300 Rivercrest Boulevard, Allen TX 75002, USA
TELEPHONE: +1 972 727 0400
FAX: +1 972 727 0515
EMAIL: steve_payne@allenisd.org
WEBSITE: www.ahs.allenisd.org

Amarillo High School

Status State
Programme Diploma
Diploma Coordinator Gary Biggers
Gender Coeducational
Languages English
Boarding/day Day
4225 Danbury Drive, Amarillo TX 79109, USA
TELEPHONE: +1 806 326 2002
FAX: +1 806 354 5092
EMAIL: doug.loomis@amaisd.org

Anderson Mill Elementary School

Status State
Programme PYP
PYP Coordinator Jan Zimmern
Gender Coeducational
Languages English
Boarding/day Day
10610 Salt Mill Hollow, Austin TX 78750, USA
TELEPHONE: +1 512 428 3700
FAX: +1 512 428 3790
EMAIL: rebecca_lavender@roundrockisd.org
WEBSITE: www.roundrockisd.org/andersonmill

Andy Woods Elementary School

Status State
Programme PYP
PYP Coordinator Patti Porter
Gender Coeducational
Languages English
Boarding/day Day
809 Clyde Drive, Tyler TX 75701, USA
TELEPHONE: +1 903 262 1280
FAX: +1 903 262 1281
EMAIL: connie.moore@tylerisd.org
WEBSITE: www.tylerisd.org/schools/woods/index.htm

Arlington High School

Status State
Programme Diploma
Diploma Coordinator Brenda Gilmore
Gender Coeducational
Languages English
Boarding/day Day
818 West Park Row, Arlington TX 76013, USA
TELEPHONE: +1-817-459-8100
FAX: +1-817-801-6105
EMAIL: jadams@aisd.net
WEBSITE: www.aisd.net/schools/seniorhigh/ahs/index.htm

Bellaire High School

Status State
Programme Diploma
Diploma Coordinator Ann Linsley
Gender Coeducational
Languages English
Boarding/day Day
5100 Maple Street, Houston ISD, Bellaire
TX 77401, USA
TELEPHONE: +1 713 667 2064
FAX: +1 713 295 3763
EMAIL: albcj@aol.com

Bill J Wilson Intermediate School

Status State
Programme MYP
MYP Coordinator Candy Core
3131 Fallbrook Drive, Houston TX 77038, USA
TELEPHONE: +1 281 878 0990
FAX: +1 281 878 0995
EMAIL: mholt@aldine.k12.tx.us
WEBSITE: www.aldine.k12.tx.us/schools

BRITISH SCHOOL OF HOUSTON

Status Private
Programme Diploma
Diploma Coordinator Simon Porter
Gender Coeducational
Languages English
Boarding/day Day
4211 Watonga Boulevard, Houston TX 77092,
USA
TELEPHONE: +1 202 290 9025
FAX: +1 202 290 9014
EMAIL: headbsh@britishschools.org
WEBSITE: www.britishschool.org
see full details on page 67

Coronada High School

Status State
Programme Diploma
Diploma Coordinator Patricia Lopez
Gender Coeducational
Languages English
Boarding/day Day
100 Champions Place, EPISD, El Paso
TX 79912, USA
TELEPHONE: +1 915 834 2460
WEBSITE: http://coronado.elpaso.k12.tx.us

Dallas International School

Status Private
Programme Diploma
Diploma Coordinator Adrienne Wagner
Gender Coeducational
Languages English, French
Boarding/day Day
6039 Churchill Way, Dallas TX 75230, USA
TELEPHONE: +1 972 991 6379
FAX: +1 972 991 6608
EMAIL:
pvittoz@dallasinternationalschool.org
WEBSITE: www.dallasinternationalschool.org

Denton High School

Status State
Programme Diploma
Diploma Coordinator Lynn Singletary
Gender Coeducational
Languages English
Boarding/day Day
1007 Fulton, Denton TX 76201, USA
TELEPHONE: +1 940 369 2000
FAX: +1 940 369 4953
EMAIL: dmuncy@dentonisd.org
WEBSITE: www.dentonisd.org/dentonhs/
site/default.asp

Dwight D Eisenhower High School

Status State
Programme Diploma
Diploma Coordinator Curtis Wood
Gender Coeducational
Languages English
Boarding/day Day
7922 Antoine Drive, Houston TX 77088, USA
TELEPHONE: +1 281 878 0900
FAX: +1 281 448 2936

E A Murchison Middle School

Programme MYP
MYP Coordinator Shawn La Torre
Gender Coeducational
Boarding/day Day
3700 North Hills Drive, Austin TX 78731, USA
TELEPHONE: +1 512 414 3254

Eisenhower Ninth Grade School

Status State
Programme MYP
MYP Coordinator Candy Core
3550 W Gulf Bank Road, Houston TX 77088,
USA
TELEPHONE: +1 281 878 7700
FAX: +1 281 878 7736
EMAIL: mmcgowen@aldine.k12.tx.us
WEBSITE: www.aldine.k12.tx.us/schools/
specific_campus.cfm?Campus Number=84

El Dorado High School

Status State
Programme Diploma
Diploma Coordinator Lizett Shaw
Gender Coeducational
Languages English
Boarding/day Day
12401 Edgemere, El Paso TX 79938, USA
TELEPHONE: +1 915-937-3200
EMAIL: npaugh@sisd.net
WEBSITE: www.schools.sisd.net/edhs/

Fairway Middle School

Status State
Programme MYP
MYP Coordinator Leigha Gautreaux
Gender Coeducational
Languages English
Boarding/day Day
701 Whitlow Avenue, Killeen TX 76541, USA
TELEPHONE: +1 254 501 1000/1032
EMAIL: teresa.daughtery@killeenisd.org
WEBSITE: www.killeenisd.org/schools/
middle/fms/index.html

Forest Park Magnet School of Global Studies

Status State
Programme MYP
MYP Coordinator Jerry Stuart
1515 Lake Drive, Longview TX 75601, USA
TELEPHONE: +1 903 758-9971
FAX: +1 903- 758-6964
EMAIL: mjdavis@lisd.org
WEBSITE:
www.lisd.org/forestpark/fpjump.htm

Garland High School

Status State
Programme Diploma
Diploma Coordinator Juanita Sacco
Gender Coeducational
Languages English
Boarding/day Day
310 South Garland Avenue, Garland TX 75040,
USA
TELEPHONE: +1 972 494 8492
FAX: +1 972 494 8415
EMAIL: jsmorris@garlandisd.net
WEBSITE: www.garlandowls.com

Grisham Middle School

Status State
Programme MYP
MYP Coordinator Ulrike Puryear
Gender Coeducational
Languages English
Boarding/day Day
10805 School House Lane, Austin TX 78750,
USA
TELEPHONE: +1 512 428-2650
FAX: +1 512 428-2690
WEBSITE: www.roundrockisd.org/grisham

Hirschi High School

Status State
Programme MYP
MYP Coordinator Janice Swarts
Gender Coeducational
Languages English
Boarding/day Day
3106 Borton Lane, Wichita Falls TX 76306,
USA
TELEPHONE: +1 940 716 2800
FAX: +1 940 716 2835
EMAIL: wjackson@wfisd.net
WEBSITE: www.hirschi.wfisd.net

Hirschi Math-Science Magnet School

Status State
Programme MYP, Diploma
Diploma Coordinator Elaine Beck
MYP Coordinator Danny Minniear
Gender Coeducational
Languages English
Boarding/day Day
3106 Borton Lane, Wichita Falls
TX 76306-6952, USA
TELEPHONE: +1 940 716 2800
FAX: +1 940 716 2835
EMAIL: wjackson@wfisd.net
WEBSITE: www.hirschi.wfisd.net/

Hoffman Academy
Status State
Programme MYP
MYP Coordinator Candy Core
6101 West Little York, Houston TX 77091, USA
TELEPHONE: +1 713 613 7670
FAX: +1 713 613 7675
EMAIL: rjohnson@aldine.k12.tx.us
WEBSITE: www.aldine.k12.tx.us/schools/
websites/hoffman/index.htm

Humble High School
Status State
Programme Diploma
Diploma Coordinator Elisabeth Baron
Gender Coeducational
Languages English
Boarding/day Day
1700 Wilson Road, Humble TX 77338, USA
TELEPHONE: +1 281 641 6300
FAX: +1 281 641 6517
EMAIL: raul.font@humble.k12.tx.us
WEBSITE: www.humble.k12.tx.us

IDEA College Preparatory
Status State
Programme MYP
MYP Coordinator Sandra Hughes
Gender Coeducational
Languages English
Boarding/day Day
401 South First Street, Donna TX 78537, USA
TELEPHONE: +1 956 464 0203
FAX: +1 956 544 2004
WEBSITE: www.ideapublicschools.org

Iduma Elementary School
Status State
Programme PYP
PYP Coordinator Michelle Froehlich
Gender Coeducational
Languages English
Boarding/day Day
4400 Foster Lane, Killeen TX 76549, USA
TELEPHONE: +1 254 501 2590
FAX: +1 254 526 9046
EMAIL: judy.tyson@killeenisd.org
WEBSITE: www.killeenisd.org

J L Everhart Magnet Academy of Cultural Studies
Status State
Programme PYP
PYP Coordinator Debra Wasson
Gender Coeducational
Languages English
Boarding/day Day
1000 Martin Luther King Jr Boulevard,
Longview TX 75602, USA
TELEPHONE: +1 903 758 5622
FAX: +1 903 758 7870
EMAIL: hlwatson@lisd.org
WEBSITE: www.lisd.org

James Bowie High School
Status State
Programme Diploma
Diploma Coordinator Christine Phenix
Gender Coeducational
Languages English
Boarding/day Day
2101 Highbank Drive, Arlington TX 76018,
USA
TELEPHONE: +1 682 867-4500
FAX: +1 817-472-4444
EMAIL: dsneed@aisd.net
WEBSITE: www.aisd.net/bowie

James S Hogg Middle School
Programme MYP
MYP Coordinator Jan Ace
Gender Coeducational
Boarding/day Boarding
920 South Broadway, Tyler TX 75701, USA
TELEPHONE: +1 903 262 1500

John Tyler High School
Status State
Programme MYP
MYP Coordinator Julie Fisher
Gender Coeducational
Languages English
Boarding/day Day
1120 N Northwest Loop 323, Tyler ISD,
Tyler TX 75702, USA
TELEPHONE: +1 903 531 6000
FAX: +1 903 531 6199
EMAIL: mcfarlandm@tyler.sprnet.org
WEBSITE: www.tyler.sprnet.org

Judson High School
Status State
Programme Diploma
Diploma Coordinator Kathy Huth
Gender Coeducational
Languages English
Boarding/day Day
9142 FM Road 78, Converse TX 78109, USA
TELEPHONE: +1 210 658 6251
FAX: +1 210 659 4359
EMAIL: bwilliams@judson.k12.tx.us

Killeen High School
Status State
Programme MYP, Diploma
Diploma Coordinator Leigha S Gautreaux
MYP Coordinator Leigha Gautreaux
Gender Coeducational
Languages English
Boarding/day Day
500 North 38th Street, Killeen TX 76543, USA
TELEPHONE: +1 254 501 0400
FAX: +1 254 680 2424
EMAIL: michael.sibberson@killeenisd.org
WEBSITE: www.killeenisd.org

Kirby Junior High
Status State
Programme MYP
MYP Coordinator Janice Swarts
Gender Coeducational
Languages English
Boarding/day Day
1715 Loop 11, Wichita Falls TX 76306, USA
TELEPHONE: +1 940 716 2900
FAX: +1 940 716 2915
EMAIL: dpalmore@wfisd.net

Klein Oak High School
Status State
Programme Diploma
Diploma Coordinator Linda Garner
Gender Coeducational
Languages English
Boarding/day Day
22603 Northcrest Drive, Spring TX 77389, USA
TELEPHONE: +1 834 484 5000
FAX: +1 834 484 7830
EMAIL: mbonetati@kleinisd.net
WEBSITE: http://kleinoak.kleinisd.net

L C Anderson High School
Status State
Programme Diploma
Diploma Coordinator Michelle Szabo
Gender Coeducational
Languages English
Boarding/day Day
8403 Mesa Drive, Austin TX 78759, USA
TELEPHONE: +1 512 414 2538
FAX: +1 512 338 1293
EMAIL: dhouser@austinisd.org
WEBSITE: www.andersonptsa.com

Lamar Academy
Status State
Programme Diploma
Diploma Coordinator Jeanette LaFevers
Gender Coeducational
Languages English
Boarding/day Day
1009 N 10th Street, McAllen TX 78501, USA
TELEPHONE: +1 956 632 3222
FAX: +1 956 632 3662
EMAIL: cindy_pena@mcallen.isd.tenet.edu

Lamar Primary Center
Status State
Programme PYP
PYP Coordinator Cindy Simmons
Gender Coeducational
Languages English
Boarding/day Day
2206 Lucas Avenue, Wichita Falls TX 76301,
USA
TELEPHONE: +1 940 720 3151
FAX: +1 940 720 3242
EMAIL: ganderson@wfisd.net
WEBSITE: http://lamar.wfisd.net

Lancaster High School
Status State
Programme Diploma
Diploma Coordinator Jeri Smith
Gender Coeducational
Languages English
Boarding/day Day
200 East Wintergreen Road, Lancaster TX 75134, USA
TELEPHONE: +1 972 218 1800 x5202
FAX: +1 972 218 5797
WEBSITE: www.lancasterisd.org

Lawrence D Bell High School
Status State
Programme Diploma
Diploma Coordinator Judy Chapman
Gender Coeducational
Languages English
Boarding/day Day
1601 Brown Trail, Hurst TX 76054, USA
TELEPHONE: +1 817 282 2551
FAX: +1 817 285 3200
EMAIL: bannistj@hebisd.edu
WEBSITE: www.hebisd.edu

Leander High School
Status State
Programme Diploma
Diploma Coordinator Judy Guerra
Languages English
3301 South Bagdad Road, Leander TX 78641, USA
TELEPHONE: +1 512 435 8000
FAX: +1 512 435 8011
EMAIL: todd.washburn@leanderisd.org

Lubbock High School
Status State
Programme Diploma
Diploma Coordinator Sharon Mouser
Gender Coeducational
Languages English
Boarding/day Day
2004 19th Street, Lubbock TX 79401, USA
TELEPHONE: +1 806 766 1444
FAX: +1 806 766 1469
EMAIL: dvogler@lubbockisd.org
WEBSITE: www.lubbockhigh.com

Luther Burbank High School
Status State
Programme Diploma
Diploma Coordinator Candace Michael
Gender Coeducational
Languages English
Boarding/day Day
1002 Edwards Street, San Antonio TX 78204, USA
TELEPHONE: +1 210 532 4241 x 103
EMAIL: anrodriguez@saisd.net

Mark Twain Elementary School
Status State
Programme PYP
PYP Coordinator Kathleen Blakeslee
Gender Coeducational
Boarding/day Day
7500 Braes Blvd, Houston TX 77025, USA
TELEPHONE: +1 713 295 5230
EMAIL: jdauber@houstonisd.org

Mirabeau B Lamar Senior High School
Status State
Programme MYP, Diploma
Diploma Coordinator Jon Mallam
MYP Coordinator Ted Williams
Gender Coeducational
Languages English
Boarding/day Day
3325 Westheimer Road, Houston TX 77098, USA
TELEPHONE: +1 713 522 5960
FAX: +1 713 535 3769
EMAIL: jmcswain@houstonisd.org

Northline Elementary
Status State
Programme PYP
PYP Coordinator Carlos Soto
Gender Coeducational
Languages English
Boarding/day Day
821 E Witcher Ln, Houston TX 77076, USA
TELEPHONE: +1 713 696 2890
FAX: +1 713 696 2894
EMAIL: bdoyle@houstonisd.org
WEBSITE: http://es.houstonisd.org/northlinees

Odessa High School
Status State
Programme Diploma
Diploma Coordinator Mary Neff
Gender Coeducational
Languages English
Boarding/day Day
PO Box 3912, Odessa TX 79761, USA
TELEPHONE: +1 432 337 6655
EMAIL: leachre@ector-county.k12.tx.us
WEBSITE: www.ector-county.k12.tx.us/schools/ODE/

Oran Roberts Elementary School
Status State
Programme PYP
PYP Coordinator Stephanie Walton
Gender Coeducational
Boarding/day Day
6000 Greenbriar Drive, Houston TX 77030, USA
TELEPHONE: +1 713 295 5272
EMAIL: ssarabia@houstonisd.org

Peebles Elementary School
Status State
Programme PYP
PYP Coordinator Lynn Hobson
Gender Coeducational
Languages English
Boarding/day Day
1800 WS Young Drive North, Killeen TX 76543, USA
TELEPHONE: +1 254 501-2120
FAX: +1 254- 519-5631
EMAIL: gayle.dudley@killeenisd.org
WEBSITE: www.killeenisd.org

Plano East Senior High School
Status State
Programme Diploma
Diploma Coordinator Rick Fernandez
Gender Coeducational
Languages English
Boarding/day Day
3000 Los Rios Boulevard, Plano TX 75074, USA
TELEPHONE: +1 469-752-9000
FAX: +1 469-752-9001
EMAIL: kmcdona@pisd.edu
WEBSITE: www.k-12.pisd.edu/schools/planoeast/ib/ib.htm

R E Good Elementary School
Status State
Programme PYP
PYP Coordinator Jessica Ryckman
Gender Coeducational
Languages English
Boarding/day Day
1012 Study Lane, Carrollton TX 75006, USA
TELEPHONE: +1 972 968 1900
FAX: +1 972 968
EMAIL: coneyl@cfbisd.edu
WEBSITE: www.cfbisd.edu/schools/goo/index.htm

Ranchview High School
Status State
Programme Diploma
Diploma Coordinator Erin Frye
Gender Coeducational
Languages English
Boarding/day Day
8401 East Valley Ranch Parkway, Irving TX 75063, USA
TELEPHONE: +1 972 968 5000
FAX: +1 972 968 5010
EMAIL: fryee@cfbisd.edu
WEBSITE: www.ranchviewcs.org/ranchviewwebsite

Rancier Middle School
Status State
Programme MYP
MYP Coordinator Leigha Gautreaux
Gender Coeducational
Languages English
Boarding/day Day
3301 Hillard Avenue, Killeen TX 76543, USA
TELEPHONE: +1 254 501 1250
EMAIL: corbett.lawler@killeenisd.org

Rice Elementary School
Status State
Programme PYP
PYP Coordinator Latricia Sutton
Gender Coeducational
Languages English
Boarding/day Day
409 Carriage Drive, Tyler TX 75703, USA
TELEPHONE: +1 903 262 2555
FAX: +1 903 262 2556
EMAIL: vicki.neill@tylerisd.org
WEBSITE: www.tylerisd.org

River Oaks Elementary School
Status State
Programme PYP
PYP Coordinator Liz Goodman
Gender Coeducational
Languages English
Boarding/day Day
2008 Kirby Drive, Houston TX 77019, USA
TELEPHONE: +1 713 942 1460
FAX: +1 713 942 1463
EMAIL: kmcbride@houstonisd.org
WEBSITE: www.es.houstonisd.org/riveroakses

Robert E Lee High School
Status State
Programme Diploma
Diploma Coordinator Becky Martin
Gender Coeducational
Languages English
Boarding/day Day
411 ESE Loop 323, Tyler TX 75703, USA
TELEPHONE: +1 903 262 2625
FAX: +1 903 262 2630
EMAIL: roger.mcadoo@tylerisd.org
WEBSITE: www.tylerisd.org/Schools/REL

Samuel Clemens High School
Status State
Programme Diploma
Diploma Coordinator Susan Shires
Gender Coeducational
Languages English
Boarding/day Day
1001 Elbel Road, Schertz TX 78154, USA
TELEPHONE: +1 210 945 6100
EMAIL: jbryan@scuc.txed.net
WEBSITE: www.scuc.txed.net

Samuel L Martin Middle School
Status State
Programme MYP
MYP Coordinator Jim Jupp
Gender Coeducational
Languages English
Boarding/day Day
1601 Haskell Street, Austin TX 78702, USA
TELEPHONE: +1 512 414-3243
FAX: +1 512 320-0125
EMAIL: rvizcain@austinisd.org
WEBSITE: www.austinisd.org

Shotwell Middle School
Status State
Programme MYP
MYP Coordinator Candy Core
6515 Trail Valley Way, Houston TX 77086, USA
TELEPHONE: +1 281 878 0960
FAX: +1 281 591 8564
EMAIL: wwalker@aldine.k12.tx.us
WEBSITE: www.aldine.k12.tx.us/schools

Sidney Lanier Middle School
Programme MYP
MYP Coordinator Mary Ellen Wolf
Gender Coeducational
Boarding/day Boarding
MYP, 3325 Westheimer, Houston Independent School Dis, Houston TX 77098, USA
TELEPHONE: +1 713 522 5960
EMAIL: jmcswain@houstonisd.org

Spicewood Elementary School
Status State
Programme PYP
PYP Coordinator Amanda Allen
Gender Coeducational
Languages English
Boarding/day Day
11601 Olson Drive, Austin TX 78750, USA
TELEPHONE: +1 512 428 3600
FAX: +1 512 428 3690
EMAIL: beth_june@roundrockisd.org
WEBSITE: www.roundrockisd.org

St Alcuin Montessori School
Status Private
Programme MYP
MYP Coordinator Susie Demarest
Gender Coeducational
Languages English
Boarding/day Day
6144 Churchill Way, Dallas TX 75230, USA
TELEPHONE: +1 972 239 1745
FAX: +1 972 934 8727
EMAIL: shaun@saintalcuin.org
WEBSITE: www.saintalcuin.org

St Paul's Episcopal Day School
Status Private
Programme PYP
PYP Coordinator Karol Daniel
Gender Coeducational
Languages English
Boarding/day Day
517 Columbus Avenue, Waco TX 76701, USA
TELEPHONE: +1 254 753-0246
EMAIL: mghee@stpaulsschoolwaco.com
WEBSITE: www.stpaulsschoolwaco.com/

Stony Point High School
Status State
Programme Diploma
Diploma Coordinator Bradly Harper
Gender Coeducational
Languages English
Boarding/day Day
1801 Bowman Road, Round Rock TX 78664, USA
TELEPHONE: +1 512 428 7000
WEBSITE: http://209.184.141.5/stonypoint

Temple High School
Status State
Programme Diploma
Diploma Coordinator Jason Bullock
Gender Coeducational
Languages English
Boarding/day Day
415 North 31st Street, Temple TX 76504, USA
TELEPHONE: +1 254 791 6301
FAX: +1 254 791 6593
EMAIL: jj.villarreal@tisd.org

THE AWTY INTERNATIONAL SCHOOL
Status Private
Programme Diploma
Diploma Coordinator Carol Case PhD
Gender Coeducational
Languages English
Boarding/day Day
7455 Awty School Lane, Houston TX 77055-7222, USA
TELEPHONE: +1 713 686 4850
FAX: +1 713 686 1351
EMAIL: admissions@awty.org
WEBSITE: www.awty.org
see full details on page 146

The North Hills School
Status State
Programme PYP, Diploma
Diploma Coordinator Charles Ryder
PYP Coordinator Kathleen Carnes
Gender Coeducational
Languages English
Boarding/day Day
606 East Royal Lane, Irving TX 75039, USA
TELEPHONE: +1 972 501 0645
FAX: +1 972 501 9459
EMAIL: chuisman@uplifteducation.org
WEBSITE: www.tnhs.org

The Westwood School
Status Private
Programme MYP
MYP Coordinator Heather Lourcey
Gender Coeducational
Languages English
Boarding/day Day
14340 Proton Road, Dallas TX 75244, USA
TELEPHONE: +1 972 239 8598
FAX: +1 972 239 1028
EMAIL: pambutler@westwoodschool.org
WEBSITE: www.westwoodschool.org

Trinity High School
Status State
Programme Diploma
Diploma Coordinator Thomas Newman
Gender Coeducational
Languages English
500 North Industrial, Euless TX 76039, USA
TELEPHONE: +1 817 571 0271
FAX: +1 817 354 3322
EMAIL: cargilea@hebisd.edu

Washington Jackson Elementary Magnet School
Status State
Programme PYP
PYP Coordinator Stephanie Eubanks
Gender Coeducational
Languages English
Boarding/day Day
1300 Harding Street, Wichita Falls TX 76301, USA
TELEPHONE: +1 940 720 3145
FAX: +1 940 720 3168
EMAIL: tcallaway@wfisd.net
WEBSITE: www.wfisd.net/washingtonjackson

Westchester Academy for International Studies
Status State
Programme Diploma
Diploma Coordinator Stephen Shearer
Gender Coeducational
Languages English
Boarding/day Day
901 Yorkchester, Houston TX 77079, USA
TELEPHONE: +1 713 365 5678
EMAIL: butlerp@springbranchisd.com
WEBSITE: http://wais2.springbranchisd.com

Westlake Academy
Status State
Programme PYP, MYP, Diploma
Diploma Coordinator David Jenkins
MYP Coordinator David Jenkins
PYP Coordinator Claudia Ourthe-Cabale
Gender Coeducational
Languages English
Boarding/day Day
2600 Ottinger Road, Westlake TX 76262, USA
TELEPHONE: +1 817 4905757
FAX: +1 817 4905758
EMAIL: info@westlakeacademy.org
WEBSITE: www.westlakeacademy.org

Westwood High School
Status State
Programme Diploma
Diploma Coordinator Kathryn Fleming
Gender Coeducational
Languages English
Boarding/day Day
Administration, 12400 Mellow Meadow Drive, Round Rock, Austin TX 78750, USA
TELEPHONE: +1 512 464 4087
EMAIL: rebecca_donald@roundrockisd.org

Utah

Bountiful High School
Status State
Programme Diploma
Diploma Coordinator Sue Baylis
Gender Coeducational
Languages English
Boarding/day Day
695 South Orchard Drive, Bountiful UT 84010, USA
TELEPHONE: +1-801-402-3900
EMAIL: rastle@dsdmail.net
WEBSITE: www.davis.k12.ut.us/bhs

Clearfield High School
Status State
Programme Diploma
Diploma Coordinator Rebecca Van Dyke
Gender Coeducational
Languages English
Boarding/day Day
931 South 1000 East, Clearfield UT 84015, USA
TELEPHONE: +1 801-408-8200
FAX: +1-801-402-8201
EMAIL: mtimothy@dsdmail.net
WEBSITE: http://chs.davis.k12.ut.us

Ecker Hill International School
Status State
Programme MYP
MYP Coordinator Jamie Duis
Gender Coeducational
Languages English
Boarding/day Day
2465 West Kilby Road, Park City UT 84098, USA
TELEPHONE: +1 435 645 5610
FAX: +1 435 645 5619
EMAIL: gproffit@pcschools.us
WEBSITE: http://ehms.pcschools.us

Hillcrest High School
Status State
Programme Diploma
Diploma Coordinator Victoria Brinton
Gender Coeducational
Languages English
7350 South 900 East, Midvale UT 84047, USA
TELEPHONE: +1 801 256 5484
FAX: +1 801 256 5483
EMAIL: victoria.brinton@jordan.k12.ut.us

Hunter High School
Status State
Programme Diploma
Diploma Coordinator Christopher Krueger
Gender Coeducational
Languages English
Boarding/day Day
4200 South 5600 West, West Valley City UT 84120, USA
TELEPHONE: +1 801 685 6501
FAX: +1 801 685 5362
EMAIL: maile.loo@granite.k12.ut.us
WEBSITE: www.granite.k12.ut.us/hunter_high/

Provo High School
Status State
Programme Diploma
Diploma Coordinator Lori Rich
Gender Coeducational
Languages English
Boarding/day Day
1125 North University Avenue, Provo UT 84604, USA
TELEPHONE: +1 801 373 6550
FAX: +1 801 374 4880
EMAIL: samray@provo.edu
WEBSITE: www.phs.provo.edu

Skyline High School
Status State
Programme Diploma
Diploma Coordinator Ruth Dallas
Gender Coeducational
Languages English
Boarding/day Day
3251 East 3760 South, Salt Lake City UT 84109, USA
TELEPHONE: +1 801 273-2080
EMAIL: ruth.dallas@granite.k12.ut.us
WEBSITE: www.skyline.granite.k12.ut.us

Treasure Mountain International School
Status State
Programme MYP
MYP Coordinator Jamie Duis
Gender Coeducational
Languages English
Boarding/day Day
2530 Kearns Boulevard, Park City UT 84060, USA
TELEPHONE: +1 435 645 5649
FAX: +1 435 645 5649
EMAIL: boc@pcschools.us
WEBSITE: http://tmms.pcschools.us

West High School
Status State
Programme Diploma
Diploma Coordinator Connie Jeanne Larsen
Gender Coeducational
Languages English
Boarding/day Day
241 North 300 West, Salt Lake City UT 84103, USA
TELEPHONE: +1 801 578 8500
FAX: +1 801 578 8524
EMAIL: margery.parker@slc.k12.ut.us
WEBSITE: www.slc.k12.ut.us/sites/west

Virginia

Annandale High School
Status State
Programme MYP, Diploma
Diploma Coordinator Erin Albright
MYP Coordinator Marylynn Archer
Gender Coeducational
Languages English
Boarding/day Day
4700 Medford Drive, Annandale VA 22003, USA
TELEPHONE: +1 703 642 4105
FAX: +1 703 642 4197
EMAIL: John.Ponton@fcps.edu
WEBSITE: www.fcps.edu/Annandale HS/

Atlee High School
Status State
Programme Diploma
Diploma Coordinator Bonnie McLaughlin
Gender Coeducational
Languages English
Boarding/day Day
9414 Atlee Station Road, Mechanicsville
VA 23116, USA
TELEPHONE: +1 804 723 2100
FAX: +1 804 723 2103
EMAIL: vdagostino@hcps.us

Breckinridge Middle School
Programme MYP
MYP Coordinator Anne Sphar
Gender Coeducational
Boarding/day Day
3901 Williamson Road, Roanoke City,
Roanoke VA 24012, USA
TELEPHONE: +1 540 853 2251
EMAIL: ajones@rcps.info
WEBSITE: www.rcps.info

Carlisle School
Status Private
Programme MYP, Diploma
Diploma Coordinator Nancy Thomas
MYP Coordinator Gayle Jessee
Gender Coeducational
Languages English
Boarding/day Day
PO Box 5388, Martinsville VA 24115, USA
TELEPHONE: +1 276-632-7288
FAX: +1 276-632-9545
EMAIL: simonow@carlisleschool.org
WEBSITE: www.carlisleschool.org

Clarke County High School
Status State
Programme Diploma
Diploma Coordinator Shaaron Loveless
Gender Coeducational
Languages English
Boarding/day Day
240 Westwood Road, Berryville VA 22611, USA
TELEPHONE: +1 540 955 6130
FAX: +1 540 955-6139
EMAIL: ballf@clarke.k12.va.us
WEBSITE: http://cchs.clarke.k12.va.us/

Dutrow Elementary School
Status State
Programme PYP
PYP Coordinator Marguerite A Pittman
Gender Coeducational
Languages English
Boarding/day Day
60 Curtis Tignor Road, Newport News
VA 23608, USA
TELEPHONE: +1 757 886 7760
EMAIL: marguerite.pittman@nn.k12.va.us
WEBSITE: http://dutrow.nn.k12.va.us

Edgar Allen Poe Middle School
Programme MYP
MYP Coordinator Virginia Hale
Gender Coeducational
Boarding/day Day
7000 Cindy Lane, Annandale VA 2203, USA
TELEPHONE: +1 703 813 3800
EMAIL: june.monterio@fcps.edu
WEBSITE: www.fcps.edu/poems

Ellen Glasgow Middle School
Programme MYP
MYP Coordinator Robert Harrison
Gender Coeducational
Boarding/day Day
Fairfax County Public Schools, 4101 Fairfax
Parkway, Alexandria VA 22312, USA
TELEPHONE: +1 703 813 8700
EMAIL: deirdre.lavery@fcps.edu
WEBSITE: www.fcps.edu/glasgowms/ibmyp

Fleming-Ruffner Magnet Center/Fleming High School
Status State
Programme MYP, Diploma
Diploma Coordinator Katrina Landon
MYP Coordinator Katrina Landon
Gender Coeducational
Languages English
Boarding/day Day
3649 Ferncliff Avenue, NW, Roanoke
VA 24017, USA
TELEPHONE: +1 540 853 6228
EMAIL: swillis@roanoke.k12.va.us

Fleming-Ruffner Magnet Center/Fleming HS
Programme MYP
MYP Coordinator Katrina Landon
Gender Coeducational
Boarding/day Boarding
3649 Ferncliff Road, Roanoke VA 24017, USA
TELEPHONE: +1 540-853-1583
EMAIL: hcarr@roanoke.k12.va.us

Galileo Magnet High School
Status State
Programme MYP, Diploma
Diploma Coordinator Kathy Renyer
MYP Coordinator Kathy Renyer
Gender Coeducational
Languages English
Boarding/day Day
230 South Ridge Road, Danville VA 24541,
USA
TELEPHONE: +1 434 773 8186
FAX: +1 434 773 8188
EMAIL: wlawrenc@mail.dps.k12.va.us
WEBSITE: http://web.dps.k12.va.us/galileo

Gar-Field Senior High School
Status State
Programme MYP, Diploma
Diploma Coordinator Brian Bassett
MYP Coordinator Della Gordon
Gender Coeducational
Languages English
Boarding/day Day
14000 Smoketown Road, Woodbridge
VA 22192, USA
TELEPHONE: +1 703 730 7000
FAX: +1 703 730 7197
EMAIL: bassetbm@pwcs.edu
WEBSITE: www.ibatgf.com

George C Marshall High School
Status State
Programme Diploma
Diploma Coordinator Connie Wineland
Gender Coeducational
Languages English
Boarding/day Day
7731 Leesburg Pike, Falls Church VA 22043,
USA
TELEPHONE: +1 703 714 5402
FAX: +1 703 714 5497
EMAIL: jay.pearson@fcps.edu
WEBSITE: www.fcps.edu/marshallhs

George H Moody Middle School
Programme MYP
MYP Coordinator Sharon Pope
Gender Coeducational
Boarding/day Boarding
302 Azalea Avenue, Richmond VA 23227, USA
TELEPHONE: +1 804-228-2700
FAX: +1 804-228-2755
EMAIL: rvschwab@henrico.k12.va.us

George Mason High School
Status State
Programme Diploma
Diploma Coordinator Brian Dickson
Gender Coeducational
Languages English
Boarding/day Day
7124 Leesburg Pike, Falls Church VA 22043,
USA
TELEPHONE: +1 703 248 5505
FAX: +1 703 533 8854
EMAIL: rwsnee@fccps.k12.va.us
WEBSITE: www.fccps.k12.va.us/gm

Granby High School
Status State
Programme Diploma
Diploma Coordinator Lynette Corley
Gender Coeducational
Languages English
Boarding/day Day
7101 Granby Street, Norfolk VA 23505, USA
TELEPHONE: +1 757 451 4110
FAX: +1 757 451 4118
EMAIL: tdaughtrey@nps.k12.va.us
WEBSITE:
www.nps.k12.va.us/Schools/GranbyHS

Hampton High School
Status State
Programme Diploma
Diploma Coordinator Elizabeth Carey
Gender Coeducational
Languages English
Boarding/day Day
1491 W Queen Street, Hampton City Schools,
Hampton VA 23669, USA
TELEPHONE: +1 757 825-4430
FAX: +1 757 825 1036
EMAIL: awoods@sbo.hampton.k12.va.us
WEBSITE: www.sbo.hampton.k12.va.us

Hanover High School
Status State
Programme Diploma
Diploma Coordinator Wanda Bibb
Gender Coeducational
Languages English
Boarding/day Day
10307 Chamberlayne Road, Mechanicsville
VA 23116, USA
TELEPHONE: +1 804 723 3700
FAX: +1 804 723 3750
EMAIL: ccash@hcps.us
WEBSITE: http://hcps2.hanover.k12.va.us/hhs

Henrico High School
Status State
Programme MYP, Diploma
Diploma Coordinator Sharon Pope
MYP Coordinator Sharon Pope
Gender Coeducational
Languages English
Boarding/day Day
302 Azalea Avenue, Richmond VA 23227, USA
TELEPHONE: +1 804 228 2700
FAX: +1 804 228 2755
EMAIL: whparker@henrico.k12.va.us

Highland Park Learning Center
Status State
Programme PYP
PYP Coordinator Patricia Watts
Gender Coeducational
Boarding/day Day
1212 5th Street SW, Roanoke VA 24015, USA
TELEPHONE: +1 540 853 2963
EMAIL: ddoss@mail.roanoke.va.us
WEBSITE: www.roanoke.k12.va.us

James River Elementary School
Status State
Programme PYP
PYP Coordinator Janet Parker
Gender Coeducational
Languages English
Boarding/day Day
8901 Pocahontas Trail, Williamsburg
VA 23185, USA
TELEPHONE: +1 757 887 1768
FAX: +1 757 887 2162
EMAIL: gastond@wjcc.k12.va.us
WEBSITE: www.wjcc.k12.va.us/jr/

**James W Robinson, Jr Secondary
School**
Status State
Programme Diploma
Diploma Coordinator Faye Brenner
Gender Coeducational
Languages English
Boarding/day Day
5035 Sideburn Road, Fairfax County Public
Schools, Fairfax VA 22032, USA
TELEPHONE: +1 703 426 2100
FAX: +1 703 426 2197
EMAIL: dan.meier@fcps.edu
WEBSITE: www.fcps.edu/robinsonss

JEB Stuart High School
Status State
Programme MYP, Diploma
Diploma Coordinator Mark Rogers
MYP Coordinator Robert Harrison
Gender Coeducational
Languages English
Boarding/day Day
3301 Peace Valley Lane, Falls Church
VA 22044, USA
TELEPHONE: +1 703 824 3900
FAX: +1 703 824 3997
EMAIL: mel.riddile@fcps.edu

Langston Hughes Middle School
Programme MYP
MYP Coordinator James Andrew Albright
Gender Coeducational
Boarding/day Boarding
11401 Ridge Heights Road, Reston VA 20191,
USA
TELEPHONE: +1 703 715 3600
EMAIL: debbie.jackson@fcps.edu

Lee-Davis High School
Status State
Programme Diploma
Diploma Coordinator Lesa Berlinghoff
Gender Coeducational
Languages English
Boarding/day Day
7052 Mechanicsville Pike, Hanover County,
Mechanicsville VA 23111-3629, USA
TELEPHONE: +1 804 723 2200
FAX: +1 804 723 2202
EMAIL: sbjones@hcps3.hanover.k12.va.us
WEBSITE: www.hanover.k12.va.us

Lucille Brown Middle School
Programme MYP
MYP Coordinator Jennifer Hart
Gender Coeducational
Boarding/day Day
6300 Jahnke Road, Richmond VA 23225, USA
TELEPHONE: +1 804 319 3013
FAX: +1 804 319 3009
EMAIL: dlewis2@richmond.k12.va.us
WEBSITE: www.richmond.k12.va.us/lucilleib

Martinsville High School
Status State
Programme Diploma
Diploma Coordinator Jean K Smith
Gender Coeducational
Languages English
Boarding/day Day
351 Commonwealth Boulevard, Martinsville
VA 24112, USA
TELEPHONE: +1 276 632 9755
FAX: +1 276 632 1516
EMAIL: jsmith@martinsville.k12.va.us

Meadowbrook High School
Status State
Programme Diploma
Diploma Coordinator Carolyn Henly
Gender Coeducational
Languages English
Boarding/day Day
4901 Cogbill Road, Richmond VA 23234, USA
TELEPHONE: +1 804 743 3675
FAX: +1 804 743 3686
EMAIL: cornelius_fletcher@ccpsnet.net
WEBSITE: www.chesterfield.k12.va.us/
schools/meadowbrook_hs

Midlothian High School
Status State
Programme Diploma
Diploma Coordinator Donna Crane
Gender Coeducational
Languages English
Boarding/day Day
401 Charter Colony Parkway, Chesterfield
County, Midlothian VA 23114, USA
TELEPHONE: +1 804 378-2440
EMAIL: christine_wilson@ccpsnet.net
WEBSITE: www.chesterfield.k12.va.us/
schools/midlothian_hs

Mills E Godwin Middle School
Programme MYP
MYP Coordinator M Patricia Moss
Gender Coeducational
Boarding/day Boarding
14800 Darbydale Avenue, Woodbridge
VA 22193, USA
TELEPHONE: +1 703 670 6166

Mount Vernon High School
Status State
Programme MYP, Diploma
Diploma Coordinator Valerie Caveney
MYP Coordinator Mary Fee
Gender Coeducational
Languages English
Boarding/day Day
8515 Old Mount Vernon Road, Alexandria
VA 22309, USA
TELEPHONE: +1 703 619 3258
FAX: +1 703 619-3197
EMAIL: nardos.king@fcps.edu
WEBSITE: www.fcps.edu/mtvernonhs

Mountain View High School
Status State
Programme Diploma
Diploma Coordinator Susan Easter
Gender Coeducational
Languages English
Boarding/day Day
2135 Mountain View Road, Stafford VA 22556, USA
TELEPHONE: +1 540 658 6840
FAX: +1 540 658 6860
EMAIL: jstemple@staffordschools.net
WEBSITE: www.mountainviewhs.net

O W Holmes Middle School
Programme MYP
MYP Coordinator Virginia Hale
Gender Coeducational
Boarding/day Day
6525 Montrose Street, Alexandria VA 22312, USA
TELEPHONE: +1 703 658 5900
EMAIL: roberto.pamas@fcps.edu
WEBSITE: www.fcps.edu/holmesms

Oscar F Smith High School
Status State
Programme Diploma
Diploma Coordinator Kerri Lancaster
Gender Coeducational
Languages English
Boarding/day Day
1994 Tiger Drive, Chesapeake VA 23320, USA
TELEPHONE: +1 757 548 0696
FAX: +1 757 548 0531
EMAIL: andrejma@cps.k12.va.us
WEBSITE: www.eclipse.cps.k12.va.us/schools/osh

Patrick Henry High School
Status State
Programme Diploma
Diploma Coordinator Anita Barnhart
Gender Coeducational
Languages English
12449 West Patrick Henry Road, Ashland VA 23005, USA
TELEPHONE: +1 804 365 8011
FAX: +1 804 365 8027
EMAIL: ibphhs@hanover.k12.va.us

Paul D Burbank Elementary School
Status State
Programme PYP
PYP Coordinator Jane Austin
40 Tide Mill Lane, Hampton VA 23666, USA

Plaza Middle School
Programme MYP
MYP Coordinator Barbara Winn
Gender Coeducational
Boarding/day Day
3080 South Lynnhaven Road, Virginia Beach VA 23452, USA
TELEPHONE: +1 757 431 4060
EMAIL: awarren@bvcps.k12.va.us
WEBSITE: www.plazams.vbschools.com

Princess Anne High School
Status State
Programme MYP, Diploma
Diploma Coordinator Helen T Cox
MYP Coordinator Barbara Winn
Gender Coeducational
Languages English
Boarding/day Day
4400 Virginia Beach Boulevard, Virginia Beach VA 23462-3198, USA
TELEPHONE: +1 757 473 5000
FAX: +1 757 473 5004
EMAIL: pat.griffin@vbschools.com
WEBSITE: www.princessannehs.vbschools.com

Randolph Elementary School
Status State
Programme PYP
PYP Coordinator Linda Smith
Gender Coeducational
Boarding/day Day
1306 S Quincy Street, Arlington VA 22204, USA
TELEPHONE: +1 703 228 5830
EMAIL: rbostick@arlington.k12.va.us

Robert E Lee Senior High School
Status State
Programme Diploma
Diploma Coordinator Frank Carbo
Gender Coeducational
Languages English
Boarding/day Day
6540 Franconia Road, Fairfax County, Springfield VA 22150, USA
TELEPHONE: +1 703 924 8300
FAX: +1 703 924 8397
EMAIL: donald.thurston@fcps.edu
WEBSITE: www.fcps.edu/leehs

Saint Mary's Catholic School
Status Private
Programme MYP
MYP Coordinator Robin Rooks
Gender Coeducational
Languages English
Boarding/day Day
9501 Gayton Road, Richmond VA 23229, USA
TELEPHONE: +1 804 740 1048
FAX: +1 804 740 1310
EMAIL: tdertinger@saintmary.org
WEBSITE: www.saintmary.org

Salem High School
Status State
Programme Diploma
Diploma Coordinator Jane Sandel
Gender Coeducational
Languages English
Boarding/day Day
400 Spartan Drive, Salem VA 24153, USA
TELEPHONE: +1 540 387 2437
FAX: +1 540 387 2543
EMAIL: jhall@salem.k12.va.us
WEBSITE: www.salem.k12.va.us

South Lakes High School
Status State
Programme MYP, Diploma
Diploma Coordinator Anne Stowe
MYP Coordinator James A Albright
Gender Coeducational
Languages English
Boarding/day Day
11400 South Lakes Drive, Reston VA 20191, USA
TELEPHONE: +1 703 715 4500
FAX: +1 703 715 4597
EMAIL: bruce.butler@fcps.edu

Stonewall Jackson High School
Status State
Programme MYP, Diploma
Diploma Coordinator Susan Watts
MYP Coordinator Julie Chamberlain
Gender Coeducational
Languages English
Boarding/day Day
8820 Rixlew Lane, Manassas VA 20109-3799, USA
TELEPHONE: +1 703 365-2900
FAX: +1 703 365-6984
EMAIL: huckesdj@pwcs.edu
WEBSITE: www.sjraiders.org

Stonewall Jackson Middle School
Programme MYP
MYP Coordinator Julie Chamberlain
Gender Coeducational
Boarding/day Boarding
10100 Lomond Drive, Manassas VA 20109, USA
TELEPHONE: +1 703 361 3185

Stuart M Belville Middle School
Status State
Programme MYP
MYP Coordinator Della Gordon
Gender Coeducational
Languages English
Boarding/day Day
7901 Dale Boulevard, Woodbridge VA 22193, USA
TELEPHONE: +1 703 878 2593
FAX: +1 703 730 1274
EMAIL: graziadj@pwcs.edu
WEBSITE: www.pwcs.edu/beville/

Thomas Alva Edison High School
Status State
Programme Diploma
Diploma Coordinator Linda Blair
Gender Coeducational
Languages English
Boarding/day Day
5801 Franconia Road, Alexandria VA 22310, USA
TELEPHONE: +1 703 924 8007
FAX: +1703 924 8097
EMAIL: gcroghan@fcps.edu
WEBSITE: www.fcps.k12.va.us/edisonhs

Thomas Jefferson High School
Status State
Programme MYP, Diploma
Diploma Coordinator Jennifer Hart
MYP Coordinator Jennifer Hart
Gender Coeducational
Languages English
Boarding/day Day
4100 West Grace Street, Richmond VA 23230,
USA
TELEPHONE: +1 804 780 6028
EMAIL: bulschmi@richmond.k12.va.us
WEBSITE:
www.richmond.k12.va.us./ib_jefferson

Thomas Jefferson Middle School
Status State
Programme MYP
MYP Coordinator Ellen Smith
Gender Coeducational
Languages English
Boarding/day Day
125 S Old Glebe Road, Arlington VA 22204,
USA
TELEPHONE: +1 703 228 5900
FAX: +1 703 979 3744
EMAIL: smonde@arlington.k12.va.us
WEBSITE: www.jefferson.arlington.k12.va.us

Trinity Episcopal School
Status Private
Programme Diploma
Diploma Coordinator Vivian Hiedemann
Gender Coeducational
Languages English
Boarding/day Day
3850 Pittaway Road, Richmond VA 23235,
USA
TELEPHONE: +1 804 272 5864
FAX: +1 804 323 1335
EMAIL: toma@trinityes.org
WEBSITE: www.trinityes.org

Virginia High School
Status State
Programme Diploma
Diploma Coordinator Brenda Carroll
Gender Coeducational
Languages English
1200 Long Crescent Drive, Bristol VA 24201,
USA
TELEPHONE: +1 276 821 5855
FAX: +1 276 821 5851
EMAIL: idanko@bristolvaschools.org

Walt Whitman Middle School
Status State
Programme MYP
MYP Coordinator Mary Fee
Gender Coeducational
Languages English
Boarding/day Day
2500 Parkers Lane, Alexandria VA 22306, USA
TELEPHONE: +1 703 660 2400
FAX: +1 703 660-2497
EMAIL: oldavis@fcps.edu

Warwick High School
Status State
Programme Diploma
Diploma Coordinator Carol Kennedy
Gender Coeducational
Languages English
Boarding/day Day
51 Copeland Lane, Newport News
VA 23601-2399, USA
TELEPHONE: +1 757 591 4700
FAX: +1 757 596 7415
EMAIL: gene.jones@.nn.k12.va.us
WEBSITE:
http://whsunix.warwick.nn.k12.va.us

Washington-Lee High School
Status State
Programme Diploma
Diploma Coordinator Marilyn Leeb
Gender Coeducational
Languages English
Boarding/day Day
1300 North Quincy Street, Arlington VA 22201,
USA
TELEPHONE: +1 703 228 6200
FAX: +1 703 527 5918
EMAIL: groberts@arlington.k12.va.us
WEBSITE: www.washlee.arlington.k12.va.us

Westwood Magnet Middle school
Programme MYP
MYP Coordinator Kathy Renyer
Gender Coeducational
500 Apollo Avenue, Danville VA 24541, USA
TELEPHONE: +1 434 797 8860
WEBSITE: http://web.dps.k12.va.us/galileo

York High School
Status State
Programme Diploma
Diploma Coordinator Gerry Tylavsky
Gender Coeducational
Languages English
Boarding/day Day
9300 George Washington, Memorial Highway,
Yorktown VA 23692, USA
TELEPHONE: +1 757 898 0354
FAX: +1 757 898 8235
EMAIL: rhart@ycsd.york.va.us

Washington

A C Davis High School
Status State
Programme Diploma
Diploma Coordinator Steve McKenna
Gender Coeducational
Languages English
Boarding/day Day
212 South 6th Avenue, Yakima WA 98902,
USA
TELEPHONE: +1 509 573 2501
FAX: +1 509 573 2525
EMAIL: maras.lee@ysd.wednet.edu

Capital High School
Status State
Programme Diploma
Diploma Coordinator Diane Rae
Gender Coeducational
Languages English
Boarding/day Day
2707 Conger Avenue, Olympia
WA 98502-4590, USA
TELEPHONE: +1 360 753 8880
FAX: +1 360 596 8001
EMAIL: tpoff@osd.wednet.edu

Chief Sealth High School
Status State
Programme Diploma
Diploma Coordinator Laura Robb
Gender Coeducational
Languages English
Boarding/day Day
2600 SW Thistle, Seattle WA 98126, USA
TELEPHONE: +1 206 252 8550
FAX: +1 206 252 8551
EMAIL: jboyd@seattleschools.org
WEBSITE:
www.seattleschools.org/schools/chiefsealth

Columbia River High School
Status State
Programme Diploma
Diploma Coordinator Heidi Lohnes
Gender Coeducational
Languages English
Boarding/day Day
800 North West 99th Street, Vancouver
WA 98665, USA
TELEPHONE: +1 360 313 3900
FAX: +1 360 313 3901
EMAIL: mstromme@vansd.org

Edmunds-Woodway High School
Status State
Programme Diploma
Diploma Coordinator Kathy Ludgate
Gender Coeducational
Languages English
Boarding/day Day
7600 212th St South West, Edmonds
WA 98026, USA
TELEPHONE: +1 425 670 7977
FAX: +1 425 670 7929
EMAIL: weissa@edmonds.wednet.edu

Harbour Pointe Middle School
Programme MYP
MYP Coordinator Kathleen Church
Gender Coeducational
Boarding/day Day
5000 Harbour Pointe Blvd, Mulilteo
WA 98275, USA
TELEPHONE: +1 425 356 6658
EMAIL: cannonnl@mukilteo.wednet.edu
WEBSITE:
http://schools.mukilteo.wednet.edu/hp

Henry Foss High School
Status State
Programme Diploma
Diploma Coordinator Dianne S Bradley
Gender Coeducational
Languages English
Boarding/day Day
Henry Foss High School, 2112 South Tyler Street, Tacoma WA 98405, USA
TELEPHONE: +1 253 571 2300
FAX: +1 253 571 7466
EMAIL: sschaus@tacoma.k12.wa.us

Highland Middle School
Status State
Programme MYP
MYP Coordinator Jane Van Ryn
Gender Coeducational
Languages English
Boarding/day Day
15027 NE Bel-Red Road, Bellevue WA 98007, USA
TELEPHONE: +1 425 456 6400
FAX: +1 425 456 6499
EMAIL: wellingtond@bsd405.org

Inglemoor High School
Status State
Programme Diploma
Diploma Coordinator Jeanie Yocum
Gender Coeducational
Languages English
Boarding/day Day
15500 Simonds Road NE, Kenmore WA 98028, USA
TELEPHONE: +1 425 489 6501
FAX: +1 425 489 6593
EMAIL: vsherwood@nsd.org

Ingraham High School
Status State
Programme Diploma
Diploma Coordinator Guy Thomas
Languages English
1819 North 135th Street, Seattle WA 98133-7709, USA
TELEPHONE: +1 206 252 3923
FAX: +1 206 252 3881
EMAIL: gathomas1@seattleschools.org

Interlake High School
Status State
Programme MYP, Diploma
Diploma Coordinator Michael O'Byrne
MYP Coordinator Jane Van Ryn
Gender Coeducational
Languages English
Boarding/day Day
16245 NE 24th Street, Bellevue WA 98008, USA
TELEPHONE: +1 425 456 7200
FAX: +1 425 456 7215
EMAIL: collinssl@bsd405.org

Kennewick High School
Status State
Programme Diploma
Diploma Coordinator Twila Wood
Gender Coeducational
Languages English
Boarding/day Day
500 South Dayton Street, Kennewick WA 99336, USA
TELEPHONE: +1 509 222-6475
FAX: +1 509 585 3216
EMAIL: andeja@ksd.org

Kent-Meridian High School
Status State
Programme Diploma
Diploma Coordinator Donald Hauck
Gender Coeducational
Languages English
10020 SE 256th Street, Kent WA 98031, USA
TELEPHONE: +1 253 373 7405
FAX: +1 253 373 7411
EMAIL: ddorn@kent.k12.wa.us

Mt Rainer High School
Status State
Programme Diploma
Diploma Coordinator Chris Wilder
Gender Coeducational
Languages English
Boarding/day Day
22450 19th Ave South, Des Moines WA 98198, USA
TELEPHONE: +1 206 631 7000
EMAIL: pacet@hsd401.org

Skyline High School
Status State
Programme Diploma
Diploma Coordinator Marion Makin
Gender Coeducational
Languages English
Boarding/day Day
1122 228th Avenue SE, Issaquah School District, Sammamish WA 98075-6914, USA
TELEPHONE: +1 425 837 7700
FAX: +1 425 837 7705
EMAIL: younge@issaquah.wednet.edu
WEBSITE: www.shs.issaquah.wednet.edu

South Charleston High School
Status State
Programme Diploma
Diploma Coordinator Edward Booten
Gender Coeducational
Languages English
Boarding/day Day
One Eagle Way, South Charleston WA 25309, USA
TELEPHONE: +1 304 766 0352
FAX: +1 304 768 4663
EMAIL: wwalton@access.k12.wv.us

Sumner High School
Status State
Programme Diploma
Diploma Coordinator Chris Prestin
Gender Coeducational
Languages English
Boarding/day Day
1707 Main Street, Sumner WA 98390, USA
TELEPHONE: +1 253 891 5500
FAX: +1 253 891 5585
EMAIL: bill_gaines@sumner.wednet.edu
WEBSITE: www.sumner.wednet.edu

Thomas Jefferson High School
Status State
Programme Diploma
Diploma Coordinator Carol Lee
Gender Coeducational
Languages English
Boarding/day Day
4248 South 288th Street, Auburn WA 98001, USA
TELEPHONE: +1 253 945 5600
FAX: +1 253-945-5656

Wisconsin

Catholic Memorial High School
Status Private
Programme Diploma
Diploma Coordinator John Burke
Gender Coeducational
Languages English
Boarding/day Day
601 East College Avenue, Waukesha WI 53186, USA
TELEPHONE: +1 262 542 7101
EMAIL: mschmitt@catholicmemorial.net
WEBSITE: www.catholicmemorial.net

Darrell Lynn Hines College Preparatory Academy of Excellence
Status State
Programme PYP
PYP Coordinator Precious Washington
Gender Coeducational
Boarding/day Day
7151 North 86th Street, Milwaukee WI 53224, USA
TELEPHONE: +1 414 358 3542
EMAIL: bhorton@dlha.org

Jerome I Case High School
Status State
Programme Diploma
Diploma Coordinator Patty Hammes
Gender Coeducational
Languages English
Boarding/day Day
7345 Washington Avenue, Racine WI 53406, USA
TELEPHONE: +1 262 619 4210
FAX: +1 262 619 4259

John Marshall High School
Status State
Programme Diploma
Diploma Coordinator James R Kroll
Gender Coeducational
Languages English
Boarding/day Day
4141 N 64th Street, Milwaukee WI 53216, USA
TELEPHONE: +1 414 393 2300
FAX: +1 414 393 2315
EMAIL: armourpe@milwaukee.k12.wi.us
WEBSITE: www.milwaukee.k12.wi.us

Lincoln High School
Status State
Programme Diploma
Diploma Coordinator Deborah Douglas
Gender Coeducational
Languages English
Boarding/day Day
1433 South Eighth Street, Manitowoc
WI 54220, USA
TELEPHONE: +1 920 683 4761
FAX: +1 920 683 4845
EMAIL: shawk@mpsd.k12.wi.us
WEBSITE: http://mpsd.k12.wi.us

Madison Country Day School
Status Private
Programme Diploma
Diploma Coordinator Mark Childs
Gender Coeducational
Languages English
Boarding/day Day
5606 River Road, Waunakee WI 53597, USA
TELEPHONE: +1 608 850 6000
FAX: +1 608 850 6006
EMAIL: lfelker@madisoncountryday.org
WEBSITE: www.madisoncountryday.org

Madison University High School
Status State
Programme Diploma
Diploma Coordinator Jay Bullock
Gender Coeducational
Languages English
Boarding/day Day
8135 West Florist Avenue, Milwaukee Public
Schools, Milwaukee WI 53218, USA
TELEPHONE: +1 414 393-6100
FAX: +1 414 393-6170
EMAIL: 022@mail.milwaukee.k12.wi.us
WEBSITE:
www2.milwaukee.k12.wi.us/madison

Notre Dame de la Baie Academy
Status Private
Programme Diploma
Diploma Coordinator Brenda Brayko
Gender Coeducational
Languages English
Boarding/day Day
610 Maryhill Drive, Green Bay WI 54303, USA
TELEPHONE: +1 920 429 6100
FAX: +1 920 429 6168
EMAIL: dradecki@notredameacademy.com
WEBSITE: www.NotreDameAcademy.com

Oconomowoc High School
Status State
Programme Diploma
Diploma Coordinator Carrie Schultz
Gender Coeducational
Boarding/day Day
641 East Forest Street, Oconomowoc
WI 53066-3888, USA
TELEPHONE: +1 262 560 3100
EMAIL: joseph.moylan@oasd.k12.wi.us
WEBSITE: www.oasd.k12.wi.us

Ronald Wilson Reagan College Preparatory High School
Status State
Programme Diploma
Diploma Coordinator M E McCormack-Mervis
Gender Coeducational
Languages English
Boarding/day Day
4965 South 20 Street, Milwaukee WI 53221,
USA
TELEPHONE: +1 414-304-6100
FAX: +1 414-304-6115
EMAIL: juldamato@aol.com
WEBSITE: www.milwaukee.k12.wi.us/pages/
mps/school/highs/reagan

Rufus King High School
Status State
Programme Diploma
Diploma Coordinator Mavis Roesch
Gender Coeducational
Languages English
Boarding/day Day
1801 West Olive Street, Milwaukee WI 53209,
USA
TELEPHONE: +1 414 267 0705
FAX: +1 414 267 0715
EMAIL:
meuleraw@mail.milwaukee.K12.wi.us
WEBSITE: www.milwaukee.k12.wi.us/king/

Wausau East High School
Status State
Programme Diploma
Diploma Coordinator Joyce Griese
Gender Coeducational
Languages English
Boarding/day Day
2607 N 18th Street, Wausau WI 54403, USA
TELEPHONE: +1 715 261 3500
FAX: +1 715 845 2913
EMAIL: bpeck@wausau.k12.wi.us
WEBSITE: www.wausau.k12.wi.us/east/

Wyoming

Cheyenne East High School
Status State
Programme Diploma
Diploma Coordinator Brian Madland
Gender Coeducational
Languages English
Boarding/day Day
2800 E Pershing Blvd, Cheyenne WY 82001,
USA
TELEPHONE: +1 307 771 2663 ext 108
FAX: +1 307 771 2352
EMAIL: mirichs@laramie1.k12.wy.us
WEBSITE: www.east.laramie1.k12.wy.us

Natrona County High School
Status State
Programme Diploma
Diploma Coordinator Margo Nokes
Gender Coeducational
Languages English
930 Elm Street, Casper WY 82601, USA
TELEPHONE: +1 307 233 1511
FAX: +1 307 233 1507
EMAIL: dean_kelly@ncsd.k12.wy.us

VIRGIN ISLANDS

Cedar International School
Status Private
Programme MYP, Diploma
Diploma Coordinator Andrew Jenkinson
MYP Coordinator Zachary Pascoe
Gender Coeducational
Languages English
Boarding/day Day
PMB 5000, PO Box 8309, Cruz Bay 00831,
Virgin Islands
TELEPHONE: +1 284 494 5262
FAX: +1 284 495 9695
EMAIL: cedaradmin@cedarschoolbvi.com
WEBSITE: www.cedarschoolbvi.com

APPENDICES

1. Addresses of all IB Offices
2. IB Associations Around the World
3. University Acknowledgment
4. University Scholarships for IB Diploma Holders
5. Diploma Programme Subjects Offered in 2008
6. Country Representation

1. Addresses of all IB Offices

IB HEADQUARTERS

International Baccalaureate
Route des Morillons 15
Grand-Saconnex, Genève
CH-1218
SWITZERLAND
Phone: +41 22 791 7740
Fax: +41 22 791 0277
Email: ibhq@ibo.org

CURRICULUM AND ASSESSMENT CENTRE

International Baccalaureate
Peterson House, Malthouse Avenue
Cardiff Gate
Cardiff, Wales
CF23 8GL
UNITED KINGDOM
Phone: +44 29 2054 7777
Fax: +44 29 2054 7778
Email:ibca@ibo.org

IB RESEARCH TEAM

Department of Education
University of Bath
Claverton Down, Bath
England
BA2 7AY
UNITED KINGDOM
Phone: +44 1225 383279
Fax: +44 1225 383277
Email:ibru@ibo.org

REGIONAL OFFICES

Africa/Europe/Middle East

Andrew Bollington
Regional director

IB Africa/Europe/Middle East
Route des Morillons 15
Grand-Saconnex, Genève
CH-1218
SWITZERLAND
Phone: +41 22 791 7740
Fax: +41 22 791 0277
Email:ibaem@ibo.org

Latin America

Marta Federico de Rodger
Regional director

IB Latin America
San Vladimiro 3056 – 2do.piso
San Isidro – B1642GMB
Provincia de Buenos Aires
ARGENTINA
Phone: +54 114 766 3900
Fax: +54 114 766 3900
Email:ibla@ibo.org

North America and the Caribbean

Drew Deutsch
Regional director

IB North America
475 Riverside Drive, 16th Floor
New York
NY 10115
USA
Phone: +1 212 696 4464
Fax: +1 212 889 9242
Email:ibna@ibo.org

Vancouver

Bob Poole
Head of Vancouver office and recognition services

1661 West 2nd Avenue, Suite 202
Vancouver
BC, V6J 1H3
CANADA
Phone: +1 604 733 8980
Fax: +1 604 733 8970
Email: vancouver@ibo.org

Asia-Pacific

Judith Guy
Regional director

IB Asia-Pacific
15 Hoe Chiang Road
11-04/06 Tower Fifteen
Singapore
089316
REPUBLIC OF SINGAPORE
Phone: +65 6 776 0249
Fax: +65 6 776 4369
Email: ibap@ibo.org

Australasia

Greg Valentine
Regional representative

6/481 - 483 Parramatta Road
Leichhardt
Sydney
NSW 2040
AUSTRALIA
Phone: +61 2 9564 2722
Fax: +61 2 9564 2733
Email: ibapaus@ibo.org

China and Mongolia

Wang Hong
Regional representative

Beijing World Youth Academy
#40 Liang Ma Qiao Road, Chaoyang District
Beijing
100016
PR CHINA
Phone: +86 10 6465 4176
Fax: +86 10 6461 7717
Email: china@ibo.org

Japan

Kyoko Bernard
Regional representative

Tamagawa University Research Institute
6-1-1 Tamagawa Gakuen
Machida, Tokyo
194-8610
JAPAN
Phone: +81 42 739 8450
Fax: +81 42 739 8929
Email: japan@ibo.org

South Asia

Farzana Dohadwalla
Regional representative

Al Madrasa
Taheri Manzil, ground floor
Nesbit Road, Mazagaon
Mumbai
400010
INDIA
Phone: +91 22 2374 6007
Fax: +91 22 2374 6007
Email: sasia@ibo.org

2. IB Associations Around the World

There are formal and/or informal associations for IB schools in the following countries. The associations in countries which are marked with an asterisk (*) also include the membership of non-IB schools:

CIS (Commonwealth of Independent States)
Germany *
Kenya
Middle East
Nordic countries (all); each Nordic country
Poland

Switzerland *
South Africa
Spain
The Netherlands *
Turkey
UK

Asia-Pacific regional associations

Association of Schools in Japan and Korea (AIBSIKJK)	East Asia	Gwyn Underwood Chair Email: gunderwood@senri.ed.jp
Association of IB Schools in Japan and Korea (AIBSIJK)	East Asia	Peter Heimer Co-Chair Email: gunderwood@senri.ed.jp
Association of Australasian IB Schools (AAIBS)	Australasia	Chris Rebbeck Chair of Standing Committee Email: srebchr@bhs.sa.edu.au
Association of Australasian IB Schools (AAIBS)	Australasia	Jeff Burn Treasurer of Standing Committee Email: jburn@shc.melb.catholic.edu.au
Association of Australasian IB Schools (AAIBS)	Australasia	Briony Morath Secretary of Standing Committee Email: bmorath@mlc.nsw.edu.au
IB Schools of China and Mongolia (IBSCM)	China/Mongolia	To be confirmed, for enquiries contact: Wang Hong, IB Asia Pacific Regional Reprentative, China & Mongolia Email: china@ibo.org
Philippines Association	South-East Asia	Kristi Pozon Email: kpozon@brent.edu.ph
Singapore Informal Association	Singapore	Julian Whiteley Head – UWCSEA Email: head@uwcsea.edu.sg
South Asia IB Schools Association (SAIBSA)	South Asia	Anurag Sangal HOD Chinmaya Residential School Email: principal@cirschool.org

Regional Networks (non-official status)	Region	Contact
East Asia MYP Network (Japan and Korea)	East Asia	Gwyn Underwood Chair Email: gunderwood@senri.ed.jp
East Asia PYP Network Group (Japan and Korea)	East Asia	Terance Tiplady PYP coordinator, K International School, Tokyo Email: pyp_co@kist.ed.jp
Hong Kong Network	China	Scott Jackson Principal Kingston International School Email: scott.jackson@kingston.edu.hk
IBAP LIS (Libary & Information Specialists)	Asia Pacific	Jane Viner Chair Email: vinermj@mlc.vic.edu.au
IBAP LIS (Libary & Information Specialists)	Asia Pacific	Yvonne Bartlett Secretary
IBSAT NETWORK (IB South Australia Teacher-librarians Network)	Australia	Email: vinermj@mic.vic.edu.au
Indonesia DP Hub – DP	South-East Asia	Richard Henry Acting Head, Sekolah Global Jaya, Indonesia Email: richard@globaljaya.com
Indonesia Network – Dunia PYP	South-East Asia	Andrew Bradtke Coordinator Email: bradtke.andrew@sph.ac.id
Indonesia Network – Dunia PYP	South-East Asia	Midah Secretary Email: sidneymd75@yahoo.com
NSW/ACT Principals	Australasia	Christopher Daunt Watney Email: cdaunt@redlands.nsw.edu.au
NSW/ACT Coordinators	Australasia	Antony Mayrhofer Diploma Coordinator St Paul's Grammar School, Penrith Email: amayrhofer@stpauls.nsw.edu.au

Regional Networks (non-official status)	Region	Contact
Queensland PYP Network	Australasia	Meryl Siggs Email: meryl.siggs@tlc.qld.edu.au
Singapore Network	South-East Asia	Alison Osborne Email: aosborne@cis.edu.sg
SA Principals of IB Schools – SASSIPA	Australasia	Panayoula Parha Chair Email: panayoula.parha@nmhs.sa.edu.au
South Australian DP Coordinators	Australasia	Chris Taylor Diploma coordinator, St Peter's College Email: ctaylor@stpeters.sa.edu.au
South Australian MYP	Australasia	Chris Rebbeck Email: srebchr@bhs.sa.edu.au
South Australian Network	Australasia	Linda Douglas Email: douglas@annesley.sa.edu.au
Thailand DP Network	South-East Asia	Mike Smith Diploma coordinator Bangkok Patana School, Thailand Email: ibcoordinator@patana.ac.th
Victorian PYP Support Network	Australasia	Colleen Moore PYP coordinator, South Auburn Primary School, Melbourne Email: moore.colleen.a@edumail.vic.gov.au
Victorian DP Coordinators	Australasia	David Hamer Diploma coordinator Carey Baptist, Melbourne Email: david.hamer@carey.vic.edu.au
Victorian Principals	Australasia	Sylvia Walton Email: swalton@tintern.vic.edu.au

IB Latin America Associations

Name	Country	Contact
Asociación Mexicana de Colegios Autorizados por la Organización del Bachillerato Internacional (AMEXCAOBI)	México	Lourdes Córdoba de Aburto President Email: laburto@avantel.net
Asociación ecuatoriana de cordinadores de colegios B.I. (ASECCBI)	Ecuador	Gustavo Ramos President Email: katbelo@punto.net.ec
Asociacion de Colegios del Bachillerato Internacional del Rio de la Plata (ACBIRP)	Argentina	Mabel Maria Mazzini de Manzitti President Email: mabelmarymanzitti@ciudad.com.ar
Asociación Andina de Colegios de Bachillerato Internacional (AACBI)	Colombia	Maureen Fleming de Pérez President Email: headofib@englishschool.edu.co
Asociación chilena del Bachillerato Internacional (ACHBI)	Chile	Peter Lacey President Email: headmaster@craighouse.cl

IB NORTH AMERICA AND THE CARIBBEAN
SUB-REGIONAL GROUP CONTACT INFORMATION

Please see the sub-regional associations website (www.ibo.org/ibna/subregions/) for more detailed contact information.

Group Name	Areas Represented	Contact
Guild of IB Schools of the Northeast	New York, New Jersey, Rhode Island, Massachusetts, Connecticut, East Pennsylvania, Maine, New Hampshire, Vermont	Anthony Foster Email: afoster@dwight.edu Tel: +1 212 724 7235 Web: www.commack.k12.ny.us/chs/gibs/
Mid Atlantic Regional Coalition of IB Schools	Virginia, Delaware, Maryland, Washington DC, West Virginia	Linda Hutchinson Email: lhutchin@sbo.hampton.k12.va.us Tel: +1 757 727 2119 Web: www.ibmidatlantic.org
IB Schools of North Carolina	North Carolina	Ron Owens Email: rowens@lenoir.k12.nc.us Tel: +1 252 527 8067 ext 419 or 251
South Carolina IB Schools	South Carolina	Carol Ann Blackmon Email: cblackmo@greenville.k12.sc.us Tel: +1 864 236 1017
IB Georgia	Georgia, Mississippi (interim)	Nancy Tuomi Email: nancy_h_tuomi@fc.dekalb.k12.ga.us Tel: +1 678 676 0213
Florida League of IB Schools	Florida, Louisiana	Vicki Murphy Email: vickimurphy907@yahoo.com Tel: +1 386 322 6272 Web: www.flibs.org
Ohio League of IB Schools	Ohio, West Pennsylvania	Cynthia Ballheim Email: ballheimcj@aol.com Tel: +1 614 487 5240 ext 136
Great Lakes IB Schools	Wisconsin, Indiana, Kentucky, Illinois	Mary Enda Tookey Email: tokkeyme@yahoo.com Tel: +1 773 534 8149
IB Minnesota	Minnesota	Ann Swanson Email: ann.swanson@minnetonka.k12.mn.us Tel: +1 952 401 5897

Group Name	Areas Represented	Contact
Midwest IB Schools	Nebraska, Kansas, Oklahoma, Missouri, Iowa	Jane Reed Email: jreed@nkcsd.k12.mo.us Tel: +1 816 413 6030 Web: www.midwestib.org
Texas IB Schools	Texas	Jeanette Lafevers Email: jeanete.lafevers@mcallenisd.net Tel: +1 956 632 2825 Web: www.texasibschools.org
IB Association of Rocky Mountain Schools	Wyoming, Colorado, New Mexico	Dorsee Johnson-Tucker Email: djohnson@jeffco.k12.co.us Tel: +1 303 982 7102 Web: www.ibarms.org
Arizona League of IB Schools	Arizona	Cathy Flesner Email: cflesner@pvschools.net Tel: +1 480 419 4511
California IB Organization	California, Nevada, Hawaii	Diana Cinatl Email: diana.cinatl@dsusd.us Tel: +1 760 345 3689 Web: www.c-ibo.org
Northwest IB Association	Washington, Oregon, Montana, Idaho, Alaska	Chuck Chamberlain Email: chamberlain_chuck@salkeiz.k12.or.us Tel: +1 503 399 3252 Web: www.northwestib.org
Arkansas League of IB Schools	Arkansas	Paula Redding Email: reddingp@hssd.net Tel: +1 501 624 5286 Web: http://ib.hssd.net/ALIBS.htm
IB Schools of Utah	Utah	Connie Jeanne Larsen Email: conniejeanne.larsen@slc.k12.ut.us Tel: +1 801 578 8500
Tennessee IB Association	Tennessee	Mary Catherine Bradshaw Email: marycatbrad@yahoo.com Tel: +1 615 298 8400
Alberta IB	Alberta	Diane Fischer Email: diane.fischer@epsb.ca Tel: +1 780 413 2700

Group Name	Areas Represented	Contact
Supporters of IB Schools of Michigan	Michigan	Ric Perry Email: rperry@portageps.org Tel: +1 269 323 5161
IB Schools of Alabama	Alabama	Sherel Perry Email: sperry@auburnschools.org Tel: +1 334 887 4983
Atlantic Canada IB Organization	Newfoundland, New Brunswick, Nova Scotia, Prince Edward Island, Bermuda	Laura Brock Email: lbrock@hgs.ns.ca Tel: +1 902 422 6497
Société des établissements du Baccalauréat Internationale-au Québec	Québec	Louis Bouchard Email: louisbourchard@sebiq.ca Tel: +1 450 679 6618 Web: www.sebiq.ca
IB Schools of Ontario	Ontario	Lee Roe-Etter Email: minibear@sympatico.ca Tel: +1 905 453 9220 Web: www.ibso.ca
IB Prairie Organization	Manitoba, Saskatchewan	Sharad Srivastava Email: ssrivastava@sjsd.net Tel: +1 204 888 0684 Web: www.westwood.sjsd.net/IBPO
IB British Columbia Society	British Columbia	Lynn Gibson Email: lgibson@sd35.bc.ca Tel: +1 604 888 3033 Web: www.ibbc.ca

3: University Acknowledgment

The IB diploma is a passport to higher education. Universities around the world welcome the unique characteristics of IB Diploma Programme students and recognize the way in which the programme helps to prepare students for university level education.

IB students routinely gain admission to some of the best known universities in the world. Most of these institutions have established recognition policies for the IB diploma.

The IB encourages governments to define a policy that details how IB diploma credentials are treated for admission, credit and placement at universities and colleges.

The following list contains the names of the universities that according to IB records have a stated IB recognition policy. This list is not necessarily complete as other universities may recognize the IB diploma but have not alerted the IB to their recognition policy.

IB AFRICA, EUROPE & MIDDLE EAST

AUSTRIA
Johannes-Kepler-Universität Linz
Karl-Franzens Universität Graz
Leopold-Franzens-Universität Innsbruck
Technische Universität Graz
Universität Wien (University of Vienna)

BELGIUM
Facultés Universitaires Saint-Louis
Universiteit Antwerpen
Université Libre de Bruxelles
Université de Liège
Universteit Antwerpen – RUCA
Vesalius College v.z.w.

BOSNIA/HERZEG
University of Sarajevo

CZECH REPUBLIC
University of Economics, Prague
University of Ostrava
University of South Bohemia
Univerzita Karlova

DENMARK
Aalborg University
Copenhagen Business School
Lyngby Uddannelsescenter/Lyngby Business Academy
Odense University
Roskilde University
The Royal Danish School of Pharmacy
The Technical University of Denmark
The University of Copenhagen

EGYPT
The American University in Cairo

FINLAND
Åbo Akademi
Helsinki School of Economics and Business Administration
Helsinki University of Technology
Swedish School of Economics and Business Administration
Tampere University of Technology
University of Helsinki (Helsingin Yliopisto)
University of Jyväskylä
University of Kuopio
University of Oulu
University of Tampere
University of Turku
University of Vaasa

FRANCE
Université de Bretagne Occidentale
Université de Franche-Comté
Université de Paris VII
Université de Paris X Nanterre
Université Joseph Fourier Grenoble I
Université Panthéon-Assas Paris II
Université Pierre Mendes France Grenoble II

GERMANY
Albert-Ludwigs-Universität Freiburg
Ausländerstudienkolleg (ASK) Konstanz
Bayerische Julius-Maximilians-Universität Würzburg
Christian-Albrechts-Universität zu Kiel
Eberhard-Karls-Universität Tübingen
Humboldt-Universität zu Berlin
Jacobs University Bremen GmBH
Johann Wolfgang Goethe-Universität Frankfurt
Ruprecht-Karls-Universität Heidelberg

Technische Universität Berlin
Technische Universität Hamburg-Harburg
Technische Universität München
Universität Hamburg

GHANA
University of Science and Technology

GREECE
University of Patras

HUNGARY
Janus Pannonius University
Pecs University Medical School
Semmelweis University of Medicine
University Medical School of Debrecen

ICELAND
University of Iceland/Haskoli Islands

IRELAND
National University of Ireland (NUI), Maynooth
Royal College of Surgeons in Ireland
University College Cork
University College Dublin
University of Dublin – Trinity College

ISRAEL
Hebrew University of Jerusalem
Technion – Israel Institute of Technology

ITALY
Bocconi University
Libero Instituto Universitario Carlo Cattaneo
Università Commerciale Luigi Bocconi
Universitá degli Studi Firenze

JORDAN
Ministry of Education
The University of Jordan

KENYA
University of Nairobi

LEBANON
American University College of Science and Technology
American University of Beirut
University of Balamand

LESOTHO
National University of Lesotho

LITHUANIA
Vilnius University

MALTA
University of Malta

NETHERLANDS
Delft University of Technology
Erasmus University Rotterdam
Leiden University
Open University of the Netherlands
University of Amsterdam
University of Nijmegen
Utrecht University
Wageningen Agricultural University

NORWAY
Norwegian School of Management
The Norwegian University of Science and Technology
        (NTNU)
University of Bergen
University of Oslo
University of Stavanger
University of Tromsö

POLAND
Kasimir Pulaski Technical University of Radom
Medical University of Gdansk
Poznan University of Technology
Technical University of Lodz
Technical University of Lublin
The Catholic University of Lublin
University of Gdansk
University of Lodz
Wroclaw University

PORTUGAL
Escola Superior de Design (IADE)
Instituto Superior Técnico (IST)
Universidade Católica Portuguesa

RUSSIAN FEDERATION
Lomonosov Moscow State University
Plekhanov Russian Academy of Economics

SLOVENIA
University of Ljubljana

SOUTH AFRICA
Rhodes University
University of Cape Town
University of Natal
University of Port Elizabeth
University of South Africa (UNISA)
University of Witwatersrand

SPAIN
St Louis University

SWAZILAND
University of Swaziland

SWEDEN
Beckmans Designhögskola
Blekinge Tekniska Högskola
Chalmers University of Technology
Göteborg University
Handelshögskolan i Stockholm
Karlstad University
Karolinska Institute
Linköpings universitet
Lund University
Mitthogskolan
The Royal Institute of Technology
Umeå University
University of Stockholm
Uppsala University
Växjö Universitet

SWITZERLAND
Ecole polytechnique fédérale de Lausanne
Eidgenössische Technische Hochschule Zürich (ETH Zürich)
Hochschule für Gestaltung & Kunst Luzern
International University in Geneva (IUG)
Universität Basel
Universität Bern
Universität Zürich
Université de Fribourg
Université de Genève
Université de Lausanne
Université de Neuchâtel
University IFM
Universitat Luzern
Webster University

TURKEY
Marmara University
Yeditepe University

UAE
American University of Sharjah
Dubai Aerospace Enterprise University

UK
Aston University
Bournemouth University
Brunel University
Cardiff University
Colchester Institute
Courtauld Institute of Art
Coventry University
De Montfort University
Heriot-Watt University
Imperial College London
Keele University

Kent Institute of Art and Design
Kingston University
Lancaster University
Liverpool Hope University
Liverpool John Moores University
London Metropolitan University
London School of Economics and Political Science
Loughborough University
Manchester Metropolitan University
Middlesex University
Napier University
Oxford Brookes University
Oxford University
Queen's University
Richmond, The American International University
       in London
Robert Gordon University
Royal Free Hospital School of Medicine
Royal Holloway
School of Oriental and African Studies
School of Pharmacy
St George's, (University of London)
St. Bartholomew's & Royal London School
       of Medicine & Dentistry
Staffordshire University
Suffolk College
Swansea Institute of Higher Education
The Nottingham Trent University
The Queen's University of Belfast
The Royal Veterinary College
The University of Aberdeen
The University of Cambridge
The University of Edinburgh
The University of Leeds
The University of Manchester
The University of Reading
University College Chichester
University College London
University of Bath
University of Bedfordshire
University of Birmingham
University of Bradford
University of Brighton
University of Bristol
University of Buckingham
University of Buckingham, Faculty of International Studies
University of Central Lancashire
University of Derby
University of Dundee
University of Durham
University of East Anglia (UEA)
University of East London
University of Essex
University of Exeter
University of Glamorgan
University of Glasgow

University of Greenwich
University of Hull
University of Kent
University of Leicester
University of Liverpool
University of Newcastle
University of Salford
University of Sheffield
University of Southampton
University of St Andrews
University of Stirling
University of Strathclyde
University of Surrey
University of Sussex
University of Testing
University of Ulster
University of Wales College, Newport
University of Wales Institute, Cardiff (UWIC)
University of Wales Swansea
University of Wales, Aberystwyth
University of Wales, Bangor
University of Wales, Lampeter
University of Warwick
University of Wolverhampton
University of York
University of the West of England, Bristol
Warrington Collegiate Institute
West Herts College

IB ASIA PACIFIC

AUSTRALIA
Australian Catholic University
Australian Defence Force Academy
Australia National University
Bond University
Central Queensland University
Charles Darwin University
Curtin University of Technology
Deakin University
Edith Cowan University
Flinders University
Griffith University
International College of Hotel Management
James Cook University
La Trobe University
Macquarie University
Melbourne Institute of Business and Technology
Monash University
Murdoch University
Queensland University of Technology
Raffles College of Design and Commerce
Southern Cross University
University of Melbourne
University of Newcastle
University of New England

University of New South Wales
University of Notre Dame Australia (Sydney)
University of Queensland
University of South Australia
University of Southern Queensland
University of Sydney
University of Tasmania
University of Technology – Sydney
University of the Sunshine Coast
University of Western Australia
University of Western Sydney
University of Wollongong

FIJI
University of the South Pacific

HONG KONG-SAROC
Hong Kong Baptist College
Lingnan University
The Chinese University of Hong Kong
The City University of Hong Kong
The Hong Kong Polytechnic University
The Hong Kong University of Science and Technology

INDONESIA
Gandhi Institute of Business and Technology
Universitas Pelita Harapan

JAPAN
Aichi Gakuin Daigaku (Aichi Gakuin University)
Aichi Gakusen Daigaku (Aichi Gakusen University)
Aichi Kenritsu Kango Daigaku
(Aichi Prefectural College of Nursing & Health)
Aichi Kyoiku Daigaku (Aichi University of Education)
Ajia Daigaku (Asia University)
Aomori Koritsu Daigaku (Aomori Public College)
Aoyama Gakui Gakuin Daigaku
(Aoyama Gakuin University)
Asahi Daigaku (Asahi University)
Asahikawa Daigaku (Asahikawa University)
Asahikawa Ika Daigaku (Asahikawa Medical College)
Atomi Gakuen Joshi Daigaku (Atomi College)
Azabu Daigaku (Azabu University)
Baika Joshi Daigaku (Baika Women's College)
Baiko Jo Gakuin Daigaku (Baiko Jo Gakuin University)
Beppu Daigaku (Beppu University)
Bukkyo Daigaku (Bukkyo University)
Bunkyo Daigaku (Bunkyo University)
Chiba Daigaku (Chiba University)
Chiba Keizai Daigaku (Chiba Keizai University)
Chubu Daigaku (Chubu University)
Chuo Daigaku (Chuo University)
Chuo Gakuin Daigaku (Chuogakuin University)
Daito Bunka Daigaku (Daito Bunka University)
Denki Tsushin Daigaku
(The University of Electro-Communications)

Dokkyo Daigaku (Dokkyo University)
Ehime Daigaku (Ehime University)
Ferisu Joshigakuin Daigaku (Ferris University)
Fukui Daigaku (Fukui University)
Fukui Kenritsu Daigaku (Fukui Prefectural University)
Fukuoka Daigaku (Fukuoka University)
Fukuoka Joshi Daigaku (Fukuoka Women's University)
Fukuoka Kenritsu Daigaku (Fukuoka Prefectural University)
Fukushima Kenritsu Ika Daigaku
      (Fukushiama Medical College)
Gakushuin Daigaku (Gakushuin University)
Gifu Keizai Daigaku (Gifu Keizai University)
Gufu Daigaku (Gifu University)
Gunma Daigaku (Gunma University)
Hakuo Daigaku (Hakuoh University)
Hamamatsu Ika Daigaku
      (Hamamatsu University School of Medicine)
Hannan Daigaku (Hannan University)
Heisei Kokusai Daigaku (Heisei International University)
Hijiyama Daigaku (Hijiyama University)
Himeji Dokkyo Daigaku (Himeji Dokkyo University)
Himeji Kogyo Daigaku (Himeji Institute of Technology)
Hirosaki Gakuin Daigaku (Hirosaki Gakuin College)
Hiroshima Daigaku (Hiroshima University)
Hiroshima Jogakuin Daigaku
      (Hiroshima Jogakuin University)
Hiroshima Joshi Daigaku (Hiroshima Women's University)
Hiroshima Kenritsu Daigaku
      (Hiroshima Prefectural University)
Hiroshima Kogyo Daigaku
      (Hiroshima Institute of Technology)
Hitotsubashi Daigaku (Hitotsubashi University)
Hokkaido Daigaku (Hokkaido University)
Hokkaido Joho Daigaku (Hokkaido Information University)
Hokkaido Kyoiku Daigaku
      (Hokkaido University of Education)
Hokkaido Tokai Daigaku (Hokkaido Tokai University)
Hokkaigakuen Daigaku (Hokkai-Gakuen University)
Hokusei Gakuen Daigaku (Hokusei Gakuen University)
Hosei Daigaku (Hosei University)
Hyogo Kenritsu Kango Daigaku
      (College of Nursing Art and Science)
Hyogo Kyoiku Daigaku
      (Hyogo University of Teacher Education)
Ibaraki Kirisutokyo Daigaku (Ibaraki Christian College)
Jissen Joshi Daigaku (Jissen Women's University)
Jochi Daigaku Ichigaya Kyampasu
Jochi Daigaku Yotsuya Kyampasu
Josai Daigaku (Josai University)
Josai Kokusai Daigaku (Josai International University)
Joshi Bijutsu Daigaku (Women's College of Fine Arts)
Kagawa Daigaku (Kagawa University)
Kagoshima Daigaku (Kagoshima University)
Kagoshima Joshi Daigaku (Kagoshima Women's College)
Kanagawa Daigaku (Kanagawa University)
Kanazawa Daigaku (Kanazawa University)

Kanoya Taiiku Daigaku
      (National Institute of Fitness and Sport)
Kansai Daigaku (Kansai University)
Kansai Gaikokugo Daigaku (Kansai Gaidai University)
Kanto Gakuin Daigaku (Kanto Gakuin University)
Kassui Joshi Daigaku (Kassui Women's University)
Kawamura Gakuen Joshi Daigaku
      (Kawamura Gakuen Woman's University)
Keiai Daigaku (Keiai University)
Keio Gijuku Daigaku (Keio University)
Keio Gijuku Daigaku Shonan Fujisawa Kyampasu
Keisen Jogakuen Daigaku (Keisen Jogakuen College)
Keiwa Gakuen Daigaku (Keiwa College)
Kinjo Gakuin Daigaku (Kinjo Gakuin University)
Kinki Daigaku (Kinki University)
Kitami Kogyo Daigaku (Kitami Institute of Technology)
Kitasato Daigaku (Kitasato University)
Kobe Daigaku (Kobe University)
Kobe Gakuin Daigaku (Kobe Gakuin University)
Kobe Geijutsu Koka Daigaku (Kobe Design University)
Kobe Jogakuin Daigaku (Kobe College)
Kobe Kokusai Daigaku (Kobe International University)
Kobe Shoka Daigaku (Kobe University of Commerce)
Kobe Shosen Daigaku
      (Kobe University of Mercantile Marine)
Kobeshi Gaikokugo Daigaku
      (Kobe City University of Foreign Studies)
Kochi Daigaku (Kochi University)
Kokugakuin Daigaku (Kokugakuin University)
Kokushikan Daigaku (Kokushikan University)
Komazawa Daigaku (Komazawa University)
Konan Daigaku (Konan University)
Koshien Daigaku (Koshien University)
Kumamoto Daigaku (Kumamoto University)
Kumamoto Kenritsu Daigaku
      (Prefectural University of Kumamoto)
Kwansei Gakuin University
Kyorin Daigaku (Kyorin University)
Kyoritsu Joshi Daigaku (Kyoritsu Women's University)
Kyoto Daigaku (Kyoto University)
Kyoto Gaikokugo Daigaku
      (Kyoto University of Foreign Studies)
Kyoto Gakuen Daigaku (Kyoto Gakuen University)
Kyoto Kogei Sen'i Daigaku (Kyoto Institute of Technology)
Kyoto Seika Daigaku (Kyoto Seika University)
Kyoto Tachibana Joshi Daigaku
      (Kyoto Tachibana Women's University)
Kyushu Daigaku (Kyushu University)
Kyushu Geijutsu Koka Daigaku
      (Kyushu Instutute of Design)
Kyushu Kogyo Daigaku (Kyushu Institute of Technology)
Kyushu Sangyo Daigaku (Kyushu Sangyo University)
Kyushu Tokai Daigaku (Kyushu Tokai University)
Matsuyama Shinonome Joshi Daigaku
      (Matsuyama Shinonome College)
Meiji Daigaku (Meiji University)

Meiji Gakuin Daigaku (Meiji Gakuin University)
Meijo Daigaku (Meijo University)
Meikai Daigaku (Meikai University)
Mejiro Daigaku (Mejiro University)
Mie Daigaku (Mie University)
Miyazaki Daigaku (Miyazaki University)
Miyazaki Koritsu Daigaku (Miyazaki Municipal University)
Momoyama Gakuin Daigaku (St. Andrew's University)
Morioka Daigaku (Morioka College)
Muroran Kogyo Daigaku (Muroran Institute of Technology)
Musashi Daigaku (Musashi University)
Musashi Kogyo Daigaku (Musashi Institute of Technology)
Nagaoka Gijutsu Kagaku Daigaku
    (Nagaoka University of Technology)
Nagasaki Daigaku (Nagasaki University)
Nagoya Daigaku (Nagoya University)
Nagoya Gakuin Daigaku (Nagoya Gakuin University)
Nagoya Shiritsu Daigaku (Nagoya City University)
Nakamura Gakuen Daigaku
    (Nakamura Gakuen University)
Nanzan Daigaku (Nanzan University)
Nara Joshi Daigaku (Nara Women's University)
Nara Sangyo Daigaku (Nara Sangyo University)
Naruto Kyoiku Daigaku (Naruto University of Education)
Nihon Daigaku (Nihon University)
Nihon Fukushi Daigaku (Nihon Fukushi University)
Niigata Daigaku (Niigata University)
Niigata Sangyo Daigaku (Niigata Institute of Technology)
Nippon Bunri Daigaku (Nippon Bunri University)
Nishinippon Kogyo Daigaku
    (Nishinippon Instutute of Technology)
Notorudamu Seishin Joshi Daigaku
    (Notre Dame Seishin University)
Obihiro Chikusan Daigaku
    (Obihiro University of Agriculture)
Obirin Daigaku (Obirin University)
Oita Daigaku (Oita University)
Okayama Daigaku (Okayama University)
Okayama Kenritsu Daigaku
    (Okayama Prefectural University)
Okinawa Kokusai Daigaku
    (Okinawa International University)
Osaka Daigaku (Osaka University)
Osaka Denki Tsushin Daigaku (Osaka Electro-
    Communication University)
Osaka Furitsu Daigaku (Osaka Prefecture University)
Osaka Gaikokugo Daigaku
    (Osaka University of Foreign Studies)
Osaka Joshi Daigaku (Osaka Women's University)
Osaka Kogyo Daigaku (Osaka Institute of Technology)
Osaka Kokusai Daigaku (Osaka International University)
Otaru Shoka Daigaku (Otaru University of Commerce)
Otemon Gakuin Daigaku (Otemon Gakuin University)
Otsuma Joshi Daigaku (Otsuma Women's University)
Ou Daigaku (Ohu University)
Puru Gakuin Daigaku (Pool Gakuin University)

Reitaku Daigaku (Reitaku University)
Rikkyo Daigaku (Rikkyo University)
Rissho Daigaku (Rissho University)
Ritsumeikan Daigaku (Ritsumeikan University)
Ruteru Gakuin Daigaku (Japan Lutheran College)
Ryukyu Daigaku (University of the Ryukyus)
Ryutsu Kagaku Daigaku
Saga Daigaku (Saga University)
Saga Ika Daigaku (Saga Medical School)
Saitama University
Sanno Daigaku (Sanno College, Isehara)
Sapporo Daigaku (Sapporo University)
Sapporo Kokusai Daigaku (Sapporo Kokusai University)
Seigakuin Daigaku (Seigakuin University)
Seikei Daigaku (Seikei University)
Seinan Gakuin Daigaku (Seinan Gakuin University)
Seisen Joshi Daigaku (Seisen University)
Seishin Joshi Daigaku (University of the Sacred Heart)
Seitoku Daigaku (Seitoku University)
Senshu Daigaku (Senshu University)
Setsunan Daigaku (Setsunan University)
Shibaura Kogyo Daigaku (Shibaura Institute of Technology)
Shiga Daigaku (Shiga University)
Shiga Kenritsu Daigaku (The University of Shiga Prefecture)
Shikoku Daigaku (Shikoku University)
Shimane Daigaku (Shimane University)
Shimonoseki Shiritsu Daigaku
    (Shimonoseki City University)
Shinshu Daigaku (Shinshu University)
Shitennoji Kokusai Bukkyo Daigaku
    (International Buddhist University)
Shizukoka Kenritsu Daigaku (University of Shizuoka)
Shizuoka Daigaku (Shizuoka University)
Shotoku Gakuen Gifu Kyoiku Daigaku
Shujitsu Joshi Daigaku (Shujitsu Women's University)
Shukutoku Daigaku (Shukutoku University)
Soai Daigaku (Soai University)
Soka Daigaku (Soka University)
Sugiyama Jogakuen Daigaku
    (Sugiyama Jogakuen University)
Surugadai Daigaku (Surugadai University)
Suzuka Kokusai Daigaku (Suzuka International University)
Takachiho Shoka Daigaku (Takachiho University)
Takasaki Keizai Daigaku
    (Takasaki City University of Economics)
Takushoku Daigaku (Takushoku University)
Tamagawa Daigaku (Tamagawa University)
Teikyo Daigaku (Teikyo University)
Tenri Daigaku (Tenri University)
Tezukayama Daigaku (Tezukayama University)
Tohoku Daigaku (Tohoku University)
Tohoku Gakuin Daigaku (Tohoku Gakuin University)
Tohoku Geijutsu Koka Daigaku
    (Tohoku University of Art and Design)
Tokai Daigaku (Tokai University)
Tokoha Gakuen Daigaku (Tokoha-Gakuen University)

Tokoha Gakuen Hamamatsu Daigaku
(Tokoha-Gakuen Hamamatsu University)
Tokushima Daigaku (The University of Tokushima)
Tokyo Daigaku (The University of Tokyo)
Tokyo Gaikokugo Daigaku
(Tokyo University of Foreign Studies)
Tokyo Gakugei Daigaku (Tokyo Gakugei University)
Tokyo Joshi Daigaku (Tokyo Woman's Christian University)
Tokyo Junshin Joshi Daigaku
(Tokyo Junshin Women's University)
Tokyo Kasei Daigaku (Tokyo Kasei University)
Tokyo Kasei Gakuin Daigaku
(Tokyo Kasei Gakuin University)
Tokyo Kasei Gakuin Tsukuba Joshi Daigaku
Tokyo Keizai Daigaku (Tokyo Keizai University)
Tokyo Kogei Daigaku (Tokyo Institute of Polytechnics)
Tokyo Kogyo Daigaku (Tokyo Institute of Technology)
Tokyo Kokusai Daigaku (Tokyo International University)
Tokyo Noko Daigaku
(Tokyo University of Agriculture and Technology)
Tokyo Seitoku Daigaku (Tokyo Seitoku University)
Tokyo Shosen Daigaku
(Tokyo University of Mercantile Marine)
Tokyo Suisan Daigaku (Tokyo University of Fisheries)
Tokyo Toritsu Daigaku (Tokyo Metropolitan University)
Tokyo University of Science (Tokyo Rika Daigaku)
Tottori Daigaku (Tottori University)
Toyama Daigaku (Toyama University)
Toyama Ika Yakka Daigaku (Toyama Medical and
Pharmaceutical University)
Toyo Daigaku (Toyo University)
Toyo Eiwa Jogakuin Daigaku
(Toyo Eiwa Women's University)
Toyohashi Gijutsu Kagaku Daigaku
(Toyohashi University of Technology)
Tsukuba Daigaku (University of Tsukuba)
Tsukuba Kokusai Daigaku
(Tsukuba International University)
Ueno Gakuen Daigaku (Ueno Gakuen University)
Utsunomiya Daigaku (Utsunomiya University)
Wakayama Daigaku (Wakayama University)
Wako Daigaku (Wako University)
Waseda Daigaku (Waseda University)
Yamaguchi Daigaku (Yamaguchi University)
Yamanashi Daigaku (Yamanashi University)
Yamanashi Ika Daigaku (Yamanashi Medical University)
Yokkaichi Daigaku (Yokkaichi University)
Yokohama Kokuritsu Daigaku
(Yokohama National University)
Yokohama Shiritsu Daigaku (Yokohama City University)

MALAYSIA
International Islamic University
International Medical University
Universiti Malaya
Universiti Tenaga Nasional

NEW ZEALAND
Auckland University of Technology
Lincoln University
Massey University
University of Auckland
University of Canterbury
University of Otago
University of Waikato
Victoria University of Wellington

PHILIPPINES
Assumption College
Ateneo de Manila University
De La Salle University
The University of the Philippines
University of Santo Tomas

SINGAPORE
Nanyang Technological University
National University of Singapore
Singapore Management University

SOUTH KOREA
Seoul National University
Yonsei University

IB LATIN AMERICA

ARGENTINA
Escuela Superior Técnica del Ejército Argentino
Instituto Tecnológico de Buenos Aires (ITBA)
Instituto Universitario CEMIC
International Buenos Aires Hotel & Restaurant School
(IBAHRS)
Lincoln University College
Ott College
Pontificia Universidad Católica Argentina
Universidad Argentina de la Empresa
Universidad Austral
Universidad Blas Pascal
Universidad Favaloro
Universidad Maimónide
Universidad Siglo 21
Universidad de Belgrano
Universidad de San Andrés
Universidad del Salvador
Universidad del Salvador – Campus Nuestra Señora del Pilar
Universidad del CEMA

BRAZIL
Pontificia Universidad Catolica do Paraná

CHILE
Pontificia Universidad Católica de Chile
Universidad Adolfo Ibañez

Universidad Andrés Bello
Universidad Católica de Valparaíso
Universidad Central de Chile
Universidad Finis Terrae
Universidad Gabriela Mistral
Universidad Internacional SEK-Chile
Universidad La República
Universidad Mayor
Universidad Metropolitana de Ciencias de la Educación
Universidad San Sebastián
Universidad de Artes, Ciencias Comunicación, UNIACC
Universidad de La Serena
Universidad de Viña del Mar
Universidad del Bío-Bío
Universidad del Desarrollo
Universidad de los Andes
Universidad del Pacífico
Universidad Técnica Federico Santa María

COLOMBIA
Colegio de Estudios Superiores de Administración
Escuela de Ingeniería de Antioquía
Instituto de Ciencias de la Salud
Politécnico Grancolombiano
Pontificia Universidad Javeriana
Universidad Antonio Nariño
Universidad EAFIT
Universidad Externado de Colombia
Universidad de Bogotá Jorge Tadeo Lozano
Universidad Pontificia Bolivariana
Universidad de la Sabana
Universidad de los Andes
Universidad del Rosario
Universidad del Norte de Barranquilla

COSTA RICA
Universidad Internacional de las Américas
Universidad de Costa Rica

ECUADOR
Blue Hill college
Pontificia Universidad Católica del Ecuador
Universidad Casa Grande
Universidad Internacional SEK Ecuador
Universidad San Francisco de Quito
Universidad de Especialidades Espíritu Santo (UEES)
Universidad de las Américas
Universidad del Pacífico – Escuela de Negocios
Universidad Santa María de Chile – Campus Guayaquil

EL SALVADOR
Universidad Albert Einstein
Universidad Dr José Matías Delgado
Universidad Tecnológica

GUATEMALA
Universidad Francisco Marroquín
Universidad Rafael Landívar
Universidad del Valle de Guatemala

MEXICO
Benemérita Universidad Autónoma de Puebla
Escuela Bancaria y Comercial, S.C.
Instituto Tecnológico y de Estudios Superiores de Monterrey
Universidad Autónoma de Baja California
Universidad Nacional Autónoma de México
Universidad de las Américas, Puebla
Universidad de Monterrey (UDEM)

NICARAGUA
Ave María College of the Americas
Universidad Americana (UAM)
Universidad Centroamericana de Nicaragua
Universidad Nacional Autónoma de Nicaragua, León

PANAMA
Florida State University – Panama Branch
Universidad Santa María la Antigua

PARAGUAY
Universidad Americana
Universidad Católica Nuestra Señora de la Asunción
Universidad Columbia del Paraguay
Universidad del Norte

PERU
Escuela Naval del Perú
Instituto Peruano de Publicidad
Pontificia Universidad Católica del Perú
Universidad Científica del Sur
Universidad Femenina del Sagrado Corazón (UNIFE)
Universidad Nacional Agraria La Molina
Universidad Nacional Federico Villarreal
Universidad Nacional de Ingeniería
Universidad Peruana Cayetano Heredia
Universidad Peruana de Ciencias Aplicadas
Universidad Privada del Norte
Universidad Ricardo Palma
Universidad San Ignacio de Loyola
Universidad de Lima
Universidad de Piura
Universidad de San Martín de Porres
Universidad del Pacífico

URUGUAY
Universidad Católica del Uruguay
Universidad ORT Uruguay
Universidad de la República

IB NORTH AMERICA & CARIBBEAN

BERMUDA
Bermuda College

CANADA
Acadia University
Alberta College of Art & Design
Algoma University College
Algonquin College
Ambrose University College
Art Institute of Vancouver (Burnaby), The
Association of Universities & Colleges of Canada
Athabasca University
Bethany Bible College
Bishop's University
Brandon University
Brescia College
Briercrest College and Seminary
British Columbia Institute of Technology
Brock University
Camosun College – Interurban Campus
Camosun College – Lansdowne Campus
Canadian Mennonite University
Canadian Merit Scholarship Foundation
Canadian University College
Canadore College
Cape Breton University
Capernwray Harbour Bible Centre
Capilano College
Carleton University
Centennial College
College of New Caledonia
Collège universitaire de Saint-Boniface
Columbia College – Vancouver
Concordia University – Montréal
Concordia University College of Alberta
Conestoga College
Covenant Bible College
Dalhousie University
Dalhousie University – Faculty of Medicine
Dawson College
DeVry Institute of Technology – Calgary
Department of Education (Newfoundland & Labrador)
Douglas College
École Polytechnique de Montréal
Emily Carr Institute of Art and Design
Faculte Saint-Jean of the University of Alberta
Fanshawe College
George Brown College
Georgian College
Glendon College
Glenn Gould Professional School
        (Royal Conservatory of Music)
Grande Prairie Regional College

Grant MacEwan College
HEC Montréal
Holland College
Humber College Institute
        of Technology & Advanced Learning
Huron University College
IB Vancouver (Lesley)
IB Vancouver (Sandra)
International Academy of Design and Technology
Keyano College
King's University College – Ontario
King's University College, The – Alberta
Klondike Institute of Art & Culture
Kwantlen University College – Surrey
Lakehead University
Lakeland College
Langara College
Laurentian University
Lethbridge College
Loyalist College
Malaspina University-College
Marianopolis College
Marine Institute of Memorial University of Newfoundland
McGill University
McGill University – Faculty of Engineering
McGill University – Faculty of Law
McGill University – Faculty of Medicine
McGill University – Faculty of Music
McGill University – School of Nutrition
McMaster University
Medicine Hat College
Memorial University of Newfoundland
Memorial University of Newfoundland – Faculty of Medicine
Montréal Neurological Institute & Hospital
Mount Allison University
Mount Royal College
Mount Saint Vincent University
National Theatre School of Canada
Nipawin Bible College
Nipissing University
Northern Alberta Institute of Technology
Nova Scotia Agricultural College
Nova Scotia College of Art and Design
Olds College
Ontario College Application Service (OCAS)
Ontario College of Art and Design
Peace River Bible Institute
Prairie Bible College
Providence College & Theological Seminary
Queen's University
Queen's University – School of Medicine
Quest University Canada
Red Deer College
Red River College
Redeemer University College
Richard Ivey School of Business

Rocky Mountain College – Calgary
Royal Military College of Canada
Ryerson University
SIAST Kelsey Campus
SIAST Wascana Campus
Saint Mary's University
Sauder School of Business at University of British Columbia
Selkirk College
Seneca College of Applied Arts and Technology
Sheridan Institute of Technology and Advanced Learning
Simon Fraser University
Southern Alberta Institute of Technology
St. Francis Xavier University
St. Jerome's University
St. Mary's College – Alberta
St. Paul University
St. Thomas University
Taylor University College & Seminary
Thompson Rivers University
Trent University
Trinity Western University
University College of the Fraser Valley
University of Alberta
University of Alberta – Augustana Campus
University of Alberta – Faculty of Medicine & Dentistry
University of British Columbia
University of British Columbia – Medicine
University of British Columbia – Okanagan
University of Calgary
University of Calgary – Faculty of Medicine
University of Guelph
University of Guelph – Humber
University of King's College
University of Lethbridge
University of Manitoba
University of Manitoba – Faculty of Medicine
University of New Brunswick – Fredericton
University of New Brunswick – St.John
University of Northern British Columbia
University of Ontario Institute of Technology
University of Ottawa
University of Ottawa – Faculty of Medicine
University of Prince Edward Island
University of Regina
University of Saskatchewan
University of Saskatchewan – College of Medicine
University of St. Michael's College
University of Toronto
University of Toronto – Faculty of Medicine
University of Victoria
University of West Ontario
   – Schulich School of Medicine/Dentistry
University of Waterloo
University of Western Ontario
University of Windsor
University of Winnipeg

Université Laval
Université Sainte-Anne
Université de Moncton
Université de Montréal
Université de Sherbrooke
Université du Québec a Montréal
Université du Québec à Hull
Université du Québec à Rimouski
Université du Québec à Trois-Rivières
Vancouver Community College – Broadway
Vancouver Community College – downtown
Vancouver Film School
Vanguard College
Victoria Conservatory of Music
West Island College – Class Afloat
Western Christian College
Western College of Veterinary Medicine
Wilfrid Laurier University
York University

CAYMAN ISLANDS
Ministry of Education – Grand Cayman

DOMINICAN REPUBLIC
Instituto Tecnológico de Santa Domingo

PUERTO RICO
Antillean Adventist University
Inter-American University of PR, School of Optometry

UNITED STATES
AMCAS – American Medical College Application Service
Abilene Christian University
Academy of Art University
Academy of Couture Art
Adams State College
Adelphi University
Agnes Scott College
Aims Community College – Greeley
Alabama Agricultural and Mechanical University
Alabama State University
Alaska Pacific University
Albany College of Pharmacy
Albion College
Albright College
Alcorn State University
Alderson-Broaddus College
Alfred University
All Saints University of Medicine, Aruba
Allegheny College
Allen County Community College
Alma College
Alpena Community College
Alverno College
Alvin Community College
Amarillo College

American Academy of Art
American Academy of Dramatic Arts
American InterContinental University – Illinois
American International College
American International University in London – Boston
American Musical & Dramatic Academy
American River College
American University
American University in Cairo – US Office
American University of Antigua College of Medicine
American University of Paris – US Office
Amherst College
Anderson University
Andrews University
Angelina College
Angelo State University
Anne Arundel Community College
Anoka-Ramsey Community College
Antelope Valley College
Antioch College
Appalachian Bible College
Appalachian State University
Arapahoe Community College
Arcadia University
Argosy University – Eagan
Arizona State University
Arizona Western College
Arkansas State University
Arkansas Tech University
Armstrong Atlantic State University
Art Academy of Cincinnati
Art Center College of Design
Art Institute of Atlanta, The
Art Institute of Boston, The
Art Institute of California – Los Angeles, The
Art Institute of California – Orange County
Art Institute of California – San Diego, The
Art Institute of California – San Francisco, The
Art Institute of Charlotte, The
Art Institute of Colorado, The
Art Institute of Dallas, The
Art Institute of Fort Lauderdale, The
Art Institute of Philadelphia, The
Art Institute of Phoenix
Art Institute of Pittsburgh, The
Art Institute of Portland, The
Art Institute of Seattle, The
Art Institute of Washington, The
Asbury College
Asheville-Buncombe Community College
Ashford University
Ashland University
Assumption College
Athens Technical College
Atlantic Union College
Auburn University

Augsburg College
Augusta State University
Augustana College – Illinois
Augustana College – South Dakota
Austin College
Austin Community College
Austin Peay State University
Ave Maria University
Averett University
Avila University
Azusa Pacific University
Babson College
Bacone College
Baker College
Bakersfield College
Baldwin-Wallace College
Ball State University
Baltimore International College
Baptist Bible College West
Baptist College of Florida
Baptist Health Schools – Little Rock
Barclay College
Bard College
Barnard College
Barry University
Barton College
Bastyr University
Bates College
Baylor University
Beach College
Becker College
Belhaven College
Bellarmine University
Bellevue Community College
Belmont Abbey College
Belmont University
Beloit College
Bemidji State University
Benedictine College
Benedictine University
Bennett College for Women
Bennington College
Bentley University
Berea College
Berkeley College – Midtown Manhattan
Berklee College of Music
Berry College
Bethany College – Kansas
Bethany College – West Virginia
Bethany Lutheran College
Bethany University – Santa Cruz
Bethel College – North Newton
Bethel University – St. Paul
Bethune-Cookman University
Biola University
Birmingham-Southern College

Blackburn College
Blinn College – Bryan
Bloomfield College
Blue River Community College
Bluffton University
Board of Regents – University of Georgia System
Bob Jones University
Boise State University
Boston College
Boston University
Bowdoin College
Bowling Green State University
Bradford College
Bradley University
Brandeis University
Brazosport College
Brenau University
Brescia University
Brevard College
Brevard Community College
Brewton-Parker College
Briar Cliff University
Briarcliffe College – Bethpage
Bridgewater College
Bridgewater State College
Brigham Young University – Hawaii
Brigham Young University – Idaho
Brigham Young University – Utah
Brooks Institute of Photography
Brown University
Bryan College
Bryant & Stratton College – Virginia Beach
Bryant University
Bryn Mawr College
Bucknell University
Buena Vista University
Burlington County College
Butera School of Art
Butler County Community College
Butler University
CUNY – Baruch College
CUNY – Borough of Manhattan Community College
CUNY – Brooklyn College
CUNY – City College of New York
CUNY – Hunter College
CUNY – John Jay College of Criminal Justice
CUNY – Lehman College
CUNY – Macaulay Honors College at Hunter College
CUNY – Queens College
CUNY – Queensborough Community College
CUNY – The Sophie Davis School of Biomedical Education
CUNY – York College
Cabrillo College
Caldwell College
California Baptist University
California College of the Arts

California Institute of Integral Studies
California Institute of Technology
California Institute of the Arts
California Lutheran University
California Maritime Academy
California Polytechnic State University – San Luis Obispo
California State Polytechnic University – Pomona
California State University – Bakersfield
California State University – Channel Islands
California State University – Chico
California State University – Dominguez Hills
California State University – East Bay
California State University – Fresno
California State University – Fullerton
California State University – Long Beach
California State University – Los Angeles
California State University – Northridge
California State University – Sacramento
California State University – San Bernardino
California State University – San Marcos
California State University – Stanislaus
Calvin College
Camden County College
Campbell University
Campbellsville University
Canada College
Canisius College
Cape Cod Community College
Capital College
Capital University
Cardinal Stritch University
Carleton College
Carlow University
Carnegie Mellon University
Carroll College – Montana
Carroll College – Wisconsin
Carson-Newman College
Carthage College
Case Western Reserve University
Castleton State College
Catawba College
Catholic University of America
Cedar Crest College
Cedarville University
Centenary College – New Jersey
Centenary College of Louisiana
Central College
Central Connecticut State University
Central Florida Community College
Central Methodist University
Central Piedmont Community College
Central State University
Central Texas College
Central Washington University
Centre College
Cerro Coso Community College

Chadron State College
Chaminade University of Honolulu
Champlain College
Chapman University
Charleston Southern University
Chatham College
Chemeketa Community College
Cheyney University of Pennsylvania
Chicago State University
Chowan University
Christendom College
Christian Brothers University
Christopher Newport University
Cisco Junior College
City College of San Francisco
Clackamas Community College
Claremont McKenna College
Clarendon College
Clarion University of Pennsylvania
Clark Atlanta University
Clark University
Clarke College
Clarkson University
Clayton College and State University
Clearwater Christian College
Clemson University
Cleveland Institute of Art
Cleveland Institute of Music
Clinch Valley College
Coastal Carolina University
Coe College
Coker College
Colburn School, The
Colby College
Colby-Sawyer College
Colgate University
College for Creative Studies
College of Charleston
College of DuPage
College of Eastern Utah
College of Idaho
College of Mount St. Joseph
College of Mount St. Vincent
College of New Jersey
College of Notre Dame of Maryland
College of Saint Benedict
College of Saint Elizabeth
College of Saint Rose
College of San Mateo
College of Santa Fe
College of St. Catherine
College of St. Joseph
College of St. Scholastica
College of William and Mary
College of Wooster
College of the Atlantic

College of the Canyons – Valencia campus
College of the Holy Cross
Collin County Community College
Colorado Christian University
Colorado College
Colorado School of Mines
Colorado State University – Fort Collins
Colorado State University – Pueblo
Columbia Basin College
Columbia College – Chicago
Columbia College – Missouri
Columbia College – South Carolina
Columbia International University – Bible College
Columbia Union College
Columbia University – Columbia College
Columbia University – Fu Foundation School of Engineering
Columbus College of Art and Design
Columbus State Community College
Columbus State University
Community College of Allegheny County
                – Allegheny Campus
Community College of Baltimore County – Essex
Community College of Philadelphia
Conception Seminary College
Concordia College
Concordia University – Austin
Concordia University – Chicago
Concordia University – Irvine
Concordia University – Mequon
Concordia University – Portland
Concordia University – Seward
Concordia University – St. Paul
Connecticut College
Converse College
Cooper Union for the Advancement of Science & Art
Coppin State University
Corban College and Graduate School
Corcoran College of Art & Design
Cornell College
Cornell University
Cornell University – College of Engineering
Cornish College of the Arts
Cottey College
County College of Morris
Covenant College
Creighton University
Crichton College
Crossroads College
Crown College
Culver-Stockton College
Curry College
Cushing Academy
Cy-Fair College
D'Youville College
Dakota Wesleyan University
Dallas Baptist University

Dallas Christian College
Dalton State College
Dana College – Nebraska
Danville Community College
Dartmouth College
Darton College
Davidson College
Davis College – New York
Daytona Beach Community College
De Anza College
DeKalb Technical College – Clarkston
DePaul University
DePauw University
DeSales University – Center Valley Campus
DeVry Institute of Technology – Kansas City
DeVry Institute of Technology – Long Island City
DeVry University – Alpharetta
DeVry University – Chicago
DeVry University – Decatur
DeVry University – McLean
DeVry University – Sherman Oaks
Dean College
Deep Springs College
Defiance College
Delaware College of Art and Design
Delaware State University
Delaware Valley College
Delta College
Denison University
Dickinson College
DigiPen Institute of Technology
Doane College
Dominican College – Orangeburg
Dominican University – River Forest
Dominican University of California
Dordt College
Dowling College – Brookhaven Campus
Drake University
Drew University
Drexel University
Drury University
Duke University
Duquesne University
Earlham College
East Carolina University
East Los Angeles College
East Mississippi Community College
        – Columbus Air Force Base
East Stroudsburg University
East Tennessee State University
East Texas Baptist University
Eastern Connecticut State University
Eastern Illinois University
Eastern Mennonite University
Eastern Michigan University
Eastern Oregon University

Eastern University – Pennsylvania
Eastern Washington University
Eastfield College
Eckerd College
Edgewood College
Edinboro University of Pennsylvania
Edison Community College
El Centro College
El Paso Community College
Elizabeth City State University
Elizabethtown College
Ellis Hospital School of Nursing
Elmhurst College
Elmira College
Elms College
Elon University
Embry-Riddle Aeronautical University – Florida
Emerson College
Emmanuel College – Boston
Emmanuel College – Franklin Springs
Emory & Henry College
Emory University
Emporia State University
Endicott College
Erskine College
Eternity Bible College
Eugene Bible College
Eugene Lang College – the New School for Liberal Arts
Eureka College
Evangel University
Evergreen State College
Evergreen Valley College
Fairleigh Dickinson University – College at Florham
Fairleigh Dickinson University – Teaneck
Fairmont State University
Fashion Institute of Technology
Faulkner University
Fayetteville State University
Fayetteville Technical Community College
Ferris State University
Ferrum College
Fisher College
Fisk University
Fitchburg State College
Flathead Valley Community College – Kalispell
Florida A&M University
Florida Atlantic University – Boca Raton
Florida Atlantic University – Wilkes Honors College
Florida Bright Futures Scholarship Program
Florida Christian College
Florida College
Florida Community College at Jacksonville – Kent
Florida Gulf Coast University
Florida Hospital College of Health Sciences
Florida Institute of Technology
Florida International University

Florida Memorial University
Florida Metropolitan University – Melbourne campus
Florida Southern College
Florida State University
Fordham University
Fort Hays State University
Fort Valley State University
Francis Marion University
Franciscan University of Steubenville
Franklin College
Franklin College Switzerland – US Admissions
Franklin Pierce College
Franklin University
Franklin and Marshall College
Free Gospel Bible Institute
Free Will Baptist Bible College
Freed-Hardeman University
Fresno Pacific University
Friends University
Front Range Community College – Westminster Campus
Frostburg State University – Maryland
Full Sail Real World Education
Furman University
Gainesville State College
Gannon University
Gardner-Webb University
Genesee Community College
Geneva College
George Fox University
George Mason University
George Washington University
Georgetown College
Georgetown University
Georgia Baptist College of Nursing of Mercer University
Georgia College and State University
Georgia Institute of Technology
Georgia Military College – Milledgeville
Georgia Perimeter College – Atlanta
Georgia Southern University
Georgia Southwestern State University
Georgia State University
Germanna Community College
Gettysburg College
Gibbs College – Vienna
Golden Gate University
Goldey-Beacom College
Gonzaga University
Gordon College – Georgia
Gordon College – Massachusetts
Goshen College
Goucher College
Grace College and Seminary
Graceland University
Grambling State University
Grand Canyon University
Grand Valley State University

Green River Community College
Greensboro College
Greenville College
Greenville Technical College
Grinnell College
Grove City College
Guilford College
Gulf Coast Community College
Gustavus Adolphus College
Hagerstown Community College
Hamilton College
Hamline University
Hampden-Sydney College
Hampshire College
Hampton University
Hannibal La-Grange College
Hanover College
Hardin-Simmons University
Harding University
Harford Community College
Hargrave Military Academy
Harold Washington College
Hartwick College
Harvard Divinity School
Harvard University
Harvey Mudd College
Haskell Indian Nations University
Hastings College
Haverford College
Hawaii Pacific University
Heidelberg College – Ohio
Hendrix College
Hennepin Technical College – Brooklyn Park Campus
Herkimer County Community College
Herron School of Art and Design
High Point University
High Tech Institute – Irving
High Tech Institute – St. Louis Park
Hill College
Hillsborough Community College – Tampa
Hillsdale College
Hillsdale Free Will Baptist College
Hinds Community College
Hiram College
Hobart and William Smith Colleges
Hofstra University
Hollins University
Holy Family University – Newtown
Holy Names University
Holyoke Community College
Hood College
Hope College
Hope International University
Hope Medical Institute
Houghton College
Houston Baptist University

Houston Community College System
Howard Community College – Maryland
Howard Payne University
Howard University
Humboldt State University
Huntington University
Huston-Tillotson University
ITT Technical Institute – Eden Prairie
Illinois College
Illinois Insitute of Art – Schaumburg
Illinois Institute of Art – Chicago
Illinois Institute of Technology
Illinois State University
Illinois Wesleyan University
Indian River Community College
Indiana Institute of Technology
Indiana State University
Indiana University – Bloomington
Indiana University – Jacobs School of Music
Indiana University – Purdue University Fort Wayne
Indiana University – Purdue University at Indianapolis
Indiana University – South Bend
Indiana University of Pennsylvania
Indiana Wesleyan University
Inver Hills Community College
Iona College
Iowa State University
Ithaca College
J. Sargeant Reynolds Community College
Jacksonville University
James Madison University
Jamestown College
Jewish Theological Seminary
John Brown University
John Carroll University
Johns Hopkins University
Johnson & Wales University – Charlotte
Johnson Bible College
Johnson C. Smith University
Johnson and Wales University – North Miami
Johnson and Wales University – Providence
Judson College – Alabama
Judson University – Illinois
Julliard School, The
Juniata College
Kalamazoo College
Kalamazoo Valley Community College
        – Texas Township Campus
Kansas State University
Kansas Wesleyan University
Kean University
Kellogg Community College
Kendall College
Kendall College of Art and Design
Kennesaw State University
Kent State University

Kentucky Christian University
Kentucky Wesleyan College
Kenyon College
Kettering University
Kilgore College
King College
King's College – Pennsylvania
Kingwood College
Knox College
Knoxville College
La Salle University
La Sierra University
LaGrange College
LaRoche College
Laboratory Institute of Merchandising
Lafayette College
Lake City Community College
Lake Erie College
Lake Forest College
Lake Superior State University
Lamar University
Lander University
Landmark College
Lane College
Laredo Community College
Lasell College
Lawrence University
Le Moyne College
LeTourneau University
Lee University
Lees-McRae College
Lehigh University
Lenoir-Rhyne College
Lesley University
Lewis University
Lewis and Clark College
Lewis-Clark State College
Liberty University
Life University
Limestone College
Lincoln Memorial University
Lindenwood University
Linfield College – McMinnville
Linfield College – Portland
Lipscomb University
Loma Linda University
Long Island University – C.W. Post Campus
Long Island University – Brooklyn Campus
Longview Community College
Longwood University
Loras College
Lord Fairfax Community College
Los Angeles Film School, The
Louisburg College
Louisiana State University
Louisiana State University – Agricultural and Mech. College

Loyola College – Maryland
Loyola Marymount University
Loyola University – Chicago
Loyola University – New Orleans
Lubbock Christian University
Luther College
Lynchburg College
Lynn University
Lyon College
MacMurray College
Macalester College
Macomb Community College
Macon State College
Malone College – Ohio
Manatee Community College
Manchester College
Manhattan Christian College
Manhattanville College
Mankato State University
Mansfield University of Pennsylvania
Maple Woods Community College
Marian College
Marietta College
Marist College
Marlboro College
Marquette University
Mars Hill College
Marshall University
Martin Luther College
Mary Baldwin College
Maryland Bible College & Seminary
Maryland Institute College of Art (MICA)
Marylhurst University
Marymount College – Palos Verdes
Marymount Manhattan College
Marymount University
Maryville College
Marywood University
Massachusetts College of Art
Massachusetts College of Pharmacy and Health Sciences
Massachusetts Institute of Technology
Master's College, The
Mayville State University
McDaniel College
McMurry University
McPherson College
Memphis College of Art
Menlo College
Mercer University
Mercy College
Mercyhurst College – Pennsylvania
Meredith College
Merrimack College
Mesa State College
Messiah College
Methodist University

Metropolitan Community College
Metropolitan State College of Denver
Metropolitan State University – St. Paul
Miami International University of Art & Design
Miami University – Ohio
Michigan State University
Michigan Technological University
Mid-America Nazarene University
Middle Georgia College
Middle Tennessee State University
Middlebury College
Middlesex County College
Midland College
Midwestern State University
Millersville University
Milligan College
Millikin University
Mills College
Millsaps College
Milwaukee School of Engineering
Minneapolis College of Art and Design
Minneapolis Community and Technical College
Minnesota School of Business – Brooklyn Center
Minnesota School of Business – Richfield
Minnesota State University – Moorhead
Minot State University
Mission College
Mississippi College
Mississippi State University
Missouri Baptist University
Missouri Southern State University
Missouri State University
Missouri University of Science and Technology
Missouri Western State University
Modesto Junior College
Molloy College
Monmouth College
Monmouth University
Monroe Community College – Rochester
Montana State University – Billings
Montana State University – Bozeman
Montclair State University
Montgomery College – Rockville
Montgomery College – Texas
Montreat College – Main Campus
Moody Bible Institute
Moore College of Art and Design
Moravian College
Morehead State University
Morehouse College
Morgan State University
Morris Brown College
Mount Holyoke College
Mount Mary College
Mount Saint Mary College – New York
Mount Sinai School of Medicine

Mount St. Mary's College – Los Angeles
Mount St. Mary's University – Emmitsburg
Mount Union College
Mount Vernon Nazarene University
Mountain Empire Community College
Mountain State University – Beckley
Mt. San Antonio College
Muhlenberg College
Multnomah Bible College and Biblical Seminary
Murray State University
Muskingum College
NCAA – Eligibility Center
Napa Valley College
Nashville State Community College
Nassau Community College
National American University – Rapid City
Navarro College
Nazareth College of Rochester
Nebraska Wesleyan University
Neumann College
Neumont University – Utah
New College of Florida
New England College
New England College of Optometry
New England Culinary Institute
New England Institute of Art
New England Institute of Technology
New England School of Photography
New Jersey City University
New Jersey Institute of Technology
New Mexico Institute of Mining & Technology (NM Tech)
New River Community College
New School for Jazz and Contemporary Music, The
New School for Social Research
New Tribes Bible Institute
New York Film Academy
New York University
New York University – Gallatin School
New York University – Tisch School of the Arts
Newberry College
Niagara University
Nicholls State University
Norfolk State University
North Carolina Agricultural and Technical State University
North Carolina Central University
North Carolina School of the Arts
North Carolina State University
North Carolina Wesleyan College
North Central College
North Central Texas College
North Central University
North Dakota State University
North Dakota University System
North Georgia College & State University
North Greenville University
North Harris College

North Harris Montgomery Community College District
North Hennepin Community College
North Idaho College
North Lake College
North Park University
Northeastern Illinois University
Northeastern State University
Northeastern University
Northern Arizona University
Northern Illinois University
Northern Kentucky University
Northern Michigan University
Northern Virginia Community College – Alexandria
Northern Virginia Community College – Annandale
Northern Virginia Community College – Loudoun
Northern Virginia Community College – Manassas
Northern Virginia Community College
    – Medical Ed. Campus
Northern Virginia Community College – Woodbridge
Northland College
Northwest Arkansas Community College
Northwest Christian University
Northwest College
Northwest Missouri State University
Northwest Nazarene University
Northwest University
Northwest Vista College
Northwestern College – Minnesota
Northwestern University – Illinois
Northwood University
Norwich University
Notre Dame College – Ohio
Notre Dame de Namur University
Nova Southeastern University
Nyack College
Oak Hills Christian College
Oakland University
Oakwood College
Oberlin College
Occidental College
Oglethorpe University
Ohio Dominican University
Ohio Northern University
Ohio State University – Columbus
Ohio University
Ohio Valley University
Ohio Wesleyan University
Okaloosa-Walton Community College
Oklahoma Baptist University
Oklahoma Christian University
Oklahoma City University
Oklahoma Panhandle State University
Oklahoma State University
Old Dominion University
Olin College
Olivet College

Olivet Nazarene University
Olympic College
Oral Roberts University
Oregon Institute of Technology
Oregon State University
Otis College of Art & Design
Ottawa University – Kansas
Otterbein College
Ouachita Baptist University
Our Lady of the Lake University
Oxford College of Emory University
Ozark Christian College
Ozarks Technical Community College
Pace University
Pacific Lutheran University
Pacific Northwest College of Art
Pacific Union College
Pacific University
Paine College
Palm Beach Atlantic University
Palm Beach Community College
Palo Alto College
Palomar College
Paradise Valley Community College
Park College
Parsons New School of Design
Pasco-Hernando Community College – West Campus
Passaic County Community College
Patrick Henry Community College
Paul Smith's College
Peabody Institute of the Johns Hopkins University
Peace College
Penn Valley Community College
Pennsylvania State University – Altoona
Pennsylvania State University – Beaver
Pennsylvania State University – Berks Campus
Pennsylvania State University – University Park
Pennsylvania State University at Erie
Pensacola Junior College
Pepperdine University
Pfeiffer University
PharmCAS
Philadelphia Biblical University
Philadelphia College of Textiles and Science
Piedmont College
Pierce College – Los Angeles
Pikes Peak Community College
Pine Manor College
Pittsburg State University
Pitzer College
Point Loma Nazarene University
Point Park University
Polytechnic University
Pomona College
Portland State University
Post University

Prairie View A&M University
Pratt Institute
Pratt Munson-Williams-Proctor Arts Institute
Presbyterian College
Prescott College
Prince George's Community College
Princeton University
Principia College
Providence College
Pueblo Community College – Pueblo Campus
Pulaski Technical College
Purdue University – Calumet
Purdue University – North Central
Purdue University – West Lafayette
Queens University of Charlotte
Quincy University
Quinnipiac University
Radford University
Ramapo College of New Jersey
Randolph College – Lynchburg
Randolph-Macon College – Ashland
Rappahannock Community College
Raritan Valley Community College
Rasmussen College – Pasco County Campus
Redstone College of Aviation Technology – Denver
Reed College
Regent University
Regis College
Regis University
Reinhardt College
Rensselaer Polytechnic Institute
Rhodes College
Rice University
Richard Bland College
Richard Stockton College of New Jersey
Richland College
Rider University
Ridgewater College
Ringling School of Art and Design
Ripon College
Riverside Community College
Rivier College
Roanoke College
Robert Morris College – Chicago
Robert Morris University – Moon Township
Roberts Wesleyan College
Rochester Institute of Technology
Rockford College
Rockhurst College
Rocky Mountain College – Billings
Rocky Mountain College of Art and Design
Roger Williams University
Rollins College
Roosevelt University
Rosalind Franklin University
Rose-Hulman Institute of Technology

Rosemont College
Rowan University
Russell Sage College
Rutgers – The State University of New Jersey
SUNY – Binghamton University
SUNY – Broome Community College
SUNY – College at Brockport
SUNY – College at Cortland
SUNY – College at Fredonia
SUNY – College at Geneseo
SUNY – College at Old Westbury
SUNY – College at Oneonta
SUNY – College at Oswego
SUNY – College at Plattsburgh
SUNY – College at Potsdam
SUNY – College of Technology at Alfred
SUNY – Columbia-Greene Community College
SUNY – Empire State College
SUNY – Farmingdale State College
SUNY – Finger Lakes Community College
SUNY – Fulton Montgomery Community College
SUNY – Maritime College
SUNY – New Paltz
SUNY – North Country Community College
SUNY – Onondaga Community College
SUNY – Orange County Community College
SUNY – Purchase College
SUNY – Rockland Community College
SUNY – Stony Brook University
SUNY – Suffolk County Community College
SUNY – Tompkins Cortland Community College
SUNY – Ulster County Community College
SUNY – University at Albany
SUNY – University at Buffalo
SUNY – Westchester Community College
Sacred Heart University
Sage College of Albany
Saginaw Valley State University
Saint Anselm College
Saint Francis University
Saint John's University - Minnesota
Saint Joseph College
Saint Joseph Seminary College
Saint Leo University
Saint Louis University – MO
Saint Martin's University
Saint Mary's College – Notre Dame
Saint Mary's College of California
Saint Mary's University of Minnesota
Saint Michael's College
Saint Paul College
Saint Peter's College
Saint Thomas University
Saint Vincent College
Salem College
Salem State College

Salem-Teikyo University
Salisbury University
Salt Lake Community College
Salve Regina University
Sam Houston State University
Samford University
San Antonio College
San Diego Mesa College
San Diego State University
San Diego State University – Imperial Valley Campus
San Francisco Art Institute
San Francisco State University
San Jacinto College
San Joaquin Delta College
San Jose City College
San Jose State University
Santa Clara University
Santa Fe Community College
Santa Monica College
Sarah Lawrence College
Savannah College of Art and Design – Atlanta
Savannah College of Art and Design – Savannah
Savannah State University
Schenectady County Community College
Schiller International University
School of Fashion Design – Boston
School of the Art Institute of Chicago
School of the Museum of Fine Arts
Schreiner University
Scripps College
Seaton Hill University
Seattle Central Community College
Seattle Pacific University
Seattle University
Seminole Community College
Seton Hall University
Sewanee – The University of the South
Shaw University
Shawnee State University
Shenandoah University
Shepherd University
Shimer College
Shorter College
Siena College
Sierra College
Simmons College
Simpson College
Simpson University
Skidmore College
Slippery Rock University
Smith College
Soka University of America
South Carolina State University
South Dakota School of Mines and Technology
South Dakota State University
South Georgia College

South Puget Sound Community College
South Texas College
South University – Pittsburgh
Southampton College, LIU
Southeast Missouri State University
Southeastern University
Southern Adventist University
Southern Baptist Theological Seminary, The
Southern Illinois University – Carbondale
Southern Illinois University – Edwardsville
Southern Maine Community College
Southern Methodist University
Southern Nazarene University
Southern Oregon University
Southern Polytechnic State University
Southern Utah University
Southern Vermont College
Southern Virginia University
Southern Wesleyan University
Southwest Baptist University
Southwest Minnesota State University
Southwest State University
Southwestern Adventist University
Southwestern Assemblies of God University
Southwestern College
Southwestern University
Spalding University
Spartanburg Methodist College
Spelman College
Spring Arbor University
Spring Hill College
Springfield Technical Community College
St. Ambrose University
St. Andrews Presbyterian College
St. Augustine College – Chicago
St. Bonaventure University
St. Catharine College
St. Cloud State University
St. Edward's University
St. Francis College
St. Gregory's University
St. John Fisher College
St. John Vianney College Seminary
St. John's College – New Mexico
St. John's College – Maryland
St. John's University – New York
St. Joseph's College – New York
St. Joseph's University
St. Lawrence University
St. Mary's College of Maryland
St. Mary's University – San Antonio
St. Norbert College
St. Olaf College
St. Philip's College
St. Thomas Aquinas College – New York
St. Thomas Aquinas Seminary

St. Xavier University
Stanford University
Stark State College of Technology
Stephen F. Austin State University
Stephens College
Sterling College
Stetson University
Stevens Institute of Technology
Stillman College
Stonehill College
Stratford University
Strayer University
Suffolk University
Sul Ross State University – Alpine
Susquehanna University
Swarthmore College
Sweet Briar College
Syracuse University
Tabor College
Tacoma Community College
Tallahasse Community College
Tarleton State University
Tarrant County College
Taylor University – Fort Wayne
Taylor University – Indianapolis
Taylor University – Upland
Teikyo Post University
Temple College
Temple University
Tennessee State University
Tennessee Technological University
Tennessee Temple University
Texas A&M International University
Texas A&M University – College Station
Texas A&M University – Commerce
Texas A&M University – Corpus Christi
Texas A&M University – Galveston
Texas A&M University – Kingsville
Texas A&M University – Texarkana
Texas Christian University
Texas Lutheran University
Texas Southern University
Texas State University – San Marcos
Texas Tech University
Texas Wesleyan University
Texas Woman's University
The Citadel – The Military College of South Carolina
Thiel College
Thomas Aquinas College
Thomas Edison State College
Thomas More College
Thomas Nelson Community College
Tidewater Community College – Norfolk
Tidewater Community College – Virginia Beach
Tiffin University
Toccoa Falls College

Tomball College
Tougaloo College
Towson University
Transylvania University
Trevecca Nazarene University
Tri-County Technical College
Tri-State University
Trinity Christian College
Trinity College
Trinity International University
Trinity University
Trinity Washington University
Troy University – Montgomery Campus
Troy University – Troy Campus
Truckee Meadows Community College
Truett-McConnell College
Truman State University
Tufts University
Tulane University
Tulsa Community College
Tusculum College
Tuskegee University
Tyler Junior College
Union College – Kentucky
Union College – Nebraska
Union College – New York
Union County College – Cranford
Union University
United States Air Force Academy
United States International University
United States Military Academy
United States Naval Academy

Unity College
Universal Technical Institute – Houston
Universal Technical Institute – Pennsylvania
University of Akron
University of Alabama – Huntsville
University of Alabama – Tuscaloosa
University of Alabama at Birmingham
University of Alaska – Anchorage
University of Alaska – Fairbanks
University of Arizona – Tucson
University of Arkansas at Fayetteville
University of Arkansas at Fort Smith
University of Arkansas at Little Rock
University of Baltimore
University of California – Berkeley
University of California – Davis
University of California – Irvine
University of California – Los Angeles
University of California – Merced
University of California – Office of the President
University of California – Riverside
University of California – San Diego
University of California – San Francisco
University of California – San Francisco, Sch. of Dentistry
University of California – Santa Barbara
University of California – Santa Cruz
University of Central Arkansas
University of Central Florida
University of Central Missouri
University of Central Oklahoma – Edmond
University of Charleston

4: University Scholarships for IB Diploma Holders

As at September 2008
The following universities offer scholarships for recipients of the IB diploma. They are listed by country.

Australia
Queensland Institute of Technology

Canada
Acadia University, NS
Bishop's University, QC
Brandon University, MB
Brock University, ON
Capilano College, BC
Carleton University, ON
Concordia University College of Alberta, AB
Dalhousie, NS
Laurentian University, ON
McMaster University, ON
Memorial University of Newfoundland, NF
Mount Allison University, NB
Mount Saint Vincent University, NS
Ontario College of Art & Design, ON
Saint Mary's University, NS
Simon Fraser University, BC
St. Francis Xavier, NS
St. Thomas University, NB
Trent University, ON
Université de Moncton, NB
Université de Montréal QC
University of Alberta, Edmonton, AB
University of British Columbia, BC
University of Calgary, AB
University of Guelph, ON
University of Manitoba, MB
University of New Brunswick (St. John), NB
University of Ottawa, ON
University of Prince Edward Island, PE
University of Toronto, ON
University of Victoria, BC
University of Waterloo, ON
University of Western Ontario, ON
University of Winnipeg, SK
York University, ON

Germany
International University of Bremen

France
American University of Paris

United Kingdom

Richmond – the American International
    University, London
University of Birmingham
University of Buckingham
University of East Anglia
University of Reading
University of Sheffield

United States
Albertson College of Idaho, ID
American University of Paris, FR
Art Institute of Ft. Lauderdale, FL
Barry University, FL
Beacon College, FL
Belhaven College, FL
Bethune-Cookman College, FL
Brevard Community College, FL
Central Florida Community College, FL
Chipola Community College, FL
Clearwater Christian College, FL
College of Notre Dame, CA
Daytona Beach Community College
Defiance College, IN
Drury University, MO
Eckerd College, FL
Edward Waters College, FL
Embry Riddle Aeronautical College, FL
Flagler College, FL
Florida Agricultural & Mechanical, FL
Florida Atlantic University, FL
Florida Atlantic University – Wilkes Honors
    College, FL

Florida College, FL
Florida Community College Jacksonville, FL
Florida Gulf Coast University, FL
Florida Hospital College of Health Sciences, FL
Florida Institute of Technology, FL
Florida International University, FL
Florida Memorial College, FL
Florida Metropolitan University, FL
Florida Southern College, FL
Florida State University, FL
Full Sail Real World Education, FL
Gulf Coast Community College, FL
Hillsborough Community College, FL
Indian River Community College, FL
International Academy of Design and Technology
        – Orlando, FL
International Academy of Design and Technology
        – Tampa, FL
International College, FL
Jacksonville University, FL
Lake City Community College, FL
Lynn University, FL
Manatee Community College, FL
Manatee Community College
        – Venice Campus, FL
Meredith College, SC
Mesa State College, CO
Miami Dade College – Kendall College, FL
Michigan Technological University, MI
Midwestern State University, TX
New College of Florida, FL
New England College, ME
Notre Dame de Namur University, CA
Nova Southeastern University, FL
Okaloosa-Walton College, FL
Oregon State University, OR
Palm Beach Atlantic College, FL
Pensacola Junior College, FL
Ringling School of Art & Design, FL
Rollins College, FL
Saint Mary's University, NS
Santa Fe Community College, FL
Schiller International University, FL
Seminole Community College, FL
Southeastern College, FL
Southern Methodist University, TX
St. Johns River Community College, FL
St. Leo University, FL

St. Thomas University, FL
Stetson University, FL
Tallahassee Community College, FL
The Art Institute of Tampa, FL
The Baptist College of Florida, FL
University of Central Florida, FL
University of Florida, FL (for IB diploma holders
        from United World Colleges)
University of Miami, FL
University of North Florida, FL
University of Rochester, NY
University of South Florida, FL
University of Tampa, FL
University of Tulsa, OK
University of West Florida, FL
Wabash College, IN
Warner Southern College, FL
Webber International University, FL
Webster College – Holiday, FL
Webster College – Ocala, FL

Please note

- The scholarships vary in size. Some are modest; others are substantial. Please check universities' websites and contact university officials for more detailed information about a particular scholarship.
- The IB diploma is recognized by universities worldwide. These universities, including those that do not offer scholarships for IB students, often look favourably on applications from IB graduates. They may offer other types of scholarships for which IB graduates are encouraged to apply.
- In many cases, universities with low tuition fees do not offer scholarships of any type because financial assistance is unnecessary. However, they may recognize the IB diploma and even be particularly interested in IB students.
- The list is not exhaustive and is regularly revised as new information is received from universities.
- The IB does not in any way endorse the universities listed.

5: Diploma Programme Subjects Offered in 2008 (May and November sessions)

Group 1 – Language A1
Language A1 HL*
Language A1 SL*

Group 2 – Second language
Classical languages HL
Classical languages SL
Language A2 HL*
Language A2 SL*
Language *ab initio* SL*
Language B HL*
Language B SL*

Group 3 – Individuals and societies
Business and management HL
Business and management SL
Economics HL
Economics SL
Geography HL
Geography SL
History SL
History: Africa HL
History: Americas HL
History: E and SE Asia and Oceania HL
History: Europe HL
History: South Asia and the Middle East HL
Information technology in a global society HL
Information technology in a global society SL
Islamic history HL
Islamic history SL
Philosophy HL
Philosophy SL
Psychology HL
Psychology SL
Social and cultural anthropology HL
Social and cultural anthropology SL

Group 4 – Experimental sciences
Biology HL
Biology SL
Chemistry HL
Chemistry SL
Design technology HL
Design technology SL
Environmental systems SL
Environmental systems and societies SL (pilot)
Physics HL
Physics SL

Group 5 – Mathematics and computer science
Computer science HL
Computer science SL
Further mathematics SL
Mathematical studies SL
Mathematics HL: discrete mathematics
Mathematics HL: series and differential equations
Mathematics HL: sets, relations and groups
Mathematics HL: statistics and probability
Mathematics SL

Group 6 – The arts
Music HL
Music SL composition
Music SL group
Music SL solo
Theatre arts HL
Theatre arts SL
Visual arts HL
Visual arts SL option A
Visual arts SL option B

Core requirements
Theory of knowledge
Extended essay
Creativity, action, service

*Languages offered

A1

Afrikaans HL/SL (only November)
Amharic
Arabic
Bosnian
Bulgarian
Catalan
Chinese
Croatian
Czech
Danish
Dutch
English
Finnish
French
German
Hebrew
Hindi
Hungarian
Indonesian
Italian
Japanese
Korean
Latvian
Lithuanian
Macedonian
Malay
Modern Greek
Nepali
Norwegian
Persian
Pilipino
Polish
Portuguese
Russian
Serbian
Sesotho
Sinhalese
Siswati SL (only November)
Slovak
Slovene
Spanish
Swahili
Swedish
Thai
Turkish
Welsh

A2

Arabic
Chinese
Dutch
English
French
German
Japanese
Modern Greek
Norwegian
Pilipino
Portuguese
Russian
Spanish
Swedish
Thai

B

Arabic
Danish
Dutch
English
Finnish
French
German
Hebrew (SL only)
Hindi
Indonesian
Italian
Japanese
Korean
Malay (SL November only)
Mandarin
Modern Greek (SL only)
Norwegian
Portuguese
Russian
Spanish
Swahili (only November)
Swedish
Tamil (SL November only)

Ab initio

Arabic
French
German
Indonesian
Italian
Japanese
Malay
Mandarin
Russian
Spanish
Swahili

6: Country Representation

Total number of IB schools by country

Country	IB World Schools	Programmes		
		PYP	MYP	DP
ANGOLA	1	1	1	1
ARGENTINA	45	7	5	43
AUSTRALIA	117	43	47	56
AUSTRIA	4	1	1	4
AZERBAIJAN	1	1	1	1
BAHAMAS	3	2	1	3
BAHRAIN	8	1	0	8
BANGLADESH	2	1	1	2
BARBADOS	1	1	0	0
BELGIUM	6	1	1	5
BERMUDA	3	0	1	2
BOLIVIA	2	0	0	2
BOSNIA AND HERZEGOVINA	3	0	1	3
BOTSWANA	1	1	0	1
BRAZIL	13	5	1	11
BRUNEI DARUSSALAM	1	0	0	1
BULGARIA	4	0	0	4
CAMBODIA	1	1	1	1
CANADA	265	37	129	122
CAYMAN ISLANDS	1	0	0	1
CHILE	17	3	4	16
CHINA	39	10	16	33
COLOMBIA	20	4	3	19
COSTA RICA	7	0	0	7
CROATIA	4	0	2	3
CUBA	1	0	0	1

Country	IB World Schools	Programmes		
		PYP	MYP	DP
CYPRUS	3	0	0	3
CZECH REPUBLIC	4	0	0	4
DENMARK	10	2	2	9
DOMINICAN REPUBLIC	1	0	0	1
ECUADOR	23	1	3	22
EGYPT	6	2	2	6
EL SALVADOR	3	0	0	3
ESTONIA	1	1	0	1
ETHIOPIA	3	0	0	3
FIJI	2	2	2	2
FINLAND	16	3	4	14
FRANCE	10	2	1	10
GERMANY	33	12	7	31
GHANA	3	1	1	3
GREECE	13	1	0	13
GUAM	1	0	0	1
GUATEMALA	4	0	1	4
HONDURAS	1	0	0	1
HONG KONG	19	7	3	14
HUNGARY	4	0	0	4
ICELAND	1	0	0	1
INDIA	49	12	6	45
INDONESIA	24	16	10	17
IRAN, ISLAMIC REPUBLIC OF	1	0	0	1
IRELAND	1	0	0	1
ISRAEL	1	0	0	1
ITALY	17	4	3	15
JAMAICA	2	0	0	2
JAPAN	14	8	4	11
JORDAN	8	0	3	7
KAZAKHSTAN	5	4	5	1
KENYA	5	1	0	5

Country	IB World Schools	Programmes		
		PYP	MYP	DP
KOREA, REPUBLIC OF	3	1	0	3
KUWAIT	2	1	1	2
LAO, PEOPLE'S DEMOCRATIC REPUBLIC OF	1	0	0	1
LATVIA	3	2	1	2
LEBANON	5	2	0	4
LESOTHO	1	0	0	1
LITHUANIA	2	0	0	2
LUXEMBOURG	3	0	0	3
MACEDONIA, THE FORMER YUGOSLAV REPUBLIC OF	2	0	0	2
MALAWI	1	0	0	1
MALAYSIA	6	1	0	6
MALTA	1	0	0	1
MAURITIUS	3	1	0	2
MEXICO	67	30	19	46
MONACO	1	1	1	1
MONGOLIA	1	1	1	1
MOROCCO	4	0	2	3
MOZAMBIQUE	1	0	0	1
NAMIBIA	1	1	0	1
NETHERLANDS	16	2	8	14
NETHERLANDS ANTILLES	1	0	0	1
NEW ZEALAND	11	4	0	8
NICARAGUA	2	0	0	2
NIGERIA	3	1	0	2
NORWAY	23	3	5	18
OMAN	2	1	1	2
PAKISTAN	1	0	1	1
PALESTINIAN TERRITORY, OCCUPIED	1	0	0	1
PANAMA	1	0	0	1
PAPUA NEW GUINEA	1	0	0	1

Country	IB World Schools	Programmes		
		PYP	MYP	DP
PARAGUAY	1	0	1	1
PERU	17	5	6	17
PHILIPPINES	8	1	1	7
POLAND	28	0	2	28
PORTUGAL	5	1	1	5
QATAR	6	1	1	6
ROMANIA	2	2	1	1
RUSSIAN FEDERATION	15	4	8	12
RWANDA	1	0	0	1
SAUDI ARABIA	3	0	0	3
SENEGAL	1	0	0	1
SERBIA	3	1	1	3
SINGAPORE	15	6	5	13
SLOVAKIA	3	0	0	3
SLOVENIA	3	1	2	2
SOUTH AFRICA	2	0	0	2
SPAIN	45	2	7	44
SRI LANKA	2	1	1	2
SUDAN	1	1	0	1
SWAZILAND	1	0	0	1
SWEDEN	36	5	6	31
SWITZERLAND	29	13	8	24
SYRIAN ARAB REPUBLIC	1	1	0	1
TAIWAN	2	0	0	2
TANZANIA, UNITED REPUBLIC OF	4	3	3	3
THAILAND	14	4	4	14
TOGO	2	0	0	2
TUNISIA	1	0	0	1
TURKEY	25	6	6	21
UGANDA	3	1	1	3
UKRAINE	2	1	1	2
UNITED ARAB EMIRATES	11	2	1	10

Country	IB World Schools	Programmes		
		PYP	MYP	DP
UNITED KINGDOM	139	8	7	134
UNITED STATES	919	146	272	615
URUGUAY	7	1	3	5
UZBEKISTAN	1	0	0	1
VENEZUELA	10	1	2	9
VIETNAM	4	2	2	4
VIRGIN ISLANDS, BRITISH	1	0	0	1
ZAMBIA	2	2	1	2
ZIMBABWE	2	1	0	2
Total schools:	2405	474	666	1781
in total number of countries:	129	77	70	128

INDEX

An index of all IB World Schools listed alphabetically.

O

P

X

Y

Z

NOTES

NOTES

NOTES

NOTES